SELECTED ESSAYS OF
WILLIAM
HAZLITT
1778 : 1830

EDITED BY
GEOFFREY KEYNES
F.R.C.S.

1934

CONTENTS

ON LIFE IN GENERAL

ON WRITERS AND WRITING

a *

INTRODUCTION

WILLIAM HAZLITT was born on April 10, 1778, and died a hundred years ago on September 18, 1830. His father, the Rev. William Hazlitt, was a Unitarian minister, who in 1778 had been preaching for eight years at the Chapel in Maidstone. He was the son of a poor Irish farmer, and after preparing for the ministry at Glasgow University had married in 1766 the daughter of an ironmonger at Wisbeach in Cambridgeshire. William was their fourth child and his early years were somewhat chequered, as the family moved from place to place in search of a permanent home. In 1784 they had gone to America, where the elder Hazlitt had founded the first Unitarian Church at Boston. In 1787 they returned to England, and it was at Wem in Shropshire that William Hazlitt first had a settled home and systematic education. He was described at the age of about ten as " one of the most entertaining and prepossessing children ever seen," but by the time he was twelve he had lost his social charms, and, as adolescence approached, his rather resentful attitude towards the world, which ever after characterised him, began to make its appearance.

In 1793, at the age of fifteen, he was sent to London to complete his education at Hackney College. He lived with his elder brother John in Long Acre, and immediately began to develop, too intensely for health of mind and body, his faculties of thought and composition, elaborating a treatise on a *Project for a New Theory of Civil and Criminal Legislation*, which he presented to his tutor in place of the theme that had been set. He had been sent to Hackney College with the object of preparing him for the Unitarian ministry, but he developed such a distaste for this that the project was after three years reluctantly abandoned, and he returned to Wem in 1796. Here, apparently for about two years, he was allowed to indulge to his heart's content his passion for reading which from an early age he had already exercised to a limited extent. He now became steeped in all the best literature of his own and earlier times, and laid the foundations of the immense knowledge of the work of other writers which he so constantly and brilliantly displayed in his own. In 1798 occurred his first meeting with Coleridge, described in his essay on " My First Acquaintance with Poets," and this led to his visiting Coleridge at Nether Stowey in the summer of the same year, where he also met Wordsworth.

Early in 1799 Hazlitt became acquainted with Henry Crabb Robinson, the diarist, who described him as " struggling against a great difficulty of expression." So great did he find this difficulty to be, that he turned at this time away from writing towards painting, and this course was strengthened by the fact that his elder brother John was already established in London as a painter and had exhibited pictures at Somerset House in 1798. At the same time William Hazlitt began to be acquainted with the old masters and this helped to turn his thoughts more strongly towards this form of expression. The painting of his first picture is described in the essay " On the Pleasure of Painting," and also the portrait of his father, which was exhibited at Somerset House in 1802. In this year he visited Paris, his chief objective being the picture galleries of the Louvre, where he made copies of the great masters. In 1803 Hazlitt renewed his acquaintance with Coleridge and Wordsworth, though he met Wordsworth only once again after this year. In the course of this visit to the Lakes, he painted portraits of both the poets; he also became involved in an affair of the heart which filled Wordsworth with an idea that he was unworthy, and probably accounted for the coolness of their relations ever afterwards. It was early in the year 1804 that Hazlitt first met Lamb, who remained one of the most intimate and staunchest of his friends until his death. Hazlitt's portrait of Lamb, now in the National Portrait Gallery, was painted in the same year and remains as the proof of his real proficiency as a painter—it proves, indeed, that he was no

mere amateur, and that he might have reached considerable heights in this art had he so chosen. At this point,
however, he felt impelled to return to his early passion for
philosophical thought, and in 1805 his first book, *An Essay
on the Principles of Human Action*, was published. This
was followed in 1806 by a political pamphlet, *Free
Thoughts on Public Affairs*, and in 1807 by three books,
philosophical and political, in one of which he attacked
Malthus's *Essay on Population*, so that his literary activities
seem to have occupied the greater part of his thoughts. By
this date, indeed, he had convinced himself that he was no
painter, but that thinking and writing were to be his
chosen path, and henceforth, with one brief intermission,
his activities centred round this occupation.

Meanwhile he had been forming an attachment to Sarah
Stoddart, a friend of the Lambs, and in May, 1808, they
were married, though not without difficulties over marriage settlements and other details. They went first to
live at Winterslow, a favourite retreat of Hazlitt's, on
Salisbury Plain, and there he developed his literary projects, a *History of English Philosophy*, an *English Grammar*,
and a *Life of Holcroft*. The first of these was afterwards
abandoned, but the other two were published in 1810 and
1816. Among the events of the year 1809 were the birth
and death of Hazlitt's first child, and a visit by the Lambs
to Winterslow in October. Meanwhile, other literary projects had been formed and given up, and in 1810 Hazlitt
returned for a time to painting in default of literary
success. In 1811, indeed, he went back to live in London,
and again attempted to follow the profession of portrait
painting, but a few months later this was again abandoned
and for the last time. Hazlitt returned to Winterslow,
where, in September, his son William was born. Lamb
wished the child might be like his father, but " with something a better temper and a smoother head of hair," a wish
which gives in a few words an impression of the father's
personality, his rough exterior and his sincere, uncompromising, somewhat touchy mind. In the latter part of
the year he was for a time actually penniless and very
miserable, but was planning a course of lectures on philosophical subjects which were again to set him on his feet.

These lectures were delivered in the first four months
of 1812, and it may be gathered from the entries in the
diary of his friend Crabb Robinson, that after a poor
start they gave considerable satisfaction to his audience.
Towards the end of the same year, through the intervention of Lamb, he obtained a position as reporter for
the *Morning Chronicle*, and for twelve months worked in
the gallery of the House of Commons for a salary of four
guineas a week—earning for the first time a steady, if
modest, income.

Having served his apprenticeship in the reporters'
gallery, Hazlitt entered in 1813, at the age of thirty-five,
upon the true work of his life, that of essayist, journalist,
and critic. As a dramatic critic he rapidly came to have
considerable influence upon contemporary opinion of the
theatre, and five years later he published his collected
criticisms in the *View of the English Stage*, the pages of
which form a comprehensive account of the stage during
the years 1813–1818. In spite of his success and obvious
power as a journalist, Perry, the editor of the *Morning
Chronicle*, found him uncongenial, and they parted company towards the end of 1814, Hazlitt regarding himself
as slighted and affronted by Perry's behaviour. He had,
however, now established his position as a journalist, and
he had no difficulty henceforth in finding editors who
would accept almost anything that he wrote. In 1812
he had met Leigh Hunt at Lamb's house, and Hunt's
Examiner was one of the papers to which he made many
contributions from 1814 to 1817, and at longer intervals,
until 1828. His criticisms embraced politics, literature,
art, and the stage, and in 1815 Hunt and Hazlitt together
wrote the " Round Table " series of miscellaneous essays,
which by themselves establish Hazlitt's position as one of
the chief essayists of the nineteenth century. He wrote
also for the *Champion* and the *Edinburgh Review*, to which
his first contribution was an important essay on " Standard
Essays and Romances." Meanwhile, Hazlitt had been
hardly hit by an event in world politics—Napoleon's
defeat at Waterloo. Napoleon had been Hazlitt's idol,
and B. R. Haydon, the painter, records that his fall
reduced Hazlitt to a state of prostration and even chronic

intoxication—though Haydon's lurid account must be taken with a grain of salt.

During 1816 and 1817 Hazlitt was busily occupied with his journalistic work. His opinions, always expressed forcibly and fearlessly, involved him in various quarrels with his friends, especially the Lake Poets, and also laid him open to the attacks of the *Quarterly Review*. This was the day of journalistic and literary battles; invective was given and taken, and reputations actually suffered, so that the souring of Hazlitt's temper may perhaps be attributed in some degree to the hostility which his writings so frequently aroused. During the winter of 1816–17 he also wrote his *Characters of Shakespear's Plays*, the first of his books to prove an immediate success with the public.

In 1817 Hazlitt joined the staff of the *Times* as Dramatic Critic for a few months, but according to his own statement was forced to quit this post " by want of health and leisure." Of his lack of health up to this date not much has been recorded, though it is probable that his addiction to strong tea was contributing to the chronic gastric trouble which accentuated his natural irritability and eventually caused his death. His lack of leisure was due in part to the preparation of his *Lectures on the English Poets*, which he began to deliver at the Surrey Institution in January, 1818, and which were published in book form in the same year. During the first half of 1818 he was also contributing to a new periodical, *The Yellow Dwarf*, edited by John Hunt, but this survived only for a few months, and for the rest of the year his work appeared chiefly in Constable's *Edinburgh Magazine*. Recently Shelley and Keats had been added to the circle of his friends, and it is clear, from several remarks, that Keats at any rate was his sincere admirer. Their books bore the imprint of the same publishers, Taylor and Hessey, and advertisements of their writings appeared in each other's books. With these and other friendships and his literary work, Hazlitt's time was full, until in the autumn of 1818 he paid another visit to Winterslow. Meanwhile, the battle of the Quarterlies raged and insult flew, so that eventually Hazlitt was forced to bring an action against *Blackwood's Magazine*, which was settled out of court in Hazlitt's favour.

In November of 1818 he was delivering his second course of lectures on the *English Comic Writers,* which were published as a book in 1819. The lectures were criticised adversely by Crabb Robinson, but Leigh Hunt voiced other contemporary opinion in their favour. Early in 1819 Hazlitt also published his *Letter to William Gifford,* the editor of the *Quarterly Review,* and in this he allowed himself to indulge in much well-spiced invective. In addition, he collected his political writings in a volume of *Political Essays,* and determined thereafter to abstain from further journalism of a political nature. He then prepared his next course of lectures on *The Dramatic Literature of the Age of Elizabeth;* these were delivered in November and December, and published in January, 1820. During the next two years Hazlitt was frequently at Winterslow, engaged in writing essays for John Scott's *London Magazine.* Some of his best essays appeared in this periodical, and were afterwards collected in his two most famous books, the *Table Talk,* published in 1821–22, and the *Plain Speaker,* published in 1826. For a short time, owing to the sudden death of Scott, Hazlitt acted as editor of the *London Magazine,* but he did not remain long in London, returning soon to Winterslow. At the end of the year 1821 he wrote one of his most celebrated essays on " The Fight," having journeyed to Hungerford in Berkshire to see the contest between the prize-fighters Neate and Hickman.

Little has been recorded of Hazlitt's domestic life during these years, but it is at least certain that his marriage had been a failure. Since the end of 1819 he had lived apart from his wife, and in August, 1820, he made his town lodging at 9 Southampton Buildings. Here he met Sarah Walker, the daughter of his landlord, and here was enacted the tragi-comedy of his deep love for this girl, which he exposed so remorselessly in the *Liber Amoris,* published in 1823. He hoped at first to marry Sarah Walker, but for this it was necessary to obtain a divorce from his wife. To this end he journeyed to Scotland, stopping for the month of February, 1822, at Renton Inn, Berwickshire, in order to write a series of essays for Colburn's *New Monthly Magazine.* In March he went to Edinburgh where the divorce proceedings were instituted. After visits to Glasgow and the Highlands he returned to London in May, but was again in Edinburgh at the end of the month, and in June the divorce proceedings were completed. By September it was common knowledge that he had been deceived by Sarah Walker, and the intensity of his sufferings is obvious through all the absurdities of the *Liber Amoris*. For several months he was unable to work, and it was not until November that articles from his pen again appeared in the *London Magazine*.

His next venture was participation with Byron and Leigh Hunt in their abortive periodical, *The Liberal*, and to this he contributed five essays in 1822. In 1823, while still under the shadow of his emotional disaster, he produced his volume of *Characteristics : in the Manner of Rochefoucauld's Maxims*. At the beginning of 1823 he was still reluctant to publish the *Liber Amoris*, but the girl was still burdening his mind, and his biographer suggests that the publication was finally decided upon in order to " burn her out of his thoughts." When this had been done he was again able to go on with his essay-writing; the rest of the year was spent at Winterslow, and here he began the series of character sketches printed in 1825 in *The Spirit of the Age*.

In 1824 Hazlitt returned to London. His friendship with Lamb had been temporarily in abeyance, but it was now renewed and together they compiled the volume of *Select Poets of Great Britain*. Hazlitt also completed his *Sketches of the Principal Picture Galleries in England*.

In April, 1824, he married his second wife, probably in Edinburgh, and while in Scotland met William Bewick who made a chalk drawing of his head and shoulders. Information concerning the second Mrs. Hazlitt is very scanty, but it is stated that they first met in a stage coach, that she was the widow of a barrister, and was " worth £300 a year." Hazlitt's financial situation was therefore greatly eased by this alliance, and it made possible a prolonged stay abroad. In September, 1824, they went to Paris where they spent three months, Hazlitt visiting the Louvre and writing several essays. In January, 1825, they proceeded to Italy, and Hazlitt described his journey in his

Notes of a Journey through France and Italy, published in
the same year. Some weeks were spent in Switzerland, and
they finally returned to England in October, 1825.

In 1826 Hazlitt was completing the two volumes of
collected essays published in May of that year, entitled
The Plain Speaker. He was also visiting Northcote and
" writing up " their conversations; these appeared as
articles in various periodicals during this year, and afterwards they were gathered together for publication in the
volume of *Conversations of Northcote* in 1830, shortly
before his death. Towards the end of 1826 Hazlitt went
again to France in connexion with his last and most
ambitious project, the *Life of Napoleon,* wishing to gather
his material as far as possible first-hand, and probably the
greater part of the first two volumes of this work was
actually written in Paris. During this period he also wrote
many essays for the London periodicals. In the autumn of
1827 he returned to London with his son. The second
Mrs. Hazlitt remained in France, and she and her husband
never met again. The parting seems not to have been
expected by Hazlitt and to have been occasioned (according to Crabb Robinson) by the " ill-conduct of the boy,"
who was the champion of his mother, the first Mrs.
Hazlitt, and did not disguise from his stepmother the
indignation which he felt.

After returning to England Hazlitt soon turned for his
usual solace to Winterslow, and here he wrote essays and
prepared the first two volumes of the *Life of Napoleon* for
the press, which were published in January, 1828. For a
brief period after this Hazlitt returned to London and re-
resumed his work as dramatic critic for the *Examiner.*
During the summer he was again in Paris, working for the
second half of the *Life of Napoleon,* and in the autumn he
returned to Winterslow.

In 1828 Hazlitt had written and published his " Farewell
to Essay Writing," but it was still necessary to earn an
income, and so perforce he had again to turn his hand to
journalism. He accordingly wrote many further essays and
continued to record his conversations with Northcote,
most of the writings appearing in the *Atlas.* The necessity
for this return to journalism became the greater owing to

the bankruptcy of the publisher of the first two volumes of the *Life of Napoleon* before the author had been paid. The two final volumes were then taken over by another house, and were published in 1830.

Meanwhile Hazlitt was finding his chief recreation in the theatre, in spite of the fact that he was becoming increasingly ill. For many years he had suffered from gastric trouble, and he now developed cancer of the stomach, which rapidly sapped his strength. He died on September 18, 1830, aged 52, his last words, as reported by his son, being, "Well, I have had a happy life." On the 23rd he was buried at St. Anne's, Soho.

T H E foregoing sketch of the main facts[1] of Hazlitt's life is intended to be but a plain statement, a background against which the Hazlitt, who reveals himself in the following selection from his writings, may stand out as a living figure. He was often at his best when being deliberately auto-biographical, or when using his own experiences to illustrate his subject, and the present selection has been made with an eye to this element in his work. Apart from his use of autobiography, his personal crotchets stick out like the quills of a porcupine from nearly every article, essay, or lecture that he wrote. He never ceased to be aware of himself, no matter of what subject he might be treating. It is clear from the written opinions of his contemporaries that he was universally regarded as "difficult." Scarcely any of his friendships remained unclouded for long periods —even Lamb suffered several eclipses—for none could brook the uncompromising directness with which Hazlitt looked upon life and upon the shortcomings of his friends. "He blowed us up," as poor Lamb said in 1814, his offence on that occasion being "political indifference"! It is easy for us to realize at this distance of time that Hazlitt's ruling passion was the search for truth and that no personal relationships were ever allowed to stand in its way. It was difficult for his friends to regard this quite so dispassionately as we can, though they loved him for his sensitiveness, generosity, and honesty of purpose. Further

---

[1] Taken from *The Life of William Hazlitt*, by P. P. Howe, London, Secker, 1928.

than this, it seems clear that Hazlitt added to his directness and fearlessness a certain irritability of temperament,
which was constantly accentuated by the events of his life
and by his personal habits. At the outset of his career
he experienced successive disappointments. Hard work
seemed always to result only in failure, and he was writer,
painter, and again writer, painter, before deciding finally
to be writer. Afterwards he was relatively successful in
this course, and came to have considerable influence with
his pen; but at many points in his career he was subjected to ferocious and sometimes inexplicable personal
attacks, all of which tended to embitter his mind and to
assist in the acidulation of his writings. To this was added
the constant drinking of a great deal of strong tea; this by
its natural properties could only increase his inherent
irritability and doubtless started the chronic indigestion
which was in itself a source of irritation. All these things
aroused in him a spirit of resentfulness which is constantly
showing itself in his work, though for the reader it adds a
pleasant spice rather than any sort of discomfort.

This quality, added to his sincerity and idealism, gives
Hazlitt's writings an unusual taste—a tang which prevents
them from being more than very occasionally dull. Every
essay is a human document and conveys its message
almost directly, as it seems, from Hazlitt's mouth to the
reader's ear, the impression being strengthened by the
conversational quality of his writing. He is constantly
thinking aloud, and his manner of thinking is racy, vigorous, virile. Of digressions there are many, but they add
point to rather than blunt the effect of the main thesis, and
no one can regret them. His style, being conversational, is
never forced. He is carried away on the current of his
thoughts, and never has recourse to any laboured originality which would indeed be foreign to the fearless sincerity
of his mind.

Widely as he was read during his lifetime, his reputation
suffered some dimming during succeeding decades, but he
has never been totally neglected. His writing appeals to
no special coterie or period, but is of permanent value
to mankind in general. He possessed the secret of being
able to be interesting though " ordinary," for the vigour

of his intellect needed no special qualities of style, no conscious artistry, to assist in the conveying of its message. This quality of permanence in Hazlitt's writings has greatly enhanced his influence since his death, and it is probable that " opinion " at the present time on art and literature is more affected by him than can be easily realized or assessed. His persistent championship of Keats in the face of contemporary criticism is an example of the sureness of his judgment, and, except for his remarkable lapse in placing Macpherson's Ossian alongside Shakespear and Milton, it is difficult to find serious mistakes even by the standard of a hundred years later.

To Hazlitt, therefore, the man-in-the-street may turn to-day for intellectual enjoyment and enlightenment; in his analysis of the personalities and events of a hundred years ago, in his confessions of his own prejudices and predilections, he has condensed the experiences of succeeding generations. He is not " out-of-date," and does not become stale.

A NUMBER of smaller selections from Hazlitt's essays have been published in recent years, and a few of his best essays have been printed many times in these; but not since the publication of Alexander Ireland's selection in 1889 has the attempt been made to cover so large a field as in the present volume. The range of Hazlitt's intellectual attainments was so wide that it would not be possible to do it justice in a volume of smaller compass, and even here it has been necessary to refrain from including many pieces which would have added to its value. As will be evident from the facts of Hazlitt's life, it is necessary to present him, if possible, as student of human nature, speculative philosopher, painter, politician, dramatic critic, historian, literary critic, and journalist. The sections into which the selection is roughly divided do not form water-tight compartments. Hazlitt in his writings was first and foremost a student of human nature, but his eager pursuit of every hare that showed itself frequently led him into digressions upon special subjects, and similarly his more specialised essays were constantly breaking light upon questions of general conduct. As a consequence of this, the first section on " Life in General " is by far the largest, and reflects from most of the many facets which his intellect exhibited. It includes essays from all the more important general collections, extracts from his book of aphorisms, *Characteristics*, from the *Liber Amoris*, from his travel book, and from his chief historical work, the *Life of Napoleon*. The section on " Writers and Writing " exhibits him as lecturer and literary critic, with extracts from his books on the *English Poets*, the *English Comic Writers*, and the *Dramatic Literature of the Age of Elizabeth*. It also includes some of his most celebrated essays, particularly that on his early impressions of the Lake Poets, and his discussion with Lamb and others on " persons one would wish to have seen."

In connexion with the third section on " Painters and Painting," I have deliberately referred above to Hazlitt as a painter instead of as an art-critic. He wrote on art as a painter, with all the warmth and vision of the artist, rather than from the academic standpoint of the critic. That he really was a painter, his portrait of Lamb is almost sufficient proof by itself, and it suggests that he has never quite received his due as a creator in that branch of art. Unfortunately, so few of his paintings are extant, that this impression cannot be verified. His descriptions of separate galleries are perhaps of less general interest at the present time, and so his *Picture Galleries in England* is represented only by " The Dulwich Gallery," chosen partly for its pleasant opening passages and partly because the contents of this gallery still remain almost the same as when he saw it.

In the fourth section, " On Actors and Acting," the selection is necessarily very brief. Dramatic criticisms are of interest at the moment when they are written and afterwards to students of dramatic history. To the general reader they have little appeal.

In the fifth section on " Characters," Hazlitt is presented as the student of human nature in detail, the careful dissector of individuals and types. As politician and historian he is represented in the first section by the essay on " The Spirit of Monarchy," and the extracts from *The Life of Napoleon*. As metaphysician he is represented scarcely at all. There were too many other good things crying out to be included to permit of the inclusion of anything from such a work as the *Essay on the Principles of Human Action*.

For the omission of some celebrated essays, such as " The Indian Jugglers " and " Merrie England," I make no apology. I have everywhere followed my own preferences, in some instances fortified by the valued advice of Mr. P. P. Howe and Mr. Richard Jennings.

The text of this selection has been taken as far as possible from sources authorized by Hazlitt himself, that is to say, from the final edition of the books published in his life-time. Some essays, however, which had not been collected by him, have been taken from volumes published after his death by his son. In one case (" Of Persons one would wish to have seen ") reference has also been made to the magazine in which the essay was first printed, as the names of the characters taking part in the conversation were supplied by the younger Hazlitt in the *Literary Remains* and were not always correctly given. Throughout the book the system has been to put within square brackets anything not appearing in Hazlitt's original text. The references which accompany the headings to the essays are to their first appearances, in periodicals or elsewhere, in order to fix as nearly as possible the dates when they were composed. The volumes of collected essays naturally contained many which had first been published several years earlier, so that references to these volumes would be misleading, though they will be found recorded in the Contents list.

Some editors have found a difficulty in Hazlitt's use of quotations in that he so frequently mis-quoted. In the present selection I have usually made no attempt to improve upon his version. Like many other prolific writers he took his quotations in his stride, often depending solely on his memory, and when they have taken their place so naturally in their context I am content to leave them as they are. In one instance only I have departed from this. In the essay, " Of Persons one would wish to have seen," there is a long quotation from Donne (p. 526), and reference is made in the context to the value of the old spelling; here, therefore, I have reproduced the original text of 1633.

The small number of footnotes other than those added by the author himself are indicated by the initials W. H., jun., W. C. H., or Ed., according to whether they were supplied by Hazlitt's son or grandson, or the present editor. A more fully annotated and more critical text will be found in Mr. P. P. Howe's revised issue of Waller and Glover's *Complete Works*.

Although I have taken the text from the original sources with which it has been carefully compared, I have not felt it necessary to be absolutely consistent in following the original spelling and punctuation. Both have been for the most part reproduced, but as these details probably represent the printer's whim as much as the author's, I have occasionally allowed myself to alter them. I have, in fact, endeavoured to make the text accurate in all important particulars, and to retain as much of its original typographical flavour as seemed judicious. Mr. P. P. Howe has kindly looked over the proof sheets, but if any errors remain, the responsibility for them rests on no one's shoulders but my own.

GEOFFREY KEYNES

Sept., 1930.

ON LIFE

IN GENERAL

ON THE LOVE OF THE COUNTRY

(THE EXAMINER, NOV. 27, 1814)

To the Editor of the Round Table

SIR,

I do not know that any one has ever explained satisfactorily the true source of our attachment to natural objects, or of that soothing emotion which the sight of the country hardly ever fails to infuse into the mind. Some persons have ascribed this feeling to the natural beauty of the objects themselves, others to the freedom from care, the silence and tranquillity which scenes of retirement afford—others to the healthy and innocent employments of a country life—others to the simplicity of country manners—and others to different causes ; but none to the right one. All these causes may, I believe, have a share in producing this feeling; but there is another more general principle, which has been left untouched, and which I shall here explain, endeavouring to be as little sentimental as the subject will admit.

Rousseau, in his *Confessions*, (the most valuable of all his works,) relates, that when he took possession of his room at Annecy, at the house of his beloved mistress and friend, he found that he could see " a little spot of green " from his window, which endeared his situation the more to him, because, he says, it was the first time he had had this object constantly before him since he left Boissy, the place where he was at school when a child[1]. Some such feeling as that here described will be found lurking at the bottom of all our attachments of this sort. Were it not for the recollections habitually associated with them, natural objects could not interest the mind in the manner

---

[1] Pope also declares that he had a particular regard for an old post which stood in the court-yard before the house where he was brought up.

they do. No doubt, the sky is beautiful; the clouds sail majestically along its bosom; the sun is cheering; there is something exquisitely graceful in the manner in which a plant or tree puts forth its branches; the motion with which they bend and tremble in the evening breeze is soft and lovely; there is music in the babbling of a brook; the view from the top of a mountain is full of grandeur; nor can we behold the ocean with indifference. Or, as the Minstrel sweetly sings—

> " Oh how can'st thou renounce the boundless store
> Of charms which Nature to her votary yields !
> The warbling woodland, the resounding shore,
> The pomp of groves, and garniture of fields ;
> All that the genial ray of morning gilds,
> And all that echoes to the song of even,
> All that the mountain's sheltering bosom shields,
> And all the dread magnificence of heaven,
> Oh how can'st thou renounce, and hope to be
>   forgiven ! "

It is not, however, the beautiful and magnificent alone that we admire in Nature; the most insignificant and rudest objects are often found connected with the strongest emotions; we become attached to the most common and familiar images as to the face of a friend whom we have long known, and from whom we have received many benefits. It is because natural objects have been associated with the sports of our childhood, with air and exercise, with our feelings in solitude, when the mind takes the strongest hold of things, and clings with the fondest interest to whatever strikes its attention; with change of place, the pursuit of new scenes, and thoughts of distant friends; it is because they have surrounded us in almost all situations, in joy and in sorrow, in pleasure and in pain; because they have been one chief source and nourishment of our feelings, and a part of our being, that we love them as we do ourselves.

There is, generally speaking, the same foundation for our love of Nature as for all our habitual attachments, namely, association of ideas. But this is not all. That which distinguishes this attachment from others is the transferable nature of our feelings with respect to physical objects; the associations connected with any one object extending to the whole class. My having been attached to any particular person does not make me feel the same attachment to the next person I may chance to meet; but, if I have .once associated strong feelings of delight with the objects of natural scenery, the tie becomes indissoluble, and I shall ever after feel the same attachment to other objects of the same sort. I remember when I was abroad, the trees, and grass, and wet leaves, rustling in the walks of the Thuilleries, seemed to be as much English, to be as much the same trees and grass, that I had always been used to, as the sun shining over my head was the same sun which I saw in England; the faces only were foreign to me. Whence comes this difference? It arises from our always imperceptibly connecting the idea of the individual with man, and only the idea of the class with natural objects. In the one case, the external appearance or physical structure is the least thing to be attended to; in the other, it is every thing. The springs that move the human form, and make it friendly or adverse to me, lie hid within it. There is an infinity of motives, passions, and ideas, contained in that narrow compass, of which I know nothing, and in which I have no share. Each individual is a world to himself, governed by a thousand contradictory and wayward impulses. I can, therefore, make no inference from one individual to another; nor can my habitual sentiments, with respect to any individual, extend beyond himself to others. But it is otherwise with respect to Nature. There is neither hypocrisy, caprice, nor mental reservation in her favours. Our intercourse with her is not liable to accident or change, interruption or disappointment. She smiles on us still the same. Thus, to give an obvious instance, if I have once enjoyed the cool shade of a tree, and been lulled into a deep repose by the sound of a brook running at its feet, I am sure that wherever I can find a tree and a brook, I can enjoy the same pleasure again. Hence, when I imagine these objects, I can easily form a mystic personification of the friendly power that inhabits them, Dryad or Naiad, offering its cool fountain or its tempting shade. Hence the origin of the Grecian mythology. All objects of the same kind being the same, not only in their appearance, but in their practical uses, we habitually confound them together under the same general idea; and, whatever fondness we may have conceived for one, is immediately placed to the common account. The most opposite kinds and remote trains of feeling gradually go to enrich the same sentiment; and in our love of Nature, there is all the force of individual attachment, combined with the most airy abstraction. It is this circumstance which gives that refinement, expansion, and wild interest to feelings of this sort, when strongly excited, which every one must have experienced who is a true lover of Nature. The sight of the setting sun does not affect me so much from the beauty of the object itself, from the glory kindled through the glowing skies, the rich broken columns of light, or the dying streaks of day, as that it indistinctly recalls to me numberless thoughts and feelings with which, through many a year and season, I have watched his bright descent in the warm summer evenings, or beheld him struggling to cast a " farewel sweet " through the thick clouds of winter. I love to see the trees first covered with leaves in the spring, the primroses peeping out from some sheltered bank, and the innocent lambs running races on the soft green turf; because, at that birth-time of Nature, I have always felt sweet hopes and happy wishes—which have not been fulfilled! The dry reeds rustling on the side of a stream,—the woods swept by the loud blast,—the dark massy foliage of autumn,—the grey trunks and naked branches of the trees in winter,—the sequestered copse and wide extended heath,—the warm sunny showers, and December snows,—have all charms for me; there is no object, however trifling or rude, that has not, in some mood or other, found the way to my heart; and I might say, in the words of the poet,

> " To me the meanest flower that blows can give
> Thoughts that do often lie too deep for tears."

Thus Nature is a kind of universal home, and every object it presents to us an old acquaintance with unaltered looks.

> ——" Nature did ne'er betray
> The heart that lov'd her, but through all the years
> Of this our life, it is her privilege
> To lead from joy to joy."

For there is that consent and mutual harmony among all her works, one undivided spirit pervading them throughout, that, if we have once knit ourselves in hearty fellowship to any of them, they will never afterwards appear as strangers to us, but, which ever way we turn, we shall find a secret power to have gone out before us, moulding them into such shapes as fancy loves, informing them with life and sympathy, bidding them put on their festive looks and gayest attire at our approach, and to pour all their sweets and choicest treasures at our feet. For him, then, who has well acquainted himself with Nature's works, she wears always one face, and speaks the same well-known language, striking on the heart, amidst unquiet thoughts and the tumult of the world, like the music of one's native tongue heard in some far-off country.

We do not connect the same feelings with the works

of art as with those of Nature, because we refer them to man, and associate with them the separate interests and passions which we know belong to those who are the authors or possessors of them. Nevertheless, there are some such objects, as a cottage, or a village church, which excite in us the same sensations as the sight of Nature, and which are, indeed, almost always included in descriptions of natural scenery.

> " Or from the mountain's sides
> View wilds and swelling floods,
> And hamlets brown, and dim-discover'd spires,
> And hear their simple bell."

Which is in part, no doubt, because they are surrounded with natural objects, and, in a populous country, inseparable from them; and also because the human interest they excite relates to manners and feelings which are simple, common, such as all can enter into, and which, therefore, always produce a pleasing effect upon the mind.

ON THE LOVE OF LIFE

(THE EXAMINER, JAN. 15, 1815)

IT is our intention, in the course of these papers, occasionally to expose certain vulgar errors, which have crept into our reasonings on men and manners. Perhaps one of the most interesting of these, is that which relates to the source of our general attachment to life. We are not going to enter into the question, whether life is, on the whole, to be regarded as a blessing, though we are by no means inclined to adopt the opinion of that sage, who thought " that the best thing that could have happened to a man was never to have been born, and the next best to have died the moment after he came into existence."

The common argument, however, which is made use of
to prove the value of life, from the strong desire which
almost every one feels for its continuance, appears to be
altogether inconclusive. The wise and the foolish, the
weak and the strong, the lame and the blind, the prisoner
and the free, the prosperous and the wretched, the
beggar and the king, the rich and the poor, the young
and the old, from the little child who tries to leap over
his own shadow, to the old man who stumbles blindfold
on his grave, all feel this desire in common. Our notions
with respect to the importance of life, and our attachment
to it, depend on a principle, which has very little to do
with its happiness or its misery.

The love of life is, in general, the effect not of our
enjoyments, but of our passions. We are not attached to
it so much for its own sake, or as it is connected with
happiness, as because it is necessary to action. Without
life there can be no action—no objects of pursuit—no
restless desires—no tormenting passions. Hence it is
that we fondly cling to it—that we dread its termination
as the close, not of enjoyment, but of hope. The proof
that our attachment to life is not absolutely owing to the
immediate satisfaction we find in it, is, that those persons
are commonly found most loath to part with it who have
the least enjoyment of it, and who have the greatest
difficulties to struggle with, as losing gamesters are the
most desperate. And farther, there are not many persons
who, with all their pretended love of life, would not, if it
had been in their power, have melted down the longest
life to a few hours. "The school-boy," says Addison,
" counts the time till the return of the holidays; the minor
longs to be of age; the lover is impatient till he is
married."—"Hope and fantastic expectations spend
much of our lives; and while with passion we look for a
coronation, or the death of an enemy, or a day of joy,
passing from fancy to possession without any intermediate

B

notices, we throw away a precious year." JEREMY TAYLOR.
—We would willingly, and without remorse, sacrifice
not only the present moment, but all the interval (no
matter how long) that separates us from any favourite
object. We chiefly look upon life, then, as the means to
an end. Its common enjoyments and its daily evils are
alike disregarded for any idle purpose we have in view.
It should seem as if there were a few green sunny spots
in the desert of life, to which we are always hastening
forward: we eye them wistfully in the distance, and care
not what perils or suffering we endure, so that we arrive
at them at last. However weary we may be of the same
stale round—however sick of the past—however hopeless
of the future—the mind still revolts at the thought of
death, because the fancied possibility of good, which
always remains with life, gathers strength as it is about
to be torn from us for ever, and the dullest scene looks
bright compared with the darkness of the grave. Our
reluctance to part with existence evidently does not
depend on the calm and even current of our lives, but on
the force and impulse of the passions. Hence that
indifference to death which has been sometimes remarked
in people who lead a solitary and peaceful life in remote
and barren districts. The pulse of life in them does not
beat strong enough to occasion any violent revulsion of
the frame when it ceases. He who treads the green
mountain turf, or he who sleeps beneath it, enjoys an
almost equal quiet. The death of those persons has
always been accounted happy, who had attained their
utmost wishes, who had nothing left to regret or to desire.
Our repugnance to death increases in proportion to our consciousness of having lived in vain—to the violence of our
efforts, and the keenness of our disappointments—and to
our earnest desire to find in the future, if possible, a rich
amends for the past. We may be said to nurse our
existence with the greatest tenderness, according to the

pain it has cost us; and feel at every step of our varying progress the truth of that line of the poet—

"An ounce of sweet is worth a pound of sour."

The love of life is in fact the sum of all our passions and of all our enjoyments; but these are by no means the same thing, for the vehemence of our passions is irritated, not less by disappointment than by the prospect of success. Nothing seems to be a match for this general tenaciousness of existence, but such an extremity either of bodily or mental suffering as destroys at once the power both of habit and imagination. In short, the question, whether life is accompanied with a greater quantity of pleasure or pain, may be fairly set aside as frivolous, and of no practical utility; for our attachment to life depends on our interest in it; and it cannot be denied that we have more interest in this moving, busy scene, agitated with a thousand hopes and fears, and checkered with every diversity of joy and sorrow, than in a dreary blank. To be something is better than to be nothing, because we can feel no interest in *nothing*. Passion, imagination, self-will, the sense of power, the very consciousness of our existence, bind us to life, and hold us fast in its chains, as by a magic spell, in spite of every other consideration. Nothing can be more philosophical than the reasoning which Milton puts into the mouth of the fallen angel:

> ——" And that must end us, that must be our cure,
> To be no more ; sad cure : for who would lose,
> Though full of pain, this intellectual being,
> Those thoughts that wander through eternity,
> To perish rather, swallow'd up and lost
> In the wide womb of uncreated night,
> Devoid of sense and motion ? "

Nearly the same account may be given in answer to the question which has been asked, *Why so few tyrants kill themselves?* In the first place, they are never satisfied with the mischief they have done, and cannot quit their hold of power, after all sense of pleasure is fled. Besides, they absurdly argue from the means of happiness placed within their reach to the end itself; and, dazzled by the pomp and pageantry of a throne, cannot relinquish the persuasion that they *ought* to be happier than other men. The prejudice of opinion, which attaches us to life, is in them stronger than in others, and incorrigible to experience. The Great are life's fools—dupes of the splendid shadows that surround them, and wedded to the very mockeries of opinion.

Whatever is our situation or pursuit in life, the result will be much the same. The strength of the passion seldom corresponds to the pleasure we find in its indulgence. The miser " robs himself to increase his store "; the ambitious man toils up a slippery precipice only to be tumbled headlong from its height; the lover is infatuated with the charms of his mistress, exactly in proportion to the mortifications he has received from her. Even those who succeed in nothing, who, as it has been emphatically expressed—

> ——" Are made desperate by too quick a sense
> Of constant infelicity ; cut off
> From peace like exiles, on some barren rock,
> Their life's sad prison, with no more of ease,
> Than sentinels between two armies set ; "

are yet as unwilling as others to give over the unprofitable strife : their harassed feverish existence refuses rest, and frets the languor of exhausted hope into the torture of unavailing regret. The exile, who has been unexpectedly restored to his country and to liberty, often finds his courage fail with the accomplishment of all his wishes, and the struggle of life and hope ceases at the same instant.

We once more repeat, that we do not, in the foregoing

remarks, mean to enter into a comparative estimate of the value of human life, but merely to shew, that the strength of our attachment to it is a very fallacious test of its happiness.

ON THE IGNORANCE OF THE LEARNED

(EDINBURH MAGAZINE, JULY, 1818)

" For the more languages a man can speak,
   His talent has but sprung the greater leak:
   And, for the industry he has spent upon't,
   Must full as much some other way discount.
   The Hebrew, Chaldee, and the Syriac,
   Do, like their letters, set men's reason back,
   And turn their wits that strive to understand it
   (Like those that write the characters) left-handed.
   Yet he that is but able to express
   No sense at all in several languages,
   Will pass for learneder than he that's known
   To speak the strongest reason in his own."
                                               BUTLER.

THE description of persons who have the fewest ideas of all others are mere authors and readers. It is better to be able neither to read nor write than to be able to do nothing else. A lounger who is ordinarily seen with a book in his hand is (we may be almost sure) equally without the power or inclination to attend either to what passes around him or in his own mind. Such a one may be said to carry his understanding about with him in his pocket, or to leave it at home on his library shelves. He is afraid of venturing on any train of reasoning, or of striking out any observation that is not mechanically suggested to him by passing his eyes over certain legible characters;

shrinks from the fatigue of thought, which, for want of practice, becomes insupportable to him; and sits down contented with an endless, wearisome succession of words and half-formed images, which fill the void of the mind, and continually efface one another. Learning is, in too many cases, but a foil to common sense; a substitute for true knowledge. Books are less often made use of as " spectacles " to look at nature with, than as blinds to keep out its strong light and shifting scenery from weak eyes and indolent dispositions. The book-worm wraps himself up in his web of verbal generalities, and sees only the glimmering shadows of things reflected from the minds of others. Nature *puts him out*. The impressions of real objects, stripped of the disguises of words and voluminous roundabout descriptions, are blows that stagger him; their variety distracts, their rapidity exhausts him; and he turns from the bustle, the noise, and glare, and whirling motion of the world about him (which he has not an eye to follow in its fantastic changes, nor an understanding to reduce to fixed principles), to the quiet monotony of the dead languages, and the less startling and more intelligible combinations of the letters of the alphabet. It is well, it is perfectly well. " Leave me to my repose," is the motto of the sleeping and the dead. You might as well ask the paralytic to leap from his chair and throw away his crutch, or, without a miracle, to " take up his bed and walk," as expect the learned reader to throw down his book and think for himself. He clings to it for his intellectual support; and his dread of being left to himself is like the horror of a vacuum. He can only breathe a learned atmosphere, as other men breathe common air. He is a borrower of sense. He has no ideas of his own, and must live on those of other people. The habit of supplying our ideas from foreign sources " enfeebles all internal strength of thought," as a course of dram-drinking destroys the tone of the stomach.

The faculties of the mind, when not exerted, or when cramped by custom and authority, become listless, torpid, and unfit for the purposes of thought or action. Can we wonder at the languor and lassitude which is thus produced by a life of learned sloth and ignorance; by poring over lines and syllables that excite little more idea or interest than if they were the characters of an unknown tongue, till the eye closes on vacancy, and the book drops from the feeble hand! I would rather be a wood-cutter, or the meanest hind, that all day " sweats in the eye of Phœbus, and at night sleeps in Elysium," than wear out my life so, 'twixt dreaming and awake. The learned author differs from the learned student in this, that the one transcribes what the other reads. The learned are mere literary drudges. If you set them upon original composition, their heads turn, they don't know where they are. The indefatigable readers of books are like the everlasting copiers of pictures, who, when they attempt to do anything of their own, find they want an eye quick enough, a hand steady enough, and colours bright enough, to trace the living forms of nature.

Any one who has passed through the regular grada-tions of a classical education, and is not made a fool by it, may consider himself as having had a very narrow escape. It is an old remark, that boys who shine at school do not make the greatest figure when they grow up and come out into the world. The things, in fact, which a boy is set to learn at school, and on which his success depends, are things which do not require the exercise either of the highest or the most useful faculties of the mind. Memory (and that of the lowest kind) is the chief faculty called into play in conning over and repeating lessons by rote in grammar, in languages, in geography, arithmetic, etc., so that he who has the most of this technical memory, with the least turn for other things, which have a stronger and more

natural claim upon his childish attention, will make
the most forward school-boy. The jargon containing
the definitions of the parts of speech, the rules for
casting up an account, or the inflections of a Greek
verb, can have no attraction to the tyro of ten years
old, except as they are imposed as a task upon him by
others, or from his feeling the want of sufficient relish
or amusement in other things. A lad with a sickly
constitution and no very active mind, who can just
retain what is pointed out to him, and has neither
sagacity to distinguish nor spirit to enjoy for himself,
will generally be at the head of his form. An idler at
school, on the other hand, is one who has high health
and spirits, who has the free use of his limbs, with all
his wits about him, who feels the circulation of his blood
and the motion of his heart, who is ready to laugh and
cry in a breath, and who had rather chase a ball or a
butterfly, feel the open air in his face, look at the fields
or the sky, follow a winding path, or enter with eagerness
into all the little conflicts and interests of his acquaintances and friends, than doze over a musty spelling-book,
repeat barbarous distichs after his master, sit so many
hours pinioned to a writing-desk, and receive his reward
for the loss of time and pleasure in paltry prize-medals
at Christmas and Midsummer. There is indeed a degree
of stupidity which prevents children from learning the
usual lessons, or ever arriving at these puny academic
honours. But what passes for stupidity is much oftener
a want of interest, of a sufficient motive to fix the attention and force a reluctant application to the dry and unmeaning pursuits of school-learning. The best capacities
are as much above this drudgery as the dullest are beneath
it. Our men of the greatest genius have not been most
distinguished for their acquirements at school or at the
university.

" Th' enthusiast Fancy was a truant ever. "

Gray and Collins were among the instances of this way-ward disposition. Such persons do not think so highly of the advantages, nor can they submit their imaginations so servilely to the trammels of strict scholastic discipline. There is a certain kind and degree of intellect in which words take root, but into which things have not power to penetrate. A mediocrity of talent, with a certain slenderness of moral constitution, is the soil that produces the most brilliant specimens of successful prize-essayists and Greek epigrammatists. It should not be forgotten that the least respectable character among modern politicians was the cleverest boy at Eton.

Learning is the knowledge of that which is not generally known to others, and which we can only derive at second-hand from books or other artificial sources. The knowledge of that which is before us, or about us, which appeals to our experience, passions, and pursuits, to the bosoms and businesses of men, is not learning. Learning is the knowledge of that which none but the learned know. He is the most learned man who knows the most of what is farthest removed from common life and actual observation, that is of the least practical utility, and least liable to be brought to the test of experience, and that, having been handed down through the greatest number of intermediate stages, is the most full of uncertainty, difficulties, and contradictions. It is seeing with the eyes of others, hearing with their ears, and pinning our faith on their understandings. The learned man prides himself in the knowledge of names and dates, not of men or things. He thinks and cares nothing about his next-door neighbours, but he is deeply read in the tribes and castes of the Hindoos and Calmuc Tartars. He can hardly find his way into the next street, though he is acquainted with the exact dimensions of Constantinople and Pekin. He does not know whether his oldest acquaintance is a knave or a fool,

B *

but he can pronounce a pompous lecture on all the principal characters in history. He cannot tell whether an object is black or white, round or square, and yet he is a professed master of the laws of optics and the rules of perspective. He knows as much of what he talks about as a blind man does of colours. He cannot give a satisfactory answer to the plainest question, nor is he ever in the right in any one of his opinions upon any one matter of fact that really comes before him, and yet he gives himself out for an infallible judge on all those points, of which it is impossible that he or any other person living should know anything but by conjecture. He is expert in all the dead and in most of the living languages; but he can neither speak his own fluently, nor write it correctly. A person of this class, the second Greek scholar of his day, undertook to point out several solecisms in Milton's Latin style; and in his own performance there is hardly a sentence of common English. Such was Dr. ——. Such is Dr. ——. Such was not Porson. He was an exception that confirmed the general rule,—a man that, by uniting talents and knowledge with learning, made the distinction between them more striking and palpable.

A mere scholar, who knows nothing but books, must be ignorant even of them. "Books do not teach the use of books." How should he know anything of a work who knows nothing of the subject of it? The learned pedant is conversant with books only as they are made of other books, and those again of others, without end. He parrots those who have parroted others. He can translate the same word into ten different languages, but he knows nothing of the *thing* which it means in any one of them. He stuffs his head with authorities built on authorities, with quotations quoted from quotations, while he locks up his senses, his understanding, and his heart. He is unacquainted with

the maxims and manners of the world; he is to seek
in the characters of individuals. He sees no beauty
in the face of nature or of art. To him " the mighty
world of eye and ear " is hid; and " knowledge," except at
one entrance, " quite shut out." His pride takes part
with his ignorance; and his self-importance rises with
the number of things of which he does not know the
value, and which he therefore despises as unworthy of
his notice. He knows nothing of pictures,—" of the
colouring of Titian, the grace of Raphael, the purity of
Domenichino, the *corregioscity* of Correggio, the learning of Poussin, the airs of Guido, the taste of the Caracci,
or the grand contour of Michael Angelo,"—of all those
glories of the Italian and miracles of the Flemish school,
which have filled the eyes of mankind with delight, and
to the study and imitation of which thousands have in
vain devoted their lives. These are to him as if they
had never been, a mere dead letter, a by-word; and
no wonder, for he neither sees nor understands their
prototypes in nature. A print of Rubens' Watering-
place, or Claude's Enchanted Castle, may be hanging
on the walls of his room for months without his once
perceiving them; and if you point them out to him he
will turn away from them. The language of nature,
or of art (which is another nature), is one that he does
not understand. He repeats indeed the names of
Apelles and Phidias, because they are to be found in
classic authors, and boasts of their works as prodigies,
because they no longer exist; or when he sees the finest
remains of Grecian art actually before him in the Elgin
Marbles, takes no other interest in them than as they
lead to a learned dispute, and (which is the same thing)
a quarrel about the meaning of a Greek particle. He
is equally ignorant of music; he " knows no touch of
it," from the strains of the all-accomplished Mozart to
the shepherd's pipe upon the mountain. His ears are

nailed to his books; and deadened with the sound of
the Greek and Latin tongues, and the din and smithery
of school-learning. Does he know anything more of
poetry? He knows the number of feet in a verse, and
of acts in a play; but of the soul or spirit he knows
nothing. He can turn a Greek ode into English, or a
Latin epigram into Greek verse; but whether either is
worth the trouble he leaves to the critics. Does he
understand " the act and practique part of life " better
than " the theorique "? No. He knows no liberal or
mechanic art, no trade or occupation, no game of skill
or chance. Learning " has no skill in surgery," in
agriculture, in building, in working in wood or in iron;
it cannot make any instrument of labour, or use it when
made; it cannot handle the plough or the spade, or the
chisel or the hammer; it knows nothing of hunting or
hawking, fishing or shooting, of horses or dogs, of
fencing or dancing, or cudgel-playing, or bowls, or
cards, or tennis, or anything else. The learned professor of all arts and sciences cannot reduce any one
of them to practice, though he may contribute an
account of them to an Encyclopedia. He has not the
use of his hands or of his feet; he can neither run,
nor walk, nor swim; and he considers all those who
actually understand and can exercise any of these arts
of body or mind as vulgar and mechanical men,—
though to know almost any one of them in perfection
requires long time and practice, with powers originally
fitted, and a turn of mind particularly devoted to them.
It does not require more than this to enable the learned
candidate to arrive, by painful study, at a doctor's degree
and a fellowship, and to eat, drink, and sleep the rest
of his life!

The thing is plain. All that men really understand
is confined to a very small compass; to their daily affairs
and experience; to what they have an opportunity to

know, and motives to study or practise. The rest is
affectation and imposture. The common people have
the use of their limbs; for they live by their labour or
skill. They understand their own business and the
characters of those they have to deal with; for it is
necessary that they should. They have eloquence to
express their passions, and wit at will to express their
contempt and provoke laughter. Their natural use of
speech is not hung up in monumental mockery, in
an obsolete language; nor is there sense of what is
ludicrous, or readiness at finding out allusions to express
it, buried in collections of *Anas*. You will hear more
good things on the outside of a stage-coach from London
to Oxford than if you were to pass a twelvemonth with
the undergraduates, or heads of colleges, of that famous
university; and more *home* truths are to be learnt from
listening to a noisy debate in an alehouse than from
attending to a formal one in the House of Commons.
An elderly country gentlewoman will often know more
of character, and be able to illustrate it by more amusing anecdotes taken from the history of what has been
said, done, and gossiped in a country town for the last
fifty years, than the best blue-stocking of the age will
be able to glean from that sort of learning which consists
in an acquaintance with all the novels and satirical
poems published in the same period. People in towns,
indeed, are woefully deficient in a knowledge of character,
which they see only *in the bust*, not as a whole-length.
People in the country not only know all that has
happened to a man, but trace his virtues or vices, as
they do his features, in their descent through several
generations, and solve some contradiction in his behaviour by a cross in the breed half a century ago. The
learned know nothing of the matter, either in town or
country. Above all, the mass of society have common
sense, which the learned in all ages want. The vulgar

are in the right when they judge for themselves; they are wrong when they trust to their blind guides. The celebrated nonconformist divine, Baxter, was almost stoned to death by the good women of Kidderminster, for asserting from the pulpit that " hell was paved with infants' skulls "; but, by the force of argument, and of learned quotations from the Fathers, the reverend preacher at length prevailed over the scruples of his congregation, and over reason and humanity.

Such is the use which has been made of human learning. The labourers in this vineyard seem as if it was their object to confound all common sense, and the distinctions of good and evil, by means of traditional maxims and preconceived notions taken upon trust, and increasing in absurdity with increase of age. They pile hypothesis on hypothesis, mountain high, till it is impossible to come at the plain truth on any question. They see things, not as they are, but as they find them in books, and " wink and shut their apprehensions up," in order that they may discover nothing to interfere with their prejudices or convince them of their absurdity. It might be supposed that the height of human wisdom consisted in maintaining contradictions and rendering nonsense sacred. There is no dogma, however fierce or foolish, to which these persons have not set their seals, and tried to impose on the understandings of their followers, as the will of Heaven, clothed with all the terrors and sanctions of religion. How little has the human understanding been directed to find out the true and useful! How much ingenuity has been thrown away in the defence of creeds and systems! How much time and talents have been wasted in theological controversy, in law, in politics, in verbal criticism, in judicial astrology, and in finding out the art of making gold! What actual benefit do we reap from the writings of a Laud or a Whitgift, or of Bishop Bull or Bishop Waterland, or

Prideaux' Connections, or Beausobre, or Calmet, or St. Augustine, or Puffendorf, or Vattel, or from the more literal but equally learned and unprofitable labours of Scaliger, Cardan, and Scioppius? How many grains of sense are there in their thousand folio or quarto volumes? What would the world lose if they were committed to the flames to-morrow? Or are they not already " gone to the vault of all the Capulets "? Yet all these were oracles in their time, and would have scoffed at you or me, at common sense and human nature, for differing with them. It is our turn to laugh now.

To conclude this subject. The most sensible people to be met with in society are men of business and of the world, who argue from what they see and know, instead of spinning cobweb distinctions of what things ought to be. Women have often more of what is called *good sense* than men. They have fewer pretensions; are less implicated in theories; and judge of objects more from their immediate and involuntary impression on the mind, and, therefore, more truly and naturally. They cannot reason wrong; for they do not reason at all. They do not think or speak by rule; and they have in general more eloquence and wit, as well as sense, on that account. By their wit, sense, and eloquence together, they generally contrive to govern their husbands. Their style, when they write to their friends (not for the booksellers), is better than that of most authors.— Uneducated people have most exuberance of invention and the greatest freedom from prejudice. Shakespear's was evidently an uneducated mind, both in the freshness of his imagination and in the variety of his views; as Milton's was scholastic, in the texture both of his thoughts and feelings. Shakespear had not been accustomed to write themes at school in favour of virtue or against vice. To this we owe the unaffected but healthy tone of his dramatic morality. If we wish to know the force of human genius we should read Shakespear. If we wish to see the insignificance of human learning we may study his commentators.

ON LIVING TO ONE'S-SELF

(WRITTEN AT WINTERSLOW HUT, JANUARY 18-19, 1821)

> " Remote, unfriended, melancholy, slow,
> Or by the lazy Scheldt or wandering Po."

I NEVER was in a better place or humour than I am at present for writing on this subject. I have a partridge getting ready for my supper, my fire is blazing on the hearth, the air is mild for the season of the year, I have had but a slight fit of indigestion to-day (the only thing that makes me abhor myself), I have three hours good before me, and therefore I will attempt it. It is as well to do it at once as to have it to do for a week to come.

If the writing on this subject is no easy task, the thing itself is a harder one. It asks a troublesome effort to ensure the admiration of others: it is a still greater one to be satisfied with one's own thoughts. As I look from the window at the wide bare heath before me, and through the misty moonlight air see the woods that wave over the top of Winterslow,

> "While Heav'n's chancel-vault is blind with sleet,"

my mind takes its flight through too long a series of years, supported only by the patience of thought and secret yearnings after truth and good, for me to be at a loss to understand the feeling I intend to write about; but I do not know that this will enable me to convey it more agreeably to the reader.

Lady G[randison], in a letter to Miss Harriet Byron, assures her that " her brother Sir Charles lived to himself "; and Lady L. soon after (for Richardson was never tired of a good thing) repeats the same observation; to which Miss Byron frequently returns in her answers to both sisters, " For you know Sir Charles lives to himself," till at length it passes into a proverb among the fair correspondents. This is not, however, an example of what I understand by *living to one's-self,* for Sir Charles Grandison was indeed always thinking of himself; but by this phrase I mean never thinking at all about one's-self, any more than if there was no such person in existence. The character I speak of is as little of an egotist as possible: Richardson's great favourite was as much of one as possible. Some satirical critic has represented him in Elysium " bowing over the *faded* hand of Lady Grandison " (Miss Byron that was)—he ought to have been represented bowing over his own hand, for he never admired any one but himself, and was the God of his own idolatry.—Neither do I call it living to one's-self to retire into a desert (like the saints and martyrs of old) to be devoured by wild beasts, nor to descend into a cave to be considered as a hermit, nor to get to the top of a pillar or rock to do fanatic penance and be seen of all men. What I mean by living to one's-self is living in the world, as in it, not of it: it is as if no one knew there was such a person, and you wished no one to know it: it is to be a silent spectator of the mighty scene of things, not an object of attention or curiosity in it; to take a thoughtful, anxious interest in what is passing in the world, but not to feel the slightest inclination to make or meddle with it. It is such a life as a pure spirit might be supposed to lead, and such an interest as it might take in the affairs of men: calm, contemplative, passive, distant, touched with pity for their sorrows, smiling at their follies without bitterness, sharing their affections, but not troubled by their passions, not seeking their notice, nor once dreamt of by them. He who lives wisely to himself and to his own heart looks at the busy world through the loop-holes of retreat, and does not want to mingle in the fray. " He hears the tumult, and is still." He is not able to mend it, nor willing to mar it. He sees enough in the universe to interest him without putting himself forward to try what he can do to fix the eyes of the universe upon him. Vain the attempt! He reads the clouds, he looks at the stars, he watches the return of the seasons, the falling leaves of autumn, the perfumed breath of spring, starts with delight at the note of a thrush in a copse near him, sits by the fire, listens to the moaning of the wind, pores upon a book, or discourses the freezing hours away, or melts down hours to minutes in pleasing thought. All this while he is taken up with other things, forgetting himself. He relishes an author's style without thinking of turning author. He is fond of looking at a print from an old picture in the room, without teasing himself to copy it. He does not fret himself to death with trying to be what he is not, or to do what he cannot. He hardly knows what he is capable of, and is not in the least concerned whether he shall ever make a figure in the world. He feels the truth of the lines—

> " The man whose eye is ever on himself,
>   Doth look on one, the least of nature's works ;
>   One who might move the wise man to that scorn
>   Which wisdom holds unlawful ever."

He looks out of himself at the wide, extended prospect of nature, and takes an interest beyond his narrow pretensions in general humanity. He is free as air, and independent as the wind. Woe be to him when he first begins to think what others say of him. While a man is contented with himself and his own resources, all is well. When he undertakes to play a part on the stage, and to persuade the world to think more about him than they do about themselves, he is got into a track where he will find nothing but briars and thorns, vexation and disappointment. I can speak a little to this point. For many years of my life I did nothing but think. I had nothing else to do but solve some knotty point, or dip in some abstruse author, or look at the sky, or wander by the pebbled sea-side—

"To see the children sporting on the shore,
    And hear the mighty waters rolling evermore "

I cared for nothing, I wanted nothing. I took my time to consider whatever occurred to me, and was in no hurry to give a sophistical answer to a question— there was no printer's devil waiting for me. I used to write a page or two perhaps in half a year; and remember laughing heartily at the celebrated experimentalist Nicholson, who told me that in twenty years he had written as much as would make three hundred octavo volumes. If I was not a great author, I could read with ever fresh delight, " never ending, still beginning," and had no occasion to write a criticism when I had done. If I could not paint like Claude, I could admire " the witchery of the soft blue sky " as I walked out, and was satisfied with the pleasure it gave me. If I was dull, it gave me little concern: if I was lively, I indulged my spirits. I wished well to the world, and believed as favourably of it as I could. I was like a stranger in a foreign land, at which I looked with wonder, curiosity, and delight, without expecting to be an object of attention in return. I had no relations to the state, no duty to perform, no ties to bind me to others: I had neither friend nor mistress, wife nor child. I lived in a world of con- templation, and not of action.

This sort of dreaming existence is the best. He who quits it to go in search of realities generally barters repose for repeated disappointments and vain regrets. His time, thoughts, and feelings are no longer at his own disposal. From that instant he does not survey the objects of nature as they are in themselves, but looks asquint at them to see whether he cannot make them the instruments of his ambition, interest, or pleasure; for a candid, undesigning, undisguised simplicity of character, his views become jaundiced, sinister, and double: he takes no farther interest in the great changes of the world but as he has a paltry share in producing them: instead of opening his senses, his understanding, and his heart to the resplendent fabric of the universe, he holds a crooked mirror before his face, in which he may admire his own person and pretensions, and just glance his eye aside to see whether others are not admiring him too. He no more exists in the impression which " the fair variety of things " makes upon him, softened and subdued by habitual contemplation, but in the feverish sense of his own upstart self-importance. By aiming to fix, he is become the slave of opinion. He is a tool, a part of a machine that never stands still, and is sick and giddy with the ceaseless motion. He has no satisfaction but in the reflection of his own image in the public gaze—but in the repetition of his own name in the public ear. He himself is mixed up with and spoils everything. I wonder Buonaparte was not tired of the N. N.'s stuck all over the Louvre and throughout France. Goldsmith (as we all know), when in Holland, went out into a balcony with some handsome Englishwomen, and on their being applauded by the spectators, turned round and said peevishly, " There are places where I also am admired." He could not give the craving appetite of an author's vanity one day's respite. I have seen a celebrated talker of our own time turn pale and go out

of the room when a showy-looking girl has come into
it, who for a moment divided the attention of his hearers.—
Infinite are the mortifications of the bare attempt to
emerge from obscurity; numberless the failures; and
greater and more galling still the vicissitudes and tormenting accompaniments of success—

> "Whose top to climb
> Is certain falling, or so slippery, that
> The fear's as bad as falling."

"Would to God," exclaimed Oliver Cromwell, when he
was at any time thwarted by the Parliament, "that I
had remained by my woodside to tend a flock of sheep,
rather than have been thrust on such a government as
this!" When Buonaparte got into his carriage to proceed on his Russian expedition, carelessly twirling his
glove, and singing the air, "Malbrook to the wars is
going," he did not think of the tumble he has got
since, the shock of which no one could have stood but
himself. We see and hear chiefly of the favourites of
Fortune and the Muse, of great generals, of first-rate
actors, of celebrated poets. These are at the head;
we are struck with the glittering eminence on which
they stand, and long to set out on the same tempting
career,—not thinking how many discontented half-pay
lieutenants are in vain seeking promotion all their
lives, and obliged to put up with "the insolence of
office, and the spurns which patient merit of the unworthy takes"; how many half-starved strolling players
are doomed to penury and tattered robes in country
places, dreaming to the last of a London engagement;
how many wretched daubers shiver and shake in the
ague-fit of alternate hopes and fears, waste and pine
away in the atrophy of genius, or else turn drawing-
masters, picture-cleaners, or newspaper-critics; how
many hapless poets have sighed out their souls to the
Muse in vain, without ever getting their effusions

farther known than the Poet's Corner of a country
newspaper, and looked and looked with grudging,
wistful eyes at the envious horizon that bounded their
provincial fame!—Suppose an actor, for instance,
" after the heart-aches and the thousand natural pangs
that flesh is heir to," *does* get at the top of his profession, he can no longer bear a rival near the throne;
to be second or only equal to another is to be nothing:
he starts at the prospect of a successor, and retains the
mimic sceptre with a convulsive grasp: perhaps as he
is about to seize the first place which he has long had
in his eye, an unsuspected competitor steps in before
him, and carries off the prize, leaving him to commence
his irksome toil again. He is in a state of alarm at
every appearance or rumour of the appearance of a
new actor: " a mouse that takes up its lodging in a cat's
ear "[1] has a mansion of peace to him: he dreads every
hint of an objection, and least of all can forgive praise
mingled with censure: to doubt is to insult; to discriminate is to degrade: he dare hardly look into a
criticism unless some one has *tasted* it for him, to see
that there is no offence in it: if he does not draw
crowded houses every night, he can neither eat nor
sleep; or if all these terrible inflictions are removed,
and he can " eat his meal in peace," he then becomes
surfeited with applause and dissatisfied with his profession: he wants to be something else, to be distinguished as an author, a collector, a classical scholar,
a man of sense and information, and weighs every
word he utters, and half retracts it before he utters
it, lest if he were to make the smallest slip of the tongue
it should get buzzed abroad that *Mr. —— was only
clever as an actor !* If ever there was a man who did not
derive more pain than pleasure from his vanity, that man,
says Rousseau, was no other than a fool. A country

[1] Webster's *Duchess of Malfy*.

gentleman near Taunton spent his whole life in making some hundreds of wretched copies of second-rate pictures, which were bought up at his death by a neighbouring baronet, to whom

" Some Demon whisper'd, L——, have a taste ! "

A little Wilson in an obscure corner escaped the man of *virtù*, and was carried off by a Bristol picture-dealer for three guineas, while the muddled copies of the owner of the mansion (with the frames) fetched thirty, forty, sixty, a hundred ducats a piece. A friend of mine found a very fine Canaletti in a state of strange disfigurement, with the upper part of the sky smeared over and fantastically variegated with English clouds; and on inquiring of the person to whom it belonged whether something had not been done to it, received for answer " that a gentleman, a great artist in the neighbourhood, had retouched some parts of it." What infatuation! Yet this candidate for the honours of the pencil might probably have made a jovial fox-hunter or respectable justice of the peace if he could only have stuck to what nature and fortune intended him for. Miss —— can by no means be persuaded to quit the boards of the theatre at ——, a little country town in the West of England. Her salary has been abridged, her person ridiculed, her acting laughed at; nothing will serve—she is determined to be an actress, and scorns to return to her former business as a milliner. Shall I go on? An actor in the same company was visited by the apothecary of the place in an ague-fit, who, on asking his landlady as to his way of life, was told that the poor gentleman was very quiet and gave little trouble, that he generally had a plate of mashed potatoes for his dinner, and lay in bed most of his time, repeating his part. A young couple, every way amiable and deserving, were to have been

married, and a benefit-play was bespoke by the officers
of the regiment quartered there, to defray the expense
of a license and of the wedding-ring, but the profits of
the night did not amount to the necessary sum, and
they have, I fear, " virgined it e'er since "! Oh for the
pencil of Hogarth or Wilkie to give a view of the
comic strength of the company at ——, drawn up in
battle-array in the *Clandestine Marriage,* with a *coup
d'œil* of the pit, boxes, and gallery, to cure for ever
the love of the *ideal,* and the desire to shine and make
holiday in the eyes of others, instead of retiring within
ourselves and keeping our wishes and our thoughts at
home!—Even in the common affairs of life, in love,
friendship, and marriage, how little security have we
when we trust our happiness in the hands of others!
Most of the friends I have seen have turned out the
bitterest enemies, or cold, uncomfortable acquaintance.
Old companions are like meats served up too often,
that lose their relish and their wholesomeness. He
who looks at beauty to admire, to adore it, who reads
of its wondrous power in novels, in poems, or in plays,
is not unwise; but let no man fall in love, for from
that moment he is " the baby of a girl." I like very well
to repeat such lines as these in the play of *Mirandola*—

> " With what a waving air she goes
> Along the corridor ! How like a fawn !
> Yet statelier. Hark ! No sound, however soft,
> Nor gentlest echo telleth when she treads,
> But every motion of her shape doth seem
> Hallowed by silence."

But however beautiful the description, defend me from
meeting with the original!

> " The fly that sips treacle
> Is lost in the sweets ;
> So he that tastes woman
> Ruin meets."

The song is Gay's, not mine, and a bitter-sweet it is.—
How few out of the infinite number of those that marry
and are given in marriage, wed with those they would
prefer to all the world; nay, how far the greater
proportion are joined together by mere motives of
convenience, accident, recommendation of friends, or
indeed not unfrequently by the very fear of the event,
by repugnance and a sort of fatal fascination: yet the
tie is for life, not to be shaken off but with disgrace or
death: a man no longer lives to himself, but is a body
(as well as mind) chained to another, in spite of himself—

> " Like life and death in disproportion met."

So Milton (perhaps from his own experience) makes
Adam exclaim, in the vehemence of his despair,

> " For either
> He never shall find out fit mate, but such
> As some misfortune brings him or mistake;
> Or whom he wishes most shall seldom gain
> Through her perverseness, but shall see her gain'd
> By a far worse ; or if she love, withheld
> By parents ; or his happiest choice too late
> Shall meet, already link'd and wedlock-bound
> To a fell adversary, his hate and shame ;
> Which infinite calamity shall cause
> To human life, and household peace confound."

If love at first sight were mutual, or to be conciliated
by kind offices; if the fondest affection were not so
often repaid and chilled by indifference and scorn; if
so many lovers both before and since the madman in
Don Quixote had not " worshipped a statue, hunted the
wind, cried aloud to the desert "; if friendship were
lasting; if merit were renown, and renown were health,
riches, and long life; or if the homage of the world
were paid to conscious worth and the true aspirations
after excellence, instead of its gaudy signs and outward

trappings; then indeed I might be of opinion that it is
better to live to others than one's-self; but as the case
stands, I incline to the negative side of the question[1].—

> " I have not loved the world, nor the world me ;
> I have not flattered its rank breath, nor bow'd
> To its idolatries a patient knee—
> Nor coin'd my cheek to smiles—nor cried aloud
> In worship of an echo ; in the crowd
> They could not deem me one of such ; I stood
> Among them, but not of them ; in a shroud
> Of thoughts which were not their thoughts, and still could,
> Had I not filed my mind which thus itself subdued.
>
> I have not loved the world, nor the world me—
> But let us part fair foes ; I do believe,
> Though I have found them not, that there may be
> Words which are things—hopes which will not deceive,
> And virtues which are merciful nor weave
> Snares for the failing : I would also deem
> O'er others' griefs that some sincerely grieve ;
> That two, or one, are almost what they seem—
> That goodness is no name, and happiness no dream."

Sweet verse embalms the spirit of sour misanthropy:
but woe betide the ignoble prose-writer who should thus
dare to compare notes with the world, or tax it roundly
with imposture.

If I had sufficient provocation to rail at the public,
as Ben Jonson did at the audience in the Prologues to
his plays, I think I should do it in good set terms,
nearly as follows:—There is not a more mean, stupid,

---

[1] Shenstone and Gray were two men, one of whom pretended to live to himself, and the other really did so. Gray
shrunk from the public gaze (he did not even like his portrait
to be prefixed to his works) into his own thoughts and indolent
musings; Shenstone affected privacy, that he might be sought
out by the world; the one courted retirement in order to
enjoy leisure and repose, as the other coquetted with it, merely
to be interrupted with the importunity of visitors and the
flatteries of absent friends.

dastardly, pitiful, selfish, spiteful, envious, ungrateful animal than the Public. It is the greatest of cowards, for it is afraid of itself. From its unwieldy, overgrown dimensions, it dreads the least opposition to it, and shakes like isinglass at the touch of a finger. It starts at its own shadow, like the man in the Hartz mountains, and trembles at the mention of its own name. It has a lion's mouth, the heart of a hare, with ears erect and sleepless eyes. It stands "listening its fears." It is so in awe of its own opinion that it never dares to form any, but catches up the first idle rumour, lest it should be behind-hand in its judgment, and echoes it till it is deafened with the sound of its own voice. The idea of what the public will think prevents the public from ever thinking at all, and acts as a spell on the exercise of private judgment, so that, in short, the public ear is at the mercy of the first impudent pretender who chooses to fill it with noisy assertions, or false surmises, or secret whispers. What is said by one is heard by all; the supposition that a thing is known to all the world makes all the world believe it, and the hollow repetition of a vague report drowns the "still, small voice" of reason. We may believe or know that what is said is not true: but we know or fancy that others believe it,—we dare not contradict or are too indolent to dispute with them, and therefore give up our internal, and, as we think, our solitary conviction to a sound without substance, without proof, and often without meaning. Nay more, we may believe and know not only that a thing is false, but that others believe and know it to be so, that they are quite as much in the secret of the imposture as we are, that they see the puppets at work, the nature of the machinery, and yet if any one has the art or power to get the management of it, he shall keep possession of the public ear by virtue of a cant phrase or nickname, and by dint of

effrontery and perseverance make all the world believe
and repeat what all the world know to be false. The
ear is quicker than the judgment. We know that
certain things are said; by that circumstance alone,
we know that they produce a certain effect on the
imagination of others, and we conform to their prejudices
by mechanical sympathy, and for want of sufficient
spirit to differ with them. So far then is public opinion
from resting on a broad and solid basis, as the aggregate of thought and feeling in a community, that it
is slight and shallow and variable to the last degree
—the bubble of the moment—so that we may safely
say the public is the dupe of public opinion, not its
parent. The public is pusillanimous and cowardly,
because it is weak. It knows itself to be a great dunce,
and that it has no opinions but upon suggestion. Yet
it is unwilling to appear in leading-strings, and would
have it thought that its decisions are as wise as they
are weighty. It is hasty in taking up its favourites,
more hasty in laying them aside, lest it should be
supposed deficient in sagacity in either case. It is
generally divided into two strong parties, each of which
will allow neither common sense nor common honesty
to the other side. It reads the *Edinburgh* and *Quarterly*
Reviews, and believes them both—or if there is a doubt,
malice turns the scale. Taylor and Hessey told me
that they had sold nearly two editions of the *Characters*
of Shakespear's Plays in about three months, but that
after the Quarterly Review of them came out they never
sold another copy. The public, enlightened as they are,
must have known the meaning of that attack as well
as those who made it. It was not ignorance then,
but cowardice, that led them to give up their own
opinion. A crew of mischievous critics at Edinburgh
having affixed the epithet of the *Cockney School* to one
or two writers born in the metropolis, all the people

in London became afraid of looking into their works, lest they too should be convicted of cockneyism. Oh, brave public! This epithet proved too much for one of the writers in question, and stuck like a barbed arrow in his heart. Poor Keats! What was sport to the town was death to him. Young, sensitive, delicate, he was like

> " A bud bit by an envious worm,
> Ere he could spread his sweet leaves to the air
> Or dedicate his beauty to the sun ; "

and unable to endure the miscreant cry and idiot laugh, withdrew to sigh his last breath in foreign climes. The public is as envious and ungrateful as it is ignorant, stupid, and pigeon-livered—

> " A huge-sized monster of ingratitudes."

It reads, it admires, it extols, only because it is the fashion, not from any love of the subject or the man. It cries you up or runs you down out of mere caprice and levity. If you have pleased it, it is jealous of its own involuntary acknowledgment of merit, and seizes the first opportunity, the first shabby pretext, to pick a quarrel with you, and be quits once more. Every petty caviller is erected into a judge, every tale-bearer is implicitly believed. Every little low paltry creature that gaped and wondered, only because others did so, is glad to find you (as he thinks) on a level with himself. An author is not then, after all, a being of another order. Public admiration is forced, and goes against the grain. Public obloquy is cordial and sincere: every individual feels his own importance in it. They give you up bound hand and foot into the power of your accusers. To attempt to defend yourself is a high crime and misdemeanour, a contempt of court, an extreme piece of impertinence. Or if you prove every charge unfounded, they never think of retracting their

error or making you amends. It would be a compromise of their dignity; they consider themselves as
the party injured, and resent your innocence as an
imputation on their judgment. The celebrated Bub
Doddington, when out of favour at court, said " he
would not *justify* before his sovereign: it was for
Majesty to be displeased, and for him to believe himself in the wrong! " The public are not quite so modest.
People already begin to talk of the Scotch Novels
as overrated. How then can common authors be supposed to keep their heads long above water? As a
general rule, all those who live by the public starve,
and are made a by-word and a standing jest into the
bargain. Posterity is no better (not a bit more enlightened
or more liberal), except that you are no longer in their
power, and that the voice of common fame saves them the
trouble of deciding on your claims. The public now are
the posterity of Milton and Shakespear. Our posterity will
be the living public of a future generation. When a man
is dead, they put money in his coffin, erect monuments
to his memory, and celebrate the anniversary of his
birthday in set speeches. Would they take any notice
of him if he were living? No!—I was complaining of
this to a Scotchman who had been attending a dinner
and a subscription to raise a monument to Burns. He
replied, he would sooner subscribe twenty pounds to
his monument than have given it him while living; so
that if the poet were to come to life again, he would
treat him just as he was treated in fact. This was an
honest Scotchman. What *he* said, the rest would do.

Enough: my soul, turn from them, and let me try
to regain the obscurity and quiet that I love, " far from
the madding strife," in some sequestered corner of my
own, or in some far-distant land! In the latter case,
I might carry with me as a consolation the passage in
Bolingbroke's *Reflections on Exile*, in which he describes

in glowing colours the resources which a man may
always find within himself, and of which the world
cannot deprive him:—

" Believe me, the providence of God has established
such an order in the world, that of all which belongs to
us the least valuable parts can alone fall under the
will of others. Whatever is best is safest; lies out of
the reach of human power; can neither be given nor
taken away. Such is this great and beautiful work of
nature, the world. Such is the mind of man, which
contemplates and admires the world, whereof it makes
the noblest part. These are inseparably ours, and as
long as we remain in one we shall enjoy the other.
Let us march therefore intrepidly wherever we are led
by the course of human accidents. Wherever they
lead us, on what coast soever we are thrown by them,
we shall not find ourselves absolutely strangers. We
shall feel the same revolution of seasons, and the same
sun and moon[1] will guide the course of our year. The
same azure vault, bespangled with stars, will be everywhere spread over our heads. There is no part of the
world from whence we may not admire those planets
which roll, like ours, in different orbits round the same
central sun; from whence we may not discover an
object still more stupendous, that army of fixed stars
hung up in the immense space of the universe, innumerable suns whose beams enlighten and cherish the
unknown worlds which roll around them; and whilst
I am ravished by such contemplations as these, whilst
my soul is thus raised up to heaven, it imports me little
what ground I tread upon."

[1] Plut. of Banishment. He compares those who cannot live
out of their own country to the simple people who fancied the
moon of Athens was a finer moon than that of Corinth.
   Labentem cœlo quæ ducitis annum.—VIRG. *Georg.*

ON READING OLD BOOKS

(LONDON MAGAZINE, FEB., 1821)

I HATE to read new books. There are twenty or thirty volumes that I have read over and over again, and these are the only ones that I have any desire ever to read at all. It was a long time before I could bring myself to sit down to the *Tales of My Landlord*, but now that author's works have made a considerable addition to my scanty library. I am told that some of Lady Morgan's are good, and have been recommended to look into *Anastasius;* but I have not yet ventured upon that task. A lady, the other day, could not refrain from expressing her surprise to a friend, who said he had been reading *Delphine:*[1]—she asked,—If it had not been published some time back? Women judge of books as they do of fashions or complexions, which are admired only " in their newest gloss." That is not my way. I am not one of those who trouble the circulating libraries much, or pester the booksellers for mail-coach copies of standard periodical publications. I cannot say that I am greatly addicted to black-letter, but I profess myself well versed in the marble bindings of Andrew Millar in the middle of the last century; nor does my taste revolt at Thurlow's *State Papers*, in russia leather; or an ample impression of Sir William Temple's *Essays*, with a portrait after Sir Godfrey Kneller in front. I do not think altogether the worse of a book for having survived the author a generation or two. I have more confidence in the dead than the living. Contemporary writers may generally be divided into two classes—one's friends or one's foes. Of the first we are compelled to think too well, and of the last we are disposed to think too ill, to receive much genuine pleasure from the perusal, or to judge fairly of the merits of either. One candidate for literary fame, who happens to be of our acquaintance, writes finely, and like a man of genius; but

[1] Madame de Staël's novel.

unfortunately has a foolish face, which spoils a delicate passage:—another inspires us with the highest respect for his personal talents and character, but does not quite come up to our expectations in print. All these contradictions and petty details interrupt the calm current of our reflections. If you want to know what any of the authors were who lived before our time, and are still objects of anxious inquiry, you have only to look into their works. But the dust and smoke and noise of modern literature have nothing in common with the pure, silent air of immortality.

When I take up a work that I have read before (the oftener the better) I know what I have to expect. The satisfaction is not lessened by being anticipated. When the entertainment is altogether new, I sit down to it as I should to a strange dish,—turn and pick out a bit here and there, and am in doubt what to think of the composition. There is a want of confidence and security to second appetite. New-fangled books are also like made-dishes in this respect, that they are generally little else than hashes and *rifaccimenti* of what has been served up entire and in a more natural state at other times. Besides, in thus turning to a well-known author, there is not only an assurance that my time will not be thrown away, or my palate nauseated with the most insipid or vilest trash, —but I shake hands with, and look an old, tried, and valued friend in the face,—compare notes, and chat the hours away. It is true, we form dear friendships with such ideal guests—dearer, alas! and more lasting, than those with our most intimate acquaintance. In reading a book which is an old favourite with me (say the first novel I ever read) I not only have the pleasure of imagination and of a critical relish of the work, but the pleasures of memory added to it. It recalls the same feelings and associations which I had in first reading it, and which I can never have again in any other way. Standard

c

productions of this kind are links in the chain of our
conscious being. They bind together the different
scattered divisions of our personal identity. They are
landmarks and guides in our journey through life. They
are pegs and loops on which we can hang up, or from
which we can take down, at pleasure, the wardrobe of a
moral imagination, the relics of our best affections, the
tokens and records of our happiest hours. They are " for
thoughts and for remembrance! " They are like For-
tunatus's Wishing-Cap—they give us the best riches—
those of Fancy; and transport us, not over half the globe,
but (which is better) over half our lives, at a word's
notice!

My father Shandy solaced himself with Bruscambille.
Give me for this purpose a volume of *Peregrine Pickle*
or *Tom Jones*. Open either of them anywhere—at the
Memoirs of Lady Vane, or the adventures at the masquerade with Lady Bellaston, or the disputes between
Thwackum and Square, or the escape of Molly Seagrim,
or the incident of Sophia and her muff, or the edifying
prolixity of her aunt's lecture—and there I find the same
delightful, busy, bustling scene as ever, and feel myself
the same as when I was first introduced into the midst of
it. Nay, sometimes the sight of an odd volume of these
good old English authors on a stall, or the name lettered
on the back among others on the shelves of a library,
answers the purpose, revives the whole train of ideas,
and sets " the puppets dallying." Twenty years are struck
off the list, and I am a child again. A sage philosopher,
who was not a very wise man, said, that he should like
very well to be young again, if he could take his experience
along with him. This ingenious person did not seem to
be aware, by the gravity of his remark, that the great
advantage of being young is to be without this weight of
experience, which he would fain place upon the shoulders
of youth, and which never comes too late with years.

Oh! what a privilege to be able to let this hump, like
Christian's burthen, drop from off one's back, and transport oneself, by the help of a little musty duodecimo, to
the time when " ignorance was bliss," and when we first
got a peep at the raree-show of the world, through the
glass of fiction—gazing at mankind, as we do at wild
beasts in a menagerie, through the bars of their cages,—
or at curiosities in a museum, that we must not touch!
For myself, not only are the old ideas of the contents of
the work brought back to my mind in all their vividness,
but the old associations of the faces and persons of those
I then knew, as they were in their life-time—the place
where I sat to read the volume, the day when I got it, the
feeling of the air, the fields, the sky—return, and all my
early impressions with them. This is better to me—
those places, those times, those persons, and those feelings
that come across me as I retrace the story and devour the
page, are to me better far than the wet sheets of the last
new novel from the Ballantyne press, to say nothing of
the Minerva press in Leadenhall Street. It is like visiting
the scenes of early youth. I think of the time " when
I was in my father's house, and my path ran down with
butter and honey,"—when I was a little, thoughtless
child, and had no other wish or care but to con my daily
task, and be happy!—*Tom Jones*, I remember, was the
first work that broke the spell. It came down in numbers
once a fortnight, in Cooke's pocket-edition, embellished
with cuts. I had hitherto read only in school-books, and
a tiresome ecclesiastical history (with the exception of
Mrs. Radcliffe's *Romance of the Forest*): but this had a
different relish with it,—" sweet in the mouth," though
not " bitter in the belly." It smacked of the world I lived
in, and in which I was to live—and showed me groups,
" gay creatures " not " of the element," but of the earth;
not " living in the clouds," but travelling the same road
that I did;—some that had passed on before me, and others

that might soon overtake me. My heart had palpitated
at the thoughts of a boarding-school ball, or gala-day at
Midsummer or Christmas: but the world I had found
out in Cooke's edition of the *British Novelists* was to me
·a dance through life, a perpetual gala-day. The sixpenny
numbers of this work regularly contrived to leave off
just in the middle of a sentence, and in the nick of a
story, where Tom Jones discovers Square behind the
blanket; or where Parson Adams, in the inextricable
confusion of events, very undesignedly gets to bed to
Mrs. Slip-slop. Let me caution the reader against this
impression of Joseph Andrews; for there is a picture of
Fanny in it which he should not set his heart on, lest he
should never meet with anything like it; or if he should,
it would, perhaps, be better for him that he had not.
It was just like —— ——! With what eagerness I used
to look forward to the next number, and open the prints!
Ah! never again shall I feel the enthusiastic delight with
which I gazed at the figures, and anticipated the story
and adventures of Major Bath and Commodore Trunnion,
of Trim and my Uncle Toby, of Don Quixote and Sancho
and Dapple, of Gil Blas and Dame Lorenza Sephora, of
Laura and the fair Lucretia, whose lips open and shut
like buds of roses. To what nameless ideas did they give
rise,—with what airy delights I filled up the outlines, as
I hung in silence over the page!—Let me still recall
them, that they may breathe fresh life into me, and that
I may live that birthday of thought and romantic pleasure
over again! Talk of the *ideal!* This is the only true ideal
—the heavenly tints of Fancy reflected in the bubbles
that float upon the spring-tide of human life.

> " O Memory ! shield me from the world's poor strife,
> And give those scenes thine everlasting life ! "

The paradox with which I set out is, I hope, less
startling than it was; the reader will, by this time, have

been let into my secret. Much about the same time, or I believe rather earlier, I took a particular satisfaction in reading *Chubb's Tracts*,[1] and I often think I will get them again to wade through. There is a high gusto of polemical divinity in them; and you fancy that you hear a club of shoemakers at Salisbury, debating a disputable text from one of St. Paul's Epistles in a workmanlike style, with equal shrewdness and pertinacity. I cannot say much for my metaphysical studies, into which I launched shortly after with great ardour, so as to make a toil of a pleasure. I was presently entangled in the briars and thorns of subtle distinctions,—of " fate, free-will, foreknowledge absolute," though I cannot add that " in their wandering mazes I found no end; " for I did arrive at some very satisfactory and potent conclusions; nor will I go so far, however ungrateful the subject might seem, as to exclaim with Marlowe's Faustus— " Would I had never seen Wittenberg, never read book " —that is, never studied such authors as Hartley, Hume, Berkeley, &c. Locke's *Essay on the Human Understanding* is, however, a work from which I never derived either pleasure or profit; and Hobbes, dry and powerful as he is, I did not read till long afterwards. I read a few poets, which did not much hit my taste,—for I would have the reader understand, I am deficient in the faculty of imagination; but I fell early upon French romances and philosophy, and devoured them tooth-and-nail. Many a dainty repast have I made of the *New Eloise;*—the description of the kiss; the excursion on the water; the letter of St. Preux, recalling the time of their first loves; and the account of Julia's death; these I read over and over again with unspeakable delight and wonder. Some years after, when I met with this work again, I found I had lost nearly my whole relish for it (except some few parts),

---

[1] By Thomas Chubb, on political and religious subjects, published between 1732 and 1745—W. C. H.

and was, I remember, very much mortified with the change
in my taste, which I sought to attribute to the smallness
and gilt edges of the edition I had bought, and its being
perfumed with rose-leaves. Nothing could exceed the
gravity, the solemnity with which I carried home and
read the Dedication to the *Social Contract*, with some
other pieces of the same author, which I had picked up
at a stall in a coarse leathern cover. Of the *Confessions*
I have spoken elsewhere, and may repeat what I have
said—" Sweet is the dew of their memory, and pleasant
the balm of their recollection!" Their beauties are not
" scattered like stray-gifts o'er the earth," but sown
thick on the page, rich and rare. I wish I had never read
the *Emilius*, or read it with less implicit faith. I had no
occasion to pamper my natural aversion to affectation or
pretence, by romantic and artificial means. I had better
have formed myself on the model of Sir Fopling Flutter.
There is a class of persons whose virtues and most shining
qualities sink in, and are concealed by, an absorbent
ground of modesty and reserve; and such a one I do,
without vanity, profess myself.[1] Now these are the very
persons who are likely to attach themselves to the character of Emilius, and of whom it is sure to be the bane.
This dull, phlegmatic, retiring humour is not in a fair
way to be corrected, but confirmed and rendered desperate, by being in that work held up as an object of
imitation, as an example of simplicity and magnanimity—
by coming upon us with all the recommendations of
novelty, surprise, and superiority to the prejudices of the
world—by being stuck upon a pedestal, made amiable,
dazzling, a *leurre de dupe!* The reliance on solid worth

[1] Nearly the same sentiment was wittily and happily expressed by a friend, who had some lottery puffs, which he had
been employed to write, returned on his hands for their too
great severity of thought and classical terseness of style, and
who observed on that occasion, that " Modest merit never can
succeed ! "

which it inculcates, the preference of sober truth to gaudy tinsel, hangs like a mill-stone round the neck of the imagination—" a load to sink a navy "—impedes our progress, and blocks up every prospect in life. A man, to get on, to be successful, conspicuous, applauded, should not retire upon the centre of his conscious resources, but be always at the circumference of appearances. He must envelop himself in a halo of mystery— he must ride in an equipage of opinion—he must walk with a train of self-conceit following him—he must not strip himself to a buff-jerkin, to the doublet and hose of his real merits, but must surround himself with a *cortège* of prejudices, like the Signs of the Zodiac—he must seem anything but what he is, and then he may pass for anything he pleases. The world love to be amused by hollow professions, to be deceived by flattering appearances, to live in a state of hallucination; and can forgive everything but the plain, downright, simple honest truth —such as we see it chalked out in the character of Emilius.—To return from this digression, which is a little out of place here.

Books have in a great measure lost their power over me; nor can I revive the same interest in them as formerly. I perceive when a thing is good, rather than feel it. It is true,

" Marcian Colonna is a dainty book ; "[1]

and the reading of Mr. Keats's *Eve of Saint Agnes* lately made me regret that I was not young again. The beautiful and tender images there conjured up, " come like shadows —so depart." The " tiger-moth's wings," which he has spread over his rich poetic blazonry, just flit across my fancy; the gorgeous twilight window which he has painted over again in his verse, to me " blushes " almost in vain

[1] *Marcian Colonna* is the title of a dramatic piece by Barry Cornwall (B. W. Procter).—W. C. H.

" with blood of queens and kings." I know how I should
have felt at one time in reading such passages; and that
is all. The sharp luscious flavour, the fine *aroma* is fled,
and nothing but the stalk, the bran, the husk of literature
is left. If any one were to ask me what I read now, I
might answer with my Lord Hamlet in the play—
" Words, words, words."—" What is the matter? "—
" *Nothing!* "—They have scarce a meaning. But it was
not always so. There was a time when to my thinking,
every word was a flower or a pearl, like those which
dropped from the mouth of the little peasant-girl in the
Fairy tale, or like those that fall from the great preacher
in the Caledonian Chapel! I drank of the stream of
knowledge that tempted, but did not mock my lips, as of
the river of life, freely. How eagerly I slaked my thirst
of German sentiment, " as the hart that panteth for the
water-springs "; how I bathed and revelled, and added
my floods of tears to Goëthe's *Sorrows of Werter*, and to
Schiller's *Robbers*—

" Giving my stock of more to that which had too much ! "

I read and assented with all my soul to Coleridge's fine
Sonnet, beginning—

" Schiller ! that hour I would have wish'd to die,
    If through the shuddering midnight I had sent,
    From the dark dungeon of the tow'r time-rent,
    That fearful voice, a famish'd father's cry ! "

I believe I may date my insight into the mysteries of
poetry from the commencement of my acquaintance with
the authors of the *Lyrical Ballads;* at least, my discrimination of the higher sorts—not my predilection for such
writers as Goldsmith or Pope: nor do I imagine they will
say I got my liking for the Novelists, or the comic writers,
—for the characters of Valentine, Tattle or Miss Prue,
from them. If so, I must have got from them what they
never had themselves. In points where poetic diction

and conception are concerned, I may be at a loss, and
liable to be imposed upon: but in forming an estimate of
passages relating to common life and manners, I cannot
think I am a plagiarist from any man.   I there "know
my cue without a prompter." I may say of such studies,
Intus et in cute. I am just able to admire those literal
touches of observation and description which persons
of loftier pretensions overlook and despise.   I think
I comprehend something of the characteristic part of
Shakespeare; and in him indeed, all is characteristic, even
the nonsense and poetry.   I believe it was the celebrated
Sir Humphrey Davy who used to say, that Shakespeare
was rather a metaphysician than a poet.   At any rate, it
was not ill said.   I wish that I had sooner known the
dramatic writers contemporary with Shakespeare; for in
looking them over about a year ago, I almost revived my
old passion for reading, and my old delight in books,
though they were very nearly new to me.   The Periodical
Essayists I read long ago.   The *Spectator* I liked extremely: but the *Tatler* took my fancy most.   I read the
others soon after, the *Rambler,* the *Adventurer,* the
World, the *Connoisseur:* I was not sorry to get to the end
of them, and have no desire to go regularly through
them again.   I consider myself a thorough adept in
Richardson.   I like the longest of his novels best, and
think no part of them tedious; nor should I ask to have
anything better to do than to read them from beginning
to end, to take them up when I chose, and lay them
down when I was tired, in some old family mansion in
the country, till every word and syllable relating to the
bright Clarissa, the divine Clementina, the beautiful
Pamela, " with every trick and line of their sweet favour,"
were once more " graven in my heart's table."[1]   I have

[1] During the peace of Amiens, a young English officer, of the
name of Lovelace, was presented at Buonaparte's levee. Instead of the usual question, " Where have you served, Sir ? "

a sneaking kindness for Mackenzie's *Julia de Roubigné*—for the deserted mansion, and straggling gilliflowers on the mouldering garden-wall; and still more for his *Man of Feeling;* not that it is better, nor so good; but at the time I read it, I sometimes thought of the heroine, Miss Walton, and of Miss —— together, and " that ligament, fine as it was, was never broken ! "—One of the poets that I have always read with most pleasure, and can wander about in for ever with a sort of voluptuous indolence, is Spenser; and I like Chaucer even better. The only writer among the Italians I can pretend to any knowledge of, is Boccaccio, and of him I cannot express half my admiration. His story of the Hawk I could read and think of from day to day, just as I would look at a picture of Titian's !

I remember, as long ago as the year 1798, going to a neighbouring town (Shrewsbury, where Farquhar has laid the plot of his *Recruiting Officer*) and bringing home with me, " at one proud swoop," a copy of Milton's *Paradise Lost,* and another of Burke's *Reflections on the French Revolution*—both which I have still; and I still recollect, when I see the covers, the pleasure with which I dipped into them as I returned with my double prize. I was set up for one while. That time is past " with all its giddy raptures ": but I am still anxious to preserve its memory, " embalmed with odours."—With respect to the first of these works, I would be permitted to remark here in passing, that it is a sufficient answer to the German criticism which has since been started against the character of Satan (viz., that it is not one of disgusting

the First Consul immediately addressed him, " I perceive your name, Sir, is the same as that of the hero of Richardson's Romance ! " Here was a Consul. The young man's uncle, who was called Lovelace, told me this anecdote while we were stopping together at Calais. I had also been thinking that his was the same name as that of the hero of Richardson's Romance. This is one of my reasons for liking Buonaparte.

deformity, or pure, defecated malice) to say that Milton
has there drawn, not the abstract principle of evil, not
a devil incarnate, but a fallen angel. This is the Scriptural
account, and the poet has followed it. We may safely
retain such passages as that well-known one—

> ——" His form had not yet lost
> All her original brightness; nor appear'd
> Less than archangel ruin'd ; and the excess
> Of glory obscur'd "—

for the theory, which is opposed to them, " falls flat upon
the grunsel edge, and shames its worshippers." Let us
hear no more, then, of this monkish cant, and bigoted
outcry for the restoration of the horns and tail of the
devil!—Again, as to the other work, Burke's *Reflections*,
I took a particular pride and pleasure in it, and read it to
myself and others for months afterwards. I had reason
for my prejudice in favour of this author. To understand
an adversary is some praise: to admire him is more.
I thought I did both: I knew I did one. From the first
time I ever cast my eyes on anything of Burke's (which
was an extract from his *Letter to a Noble Lord* in a three-
times-a-week paper, the *St. James's Chronicle*, in 1796),
I said to myself, " This is true eloquence: this is a man
pouring out his mind on paper." All other style seemed
to me pedantic and impertinent. Dr. Johnson's was
walking on stilts; and even Junius's (who was at that
time a favourite with me) with all his terseness, shrunk
up into little antithetic points and well-trimmed sentences.
But Burke's style was forked and playful as the lightning,
crested like the serpent. He delivered plain things on a
plain ground; but when he rose, there was no end of his
flights and circumgyrations—and in this very Letter,
" he, like an eagle in a dove-cot, fluttered *his* Volscians "
(the Duke of Bedford and the Earl of Lauderdale[1]) " in

---

[1] He is there called " Citizen Lauderdale." Is this the
present Earl [1826] ?

Corioli." I did not care for his doctrines. I was then, and am still, proof against their contagion; but I admired the author, and was considered as not a very staunch partisan of the opposite side, though I thought myself that an abstract proposition was one thing—a masterly transition, a brilliant metaphor, another. I conceived, too, that he might be wrong in his main argument, and yet deliver fifty truths in arriving at a false conclusion. I remember Coleridge assuring me, as a poetical and political set-off to my sceptical admiration, that Wordsworth had written an *Essay on Marriage*, which, for manly thought and nervous expression, he deemed incomparably superior. As I had not, at that time, seen any specimens of Mr. Wordsworth's prose style, I could not express my doubts on the subject. If there are greater prose-writers than Burke, they either lie out of my course of study, or are beyond my sphere of comprehension. I am too old to be a convert to a new mythology of genius. The niches are occupied, the tables are full. If such is still my admiration of this man's misapplied powers, what must it have been at a time when I myself was in vain trying, year after year, to write a single Essay, nay, a single page or sentence; when I regarded the wonders of his pen with the longing eyes of one who was dumb and a changeling; and when to be able to convey the slightest conception of my meaning to others in words, was the height of an almost hopeless ambition! But I never measured others' excellences by my own defects: though a sense of my own incapacity, and of the steep, impassable ascent from me to them, made me regard them with greater awe and fondness. I have thus run through most of my early studies and favourite authors, some of whom I have since criticized more at large. Whether those observations will survive me, I neither know nor do I much care: but to the works themselves, " worthy of all acceptation," and to the feelings they have always excited

in me since I could distinguish a meaning in language,
nothing shall ever prevent me from looking back with
gratitude and triumph. To have lived in the cultivation
of an intimacy with such works, and to have familiarly
relished such names, is not to have lived quite in vain.

There are other authors whom I have never read, and
yet whom I have frequently had a great desire to read,
from some circumstance relating to them. Among them
is Lord Clarendon's *History of the Grand Rebellion,* after
which I have a hankering, from hearing it spoken of by
good judges—from my interest in the events, and knowledge of the characters from other sources, and from
having seen fine portraits of most of them. I like to read
a well-penned character, and Clarendon is said to have
been a master in his way. I should like to read Froissart's
Chronicles, Holinshed and Stowe, and Fuller's *Worthies.*
I intend, whenever I can, to read Beaumont and Fletcher
all through. There are fifty-two of their plays, and I
have only read a dozen or fourteen of them. *A Wife for
a Month* and *Thierry and Theodoret* are, I am told,
delicious, and I can believe it. I should like to read the
speeches in *Thucydides,* and Guicciardini's *History of
Florence,* and *Don Quixote* in the original. I have often
thought of reading the *Loves of Persiles and Sigismunda,*
and the *Galatea* of the same author. But I somehow
reserve them like " another Yarrow." I should also like
to read the last new novel (if I could be sure it was so)
of the Author of *Waverley:*—no one would be more glad
than I to find it the best!

ON PERSONAL CHARACTER

(L O N D O N   M A G A Z I N E ,   M A R C H ,   1 8 2 1)

" Men palliate and conceal their original qualities, but do
not extirpate them."—MONTAIGNE'S *Essays*.

N O one ever changes his character from the time he is
two years old; nay, I might say, from the time he is two
hours old. We may, with instruction and opportunity,
mend our manners, or else alter for the worse,—" as the
flesh and fortune shall serve "; but the character, the
internal, original bias, remains always the same, true to
itself to the very last—

> " And feels the ruling passion strong in death ! "

A very grave and dispassionate philosopher (the late
celebrated chemist, Mr. Nicholson) was so impressed
with the conviction of the instantaneous commencement
and development of the character with the birth, that he
published a long and amusing article in the *Monthly
Magazine*, giving a detailed account of the progress,
history, education, and tempers of two twins, up to the
period of their being *eleven days old*. This is, perhaps,
considering the matter too curiously, and would amount
to a species of horoscopy, if we were to build on such
premature indications; but the germ no doubt is there,
though we must wait a little longer to see what form it
takes. We need not in general wait long. The Devil
soon betrays the cloven foot; or a milder and better
spirit appears in its stead. A temper sullen or active, shy
or bold, grave or lively, selfish or romantic, (to say nothing
of quickness or dullness of apprehension) is manifest
very early ; and imperceptibly but irresistibly moulds
our inclinations, habits, and pursuits through life. The
greater or less degree of animal spirits,—of nervous
irritability,—the complexion of the blood,—the proportion of " hot, cold, moist, and dry, four champions fierce

that strive for mastery,"—the Saturnine or the Mercurial,
—the disposition to be affected by objects near, or at a
distance, or not at all,—to be struck with novelty, or
to brood over deep-rooted impressions,—to indulge in
laughter or in tears, the leaven of passion or of prudence
that tempers this frail clay, is born with us and never
quits us. " It is not in our stars," in planetary influence,
but neither is it owing " to ourselves, that we are thus
or thus." The accession of knowledge, the pressure of
circumstances, favourable or unfavourable, does little
more than minister occasion to the first predisposing bias
—than assist, like the dews of heaven, or retard, like the
nipping north, the growth of the seed originally sown in
our constitution—than give a more or less decided
expression to that personal character, the outlines of
which nothing can alter. What I mean is, that Blifil and
Tom Jones, for instance, by changing places, would
never have changed characters. The one might, from
circumstances, and from the notions instilled into him,
have become a little less selfish, and the other a little less
extravagant; but with a trifling allowance of this sort,
taking the proposition *cum grano salis*, they would have
been just where they set out. Blifil would have been
Blifil still, and Jones what nature intended him to be.
I have made use of this example without any apology for
its being a fictitious one, because I think good novels are
the most authentic as well as most accessible repositories
of the natural history and philosophy of the species.

I shall not borrow assistance or illustration from the
organic system of Doctors Gall and Spurzheim, which
reduces this question to a small compass and very distinct
limits, because I do not understand or believe in it: but
I think those who put faith in physiognomy at all, or
imagine that the mind is stamped upon the countenance,
must believe that there is such a thing as an essential
difference of character in different individuals. We do

not change our features with our situations; neither do we change the capacities or inclinations which lurk beneath them. A flat face does not become an oval one, nor a pug nose a Roman one, with the acquisition of an office, or the addition of a title. So neither is the pert, hard, unfeeling outline of character turned from selfishness and cunning to openness and generosity by any softening of circumstances. If the face puts on an habitual smile in the sunshine of fortune, or if it suddenly lowers in the storms of adversity, do not trust too implicitly to appearances; the man is the same at bottom. The designing knave may sometimes wear a vizor, or, " to beguile the time, look like the time "; but watch him narrowly, and you will detect him behind his mask! We recognize, after a length of years, the same well-known face that we were formerly acquainted with, changed by time, but the same in itself; and can trace the features of the boy in the full-grown man. Can we doubt that the character and thoughts have remained as much the same all that time; have borne the same image and superscription; have grown with the growth, and strengthened with the strength? In this sense, and in Mr. Wordsworth's phrase, " the child's the father of the man " surely enough. The same tendencies may not always be equally visible, but they are still in existence, and break out, whenever they dare and can, the more for being checked. Again, we often distinctly notice the same features, the same bodily peculiarities, the same look and gestures, in different persons of the same family; and find this resemblance extending to collateral branches and through several generations, showing how strongly nature must have been warped and biassed in that particular direction at first. This pre-determination in the blood has its caprices too, and wayward as well as obstinate fits. The family-likeness sometimes skips over the next of kin or the nearest branch, and reappears in all

its singularity in a second or third cousin, or passes over
the son to the grandchild. Where the pictures of the
heirs and successors to a title or estate have been preserved
for any length of time in Gothic halls and old-fashioned
mansions, the prevailing outline and character does not
wear out, but may be traced through its numerous
inflections and descents, like the winding of a river
through an expanse of country, for centuries. The ancestor of many a noble house has sat for the portraits of
his youthful descendants; and still the soul of " Fairfax
and the starry Vere," consecrated in Marvel's verse, may
be seen mantling in the suffused features of some young
court-beauty of the present day. The portrait of Judge
Jeffries, which was exhibited lately in the Gallery in Pall
Mall—young, handsome, spirited, good-humoured, and
totally unlike, at first view, what you would expect from
the character—was an exact likeness of two young men
whom I knew some years ago, the living representatives
of that family. It is curious that, consistently enough
with the delineation in the portrait, old Evelyn should
have recorded in his *Memoirs*, that " he saw the Chief-
Justice Jeffries in a large company the night before, and
that he thought he laughed, drank and danced too much
for a man who had that day condemned Algernon Sidney
to the block." It is not always possible to foresee the
tiger's spring, till we are in his grasp; the fawning, cruel
eye dooms its prey, while it glitters! Features alone do
not run in the blood; vices and virtues, genius and folly
are transmitted through the same sure but unseen
channel. There is an involuntary, unaccountable family
character, as well as family face; and we see it manifesting
itself in the same way, with unbroken continuity, or by
fits and starts. There shall be a regular breed of misers,
of incorrigible old *hunkses* in a family, time out of mind;
or the shame of the thing, and the hardships and restraint
imposed upon him while young, shall urge some desperate

spendthrift to wipe out the reproach upon his name by a course of extravagance and debauchery; and his immediate successors shall make his example an excuse for relapsing into the old jog-trot incurable infirmity, the grasping and pinching disease of the family again.[1] A person may be indebted for a nose or an eye, for a graceful carriage or a voluble discourse, to a great-aunt or uncle, whose existence he has scarcely heard of; and distant relations are surprised, on some casual introduction, to find each other an *alter idem*. Country cousins, who meet after they are grown up for the first time in London, often start at the likeness,—it is like looking at themselves in the glass—nay, they shall see, almost before they exchange a word, their own thoughts (as it were) staring them in the face, the same ideas, feelings, opinions, passions, prejudices, likings and antipathies; the same turn of mind and sentiment, the same foibles, peculiarities, faults, follies, misfortunes, consolations, the same self, the same everything! And farther, this coincidence shall take place and be most remarkable, where not only no intercourse has previously been kept up, not even by letter or by common friends, but where the different branches of a family have been estranged for long years, and where the younger part in each have been brought up in totally different situations, with different studies, pursuits, expectations and opportunities. To assure me that this is owing to circumstances, is to assure me of a gratuitous absurdity, which you cannot know,

[1] " I know at this time a person of vast estate, who is the immediate descendant of a fine gentleman, but the great-grandson of a broker, in whom his ancestor is now revived. He is a very honest gentleman in his principles, but cannot for his blood talk fairly : he is heartily sorry for it; but he cheats by constitution, and overreaches by instinct."—See this subject delightfully treated in the 75th Number of the *Tatler*, in an account of Mr. Bickerstaff's pedigree, on occasion of his sister's marriage.

and which I shall not believe. It is owing, not to circumstances, but to the force of kind, to the stuff of which our blood and humours are compounded being the same. Why should I and an old hair-brained uncle of mine fasten upon the same picture in a Collection, and talk of it for years after, though one of no particular " mark or likelihood " in itself, but for something congenial in the look to our own humour and way of seeing nature? Why should my cousin L—— and I fix upon the same book, *Tristram Shandy*—without comparing notes, have it " doubled down and dog-eared " in the same places, and live upon it as a sort of food that assimilated with our natural dispositions?—" Instinct, Hal, instinct! " They are fools who say otherwise, and have never studied nature or mankind, but in books and systems of philosophy. But, indeed, the colour of our lives is woven into the fatal thread at our births: our original sins, and our redeeming graces are infused into us; nor is the bond, that confirms our destiny, ever cancelled.

> " Beneath the hills, amid the flowery groves,
> The generations are prepar'd ; the pangs,
> The internal pangs, are ready ; the dread strife
> Of poor humanity's afflicted will
> Struggling in vain with ruthless destiny."

The " winged wounds " that rankle in our breasts to our latest day, were planted there long since, ticketed and labelled on the outside in small but indelible characters, written in our blood, " like that ensanguined flower inscribed with woe: " we are in the toils from the very first, hemmed in by the hunters; and these are our own passions, bred of our brain and humours, and that never leave us, but consume and gnaw the heart in our short lifetime, as worms wait for us in the grave!

Critics and authors, who congregate in large cities, and see nothing of the world but a sort of phantasmagoria, to whom the numberless characters they meet in the course of a few hours are fugitive " as the flies of a summer," evanescent as the figures in a *camera obscura*, may talk very learnedly, and attribute the motions of the puppets to circumstances of which they are confessedly in total ignorance. They see character only in the bust, and have not room (for the crowd) to study it as a whole length, that is, as it exists in reality. But those who trace things to their source, and proceed from individuals to generals, know better. School-boys, for example, who are early let into the secret, and see the seeds growing, are not only sound judges, but true prophets of character; so that the nick-names they give their playfellows usually stick by them ever after. The gossips in country-towns, also, who study human nature, not merely in the history of the individual, but in the genealogy of the race, know the comparative anatomy of the minds of a whole neighbour-hood to a tittle, where to look for marks and defects—explain a vulgarity by a cross in the breed, or a foppish air in a young tradesman by his grandmother's marriage with a dancing-master, and are the only practical con-jurors and expert decypherers of the determinate lines of true or supposititious character.

The character of women (I should think it will at this time of day be granted) differs essentially from that of men, not less so than their shape or the texture of their skin. It has been said indeed, " Most women have no character at all,"—and on the other hand, the fair and eloquent Authoress of the *Rights of Women* was for estab-lishing the masculine pretensions and privileges of her sex on a perfect equality with ours. I shall leave Pope and Mary Wolstonecraft to settle that point between them. I should laugh at any one who told me that the European, the Asiatic, and the African character were the same. I no more believe it than I do that black is the same colour as white, or that a straight line is a crooked one. We see in whole nations and large classes the physiognomies, and I should suppose ("not to speak it profanely") the general characters of different animals with which we are acquainted, as of the fox, the wolf, the hog, the goat, the dog, the monkey; and I suspect this analogy, whether perceived or not, has as prevailing an influence on their habits and actions as any theory of moral sentiments taught in the schools. Rules and precautions may, no doubt, be applied to counteract the excesses and overt demonstrations of any such characteristic infirmity; but still the disease will be in the mind, an impediment, not a help to virtue. An exception is usually taken to all national or general reflections, as unjust and illiberal, because they cannot be true of every individual. It is not meant that they are; and besides, the same captious objection is not made to the handsome things that are said of whole bodies and classes of men. A lofty panegyric, a boasted virtue will fit the inhabitants of an entire district to a hair; the want of strict universality, of philosophical and abstract truth, is no difficulty here; but if you hint at an obvious vice or defect, this is instantly construed into a most unfair and partial view of the case, and each defaulter throws the imputation from himself and his country with scorn. Thus you may praise the generosity of the English, the prudence of the Scotch, the hospitality of the Irish, as long as you please, and not a syllable is whispered against these sweeping expressions of admiration; but reverse the picture, hold up to censure, or only glance at the unfavourable side of each character (and they themselves admit that they have a distinguishing and generic character as a people), and you are assailed by the most violent clamours, and a confused Babel of noises, as a disseminator of unfounded prejudices, or a libeller of human nature. I am sure there is nothing reasonable in this.—Harsh and disagreeable qualities wear out in nations, as in individuals, from time and intercourse with the world; but it is at the expense

of their intrinsic excellences. The vices of softness
and effeminacy sink deeper with age, like thorns in the
flesh. Single acts or events often determine the fate of
mortals, yet may have nothing to do with their general
deserts or failings. He who is said to be cured of any
glaring infirmity may be suspected never to have had it;
and lastly, it may be laid down as a general rule, that
mankind improve, by means of luxury and civilization,
in social manners, and become more depraved in what
relates to personal habits and character. There are few
nations, as well as few men (with the exception of tyrants),
that are cruel and voluptuous, immersed in pleasure, and
bent on inflicting pain on others, at the same time.
Ferociousness is the characteristic of barbarous ages,
licentiousness of more refined periods.[1]

I shall not undertake to decide exactly how far the
original character may be modified by the general progress
of society, or by particular circumstances happening to
the individual; but I think the alteration (be it what it
may) is more apparent than real, more in conduct than
in feeling. I will not deny, that an extreme and violent
difference of circumstances (as that between the savage
and civilized state) will supersede the common distinctions
of character, and prevent certain dispositions and sentiments from ever developing themselves. Yet with reference to this, I would observe, in the first place, that in
the most opposite ranks and conditions of life, we find
qualities shewing themselves, which we should have
least expected—grace in a cottage, humanity in a bandit,
sincerity in courts; and secondly, in ordinary cases, and
in the mixed mass of human affairs, the mind contrives
to lay hold of those circumstances and motives which

---

[1] *Fideliter didicisse ingenuas artes
Emollit mores, nec sinit esse feros.*

The same maxim does not establish the purity of morals
that infers their mildness.

suit its own bias and confirm its natural disposition, whatever it may be, gentle or rough, vulgar or refined. spirited or cowardly, open-hearted or cunning. The will is not blindly impelled by outward accidents, but selects the impressions by which it chooses to be governed, with great dexterity and perseverance. Or the machine may be at the disposal of fortune: the man is still his own master. The soul, under the pressure of circumstances, does not lose its original spring, but, as soon as the pressure is removed, recoils with double violence to its first position. That which any one has been long learning unwillingly, he unlearns with proportionable eagerness and haste. Kings have been said to be incorrigible to experience. The maxim might be extended, without injury, to the benefit of their subjects; for every man is a king (with all the pride and obstinacy of one) in his own little world. It is only lucky that the rest of the species are not answerable for his caprices! We laugh at the warnings and advice of others; we resent the lessons of adversity, and lose no time in letting it appear that we have escaped from its importunate hold. I do not think, with every assistance from reason and circumstances, that the slothful ever becomes active, the coward brave, the headstrong prudent, the fickle steady, the mean generous, the coarse delicate, the ill-tempered amiable, or the knave honest; but that the restraint of necessity and appearances once taken away, they would relapse into their former and real character again:—*Cucullus non facit monachum.* Manners, situation, example, fashion, have a prodigious influence on exterior deportment. But do they penetrate much deeper? The thief will not steal by day; but his having this command over himself does not do away his character or calling. The priest cannot indulge in certain irregularities; but unless his pulse beats temperately from the first, he will only be playing a part through life. Again, the soldier cannot shrink from his duty in a dastardly manner; but if he has not naturally steady nerves and strong resolution— except in the field of battle, he may be fearful as a woman, though covered with scars and honour. The judge must be disinterested and above suspicion; yet should he have from nature an itching palm, an eye servile and greedy of office, he will somehow contrive to indemnify his private conscience out of his public principle, and husband a reputation for legal integrity, as a stake to play the game of political profligacy with more advantage! There is often a contradiction in character, which is composed of various and unequal parts; and hence there will arise an appearance of fickleness and inconsistency. A man may be sluggish by the father's side, and of a restless and uneasy temper by the mother's; and he may favour either of these inherent dispositions according to circumstances. But he will not have changed his character, any more than a man who sometimes lives in one apartment of a house and then takes possession of another, according to whim or convenience, changes his habitation. The simply phlegmatic never turns to the truly " fiery quality." So, the really gay or trifling never become thoughtful and serious. The light-hearted wretch takes nothing to heart. He, on whom (from natural carelessness of disposition) " the shot of accident and dart of chance " fall like drops of oil on water, so that he brushes them aside with heedless hand and smiling face, will never be roused from his volatile indifference to meet inevitable calamities. He may try to laugh them off, but will not put himself to any inconvenience to prevent them. I know a man that, if a tiger were to jump into his room, would only play off some joke, some " quip, or crank, or wanton wile " upon him. Mortifications and disappointments may break such a person's heart; but they will be the death of him ere they will make him provident of the future, or willing to forego one idle gratification of the passing moment for any consideration whatever. The dilatory man never becomes punctual. Resolution is of no avail; for the very essence of the character consists in this, that the present impression is of more efficacy than any previous resolution. I have heard it said of a celebrated writer, that if he had to get a reprieve from the gallows for himself or a friend (with leave be it spoken), and was to be at a certain place at a given time for this purpose, he would be a quarter of an hour behind-hand. What is to be done in this case? Can you talk or argue a man out of his humour? You might as well attempt to talk or argue him out of a lethargy, or a fever. The disease is in the blood: you may see it (if you are a curious observer) meandering in his veins, and reposing on his eyelids! Some of our foibles are laid in the constitution of our bodies; others in the structure of our minds, and both are irremediable. The vain man, who is full of himself, is never cured of his vanity, but looks for admiration to the last, with a restless, suppliant eye, in the midst of contumely and contempt; the modest man never grows vain from flattery, or unexpected applause, for he sees himself in the diminished scale of other things. He will not " have his nothings monstered." He knows how much he himself wants, how much others have; and till you can alter this conviction in him, or make him drunk by infusing some new poison, some celestial *ichor* into his veins, you cannot make a coxcomb of him. He is too well aware of the truth of what has been said, that " the wisest amongst us is a fool in some things, as the lowest amongst men has some just notions, and therein is as wise as Socrates; so that every man resembles a statue made to stand against a wall, or in a niche; on one side it is a Plato, an Apollo, a Demosthenes; on the other, it is a rough, unformed piece of stone."[1] Some persons of my acquaintance, who think themselves *teres et rotundus*, and armed at all

[1] Richardson's Works, *On the Science of a Connoisseur*, p. 212.

points with perfections, would not be much inclined to give in to this sentiment, the modesty of which is only equalled by its sense and ingenuity. The man of sanguine temperament is seldom weaned from his castles in the air; nor can you, by virtue of any theory, convert the cold, careful calculator into a wild enthusiast. A self-tormentor is never satisfied, come what will. He always apprehends the worst, and is indefatigable in conjuring up the apparition of danger. He is uneasy at his own good fortune, as it takes from him his favourite topic of repining and complaint. Let him succeed to his heart's content in all that is reasonable or important, yet if there is any one thing (and *that* he is sure to find out) in which he does not get on, this embitters all the rest. I know an instance. Perhaps it is myself. Again, a surly man, in spite of warning, neglects his own interest, and will do so, because he has more pleasure in disobliging you than in serving himself. "A friendly man will show himself friendly " to the last; for those who are said to have been spoiled by prosperity were never really good for anything. A good-natured man never loses his native happiness of disposition: good temper is an estate for life; and a man born with common sense rarely turns out a very egregious fool. It is more common to see a fool become wise, that is, set up for wisdom, and be taken at his word by fools. We frequently judge of a man's intellectual pretensions by the number of books he writes; of his eloquence, by the number of speeches he makes; of his capacity for business, by the number of offices he holds. These are not true tests. Many a celebrated author is a known blockhead (between friends); and many a minister of state, whose gravity and self-importance pass with the world for depth of thought and weight of public care, is a laughing-stock to his very servants and dependents.[1]

[1] The reputation is not the man. Yet all true reputation begins and ends in the opinion of a man's intimate

The talents of some men, indeed, which might not otherwise have had a field to display themselves, are called
out by extraordinary situations, and rise with the occasion;
but for all the routine and mechanical preparation, the
pomp and parade and big looks of great statesmen, or
what is called merely *filling office*, a very shallow capacity,
with a certain immovableness of countenance, is, I should
suppose, sufficient, from what I have seen. Such political
machines are not so good as the Mock-Duke in the
Honeymoon. As to genius and capacity for the works of
art and science, all that a man really excels in is his
own and incommunicable; what he borrows from others
he has in an inferior degree, and it is never what his fame
rests on. Sir Joshua observes, that Raphael, in his latter
pictures, shewed that he had learnt in some measure the
colouring of Titian. If he had learnt it quite, the merit
would still have been Titian's; but he did not learn it,
and never would. But his expression (his glory and his
excellence) was what he had within himself, first and last;
and this it was that seated him on the pinnacle of fame,
a pre-eminence that no artist, without an equal warrant
from nature and genius, will ever deprive him of. With
respect to indications of early genius for particular things,
I will just mention, that I myself know an instance of
a little boy, who could catch the hardest tunes, when
between two and three years old, without any assistance
but hearing them played on a hand-organ in the street;

friends. He *is* what they think him, and in the last result will
be thought so by others. Where there is no solid merit to bear
the pressure of personal contact, fame is but a vapour raised by
accident or prejudice, and will soon vanish like a vapour or
a noisome stench. But he who appears to those about him what
he would have the world think him, from whom every one
that approaches him in whatever circumstances brings something away to confirm the loud rumour of the popular voice,
is alone great in spite of fortune. The malice of friendship, the
littleness of curiosity, is as severe a test as the impartiality and
enlarged views of history.

and who followed the exquisite pieces of Mozart, played to him for the first time, so as to fall in like an echo at the close. Was this accident, or education, or natural aptitude? I think the last. All the presumptions are for it, and there are none against it.

In fine, do we not see how hard certain early impressions, or prejudices acquired later, are to overcome? Do we not say habit is a second nature? And shall we not allow the force of nature itself? If the real disposition is concealed for a time and tampered with, how readily it breaks out with the first excuse or opportunity! How soon does the drunkard forget his resolution and constrained sobriety, at sight of the foaming tankard and blazing hearth! Does not the passion for gaming, in which there had been an involuntary pause, return like a madness all at once? It would be needless to offer instances of so obvious a truth. But if this superinduced nature is not to be got the better of by reason or prudence, who shall pretend to set aside the original one by prescription and management? Thus, if we turn to the characters of women, we find that the shrew, the jilt, the coquette, the wanton, the intriguer, the liar, continue all their lives the same. Meet them after the lapse of a quarter or half a century, and they are still infallibly at their old work. No rebuke from experience, no lessons of misfortune, make the least impression on them. On they go; and, in fact, they can go on in no other way. They try other things, but it will not do. They are like fish out of water, except in the element of their favourite vices. They might as well not be, as cease to be what they are by nature and custom. " Can the Ethiopian change his skin, or the leopard his spots? " Neither do these wretched persons find any satisfaction or consciousness of their power, but in being a plague and a torment to themselves and every one else as long as they can. A good sort of woman is a character more rare than any of these, but it is equally durable. Look at the head of Hogarth's Idle Apprentice in the boat, holding up his fingers as horns at Cuckold's Point, and ask what penitentiary, what prison-discipline, would change the form of his forehead, " villainous low," or the conceptions lurking within it? Nothing:—no mother's fearful warnings,—nor the formidable precautions of that wiser and more loving mother, his country! That fellow is still to be met with somewhere in our time. Is he a spy, a jack-ketch, or an underling of office? In truth, almost all the characters in Hogarth are of the class of incorrigibles; so that I often wonder what has become of some of them. Have the worst of them been cleared out, like the breed of noxious animals? Or have they been swept away, like locusts, in the whirlwind of the French Revolution? Or has Mr. Bentham put them into his Panopticon; from which they have come out, so that nobody knows them, like the chimney-sweeper boy at Sadler's Wells, that was thrown into a cauldron and came out a little dapper volunteer? I will not deny that some of them may, like Chaucer's characters, have been modernized a little; but I think I could re-translate a few of them into their mother tongue, the original honest *black-letter*. We may refine, we may disguise, we may equivocate, we may compound for our vices, without getting rid of them; as we change our liquors, but do not leave off drinking. We may, in this respect, look forward to a decent and moderate, rather than a thorough and radical reform. Or (without going deep into the political question) I conceive we may improve the mechanism, if not the texture of society; that is, we may improve the physical circumstances of individuals and their general relations to the State, though the internal character, like the grain in wood, or the sap in trees, that still rises, bend them how you will, may remain nearly the same. The clay that the potter uses may be of the same quality, coarse or fine in itself, though he may mould it into vessels of very different shape or beauty. Who shall alter the stamina of national character by any systematic process? Who shall make the French respectable, or the English amiable? Yet the Author of *The Year* 2500[1] has done it! Suppose public spirit to become the general principle of action in the community—how would it shew itself? Would it not then become the fashion, like loyalty, and have its apes and parrots, like loyalty? The man of principle would no longer be distinguished from the crowd, the *servum pecus imitatorum*. There is a cant of democracy as well as of aristocracy; and we have seen both triumphant in our day. The Jacobin of 1794 was the Anti-Jacobin of 1814. The loudest chaunters of the Pæans of liberty were the loudest applauders of the restored doctrine of Divine Right. They drifted with the stream, they sailed before the breeze in either case. The politician was changed; the man was the same, the very same!—But enough of this.

I do not know any moral to be deduced from this view of the subject but one, namely, that we should mind our own business, cultivate our good qualities, if we have any, and irritate ourselves less about the absurdities of other people, which neither we nor they can help. I grant there is something in what I have said which might be made to glance towards the doctrines of original sin, grace, election, reprobation, or the Gnostic principle that acts did not determine the virtue or vice of the character; and in those doctrines, so far as they are deducible from what I have said, I agree—but always with a salvo.

[1] Mercier.

ON GOING A JOURNEY

(NEW MONTHLY MAGAZINE, JAN., 1822)

O N E of the pleasantest things in the world is going a journey; but I like to go by myself. I can enjoy society in a room; but out of doors, nature is company enough for me. I am then never less alone that when alone.

> " The fields his study, nature was his book."

I cannot see the wit of walking and talking at the same time. When I am in the country I wish to vegetate like the country. I am not for criticizing hedge-rows and black cattle. I go out of town in order to forget the town and all that is in it. There are those who for this purpose go to watering-places, and carry the metropolis with them. I like more elbow-room and fewer incumbrances. I like solitude, when I give myself up to it, for the sake of solitude; nor do I ask for

> " a friend in my retreat,
> Whom I may whisper solitude is sweet."

The soul of a journey is liberty, perfect liberty, to think, feel, do, just as one pleases. We go a journey chiefly to be free of all impediments and of all inconveniences; to leave ourselves behind, much more to get rid of others. It is because I want a little breathing-space to muse on indifferent matters, where Contemplation

> " May plume her feathers and let grow her wings,
> That in the various bustle of resort
> Were all too ruffled, and sometimes impair'd,"

that I absent myself from the town for a while, without feeling at a loss the moment I am left by myself. Instead of a friend in a post-chaise or in a Tilbury, to exchange good things with, and vary the same stale

topics over again, for once let me have a truce with
impertinence. Give me the clear blue sky over my
head, and the green turf beneath my feet, a winding
road before me, and a three hours' march to dinner—
and then to thinking! It is hard if I cannot start some
game on these lone heaths. I laugh, I run, I leap, I
sing for joy. From the point of yonder rolling cloud
I plunge into my past being, and revel there, as the
sun-burnt Indian plunges headlong into the wave that
wafts him to his native shore. Then long-forgotten
things, like "sunken wrack and sumless treasuries,"
burst upon my eager sight, and I begin to feel, think,
and be myself again. Instead of an awkward silence,
broken by attempts at wit or dull common-places, mine
is that undisturbed silence of the heart which alone is
perfect eloquence. No one likes puns, alliterations,
antitheses, argument, and analysis better than I do;
but I sometimes had rather be without them. "Leave,
oh, leave me to my repose!" I have just now other
business in hand, which would seem idle to you, but is
with me "very stuff of the conscience." Is not this wild
rose sweet without a comment? Does not this daisy
leap to my heart set in its coat of emerald? Yet if I
were to explain to you the circumstance that has so
endeared it to me, you would only smile. Had I not
better then keep it to myself, and let it serve me to
brood over, from here to yonder craggy point, and
from thence onward to the far-distant horizon? I
should be but bad company all that way, and therefore
prefer being alone. I have heard it said that you may,
when the moody fit comes on, walk or ride on by yourself, and indulge your reveries. But this looks like a
breach of manners, a neglect of others, and you are
thinking all the time that you ought to rejoin your
party. "Out upon such half-faced fellowship," say I.
I like to be either entirely to myself, or entirely at the

disposal of others; to talk or be silent, to walk or sit still, to be sociable or solitary. I was pleased with an observation of Mr. Cobbett's, that " he thought it a bad French custom to drink our wine with our meals, and that an Englishman ought to do only one thing at a time." So I cannot talk and think, or indulge in melancholy musing and lively conversation by fits and starts. " Let me have a companion of my way," says Sterne, " were it but to remark how the shadows lengthen as the sun declines." It is beautifully said; but, in my opinion, this continual comparing of notes interferes with the involuntary impression of things upon the mind, and hurts the sentiment. If you only hint what you feel in a kind of dumb show, it is insipid: if you have to explain it, it is making a toil of a pleasure. You cannot read the book of nature without being perpetually put to the trouble of translating it for the benefit of others. I am for this synthetical method on a journey in preference to the analytical. I am content to lay in a stock of ideas then, and to examine and anatomise them afterwards. I want to see my vague notions float like the down of the thistle before the breeze, and not to have them entangled in the briars and thorns of controversy. For once, I like to have it all my own way; and this is impossible unless you are alone, or in such company as I do not covet. I have no objection to argue a point with any one for twenty miles of measured road, but not for pleasure. If you remark the scent of a bean-field crossing the road, perhaps your fellow-traveller has no smell. If you point to a distant object, perhaps he is short-sighted, and has to take out his glass to look at it. There is a feeling in the air, a tone in the colour of a cloud, which hits your fancy, but the effect of which you are unable to account for. There is then no sympathy, but an uneasy craving after it, and a dissatis-

D

faction which pursues you on the way, and in the end probably produces ill-humour. Now I never quarrel with myself, and take all my own conclusions for granted till I find it necessary to defend them against objections. It is not merely that you may not be of accord on the objects and circumstances that present themselves before you—these may recall a number of objects, and lead to associations too delicate and refined to be possibly communicated to others. Yet these I love to cherish, and sometimes still fondly clutch them, when I can escape from the throng to do so. To give way to our feelings before company seems extravagance or affectation; and, on the other hand, to have to unravel this mystery of our being at every turn, and to make others take an equal interest in it (otherwise the end is not answered), is a task to which few are competent. We must " give it an understanding, but no tongue." My old friend C[oleridge], however, could do both. He could go on in the most delightful explanatory way over hill and dale a summer's day, and convert a landscape into a didactic poem or a Pindaric ode. " He talked far above singing." If I could so clothe my ideas in sounding and flowing words, I might perhaps wish to have some one with me to admire the swelling theme; or I could be more content, were it possible for me still to hear his echoing voice in the woods of All-Foxden.[1] They had " that fine madness in them which our first poets had " ; and if they could have been caught by some rare instrument, would have breathed such strains as the following:—

> " Here be woods as green
> As any, air likewise as fresh and sweet
> As when smooth Zephyrus plays on the fleet
> Face of the curled streams, with flow'rs as many
> As the young spring gives, and as choice as any ;

[1] Near Nether-Stowey, Somersetshire, where Hazlitt visited Coleridge in 1798. (Ed.)

Here be all new delights, cool streams and wells,
Arbours o'ergrown with woodbine, caves and dells ;
Choose where thou wilt, whilst I sit by and sing,
Or gather rushes to make many a ring
For thy long fingers ; tell thee tales of love,
How the pale Phœbe, hunting in a grove,
First saw the boy Endymion, from whose eyes
She took eternal fire that never dies ;
How she convey'd him softly in a sleep,
His temples bound with poppy, to the steep
Head of old Latmos, where she stoops each night,
Gilding the mountain with her brother's light,
To kiss her sweetest."

Fletcher's *Faithful Shepherdess*.

Had I words and images at command like these, I would attempt to wake the thoughts that lie slumbering on golden ridges in the evening clouds: but at the sight of nature my fancy, poor as it is, droops and closes up its leaves, like flowers at sunset. I can make nothing out on the spot:—I must have time to collect myself.

In general, a good thing spoils out-of-door prospects: it should be reserved for Table-talk. L[amb] is for this reason, I take it, the worst company in the world out of doors; because he is the best within. I grant, there is one subject on which it is pleasant to talk on a journey; and that is, what one shall have for supper when we get to our inn at night. The open air improves this sort of conversation or friendly altercation, by setting a keener edge on appetite. Every mile of the road heightens the flavour of the viands we expect at the end of it. How fine it is to enter some old town, walled and turreted, just at approach of night-fall, or to come to some straggling village, with the lights streaming through the surrounding gloom; and then, after inquiring for the best entertainment that the place affords, to " take one's ease at one's inn "! These eventful moments in our lives' history are too precious, too full of solid, heart-felt happiness to be frittered and dribbled away in imperfect sympathy. I would have them all to myself, and drain them to the last drop: they will do to talk of or to write about afterwards. What a delicate speculation it is, after drinking whole goblets of tea—

" The cups that cheer, but not inebriate,"

and letting the fumes ascend into the brain, to sit considering what we shall have for supper—eggs and a rasher, a rabbit smothered in onions, or an excellent veal-cutlet! Sancho in such a situation once fixed upon cow-heel; and his choice, though he could not help it, is not to be disparaged. Then, in the intervals of pictured scenery and Shandean contemplation, to catch the preparation and the stir in the kitchen [getting ready for the gentleman in the parlour][1]. *Procul, O procul este profani!* These hours are sacred to silence and to musing, to be treasured up in the memory, and to feed the source of smiling thoughts hereafter. I would not waste them in idle talk; or if I must have the integrity of fancy broken in upon, I would rather it were by a stranger than a friend. A stranger takes his hue and character from the time and place; he is a part of the furniture and costume of an inn. If he is a Quaker, or from the West Riding of Yorkshire, so much the better. I do not even try to sympathise with him, and he breaks no squares. [How I love to see the camps of the gypsies, and to sigh my soul into that sort of life. If I express this feeling to another, he may qualify and spoil it with some objection.][1] I associate nothing with my travelling companion but present objects and passing events. In his ignorance of me and my affairs, I in a manner forget myself. But a friend reminds one of other things, rips up old grievances, and destroys the abstraction of the scene. He comes in ungraciously between us and our imaginary

[1] Added from the Author's MS. by W. C. H.

character. Something is dropped in the course of conversation that gives a hint of your profession and pursuits; or from having some one with you that knows the less sublime portions of your history, it seems that other people do. You are no longer a citizen of the world; but your "unhoused free condition is put into circumscription and confine." The *incognito* of an inn is one of its striking privileges—"lord of one's self, uncumber'd with a name." Oh! it is great to shake off the trammels of the world and of public opinion—to lose our importunate, tormenting, everlasting personal identity in the elements of nature, and become the creature of the moment, clear of all ties—to hold to the universe only by a dish of sweet-breads, and to owe nothing but the score of the evening—and no longer seeking for applause and meeting with contempt, to be known by no other title than *the Gentleman in the parlour!* One may take one's choice of all characters in this romantic state of uncertainty as to one's real pretensions, and become indefinitely respectable and negatively right-worshipful. We baffle prejudice and disappoint conjecture; and from being so to others, begin to be objects of curiosity and wonder even to ourselves. We are no more those hackneyed common-places that we appear in the world; an inn restores us to the level of nature, and quits scores with society! I have certainly spent some enviable hours at inns—sometimes when I have been left entirely to myself, and have tried to solve some metaphysical problem, as once at Witham-common, where I found out the proof that likeness is not a case of the association of ideas—at other times, when there have been pictures in the room, as at St. Neot's (I think it was), where I first met with Gribelin's engravings of the Cartoons, into which I entered at once, and at a little inn on the borders of Wales, where there happened to be hanging some of Westall's drawings, which I compared triumphantly (for a theory that I had, not for the admired artist) with the figure of a girl who had ferried me over the Severn, standing up in the boat between me and the twilight—at other times I might mention luxuriating in books, with a peculiar interest in this way, as I remember sitting up half the night to read *Paul and Virginia,* which I picked up at an inn at Bridgewater, after being drenched in the rain all day; and at the same place I got through two volumes of Madame D'Arblay's *Camilla.* It was on the tenth of April, 1798, that I sat down to a volume of the *New Eloise,* at the inn at Llangollen, over a bottle of sherry and a cold chicken. The letter I chose was that in which St. Preux describes his feelings as he first caught a glimpse from the heights of the Jura of the Pays de Vaud, which I had brought with me as a *bon bouche* to crown the evening with. It was my birth-day, and I had for the first time come from a place in the neighbourhood to visit this delightful spot. The road to Llangollen turns off between Chirk and Wrexham; and on passing a certain point you come all at once upon the valley, which opens like an amphitheatre, broad, barren hills rising in majestic state on either side, with " green upland swells that echo to the bleat of flocks " below, and the river Dee babbling over its stony bed in the midst of them. The valley at this time " glittered green with sunny showers," and a budding ash-tree dipped its tender branches in the chiding stream. How proud, how glad I was to walk along the high road that overlooks the delicious prospect, repeating the lines which I have just quoted from Mr. Coleridge's poems! But besides the prospect which opened beneath my feet, another also opened to my inward sight, a heavenly vision, on which were written, in letters large as Hope could make them, these four words, LIBERTY, GENIUS, LOVE, VIRTUE; which have since faded into the light of common day, or mock my idle gaze.

"The beautiful is vanished, and returns not."

Still I would return some time or other to this enchanted spot; but I would return to it alone. What other self could I find to share that influx of thoughts, of regret, and delight, the fragments of which I could hardly conjure up to myself, so much have they been broken and defaced. I could stand on some tall rock, and overlook the precipice of years that separates me from what I then was. I was at that time going shortly to visit the poet whom I have above named. Where is he now? Not only I myself have changed; the world which was then new to me, has become old and incorrigible. Yet will I turn to thee in thought, O sylvan Dee, in joy, in youth and gladness as thou then wert; and thou shalt always be to me the river of Paradise, where I will drink of the waters of life freely!

There is hardly anything that shows the short-sightedness or capriciousness of the imagination more than travelling does. With change of place we change our ideas; nay, our opinions and feelings. We can by an effort indeed transport ourselves to old and long-forgotten scenes, and then the picture of the mind revives again; but we forget those that we have just left. It seems that we can think but of one place at a time. The canvas of the fancy is but of a certain extent, and if we paint one set of objects upon it, they immediately efface every other. We cannot enlarge our conceptions, we only shift our point of view. The landscape bares its bosom to the enraptured eye, we take our fill of it, and seem as if we could form no other image of beauty or grandeur. We pass on, and think no more of it: the horizon that shuts it from our sight, also blots it from our memory like a dream. In

travelling through a wild barren country I can form
no idea of a woody and cultivated one. It appears to
me that all the world must be barren, like what I see
of it. In the country we forget the town, and in town
we despise the country. " Beyond Hyde Park," says
Sir Topling Flutter, " all is a desert." All that part of
the map that we do not see before us is a blank. The
world in our conceit of it is not much bigger than a
nutshell. It is not one prospect expanded into another,
county joined to county, kingdom to kingdom, lands
to seas, making an image voluminous and vast;—the
mind can form no larger idea of space than the eye
can take in at a single glance. The rest is a name
written in a map, a calculation of arithmetic. For
instance, what is the true signification of that immense
mass of territory and population known by the name
of China to us? An inch of pasteboard on a wooden
globe, of no more account than a China orange! Things
near us are seen of the size of life: things at a distance
are diminished to the size of the understanding. We
measure the universe by ourselves, and even comprehend
the texture of our being only piece-meal. In this way,
however, we remember an infinity of things and places.
The mind is like a mechanical instrument that plays a
great variety of tunes, but it must play them in succession. One idea recalls another, but it at the same time
excludes all others. In trying to renew old recollections, we cannot as it were unfold the whole web of our
existence; we must pick out the single threads. So in
coming to a place where we have formerly lived, and
with which we have intimate associations, every one
must have found that the feeling grows more vivid the
nearer we approach the spot, from the mere anticipation of the actual impression: we remember circumstances, feelings, persons, faces, names that we had not
thought of for years; but for the time all the rest of

the world is forgotten!—To return to the question I have
quitted above:

I have no objection to go to see ruins, aqueducts,
pictures, in company with a friend or a party, but
rather the contrary, for the former reason reversed.
They are intelligible matters, and will bear talking
about. The sentiment here is not tacit, but communicable and overt. Salisbury Plain is barren of criticism,
but Stonehenge will bear a discussion antiquarian,
picturesque, and philosophical. In setting out on a
party of pleasure, the first consideration always is where
we shall go to: in taking a solitary ramble, the question
is what we shall meet with by the way. " The mind
is its own place "; nor are we anxious to arrive at the
end of our journey. I can myself do the honours indifferently well to works of art and curiosity. I once took a
party to Oxford with no mean *éclat*—shewed them that
seat of the Muses at a distance,

" With glistering spires and pinnacles adorn'd—"

descanted on the learned air that breathes from the
grassy quadrangles and stone walls of halls and colleges
—was at home in the Bodleian; and at Blenheim quite
superseded the powdered Cicerone that attended us,
and that pointed in vain with his wand to common-
place beauties in matchless pictures. As another exception to the above reasoning, I should not feel confident
in venturing on a journey in a foreign country without
a companion. I should want at intervals to hear the
sound of my own language. There is an involuntary
antipathy in the mind of an Englishman to foreign
manners and notions that requires the assistance of
social sympathy to carry it off. As the distance from
home increases, this relief, which was at first a luxury,
becomes a passion and an appetite. A person would
almost feel stifled to find himself in the deserts of

D *

Arabia without friends and countrymen: there must be allowed to be something in the view of Athens or old Rome that claims the utterance of speech; and I own that the Pyramids are too mighty for any single contemplation. In such situations, so opposite to all one's ordinary train of ideas, one seems a species by one's-self, a limb torn off from society, unless one can meet with instant fellowship and support.—Yet I did not feel this want or craving very pressing once, when I first set my foot on the laughing shores of France. Calais was peopled with novelty and delight.. The confused, busy murmur of the place was like oil and wine poured into my ears; nor did the mariners' hymn, which was sung from the top of an old crazy vessel in the harbour, as the sun went down, send an alien sound into my soul. I only breathed the air of general humanity. I walked over " the vine-covered hills and gay regions of France," erect and satisfied; for the image of man was not cast down and chained to the foot of arbitrary thrones: I was at no loss for language, for that of all the great schools of painting was open to me. The whole is vanished like a shade. Pictures, heroes, glory, freedom, all are fled: nothing remains but the Bourbons and the French people!—There is undoubtedly a sensation in travelling into foreign parts that is to be had nowhere else; but it is more pleasing at the time than lasting. It is too remote from our habitual associations to be a common topic of discourse or reference, and, like a dream or another state of existence, does not piece into our daily modes of life. It is an animated but a momentary hallucination. It demands an effort to exchange our actual for our ideal identity; and to feel the pulse of our old transports revive very keenly, we must " jump " all our present comforts and connexions. Our romantic and itinerant character is not to be domesticated. Dr.

Johnson remarked how little foreign travel added to the facilities of conversation in those who had been abroad. In fact, the time we have spent there is both delightful, and in one sense instructive; but it appears to be cut out of our substantial, downright existence, and never to join kindly on to it. We are not the same, but another, and perhaps more enviable individual, all the time we are out of our own country. We are lost to ourselves, as well as our friends. So the poet somewhat quaintly sings,

> "Out of my country and myself I go."

Those who wish to forget painful thoughts, do well to absent themselves for a while from the ties and objects that recall them; but we can be said only to fulfil our destiny in the place that gave us birth. I should on this account like well enough to spend the whole of my life in travelling abroad, if I could anywhere borrow another life to spend afterwards at home!

THE FIGHT

(NEW MONTHLY MAGAZINE, FEB., 1822)

> ——"The *fight*, the *fight's* the thing,
> Wherein I'll catch the conscience of the king."

Where there's a will, there's a way.—I said so to myself, as I walked down Chancery lane, about half-past six o'clock on Monday the 10th of December, to inquire at Jack Randall's where the fight the next day was to be; and I found "the proverb" nothing "musty" in the present instance. I was determined to see this fight, come what would, and see it I did, in great style. It was my *first fight,* yet it more than answered my expectations.

Ladies! it is to you I dedicate this description; nor let it seem out of character for the fair to notice the exploits of the brave. Courage and modesty are the old English virtues; and may they never look cold and askance on one another! Think, ye fairest of the fair, loveliest of the lovely kind, ye practisers of soft enchantment, how many more ye kill with poisoned baits than ever fell in the ring; and listen with subdued air and without shuddering, to a tale tragic only in appearance, and sacred to the FANCY!

I was going down Chancery lane, thinking to ask at Jack Randall's where the fight was to be, when looking through the glass-door of the *Hole in the Wall*, I heard a gentleman asking the same question *at* Mrs. Randall, as the author of *Waverley* would express it. Now Mrs. Randall stood answering the gentleman's question, with the authenticity of the lady of the Champion of the Light Weights. Thinks I, I'll wait till this person comes out, and learn from him how it is. For to say a truth, I was not fond of going into this house of call for heroes and philosophers, ever since the owner of it (for Jack is no gentleman) threatened once upon a time to kick me out of doors for wanting a mutton-chop at his hospitable board, when the conqueror in thirteen battles was more full of *blue ruin* than of good manners. I was the more mortified at this repulse, inasmuch as I had heard Mr. James Simpkins, hosier in the Strand, one day when the character of the *Hole in the Wall* was brought in question, observe—" The house is a very good house, and the company quite genteel: I have been there myself!" Remembering this unkind treatment of mine host, to which mine hostess was also a party, and not wishing to put her in unquiet thoughts at a time jubilant like the present, I waited at the door, when, who should issue forth but my friend Joe Toms, and turning suddenly up Chancery lane with that quick jerk and impatient stride

which distinguishes a lover of the FANCY, I said, " I'll be
hanged if that fellow is not going to the fight, and is on
his way to get me to go with him." So it proved in effect,
and we agreed to adjourn to my lodgings to discuss
measures with that cordiality which makes old friends
like new, and new friends like old, on great occasions.
We are cold to others only when we are dull in ourselves
and have neither thoughts nor feelings to impart to them.
Give a man a topic in his head, a throb of pleasure in his
heart, and he will be glad to share it with the first person
he meets. Toms and I, though we seldom meet, were an
alter idem on this memorable occasion, and had not an
idea that we did not candidly impart; and " so carelessly
did we fleet the time," that I wish no better, when there
is another fight, than to have him for a companion on
my journey down, and to return with my friend Jack
Pigott, talking of what was to happen or of what did
happen, with a noble subject always at hand, and liberty
to digress to others whenever they offered. Indeed, on
my repeating the lines from Spenser in an involuntary
fit of enthusiasm,

" What more felicity can fall to creature,
Than to enjoy delight with liberty ? "

my last-named ingenious friend stopped me by saying
that this, translated into the vulgate, meant " *Going to
see a fight.*"

Joe Toms and I could not settle about the method of
going down. He said there was a caravan, he understood,
to start from Tom Belcher's at two, which would go
there *right out* and back again the next day. Now I never
travel all night, and said I should get a cast to Newbury
by one of the mails. Joe swore the thing was impossible,
and I could only answer that I had made up my mind to
it. In short, he seemed to me to waver, said he only
came to see if I was going, had letters to write, a cause
coming on the day after, and faintly said at parting (for

I was bent on setting out that moment)—" Well, we meet at Philippi! " I made the best of my way to Piccadilly. The mail coach stand was bare. " They are all gone," said I—" this is always the way with me—in the instant I lose the future—if I had not stayed to pour out that last cup of tea, I should have been just in time; "—and cursing my folly and ill-luck together, without inquiring at the coach-office whether the mails were gone or not, I walked on in despite, and to punish my own dilatoriness and want of determination. At any rate, I would not turn back: I might get to Hounslow, or perhaps farther, to be on my road the next morning. I passed Hyde park corner (my Rubicon), and trusted to fortune. Suddenly I heard the clattering of a Brentford stage, and the fight rushed full upon my fancy. I argued (not unwisely) that even a Brentford coachman was better company than my own thoughts (such as they were just then) and at his invitation mounted the box with him. I immediately stated my case to him—namely, my quarrel with myself for missing the Bath or Bristol mail, and my determination to get on in consequence as well as I could, without any disparagement or insulting comparison between longer or shorter stages. It is a maxim with me that stage-coaches, and consequently stage-coachmen, are respect-able in proportion to the distance they have to travel: so I said nothing on that subject to my Brentford friend. Any incipient tendency to an abstract proposition, or (as he might have construed it) to a personal reflection of this kind, was however nipped in the bud; for I had no sooner declared indignantly that I had missed the mails, than he flatly denied that they were gone along, and lo! at the instant three of them drove by in rapid, provoking, orderly succession, as if they would devour the ground before them. Here again I seemed in the contradictory situation of the man in Dryden who exclaims,

" I follow Fate, which does too hard pursue ! "

If I had stopped to inquire at the White Horse Cellar, which would not have taken me a minute, I should now have been driving down the road in all the dignified unconcern and *ideal* perfection of mechanical conveyance. The Bath mail I had set my mind upon, and I had missed it, as I miss everything else, by my own absurdity, in putting the will for the deed, and aiming at ends without employing means. " Sir," said he of the Brentford, " the Bath mail will be up presently, my brother-in-law drives it, and I will engage to stop him if there is a place empty." I almost doubted my good genius; but, sure enough, up it drove like lightning, and stopped directly at the call of the Brentford Jehu. I would not have believed this possible, but the brother-in-law of a mail-coach driver is himself no mean man. I was transferred without loss of time from the top of one coach to that of the other, desired the guard to pay my fare to the Brentford coachman for me as I had no change, was accommodated with a great coat, put up my umbrella to keep off a drizzling mist, and we began to cut through the air like an arrow. The mile-stones disappeared one after another, the rain kept off; Tom Turtle,[1] the trainer, sat before me on the coach-box, with whom I exchanged civilities as a gentleman going to the fight; the passion that had transported me an hour before was subdued to pensive regret and conjectural musing on the next day's battle; I was promised a place inside at Reading, and upon the whole, I thought myself a lucky fellow. Such is the force of imagination! On the outside of any other coach on the 10th of December, with a Scotch mist drizzling through the cloudy moonlight air, I should have been cold, comfortless, impatient, and, no doubt, wet through; but seated on the Royal mail, I felt warm and comfortable, the air did me good, the ride did me good, I was pleased with the progress we had made, and confident that all would

[1] John Thurtell, to wit. [W. H. jun.]

go well through the journey. When I got inside at
Reading, I found Turtle and a stout valetudinarian,
whose costume bespoke him one of the FANCY, and who
had risen from a three months' sick bed to get into the
mail to see the fight. They were intimate, and we fell
into a lively discourse. My friend the trainer was confined in his topics to fighting dogs and men, to bears and
badgers; beyond this he was " quite chap-fallen," had
not a word to throw at a dog, or indeed very wisely fell
asleep, when any other game was started. The whole art
of training (I, however, learnt from him,) consists in two
things, exercise and abstinence, abstinence and exercise,
repeated alternately and without end. A yolk of an egg
with a spoonful of rum in it is the first thing in a morning,
and then a walk of six miles till breakfast. This meal
consists of a plentiful supply of tea and toast and beef-
steaks. Then another six or seven miles till dinner-time,
and another supply of solid beef or mutton with a pint
of porter, and perhaps, at the utmost, a couple of glasses
of sherry. Martin trains on water, but this increases his
infirmity on another very dangerous side. The Gas-man
takes now and then a chirping glass (under the rose) to
console him, during a six weeks' probation, for the
absence of Mrs. Hickman—an agreeable woman, with
(I understand) a pretty fortune of two hundred pounds.
How matter presses on me! What stubborn things are
facts! How inexhaustible is nature and art! " It is well,"
as I once heard Mr. Richmond observe, " to see a variety."
He was speaking of cock-fighting as an edifying spectacle.
I cannot deny but that one learns more of what *is* (I do
not say of what *ought to be*) in this desultory mode of
practical study, than from reading the same book twice
over, even though it should be a moral treatise. Where
was I? I was sitting at dinner with the candidate for the
honours of the ring, " where good digestion waits on
appetite, and health on both." Then follows an hour of

social chat and native glee; and afterwards, to another
breathing over heathy hill or dale. Back to supper, and
then to bed, and up by six again—Our hero

> " Follows so the ever-running sun,
> With profitable *ardour*——"

to the day that brings him victory or defeat in the green
fairy circle. Is not this life more sweet than mine?
I was going to say; but I will not libel any life by comparing it to mine, which is (at the date of these presents)
bitter as coloquintida and the dregs of aconitum!

The invalid in the Bath mail soared a pitch above the
trainer, and did not sleep so sound, because he had
" more figures and more fantasies." We talked the hours
away merrily. He had faith in surgery, for he had had
three ribs set right, that had been broken in a *turn-up*
at Belcher's, but thought physicians old women, for they
had no antidote in their catalogue for brandy. An
indigestion is an excellent common-place for two people
that never met before. By way of ingratiating myself,
I told him the story of my doctor, who, on my earnestly
representing to him that I thought his regimen had done
me harm, assured me that the whole pharmacopeia
contained nothing comparable to the prescription he had
given me; and, as a proof of its undoubted efficacy, said,
that " he had had one gentleman with my complaint
under his hands for the last fifteen years." This anecdote
made my companion shake the rough sides of his three
great coats with boisterous laughter; and Turtle, starting
out of his sleep, swore he knew how the fight would go,
for he had had a dream about it. Sure enough the rascal
told us how the three first rounds went off, but " his
dream," like others, " denoted a foregone conclusion."
He knew his men. The moon now rose in silver state,
and I ventured, with some hesitation, to point out this
object of placid beauty, with the blue serene beyond, to

the man of science, to which his ear he " seriously inclined," the more as it gave promise *d'un beau jour* for
the morrow, and showed the ring undrenched by envious
showers, arrayed in sunny smiles. Just then, all going on
well, I thought on my friend Toms, whom I had left
behind, and said innocently, " There was a blockhead of
a fellow I left in town, who said there was no possibility
of getting down by the mail, and talked of going by a
caravan from Belcher's at two in the morning, after he
had written some letters." " Why," said he of the lapells,
" I should not wonder if that was the very person we
saw running about like mad from one coach-door to
another, and asking if any one had seen a friend of his,
a gentleman going to the fight, whom he had missed
stupidly enough by staying to write a note." " Pray,
Sir," said my fellow-traveller, " had he a plaid-cloak
on? "—" Why, no," said I, " not at the time I left him,
but he very well might afterwards, for he offered to lend
me one." The plaid-cloak and the letter decided the
thing. Joe, sure enough, was in the Bristol mail, which
preceded us by about fifty yards. This was droll enough.
We had now but a few miles to our place of destination,
and the first thing I did on alighting at Newbury, both
coaches stopping at the same time, was to call out,
" Pray, is there a gentleman in that mail of the name of
Toms? " " No," said Joe, borrowing something of the
vein of Gilpin, " for I have just got out." " Well! " says
he, " this is lucky; but you don't know how vexed I was
to miss you; for," added he, lowering his voice, " do you
know when I left you I went to Belcher's to ask about the
caravan, and Mrs. Belcher said very obligingly, she
couldn't tell about that, but there were two gentlemen
who had taken places by the mail and were gone on in a
laudau, and she could frank us. It's a pity I didn't meet
with you; we could then have got down for nothing.
But *mum's the word*." It's the devil for any one to tell

me a secret, for it is sure to come out in print. I do not care so much to gratify a friend, but the public ear is too great a temptation to me.

Our present business was to get beds and a supper at an inn; but this was no easy task. The public-houses were full, and where you saw a light at a private house, and people poking their heads out of the casement to see what was going on, they instantly put them in and shut the window, the moment you seemed advancing with a suspicious overture for accommodation. Our guard and coachman thundered away at the outer gate of the Crown for some time without effect—such was the greater noise within;—and when the doors were unbarred, and we got admittance, we found a party assembled in the kitchen round a good hospitable fire, some sleeping, others drinking, others talking on politics and on the fight. A tall English yeoman (something like Matthews in the face, and quite as great a wag)—

" A lusty man to ben an abbot able,"—

was making such a prodigious noise about rent and taxes, and the price of corn now and formerly, that he had prevented us from being heard at the gate. The first thing I heard him say was to a shuffling fellow who wanted to be off a bet for a shilling glass of brandy and water—" Confound it, man, don't be *insipid !* " Thinks I, that is a good phrase. It was a good omen. He kept it up so all night, nor flinched with the approach of morning. He was a fine fellow, with sense, wit, and spirit, a hearty body and a joyous mind, free-spoken, frank, convivial—one of that true English breed that went with Harry the Fifth to the siege of Harfleur—" standing like greyhounds in the slips," &c. We ordered tea and eggs (beds were soon found to be out of the question) and this fellow's conversation was *sauce piquante*. It did one's heart good to see him brandish his oaken towel and to hear him talk. He made mince-meat of a drunken, stupid, red-faced, quarrelsome, *frowsy* farmer, whose nose " he moralized into a thousand similes," making it out a firebrand like Bardolph's. " I'll tell you what, my friend," says he, " the landlady has only to keep you here to save fire and candle. If one was to touch your nose, it would go off like a piece of charcoal." At this the other only grinned like an idiot, the sole variety in his purple face being his little peering grey eyes and yellow teeth; called for another glass, swore he would not stand it; and after many attempts to provoke his humorous antagonist to single combat, which the other turned off (after working him up to a ludicrous pitch of choler) with great adroitness, he fell quietly asleep with a glass of liquor in his hand, which he could not lift to his head. His laughing persecutor made a speech over him, and turning to the opposite side of the room, where they were all sleeping in the midst of this " loud and furious fun," said, " There's a scene, by G-d, for Hogarth to paint. I think he and Shakespeare were our two best men at copying life." This confirmed me in my good opinion of him. Hogarth, Shakespeare and Nature, were just enough for him (indeed for any man) to know. I said, " You read Cobbett, don't you? At least," says I, " you talk just as well as he writes." He seemed to doubt this. But I said, " We have an hour to spare: if you'll get pen, ink, and paper, and keep on talking, I'll write down what you say; and if it doesn't make a capital ' Political Register,' I'll forfeit my head. You have kept me alive to-night, however. I don't know what I should have done without you." He did not dislike this view of the thing, nor my asking if he was not about the size of Jem Belcher; and told me soon afterwards, in the confidence of friendship, that " the circumstance which had given him nearly the greatest concern in his life, was Cribb's beating Jem after he had lost his eye by racket

playing."—The morning dawns; that dim but yet clear
light appears, which weighs like solid bars of metal on
the sleepless eyelids; the guests drop down from their
chambers one by one—but it was too late to think of
going to bed now (the clock was on the stroke of seven),
we had nothing for it but to find a barber's (the pole that
glittered in the morning sun lighted us to his shop), and
then a nine miles' march to Hungerford. The day was
fine, the sky was blue, the mists were retiring from the
marshy ground, the path was tolerably dry, the sitting-up
all night had not done us much harm—at least the cause
was good; we talked of this and that with amicable
difference, roving and sipping of many subjects, but still
invariably we returned to the fight. At length, a mile to
the left of Hungerford, on a gentle eminence, we saw the
ring surrounded by covered carts, gigs, and carriages, of
which hundreds had passed us on the road; Toms gave
a youthful shout, and we hastened down a narrow lane
to the scene of action.

Reader, have you ever seen a fight? If not, you have
a pleasure to come, at least if it is a fight like that between
the Gas-man and Bill Neate. The crowd was very great
when we arrived on the spot; open carriages were coming
up, with streamers flying and music playing, and the
country-people were pouring in over hedge and ditch in
all directions, to see their hero beat or be beaten.
The odds were still on Gas, but only about five to four.
Gully had been down to try Neate, and had backed him
considerably, which was a damper to the sanguine
confidence of the adverse party. About two hundred
thousand pounds were pending. The Gas says, he has
lost 3000l. which were promised him by different gentlemen if he had won. He had presumed too much on himself, which had made others presume on him. This
spirited and formidable young fellow seems to have
taken for his motto the old maxim, that " there are three

things necessary to success in life—*Impudence! Impudence! Impudence!* " It is so in matters of opinion, but not in the FANCY, which is the most practical of all things, though even here confidence is half the battle, but only half. Our friend had vapoured and swaggered too much, as if he wanted to grin and bully his adversary out of the fight. " Alas! the Bristol man was not so tamed! "—" This is *the grave-digger* " (would Tom Hickman exclaim in the moments of intoxication from gin and success, shewing his tremendous right hand), " this will send many of them to their long homes; I haven't done with them yet! " Why should he—though he had licked four of the best men within the hour, yet why should he threaten to inflict dishonourable chastisement on my old master Richmond, a veteran going off the stage and who has borne his sable honours meekly? Magnanimity, my dear Tom, and bravery, should be inseparable. Or why should he go up to his antagonist, the first time he ever saw him at the Fives Court, and measuring him from head to foot with a glance of contempt, as Achilles surveyed Hector, say to him, " What, are you Bill Neate? I'll knock more blood out of that great carcase of thine, this day fortnight, than you ever knock'd out of a bullock's! " It was not manly, 'twas not fighter-like. If he was sure of the victory (as he was not), the less said about it the better. Modesty should accompany the FANCY as its shadow. The best men were always the best behaved. Jem Belcher, the Game Chicken (before whom the Gas-man could not have lived) were civil, silent men. So is Cribb, so is Tom Belcher, the most elegant of sparrers, and not a man for every one to take by the nose. I enlarged on this topic in the mail (while Turtle was asleep), and said very wisely (as I thought) that impertinence was a part of no profession. A boxer was bound to beat his man, but not to thrust his fist, either actually or by implication, in every one's face.

Even a highwayman, in the way of trade, may blow out
your brains, but if he uses foul language at the same time,
I should say he was no gentleman. A boxer, I would
infer, need not be a blackguard or a coxcomb, more than
another. Perhaps I press this point too much on a fallen
man—Mr. Thomas Hickman has by this time learnt
that first of all lessons, " That man was made to mourn."
He has lost nothing by the late fight but his presumption;
and that every man may do as well without! By an over-
display of this quality, however, the public had been
prejudiced against him, and the *knowing-ones* were taken
in. Few but those who had bet on him wished Gas to
win. With my own prepossessions on the subject, the result
of the 11th of December appeared to me as fine a piece of
poetical justice as I had ever witnessed. The difference
of weight between the two combatants (14 stone to 12)
was nothing to the sporting men. Great, heavy, clumsy,
long-armed Bill Neate kicked the beam in the scale of
the Gas-man's vanity. The amateurs were frightened at
his big words, and thought they would make up for the
difference of six feet and five feet nine. Truly, the FANCY
are not men of imagination. They judge of what has been,
and cannot conceive of any thing that is to be. The Gas-
man had won hitherto; therefore he must beat a man half
as big again as himself—and that to a certainty. Besides,
there are as many feuds, factions, prejudices, pedantic
notions in the FANCY as in the state or in the schools.
Mr. Gully is almost the only cool, sensible man among
them, who exercises an unbiassed discretion, and is not
a slave to his passions in these matters. But enough of
reflections, and to our tale. The day, as I have said, was
fine for a December morning. The grass was wet, and
the ground miry, and ploughed up with multitudinous
feet, except that, within the ring itself, there was a spot
of virgin-green closed in and unprofaned by vulgar
tread, that shone with dazzling brightness in the mid-day

sun. For it was now noon, and we had an hour to wait.
This is the trying time. It is then the heart sickens, as
you think what the two champions are about, and how
short a time will determine their fate. After the first
blow is struck, there is no opportunity for nervous
apprehensions; you are swallowed up in the immediate
interest of the scene—but

> " Between the acting of a dreadful thing
> And the first motion, all the interim is
> Like a phantasma, or a hideous dream."

I found it so as I felt the sun's rays clinging to my back,
and saw the white wintry clouds sink below the verge of
the horizon. " So, I thought, my fairest hopes have
faded from my sight!—so will the Gas-man's glory, or
that of his adversary, vanish in an hour." The *swells*
were parading in their white box-coats, the outer ring
was cleared with some bruises on the heads and shins of
the rustic assembly (for the *cockneys* had been distanced
by the sixty-six miles); the time drew near; I had got a
good stand; a bustle, a buzz, ran through the crowd; and
from the opposite side entered Neate, between his second
and bottle-holder. He rolled along, swathed in his loose
great coat, his knock-knees bending under his huge bulk;
and, with a modest cheerful air, threw his hat into the
ring. He then just looked round, and began quietly to
undress; when from the other side there was a similar
rush and an opening made, and the Gas-man came forward with a conscious air of anticipated triumph, too
much like the cock-of-the-walk. He strutted about
more than became a hero, sucked oranges with a supercilious air, and threw away the skin with a toss of his
head, and went up and looked at Neate, which was an
act of supererogation. The only sensible thing he did
was, as he strode away from the modern Ajax, to fling
out his arms, as if he wanted to try whether they would

do their work that day. By this time they had stripped, and presented a strong contrast in appearance. If Neate was like Ajax, " with Atlantean shoulders, fit to bear " the pugilistic reputation of all Bristol, Hickman might be compared to Diomed, light, vigorous, elastic, and his back glistened in the sun, as he moved about, like a panther's hide. There was now a dead pause—attention was awe-struck. Who at that moment, big with a great event, did not draw his breath short—did not feel his heart throb? All was ready. They tossed up for the sun, and the Gas-man won. They were led up to the *scratch*— shook hands, and went at it.

In the first round every one thought it was all over. After making play a short time, the Gas-man flew at his adversary like a tiger, struck five blows in as many seconds, three first, and then following him as he staggered back, two more, right and left, and down he fell, a mighty ruin. There was a shout, and I said, " There is no standing this." Neate seemed like a lifeless lump of flesh and bone, round which the Gas-man's blows played with the rapidity of electricity or lightning, and you imagined he would only be lifted up to be knocked down again. It was as if Hickman held a sword or a fire in that right hand of his, and directed it against an unarmed body. They met again, and Neate seemed, not cowed, but particularly cautious. I saw his teeth clenched to-gether and his brows knit close against the sun. He held out both his arms at full length straight before him, like two sledge-hammers, and raised his left an inch or two higher. The Gas-man could not get over this guard —they struck mutually and fell, but without advantage on either side. It was the same in the next round; but the balance of power was thus restored—the fate of the battle was suspended. No one could tell how it would end. This was the only moment in which opinion was divided; for, in the next, the Gas-man aiming a mortal blow at his adversary's neck, with his right hand, and failing from the length he had to reach, the other returned it with his left at full swing, planted a tremendous blow on his cheek-bone and eye-brow, and made a red ruin of that side of his face. The Gas-man went down, and there was another shout—a roar of triumph as the waves of fortune rolled tumultuously from side to side. This was a settler. Hickman got up, and "grinned horrible a ghastly smile," yet he was evidently dashed in his opinion of himself; it was the first time he had ever been so punished; all one side of his face was perfect scarlet, and his right eye was closed in dingy blackness, as he advanced to the fight, less confident, but still determined. After one or two rounds, not receiving another such remembrancer, he rallied and went at it with his former impetuosity. But in vain. His strength had been weakened,—his blows could not tell at such a distance,— he was obliged to fling himself at his adversary, and could not strike from his feet; and almost as regularly as he flew at him with his right hand, Neate warded the blow, or drew back out of its reach, and felled him with the return of his left. There was little cautious sparring— no half-hits—no tapping and trifling, none of the *petit-maitreship* of the art—they were almost all knock-down blows:—the fight was a good stand-up fight. The wonder was the half-minute time. If there had been a minute or more allowed between each round, it would have been intelligible how they should by degrees recover strength and resolution; but to see two men smashed to the ground, smeared with gore, stunned, senseless, the breath beaten out of their bodies; and then, before you recover from the shock, to see them rise up with new strength and courage, stand ready to inflict or receive mortal offence, and rush upon each other "like two clouds over the Caspian"—this is the most astonishing thing of all:—this is the high and heroic state of man!

From this time forward the event became more certain every round; and about the twelfth it seemed as if it must have been over. Hickman generally stood with his back to me; but in the scuffle, he had changed positions, and Neate just then made a tremendous lunge at him, and hit him full in the face. It was doubtful whether he would fall backwards or forwards; he hung suspended for a second or two, and then fell back, throwing his hands in the air, and with his face lifted up to the sky. I never saw any thing more terrific than his aspect just before he fell. All traces of life, of natural expression, were gone from him. His face was like a human skull, a death's head, spouting blood. The eyes were filled with blood, the nose streamed with blood, the mouth gaped blood. He was not like an actual man, but like a preternatural, spectral appearance, or like one of the figures in Dante's *Inferno*. Yet he fought on after this for several rounds, still striking the first desperate blow, and Neate standing on the defensive, and using the same cautious guard to the last, as if he had still all his work to do; and it was not till the Gas-man was so stunned in the seventeenth or eighteenth round, that his senses forsook him, and he could not come to time, that the battle was declared over.[1] Ye who despise the FANCY, do something to shew as much *pluck*, or as much self-possession as this, before you assume a superiority which you have never given a single proof of by any one action in the whole course of your lives!—When the Gas-man came to himself, the first words he uttered were, " Where am I? What is the matter? "—" Nothing is the matter, Tom,—you have lost the battle, but you

---

[1] Scroggins said of the Gas-man, that he thought he was a man of that courage, that if his hands were cut off, he would still fight on with the stumps—like that of Wildrington,—
——" In doleful dumps,
Who, when his legs were smitten off,
Still fought upon his stumps."

are the bravest man alive." And Jackson whispered to him, " I am collecting a purse for you, Tom."—Vain sounds, and unheard at that moment! Neate instantly went up and shook him cordially by the hand, and seeing some old acquaintance, began to flourish with his fists, calling out, " Ah! you always said I couldn't fight— What do you think now? " But all in good humour, and without any appearance of arrogance; only it was evident Bill Neate was pleased that he had won the fight. When it was over, I asked Cribb if he did not think it was a good one? He said, " *Pretty well!* " The carrier-pigeons now mounted into the air, and one of them flew with the news of her husband's victory to the bosom of Mrs. Neate. Alas, for Mrs. Hickman!

Mais au revoir, as Sir Fopling Flutter says. I went down with Toms; I returned with Jack Pigott, whom I met on the ground. Toms is a rattle-brain; Pigott is a sentimentalist. Now, under favour, I am a sentimentalist too—therefore I say nothing, but that the interest of the excursion did not flag as I came back. Pigott and I marched along the causeway leading from Hungerford to Newbury, now observing the effect of a brilliant sun on the tawny meads or moss-coloured cottages, now exulting in the fight, now digressing to some topic of general and elegant literature. My friend was dressed in character for the occasion, or like one of the FANCY; that is, with a double portion of great coats, clogs, and over-hauls: and just as we had agreed with a couple of country-lads to carry his superfluous wearing-apparel to the next town, we were overtaken by a return post-chaise, into which I got, Pigott preferring a seat on the bar. There were two strangers already in the chaise, and on their observing they supposed I had been to the fight, I said I had, and concluded they had done the same. They appeared, however, a little shy and sore on the subject; and it was not till after several hints dropped, and questions put, that it turned out that they had missed it. One of these friends had undertaken to drive the other there in his gig: they had set out, to make sure work, the day before at three in the afternoon. The owner of the one-horse vehicle scorned to ask his way, and drove right on to Bagshot, instead of turning off at Hounslow: there they stopped all night, and set off the next day across the country to Reading, from whence they took coach, and got down within a mile or two of Hungerford, just half an hour after the fight was over. This might be safely set down as one of the miseries of human life. We parted with these two gentlemen who had been to see the fight, but had returned as they went, at Wolhampton, where we were promised beds (an irresistible temptation, for Pigott had passed the preceding night at Hungerford as we had done at Newbury), and we turned into an old bow-windowed parlour with a carpet and a snug fire; and after devouring a quantity of tea, toast, and eggs, sat down to consider, during an hour of philosophic leisure, what we should have for supper. In the midst of an Epicurean deliberation between a roasted fowl and mutton chops with mashed potatoes, we were interrupted by an inroad of Goths and Vandals—*O procul este profani*—not real flash-men, but interlopers, noisy pretenders, butchers from Tothill-fields, brokers from Whitechapel, who called immediately for pipes and tobacco, hoping it would not be disagreeable to the gentlemen, and began to insist that it was *a cross*. Pigott withdrew from the smoke and noise into another room, and left me to dispute the point with them for a couple of hours *sans intermission* by the dial. The next morning we rose refreshed; and on observing that Jack had a pocket volume in his hand, in which he read in the intervals of our discourse, I inquired what it was, and learned to my particular satisfaction that it was a volume of the *New Eloise*. Ladies, after this, will you contend that a love for the FANCY is incompatible with the

cultivation of sentiment?—We jogged on as before, my
friend setting me up in a genteel drab great coat and
green silk handkerchief (which I must say became me
exceedingly), and after stretching our legs for a few miles,
and seeing Jack Randall, Ned Turner, and Scroggins,
pass on the top of one of the Bath coaches, we engaged
with the driver of the second to take us to London for the
usual fee. I got inside, and found three other passengers.
One of them was an old gentleman with an aquiline nose,
powdered hair, and a pigtail, and who looked as if he had
played many a rubber at the Bath rooms. I said to
myself, he is very like Mr. Windham; I wish he would
enter into conversation, that I might hear what fine
observations would come from those finely-turned
features. However, nothing passed, till stopping to dine
at Reading, some inquiry was made by the company
about the fight, and I gave (as the reader may believe)
an eloquent and animated description of it. When we
got into the coach again, the old gentleman, after a graceful
exordium, said, he had, when a boy, been to a fight
between the famous Broughton and George Stevenson,
who was called the *Fighting Coachman*, in the year 1770,
with the late Mr. Windham. This beginning flattered
the spirit of prophecy within me, and riveted my attention. He went on—" George Stevenson was coachman
to a friend of my father's. He was an old man when I
saw him some years afterwards. He took hold of his own
arm and said, ' there was muscle here once, but now it
is no more than this young gentleman's.' He added,
' well, no matter; I have been here long, I am willing to
go hence, and I hope I have done no more harm than
another man.' Once," said my unknown companion,
" I asked him if he had ever beat Broughton? He said
Yes; that he had fought with him three times, and the
last time he fairly beat him, though the world did not
allow it. ' I'll tell you how it was, master. When the

seconds lifted us up in the last round, we were so exhausted that neither of us could stand, and we fell upon one another, and as Master Broughton fell uppermost, the mob gave it in his favour, and he was said to have won the battle. But the fact was, that as his second (John Cuthbert) lifted him up, he said to him, " I'll fight no more, I've had enough; " which,' says Stevenson, ' you know gave me the victory. And to prove to you that this was the case, when John Cuthbert was on his death-bed, and they asked him if there was any thing on his mind which he wished to confess, he answered, " Yes, that there was one thing he wished to set right, for that certainly Master Stevenson won that last fight with Master Broughton; for he whispered him as he lifted him up in the last round of all, that he had had enough." '

" This," said the Bath gentleman, " was a bit of human nature; " and I have written this account of the fight on purpose that it might not be lost to the world. He also stated as a proof of the candour of mind in this class of men, that Stevenson acknowledged that Broughton could have beat him in his best day; but that he (Broughton) was getting old in their last rencounter. When we stopped in Piccadilly, I wanted to ask the gentleman some questions about the late Mr. Windham, but had not courage. I got out, resigned my coat and green silk handkerchief to Pigott (loth to part with these ornaments of life), and walked home in high spirits.

P.S. Toms called upon me the next day, to ask me if I did not think the fight was a complete thing? I said I thought it was. I hope he will relish my account of it.

ON GREAT AND LITTLE THINGS

(NEW MONTHLY MAGAZINE, FEB., 1822)

> " These little things are great to little man."
>
> GOLDSMITH.

T H E great and the little have, no doubt, a real existence in the nature of things; but they both find pretty much the same level in the mind of man. It is a common measure, which does not always accommodate itself to the size and importance of the objects it represents. It has a certain interest to spare for certain things (and no more) according to its humour and capacity; and neither likes to be stinted in its allowance, nor to muster up an unusual share of sympathy, just as the occasion may require. Perhaps, if we could recollect distinctly, we should discover that the two things that have affected us most in the course of our lives have been, one of them of the greatest, and the other of the smallest possible consequence. To let that pass as too fine a speculation, we know well enough that very trifling circumstances do give us great and daily annoyance, and as often prove too much for our philosophy and forbearance, as matters of the highest moment. A lump of soot spoiling a man's dinner, a plate of toast falling in the ashes, the being disappointed of a ribbon to a cap or a ticket for a ball, have led to serious and almost tragical consequences. Friends not unfrequently fall out and never meet again for some idle misunderstanding, " some trick not worth an egg," who have stood the shock of serious differences of opinion and clashing interests in life; and there is an excellent paper in the *Tatler*, to prove that if a married couple do not quarrel about some point in the first instance not worth contesting, they will seldom find an opportunity afterwards to quarrel about a question of real importance. Grave divines, great statesmen, and deep philosophers are put out of their way by very little things: nay, discreet, worthy people, without any pretensions but to good-nature and common sense, readily surrender the happiness of their whole lives sooner than give up an opinion to which they have committed themselves, though in all likelihood it was the mere turn of a feather which side they should take in the argument. It is the being baulked or thwarted in anything that constitutes the grievance, the unpardonable affront, not the value of the thing to which we had made up our minds. Is it that we despise little things; that we are not prepared for them; that they take us in our careless, unguarded moments, and tease us out of our ordinary patience by their petty, incessant, insect warfare, buzzing about us and stinging us like gnats, so that we can neither get rid of nor grapple with them; whereas we collect all our fortitude and resolution to meet evils of greater magnitude? Or is it that there is a certain stream of irritability that is continually fretting upon the wheels of life, which finds sufficient food to play with in straws and feathers, while great objects are too much for it, either choke it up, or divert its course into serious and thoughtful interest? Some attempt might be made to explain this in the following manner.

One is always more vexed at losing a game of any sort by a single hole or ace, than if one has never had a chance of winning it. This is no doubt in part or chiefly because the prospect of success irritates the subsequent disappointment. But people have been known to pine and fall sick from holding the next number to the twenty thousand pound prize in the lottery. Now this could only arise from their being so near winning in fancy, from there seeming to be so thin a partition between them and success. When they were within one of the right number, why could they not have taken the next—it was so easy:

E

this haunts their minds and will not let them rest, notwithstanding the absurdity of the reasoning. It is that the will here has a slight imaginary obstacle to surmount to attain its end; it should appear it had only an exceedingly trifling effort to make for this purpose, that it was absolutely in its power (had it known) to seize the envied prize, and it is continually harassing itself by making the obvious transition from one number to the other, when it is too late. That is to say, the will acts in proportion to its fancied power, to its superiority over immediate obstacles. Now in little or indifferent matters there seems no reason why it should not have its own way, and therefore a disappointment vexes it the more. It grows angry according to the insignificance of the occasion, and frets itself to death about an object, merely because from its very futility there can be supposed to be no real difficulty in the way of its attainment, nor anything more required for this purpose than a determination of the will. The being baulked of this throws the mind off its balance, or puts it into what is called *a passion;* and as nothing but an act of voluntary power still seems necessary to get rid of every impediment, we indulge our violence more and more, and heighten our impatience by degrees into a sort of frenzy. The object is the same as it was, but we are no longer as we were. The blood is heated, the muscles are strained. The feelings are wound up to a pitch of agony with the vain strife. The temper is tried to the utmost it will bear. The more contemptible the object or the obstructions in the way to it, the more are we provoked at being hindered by them. It looks like witchcraft. We fancy there is a spell upon us, so that we are hampered by straws and entangled in cobwebs. We believe that there is a fatality about our affairs. It is evidently done on purpose to plague us. A demon is at our elbow to torment and defeat us in everything, even in the smallest things. We see him sitting and mocking us, and we rave and gnash our teeth at him in return. It is particularly hard that we cannot succeed in any one point, however trifling, that we set our hearts on. We are the sport of imbecility and mischance. We make another desperate effort, and fly out into all the extravagance of impotent rage once more. Our anger runs away with our reason, because, as there is little to give it birth, there is nothing to check it or recall us to our senses in the prospect of consequences. We take up and rend in pieces the mere toys of humour, as the gusts of wind take up and whirl about chaff and stubble. Passion plays the tyrant, in a grand tragi-comic style, over the Lilliputian difficulties and petty disappointments it has to encounter, gives way to all the fretfulness of grief and all the turbulence of resentment, makes a fuss about nothing because there is nothing to make a fuss about—when an impending calamity, an irretrievable loss, would instantly bring it to its recollection, and tame it in its preposterous career. A man may be in a great passion and give himself strange airs at so simple a thing as a game at ball, for instance; may rage like a wild beast, and be ready to dash his head against the wall about nothing, or about that which he will laugh at the next minute, and think no more of ten minutes after, at the same time that a good smart blow from the ball, the effects of which he might feel as a serious inconvenience for a month, would calm him directly—

> " Anon as patient as the female dove,
> His silence will sit drooping."

The truth is, we pamper little griefs into great ones, and bear great ones as well as we can. We can afford to dally and play tricks with the one, but the others we have enough to do with, without any of the wantonness and bombast of passion—without the swaggering of Pistol or the insolence of King Cambyses' vein. To great evils we submit; we resent little provocations. I have before now been disappointed of a hundred-pound job and lost half a crown at rackets on the same day, and been more mortified at the latter than the former. That which is lasting we share with the future, we defer the consideration of till to-morrow: that which belongs to the moment we drink up in all its bitterness, before the spirit evaporates. We probe minute mischiefs to the quick; we lacerate, tear, and mangle our bosoms with misfortune's finest, brittlest point, and wreak our vengeance on ourselves and it for good and all. Small pains are more manageable, more within our reach; we can fret and worry ourselves about them, can turn them into any shape, can twist and torture them how we please:—a grain of sand in the eye, a thorn in the flesh, only irritates the part, and leaves us strength enough to quarrel and get out of all patience with it: a heavy blow stuns and takes away all power of sense as well as of resistance. The great and mighty reverses of fortune, like the revolutions of nature, may be said to carry their own weight and reason along with them: they seem unavoidable and remediless, and we submit to them without murmuring as to a fatal necessity. The magnitude of the events in which we may happen to be concerned fills the mind, and carries it out of itself, as it were, into the page of history. Our thoughts are expanded with the scene on which we have to act, and lend us strength to disregard our own personal share in it. Some men are indifferent to the stroke of fate, as before and after earthquakes there is a calm in the air. From the commanding situation whence they have been accustomed to view things, they look down at themselves as only a part of the whole, and can abstract their minds from the pressure of misfortune, by the aid of its very violence. They are projected, in the explosion of events, into a different sphere, far from their ·former thoughts, purposes, and passions. The greatness of the change anticipates the slow effects of time and reflection:—they at once contemplate themselves from an immense distance, and look up with speculative wonder at the height on which they stood. Had the downfall been less complete, it would have been more galling and borne with less resignation, because there might still be a chance of remedying it by farther efforts and farther endurance—but *past cure, past hope.* It is chiefly this cause (together with something of constitutional character) which has enabled the greatest man in modern history to bear his reverses of fortune with gay magnanimity, and to submit to the loss of the empire of the world with as little discomposure as if he had been playing a game at chess.[1] This does not prove by our theory that he did not use to fly into violent passions with Talleyrand for plaguing him with bad news when things went wrong. He was mad at uncertain forebodings of disaster, but resigned to its consummation. A man may dislike impertinence, yet have no quarrel with necessity!

There is another consideration that may take off our wonder at the firmness with which the principals in great vicissitudes of fortune bear their fate, which is, that they are in the secret of its operations, and know that what to others appears chance-medley was unavoidable. The clearness of their perception of all the circumstances converts the uneasiness of doubt into certainty: they have not the qualms of conscience which their admirers have, who cannot tell how much of the event is to be attributed to the leaders, and how much to unforeseen accidents: they are aware either that the result

[1] This Essay was written in January 1821.

was not to be helped, or that they did all they could to prevent it.

> ——" Si Pergama dextra
> Defendi possent, etiam hac defensa fuissent."

It is the mist and obscurity through which we view objects that makes us fancy they might have been, or might still be otherwise.   The precise knowledge of antecedents and consequents makes men practical as well as philosophical Necessarians.—It is the want of this knowledge which is the principle and soul of gambling, and of all games of chance or partial skill. The supposition is, that the issue is uncertain, and that there is no positive means of ascertaining it. It is dependent on the turn of a die, on the tossing up of a halfpenny: to be fair it must be a lottery; there is no knowing but by the event; and it is this which keeps the interest alive, and works up the passion little short of madness. There is all the agitation of suspense, all the alternation of hope and fear, of good and bad success, all the eagerness of desire, without the possibility of reducing this to calculation, that is, of subjecting the increased action of the will to a known rule, or restraining the excesses of passion within the bounds of reason. We see no cause beforehand why the run of the cards should not be in our favour: we will hear of none afterwards why it should not have been so. As in the absence of all *data* to judge by, we wantonly fill up the blank with the most extravagant expectations, so, when all is over, we obstinately recur to the chance we had previously. There is nothing to tame us down to the event, nothing to reconcile us to our hard luck, for so we think it. We see no reason why we failed (and there was none, any more than why we should succeed)—we think that, reason apart, our will is the next best thing; we still try to have it our own way, and fret, torment, and harrow ourselves up with vain imaginations to effect impossibilities.[1] We play the game over again: we wonder how it was possible for us to fail. We turn our brain with straining at contradictions, and striving to make things what they are not, or, in other words, to subject the course of nature to our fantastical wishes. " *If it had been so —if we had done such and such a thing* "—we try it in a thousand different ways, and are just as far off the mark as ever. We appealed to chance in the first instance, and yet, when it has decided against us, we will not give in, and sit down contented with our loss, but refuse to submit to anything but reason, which has nothing to do with the matter. In drawing two straws, for example, to see which is the longest, there was no apparent necessity we should fix upon the wrong one, it was so easy to have fixed upon the other, nay, at one time we were going to do it—if we had,—the mind thus runs back to what was so possible and feasible at one time, while the thing was pending, and would fain give a bias to causes so slender and insignificant, as the skittle-player bends his body to give a bias to the bowl he has already delivered from his hand, not considering that what is once determined, be the causes ever so trivial or evanescent, is in the individual instance unalterable. Indeed, to be a great philosopher, in the practical and most important sense of the term, little more seems necessary than to be convinced of the truth of the maxim which the wise man repeated to the daughter of King Cophetua, *That if a thing is, it is*, and there is an end of it!

We often make life unhappy in wishing things to have turned out otherwise than they did, merely because

---

[1] Losing gamesters thus become desperate, because the continued and violent irritation of the will against a run of ill luck drives it to extremity, and makes it bid defiances to common sense and every consideration of prudence or self-interest.

that is possible to the imagination, which is impossible in fact. I remember, when L[amb]'s farce was damned (for damned it was, that's certain), I used to dream every night for a month after (and then I vowed I would plague myself no more about it) that it was revived at one of the minor or provincial theatres with great success, that such and such retrenchments and alterations had been made in it, and that it was thought *it might do at the other House.* I had heard indeed (this was told in confidence to L[amb]) that *Gentleman* Lewis was present on the night of its performance, and said that if he had had it, he would have made it, by a few judicious curtailments, " the most popular little thing that had been brought out for some time." How often did I conjure up in recollection the full diapason of applause at the end of the *Prologue,* and hear my ingenious friend in the first row of the pit roar with laughter at his own wit! Then I dwelt with forced complacency on some part in which it had been doing well: then we would consider (in concert) whether the long tedious opera of the *Travellers,* which preceded it, had not tired people beforehand, so that they had not spirits left for the quaint and sparkling " wit skirmishes " of the dialogue; and we all agreed it might have gone down after a tragedy, except L[amb] himself, who swore he had no hopes of it from the beginning, and that he knew the name of the hero when it came to be discovered could not be got over. *Mr. H——,* thou wert damned![1] Bright shone the morning on the play-bills that announced thy appearance, and the streets were filled with the buzz of persons asking one another if they would go to see *Mr. H——,* and answering that they would certainly; but before night the gaiety, not of the author, but of his friends and the town, was eclipsed, for

[1] At Drury Lane in 1805 (Ed.)

thou wert damned! Hadst thou been anonymous thou haply mightst have lived. But thou didst come to an untimely end for thy tricks, and for want of a better name to pass them off!

In this manner we go back to the critical minutes on which the turn of our fate, or that of any one else in whom we are interested, depended; try them over again with new knowledge and sharpened sensibility; and thus think to alter what is irrevocable, and ease for a moment the pang of lasting regret. So in a game at rackets[2] (to compare small things with great), I think if at such a point I had followed up my success, if I had not been too secure or over-anxious in another part, if I had played for such an opening—in short, if I had done anything but what I did and what has proved unfortunate in the result, the chances were all in my favour. But it is merely because I do not know what would have happened in the other case that I interpret it so readily to my own advantage. I have sometimes lain awake a whole night, trying to serve out the last ball of an interesting game in a particular corner of the court, which I had missed from a nervous feeling. Rackets (I might observe, for the sake of the uninformed reader) is, like any other athletic game, very much a thing of skill and practice; but it is also a thing of opinion, " subject to all the skyey influences." If you think you can win, you can win. Faith is necessary to victory. If you hesitate in striking at the ball, it is ten to one but you miss it. If you are apprehensive of committing some particular error (such as striking the ball *foul*) you will be nearly sure to do it. While thinking of that which you are so earnestly bent on avoiding, your

---

[1] Some of the poets in the beginning of the last century would often set out on a simile by observing, " So in Arabia have I seen a Phœnix ! " I confess my illustrations are of a more homely and humble nature.

E *

hand mechanically follows the strongest idea, and obeys the imagination rather than the intention of the striker. A run of luck is a fore-runner of success, and courage is as much wanted as skill. No one is, however, free from nervous sensations at times. A good player may not be able to strike a single stroke if another comes into the court that he has a particular dread of; and it frequently so happens that a player cannot beat another, even though he can give half the game to an equal player, because he has some associations of jealousy or personal pique against the first which he has not towards the last. *Sed hæc hactenus.* Chess is a game I do not understand, and have not comprehension enough to play at. But I believe, though it is so much less a thing of chance than science or skill, eager players pass whole nights in marching and counter-marching their men and check-mating a successful adversary, supposing that at a certain point of the game they had determined upon making a particular move instead of the one which they actually did make. I have heard a story of two persons playing at back-gammon, one of whom was so enraged at losing his match at a particular point of the game, that he took the board and threw it out of the window. It fell upon the head of one of the passengers in the street, who came up to demand instant satisfaction for the affront and injury he had sustained. The losing gamester only asked him if he understood back-gammon, and finding that he did, said, that if upon seeing the state of the game he did not excuse the extravagance of his conduct, he would give him any other satisfaction he wished for. The tables were accordingly brought, and the situation of the two contending parties being explained, the gentleman put up his sword and went away perfectly satisfied.—To return from this, which to some will seem a digression, and to others will serve as a confirmation of the doctrine I am insisting on.

It is not, then, the value of the object, but the time and pains bestowed upon it, that determines the sense and degree of our loss. Many men set their minds only on trifles, and have not a compass of soul to take an interest in anything truly great and important beyond forms and *minutiæ*. Such persons are really men of little minds, or may be complimented with the title of great children,

" Pleased with a feather, tickled with a straw."

Larger objects elude their grasp, while they fasten eagerly on the light and insignificant. They fidget themselves and others to death with incessant anxiety about nothing. A part of their dress that is awry keeps them in a fever of restlessness and impatience ; they sit picking their teeth, or paring their nails, or stirring the fire, or brushing a speck of dirt off their coats, while the house or the world tumbling about their ears would not rouse them from their morbid insensibility. They cannot sit still on their chairs for their lives, though if there were anything for them to do they would become immovable. Their nerves are as irritable as their imaginations are callous and inert. They are addicted to an inveterate habit of littleness and perversity, which rejects every other motive to action or object of contemplation but the daily, teasing, contemptible, familiar, favourite sources of uneasiness and dissatisfaction. When they are of a sanguine instead of a morbid temperament, they become *quid-nuncs* and virtuosos—collectors of caterpillars and odd volumes, makers of fishing-rods and curious in watch-chains. Will Wimble dabbled in this way, to his immortal honour. But many others have been less successful. There are those who build their fame on epigrams or epitaphs, and others who devote their lives to writing the Lord's Prayer in little. Some poets compose and sing their own verses. Which character would they have us think most highly of—the poet or the musician? The Great is One. Some there are who feel more pride in sealing a letter with a head of Homer than ever that old blind bard did in reciting his *Iliad*. These raise a huge opinion of themselves out of nothing, as there are those who shrink from their own merits into the shade of unconquerable humility. I know one person at least, who would rather be the author of an unsuccessful farce than of a successful tragedy. Repeated mortification has produced an inverted ambition in his mind, and made failure the bitter test of desert. He cannot lift his drooping head to gaze on the gaudy crown of popularity placed within his reach, but casts a pensive, riveted look downwards to the modest flowers which the multitude trample under their feet. If he had a piece likely to succeed, coming out under all advantages, he would damn it by some ill-timed, wilful jest, and lose the favour of the public, to preserve the sense of his personal identity. " Misfortune," Shakespear says, " brings a man acquainted with strange bed-fellows "; and it makes our thoughts traitors to ourselves.—It is a maxim with many—" *Take care of the pence, and the pounds will take care of themselves*." Those only put it in practice successfully who think more of the pence than of the pounds. To such, a large sum is less than a small one. Great speculations, great returns are to them extravagant or imaginary: a few hundreds a year are something *snug* and comfortable. Persons who have been used to a petty, huckstering way of life cannot enlarge their apprehensions to a notion of anything better. Instead of launching out into greater expense and liberality with the tide of fortune, they draw back with the fear of consequences, and think to succeed on a broader scale by dint of meanness and parsimony. My uncle Toby frequently caught

Trim standing up behind his chair, when he had told him to be seated. What the corporal did out of respect, others would do out of servility. The menial character does not wear out in three or four generations. You cannot keep some people out of the kitchen, merely because their grandfathers or grandmothers came out of it. A poor man and his wife walking along in the neighbourhood of Portland Place, he said to her peevishly, " What is the use of walking along these fine streets and squares? Let us turn down some alley!" He felt he should be more at home there. L[amb] said of an old acquaintance of his, that when he was young he wanted to be a tailor, but had not spirit! This is the misery of unequal matches. The woman cannot easily forget, or think that others forget, her origin; and, with perhaps superior sense and beauty, keeps painfully in the back-ground. It is worse when she braves this conscious feeling, and displays all the insolence of the upstart and affected fine lady. But shouldst thou ever, my Infelice, grace my home with thy loved presence, as thou hast cheered my hopes with thy smile, thou wilt conquer all hearts with thy prevailing gentleness, and I will shew the world what Shakespear's women were!—Some gallants set their hearts on princesses; others descend in imagination to women of quality; others are mad after opera-singers. For my part, I am shy even of actresses, and should not think of leaving my card with Madame V[estris]. I am for none of these *bonnes fortunes;* but for a list of humble beauties, servant-maids and shepherd-girls, with their red elbows, hard hands, black stockings and mob-caps, I could furnish out a gallery equal to Cowley's, and paint them half as well. Oh! might I but attempt a description of some of them in poetic prose, Don Juan would forget his Julia, and Mr. Davison might both print and publish this volume. I agree so far with Horace, and differ with Montaigne. I admire the Clementinas and

Clarissas at a distance: the Pamelas and Fannys of Richardson and Fielding make my blood tingle. I have written love-letters to such in my time, *d'un pathetique à faire fendre les rochers*, and with about as much effect as if they had been addressed to stone. The simpletons only laughed, and said that " those were not the sort of things to gain the affections." I wish I had kept copies in my own justification. What is worse, I have an utter aversion to *blue-stockings*. I do not care a fig for any woman that knows even what *an author* means. If I know that she has read anything I have written, I cut her acquaintance immediately. This sort of literary intercourse with me passes for nothing. Her critical and scientific acquirements are *carrying coals to Newcastle*. I do not want to be told that I have published such or such a work. I knew all this before. It makes no addition to my sense of power. I do not wish the affair to be brought about in that way. I would have her read my soul: she should understand the language of the heart: she should know what I am, as if she were another self! She should love me for myself alone. I like myself without any reason: I would have her do so too. This is not very reasonable. I abstract from my temptations to admire all the circumstances of dress, birth, breeding, fortune; and I would not willingly put forward my own pretensions, whatever they may be. The image of some fair creature is engraven on my inmost soul; it is on that I build my claim to her regard, and expect her to see into my heart, as I see her form always before me. Wherever she treads, pale primroses, like her face, vernal hyacinths, like her brow, spring up beneath her feet, and music hangs on every bough; but all is cold, barren, and desolate without her. Thus I feel, and thus I think. But have I ever told her so? No. Or if I did, would she understand it? No. I " hunt the wind, I worship a statue, cry aloud to the desert." To see beauty is not to be beautiful, to pine in love is not to be loved again.—I always was inclined to raise and magnify the power of Love. I thought that his sweet power should only be exerted to join together the loveliest forms and fondest hearts; that none but those in whom his Godhead shone outwardly, and was inly felt, should ever partake of his triumphs; and I stood and gazed at a distance, as unworthy to mingle in so bright a throng, and did not (even for a moment) wish to tarnish the glory of so fair a vision by being myself admitted into it. I say this was my notion once, but God knows it was one of the errors of my youth. For coming nearer to look, I saw the maimed, the blind, and the halt enter in, the crooked and the dwarf, the ugly, the old and impotent, the man of pleasure and the man of the world, the dapper and the pert, the vain and shallow boaster, the fool and the pedant, the ignorant and brutal, and all that is farthest removed from earth's fairest-born, and the pride of human life. Seeing all these enter the courts of Love, and thinking that I also might venture in under favour of the crowd, but finding myself rejected, I fancied (I might be wrong) that it was not so much because I was below, as above the common standard. I did feel, but I was ashamed to feel, mortified at my repulse, when I saw the meanest of mankind, the very scum and refuse, all creeping things and every obscene creature, enter in before me. I seemed a species by myself. I took a pride even in my disgrace; and concluded I had else-where my inheritance! The only thing I ever piqued myself upon was the writing the *Essay on the Principles of Human Action*[1]—a work that no woman ever read, or would ever comprehend the meaning of. But if I do not build my claim to regard on the pretensions I have, how can I build it on those I am totally without? Or why do I complain and expect to gather grapes

[1] Published in 1805 (Ed.)

of thorns, or figs of thistles? Thought has in me cancelled
pleasure; and this dark forehead, bent upon truth, is the
rock on which all affection has split. And thus I waste my
life in one long sigh; nor ever (till too late) beheld a gentle
face turned gently upon mine! . . . But no! not too late, if
that face, pure, modest, downcast, tender, with angel
sweetness, not only gladdens the prospect of the future,
but sheds its radiance on the past, smiling in tears. A
purple light hovers round my head. The air of love is in
the room. As I look at my long-neglected copy of the
Death of Clorinda, golden gleams play upon the canvas,
as they used when I painted it. The flowers of Hope
and Joy springing up in my mind, recall the time when
they first bloomed there. The years that are fled knock at
the door and enter. I am in the Louvre once more. The
sun of Austerlitz has not set. It still shines here—in my
heart; and he, the son of glory, is not dead, nor ever shall,
to me. I am as when my life began. The rainbow is in the
sky again. I see the skirts of the departed years. All that I
have thought and felt has not been in vain. I am not
utterly worthless, unregarded; nor shall I die and
wither of pure scorn. Now could I sit on the tomb of
Liberty, and write a Hymn to Love. Oh! if I am deceived,
let me be deceived still. Let me live in the Elysium of
those soft looks; poison me with kisses, kill me with smiles;
but still mock me with thy love![1]

Poets choose mistresses who have the fewest charms,
that they may make something out of nothing. They
succeed best in fiction, and they apply this rule to love.
They make a Goddess of any dowdy. As Don Quixote
said, in answer to the matter-of-fact remonstrances of
Sancho, that Dulcinea del Toboso answered the purpose
of signalising his valour just as well as the " fairest

---

[1] I beg the reader to consider this passage merely as a
specimen of the mock-heroic style, and as having nothing to
do with any real facts or feelings.

princess under sky;" so any of the fair sex will serve
them to write about just as well as another. They take
some awkward thing and dress her up in fine words,
as children dress up a wooden doll in fine clothes.
Perhaps a fine head of hair, a taper waist, or some other
circumstance strikes them, and they make the rest out
according to their fancies. They have a wonderful
knack of supplying deficiencies in the subjects of their
idolatry out of the storehouse of their imaginations.
They presently translate their favourites to the skies,
where they figure with Berenice's locks and Ariadne's
crown. This predilection for the unprepossessing and
insignificant, I take to arise not merely from a desire
in poets to have some subject to exercise their inventive
talents upon, but from their jealousy of any pretensions
(even those of beauty in the other sex) that might interfere
with the continual incense offered to their personal vanity.

Cardinal Mazarine never thought anything of Cardinal de Retz after he told him that he had written for
the last thirty years of his life with the same pen.
Some Italian poet going to present a copy of verses
to the Pope, and finding, as he was looking them over
in the coach as he went, a mistake of a single letter in
the printing, broke his heart of vexation and chagrin.
A still more remarkable case of literary disappointment
occurs in the history of a countryman of his, which I
cannot refrain from giving here, as I find it related.
"Anthony Codrus Urceus, a most learned and unfortunate Italian, born near Modena, 1446, was a striking
instance," says his biographer, " of the miseries men
bring upon themselves by setting their affections unreasonably on trifles. This learned man lived at Forli,
and had an apartment in the palace. His room was so
very dark that he was forced to use a candle in the
day-time; and one day, going abroad without putting
it out, his library was set on fire, and some papers which he

had prepared for the press were burned. The instant he was informed of this ill news he was affected even to madness. He ran furiously to the palace, and stopping at the door of his apartment, he cried aloud, ' Christ Jesus! what mighty crime have I committed! whom of your followers have I ever injured, that you thus rage with inexpiable hatred against me? ' Then turning himself to an image of the Virgin Mary near at hand, ' Virgin (says he), hear what I have to say, for I speak in earnest, and with a composed spirit: if I shall happen to address you in my dying moments, I humbly entreat you not to hear me, nor receive me into Heaven, for I am determined to spend all eternity in Hell!' Those who heard these blasphemous expressions endeavoured to comfort him; but all to no purpose: for, the society of mankind being no longer supportable to him, he left the city, and retired, like a savage, to the deep solitude of a wood. Some say that he was murdered there by ruffians: others, that he died at Bologna in 1500, after much contrition and penitence."

Perhaps the censure passed at the outset of the anecdote on this unfortunate person is unfounded and severe, when it is said that he brought his miseries on himself " by having set his affections unreasonably on trifles." To others it might appear so; but to himself the labour of a whole life was hardly a trifle. His passion was not a causeless one, though carried to such frantic excess. The story of Sir Isaac Newton presents a strong contrast to the last-mentioned one, who, on going into his study and finding that his dog Tray had thrown down a candle on the table, and burnt some papers of great value, contented himself with exclaiming, " Ah! Tray, you don't know the mischief you have done! " Many persons would not forgive the overturning a cup of chocolate so soon.

I remember hearing an instance some years ago of a

man of character and property, who through unexpected losses had been condemned to a long and heart-breaking imprisonment, which he bore with exemplary fortitude. At the end of four years, by the interest and exertions of friends, he obtained his discharge, with every prospect of beginning the world afresh, and had made his arrangements for leaving his irksome abode, and meeting his wife and family at a distance of two hundred miles by a certain day. Owing to the miscarriage of a letter, some signature necessary to the completion of the business did not arrive in time, and on account of the informality which had thus arisen, he could not set out home till the return of the post, which was four days longer. His spirit could not brook the delay. He had wound himself up to the last pitch of expectation; he had, as it were, calculated his patience to hold out to a certain point, and then to throw down his load for ever, and he could not find resolution to resume it for a few hours beyond this. He put an end to the intolerable conflict of hope and disappointment in a fit of excruciating anguish. Woes that we have time to foresee and leisure to contemplate break their force by being spread over a larger surface and borne at intervals; but those that come upon us suddenly, for however short a time, seem to insult us by their unnecessary and uncalled-for intrusion; and the very prospect of relief, when held out and then withdrawn from us, to however small a distance, only frets impatience into agony by tantalising our hopes and wishes; and to rend asunder the thin partition that separates us from our favourite object, we are ready to burst even the fetters of life itself!

I am not aware that any one has demonstrated how it is that a stronger capacity is required for the conduct of great affairs than of small ones. The organs of the mind, like the pupil of the eye, may be contracted or dilated to view a broader or a narrower surface, and yet find sufficient variety to occupy its attention in each. The material universe is infinitely divisible, and so is the texture of human affairs. We take things in the gross or in the detail, according to the occasion. I think I could as soon get up the budget of Ways and Means for the current year, as be sure of making both ends meet, and paying my rent at quarter-day in a paltry huckster's shop. Great objects move on by their own weight and impulse; great power turns aside petty obstacles; and he who wields it is often but the puppet of circumstances, like the fly on the wheel that said, "What a dust we raise!" It is easier to ruin a kingdom and aggrandise one's own pride and prejudices than to set up a green-grocer's stall. An idiot or a madman may do this at any time, whose word is law, and whose nod is fate. Nay, he whose look is obedience, and who understands the silent wishes of the great, may easily trample on the necks and tread out the liberties of a mighty nation, deriding their strength, and hating it the more from a consciousness of his own meanness. Power is not wisdom, it is true; but it equally ensures its own objects. It does not exact, but dispenses with talent. When a man creates this power, or new-moulds the state by sage counsels and bold enterprises, it is a different thing from overturning it with the levers that are put into his baby hands. In general, however, it may be argued that great transactions and complicated concerns ask more genius to conduct them than smaller ones, for this reason, viz. that the mind must be able either to embrace a greater variety of details in a more extensive range of objects, or must have a greater faculty of generalising, or a greater depth of insight into ruling principles, and so come at true results in that way. Buonaparte knew everything, even to the names of our cadets in the East

India service; but he failed in this, that he did not calculate the resistance which barbarism makes to refinement. He thought that the Russians could not burn Moscow, because the Parisians could not burn Paris. The French think everything must be French. The Cossacks, alas! do not conform to etiquette: the rudeness of the seasons knows no rules of politeness!— Some artists think it a test of genius to paint a large picture, and I grant the truth of this position, if the large picture contains more than a small one. It is not the size of the canvas, but the quantity of truth and nature put into it, that settles the point. It is a mistake, common enough on this subject, to suppose that a miniature is more finished than an oil-picture. The miniature is inferior to the oil-picture only because it is less finished, because it cannot follow nature into so many individual and exact particulars. The proof of which is, that the copy of a good portrait will always make a highly finished miniature (see for example Mr. Bone's enamels), whereas the copy of a good miniature, if enlarged to the size of life, will make but a very sorry portrait. Several of our best artists, who are fond of painting large figures, invert this reasoning. They make the whole figure gigantic, not that they may have room for nature, but for the motion of their brush (as if they were painting the side of a house), regarding the extent of canvas they have to cover as an excuse for their slovenly and hasty manner of getting over it; and thus, in fact, leave their pictures nothing at last but over-grown miniatures, but huge caricatures. It is not necessary in any case (either in a larger or a smaller compass) to go into the details, so as to lose sight of the effect, and decompound the face into porous and transparent molecules, in the manner of Denner, who painted what he saw through a magnifying-glass. The painter's eye need not be a microscope, but I contend that it should be a looking-glass,

bright, clear, lucid. The *little* in art begins with insignificant parts, with what does not tell in connection with
other parts. The true artist will paint not material points,
but *moral qualities*. In a word, wherever there is feeling
or expression in a muscle or a vein, there is grandeur and
refinement too.—I will conclude these remarks with an
account of the manner in which the ancient sculptors combined great and little things in such matters. " That the
name of Phidias," says Pliny, " is illustrious among all
the nations that have heard of the fame of the Olympian
Jupiter, no one doubts; but in order that those may
know that he is deservedly praised who have not even
seen his works, we shall offer a few arguments, and
those of his genius only: nor to this purpose shall we
insist on the beauty of the Olympian Jupiter, nor on
the magnitude of the Minerva at Athens, though it is
twenty-six cubits in height (about thirty-five feet), and
is made of ivory and gold; but we shall refer to the
shield, on which the battle of the Amazons is carved
on the outer side; on the inside of the same is the
fight of the Gods and Giants; and on the sandals, that
between the Centaurs and Lapithæ; so well did every
part of that work display the powers of the art. Again,
the sculptures on the pedestal he called the birth of
Pandora: there are to be seen in number thirty Gods,
the figure of Victory being particularly admirable: the
learned also admire the figures of the serpent and the
brazen sphinx, writhing under the spear. These things
are mentioned, in passing, of an artist never enough
to be commended, that it may be seen that he shewed
the same magnificence even in small things." (Pliny's
Natural History, Book 36.)

WHY DISTANT OBJECTS PLEASE

(W R I T T E N   A B O U T   1 8 2 1 – 1 8 2 2)

D I S T A N T objects please, because, in the first place, they imply an idea of space and magnitude, and because not being obtruded too close upon the eye, we clothe them with the indistinct and airy colours of fancy. In looking at the misty mountain-tops that bound the horizon, the mind is as it were conscious of all the conceivable objects and interests that lie between; we imagine all sorts of adventures in the interim; strain our hopes and wishes to reach the air-drawn circle, or to " descry new lands, rivers, and mountains," stretching far beyond it: our feelings, carried out of themselves, lose their grossness and their husk, are rarefied, expanded, melt into softness and brighten into beauty, turning to ethereal mould, sky-tinctured. We drink the air before us, and borrow a more refined existence from objects that hover on the brink of nothing. Where the landscape fades from the dull sight, we fill the thin, viewless space with shapes of unknown good, and tinge the hazy prospect with hopes and wishes and more charming fears.

> " But thou, oh Hope ! with eyes so fair,
> What was thy delighted measure ?
> Still it whisper'd promised pleasure,
> And bade the lovely scenes at distance hail ! "

Whatever is placed beyond the reach of sense and knowledge, whatever is imperfectly discerned, the fancy pieces out at its leisure; and all but the present moment, but the present spot, passion claims for its own, and brooding over it with wings outspread, stamps it with an image of itself. Passion is lord of infinite space, and distant objects please because they border on its confines and are moulded by its touch. When I was a boy, I lived within sight of a range of lofty hills, whose blue tops blending with the setting sun had often tempted my longing eyes and wandering feet. At last I put my project in execution, and on a nearer approach, instead of glimmering air woven into fantastic shapes, found them huge lumpish heaps of discoloured earth. I learnt from this (in part) to leave " Yarrow unvisited," and not idly to disturb a dream of good!

Distance of time has much the same effect as distance of place. It is not surprising that fancy colours the prospect of the future as it thinks good, when it even effaces the forms of memory. Time takes out the sting of pain; our sorrows after a certain period have been so often steeped in a medium of thought and passion, that they " unmould their essence "; and all that remains of our original impressions is what we would wish them to have been. Not only the untried steep ascent before us, but the rude, unsightly masses of our past experience presently resume their power of deception over the eye: the golden cloud soon rests upon their heads, and the purple light of fancy clothes their barren sides! Thus we pass on, while both ends of our existence touch upon Heaven! There is (so to speak) " a mighty stream of tendency " to good in the human mind, upon which all objects float and are imperceptibly borne along; and though in the voyage of life we meet with strong rebuffs, with rocks and quicksands, yet there is " a tide in the affairs of men," a heaving and a restless aspiration of the soul, by means of which, " with sails and tackle torn," the wreck and scattered fragments of our entire being drift into the port and haven of our desires! In all that relates to the affections, we put the will for the deed; so that the instant the pressure of unwelcome circumstances is removed, the mind recoils from their hold, recovers its elasticity, and re-unites itself to that image of good, which is but a reflection and configuration of its own nature. Seen in the distance, in the long perspective of waning years, the meanest incidents, enlarged and enriched by countless recollections, become interesting; the most painful, broken and softened by time, soothe. How any object that unexpectedly brings back to us old scenes and associations startles the mind! What a yearning it creates within us; what a longing to leap the intermediate space! How fondly we cling to, and try to revive the impression of all that we then were!

" Such tricks hath strong imagination ! "

In truth we impose upon ourselves, and know not what we wish. It is a cunning artifice, a quaint delusion, by which, in pretending to be what we were at a particular moment of time, we would fain be all that we have since been, and have our lives to come over again. It is not the little, glimmering, almost annihilated speck in the distance that rivets our attention and " hangs upon the beatings of our hearts ": it is the interval that separates us from it, and of which it is the trembling boundary, that excites all this coil and mighty pudder in the breast. Into that great gap in our being " come thronging soft desires " and infinite regrets. It is the contrast, the change from what we then were, that arms the half-extinguished recollection with its giant strength, and lifts the fabric of the affections from its shadowy base. In contemplating its utmost verge, we overlook the map of our existence, and re-tread, in apprehension, the journey of life. So it is that in early youth we strain our eager sight after the pursuits of manhood; and, as we are sliding off the stage, strive to gather up the toys and flowers that pleased our thoughtless childhood.

When I was quite a boy my father used to take me to the Montpelier Tea-Gardens at Walworth. Do I go

there now? - No; the place is deserted, and its borders
and its beds o'erturned. Is there, then, nothing that can

> " Bring back the hour
> Of glory in the grass, of splendour in the flower ? "

Oh! yes. I unlock the casket of memory, and draw
back the warders of the brain; and there this scene
of my infant wanderings still lives unfaded, or with
fresher dyes. A new sense comes upon me, as in a
dream; a richer perfume, brighter colours start out;
my eyes dazzle; my heart heaves with its new load of
bliss, and I am a child again. My sensations are all
glossy, spruce, voluptuous, and fine : they wear a candied
coat, and are in holiday trim. I see the beds of larkspur
with purple eyes; tall holyoaks, red and yellow; the
broad sun-flowers, caked in gold, with bees buzzing round
them; wildernesses of pinks, and hot-glowing pionies;
poppies run to seed; the sugared lily, and faint mignionette,
all ranged in order, and as thick as they can grow; the box-
tree borders; the gravel-walks, the painted alcove, the
confectionery, the clotted cream:—I think I see them now
with sparkling looks; or have they vanished while I have
been writing this description of them? No matter;
they will return again when I least think of them. All
that I have observed since, of flowers and plants, and
grass-plots, and of suburb delights, seems to me borrowed
from " that first garden of my innocence "—to be slips
and scions stolen from that bed of memory. In this
manner the darlings of our childhood burnish out in the
eye of after-years, and derive their sweetest perfume from
the first heartfelt sigh of pleasure breathed upon them,

> " Like the sweet south,
> That breathes upon a bank of violets,
> Stealing and giving odour ! "

If I have pleasure in a flower-garden, I have in a kitchen-
garden too, and for the same reason. If I see a row

of cabbage-plants, or of peas or beans coming up, I
immediately think of those which I used so carefully
to water of an evening at W[e]m, when my day's tasks
were done, and of the pain with which I saw them
droop and hang down their leaves in the morning's
sun. Again, I never see a child's kite in the air but
it seems to pull at my heart. It is to me " a thing of
life." I feel the twinge at my elbow, the flutter and
palpitation, with which I used to let go the string of
my own, as it rose in the air, and towered among the
clouds. My little cargo of hopes and fears ascended
with it; and as it made a part of my own consciousness
then, it does so still, and appears " like some gay creature
of the element," my playmate when life was young,
and twin-born with my earliest recollections. I could
enlarge on this subject of childish amusements, but
Mr. Leigh Hunt has treated it so well, in a paper in the
Indicator, on the productions of the toy-shops of the
metropolis, that if I were to insist more on it I should
only pass for an imitator of that ingenious and agreeable
writer, *and for an indifferent one into the bargain.*

Sounds, smells, and sometimes tastes, are remembered
longer than visible objects, and serve, perhaps, better
for links in the chain of association. The reason seems
to be this: they are in their nature intermittent, and
comparatively rare; whereas objects of sight are always
before us, and, by their continuous succession, drive
one another out. The eye is always open; and between
any given impression and its recurrence a second time,
fifty thousand other impressions have, in all likelihood,
been stamped upon the sense and on the brain. The other
senses are not so active or vigilant. They are but seldom
called into play. The ear, for example, is oftener courted
by silence than noise; and the sounds that break that
silence sink deeper and more durably into the mind.
I have a more present and lively recollection of certain

scents, tastes, and sounds, for this reason, than I have of mere visible images, because they are more original, and less worn by frequent repetition. Where there is nothing interposed between any two impressions, whatever the distance of time that parts them, they naturally seem to touch; and the renewed impression recalls the former one in full force, without distraction or competitor. The taste of barberries, which have hung out in the snow during the severity of a North American winter, I have in my mouth still, after an interval of thirty years; for I have met with no other taste in all that time at all like it. It remains by itself, almost like the impression of a sixth sense. But the colour is mixed up indiscriminately with the colours of many other berries, nor shall I be able to distinguish it among them. The smell of a brick-kiln carries the evidence of its own identity with it: neither is it to me (from peculiar associations) unpleasant. The colour of brickdust, on the contrary, is more common, and easily confounded with other colours. Raphael did not keep it quite distinct from his flesh-colour. I will not say that we have a more perfect recollection of the human voice than of that complex picture the human face, but I think the sudden hearing of a well-known voice has something in it more affecting and striking than the sudden meeting with the face: perhaps, indeed, this may be because we have a more familiar remembrance of the one than the other, and the voice takes us more by surprise on that account. I am by no means certain (generally speaking) that we have the ideas of the other senses so accurate and well made out as those of visible form: what I chiefly mean is, that the feelings belonging to the sensations of our other organs, when accidentally recalled, are kept more separate and pure. Musical sounds, probably, owe a good deal of their interest and romantic effect to the principle here spoken of. Were they constant, they would become indifferent, as we may find with respect to disagreeable noises, which we do not hear after a time. I know no situation more pitiable than that of a blind fiddler who has but one sense left (if we except the sense of snuff-taking[1]) and who has that stunned or deafened by his own villainous noises. Shakespear says,

" How silver-sweet sound lovers' tongues by night ! "

It has been observed in explanation of this passage, that it is because in the day-time lovers are occupied with one another's faces, but that at night they can only distinguish the sound of each other's voices. I know not how this may be; but I have, ere now, heard a voice break so upon the silence,

" To angels' 'twas most like,"

and charm the moonlight air with its balmy essence, that the budding leaves trembled to its accents. Would I might have heard it once more whisper peace and hope (as erst when it was mingled with the breath of spring), and with its soft pulsations lift winged fancy to heaven ! But it has ceased, or turned where I no more shall hear it!—Hence, also, we see what is the charm of the shepherd's pastoral reed; and why we hear him, as it were, piping to his flock, even in a picture. Our ears are fancy-stung ! I remember once strolling along the margin of a stream, skirted with willows and plashy sedges, in one of those low sheltered valleys on Salisbury Plain, where the monks of former ages had planted chapels and built hermits' cells. There was a little parish-church near, but tall elms and quivering alders hid it from my sight, when, all of a sudden, I was startled by the sound of the full organ pealing on the ear, accompanied by rustic voices and the willing choir of village-maids and children. It rose, indeed, " like an

¹ See Wilkie's Blind Fiddler.

exhalation of rich distilled perfumes." The dew from a
thousand pastures was gathered in its softness; the silence
of a thousand years spoke in it. It came upon the heart
like the calm beauty of death; fancy caught the sound, and
faith mounted on it to the skies. It filled the valley like
a mist, and still poured out its endless chant, and still it
swells upon the ear, and wraps me in a golden trance,
drowning the noisy tumult of the world!

There is a curious and interesting discussion on the
comparative distinctness of our visual and other external
impressions, in Mr. Fearn's *Essay on Consciousness*, with
which I shall try to descend from this rhapsody to the
ground of common sense and plain reasoning again.
After observing, a little before, that " nothing is more
untrue than that sensations of vision do necessarily leave
more vivid and durable ideas than those of grosser senses,"
he proceeds to give a number of illustrations in support
of this position. " Notwithstanding," he says, " the
advantages here enumerated in favour of sight, I think
there is no doubt that a man will come to forget acquaintance, and many other visible objects, noticed in mature
age, before he will in the least forget taste and smells, of
only moderate interest, encountered either in his childhood or at any time since.

" In the course of voyaging to various distant regions,
it has several times happened that I have eaten once or
twice of different things that never came in my way before
nor since. Some of these have been pleasant, and some
scarce better than insipid; but I have no reason to think
I have forgot, or much altered the ideas left by those
single impulses of taste; though here the memory of them
certainly has not been preserved by repetition. It is clear I
must have seen as well as tasted those things; and I am
decided that I remember the tastes with more precision
than I do the visual sensations.

" I remember having once, and only once, eat Kangaroo in New Holland; and having once smelled a baker's shop having a peculiar odour in the city of Bassorah. Now both these gross ideas remain with me quite as vivid as any visual ideas of those places; and this could not be from repetition, but really from interest in the sensation.

" Twenty-eight years ago, in the island of Jamaica, I partook (perhaps twice) of a certain fruit, of the taste of which I have now a very fresh idea; and I could add other instances of that period.

" I have had repeated proofs of having lost retention of visual objects, at various distances of time, though they had once been familiar. I have not, during thirty years, forgot the delicate, and in itself most trifling sensation that the palm of my hand used to convey, when I was a boy, trying the different effects of what boys call *light* and *heavy* tops; but I cannot remember within several shades of the brown coat which I left off a week ago. If any man thinks he can do better, let him take an ideal survey of his wardrobe, and then actually refer to it for proof.

" After retention of such ideas, it certainly would be very difficult to persuade me that feeling, taste, and smell can scarce be said to leave ideas, unless indistinct and obscure ones. . . .

" Show a Londoner correct models of twenty London churches, and, at the same time, a model of each, which differs, in several considerable features, from the truth, and I venture to say he shall not tell you, in any instance, which is the correct one, except by mere chance.

" If he is an architect he may be much more correct than any ordinary person: and this obviously is, because he has felt an interest in viewing these structures, which an ordinary person does not feel: and here interest is the sole reason of his remembering more correctly than his neighbour.

" I once heard a person quaintly ask another, How many trees there are in St. Paul's churchyard? The question itself indicates that many cannot answer it; and this is found to be the case with those who have passed the church a hundred times: whilst the cause is, that every individual in the busy stream which glides past St. Paul's is engrossed in various other interests.

" How often does it happen that we enter a well-known apartment, or meet a well-known friend, and receive some vague idea of visible difference, but cannot possibly find out *what* it is; until at length we come to perceive (or perhaps must be told) that some ornament or furniture is removed, altered, or added in the apartment; or that our friend has cut his hair, taken a wig, or has made any of twenty considerable alterations in his appearance. At other times we have no perception of alteration whatever, though the like has taken place.

" It is, however, certain that sight, apposited with interest, can retain tolerably exact copies of sensations, especially if not too complex, such as of the human countenance and figure. Yet the voice will convince us when the countenance will not; and he is reckoned an excellent painter, and no ordinary genius, who can make a tolerable likeness from memory. Nay, more, it is a conspicuous proof of the inaccuracy of visual ideas, that it is an effort of consummate art, attained by many years' practice, to take a strict likeness of the human countenance, even when the object is present; and among those cases where the wilful cheat of flattery has been avoided, we still find in how very few instances the best painters produce a likeness up to the life, though practice and interest join in the attempt.

" I imagine an ordinary person would find it very difficult, supposing he had some knowledge of drawing, to afford from memory a tolerable sketch of such a familiar object as his curtain, his carpet, or his dressing-

gown, if the pattern of either be at all various or irregular;
yet he will instantly tell, with precision, either if his snuff
or his wine has not the same character it had yesterday,
though both these are compounds.

" Beyond all this I may observe, that a draper who is
in the daily habit of such comparisons cannot carry in
his mind the particular shade of a colour during a second
of time; and has no certainty of tolerably matching
two simple colours, except by placing the patterns in
contact."[1]

I will conclude the subject of this Essay with observing that (as it appears to me) a nearer and more familiar
acquaintance with persons has a different and more
favourable effect than that with places or things. The
latter improve (as an almost universal rule) by being
removed to a distance: the former, generally at least,
gain by being brought nearer and more home to us.
Report or imagination seldom raises any individual so
high in our estimation as to disappoint us greatly when
we are introduced to him: prejudice and malice constantly exaggerate defects beyond the reality. Ignorance alone makes monsters or bugbears: our actual
acquaintances are all very common-place people. The
thing is, that as a matter of hearsay or conjecture, we
make abstractions of particular vices, and irritate ourselves against some particular quality or action of the
person we dislike: whereas individuals are concrete
existences, not arbitrary denominations or nicknames;
and have innumerable other qualities, good, bad, and
indifferent, besides the damning feature with which we
fill up the portrait or caricature in our previous fancies.
We can scarcely hate any one that we know. An acute
observer complained, that if there was any one to whom
he had a particular spite, and a wish to let him see it,
the moment he came to sit down with him his enmity

---

[1] *Essay on Consciousness*, p. 303.

F

was disarmed by some unforeseen circumstance. If it
was a Quarterly Reviewer, he was in other respects
like any other man. Suppose, again, your adversary
turns out a very ugly man, or wants an eye, you are
baulked in that way: he is not what you expected, the
object of your abstract hatred and implacable disgust.
He may be a very disagreeable person, but he is no
longer the same. If you come into a room where a
man is, you find, in general, that he has a nose upon
his face. "There's sympathy!" This alone is a diversion to your unqualified contempt. He is stupid, and
says nothing, but he seems to have something in him
when he laughs. You had conceived of him as a rank
Whig or Tory—yet he talks upon other subjects. You
knew that he was a virulent party-writer; but you find
that the man himself is a tame sort of animal enough.
He does not bite. That's something. In short, you
can make nothing of it. Even opposite vices balance
one another. A man may be pert in company, but he
is also dull; so that you cannot, though you try, hate
him cordially, merely for the wish to be offensive. He
is a knave. Granted. You learn, on a nearer acquaintance, what you did not know before—that he is a fool
as well; so you forgive him. On the other hand, he
may be a profligate public character, and may make no
secret of it; but he gives you a hearty shake by the
hand, speaks kindly to servants, and supports an aged
father and mother. Politics apart, he is a very honest
fellow. You are told that a person has carbuncles on
his face; but you have ocular proofs that he is sallow,
and pale as a ghost. This does not much mend the
matter; but it blunts the edge of the ridicule, and
turns your indignation against the inventor of the lie;
but he is ——, the editor of a Scotch magazine; so
you are just where you were. I am not very fond of
anonymous criticism; I want to know who the author

can be: but the moment I learn this, I am satisfied. Even —— would do well to come out of his disguise. It is the mask only that we dread and hate: the man may have something human about him! The notions, in short, which we entertain of people at a distance, or from partial representations, or from guess-work, are simple uncompounded ideas, which answer to nothing in reality: those which we derive from experience are mixed modes, the only true, and, in general, the most favourable ones. Instead of naked deformity, or abstract perfection—

" Those faultless monsters which the world ne'er saw "—

" the web of our lives is of mingled yarn, good and ill together: our virtues would be proud, if our faults whipt them not; and our vices would despair, if they were not encouraged by our virtues." This was truly and finely said long ago, by one who knew the strong and weak points of human nature; but it is what sects, and parties, and those philosophers whose pride and boast it is to classify by nicknames, have yet to learn the meaning of!

ON THE KNOWLEDGE OF CHARACTER

(WRITTEN ABOUT 1821-1822)

I T is astonishing, with all our opportunities and practice, how little we know of this subject. For myself, I feel that the more I learn, the less I understand it.

I remember, several years ago, a conversation in the *diligence* coming from Paris, in which, on its being mentioned that a man had married his wife after thirteen years' courtship, a fellow-countryman of mine observed, that "then, at least, he would be acquainted with her character"; when a Monsieur P——, inventor and proprietor of the *Invisible Girl*, made answer, "No, not at all; for that the. very next day she might turn out the very reverse of the character that she had appeared in during all the preceding time."[1] I could not help admiring the superior sagacity of the French juggler, and it struck me then that we could never be sure when we had got at the bottom of this riddle.

There are various ways of getting at a knowledge of character—by looks, words, actions. The first of these, which seems the most superficial, is perhaps the safest, and least liable to deceive: nay, it is that which mankind, in spite of their pretending to the contrary, most generally go by. Professions pass for nothing, and actions may be counterfeited; but a man cannot help his looks, "Speech," said a celebrated wit, "was given to man to conceal his thoughts." Yet I do not know that the greatest hypocrites are the least silent. The mouth of Cromwell is pursed up in the portraits of him, as if he was afraid to trust himself with words. Lord Chesterfield advises us, if we wish to know the real sentiments of the person we are conversing with, to look in his face, for he can more easily command his words than his features. A man's whole life may be a lie to himself and others; and yet a picture painted of him by a great artist would probably stamp his true character on the canvas, and betray the secret to posterity. Men's opinions were divided, in their lifetimes, about such prominent personages as Charles V and Ignatius Loyola, partly, no doubt, from passion and interest, but partly from contradictory evidence in their ostensible conduct: the spectator, who has ever seen their pictures by Titian, judges of them at once, and truly. I had rather leave a

---

[1] "It is not a year or two shows us a man."—Æmilia, in *Othello*.

good portrait of myself behind me than have a fine epitaph. The face, for the most part, tells what we have thought and felt—the rest is nothing. I have a higher idea of Donne from a rude, half-effaced outline of him prefixed to his poems than from anything he ever wrote. Cæsar's *Commentaries* would not have redeemed him in my opinion, if the bust of him had resembled the Duke of [Wellington]. My old friend Fawcett used to say, that if Sir Isaac Newton himself had lisped, he could not have thought anything of him. So I cannot persuade myself that any one is a great man who looks like a fool. In this I may be wrong.

First impressions are often the truest, as we find (not unfrequently) to our cost, when we have been wheedled out of them by plausible professions or actions. A man's look is the work of years, it is stamped on his countenance by the events of his whole life, nay, more, by the hand of nature, and it is not to be got rid of easily. There is, as it has been remarked repeatedly, something in a person's appearance at first sight which we do not like, and that gives us an odd twinge, but which is overlooked in a multiplicity of other circumstances, till the mask is taken off, and we see this lurking character verified in the plainest manner in the sequel. We are struck at first, and by chance, with what is peculiar and characteristic; also with permanent *traits* and general effect: this afterwards goes off in a set of unmeaning, common-place details. This sort of *prima facie* evidence, then, shews what a man is better than what he says or does; for it shows us the habit of his mind, which is the same under all circumstances and disguises. You will say, on the other hand, that there is no judging by appearances, as a general rule. No one, for instance, would take such a person for a very clever man without knowing who he was. Then, ten to one, he is not: he may have got the reputation, but it is a mistake. You say, there is Mr. ——, undoubtedly a person of great genius; yet, except when excited by something extraordinary, he seems half dead. He has wit at will, yet wants life and spirit. He is capable of the most generous acts, yet meanness seems to cling to every motion. He looks like a poor creature—and in truth he is one! The first impression he gives you of him answers nearly to the feeling he has of his personal identity; and this image of himself, rising from his thoughts, and shrouding his faculties, is that which sits with him in the house, walks out with him into the street, and haunts his bedside. The best part of his existence is dull, cloudy, leaden: the flashes of light that proceed from it, or streak it here and there, may dazzle others, but do not deceive himself. Modesty is the lowest of the virtues, and is a real confession of the deficiency it indicates. He who undervalues himself is justly undervalued by others. Whatever good properties he may possess are, in fact, neutralized by a " cold rheum " running through his veins, and taking away the zest of his pretensions, the pith and marrow of his performances. What is it to me that I can write these TABLE-TALKS? It is true I can, by a reluctant effort, rake up a parcel of half-forgotten observations, but they do not float on the surface of my mind, nor stir it with any sense of pleasure, nor even of pride. Others have more property in them than I have: *they* may reap the benefit, *I* have only had the pain. Otherwise, they are to me as if they had never existed; nor should I know that I had ever thought at all, but that I am reminded of it by the strangeness of my appearance, and my unfitness for everything else. Look in C[oleridge]'s face while he is talking. His words are such as might " create a soul under the ribs of death." His face is a blank. Which are we to consider as the true index of his mind? Pain, languor, shadowy remembrances, are the uneasy inmates there: his lips move mechanically!

There are people that we do not like, though we may have known them long, and have no fault to find with them, " their appearance ", as we say, " is so much against them." That is not all, if we could find it out. There is, generally, a reason for this prejudice; for nature is true to itself. They may be very good sort of people too, in their way, but still something is the matter. There is a coldness, a selfishness, a levity, an insincerity, which we cannot fix upon any particular phrase or action, but we see it in their whole persons and deportment. One reason that we do not see it in any other way may be, that they are all the time trying to conceal this defect by every means in their power. There is, luckily, a sort of *second sight* in mortals: we discern the lurking indications of temper and habit a long while before their palpable effects appear. I once used to meet with a person at an ordinary, a very civil, good-looking man in other respects, but with an odd look about his eyes, which I could not explain, as if he saw you under their fringed lids, and you could not see him again: this man was a common sharper. The greatest hypocrite I ever knew was a little, demure, pretty, modest-looking girl, with eyes timidly cast upon the ground, and an air soft as enchantment; the only circumstance that could lead to a suspicion of her true character was a cold, sullen, watery, glazed look about the eyes, which she bent on vacancy, as if determined to avoid all explanation with yours. I might have spied in their glittering, motionless surface the rocks and quicksands that awaited me below! We do not feel quite at ease in the company or friendship of those who have any natural obliquity or imperfection of person. The reason is, they are not on the best terms with themselves, and are sometimes apt to play off on others the tricks that nature has played them. This, however, is a remark that, perhaps, ought not to have been made. I know a person to whom it has been objected as a disqualification for friendship, that he never shakes you cordially by the hand. I own this is a damper to sanguine and florid temperaments, who abound in these practical demonstrations and " compliments extern." The same person who testifies the least pleasure at meeting you, is the last to quit his seat in your company, grapples with a subject in conversation right earnestly, and is, I take it, backward to give up a cause or a friend. Cold and distant in appearance, he piques himself on being the king of *good haters*, and a no less zealous partisan. The most phlegmatic constitutions often contain the most inflammable spirits— as fire is struck from the hardest flints.

And this is another reason that makes it difficult to judge of character. Extremes meet; and qualities display themselves by the most contradictory appearances. Any inclination, in consequence of being generally suppressed, vents itself the more violently when an opportunity presents itself: the greatest grossness sometimes accompanies the greatest refinement, as a natural relief, one to the other; and we find the most reserved and indifferent tempers at the beginning of an entertainment, or an acquaintance, turn out the most communicative and cordial at the end of it. Some spirits exhaust themselves at first: others gain strength by progression. Some minds have a greater facility of throwing off impressions—are, as it were, more transparent or porous than others. Thus the French present a marked contrast to the English in this respect. A Frenchman addresses you at once with a sort of lively indifference: an Englishman is more on his guard, feels his way, and is either exceedingly reserved, or lets you into his whole confidence, which he cannot so well impart to an entire stranger. Again, a Frenchman is naturally humane: an Englishman is, I should say, only friendly by habit. His virtues and his vices cost him more than they do his more gay and volatile neighbours. An Englishman is said to speak his mind more plainly than others:—yes, if it will give you pain to hear it. He does not care whom he offends by his discourse: a foreigner generally strives to oblige in what he says. The French are accused of promising more than they perform. That may be, and yet they may perform as many good-natured acts as the English, if the latter are as averse to perform as they are to promise. Even the professions of the French may be sincere at the time, or arise out of the impulse of the moment; though their desire to serve you may be neither very violent nor very lasting. I cannot think, notwithstanding, that the French are not a serious people; nay, that they are not a more reflecting people than the common run of the English. Let those who think them merely light and mercurial explain that enigma, their everlasting prosing tragedy. The English are considered as comparatively a slow, plodding people. If the French are quicker, they are also more plodding. See, for example, how highly finished and elaborate their works of art are! How systematic and correct they aim at being in all their productions of a graver cast! " If the French have a fault," as Yorick said, " it is that they are too grave." With wit, sense, cheerfulness, patience, good-nature, and refinement of manners, all they want is imagination and sturdiness of moral principle! Such are some of the contradictions in the character of the two nations, and so little does the character of either appear to have been understood! Nothing can be more ridiculous indeed than the way in which we exaggerate each other's vices and extenuate our own. The whole is an affair of prejudice on one side of the question, and of partiality on the other. Travellers who set out to carry back a true report of the case appear to lose not only the use of their understandings, but of their senses, the instant they set foot in a foreign land. The commonest facts and appearances are distorted and discoloured. They go abroad with certain preconceived

F *

notions on the subject, and they make everything answer, in reason's spite, to their favourite theory. In addition to the difficulty of explaining customs and manners foreign to our own, there are all the obstacles of wilful prepossession thrown in the way. It is not, therefore, much to be wondered at that nations have arrived at so little knowledge of one another's characters; and that, where the object has been to widen the breach between them, any slight differences that occur are easily blown into a blaze of fury by repeated misrepresentations, and all the exaggerations that malice or folly can invent!

This ignorance of character is not confined to foreign nations: we are ignorant of that of our own countrymen in a class a little below or above ourselves. We shall hardly pretend to pronounce magisterially on the good or bad qualities of strangers; and, at the same time, we are ignorant of those of our friends, of our kindred, and of our own. We are in all these cases either too near or too far off the object to judge of it properly.

Persons, for instance, in a higher or middle rank of life know little or nothing of the characters of those below them, as servants, country people, etc. I would lay it down in the first place as a general rule on this subject, that all uneducated people are hypocrites. Their sole business is to deceive. They conceive them-selves in a state of hostility with others, and stratagems are fair in war. The inmates of the kitchen and the parlour are always (as far as respects their feelings and intentions towards each other) in Hobbes's " state of nature." Servants and others in that line of life have nothing to exercise their spare talents for invention upon but those about them. Their superfluous electrical particles of wit and fancy are not carried off by those established and fashionable conductors, novels and romances. Their faculties are not buried in books, but all alive and stirring, erect and bristling like a cat's back.

Their coarse conversation sparkles with "wild wit, invention ever new." Their betters try all they can to set themselves up above them, and they try all they can to pull them down to their own level. They do this by getting up a little comic interlude, a daily, domestic, homely drama out of the odds and ends of the family failings, of which there is in general a pretty plentiful supply, or make up the deficiency of materials out of their own heads. They turn the qualities of their masters and mistresses inside out, and any real kindness or condescension only sets them the more against you. They are not to be taken in that way—they will not be baulked in the spite they have to you. They only set to work with redoubled alacrity, to lessen the favour or to blacken your character. They feel themselves like a degraded *caste*, and cannot understand how the obligations can be all on one side, and the advantages all on the other. You cannot come to equal terms with them— they reject all such overtures as insidious and hollow— nor can you ever calculate upon their gratitude or good-will, any more than if they were so many strolling Gipsies or wild Indians. They have no fellow-feeling, they keep no faith with the more privileged classes. They are in your power, and they endeavour to be even with you by trick and cunning, by lying and chicanery. In this they have nothing to restrain them. Their whole life is a succession of shifts, excuses, and expedients. The love of truth is a principle with those only who have made it their study, who have applied themselves to the pursuit of some art or science, where the intellect is severely tasked, and learns by habit to take a pride in, and to set a just value on, the correctness of its conclusions. To have a disinterested regard to truth, the mind must have contemplated it in abstract and remote questions; whereas the ignorant and vulgar are only conversant with those things in which their own interest is concerned.

All their notions are local, personal, and consequently gross and selfish. They say whatever comes uppermost —turn whatever happens to their own account—and invent any story, or give any answer that suits their purposes. Instead of being bigoted to general principles, they trump up any lie for the occasion, and the more of a *thumper* it is, the better they like it; the more unlooked-for it is, why, so much the more of a *God-send!* They have no conscience about the matter; and if you find them out in any of their manœuvres, are not ashamed of themselves, but angry with you. If you remonstrate with them, they laugh in your face. The only hold you have of them is their interest—you can but dismiss them from your employment; and *service is no inheritance.* If they effect anything like decent remorse, and hope you will pass it over, all the while they are probably trying to recover the wind of you. Persons of liberal knowledge or sentiments have no kind of chance in this sort of mixed intercourse with these barbarians in civilized life. You cannot tell, by any signs or principles, what is passing in their minds. There is no common point of view between you. You have not the same topics to refer to, the same language to express yourself. Your interests, your feelings are quite distinct. You take certain things for granted as rules of action: they take nothing for granted but their own ends, pick up all their knowledge out of their own occasions, are on the watch only for what they can catch—are

> " Subtle as the fox for prey :
> Like warlike as the wolf, for what they eat."

They have indeed a regard to their character, as this last may affect their livelihood or advancement, none as it is connected with a sense of propriety; and this sets their mother-wit and native talents at work upon a double file of expedients, to bilk their consciences, and salve their reputation. In short, you never know where to have them, any more than if they were of a different species of animals; and in trusting to them, you are sure to be betrayed and overreached. You have other things to mind; they are thinking only of you, and how to turn you to advantage. *Give and take* is no maxim here. You can build nothing on your own moderation or on their false delicacy. After a familiar conversation with a waiter at a tavern, you overhear him calling you by some provoking nickname. If you make a present to the daughter of the house where you lodge, the mother is sure to recollect some addition to her bill. It is a running fight. In fact, there is a principle in human nature not willingly to endure the idea of a superior, a sour jacobinical disposition to wipe out the score of obligation, or efface the tinsel of external advantages—and where others have the opportunity of coming in contact with us, they generally find the means to establish a sufficiently marked degree of degrading equality. No man is a hero to his valet-de-chambre, is an old maxim. A new illustration of this principle occurred the other day. While Mrs. Siddons was giving her readings of Shakespear to a brilliant and admiring drawing-room, one of the servants in the hall below was saying, " What, I find the old lady is making as much noise as ever! " So little is there in common between the different classes of society, and so impossible is it ever to unite the diversities of custom and knowledge which separate them.

Women, according to Mrs. Peachum, are " bitter bad judges " of the characters of men; and men are not much better of theirs, if we can form any guess from their choice in marriage. Love is proverbially blind. The whole is an affair of whim and fancy. Certain it is that the greatest favourites with the other sex are not those who are most liked or respected among their own. I never knew but one clever man who was what is called a *lady's man;* and he (unfortunately for the argument) happened to be a considerable coxcomb. It was by this irresistible quality, and not by the force of his genius, that he vanquished. Women seem to doubt their own judgments in love, and to take the opinion which a man entertains of his own prowess and accomplishments for granted. The wives of poets are (for the most part) mere pieces of furniture, in the room. If you speak to them of their husbands' talents or reputation in the world, it is as if you made mention of some office that they held. It can hardly be otherwise, when the instant any subject is started or conversation arises, in which men are interested, or try one another's strength, the women leave the room, or attend to something else. The qualities, then, in which men are ambitious to excel, and which ensure the applause of the world,—eloquence, genius, learning, integrity,—are not those which gain the favour of the fair. I must not deny, however, that wit and courage have this effect. Neither is youth nor beauty the sole passport to their affections.

> " The way of woman's will is hard to find,
>   Harder to hit."

Yet there is some clue to this mystery, some determining cause; for we find that the same men are universal favourites with women, as others are uniformly disliked by them. Is not the loadstone that attracts so powerfully, and in all circumstances, a strong and undisguised bias towards them, a marked attention, a conscious preference of them to every other passing object or topic? I am not sure, but I incline to think so. The successful lover is the *cavalier servente* of all nations. The man of gallantry behaves as if he had made an assignation with every woman he addresses. An argument immediately draws off my attention from the prettiest woman in the room. I accordingly succeed better in argument—than in love!—

I do not think that what is called *Love at first sight* is so great an absurdity as it is sometimes imagined to be. We generally make up our minds beforehand to the sort of person we should like,—grave or gay, black, brown, or fair; with golden tresses or with raven locks;—and when we meet with a complete example of the qualities we admire, the bargain is soon struck. We have never seen anything to come up to our newly-discovered goddess before, but she is what we have been all our lives looking for. The idol we fall down and worship is an image familiar to our minds. It has been present to our waking thoughts, it has haunted us in our dreams, like some fairy vision. Oh! thou who, the first time I ever beheld thee, didst draw my soul into the circle of thy heavenly looks, and wave enchantment round me, do not think thy conquest less complete because it was instantaneous; for in that gentle form (as if another Imogen had entered) I saw all that I had ever loved of female grace, modesty, and sweetness!

I shall not say much of friendship as giving an insight into character, because it is often founded on mutual infirmities and prejudices. Friendships are frequently taken up on some sudden sympathy, and we see only as much as we please of one another's characters afterwards. Intimate friends are not fair witnesses to character, any more than professed enemies. They cool, indeed, in time, part, and retain only a rankling grudge of past errors and oversights. Their testimony in the latter case is not quite free from suspicion.

One would think that near relations who live constantly together, and always have done so, must be pretty well acquainted with one another's characters. They are nearly in the dark about it. Familiarity confounds all traits of distinction: interest and prejudice take away the power of judging. We have no opinion on the subject, any more than of one another's faces. The Penates, the household

gods, are veiled. We do not see the features of those we
love, nor do we clearly distinguish their virtues or their
vices. We take them as they are found in the lump,—
by weight, and not by measure. We know all about the
individuals, their sentiments, history, manners, words,
actions, everything; but we know all these too much
as facts, as inveterate, habitual impressions, as clothed
with too many associations, as sanctified with too many
affections, as woven too much into the web of our hearts,
to be able to pick out the different threads, to cast up the
items of the debtor and creditor account, or to refer them
to any general standard of right and wrong. Our impressions with respect to them are too strong, too real,
too much *sui generis*, to be capable of a comparison with
anything but themselves. We hardly inquire whether
those for whom we are thus interested, and to whom we
are thus knit, are *better* or *worse* than others—the question
is a kind of profanation—all we know is, they are *more*
to us than any one else can be. Our sentiments of this
kind are rooted and grow in us, and we cannot eradicate
them by voluntary means. Besides, our judgments are
bespoke, our interests take part with our blood. If any
doubt arises, if the veil of our implicit confidence is
drawn aside by any accident for a moment, the shock is
too great, like that of a dislocated limb, and we recoil on
our habitual impressions again. Let not that veil ever be
rent entirely asunder, so that those images may be left
bare of reverential awe, and lose their religion; for nothing
can ever support the desolation of the heart afterwards.

The greatest misfortune that can happen among relations is a different way of bringing up, so as to set one
another's opinions and characters in an entirely new
point of view. This often lets in an unwelcome day-light
on the subject, and breeds schisms, coldness, and incurable
heart-burnings in families. I have sometimes thought
whether the progress of society and march of knowledge

does not do more harm in this respect, by loosening the ties of domestic attachment, and preventing those who are most interested in, and anxious to think well of one another from feeling a cordial sympathy and approbation of each other's sentiments, manners, views, etc., than it does good by any real advantage to the community at large. The son, for instance, is brought up to the Church, and nothing can exceed the pride and pleasure the father takes in him while all goes on well in this favourite direction. His notions change, and he imbibes a taste for the Fine Arts. From this moment there is an end of anything like the same unreserved communication between them. The young man may talk with enthusiasm of his "Rembrandts, Correggios, and stuff": it is all *Hebrew* to the elder; and whatever satisfaction he may feel in the hearing of his son's progress, or good wishes for his success, he is never reconciled to the new pursuit, he still hankers after the first object that he had set his mind upon. Again, the grandfather is a Calvinist, who never gets the better of his disappointment at his son's going over to the Unitarian side of the question. The matter rests here till the grandson, some years after, in the fashion of the day and "infinite agitation of men's wit," comes to doubt certain points in the creed in which he has been brought up, and the affair is all abroad again. Here are three generations made uncomfortable and in a manner set at variance by a veering point of theology, and the officious meddling of biblical critics! Nothing, on the other hand, can be more wretched or common than that upstart pride and insolent good fortune which is ashamed of its origin; nor are there many things more awkward than the situation of rich and poor relations. Happy, much happier, are those tribes and people who are confined to the same *caste* and way of life from sire to son, where prejudices are transmitted like instincts, and where the same unvarying standard of opinion and refinement blends countless generations in its improgressive, ever-lasting mould!

Not only is there a wilful and habitual blindness in near kindred to each other's defects, but an incapacity to judge from the quantity of materials, from the contra-dictoriness of the evidence. The chain of particulars is too long and massy for us to lift it or put it into the most approved ethical scales. The concrete result does not answer to any abstract theory, to any logical definition. There is black, and white, and grey, square and round—there are too many anomalies, too many redeeming points, in poor human nature, such as it actually is, for us to arrive at a smart, summary decision on it. We know too much to come to any hasty or partial conclusion. We do not pronounce upon the present act, because a hundred others rise up to contradict it. We suspend our judgments altogether, because in effect one thing unconsciously balances another; and perhaps this obstinate, pertinacious indecision would be the truest philosophy in other cases, where we dispose of the question of character easily, because we have only the smallest part of the evidence to decide upon. Real character is not one thing, but a thousand things; actual qualities do not conform to any factitious standard in the mind, but rest upon their own truth and nature. The dull stupor under which we labour in respect of those whom we have the greatest oppor-tunities of inspecting nearly, we should do well to imitate before we give extreme and uncharitable verdicts against those whom we only see in passing or at a distance. If we knew them better, we should be disposed to say less about them.

In the truth of things, there are none utterly worthless, none without some drawback on their pretensions, or some alloy of imperfection. It has been observed that a familiarity with the worst characters lessens our abhorrence of them; and a wonder is often expressed that the greatest criminals look like other men. The reason is that *they are like other men in many respects.* If a particular individual was merely the wretch we read of, or conceive in the abstract, that is, if he was the mere personified idea of the criminal brought to the bar, he would not disappoint the spectator, but would look like what he would be—a monster! But he has other qualities, ideas, feelings, nay, probably virtues, mixed up with the most profligate habits or desperate acts. This need not lessen our abhorrence of the crime, though it does of the criminal; for it has the latter effect only by shewing him to us in different points of view, in which he appears a common mortal, and not the caricature of vice we took him for, or spotted all over with infamy. I do not, at the same time, think this is a lax or dangerous, though it is a charitable view of the subject. In my opinion, no man ever answered in his own mind (except in the agonies of conscience or of repentance, in which latter case he throws the imputation from himself in another way) to the abstract idea of a *murderer.* He may have killed a man in self-defence, or " in the trade of war," or to save himself from starving, or in revenge for an injury, but always " so as with a difference," or from mixed and questionable motives. The individual, in reckoning with himself, always takes into the account the considerations of time, place, and circumstance, and never makes out a case of unmitigated, unprovoked villainy, of " pure defecated evil " against himself. There are degrees in real crimes: we reason and moralize only by names and in classes. I should be loth, indeed, to say that " whatever is, is right "; but almost every actual choice inclines to it, with some sort of imperfect, unconscious bias. This is the reason, besides the ends of secrecy, of the invention of *slang* terms for different acts of profligacy committed by thieves, pickpockets, etc. The common names suggest associations of disgust in the minds of others, which those

who live by them do not willingly recognize, and which
they wish to sink in a technical phraseology. So there is
a story of a fellow who, as he was writing down his confession of a murder, stopped to ask how the word *murder*
was spelt; this, if true, was partly because his imagination
was staggered by the recollection of the thing, and partly
because he shrunk from the verbal admission of it.
" *Amen* stuck in his throat "! The defence made by
Eugene Aram of himself against a charge of murder,
some years before, shows that he in imagination completely flung from himself the *nominal* crime imputed to
him: he might, indeed, have staggered an old man with
a blow, and buried his body in a cave, and lived ever
since upon the money he found upon him, but there was
"no malice in the case, none at all," as Peachum says.
The very coolness, subtlety, and circumspection of his
defence (as masterly a legal document as there is upon
record) prove that he was guilty of the act, as much as
they prove that he was unconscious of the *crime*.[1] In the
same spirit, and I conceive with great metaphysical truth,
Mr. Coleridge, in his tragedy of *Remorse*, makes Ordonio
(his chief character) wave the acknowledgment of his
meditated guilt to his own mind, by putting into his
mouth that striking soliloquy:

> "Say, I had lay'd a body in the sun!
> Well! in a month there swarm forth from the corse
> A thousand, nay, ten thousand sentient beings
> In place of that one man. Say I had *kill'd* him!
> Yet who shall tell me, that each one and all
> Of these ten thousand lives is not as happy
> As that one life, which being push'd aside,
> Made room for these unnumber'd."—Act ii. Sc. 2.

[1] The bones of the murdered man were dug up in an old
hermitage. On this, as one instance of the acuteness which he
displayed all through the occasion, Aram remarks, "Where
would you expect to find the bones of a man sooner than in a
hermit's cell, except you were to look for them in a cemetery?"
—See *Newgate Calendar* for the year 1758 or 9.

I am not sure, indeed, that I have not got this whole train of speculation from him; but I should not think the worse of it on that account. That gentleman, I recollect, once asked me whether I thought that the different members of a family really liked one another so well, or had so much attachment, as was generally supposed; and I said that I conceived the regard they had towards each other was expressed by the word *interest* rather than by any other, which he said was the true answer. I do not know that I could mend it now. Natural affection is not pleasure in one another's company, nor admiration of one another's qualities; but it is an intimate and deep knowledge of the things that affect those, to whom we are bound by the nearest ties, with pleasure or pain; it is an anxious, uneasy fellow-feeling with them, a jealous watchfulness over their good name, a tender and un-conquerable yearning for their good. The love, in short, we bear them is the nearest to that we bear ourselves. *Home,* according to the old saying, *is home, be it never so homely.* We love ourselves, not according to our deserts, but our cravings after good: so we love our immediate re-lations in the next degree (if not, even sometimes a higher one), because we know best what they have suffered and what sits nearest to their hearts. We are implicated, in fact, in their welfare by habit and sympathy, as we are in our own.

If our devotion to our own interests is much the same as to theirs, we are ignorant of our own characters for the same reason. We are parties too much concerned to return a fair verdict, and are too much in the secret of our own motives or situation not to be able to give a favourable turn to our actions. We exercise a liberal criticism upon ourselves, and put off the final decision to a late day. The field is large and open. Hamlet exclaims, with a noble magnanimity, " I count myself indifferent honest, and yet I could accuse me of such things!" If you could prove to a man that he is a knave, it would not make much difference in his opinion, his self-love is stronger than his love of virtue. Hypocrisy is generally used as a mask to deceive the world, not to impose on ourselves: for once detect the delinquent in his knavery, and he laughs in your face or glories in his iniquity. This at least happens except where there is a contradiction in the character, and our vices are involuntary and at variance with our convictions. One great difficulty is to distinguish ostensible motives, or such as we acknowledge to ourselves, from tacit or secret springs of action. A man changes his opinion readily, he thinks it candour: it is levity of mind. For the most part, we are stunned and stupid in judging of ourselves. We are callous by custom to our defects or excellences, unless where vanity steps in to exaggerate or extenuate them. I cannot conceive how it is that people are in love with their own persons, or astonished at their own performances, which are but a nine days' wonder to every one else. In general it may be laid down that we are liable to this twofold mistake in judging of our own talents: we, in the first place, nurse the rickety bantling, we think much of that which has cost us much pains and labour, and comes against the grain; and we also set little store by what we do with most ease to ourselves, and therefore best. The works of the greatest genius are produced almost unconsciously, with an ignorance on the part of the persons themselves that they have done anything extraordinary. Nature has done it for them. How little Shakespear seems to have thought of himself or of his fame! Yet, if " to know another well were to know one's self," he must have been acquainted with his own pretensions and character, " who knew all qualities with a learned spirit." His eye seems never to have been bent upon himself, but outwards upon nature. A man who thinks highly of himself may almost set it down that it is without reason. Milton, notwithstanding, appears to have had a high opinion of himself, and to have made it good. He was conscious of his powers, and great by design. Perhaps his tenaciousness, on the score of his own merit, might arise from an early habit of polemical writing, in which his pretensions were continually called to the bar of prejudice and party-spirit, and he had to plead not guilty to the indictment. Some men have died unconscious of immortality, as others have almost exhausted the sense of it in their life-times. Correggio might be mentioned as an instance of the one, Voltaire of the other.

There is nothing that helps a man in his conduct through life more than a knowledge of his own characteristic weaknesses (which, guarded against, become his strength), as there is nothing that tends more to the success of a man's talents than his knowing the limits of his faculties, which are thus concentrated on some practicable object. One man can do but one thing. Universal pretensions end in nothing. Or, as Butler has it, too much wit requires

"As much again to govern it."

There are those who have gone, for want of this self-knowledge, strangely out of their way, and others who have never found it. We find many who succeed in certain departments, and are yet melancholy and dissatisfied, because they failed in the one to which they first devoted themselves, like discarded lovers who pine after their scornful mistress. I will conclude with observing that authors in general overrate the extent and value of posthumous fame: for what (as it has been asked) is the amount even of Shakespear's fame? That in that very country which boasts his genius and his birth, perhaps, scarce one person in ten has ever heard of his name or read a syllable of his writings!

ON THE FEAR OF DEATH

(WRITTEN ABOUT 1821–1822)

"And our little life is rounded with a sleep."

PERHAPS the best cure for the fear of death is to reflect that life has a beginning as well as an end. There was a time when we were not: this gives us no concern—why, then, should it trouble us that a time will come when we shall cease to be? I have no wish to have been alive a hundred years ago, or in the reign of Queen Anne: why should I regret and lay it so much to heart that I shall not be alive a hundred years hence, in the reign of I cannot tell whom?

When Bickerstaff wrote his Essays I knew nothing of the subjects of them; nay, much later, and but the other day, as it were, in the beginning of the reign of George III, when Goldsmith, Johnson, Burke, used to meet at the Globe, when Garrick was in his glory, and Reynolds was over head and ears with his portraits, and Sterne brought out the volumes of *Tristram Shandy* year by year, it was without consulting me: I had not the slightest intimation of what was going on: the debates in the House of Commons on the American War, or the firing at Bunker's Hill, disturbed not me: yet I thought this no evil—I neither ate, drank, nor was merry, yet I did not complain: I had not then looked out into this breathing world, yet I was well; and the world did quite as well without me as I did without it! Why, then, should I make all this outcry about parting with it, and being no worse off than I was before? There is nothing in the recollection that at a certain time we were not come into the world that " the gorge rises at "—why should we revolt at the idea that we must one day go out of it? To die is only to be as we were before we were born; yet no one feels any remorse, or regret, or repugnance, in contemplating this last idea. It is rather a relief and disburthening of the mind: it seems to have been holiday-time with us then: we were not called to appear upon the stage of life, to wear robes or tatters, to laugh or cry, be hooted or applauded; we had lain *perdus* all this while, snug, out of harm's way; and had slept out our thousands of centuries without wanting to be waked up; at peace and free from care, in a long nonage, in a sleep deeper and calmer than that of infancy, wrapped in the softest and finest dust. And the worst that we dread is, after a short, fretful, feverish being, after vain hopes and idle fears, to sink to final repose again, and forget the troubled dream of life! . . . Ye armed men, knights templars, that sleep in the stone aisles of that old Temple church, where all is silent above, and where a deeper silence reigns below (not broken by the pealing organ), are ye not contented where ye lie? Or would you come out of your long homes to go to the Holy War? Or do ye complain that pain no longer visits you, that sickness has done its worst, that you have paid the last debt to nature, that you hear no more of the thickening phalanx of the foe, or your lady's waning love; and that while this ball of earth rolls its eternal round, no sound shall ever pierce through to disturb your lasting repose, fixed as the marble over your tombs, breathless as the grave that holds you! And thou, oh! thou, to whom my heart turns, and will turn while it has feeling left, who didst love in vain, and whose first was thy last sigh, wilt not thou too rest in peace (or wilt thou cry to me complaining from thy clay-cold bed) when that sad heart is no longer sad, and that sorrow is dead which thou wert only called into the world to feel!

It is certain that there is nothing in the idea of a pre-existent state that excites our longing like the prospect of a posthumous existence. We are satisfied to have begun life when we did; we have no ambition to have set out on our journey sooner; and feel that we have had quite enough to do to battle our way through since. We cannot say,

> " The wars we well remember of King Nine,
> Of old Assaracus and Inachus divine."

Neither have we any wish: we are contented to read of them in story, and to stand and gaze at the vast sea of time that separates us from them. It was early days then: the world was not *well-aired* enough for us: we have no inclination to have been up and stirring. We do not consider the six thousand years of the world before we were born as so much time lost to us: we are perfectly indifferent about the matter. We do not grieve and lament that we did not happen to be in time to see the grand mask and pageant of human life going on in all that period; though we are mortified at being obliged to quit our stand before the rest of the procession passes.

It may be suggested in explanation of this difference, that we know from various records and traditions what happened in the time of Queen Anne, or even in the reigns of the Assyrian monarchs, but that we have no means of ascertaining what is to happen hereafter but by awaiting the event, and that our eagerness and curiosity are sharpened in proportion as we are in the dark about it. This is not at all the case; for at that rate we should be constantly wishing to make a voyage of discovery to Greenland or to the Moon, neither of which we have, in general, the least desire to do. Neither, in truth, have we any particular solicitude to pry into the secrets of futurity, but as a pretext for prolonging our own existence. It is not so much that we care to be alive a hundred or a thousand years hence, any more than to have been alive a hundred or a thousand years ago: but the thing lies here, that we would all of us wish the present moment to last for ever. We would be as we are, and would have the world remain just as it is, to please us.

> " The present eye catches the present object "—

to have and to hold while it may; and abhors, on any terms, to have it torn from us, and nothing left in its room. It is the pang of parting, the unloosing our grasp, the breaking asunder some strong tie, the leaving some cherished purpose unfulfilled, that creates the repugnance to go, and " makes calamity of so long life," as it often is.

> " Oh ! thou strong heart !
> There's such a covenant 'twixt the world and thee
> They're loth to break ! "

The love of life, then, is an habitual attachment, not an abstract principle. Simply *to be* does not " content man's natural desire ": we long to be in a certain time, place, and circumstance. We would much rather be now, " on this bank and shoal of time," than have our choice of any future period, than take a slice of fifty or sixty years out of the Millennium, for instance. This shows that our attachment is not confined either to *being* or to *well-being;* but that we have an inveterate prejudice in favour of our immediate existence, such as it is. The mountaineer will not leave his rock, nor the savage his hut; neither are we willing to give up our present mode of life, with all its advantages and disadvantages, for any other that could be substituted for it. No man would, I think, exchange his existence with any other man, however fortunate. We had as lief *not be*, as *not be ourselves*. There are some persons of that reach of soul that they would like to live two hundred and fifty years hence, to see to what height of empire America will have grown up in that period, or whether the English constitution will last so long. These are points beyond me. But I confess I should like to live to see the downfall of the Bourbons. That is a vital question with me; and I shall like it the better the sooner it happens!

No young man ever thinks he shall die. He may believe that others will, or assent to the doctrine that

" all men are mortal " as an abstract proposition, but he
is far enough from bringing it home to himself indi-
vidually.[1] Youth, buoyant activity, and animal spirits, hold
absolute antipathy with old age as well as with death; nor
have we, in the hey-day of life, any more than in the
thoughtlessness of childhood, the remotest conception how

> " This sensible warm motion can become
>   A kneaded clod "—

nor how sanguine, florid health and vigour, shall " turn
to withered, weak, and grey." Or if in a moment of idle
speculation we indulge in this notion of the close of life
as a theory, it is amazing at what a distance it seems;
what a long, leisurely interval there is between; what
a contrast its slow and solemn approach affords to our
present gay dreams of existence! We eye the farthest
verge of the horizon, and think what a way we shall have
to look back upon, ere we arrive at our journey's end; and
without our in the least suspecting it, the mists are at our
feet, and the shadows of age encompass us. The two divisions of our lives have melted into each other: the extreme
points close and meet with none of that romantic interval
stretching out between them that we had reckoned upon;
and for the rich, melancholy, solemn hues of age, " the
sear, the yellow leaf," the deepening shadows of an
autumnal evening, we only feel a dank, cold mist, en-
circling all objects, after the spirit of youth is fled.
There is no inducement to look forward; and what is
worse, little interest in looking back to what has become
so trite and common. The pleasures of our existence
have worn themselves out, are " gone into the wastes of
time," or have turned their indifferent side to us: the
pains by their repeated blows have worn us out, and have
left us neither spirit nor inclination to encounter them
again in retrospect. We do not want to rip up old griev-

[1] "All men think all men mortal but themselves."—YOUNG.

ances, nor to renew our youth like the phœnix, nor to live our lives twice over. Once is enough. As the tree falls, so let it lie. Shut up the book and close the account once for all!

It has been thought by some that life is like the exploring of a passage that grows narrower and darker the farther we advance, without a possibility of ever turning back, and where we are stifled for want of breath at last. For myself, I do not complain of the greater thickness of the atmosphere as I approach the narrow house. I felt it more formerly,[1] when the idea alone seemed to suppress a thousand rising hopes, and weighed upon the pulses of the blood. At present I rather feel a thinness and want of support, I stretch out my hand to some object and find none, I am too much in a world of abstraction; the naked map of life is spread out before me, and in the emptiness and desolation I see Death coming to meet me. In my youth I could not behold him for the crowd of objects and feelings, and Hope stood always between us, saying, "Never mind that old fellow!" If I had lived indeed, I should not care to die. But I do not like a contract of pleasure broken off unfulfilled, a marriage with joy unconsummated, a promise of happiness rescinded. My public and private hopes have been left a ruin, or remain only to mock me. I would wish them to be re-edified. I should like to see some prospect of good to mankind, such as my life began with. I should like to leave some sterling work behind me. I should like to have some friendly hand to consign me to the grave. On these conditions I am ready, if not willing, to depart. I shall then write on my tomb—GRATEFUL AND CONTENTED! But I have thought and suffered too much to be willing to have thought and suffered in vain.—In looking

---

[1] I remember once, in particular, having this feeling in reading Schiller's *Don Carlos*, where there is a description of death, in a degree that almost stifled me.

back, it sometimes appears to me as if I had in a manner slept out my life in a dream or shadow on the side of the hill of knowledge, where I have fed on books, on thoughts, on pictures, and only heard in half-murmurs the trampling of busy feet, or the noises of the throng below. Waked out of this dim, twilight existence, and startled with the passing scene, I have felt a wish to descend to the world of realities, and join in the chase. But I fear too late, and that I had better return to my bookish chimeras and indolence once more! *Zanetto, lascia le donne, et studia la matematica.* I will think of it.

It is not wonderful that the contemplation and fear of death become more familiar to us as we approach nearer to it: that life seems to ebb with the decay of blood and youthful spirits; and that as we find everything about us subject to chance and change, as our strength and beauty die, as our hopes and passions, our friends and our affections leave us, we begin by degrees to feel ourselves mortal!

I have never seen death but once, and that was in an infant. It is years ago. The look was calm and placid, and the face was fair and firm. It was as if a waxen image had been laid out in the coffin, and strewed with innocent flowers. It was not like death, but more like an image of life! No breath moved the lips, no pulse stirred, no sight or sound would enter those eyes or ears more. While I looked at it, I saw no pain was there; it seemed to smile at the short pang of life which was over: but I could not bear the coffin-lid to be closed—it seemed to stifle me; and still as the nettles wave in a corner of the churchyard over his little grave, the welcome breeze helps to refresh me, and ease the tightness at my breast!

An ivory or marble image, like Chantry's monument of the two children, is contemplated with pure delight. Why do we not grieve and fret that the marble is not alive, or fancy that it has a shortness of breath? It never was alive; and it is the difficulty of making the transition from life to death, the struggle between the two in our imagination, that confounds their properties painfully together, and makes us conceive that the infant that is but just dead, still wants to breathe, to enjoy, and look about it, and is prevented by the icy hand of death, locking up its faculties and benumbing its senses; so that, if it could, it would complain of its own hard state. Perhaps religious considerations reconcile the mind to this change sooner than any others, by representing the spirit as fled to another sphere, and leaving the body behind it. So in reflecting on death generally, we mix up the idea of life with it, and thus make it the ghastly monster it is. We think how we should feel, not how the dead feel.

> " Still from the tomb the voice of nature cries ;
> Even in our ashes live their wonted fires ! "

There is an admirable passage on this subject in Tucker's *Light of Nature Pursued,* which I shall transcribe, as by much the best illustration I can offer of it.

" The melancholy appearance of a lifeless body, the mansion provided for it to inhabit, dark, cold, close and solitary, are shocking to the imagination; but it is to the imagination only, not the understanding; for whoever consults this faculty will see at first glance, that there is nothing dismal in all these circumstances: if the corpse were kept wrapped up in a warm bed, with a roasting fire in the chamber, it would feel no comfortable warmth therefrom; were store of tapers lighted up as soon as day shuts in, it would see no objects to divert it; were it left at large it would have no liberty, nor if surrounded with company would be cheered thereby; neither are the distorted features expressions of pain, uneasiness, or distress. This every one knows, and will readily allow upon being suggested, yet still cannot behold, nor even cast a thought upon those objects without shuddering;

for knowing that a living person must suffer grievously under such appearances, they become habitually formidable to the mind, and strike a mechanical horror, which is increased by the customs of the world around us."

There is usually one pang added voluntarily and unnecessarily to the fear of death, by our affecting to compassionate the loss which others will have in us. If that were all, we might reasonably set our minds at rest. The pathetic exhortation on country tombstones, " Grieve not for me, my wife and children dear," etc., is for the most part speedily followed to the letter. We do not leave so great a void in society as we are inclined to imagine, partly to magnify our own importance, and partly to console ourselves by sympathy. Even in the same family the gap is not so great; the wound closes up sooner than we should expect. Nay, *our room* is not unfrequently thought better than *our company*. People walk along the streets the day after our deaths just as they did before, and the crowd is not diminished. While we were living, the world seemed in a manner to exist only for us, for our delight and amusement, because it contributed to them. But our hearts cease to beat, and it goes on as usual, and thinks no more about us than it did in our lifetime. The million are devoid of sentiment, and care as little for you or me as if we belonged to the moon. We live the week over in the Sunday's paper, or are decently interred in some obituary at the month's end! It is not surprising that we are forgotten so soon after we quit this mortal stage; we are scarcely noticed while we are on it. It is not merely that our names are not known in China—they have hardly been heard of in the next street. We are hand in glove with the universe, and think the obligation is mutual. This is an evident fallacy. If this, however, does not trouble us now, it will not hereafter. A handful of dust can have no quarrel to pick with its neighbours or complaint to make against

Providence, and might well exclaim, if it had but an understanding and a tongue, " Go thy ways, old world, swing round in blue ether, voluble to every age, you and I shall no more jostle ! "

It is amazing how soon the rich and titled, and even some of those who have wielded great political power, are forgotten.

> " A little rule, a little sway,
>   Is all the great and mighty have
>   Betwixt the cradle and the grave "—

and, after its short date, they hardly leave a name behind them. " A great man's memory may, at the common rate, survive him half a year." His heirs and successors take his titles, his power, and his wealth—all that made him considerable or courted by others; and he has left nothing else behind him either to delight or benefit the world. Posterity are not by any means so disinterested as they are supposed to be. They give their gratitude and admiration only in return for benefits conferred. They cherish the memory of those to whom they are indebted for instruction and delight; and they cherish it just in proportion to the instruction and delight they are conscious they receive. The sentiment of admiration springs immediately from this ground, and cannot be otherwise than well founded.[1]

The effeminate clinging to life as such, as a general

---

[1] It has been usual to raise a very unjust clamour against the enormous salaries of public singers, actors, and so on. This matter seems reducible to a *moral equation.* They are paid out of money raised by voluntary contributions in the strictest sense ; and if they did not bring certain sums into the treasury, the Managers would not engage them. These sums are exactly in proportion to the number of individuals to whom their performance gives an extraordinary degree of pleasure. The talents of a singer, actor, etc., are therefore worth just as much as they will fetch.

G

or abstract idea, is the effect of a highly civilized and artificial state of society. Men formerly plunged into all the vicissitudes and dangers of war, or staked their all upon a single die, or some one passion, which if they could not have gratified, life became a burthen to them— now our strongest passion is to think, our chief amusement is to read new plays, new poems, new novels, and this we may do at our leisure, in perfect security, *ad infinitum*. If we look into the old histories and romances, before the *belles-lettres* neutralized human affairs and reduced passion to a state of mental equivocation, we find the heroes and heroines not setting their lives " at a pin's fee," but rather courting opportunities of throwing them away in very wantonness of spirit. They raise their fondness for some favourite pursuit to its height, to a pitch of madness, and think no price too dear to pay for its full gratification. Everything else is dross. They go to death as to a bridal bed, and sacrifice themselves or others without remorse at the shrine of love, of honour, of religion, or any other prevailing feeling. Romeo runs his " sea-sick, weary bark upon the rocks " of death the instant he finds himself deprived of his Juliet; and she clasps his neck in their last agonies, and follows him to the same fatal shore. One strong idea takes possession of the mind and over-rules every other; and even life itself, joyless without that, becomes an object of indifference or loathing. There is at least more of imagination in such a state of things, more vigour of feeling and promptitude to act, than in our lingering, languid, protracted attachment to life for its own poor sake. It is, perhaps, also better, as well as more heroical, to strike at some daring or darling object, and if we fail in that, to take the consequences manfully, than to renew the lease of a tedious, spiritless, charmless existence, merely (as Pierre says) " to lose it afterwards in some vile brawl " for some worthless object. Was there not a spirit of martyrdom as well as a spice of the reckless energy of barbarism in this bold defiance of death? Had not religion something to do with it: the implicit belief in a future life, which rendered this of less value, and embodied something beyond it to the imagination; so that the rough soldier, the infatuated lover, the valorous knight, etc., could afford to throw away the present venture, and take a leap into the arms of futurity, which the modern sceptic shrinks back from, with all his boasted reason and vain philosophy, weaker than a woman! I cannot help thinking so myself; but I have endeavoured to explain this point before, and will not enlarge farther on it here.

A life of action and danger moderates the dread of death. It not only gives us fortitude to bear pain, but teaches us at every step the precarious tenure on which we hold our present being. Sedentary and studious men are the most apprehensive on this score. Dr. Johnson was an instance in point. A few years seemed to him soon over, compared with those sweeping contemplations on time and infinity with which he had been used to pose himself. In the *still-life* of a man of letters there was no obvious reason for a change. He might sit in an arm-chair and pour out cups of tea to all eternity. Would it had been possible for him to do so! The most rational cure after all for the inordinate fear of death is to set a just value on life. If we merely wish to continue on the scene to indulge our headstrong humours and tormenting passions, we had better begone at once; and if we only cherish a fondness for existence according to the good we derive from it, the pang we feel at parting with it will not be very severe!

ON THE CONDUCT OF LIFE; OR, ADVICE TO A SCHOOL-BOY

(WRITTEN ABOUT 1822)

MY DEAR LITTLE FELLOW,

You are now going to settle at school, and may consider this as your first entrance into the world. As my health is so indifferent, and I may not be with you long, I wish to leave you some advice (the best I can) for your conduct in life, both that it may be of use to you, and as something to remember me by. I may at least be able to caution you against my own errors, if nothing else.

As we went along to your new place of destination, you often repeated that " You durst say they were a set of stupid, disagreeable people," meaning the people at the school. You were to blame in this. It is a good old rule to hope for the best. Always, my dear, believe things to be right, till you find them the contrary; and even then, instead of irritating yourself against them, endeavour to put up with them as well as you can, if you cannot alter them. You said " You were sure you should not like the school where you were going." This was wrong. What you meant was that you did not like to leave home. But you could not tell whether you should like the school or not, till you had given it a trial. Otherwise, your saying that you should not like it was determining that you would not like it. Never anticipate evils; or, because you cannot have things exactly as you wish, make them out worse than they are, through mere spite and wilfulness.

You seemed at first to take no notice of your schoolfellows, or rather to set yourself against them, because they were strangers to you. They knew as little of you as you did of them; so that this would have been a reason

for their keeping aloof from you as well, which you would
have felt as a hardship. Learn never to conceive a prejudice against others, because you know nothing of them.
It is bad reasoning, and makes enemies of half the world.
Do not think ill of them, till they behave ill to you; and
then strive to avoid the faults which you see in them.
This will disarm their hostility sooner than pique or
resentment or complaint.

I thought you were disposed to criticize the dress of
some of the boys as not so good as your own. Never
despise any one for anything that he cannot help—least
of all, for his poverty. I would wish you to keep up
appearances yourself as a defence against the idle sneers
of the world, but I would not have you value yourself
upon them. I hope you will neither be the dupe nor
victim of vulgar prejudices. Instead of saying above—
" Never despise any one for anything that he cannot
help "—I might have said, " Never despise any one at
all "; for contempt implies a triumph over and pleasure
in the ill of another. It means that you are glad and
congratulate yourself on their failings or misfortunes.
The sense of inferiority in others, without this indirect
appeal to our self-love, is a painful feeling, and not an
exulting one.

You complain since, that the boys laugh at you and do
not care about you, and that you are not treated as you
were at home. My dear, that is one chief reason for your
being sent to school, to inure you betimes to the unavoidable rubs and uncertain reception you may meet with in
life. You cannot always be with me, and perhaps it is
as well that you cannot. But you must not expect others
to show the same concern about you as I should. You
have hitherto been a spoiled child, and have been used
to have your own way a good deal, both in the house and
among your play-fellows, with whom you were too fond
of being a leader: but you have good-nature and good

sense, and will get the better of this in time. You have now got among other boys who are your equals, or bigger and stronger than yourself, and who have something else to attend to besides humouring your whims and fancies, and you feel this as a repulse or piece of injustice. But the first lesson to learn is that there are other people in the world besides yourself. There are a number of boys in the school where you are, whose amusements and pursuits (whatever they may be) are and ought to be of as much consequence to them as yours can be to you, and to which therefore you must give way in your turn. The more airs of childish self-importance you give yourself, you will only expose yourself to be the more thwarted and laughed at. True equality is the only true morality or true wisdom. Remember always that you are but one among others, and you can hardly mistake your place in society. In your father's house, you might do as you pleased: in the world, you will find competitors at every turn. You are not born a king's son to destroy or dictate to millions: you can only expect to share their fate, or settle your differences amicably with them. You already find it so at school; and I wish you to be reconciled to your situation as soon and with as little pain as you can.

It was my misfortune perhaps to be bred up among Dissenters, who look with too jaundiced an eye at others, and set too high a value on their own peculiar pretensions. From being proscribed themselves, they learn to proscribe others; and come in the end to reduce all integrity of principle and soundness of opinion within the pale of their own little communion. Those who were out of it, and did not belong to the class of *Rational Dissenters*, I was led erroneously to look upon as hardly deserving the name of rational beings. Being thus satisfied as to the select few who are " the salt of the earth," it is easy to persuade ourselves that we are at the head of them, and to fancy ourselves of more importance in the scale of true desert than all the rest of the world put together, who do not interpret a certain text of Scripture in the manner that we have been taught to do. You will (from the difference of education) be free from this bigotry, and will, I hope, avoid every thing akin to the same exclusive and narrow-minded spirit. Think that the minds of men are various as their faces—that the modes and employments of life are numberless as they are necessary—that there is more than one class of merit—that though others may be wrong in some things, they are not so in all—and that countless races of men have been born, have lived and died without ever hearing of any one of those points in which you take a just pride and pleasure—and you will not err on the side of that spiritual pride or intellectual coxcombry which has been so often the bane of the studious and learned!

I observe you have got a way of speaking of your school-fellows as " *that* Hoare, *that* Harris," and so on, as if you meant to mark them out for particular reprobation, or did not think them good enough for you. It is a bad habit to speak disrespectfully of others: for it will lead you to think and feel uncharitably towards them. Ill names beget ill blood. Even where there may be some repeated trifling provocation, it is better to be courteous, mild, and forbearing, than captious, impatient, and fretful. The faults of others too often arise out of our own ill-temper; or though they should be real, we shall not mend them, by exasperating ourselves against them. Treat your playmates, as Hamlet advises Polonius to treat the players, " according to your own dignity, rather than their deserts." If you fly out at every thing in them that you disapprove or think done on purpose to annoy you, you lie constantly at the mercy of their caprice, rudeness, or ill-nature. You should be more your own master.

Do not begin to quarrel with the world too soon: for, bad as it may be, it is the best we have to live in—here.

If railing would have made it better, it would have been reformed long ago: but as this is not to be hoped for at present, the best way is to slide through it as contentedly and innocently as we may. The worst fault it has, is want of charity: and calling *knave* and *fool* at every turn will not cure this failing. Consider (as a matter of vanity) that if there were not so many knaves and fools as we find, the wise and honest would not be those rare and shining characters that they are allowed to be; and (as a matter of philosophy) that if the world be really incorrigible in this respect, it is a reflection to make one sad, not angry. We may laugh or weep at the madness of mankind; we have no right to vilify them, for our own sakes or theirs. Misanthropy is not the disgust of the mind at human nature, but with itself; or it is laying its own exaggerated vices and foul blots at the door of others! Do not, however, mistake what I have here said. I would not have you, when you grow up, adopt the low and sordid fashion of palliating existing abuses or of putting the best face upon the worst things. I only mean that indiscriminate, unqualified satire can do little good, and that those who indulge in the most revolting speculations on human nature, do not themselves always set the fairest examples, or strive to prevent its lower degradation. They seem rather willing to reduce it to their theoretical standard. For the rest, the very outcry that is made (if sincere) shews that things cannot be quite so bad as they are represented. The abstract hatred and scorn of vice implies the capacity for virtue: the impatience expressed at the most striking instances of deformity proves the innate idea and love of beauty in the human mind. The best antidote I can recommend to you hereafter against the disheartening effect of such writings as those of Rochefoucault, Mandeville, and others, will be to look at the pictures of Raphael and Correggio. You need not be altogether ashamed, my dear little boy, of belonging to a species which could produce such faces as those; nor despair of doing something worthy of a laudable ambition, when you see what such hands have wrought! You will, perhaps, one day have reason to thank me for this advice.

As to your studies and school-exercises, I wish you to learn Latin, French, and dancing. I would insist upon the last more particularly, both because it is more likely to be neglected, and because it is of the greatest consequence to your success in life. Everything almost depends upon first impressions; and these depend (besides *person*, which is not in our power) upon two things, *dress* and *address*, which every one may command with proper attention. These are the small coin in the intercourse of life, which are continually in request; and perhaps you will find at the year's end, or towards the close of life, that the daily insults, coldness, or contempt, to which you have been exposed by a neglect of such superficial recommendations, are hardly atoned for by the few proofs of esteem or admiration which your integrity or talents have been able to extort in the course of it. When we habitually disregard those things which we know will ensure the favourable opinion of others, it shews we set that opinion at defiance, or consider ourselves above it, which no one ever did with impunity. An inattention to our own persons implies a disrespect to others, and may often be traced no less to a want of good nature than of good sense. The old maxim—*Desire to please, and you will infallibly please*—explains the whole matter. If there is a tendency to vanity and affectation on this side of the question, there is an equal alloy of pride and obstinacy on the opposite one. Slovenliness may at any time be cured by an effort of resolution, but a graceful carriage requires an early habit, and in most cases the aid of the dancing-master. I would not have you, from not knowing how to enter a room properly, stumble at the very threshold in the good graces of those on whom it is

G *

possible the fate of your future life may depend. Nothing creates a greater prejudice against any one than awkwardness. A person who is confused in manner and gesture seems to have done something wrong, or as if he was conscious of no one qualification to build a confidence in himself upon. On the other hand, openness, freedom, self-possession, set others at ease with you by shewing that you are on good terms with yourself. Grace in women gains the affections sooner, and secures them longer, than any thing else—it is an outward and visible sign of an inward harmony of soul—as the want of it in men, as if the mind and body equally hitched in difficulties and were distracted with doubts, is the greatest impediment in the career of gallantry and road to the female heart. Another thing I would caution you against is not to pore over your books till you are bent almost double—a habit you will never be able to get the better of, and which you will find of serious ill consequence. *A stoop in the shoulders* sinks a man in public and in private estimation. You are at present straight enough, and you walk with boldness and spirit. Do nothing to take away the use of your limbs, or the spring and elasticity of your muscles. As to all worldly advantages, it is to the full of as much importance that your deportment should be erect and manly as your actions.

You will naturally find out all this and fall into it, if your attention is drawn out sufficiently to what is passing around you; and this will be the case, unless you are absorbed too much in books and those sedentary studies,

" Which waste the marrow, and consume the brain."

You are, I think, too fond of reading as it is. As one means of avoiding excess in this way, I would wish you to make it a rule, never to read at meal-times, nor in company when there is any (even the most trivial) conversation going on, nor ever to let your eagerness to

learn encroach upon your play-hours. Books are but one
inlet of knowledge; and the pores of the mind, like those
of the body, should be left open to all impressions. I
applied too close to my studies, soon after I was of your
age, and hurt myself irreparably by it. Whatever may be
the value of learning, health and good spirits are of more.

I would have you, as I said, make yourself master of
French, because you may find it of use in the commerce
of life; and I would have you learn Latin, partly because
I learnt it myself, and I would not have you without any
of the advantages or sources of knowledge that I possessed—it would be a bar of separation between us—and
secondly, because there is an atmosphere round this sort
of classical ground, to which that of actual life is gross
and vulgar. Shut out from this garden of early sweetness,
we may well exclaim—

> " How shall we part and wander down
> Into a lower world, to this obscure
> And wild ? How shall we breathe in other air
> Less pure, accustom'd to immortal fruits ? "

I do not think the Classics so indispensable to the cultivation of your intellect as on another account, which I have
seen explained elsewhere, and you will have no objection
to turn with me to the passage.

" The study of the Classics is less to be regarded as an
exercise of the intellect, than as *a discipline of humanity.*
The peculiar advantage of this mode of education consists
not so much in strengthening the understanding, as in
softening and refining the taste. It gives men liberal
views; it accustoms the mind to take an interest in things
foreign to itself; to love virtue for its own sake; to prefer
fame to life, and glory to riches; and to fix our thoughts
on the remote and permanent, instead of narrow and
fleeting objects. It teaches us to believe that there is
something really great and excellent in the world, surviving all the shocks of accident and fluctuations of opinion,

and raises us above that low and servile fear, which bows
only to present power and upstart authority. Rome and
Athens filled a place in the history of mankind, which can
never be occupied again. They were two cities set on a
hill, which could not be hid; all eyes have seen them, and
their light shines like a mighty sea-mark into the abyss
of time.

> " Still green with bays each ancient altar stands,
>   Above the reach of sacrilegious hands ;
>   Secure from flames, from envy's fiercer rage,
>   Destructive war, and all-involving age.
>   Hail, bards triumphant, born in happier days,
>   Immortal heirs of universal praise !
>   Whose honours with increase of ages grow,
>   As streams roll down, enlarging as they flow ! "

It is this feeling more than any thing else which produces
a marked difference between the study of the ancient and
modern languages, and which, by the weight and importance of the consequences attached to the former,
stamps every word with a monumental firmness. By
conversing with the *mighty dead,* we imbibe sentiment
with knowledge. We become strongly attached to those
who can no longer either hurt or serve us, except through
the influence which they exert over the mind. We feel
the presence of that power which gives immortality to
human thoughts and actions, and catch the flame of
enthusiasm from all nations and ages."

Because, however, you have learnt Latin and Greek,
and can speak a different language, do not fancy yourself
of a different order of beings from those you ordinarily
converse with. They perhaps know and can do more
things than you, though you have learnt a greater variety
of *names* to express the same thing by. The great object
indeed of these studies is to be " a cure for a narrow and
selfish spirit," and to carry the mind out of its petty and
local prejudices to the idea of a more general humanity.

Do not fancy, because you are intimate with Homer and Virgil, that your neighbours who can never attain the same posthumous fame are to be despised, like those impudent valets who live in noble families and look down upon every one else. Though you are master of Cicero's Orations, think it possible for a cobbler at a stall to be more eloquent than you. " But you are a scholar, and he is not." Well, then, you have that advantage over him, but it does not follow that you are to have every other. Look at the heads of the celebrated poets and philosophers . of antiquity in the collection at Wilton, and you will say they answer to their works: but you will find others in the same collection whose names have hardly come down to us, that are equally fine, and cast in the same classic mould. Do you imagine that all the thoughts, genius, and capacity of those old and mighty nations are contained in a few odd volumes, to be thumbed by school-boys? This reflection is not meant to lessen your admiration of the great names to which you will be accustomed to look up, but to direct it to that solid mass of intellect and power, of which they were the most shining ornaments. I would wish you to excel in this sort of learning and to take a pleasure in it, because it is the path that has been chosen for you: but do not suppose that others do not excel equally in their line of study or exercise of skill, or that there is but one mode of excellence in art or nature. You have got on vastly beyond the point at which you set out; but others have been getting on as well as you in the same or other ways, and have kept pace with you. What then, you may ask, is the use of all the pains you have taken, if it gives you no superiority over mankind in general? It is this—You have reaped all the benefit of improvement and knowledge yourself; and farther, if you had not moved forwards, you would by this time have been left behind. Envy no one, disparage no one, think yourself above no one. Their demerits will not piece out your deficiencies; nor is it a waste of time and labour for you to cultivate your own talents, because you cannot bespeak a monopoly of all advantages. You are more learned than many of your acquaintance who may be more active, healthy, witty, successful in business or expert in some elegant or useful art than you; but you have no reason to complain, if you have attained the object of your ambition. Or, if you should not be able to compass this from a want of genius or parts, yet learn, my child, to be contented with a mediocrity of acquirements. You may still be respectable in your conduct, and enjoy a tranquil obscurity, with more friends and fewer enemies than you might otherwise have had.

There is one almost certain drawback on a course of scholastic study, that it unfits men for active life. The *ideal* is always at variance with the *practical*. The habit of fixing the attention on the imaginary and abstracted deprives the mind equally of energy and fortitude. By indulging our imaginations on fictions and chimeras, where we have it all our own way and are led on only by the pleasure of the prospect, we grow fastidious, effeminate, lapped in idle luxury, impatient of contradiction, and unable to sustain the shock of real adversity, when it comes; as by being taken up with abstract reasoning or remote events in which we are merely passive spectators, we have no resources to provide against it, no readiness, or expedients for the occasion, or spirit to use them, even if they occur. We must think again before we determine, and thus the opportunity for action is lost. While we are considering the very best possible mode of gaining an object, we find that it has slipped through our fingers, or that others have laid rude, fearless hands upon it. The youthful tyro reluctantly discovers that the ways of the world are not his ways, nor their thoughts his thoughts. Perhaps the old monastic institutions were not in this respect unwise, which carried on to the end of life the secluded habits and romantic associations with which it began, and which created a privileged world for the inhabitants, distinct from the common world of men and women. You will bring with you from your books and solitary reveries a wrong measure of men and things, unless you correct it by careful experience and mixed observation. You will raise your standard of character as much too high at first as from disappointed expectation it will sink too low afterwards. The best qualifier of this theoretical *mania* and of the dreams of poets and moralists (who both treat of things as *they ought to be* and not as *they are*) is in one sense to be found in some of our own popular writers, such as our Novelists and periodical Essayists. But you had, after all, better wait and see what things are than try to anticipate the results. You know more of a road by having travelled it than by all the conjectures and descriptions in the world. You will find the business of life conducted on a much more varied and individual scale than you would expect. People will be concerned about a thousand things that you have no idea of, and will be utterly indifferent to what you feel the greatest interest in. You will find good and evil, folly and discretion more mingled, and the shades of character running more into each other than they do in the ethical charts. No one is equally wise or guarded at all points, and it is seldom that any one is quite a fool. Do not be surprised, when you go out into the world, to find men talk exceedingly well on different subjects, who do not derive their information immediately from books. In the first place, the light of books is diffused very much abroad in the world in conversation and at second-hand; and besides, common sense is not a monopoly, and experience and observation are sources of information open to the man of the world as well as to the retired student. If you know more of the outline and principles, he knows more of the details and " practique part of life." A man may discuss the adventures of a campaign in which he was engaged very agreeably without having read the *Retreat of the Ten Thousand*, or give a singular account of the method of drying teas in China without being a profound chemist. It is the vice of scholars to suppose that there is no knowledge in the world but that of books. Do you avoid it, I conjure you; and thereby save yourself the pain and mortification that must otherwise ensue from finding out your mistake continually!

Gravity is one great ingredient in the conduct of life, and perhaps a certain share of it is hardly to be dispensed with. Few people can afford to be quite unaffected. At any rate, do not put your worst qualities foremost. Do not seek to distinguish yourself by being ridiculous; nor entertain that miserable ambition to be the sport and butt of the company. By aiming at a certain standard of behaviour or intellect, you will at least shew your taste and value for what is excellent. There are those who *blurt* out their good things with so little heed of what they are about that no one thinks any thing of them; as others by keeping their folly to themselves gain the reputation of wisdom. Do not, however, affect to speak only in oracles, or to deal in *bon-mots :* condescend to the level of the company, and be free and accessible to all persons. Express whatever occurs to you, that cannot offend others or hurt yourself. Keep some opinions to yourself. Say what you please of others, but never repeat what you hear said of them to themselves. If you have nothing to offer yourself, laugh with the witty, assent to the wise; they will not think the worse of you for it. Listen to information on subjects you are unacquainted with, instead of always striving to lead the conversation to some favourite one of your own. By the last method you will shine, but will not improve. I am ashamed myself ever to open my lips on any question I have ever written upon. It is much more difficult to be able to converse on an equality with a number of persons in turn, than to soar above their heads, and excite the stupid gaze of all companies by bestriding some senseless topic of your own and confounding the understandings of those who are ignorant of it. Be not too fond of argument. Indeed, by going much into company (which I do not, however, wish you to do) you will be weaned from this practice, if you set out with it. Rather suggest what remarks may have occurred to you on a subject than aim at dictating your opinions to others or at defending yourself at all points. You will learn more by agreeing in the main with others and entering into their trains of thinking, than by contradicting and urging them to extremities. Avoid singularity of opinion at well as of everything else. Sound conclusions come with practical knowledge, rather than with speculative refinements: in what we really understand, we reason but little. Long-winded disputes fill up the place of common sense and candid inquiry. Do not imagine that you will make people friends by shewing your superiority over them: it is what they will neither admit nor forgive, unless you have a high and acknowledged reputation beforehand, which renders this sort of petty vanity more inexcusable. Seek to gain the good-will of others, rather than to extort their applause; and to this end, be neither too tenacious of your own claims, nor inclined to press too hard on their weaknesses.

Do not affect the society of your inferiors in rank, nor court that of the great. There can be no real sympathy in either case. The first will consider you as a restraint upon them, and the last as an intruder or *upon sufferance*. It is not a desirable distinction to be admitted into company as a man of talents. You are a mark for invidious observation. If you say nothing or merely behave with common propriety and simplicity, you seem to have no business there. If you make a studied display of yourself, it is arrogating a consequence you have no right to. If you

are contented to pass as an indifferent person, they despise
you; if you distinguish yourself, and shew more knowledge, wit, or taste than they do, they hate you for it.
You have no alternative. I would rather be asked out to
sing than to talk. Every one does not pretend to a fine
voice, but every one fancies he has as much understanding
as another. Indeed, the secret of this sort of intercourse
has been pretty well found out. Literary men are seldom
invited to the tables of the great; they send for players
and musicians, as they keep monkeys and parrots!

I would not, however, have you run away with a notion
that the rich are knaves or that lords are fools. They are
for what I know as honest and as wise as other people.
But it is a trick of our self-love, supposing that another
has the decided advantage of us in one way, to strike a
balance by taking it for granted (as a moral antithesis)
that he must be as much beneath us in those qualities on
which we plume ourselves, and which we would appropriate almost entirely to our own use. It is hard indeed if
others are raised above us not only by the gifts of fortune,
but of understanding too. It is not to be credited. People
have an unwillingness to admit that the House of Lords
can be equal in talent to the House of Commons. So in
the other sex, if a woman is handsome, she is an idiot or
no better than she should be: in ours, if a man is worth a
million of money, he is a miser, a fellow that cannot spell
his own name, or a poor creature in some way, to bring
him to our level. This is malice, and not truth. Believe
all the good you can of every one. Do not measure others
by yourself. If they have advantages which you have not,
let your liberality keep pace with their good fortune.
Envy no one, and you need envy no one. If you have but
the magnanimity to allow merit wherever you see it—
understanding in a lord or wit in a cobbler—this temper
of mind will stand you instead of many accomplishments.
Think no man too happy. Raphael died young. Milton

had the misfortune to be blind. If any one is vain or proud, it is from folly or ignorance. Those who pique themselves excessively on some one thing, have but that one thing to pique themselves upon, as languages, mechanics, &c. I do not say that this is not an enviable delusion where it is not liable to be disturbed; but at present knowledge is too much diffused and pretensions come too much into collision for this to be long the case; and it is better not to form such a prejudice at first than to have it to undo all the rest of one's life. If you learn any two things, though they may put you out of conceit one with the other, they will effectually cure you of any conceit you might have of yourself, by shewing the variety and scope there is in the human mind beyond the limits you had set to it.

You were convinced the first day that you could not learn Latin, which now you find easy. Be taught from this, not to think other obstacles insurmountable that you may meet with in the course of your life, though they seem so at first sight.

Attend above all things to your health; or rather, do nothing wilfully to impair it. Use exercise, abstinence, and regular hours. Drink water when you are alone, and wine or very little spirits in company. It is the last that are ruinous by leading to unlimited excess. There is not the same headlong *impetus* in wine. But one glass of brandy and water makes you want another, and that other makes you want a third, and so on, in an increased proportion. Therefore no one can stop midway who does not possess the resolution to abstain altogether; for the inclination is sharpened with its indulgence. Never gamble. Or if you play for any thing, never do so for what will give you uneasiness the next day. Be not precise in these matters: but do not pass certain limits, which it is difficult to recover. Do nothing in the irritation of the moment, but take time to reflect. Because you have done one foolish thing, do not do another; nor throw away your health or reputation or comfort, to thwart impertinent advice. Avoid a spirit of contradiction, both in words and actions. Do not aim at what is beyond your reach, but at what is within it. Indulge in calm and pleasing pursuits, rather than violent excitements; and learn to conquer your own will, instead of striving to obtain the mastery of that of others.

With respect to your friends, I would wish you to choose them neither from caprice nor accident, and to adhere to them as long as you can. Do not make a surfeit of friendship, through over-sanguine enthusiasm, nor expect it to last for ever. Always speak well of those with whom you have once been intimate, or take some part of the censure you bestow on them to yourself. Never quarrel with tried friends, or those whom you wish to continue such. Wounds of this kind are sure to open again. When once the prejudice is removed that sheathes defects, familiarity only causes jealousy and distrust. Do not keep on with a mockery of friendship after the substance is gone—but part, while you can part friends. Bury the carcase of friendship: it is not worth embalming.

As to the books you will have to read by choice or for amusement, the best are the commonest. The names of many of them are already familiar to you. Read them as you grow up with all the satisfaction in your power, and make much of them. It is perhaps the greatest pleasure you will have in life, the one you will think of longest, and repent of least. If my life had been more full of calamity than it has been (much more than I hope yours will be) I would live it over again, my poor little boy, to have read the books I did in my youth.

In politics I wish you to be an honest man, but no brawler. Hate injustice and falsehood for your own sake. Be neither a martyr, nor a sycophant. Wish well to the world without expecting to see it much better than it is;

and do not gratify the enemies of liberty by putting yourself at their mercy, if it can be avoided with honour.

If you ever marry, I would wish you to marry the woman you like. Do not be guided by the recommendation of friends. Nothing will atone for or overcome an original distaste. It will only increase from intimacy; and if you are to live separate, it is better not to come together. There is no use in dragging a chain through life, unless it binds one to the object we love. Choose a mistress from among your equals. You will be able to understand her character better, and she will be more likely to understand yours. Those in an inferior station to yourself will doubt your good intentions, and misapprehend your plainest expressions. All that you swear is to them a riddle or downright nonsense. You cannot by possibility translate your thoughts into their dialect. They will be ignorant of the meaning of half you say, and laugh at the rest. As mistresses, they will have no sympathy with you; and as wives, you can have none with them. But they will do all they can to thwart you, and to retrieve themselves in their own opinion by trick and low cunning. No woman ever married into a family above herself that did not try to make all the mischief she could in it. Be not in haste to marry, nor to engage your affections, where there is no probability of a return. Do not fancy every woman you see the heroine of a romance, a Sophia Western, a Clarissa, or a Julia; and yourself the potential hero of it, Tom Jones, Lovelace, or St. Preux. Avoid this error as you would shrink back from a precipice. All your fine sentiments and romantic notions will (of themselves) make no more impression on one of these delicate creatures, than on a piece of marble. Their soft bosoms are steel to your amorous refinements, if you have no other pretensions. It is not what you think of them that determines their choice, but what they think of you. Endeavour, if you would escape lingering torments and the gnawing of the worm that dies not, to find out this, and to abide by the issue. We trifle with, make sport of, and despise those who are attached to us, and follow those that fly from us. " We hunt the wind, we worship a statue, cry aloud to the desert." Do you, my dear boy, stop short in this career, if you find yourself setting out in it, and make up your mind to this, that if a woman does not like you of her own accord, that is, from involuntary impressions, nothing you can say or do or suffer for her sake will make her, but will set her the more against you. So the song goes—

> " Quit, quit for shame ; this will not move :
>   If of herself she will not love,
>   Nothing will make her, the devil take her ! "

Your pain is her triumph; the more she feels you in her power, the worse she will treat you: the more you make it appear you deserve her regard, the more will she resent it as an imputation on her first judgment. Study first impressions above all things; for everything depends on them, in love especially. Women are armed by nature and education with a power of resisting the importunity of men, and they use this power according to their discretion. They enforce it to the utmost rigour of the law against those whom they do not like, and relax their extreme severity proportionably in favour of those that they do like, and who in general care as little about them. Hence we see so many desponding lovers and forlorn damsels. Love in women (at least) is either vanity, or interest, or fancy. It is a merely selfish feeling. It has nothing to do (I am sorry to say) with friendship, or esteem, or even pity. I once asked a girl, the pattern of her sex in shape and mind and attractions, whether she did not think Mr. Coleridge had done wrong in making the heroine of his beautiful ballad story of Geneviève take compassion on her hapless lover—

" When on the yellow forest-leaves
 A dying man he lay "—

And whether she believed that any woman ever fell in
love through a sense of compassion; and she made
answer—" Not if it was against her inclination! " I would
take the lady's word *for a thousand pound,* on this point.
Pain holds antipathy to pleasure; pity is not akin to love;
a dying man has more need of a nurse than of a mistress.
There is no forcing liking. It is as little to be fostered by
reason and good-nature, as it can be controlled by
prudence or propriety. It is a mere blind, headstrong
impulse. Least of all, flatter yourself that talents or virtue
will recommend you to the favour of the sex, in lieu of
exterior advantages. Oh! no. Women care nothing about
poets, or philosophers, or politicians. They go by a man's
looks and manner. Richardson calls them " an eye-
judging sex; " and I am sure he knew more about them
than I can pretend to do. If you run away with a pedantic
notion that they care a pin's-point about your head or
your heart, you will repent it too late. Some blue-stocking
may have her vanity flattered by your reputation or be
edified by the solution of a metaphysical problem or a
critical remark or a dissertation on the state of the nation,
and fancy that she has a taste for intellect and is an epicure
in sentiment. No true woman ever regarded anything
but her lover's person and address. Gravity will here
answer all the same purpose without understanding, gaiety
without wit, folly without good-nature, and impudence
without any other pretension. The natural and instinctive
passion of love is excited by qualities not peculiar to
artists, authors, and men of letters. It is not the jest but
the laugh that follows, not the sentiment but the glance
that accompanies it, that *tells*—in a word, the sense of
actual enjoyment that imparts itself to others, and excites
mutual understanding and inclination. Authors, on the
other hand, feel nothing spontaneously. The common

incidents and circumstances of life with which others are taken up, make no alteration in them, nor provoke any of the common expressions surprise, of joy, admiration, anger, or merriment. Nothing stirs their blood or accelerates their juices or tickles their veins. Instead of yielding to the first natural and lively impulses of things, in which they would find sympathy, they screw themselves up to some far-fetched view of the subject in order to be unintelligible. Realities are not good enough for them, till they undergo the process of imagination and reflection. If you offer them your hand to shake, they will hardly take it; for this does not amount to a proposition. If you enter their room suddenly, they testify neither surprise nor satisfaction: no new idea is elicited by it. Yet if you suppose this to be a repulse, you are mistaken. They will enter into your affairs or combat your ideas with all the warmth and vehemence imaginable, as soon as they have a subject started. But their faculty for thinking must be set in motion, before you can put any soul into them. They are intellectual dram-drinkers; and without their necessary stimulus, are torpid, dead, insensible to everything. They have great life of mind, but none of body. They do not drift with the stream of company or of passing occurrences, but are straining at some hyperbole or striking out a bye-path of their own. Follow them who list. Their minds are a sort of Herculaneum, full of old, petrified images;—are set in stereotype, and little fitted to the ordinary occasions of life.

What chance, then, can they have with women, who deal only in the pantomime of discourse, in gesticulation and the flippant bye-play of the senses, " nods and winks and wreathed smiles "; and to whom to offer a remark is an impertinence, or a reason an affront? The only way in which I ever knew mental qualities or distinction tell was in the clerical character; and women do certainly incline to this with some sort of favourable regard.

Whether it is that the sanctity of pretension piques curiosity, or that the habitual submission of their understandings to their spiritual guides subdues the will, a popular preacher generally has the choice among the *élite* of his female flock. According to Mrs. Inchbald (see her *Simple Story*) there is another reason why religious courtship is not without its charms! But as I do not intend you for the church, do not, in thinking to study yourself into the good graces of the fair, study yourself out of them, millions of miles. Do not place thought as a barrier between you and love: do not abstract yourself into the regions of truth, far from the smile of earthly beauty. Let not the cloud sit upon your brow: let not the canker sink into your heart. Look up, laugh loud, talk big, keep the colour in your cheek and the fire in your eye, adorn your person, maintain your health, your beauty, and your animal spirits, and you will pass for a fine man. But should you let your blood stagnate in some deep metaphysical question, or refine too much in your ideas of the sex, forgetting yourself in a dream of exalted perfection, you will want an eye to cheer you, a hand to guide you, a bosom to lean on, and will stagger into your grave, old before your time, unloved and unlovely. If you feel that you have not the necessary advantages of person, confidence, and manner, and that it is *up-hill* work with you to gain the ear of beauty, quit the pursuit at once, and seek for other satisfactions and consolations.

A spider, my dear, the meanest creature that crawls or lives, has its mate or fellow: but a scholar has no mate or fellow. For myself, I had courted thought, I had felt pain; and Love turned away his face from me. I have gazed along the silent air for that smile which had lured me to my doom. I no more heard those accents which would have burst upon me, like a voice from heaven. I loathed the light that shone on my disgrace. Hours, days, years, passed away; and only turned false hope to fixed despair. And as my frail bark sails down the stream of time, the God of Love stands on the shore, and as I stretch out my hands to him in vain, claps his wings, and mocks me as I pass!

There is but one other point on which I meant to speak to you, and that is the choice of a profession. This, probably, had better be left to time or accident or your own inclination. You have a very fine ear, but I have somehow a prejudice against men-singers, and indeed against the stage altogether. It is an uncertain and ungrateful soil. All professions are bad that depend on reputation, which is " as often got without merit as lost without deserving." Yet I cannot easily reconcile myself to your being a slave to business, and I shall hardly be able to leave you an independence. A situation in a public office is secure, but laborious and mechanical, and without the two great springs of life, Hope and Fear. Perhaps, however, it might ensure you a competence, and leave you leisure for some other favourite amusement or pursuit. I have said all reputation is hazardous, hard to win, harder to keep. Many never attain a glimpse of what they have all their lives been looking for, and others survive a passing shadow of it. Yet if I were to name one pursuit rather than another, I should wish you to be a good painter, if such a thing could be hoped. I have failed in this myself, and should wish you to be able to do what I have not—to paint like Claude or Rembrandt or Guido or Vandyke, if it were possible. Artists, I think, who have succeeded in their chief object, live to be old, and are agreeable old men. Their minds keep alive to the last. Cosway's spirits never flagged till after ninety, and Nollekins, though nearly blind, passed all his mornings in giving directions about some group or bust in his workshop. You have seen Mr. Northcote, that delightful specimen of the last age. With what avidity he takes up his pencil, or lays it down again to talk of numberless things! His eye has not lost its lustre, nor " paled its ineffectual fire." His body is a shadow: he himself is a pure spirit. There is a kind of immortality about this sort of ideal and visionary existence that dallies with Fate and baffles the grim monster, Death. If I thought you could make as clever an artist and arrive at such an agreeable old age as Mr. Northcote, I should declare at once for your devoting yourself to this enchanting profession; and in that reliance, should feel less regret at some of my own disappointments, and little anxiety on your account!

ON THE SPIRIT OF MONARCHY

(THE LIBERAL, JAN., 1823)

" Strip it of its externals, and what is but a *jest ?* "
Charade on the word MAJESTY.

" As for politics, I think poets are *Tories* by nature, supposing them to be by nature poets. The love of an individual person or family, that has worn a crown for many successions, is an inclination greatly adapted to the fanciful tribe. On the other hand, mathematicians, abstract reasoners, of no manner of attachment to persons, at least to the visible part of them, but prodigiously devoted to the ideas of virtue, liberty, and so forth, are generally *Whigs*. It happens agreeably enough to this maxim, that the Whigs are friends to that wise, plodding, unpoetical people, the Dutch."—*Shenstone's Letters*, 1746.

T H E Spirit of Monarchy, then, is nothing but the craving in the human mind after the Sensible and the One. It is not so much a matter of state-necessity or policy, as a natural infirmity, a disease, a false appetite in the popular feeling, which must be gratified. Man is an individual animal with narrow faculties, but infinite desires, which he is anxious to concentrate in some one object within the grasp of his imagination, and where, if he cannot be all that he wishes himself, he may at least contemplate his own pride, vanity, and passions, displayed in their most extravagant dimensions in a being no bigger and no better than himself. Each individual would (were it in his power) be a king, a God: but as he cannot, the next best thing is to see this reflex image of his self-love, the darling passion of his breast, realized, embodied out of himself in the first object he can lay his hands on for the purpose. The slave admires the tyrant, because the last *is*, what the first *would be*. He surveys himself all over in the glass of royalty. The swelling, bloated, self-importance of the one is the very counterpart and ultimate goal of the abject servility of the other. But both hate mankind for the same reason, because a respect for humanity is a diversion to their inordinate self-love, and the idea of the general good is a check to the gross intemperance of passion. The worthlessness of the object does not diminish but irritate the propensity to admire. It serves to pamper our imagination equally, and does not provoke our envy. All we want is to aggrandize our own vainglory at second hand; and the less of real superiority or excellence there is in the person we fix upon as our proxy in this dramatic exhibition, the more easily can we change places with him, and fancy ourselves as good as he. Nay, the descent favours the rise; and we heap our tribute of applause the higher, in proportion as it is a free gift. An idol is not the worse for being of coarse materials; a king should be a common-place man. Otherwise, he is superior in his own nature, and not dependent on our bounty or caprice. Man is a poetical animal, and delights in fiction. We like to have scope for the exercise of our mere will. We make kings of men, and Gods of stocks and stones: we are not jealous of the creatures of our own hands. We only want a peg or loop to hang our idle fancies on, a puppet to dress up, a lay-figure to paint from. It is " THING Ferdinand, and not KING

Ferdinand," as it was wisely and wittily observed. We ask only for the stage effect; we do not go behind the scenes, or it would go hard with many of our prejudices! We see the symbols of Majesty, we enjoy the pomp, we crouch before the power, we walk in the procession, and make part of the pageant, and we say in our secret hearts, there is nothing but accident that prevents us from being at the head of it. There is something in the mock-sublimity of thrones, wonderfully congenial to the human mind. Every man feels that he could sit there; every man feels that he could look big there; every man feels that he could bow there; every man feels that he could play the monarch there. The transition is so easy, and so delightful! The imagination keeps pace with royal state,

> " And by the vision splendid
> Is on its way attended."

The Madman in Hogarth who fancies himself a king, is not a solitary instance of this species of hallucination. Almost every true and loyal subject holds such a barren sceptre in his hand; and the meanest of the rabble, as he runs by the monarch's side, has wit enough to think— " There goes my *royal* self!" From the most absolute despot to the lowest slave there is but one step (no, not one) in point of real merit. As far as truth or reason is concerned, they might change situations to-morrow— nay, they constantly do so without the smallest loss or benefit to mankind! Tyranny, in a word, is a farce got up for the entertainment of poor human nature; and it might pass very well, if it did not so often turn into a tragedy.

We once heard a celebrated and elegant historian and a hearty Whig declare, he liked a king like George III better than such a one as Buonaparte; because, in the former case, there was nothing to overawe the imagination but birth and situation; whereas he could not so easily brook the double superiority of the other, mental as well as adventitious. So does the spirit of independence and the levelling pride of intellect join in with the servile rage of the vulgar! This is the advantage which an hereditary has over an elective monarchy: for there is no end of the dispute about precedence while merit is supposed to determine it, each man laying claim to this in his own person; so that there is no other way to set aside all controversy and heart-burnings, but by precluding moral and intellectual qualifications altogether, and referring the choice to accident, and giving the preference to a nonentity. " A good king," says Swift, " should be, in all other respects, a mere cypher."

It has been remarked, as a peculiarity in modern criticism, that the courtly and loyal make a point of crying up Mr. Young, as an actor, and equally running down Mr. Kean; and it has been conjectured in consequence that Mr. Kean was a *radical*. Truly, he is not a radical politician; but what is as bad, he is a radical actor. He savours too much of the reality. He is not a mock-tragedian, an automaton player—he is something besides his paraphernalia. He has " that within which passes shew." There is not a particle of affinity between him and the patrons of the court-writers. Mr. Young, on the contrary, is the very thing—all assumption and strut and measured pomp, full of self-importance, void of truth and nature, the mask of the characters he takes, a pasteboard figure, a stiff piece of wax-work. He fills the throne of tragedy, not like an upstart or usurper, but as a matter of course, decked out in his plumes of feathers, and robes of state, stuck into a posture, and repeating certain words by rote. Mr. Kean has a heart in his bosom, beating with human passion (a thing for the great " to fear, not to delight in! ") he is a living man, and not an artificial one. How should those, who look to the surface, and never probe deeper, endure him? He is the antithesis of a court-actor. It is the object there to

suppress and varnish over the feelings, not to give
way to them. His *overt* manner must shock them, and
be thought a breach of all decorum. They are in dread
of his fiery humours, of coming near his Voltaic Battery
—they choose rather to be roused gently from their
self-complacent apathy by the application of Metallic
Tractors. They dare not trust their delicate nerves within
the estuary of the passions, but would slumber out their
torpid existence in a calm, a Dead Sea—the air of which
extinguishes life and motion!

Would it not be hard upon a little girl, who is busy in
dressing up a favourite doll, to pull it in pieces before
her face in order to shew her the bits of wood, the
wool, and rags it is composed of? So it would be hard
upon that great baby, the world, to take any of its idols
to pieces, and shew that they are nothing but painted
wood. Neither of them would thank you, but consider
the offer as an insult. The little girl knows as well as you
do that her doll is a cheat; but she shuts her eyes to it,
for she finds her account in keeping up the deception.
Her doll is her pretty little self. In its glazed eyes, its
cherry cheeks, its flaxen locks, its finery and its baby-
house, she has a fairy vision of her own future charms,
her future triumphs, a thousand hearts led captive, and
an establishment for life. Harmless illusion! that can
create something out of nothing, can make that which
is good for nothing in itself so fine in appearance, and
clothe a shapeless piece of deal-board with the attri-
butes of a divinity! But the great world has been doing
little else but playing at *make-believe* all its life-time.
For several thousand years its chief rage was to paint
larger pieces of wood and smear them with gore and call
them Gods and offer victims to them—slaughtered
hecatombs, the fat of goats and oxen, or human sacrifices
—shewing in this its love of show, of cruelty, and
imposture; and woe to him who should " peep through the

blanket of the dark to cry, *Hold, hold.*"—*Great is Diana
of the Ephesians,* was the answer in all ages. It was in
vain to represent to them, " Your Gods have eyes but
they see not, ears but they hear not, neither do they
understand "—the more stupid, brutish, helpless, and
contemptible they were, the more furious, bigoted, and
implacable were their votaries in their behalf.[1] The
more absurd the fiction, the louder was the noise made
to hide it—the more mischievous its tendency, the more
did it excite all the phrenzy of the passions. Superstition
nursed, with peculiar zeal, her rickety, deformed, and
preposterous offspring. She passed by the nobler races
of animals even, to pay divine honours to the odious and
unclean—she took toads and serpents, cats, rats, dogs,
crocodiles, goats, and monkeys, and hugged them to her
bosom, and dandled them into deities, and set up altars
to them, and drenched the earth with tears and blood in
their defence; and those who did not believe in them
were cursed, and were forbidden the use of bread, of
fire, and water, and to worship them was piety, and their
images were held sacred, and their race became Gods
in perpetuity and by divine right. To touch them, was
sacrilege: to kill them, death, even in your own defence.
If they stung you, you must die: if they infested the land
with their numbers and their pollutions, there was no
remedy. The nuisance was intolerable, impassive, immortal. Fear, religious horror, disgust, hatred, heightened
the flame of bigotry and intolerance. There was nothing
so odious or contemptible but it found a sanctuary in
the more odious and contemptible perversity of human
nature. The barbarous Gods of antiquity reigned *in contempt of their worshippers!*

[1] " Of whatsoe'er descent his Godhead be,
    Stock, stone, or other homely pedigree,
    In his defence his servants are as bold
    As if he had been made of beaten gold."—DRYDEN.

This game was carried on through all the first ages of the world, and is still kept up in many parts of it; and it is impossible to describe the wars, massacres, horrors, miseries, and crimes, to which it gave colour, sanctity, and sway. The idea of a God, beneficent and just, the invisible maker of all things, was abhorrent to their gross, material notions. No, they must have Gods of their own making, that they could see and handle, that they knew to be nothing in themselves but senseless images, and these they daubed over with the gaudy emblems of their own pride and passions, and these they lauded to the skies, and grew fierce, obscene, frantic before them, as the representatives of their sordid ignorance and barbaric vices. TRUTH, GOOD, were idle names to them, without a meaning. They must have a lie, a palpable, pernicious lie, to pamper their crude, unhallowed conceptions with, and to exercise the untameable fierceness of their wills. The Jews were the only people of antiquity who were withheld from running headlong into this abomination; yet so strong was the propensity in them (from inherent frailty as well as neighbouring example) that it could only be curbed and kept back by the hands of Omnipotence.[1] At length, reason prevailed over imagination so far, that these brute idols and their altars were overturned: it was thought too much to set up stocks and stones, Golden Calves and Brazen Serpents, as *bona fide* Gods and Goddesses, which men were to fall down and worship at their peril—and Pope long after summed up the merits of the whole mythologic tribe in a handsome distich—

> " Gods partial, changeful, passionate, unjust,
>   Whose attributes were rage, revenge, or lust."

[1] They *would* have a king in spite of the devil. The image-worship of the Papists is a batch of the same leaven. The apishness of man's nature would not let even the Christian religion escape.

H

It was thought a bold stride to divert the course of our imaginations, the overflowings of our enthusiasm, our love of the mighty and the marvellous, from the dead to the living *subject*, and there we stick. We have got living idols, instead of dead ones; and we fancy that they are real, and put faith in them accordingly. Oh, Reason! when will thy long minority expire? It is not now the fashion to make Gods of wood and stone and brass, but we make kings of common men, and are proud of our own handy-work. We take a child from his birth, and we agree, when he grows up to be a man, to heap the highest honours of the state upon him, and to pay the most devoted homage to his will. Is there any thing in the person, " any mark, any likelihood," to warrant this sovereign awe and dread? No: he may be little better than an idiot, little short of a madman, and yet he is no less qualified for king.[2] If he can contrive to pass the College of Physicians, the Heralds' College dub

---

[2] " In fact, the argument drawn from the supposed incapacity of the people against a representative Government, comes with the worst grace in the world from the patrons and admirers of hereditary government. Surely, if government were a thing requiring the utmost stretch of genius, wisdom, and virtue to carry it on, the office of King would never even have been dreamt of as hereditary, any more than that of poet, painter, or philosopher. It is easy here ' for the son to tread in the Sire's steady steps.' It requires nothing but the will to do it. Extraordinary talents are not once looked for. Nay, a person, who would never have risen by natural abilities to the situation of churchwarden or parish beadle, succeeds by unquestionable right to the possession of a throne, and wields the energies of an empire, or decides the fate of the world with the smallest possible share of human understanding. The line of distinction which separates the regal purple from the slabbering-bib is sometimes fine indeed; as we see in the case of the two Ferdinands. Any one above the rank of an idiot is supposed capable of exercising the highest functions of royal state. Yet these are the persons who talk of the people as a swinish multi-tude, and taunt them with their want of refinement and philosophy." — *Yellow Dwarf*, p. 84

him divine. Can we make any given individual taller
or stronger or wiser than other men, or different in any
respect from what nature intended him to be? No;
but we can make a king of him. We cannot add a cubit
to the stature, or instil a virtue into the minds of monarchs
—but we can put a sceptre into their hands, a crown upon
their heads, we can set them on an eminence, we can
surround them with circumstance, we can aggrandise
them with power, we can pamper their appetites, we can
pander to their wills. We can do everything to exalt
them in external rank and station—nothing to lift them
one step higher in the scale of moral or intellectual
excellence. Education does not give capacity or temper;
and the education of kings is not especially directed to
useful knowledge or liberal sentiment. What then is the
state of the case? The highest respect of the community
and of every individual in it is paid and is due of right
there, where perhaps not an idea can take root, or a
single virtue be engrafted. Is not this to erect a standard
of esteem directly opposite to that of mind and morals?
The lawful monarch may be the best or the worst man
in his dominions, he may be the wisest or the weakest,
the wittiest or the stupidest: still he is equally entitled
to our homage as king, for it is the place and power we
bow to, and not the man. He may be a sublimation of
all the vices and diseases of the human heart; yet we are
not to say so, we dare not even think so. " Fear God, and
honour the King," is equally a maxim at all times and
seasons. The personal character of the king has nothing
to do with the question. Thus the extrinsic is set up over
the intrinsic by authority: wealth and interest lend their
countenance to gilded vice and infamy on principle, and
outward show and advantages become the symbols and
the standard of respect in despite of useful qualities or
well-directed efforts through all ranks and gradations of
society. " From the crown of the head to the sole of the

foot there is no soundness left." The whole style of moral thinking, feeling, acting, is in a false tone—is hollow, spurious, meretricious. Virtue, says Montesquieu, is the principle of republics; honour, of a monarchy. But it is " honour dishonourable, sin-bred "—it is the honour of trucking a principle for a place, of exchanging our honest convictions for a ribbon or a garter. The business of life is a scramble for unmerited precedence. Is not the highest respect entailed, the highest station filled without any possible proofs or pretensions to public spirit or public principle? Shall not the next places to it be secured by the sacrifice of them? It is the order of the day, the understood etiquette of courts and kingdoms. For the servants of the crown to presume on merit, when the crown itself is held as an heir-loom by prescription, is a kind of *lèse majesté*, an indirect attainder of the title to the succession. Are not all eyes turned to the sun of court-favour? Who would not then reflect its smile by the performance of any acts which can avail in the eye of the great, and by the surrender of any virtue, which attracts neither notice nor applause? The stream of corruption begins at the fountain-head of court-influence. The sympathy of mankind is that on which all strong feeling and opinion floats; and this sets in full in every absolute monarchy to the side of tinsel show and iron-handed power, in contempt and defiance of right and wrong. The right and the wrong are of little consequence, compared to the *in* and the *out*. The distinction between Whig and Tory is merely nominal: neither have their country one bit at heart. Phaw! we had forgot—Our British monarchy is a mixed, and the only perfect form of government; and therefore what is here said cannot properly apply to it. But MIGHT BEFORE RIGHT is the motto blazoned on the front of unimpaired and undivided Sovereignty!—

A court is the centre of fashion; and no less so, for being the sink of luxury and vice—

——" Of outward show
Elaborate, of inward less exact."

The goods of fortune, the baits of power, the indulgences
of vanity, may be accumulated without end, and the taste
for them increases as it is gratified: the love of virtue, the
pursuit of truth, grow stale and dull in the dissipation
of a court. Virtue is thought crabbed and morose,
knowledge pedantic, while every sense is pampered, and
every folly tolerated. Everything tends naturally to
personal aggrandisement and unrestrained self-will. It
is easier for monarchs as well as other men " to tread the
primrose path of dalliance " than " to scale the steep and
thorny road to heaven." The vices, when they have leave
from power and authority, go greater lengths than the
virtues; example justifies almost every excess, and " nice
customs curtesy to great kings." What chance is there
that monarchs should not yield to the temptations of
gallantry then, when youth and beauty are as wax?
What female heart can indeed withstand the attractions
of a throne—the smile that melts all hearts, the air that
awes rebellion, the frown that kings dread, the hand that
scatters fairy wealth, that bestows titles, places, honour,
power, the breast on which the star glitters, the head
circled with a diadem, whose dress dazzles with its
richness and its taste, who has nations at his command,
senates at his control, " in form and motion so express
and admirable, in action how like an angel, in apprehension how like a God; the beauty of the world, the
paragon of animals! " The power of resistance is so much
the less, where fashion extends impunity to the frail
offender, and screens the loss of character.

" Vice is undone, if she forgets her birth,
   And stoops from angels to the dregs of earth ;
   But 'tis the fall degrades her to a whore :
   Let greatness own her and she's mean no more
   Her birth, her beauty, crowds and courts confess,
   Chaste matrons praise her, and grave bishops bless.

> In golden chains the willing world she draws,
> And hers the Gospel is, and hers the laws."[1]

The air of a court is not assuredly that which is most favourable to the practice of self-denial and strict morality. We increase the temptations of wealth, of power, and pleasure a thousand-fold, while we can give no additional force to the antagonist principles of reason, disinterested integrity and goodness of heart. Is it to be wondered at that courts and palaces have produced so many monsters of avarice, cruelty, and lust? The adept in voluptuousness is not likely to be a proportionable proficient in humanity. To feed on plate or be clothed in purple, is not to feel for the hungry and the naked. He who has the greatest power put into his hands, will only become more impatient of any restraint in the use of it. To have the welfare and the lives of millions placed at our disposal, is a sort of warrant, a challenge to

---

[1] A lady of quality abroad, in allusion to the gallantries of the reigning Prince, being told, " I suppose it will be your turn next ? " said, " No, I hope not; for you know it is impossible to refuse ! " What a satire on the court and fashionables! If this be true, female virtue in the blaze of royalty is no more than the moth in the candle, or ice in the sun's ray. What will the great themselves say to it, in whom at this rate,
>   —" the same luck holds,
>   They all are subjects, courtiers, and cuckolds ! "
Out upon it ! We'll not believe it. Alas ! poor virtue, what is to become of the very idea of it, if we are to be told that every man within the precincts of a palace is an *hypothetical* cuckold, or holds his wife's virtue in trust for the Prince ? We entertain no doubt that many ladies of quality have resisted the importunities of a throne, and that many more would do so in private life, if they had the desired opportunity : nay, we have been assured by several that a king would no more be able to prevail with them than any other man ! If however there is any foundation for the above insinuation, it throws no small light on the Spirit of Monarchy, which by the supposition implies in it the *virtual* surrender of the whole sex at discretion ; and at the same time accounts perhaps for the indifference shewn by some monarchs in availing themselves of so mechanical a privilege.

squander them without mercy. An arbitrary monarch set over the heads of his fellows does not identify himself with them, or learn to comprehend their rights or sympathise with their interests, but looks down upon them as of a different species from himself, as insects crawling on the face of the earth, that he may trample on at his pleasure, or if he spares them, it is an act of royal grace;— he is besotted with power, blinded with prerogative, an alien to his nature, a traitor to his trust, and instead of being the organ of public feeling and public opinion, is an excrescence and an anomaly in the state, a bloated mass of morbid humours and proud flesh! A constitutional king, on the other hand, is a servant of the public, a representative of the people's wants and wishes, dispensing justice and mercy according to law. Such a monarch is the King of England! Such was his late, and such is his present Majesty George the IVth!—

Let us take the Spirit of Monarchy in its highest state of exaltation, in the moment of its proudest triumph— a Coronation-day. We now see it in our mind's eye; the preparation of weeks—the expectation of months—the seats, the privileged places, are occupied in the obscurity of night, and in silence—the day dawns slowly, big with the hope of Cæsar and of Rome—the golden censers are set in order, the tables groan with splendour and with luxury—within the inner space the rows of peeresses are set, and revealed to the eye decked out in ostrich feathers and pearls, like beds of lilies sparkling with a thousand dew-drops—the marshals and the heralds are in motion —the full organ, majestic, peals forth the Coronation Anthem—everything is ready—and all at once the Majesty of kingdoms bursts upon the astonished sight— his person is swelled out with all the gorgeousness of dress, and swathed in bales of silk and golden tissues—the bow with which he greets the assembled multitude, and the representatives of foreign kings, is the climax of

conscious dignity, bending gracefully on its own bosom,
and instantly thrown back into the sightless air, as if
asking no recognition in return—the oath of mutual
fealty between him and his people is taken—the fairest
flowers of female beauty precede the Sovereign, scatter-
ing roses; the sons of princes page his heels, holding up
the robes of crimson and ermine—he staggers and reels
under the weight of royal pomp, and of a nation's eyes;
and thus the pageant is launched into the open day,
dazzling the sun, whose beams seem beaten back by the
sun of royalty—there were the warrior, the statesman,
and the mitred head—there was Prince Leopold, like a
panther in its dark glossy pride, and Castlereagh, clad
in triumphant smiles and snowy satin, unstained with his
own blood—the loud trumpet brays, the cannon roars, the
spires are mad with music, the stones in the street are
startled at the presence of a king:—the crowd press on,
the metropolis heaves like a sea in restless motion, the
air is thick with loyalty's quick pants in its monarch's
arms—all eyes drink up the sight, all tongues reverberate
the sound—

> " A present deity they shout around,
> A present deity the vaulted roofs rebound ! "

What does it all amount to? A show—a theatrical
spectacle! What does it prove? That a king is crowned,
that a king is dead! What is the moral to be drawn from
it, that is likely to sink into the heart of a nation? That
greatness consists in finery, and that supreme merit is
the dower of birth and fortune! It is a form, a ceremony
to which each successor to the throne is entitled in his
turn as a matter of right. Does it depend on the inheritance of virtue, on the acquisition of knowledge in the new
monarch, whether he shall be thus exalted in the eyes of
the people? No:—to say so is not only an offence in
manners, but a violation of the laws. The king reigns in

contempt of any such pragmatical distinctions. They are
set aside, proscribed, treasonable, as it relates to the
august person of the monarch; what is likely to become
of them in the minds of the people? A Coronation over-
lays and drowns all such considerations for a generation
to come, and so far it serves its purpose well. It debauches
the understandings of the people, and makes them the
slaves of sense and show. It laughs to scorn and tramples
upon every other claim to distinction or respect. Is the
chief person in the pageant a tyrant? It does not lessen,
but aggrandise him to the imagination. Is he the king of
a free people? We make up in love and loyalty what we
want in fear. Is he young? He borrows understanding
and experience from the learning and tried wisdom of
councils and parliaments. Is he old? He leans upon the
youth and beauty that attend his triumph. Is he weak?
Armies support him with their myriads. Is he diseased?
What is health to a staff of physicians? Does he die?
The truth is out, and he is then—nothing!

There is a cant among court-sycophants of calling all
those who are opposed to them " the *rabble*," "*fellows*,"
"*miscreants*," &c. This shews the grossness of their
ideas of all true merit, and the false standard of rank and
power by which they measure everything; like footmen,
who suppose their masters must be gentlemen, and that
the rest of the world are low people. Whatever is opposed
to power, they think despicable; whatever suffers oppression they think deserves it. They are ever ready to side
with the strong, to insult and trample on the weak.
This is with us a pitiful fashion of thinking. They are
not of the mind of Pope, who was so full of the opposite
conviction, that he has even written a bad couplet to
express it:—

> " Worth makes the man, and want of it the fellow :
>   The rest is all but leather and prunella."

H *

Those lines in Cowper also must sound very puerile or old-fashioned to courtly ears:—

> " The only amaranthine flower on earth
> Is virtue ; the only lasting treasure, truth."

To this sentiment, however, we subscribe our hearts and hands. There is nothing truly liberal but that which postpones its own claims to those of propriety—or great but that which looks out of itself to others. All power is but an unabated nuisance, a barbarous assumption, an aggravated injustice, that is not directed to the common good: all grandeur that has not something corresponding to it in personal merit and heroic acts, is a deliberate burlesque, and an insult on common sense and human nature. That which is true, the understanding ratifies: that which is good, the heart owns: all other claims are spurious, vitiated, mischievous, false—fit only for those who are sunk below contempt, or raised above opinion. We hold in scorn all *right-lined* pretensions but those of rectitude. If there is offence in this, we are ready to abide by it. If there is shame, we take it to ourselves: and we hope and hold that the time will come, when all other idols but those which represent pure truth and real good, will be looked upon with the same feelings of pity and wonder that we now look back to the images of Thor and Woden!

Really, that men born to a throne (limited or un-limited) should employ the brief span of their existence here in doing all the mischief in their power, in levying cruel wars and undermining the liberties of the world, to prove to themselves and others that their pride and passions are of more consequence than the welfare of mankind at large, would seem a little astonishing, but that the fact is so. It is not our business to preach lectures to monarchs, but if we were at all disposed to attempt the ungracious task, we should do it in the words of an author who often addressed the ear of monarchs.

"A man may read a sermon," says Jeremy Taylor, "the best and most passionate that ever man preached, if he shall but enter into the sepulchres of kings. In the same Escurial where the Spanish princes live in greatness and power, and decree war or peace, they have wisely placed a cemetery where their ashes and their glory shall sleep till time shall be no more: and where *our* kings have been crowned, their ancestors lie interred, and they must walk over their grandsire's head to take his crown. There is an acre sown with royal seed, the copy of the greatest change from rich to naked, from ceiled roofs to arched coffins, from living like Gods to die like men. There is enough to cool the flames of lust, to abate the height of pride, to appease the itch of covetous desires, to sully and dash out the dissembling colours of a lustful, artificial, and imaginary beauty. There the warlike and the peaceful, the fortunate and the miserable, the beloved and the despised princes mingle their dust, and pay down their symbol of mortality, and tell all the world, that when we die our ashes shall be equal to kings, and our accounts shall be easier, and our pains for our crimes shall be less. To my apprehension, it is a sad record which is left by Athenaeus concerning Ninus, the great Assyrian monarch, whose life and death is summed up in these words: 'Ninus, the Assyrian, had an ocean of gold, and other riches more than the sand in the Caspian sea; he never saw the stars, and perhaps he never desired it; he never stirred up the holy fire among the Magi; nor touched his God with the sacred rod, according to the laws; he never offered sacrifice, nor worshipped the Deity, nor administered justice, nor spake to the people, nor numbered them; but he was most valiant to eat and drink, and having mingled his wines, he threw the rest upon the stones. This man is dead: behold his sepulchre,

and now hear where Ninus is. *Sometime I was Ninus,
and drew the breath of a living man, but now am nothing
but clay. I have nothing but what I did eat, and what I
served to myself in lust is all my portion: the wealth with
which I was blest, my enemies meeting together shall carry
away, as the mad Thyades carry a raw goat. I am gone
to Hell; and when I went thither, I carried neither gold nor
horse, nor a silver chariot. I that wore a mitre, am now a
little heap of dust!* ' "—Taylor's *Holy Living and Dying.*

LIBER AMORIS

1 8 2 3

UNALTERED LOVE

" Love is not love that alteration finds :
Oh no ! it is an ever-fixed mark,
That looks on tempests and is never shaken."

SHALL I not love her for herself alone, in spite of
fickleness and folly? To love her for her regard to me,
is not to love her, but myself. She has robbed me of
herself: shall she also rob me of my love of her? Did I
not live on her smile? Is it less sweet because it is
withdrawn from me? Did I not adore her every grace?
Does she bend less enchantingly, because she has turned
from me to another? Is my love then in the power of
fortune, or of her caprice ? No, I will have it lasting as it
is pure; and I will make a Goddess of her, and build a
temple to her in my heart, and worship her on indestructible altars, and raise statues to her: and my homage
shall be unblemished as her unrivalled symmetry of
form; and when that fails, the memory of it shall survive;
and my bosom shall be proof to scorn, as hers has been
to pity; and I will pursue her with an unrelenting love,
and sue to be her slave, and tend her steps without notice

and without reward; and serve her living, and mourn
for her when dead. And thus my love will have shewn
itself superior to her hate; and I shall triumph and then
die. This is my idea of the only true and heroic love!
Such is mine for her.

PERFECT LOVE

Perfect love has this advantage in it, that it leaves the
possessor of it nothing farther to desire. There is one
object (at least) in which the soul finds absolute content,
for which it seeks to live, or dares to die. The heart has
as it were filled up the moulds of the imagination. The
truth of passion keeps pace with and outvies the extravagance of mere language. There are no words so fine, no
flattery so soft, that there is not a sentiment beyond
them, that it is impossible to express, at the bottom of
the heart where true love is. What idle sounds the common phrases, *adorable creature, angel, divinity,* are!
What a proud reflection it is to have a feeling answering
to all these, rooted in the breast, unalterable, unutterable,
to which all other feelings are light and vain! Perfect
love reposes on the object of its choice, like the halcyon
on the wave; and the air of heaven is around it.

CHARACTERISTICS

1823

T O speak highly of one with whom we are intimate, is a
species of egotism. Our modesty as well as our jealousy
teaches us caution on this subject.

*   *   *

What makes it so difficult to do justice to others is,
that we are hardly sensible of merit, unless it falls in
with our own views and line of pursuit; and where this is

the case, it interferes with our own pretensions. To be forward to praise others, implies either great eminence, that can afford to part with applause; or great quickness of discernment, with confidence in our own judgments; or great sincerity and love of truth, getting the better of our self-love.

*   *   *

Society is a more level surface than we imagine. Wise men or absolute fools are hard to be met with, as there are few giants or dwarfs. The heaviest charge we can bring against the general texture of society is, that it is common-place; and many of those who are singular, had better be common-place. Our fancied superiority to others is in some one thing, which we think most of, because we excel in it, or have paid most attention to it; whilst we overlook their superiority to us in something else, which they set equal and exclusive store by. This is fortunate for all parties. I never felt myself superior to any one, who did not go out of his way to affect qualities which he had not. In his own individual character and line of pursuit, every one has knowledge, experience, and skill:—and who shall say which pursuit requires most, thereby proving his own narrowness and incompetence to decide? Particular talent or genius does not imply general capacity. Those who are most versatile are seldom great in any one department: and the stupidest people can generally do something. The highest pre-eminence in any one study commonly arises from the concentration of the attention and faculties on that one study. He who expects from a great name in politics, in philosophy, in art, equal greatness in other things, is little versed in human nature. Our strength lies in our weakness. The learned in books is ignorant of the world. He who is ignorant of books is often well acquainted with other things: for life is of the same length in the learned and unlearned; the mind cannot be idle; if it is not taken up with one thing, it attends to another through choice or necessity; and the degree of previous capacity in one class or another is a mere lottery.

* * *

There are few things in which we deceive ourselves more than in the esteem we profess to entertain for our friends. It is little better than a piece of quackery. The truth is, we think of them as we please—that is, as *they* please or displease us. As long as we are in good humour with them, we see nothing but their good qualities; but no sooner do they offend us than we rip up all their bad ones (which we before made a secret of, even to ourselves) with double malice. He who but now was little less than an angel of light shall be painted in the blackest colours for a slip of the tongue, " some trick not worth an egg," for the slightest suspicion of offence given or received. We often bestow the most opprobrious epithets on our best friends, and retract them twenty times in the course of a day, while the man himself remains the same. In love, which is all rhapsody and passion, this is excusable; but in the ordinary intercourse of life, it is preposterous.

* * *

It is well that there is no one without a fault; for he would not have a friend in the world. He would seem to belong to a different species.

* * *

The difficulty is for a man to rise to high station, not to fill it; as it is easier to stand on an eminence than to climb up to it. Yet he alone is truly great who is so without the aid of circumstances and in spite of fortune, who is as little lifted up by the tide of opinion, as he is depressed by neglect or obscurity, and who borrows dignity only from himself. It is a fine compliment which Pope has paid to Lord Oxford—

> " A soul supreme, in each hard instance tried,
> Above all pain, all passion, and all pride ;
> The rage of power, the blast of public breath,
> The lust of lucre, and the dread of death ! "

*　　*　　*

The greatest talents do not generally attain to the highest stations. For though high, the ascent to them is narrow, beaten, and crooked. The path of genius is free, and its own. Whatever requires the concurrence and co-operation of others, must depend chiefly on routine and an attention to rules and *minutiæ*. Success in business is therefore seldom owing to uncommon talents or original power, which is untractable and self-willed, but to the greatest degree of common-place capacity.

*　　*　　*

It is great weakness to lay ourselves open to others, who are reserved towards us. There is not only no equality in it, but we may be pretty sure they will turn a confidence, which they are so little disposed to imitate, against us.

*　　*　　*

Simplicity of character is the natural result of profound thought.

*　　*　　*

We as often repent the good we have done as the ill.

*　　*　　*

In public speaking, we must appeal either to the prejudices of others, or to the love of truth and justice. If we think merely of displaying our own ability, we shall ruin every cause we undertake. .

*　　*　　*

A person who talks with equal vivacity on every subject, excites no interest in any. *Repose* is as necessary in conversation as in a picture.

*   *   *

The best kind of conversation is that which may be called *thinking aloud*. I like very well to speak my mind on any subject (or to hear another do so) and to go into the question according to the degree of interest it naturally inspires, but not to have to get up a thesis upon every topic. There are those, on the other hand, who seem always to be practising on their audience, as if they mistook them for a DEBATING-SOCIETY, or to hold a general retainer, by which they are bound to explain every difficulty, and answer every objection that can be started. This, in private society and among friends, is not desirable. You thus lose the two great ends of conversation, which are to learn the sentiments of others, and see what they think of yours. One of the best talkers I ever knew had this defect—that he evidently seemed to be considering less what he felt on any point than what might be said upon it, and that he listened to you, not to weigh what you said, but to reply to it, like counsel on the other side. This habit gave a brilliant smoothness and polish to his general discourse, but, at the same time, took from its solidity and prominence: it reduced it to a tissue of lively, fluent, ingenious *common-places* (for original, genuine observations are like " minute drops from off the eaves," and not an incessant shower) and, though his talent in this way was carried to the very extreme of cleverness, yet I think it seldom, if ever, went beyond it.

*   *   *

A man's reputation is not in his own keeping, but lies at the mercy of the profligacy of others. Calumny

requires no proof. The throwing out malicious imputations against any character leaves a stain, which no after-
refutation can wipe out. To create an unfavourable
impression, it is not necessary that certain things should
be *true*, but that they *have been said*. The imagination
is of so delicate a texture, that even words wound it.

* * *

Want of principle is power. Truth and honesty set a
limit to our efforts, which impudence and hypocrisy
easily overleap.

* * *

In estimating the value of an acquaintance or even a
friend, we give a preference to intellectual or convivial
over moral qualities. The truth is, that in our habitual
intercourse with others, we much oftener require to be
amused than assisted. We consider less, therefore, what
a person with whom we are intimate is ready to do for
us in critical emergencies, than what he has to say on
ordinary occasions. We dispense with his services, if he
only saves us from *ennui*. In civilized society, words are
of as much importance as things.

* * *

Insignificant people are a necessary relief in society.
Such characters are extremely agreeable, and even
favourites, if they appear satisfied with the part they
have to perform.

* * *

The youth is better than the old age of friendship.

* * *

In the course of a long acquaintance we have repeated
all our good things and discussed all our favourite topics
several times over, so that our conversation becomes a
mockery of social intercourse. We might as well talk to

ourselves. The soil of friendship is worn out with constant use. Habit may still attach us to each other, but we feel ourselves fettered by it. Old friends might be compared to old married people without the tie of children.

*   *   *

We grow tired of ourselves, much more of other people. Use may in part reconcile us to our own tediousness, but we do not adopt that of others on the same paternal principle. We may be willing to tell a story twice, never to hear one more than once.

*   *   *

To be capable of steady friendship or lasting love, are the two greatest proofs, not only of goodness of heart, but of strength of mind.

*   *   *

It makes us proud when our love of a mistress is returned: it ought to make us prouder that we can love her for herself alone, without the aid of any such selfish reflection. This is the religion of love.

*   *   *

It is wonderful how often we see and hear of Shakespear's plays without being annoyed with it. Were it any other writer, we should be sick to death of the very name. But his volumes are like that of nature, we can turn to them again and again:—

> " Age cannot wither, nor custom stale
> His infinite variety."

*   *   *

The contempt of a wanton for a man who is determined to think her virtuous, is perhaps the strongest of all others. He officiously reminds her of what she ought to be; and she avenges the galling sense of lost character on the fool who still believes in it.

★　　★　　★

The only vice that cannot be forgiven is hypocrisy. The repentance of a hypocrite is itself hypocrisy.

★　　★　　★

There is less impertinence and more independence in London than in any other place in the kingdom.

★　　★　　★

To expect an author to talk as he writes is ridiculous; or even if he did, you would find fault with him as a pedant. We should *read* authors, and not converse with them.

★　　★　　★

Good and ill seem as necessary to human life as light and shade are to a picture. We grow weary of uniform success, and pleasure soon surfeits. Pain makes ease delightful; hunger relishes the homeliest food, fatigue turns the hardest bed to down; and the difficulty and uncertainty of pursuit in all cases enhance the value of possession. The wretched are in this respect fortunate, that they have the strongest yearnings after happiness; and to desire is in some sense to enjoy. If the schemes of Utopians could be realized, the tone of society would be changed from what it is, into a sort of insipid high life. There could be no fine tragedies written; nor would there be any pleasure in seeing them. We tend to this conclusion already with the progress of civilization.

★　　★　　★

It is remarkable how virtuous and generously disposed every one is at a play. We uniformly applaud what is right and condemn what is wrong, when it costs us nothing but the sentiment.

* * *

The best lessons we can learn from witnessing the folly of mankind is not to irritate ourselves against it.

* * *

Women never reason, and therefore they are (comparatively) seldom wrong. They judge instinctively of what falls under their immediate observation or experience, and do not trouble themselves about remote or doubtful consequences. If they make no profound discoveries, they do not involve themselves in gross absurdities. It is only by the help of reason and logical inference, according to Hobbes, that " man becomes excellently wise, or excellently foolish."[1]

* * *

The French are fond of reading as well as of talking. You may constantly see girls tending an apple-stall in the coldest day in winter, and reading Voltaire or Racine. Such a thing was never known in London as a barrow-woman reading Shakespear. Yet we talk of our widespread civilization, and ample provisions for the education of the poor.

* * *

An awkward Englishman has an advantage in going abroad. Instead of having his deficiency more remarked, it is less so; for all Englishmen are thought awkward alike. Any slip in politeness or abruptness of address is attributed to an ignorance of foreign manners, and you escape under the cover of the national character. Your behaviour is no more criticized than your accent. They

[1] *Leviathan.*

consider the barbarism of either as a compliment to their own superior refinement.

*   *   *

The national precedence between the English and Scotch may be settled by this, that the Scotch are always asserting their superiority over the English, while the English never say a word about their superiority over the Scotch. The first have got together a great number of facts and arguments in their own favour; the last never trouble their heads about the matter, but have taken the point for granted as self-evident.

*   *   *

There is a double aristocracy of rank and letters, which is hardly to be endured—*monstrum ingens, biforme*. A lord, who is a poet as well, regards the House of Peers with contempt as a set of dull fellows; and he considers his brother authors as a Grub-street crew. A king is hardly good enough for him to touch; a mere man of genius is no better than a worm. He alone is all-accomplished. Such people should be *sent to Coventry;* and they generally are so, through their insufferable pride and self-sufficiency.

*   *   *

A copy is never so good as an original. This would not be the case indeed, if great painters were in the habit of copying bad pictures; but as the contrary practice holds, it follows that the excellent parts of a fine picture must lose in the imitation, and the indifferent parts will not be proportionably improved by any thing substituted at a venture for them.

*   *   *

In some situations, if you say nothing, you are called dull; if you talk, you are thought impertinent or arrogant.

It is hard to know what to do in this case. The question seems to be, whether your vanity or your prudence predominates.

* * *

Wit is the rarest quality to be met with among people of education, and the most common among the uneducated.

* * *

The most perfect style of writing may be that, which treats strictly and methodically of a given subject; the most amusing (if not the most instructive) is that, which mixes up the personal character of the author with general reflection.

* * *

The seat of knowledge is in the head; of wisdom, in the heart. We are sure to judge wrong, if we do not feel right.

* * *

Fame is the inheritance not of the dead, but of the living. It is we who look back with lofty pride to the great names of antiquity, who drink of that flood of glory as of a river, and refresh our wings in it for future flight.

* * *

Those who from a constant change and dissipation of outward objects have not a moment's leisure left for their own thoughts, can feel no respect for themselves, and learn little consideration for humanity.

* * *

He will never have true friends who is afraid of making enemies.

* * *

Those people who are fond of giving trouble, like to take it; just as those who pay no attention to the comforts of others, are generally indifferent to their own. We are governed by sympathy; and the extent of our sympathy is determined by that of our sensibility.

*   *   *

No one is idle, who can do any thing.

*   *   *

Vice is man's nature: virtue is a habit—or a mask.

*   *   *

The foregoing maxim shews the difference between truth and sarcasm.

*   *   *

Those who are fond of setting things to rights, have no great objection to seeing them wrong. There is often a good deal of spleen at the bottom of benevolence.

OXFORD

(LONDON MAGAZINE, NOV., 1823)

R O M E has been called the " Sacred City ":—might not *our* Oxford be called so too? There is an air about it, resonant of joy and hope: it speaks with a thousand tongues to the heart: it waves its mighty shadow over the imagination: it stands in lowly sublimity, on the " hill of ages "; and points with prophetic fingers to the sky: it greets the eager gaze from afar, " with glistering spires and pinnacles adorned," that shine with an internal light as with the lustre of setting suns; and a dream and a glory hover round its head, as the spirits of former times, a throng of intellectual shapes, are seen retreating or advancing to the eye of memory: its streets are paved with the names of learning that can never wear out: its green quadrangles breathe the silence of thought, conscious of the weight of yearnings innumerable after the past, of loftiest aspirations for the future: Isis babbles of the Muse, its waters are from the springs of Helicon, its Christ-Church meadows, classic, Elysian fields!—We could pass our lives in Oxford without having or wanting any other idea—that of the place is enough. We imbibe the air of thought; we stand in the presence of learning. We are admitted into the Temple of Fame, we feel that we are in the sanctuary, on holy ground, and " hold high converse with the mighty dead." The enlightened and the ignorant are on a level, if they have but faith in the tutelary genius of the place. We may be wise by proxy, and studious by prescription. Time has taken upon himself the labour of thinking; and accumulated libraries leave us leisure to be dull. There is no occasion to examine the buildings, the churches, the colleges, by the rules of architecture, to reckon up the streets, to compare it with Cambridge (Cambridge lies out of the way, on one side of the world)—but woe to him who does not feel in passing through Oxford that he is in " no mean city," that he is surrounded with the monuments and lordly mansions of the mind of man, outvying in pomp and splendour the courts and palaces of princes, rising like an exhalation in the night of ignorance, and triumphing over barbaric foes, saying, " All eyes shall see me, and all knees shall bow to me! "—as the shrine where successive ages came to pay their pious vows, and slake the sacred thirst of knowledge, where youthful hopes (an endless flight) soared to truth and good, and where the retired and lonely student brooded over the historic or over fancy's page, imposing high tasks for himself, framing high destinies for man—the lamp, the mine, the well-head from whence the spark of learning was kindled, its stream flowed, its treasures were spread out through the remotest corners of the land and to distant nations. Let him then who is fond of indulging in a dream-like existence go to Oxford and stay there; let him study this magnificent spectacle, the same under all aspects, with its mental twilight tempering the glare of noon, or mellowing the silver moonlight; let him wander in her sylvan suburbs, or linger in her cloistered halls; but let him not catch the din of scholars or teachers, or dine or sup with them, or speak a word to any of the privileged inhabitants; for if he does, the spell will be broken, the poetry and the religion gone, and the palace of enchantment will melt from his embrace into thin air!

ON THE SPIRIT OF OBLIGATIONS

(NEW MONTHLY MAGAZINE, JAN., 1824)

T H E two rarest things to be met with are good sense and good-nature. For one man who judges right, there are twenty who can say good things; as there are numbers who will serve you or do friendly actions, for one who really wishes you well. It has been said, and often repeated, that "mere good-nature is a fool": but I think that the dearth of sound sense, for the most part, proceeds from the want of a real, unaffected interest in things, except as they react upon ourselves; or from a neglect of the maxim of that good old philanthropist who said, " *Nihil humani a me alienum puto.*" The narrowness of the heart warps the understanding, and makes us weigh objects in the scales of our self-love, instead of those of truth and justice. We consider not the merits of the case, or what is due to others, but the manner in which our own credit or consequence will be affected ; and adapt

our opinions and conduct to the last of these rather than
to the first. The judgment is seldom wrong where the
feelings are right; and they generally are so, provided
they are warm and sincere. He who intends others well,
is likely to advise them for the best; he who has any
cause at heart, seldom ruins it by his imprudence. Those
who play the public or their friends slippery tricks, have
in secret no objection to betray them.

One finds out the folly and malice of mankind by the
impertinence of friends—by their professions of service
and tenders of advice—by their fears for your reputation
and anticipation of what the world may say of you; by
which means they suggest objections to your enemies, and
at the same time absolve themselves from the task of
justifying your errors, by having warned you of the consequences—by the care with which they tell you ill-news,
and conceal from you any flattering circumstance—by
their dread of your engaging in any creditable attempt,
and mortification if you succeed—by the difficulties and
hindrances they throw in your way—by their satisfaction
when you happen to make a slip or get into a scrape, and
their determination to tie your hands behind you, lest
you should get out of it—by their panic-terrors at your
entering into a vindication of yourself, lest in the course
of it, you should call upon them for a certificate to your
character—by their lukewarmness in defending, by their
readiness in betraying you—by the high standard by
which they try you, and to which you can hardly ever
come up—by their forwardness to partake your triumphs,
by their backwardness to share your disgrace—by their
acknowledgment of your errors out of candour, and
suppression of your good qualities out of envy—by their
not contradicting, or by their joining in the cry against
you, lest they, too, should become objects of the same
abuse—by their playing the game into your adversaries'
hands—by always letting their imaginations take part

with their cowardice, their vanity, and selfishness against you; and thus realising or hastening all the ill consequences they affect to deplore, by spreading abroad that very spirit of distrust, obloquy, and hatred which they predict will be excited against you!

In all these pretended demonstrations of an over-anxiety for our welfare, we may detect a great deal of spite and ill-nature lurking under the disguise of a friendly and officious zeal. It is wonderful how much love of mischief and rankling spleen lies at the bottom of the human heart, and how a constant supply of gall seems as necessary to the health and activity of the mind as of the body. Yet perhaps it ought not to excite much surprise that this gnawing, morbid, acrimonious temper should produce the effect it does, when, if it does not vent itself on others, it preys upon our own comforts, and makes us see the worst side of everything, even as it regards our own prospects and tranquillity. It is the not being comfortable in ourselves, that makes us seek to render other people uncomfortable. A person of this character will advise you against a prosecution for a libel, and shake his head at your attempting to shield yourself from a shower of calumny. It is not that he is afraid you will be *nonsuited*, but that you will gain a verdict! They caution you against provoking hostility, in order that you may submit to indignity. They say that " if you publish a certain work, it will be your ruin "—hoping that it will, and by their tragical denunciations, bringing about this very event as far as it lies in their power, or at any rate, enjoying a premature triumph over you in the meantime. What I would say to any friend who may be disposed to foretell a general outcry against any work of mine, would be to request him to judge and speak of it for himself, as he thinks it deserves—and not by his overweening scruples and qualms of conscience on my account, to afford those very persons whose hostility he deprecates the cue they are to give to party-prejudice, and which they may justify by his authority.

Suppose you are about to give lectures at a Public Institution, these friends and well-wishers hope " you'll be turned out—if you preserve your principles, they are sure you will." Is it that your consistency gives them any concern ? No, but they are uneasy at your gaining a chance of a little popularity—they do not like this new feather in your cap, they wish to see it struck out, *for the sake of your character*—and when this was once the case, it would be an additional relief to them to see your character following the same road the next day. The exercise of their bile seems to be the sole employment and gratification of such people. They deal in the miseries of human life. They are always either hearing or foreboding some new grievance. They cannot contain their satisfaction, if you tell them any mortification or cross-accident that has happened to yourself; and if you complain of their want of sympathy, they laugh in your face. This would be unaccountable, but for the spirit of perversity and contradiction implanted in human nature. If things go right, there is nothing to be done—these active-minded persons grow restless, dull, vapid—life is a sleep, a sort of *euthanasia*—Let them go wrong, and all is well again; they are once more on the alert, have something to pester themselves and other people about; may wrangle on, and " make mouths at the invisible event!" Luckily, there is no want of materials for this disposition to work upon, *there is plenty of grist for the mill*. If you fall in love, they tell you (by way of consolation) it is a pity that you do not fall downstairs and fracture a limb— it would be a relief to your mind, and show you your folly. So they would reform the world. The class of persons I speak of are almost uniform grumblers and croakers against governments; and it must be confessed, governments are of great service in fostering their

humours. " Born for their use, they live but to oblige
them." While kings are left free to exercise their proper
functions, and poet-laureates make out their Mittimus to
Heaven without a warrant, they will never stop the
mouths of the censorious by changing their dispositions;
the juices of faction will ferment, and the secretions of
the State be duly performed! I do not mind when a
character of this sort meets a minister of state like an
east wind round a corner, and gives him an ague-fit; but
why should he meddle with me? Why should he tell me
I write too much, and say that I should gain reputation if
I could contrive to starve for a twelvemonth? Or if I
apply to him for a loan of fifty pounds for present necessity,
send me word back that he has too much regard for me
to comply with my request? It is unhandsome irony.
It is not friendly, 'tis not pardonable.[1]

I like real good-nature and good-will, better than I do
any offers of patronage or plausible rules for my conduct
in life. I may suspect the soundness of the last, and I
may not be quite sure of the motives of the first. People
complain of ingratitude for benefits, and of the neglect
of wholesome advice. In the first place, we pay little
attention to advice, because we are seldom thought of
in it. The person who gives it either contents himself to
lay down (*ex cathedra*) certain vague, general maxims,
and " wise saws," which we knew before; or, instead of
considering what we *ought to do*, recommends what he
himself *would do*. He merely substitutes his own will,
caprice, and prejudices for ours, and expects us to be
guided by them. Instead of changing places with us (to
see what is best to be done in the given circumstances),
he insists on our looking at the question from his point of
view, and acting in such a manner as to please him. This
is not at all reasonable; for *one man's meat*, according to

---

[1] This circumstance did not happen to me, but to an
acquaintance.

the old adage, *is another man's poison*. And it is not strange, that starting from such opposite premises, we should seldom jump in a conclusion, and that the art of giving and taking advice is little better than a game at cross-purposes. I have observed that those who are the most inclined to assist others are the least forward or peremptory with their advice; for having our interest really at heart, they consider what can, rather than what *cannot* be done, and aid our views and endeavour to avert ill consequences by moderating our impatience and allaying irritations, instead of thwarting our main design, which only tends to make us more extravagant and violent than ever. In the second place, benefits are often conferred out of ostentation or pride, rather than from true regard; and the person obliged is too apt to perceive this. People who are fond of appearing in the light of patrons will perhaps go through fire and water to serve you, who yet would be sorry to find you no longer wanted their assistance, and whose friendship cools and their good-will slackens, as you are relieved by their active zeal from the necessity of being further beholden to it. Compassion and generosity are their favourite virtues; and they countenance you, as you afford them opportunities for exercising them. The instant you can go alone, or can stand upon your own ground, you are discarded as unfit for their purpose.

This is something more than mere good-nature or humanity. A thoroughly good-natured man, a real friend, is one who is pleased at our good-fortune, as well as prompt to seize every occasion of relieving our distress. We apportion our gratitude accordingly. We are thankful for good-will rather than for services, for the motive than the *quantum* of favour received—a kind word or look is never forgotten, while we cancel prouder and weightier obligations; and those who esteem us or evince a partiality to us are those whom we still consider as our best friends. Nay, so strong is this feeling, that we extend it even to those counterfeits in friendship—flatterers and sycophants. Our self-love, rather than our self-interest, is the master-key to our affections.

I am not convinced that those are always the best-natured or the best-conditioned men, who busy themselves most with the distresses of their fellow-creatures. I do not know that those whose names stand at the head of all subscriptions to charitable institutions, and who are perpetual stewards of dinners and meetings to encourage and promote the establishment of asylums for the relief of the blind, the halt, and the orphan poor, are persons gifted with the best tempers or the kindliest feelings. I do not dispute their virtue, I doubt their sensibility. I am not here speaking of those who make a trade of the profession of humanity, or set their names down out of mere idle parade and vanity. I mean those who really enter into the details and drudgery of this sort of service, *con amore*, and who delight in surveying and in diminishing the amount of human misery. I conceive it possible, that a person who is going to pour oil and balm into the wounds of afflicted humanity, at a meeting of the Western Dispensary, by handsome speeches and by a handsome donation (not grudgingly given), may be thrown into a fit of rage that very morning by having his toast too much buttered, may quarrel with the innocent prattle and amusements of his children, cry "Pish!" at every observation his wife utters, and scarcely feel a moment's comfort at any period of his life, except when he hears or reads of some case of pressing distress that calls for his immediate interference, and draws off his attention from his own situation and feelings by the act of alleviating it. Those martyrs to the cause of humanity, in short, who run the gauntlet of the whole catalogue of unheard-of crimes and afflicting casualties, who ransack prisons, and plunge into lazar-houses and slave-ships as their daily amusement and highest luxury, must generally, I think (though not always), be prompted to the arduous task by uneasy feelings of their own, and supported through it by iron nerves. Their fortitude must be equal to their pity. I do not think Mr. Wilberforce a case in point in this argument. He is evidently a delicately-framed, nervous, sensitive man. I should suppose him to be a kind and affectionately-disposed person in all the relations of life. His weakness is too quick a sense of reputation, a desire to have the good word of all men, a tendency to truckle to power and fawn on opinion. But there are some of these philanthropists that a physiognomist has hard work to believe in. They seem made of pasteboard, they look like mere machines: their benevolence may be said to go on rollers, and they are screwed to the sticking-place by the wheels and pulleys of humanity:

> " If to their share some splendid virtues fall,
>   Look in their face, and you forget them all."

They appear so much the creatures of the head and so little of the heart, they are so cold, so lifeless, so mechanical, so much governed by calculation, and so little by impulse, that it seems the toss-up of a halfpenny, a mere turn of a feather, whether such people should become a Granville Sharp, or a Hubert in *King John*, a Howard, or a Sir Hudson Lowe!

" Charity covers a multitude of sins." Wherever it is, there nothing can be wanting; wherever it is not, all else is vain. " The meanest peasant on the bleakest mountain is not without a portion of it (says Sterne); he finds the lacerated lamb of another's flock." &c.[1] I do not think education or circumstances can ever entirely eradicate this principle. Some professions may be supposed to blunt it, but it is perhaps more in appearance than in reality. Butchers are not allowed to sit on a jury for

[1] See the passage in the *Sentimental Journey*.

I

life and death; but probably this is a prejudice: if they have the *destructive organ* in an unusual degree of expansion, they vent their sanguinary inclinations on the brute creation ; and besides, they look too jolly, rosy, and in good case (they and their wives), to harbour much cruelty in their dispositions. Neither would I swear that a man was humane merely for abstaining from animal food. A tiger would not be a lamb, though it fed on milk. Surgeons are in general thought to be unfeeling, and steeled by custom to the sufferings of humanity. They may be so, as far as relates to broken bones and bruises, but not to other things. Nor are they necessarily so in their profession; for we find different degrees of callous insensibility in different individuals. Some practitioners have an evident delight in alarming the apprehensions and cutting off the limbs of their patients: these would have been ill-natured men in any situation in life, and merely make an excuse of their profession to indulge their natural ill-humour and brutality of temper. A surgeon who is fond of giving pain to those who consult him will not spare the feelings of his neighbours in other respects; has a tendency to probe other wounds besides those of the body; and is altogether a harsh and disagreeable character. A Jack-Ketch may be known to tie the fatal noose with trembling fingers; or a jailor may have a heart softer than the walls of his prison. There have been instances of highwaymen who were proverbially gentlemen. I have seen a Bow-street officer[1] (not but that the transition is ungracious and unjust) reading Racine, and following the recitation of Talma at the door of a room which he was sent to guard. Police-magistrates, from the scenes they have to witness and the characters they come in contact with, may be supposed to lose the fine edge of delicacy and sensibility: yet they are not all alike, but differ, as one star differs from another in

[1] Lavender.

magnitude. One is as remarkable for mildness and lenity as another is notorious for harshness and severity. The late Mr. Justice Fielding was a member of this profession, which (however little accordant with his own feelings) he made pleasant to those of others. He generally sent away the disputants in that unruly region, where he presided, tolerably satisfied. I have often seen him, escaped from the noisy repulsive scene, sunning himself in the adjoining walks of St. James's Park, and with mild aspect, and lofty but unwieldy mien, eyeing the verdant glades and lengthening vistas where perhaps his childhood loitered. He had a strong resemblance to his father, the immortal author of *Tom Jones*. I never passed him that I did not take off my hat to him in spirit. I could not help thinking of Parson Adams, of Booth and Amelia. I seemed to belong by intellectual adoption to the same family, and would willingly have acknowledged my obligations to the father to the son. He had something of the air of Colonel Bath. When young, he had very excellent prospects in the law, but neglected a brief sent him by the Attorney-General, in order to attend a glee-club, for which he had engaged to furnish a rondeau. This spoiled his fortune. À man whose object is to please himself, or to keep his word to his friends, is the last man to thrive at court. Yet he looked serene and smiling to his latest breath, conscious of the goodness of his own heart, and of not having sullied a name that had thrown a light upon humanity!

There are different modes of obligation, and different avenues to our gratitude and favour. A man may lend his countenance who will not part with his money, and open his mind to us who will not draw out his purse. How many ways are there, in which our peace may be assailed, besides actual want! How many comforts do we stand in need of, besides meat and drink and clothing! Is it nothing to " administer to a mind diseased "—to heal a wounded spirit? After all other difficulties are removed, we still want some one to bear with our infirmities, to impart our confidence to, to encourage us in our *hobbies* (nay, to get up and ride behind us), and to like us with all our faults. True friendship is self-love at second-hand; where, as in a flattering mirror, we may see our virtues magnified and our errors softened, and where we may fancy our opinion of ourselves confirmed by an impartial and faithful witness. He (of all the world) creeps closest to our bosoms, into our favour and esteem, who thinks of us most nearly as we do of ourselves. Such a one is indeed the pattern of a friend, another self—and our gratitude for the blessing is as sincere, as it is hollow in most other cases! This is one reason why entire friendship is scarcely to be found except in love. There is a hardness and severity in our judgments of one another; the spirit of competition also intervenes, unless where there is too great an inequality of pretension or difference of taste to admit of mutual sympathy and respect; but a woman's vanity is interested in making the object of her choice the God of her idolatry; and in the intercourse with that sex, there is the finest balance and reflection of opposite and answering excellences imaginable! It is in the highest spirit of the religion of love in the female breast, that Lord Byron has put that beautiful apostrophe in the mouth of Anah, in speaking of her angel-lover (alas! are not the sons of men, too, when they are deified in the hearts of women, only " a little lower than the angels? ")—

> " And when I think that his immortal wings
>   Shall one day hover o'er the sepulchre
>   Of the poor child of clay that so adored him,
>   As he adored the Highest, death becomes
>   Less terrible ! "

This is a dangerous string, which I ought never to touch upon; but the shattered cords vibrate of themselves!

The difference of age, of situation in life, and an absence of all considerations of business have, I apprehend, something of the same effect in producing a refined and abstracted friendship. The person whose doors I enter with most pleasure, and quit with most regret, never did me the smallest favour. I once did him an uncalled-for service, and we nearly quarrelled about it. If I were in the utmost distress, I should just as soon think of asking his assistance, as of stopping a person on the highway. Practical benevolence is not his *forte*. He leaves the profession of that to others. His habits, his theory are against it as idle and vulgar. His hand is closed, but what of that? His eye is ever open, and reflects the universe: his silver accents, beautiful, venerable as his silver hairs, but not scanted, flow as a river. I never ate or drank in his house; nor do I know or care how the flies or spiders fare in it, or whether a mouse can get a living. But I know that I can get there what I get nowhere else—a welcome, as if one was expected to drop in just at that moment, a total absence of all respect of persons and of airs of self-consequence, endless topics of discourse, refined thoughts, made more striking by ease and simplicity of manner—the husk, the shell of humanity is left at the door, and the spirit, mellowed by time, resides within! All you have to do is to sit and listen; and it is like hearing one of Titian's faces speak. To think of worldly matters is a profanation, like that of the money-changers in the Temple; or it is to regard the bread and wine of the Sacrament with carnal eyes. We enter the enchanter's cell, and converse with the divine inhabitant. To have this privilege always at hand, and to be circled by that spell whenever we choose, with an " *Enter Sessami*," is better than sitting at the lower end of the tables of the Great, than eating awkwardly from gold plate, than drinking fulsome toasts, or being thankful for gross favours, and gross insults!

Few things tend more to alienate friendship than a want of punctuality in our engagements. I have known the breach of a promise to dine or sup to break up more than one intimacy. A disappointment of this kind rankles in the mind—it cuts up our pleasures (those rare events in human life, which ought not to be wantonly sported with!)—it not only deprives us of the expected gratification, but renders us unfit for, and out of humour with, every other; it makes us think our society not worth having, which is not the way to make us delighted with our own thoughts; it lessens our self-esteem and destroys our confidence in others; and having leisure on our hands (by being thus left alone) and sufficient provocation withal, we employ it in ripping up the faults of the acquaintance who has played us this slippery trick, and in forming resolutions to pick a quarrel with him the very first opportunity we can find. I myself once declined an invitation to meet Talma, who was an admirer of Shakespear, and who idolized Buonaparte, to keep an appointment with a person who had *forgot* it! One great art of women, who pretend to manage their husbands and keep them to themselves, is to contrive some excuse for breaking their engagements with friends for whom they entertain any respect, or who are likely to have any influence over them.

There is, however, a class of persons who have a particular satisfaction in falsifying your expectations of pleasure in their society, who make appointments for no other ostensible purpose than *not to keep them;* who think their ill-behaviour gives them an air of superiority over you, instead of placing them at your mercy; and who, in fact, in all their overtures of condescending kindness towards you, treat you exactly as if there was no such person in the world. Friendship is with them a *mono-drama,* in which they play the principal and sole part. They must needs be very imposing or amusing characters to surround themselves with a circle of friends, who find that they are to be mere cyphers. The egotism would in such instances be offensive and intolerable, if its very excess did not render it entertaining. Some individuals carry this hard, unprincipled, reckless unconsciousness of everything but themselves and their own purposes to such a pitch, that they may be compared to *automata*, whom you never expect to consult your feelings or alter their movements out of complaisance to others. They are wound up to a certain point, by an internal machinery which you do not very well comprehend; but if they perform their accustomed evolutions so as to excite your wonder or laughter, it is all very well, you do not quarrel with them, but look on at the *pantomime* of friendship while it lasts or is agreeable.

There are (I may add here) a happy few, whose manner is so engaging and delightful, that, injure you how they will, they cannot offend you. They rob, ruin, ridicule you, and you cannot find in your heart to say a word against them. The late Mr. Sheridan was a man of this kind. He *could not* make enemies. If anyone came to request the repayment of a loan from him, he borrowed more. A cordial shake of his hand was a receipt in full for all demands. He could " coin his *smile* for drachmas," cancelled bonds with *bon mots*, and gave jokes in discharge of a bill. A friend of his said, " If I pull off my hat to him in the street, it costs me fifty pounds, and if he speaks to me, it's a hundred ! "

Only one other reflection occurs to me on this subject. I used to think better of the world than I do. I thought its great fault, its original sin, was barbarous ignorance and want, which would be cured by the diffusion of civilisation and letters. But I find (or fancy I do) that as selfishness is the vice of unlettered periods and nations, envy is the bane of more refined and intellectual ones. Vanity springs out of the grave of sordid self-interest.

Men were formerly ready to cut one another's throats about the gross means of subsistence, and now they are ready to do it about reputation. The worst is, you are no better off if you fail than if you succeed. You are despised if you do not excel others, and hated if you do. Abuse or praise equally weans your friends from you. We cannot bear eminence in our own department or pursuit, and think it an impertinence in any other. Instead of being delighted with the proofs of excellence and the admiration paid to it, we are mortified with it, thrive only by the defeat of others, and live on the carcase of mangled reputation. By being tried by an *ideal* standard of vanity and affectation, real objects and common people become odious, or insipid. Instead of being raised, all is prostituted, degraded, vile. Everything is reduced to this feverish, importunate, harassing state. I'm heartily sick of it, and I'm sure I have reason if anyone has.

THE ENTRANCE INTO ITALY

(NOTES OF A JOURNEY THROUGH FRANCE AND ITALY, 6TH APRIL, 1825)

THE coach shortly after overtook us. We descended a long and steep declivity, with the highest point of Mount Cenis on our left, and a lake to the right, like a landing-place for geese. Between the two was a low, white monastery, and the barrier where we had our passports inspected, and then went forward with only two stout horses and one rider. The snow on this side of the mountain was nearly gone. I supposed myself for some time nearly on level ground, till we came in view of several black chasms or steep ravines in the side of the mountain facing us, with water oozing from it, and saw through some *galleries*, that is, massy stone-pillars knit together by thick rails of strong timber, guarding the road-side, a perpendicular precipice below, and other galleries beyond, diminished in a fairy perspective, and descending " with cautious haste and giddy cunning," and with innumerable windings and re-duplications to an interminable depth and distance from the height where we were. The men and horses with carts, that were labouring up the path in the hollow below, shewed like crows or flies. The road we had to pass was often immediately under that we were passing, and cut from the side of what was all but a precipice out of the solid rock by the broad, firm masterhand that traced and executed this mighty work. The share that art has in the scene is as appalling as the scene itself—the strong security against danger as sublime as the danger itself. Near the turning of one of the first galleries is a beautiful waterfall, which at this time was frozen into a sheet of green pendant ice—a magical transformation. Long after we continued to descend, now faster and now slower, and came at length to a small village at the bottom of a sweeping line of road, where the houses seemed like dove-cotes with the mountain's back reared like a wall behind them, and which I thought the termination of our journey. But here the wonder and the greatness began: for, advancing through a grove of slender trees to another point of the road, we caught a new view of the lofty mountain to our left. It stood in front of us, with its head in the skies, covered with snow, and its bare sides stretching far away into a valley that yawned at its feet, and over which we seemed suspended in mid-air. The height, the magnitude, the immoveableness of the objects, the wild contrast, the deep tones, the dance and play of the landscape from the change of our direction and the interposition of other striking

I *

objects, the continued recurrence of the same huge masses, like giants following us with unseen strides, stunned the sense like a blow, and yet gave the imagination strength to contend with a force that mocked it. Here immeasurable columns of reddish granite shelved from the mountain's sides; here they were covered and stained with furze and other shrubs; here a chalky cliff shewed a fir-grove climbing its tall sides, and that itself looked at a distance like a huge, branching pine-tree; beyond was a dark, projecting knoll, or hilly promontory, that threatened to bound the perspective—but, on drawing nearer to it, the cloudy vapour that shrouded it (as it were) retired, and opened another vista beyond, that, in its own unfathomed depth, and in the gradual obscurity of twilight, resembled the uncertain gloom of the background of some fine picture. At the bottom of this valley crept a sluggish stream, and a monastery or low castle stood upon its banks. The effect was altogether grander than I had any conception of. It was not the idea of height or elevation that was obtruded upon the mind and staggered it, but we seemed to be descending into the bowels of the earth—its foundations seemed to be laid bare to the centre; and abyss after abyss, a vast, shadowy, interminable space, opened to receive us. We saw the building up and framework of the world—its limbs, its ponderous masses, and mighty proportions, raised stage upon stage, and we might be said to have passed into an unknown sphere, and beyond mortal limits. As we rode down our winding, circuitous path, our baggage, (which had been taken off) moved on before us; a grey horse that had got loose from the stable followed it, and as we whirled round the different turnings in this rapid, mechanical flight, at the same rate and the same distance from each other, there seemed something like witchcraft in the scene and in our progress through it. The moon had risen, and threw its gleams across the fading twilight; the snowy tops of the mountains were blended with the clouds and stars; their sides were shrouded in mysterious gloom, and it was not till we entered Susa, with its fine old drawbridge and castellated walls, that we found ourselves on *terra firma*, or breathed common air again.   At the inn at Susa, we first perceived the difference of Italian manners; and the next day arrived at Turin, after passing over thirty miles of the straightest, flattest, and dullest road in the world. Here we stopped two days to recruit our strength and look about us.

ON THE PLEASURE OF HATING

(WRITTEN ABOUT 1826)

THERE is a spider crawling along the matted floor of the room where I sit (not the one which has been so well allegorised in the admirable *Lines to a Spider*, but another of the same edifying breed); he runs with heedless, hurried haste, he hobbles awkwardly towards me, he stops —he sees the giant shadow before him, and, at a loss whether to retreat or proceed, meditates his huge foe—but as I do not start up and seize upon the straggling caitiff, as he would upon a hapless fly within his toils, he takes heart, and ventures on with mingled cunning, impudence, and fear. As he passes me, I lift up the matting to assist his escape, am glad to get rid of the unwelcome intruder, and shudder at the recollection after he is gone. A child, a woman, a clown, or a moralist a century ago, would have crushed the little reptile to death—my philosophy has got beyond that—I bear the creature no ill-will, but still I

hate the very sight of it. The spirit of malevolence
survives the practical exertion of it. We learn to curb
our will and keep our overt actions within the bounds of
humanity, long before we can subdue our sentiments and
imaginations to the same mild tone. We give up the
external demonstration, the *brute* violence, but cannot part
with the essence or principle of hostility. We do not
tread upon the poor little animal in question (that seems
barbarous and pitiful!) but we regard it with a sort of
mystic horror and superstitious loathing. It will ask
another hundred years of fine writing and hard thinking
to cure us of the prejudice, and make us feel towards this
ill-omened tribe with something of " the milk of human
kindness," instead of their own shyness and venom.

Nature seems (the more we look into it) made up of
antipathies: without something to hate, we should lose
the very spring of thought and action. Life would turn
to a stagnant pool, were it not ruffled by the jarring
interests, the unruly passions, of men. The white streak
in our own fortunes is brightened (or just rendered visible)
by making all around it as dark as possible; so the rainbow paints its form upon the cloud. Is it pride? Is it
envy? Is it the force of contrast? Is it weakness or
malice? But so it is, that there is a secret affinity [with], a
hankering after, evil in the human mind, and that it takes
a perverse, but a fortunate delight in mischief, since it is
a never-failing source of satisfaction. Pure good soon
grows insipid, wants variety and spirit. Pain is a bitter-
sweet, which never surfeits. Love turns, with a little
indulgence, to indifference or disgust: hatred alone is
immortal. Do we not see this principle at work everywhere? Animals torment and worry one another without
mercy: children kill flies for sport: every one reads the
accidents and offences in a newspaper as the cream of the
jest: a whole town runs to be present at a fire, and the
spectator by no means exults to see it extinguished. It is

better to have it so, but it diminishes the interest; and
our feelings take part with our passions rather than with
our understandings. Men assemble in crowds, with eager
enthusiasm, to witness a tragedy: but if there were an
execution going forward in the next street, as Mr. Burke
observes, the theatre would be left empty. A strange cur
in a village, an idiot, a crazy woman, are set upon and
baited by the whole community. Public nuisances are in
the nature of public benefits. How long did the Pope,
the Bourbons, and the Inquisition keep the people of
England in breath, and supply them with nicknames to
vent their spleen upon! Had they done us any harm of
late? No: but we have always a quantity of superfluous
bile upon the stomach, and we wanted an object to let it
out upon. How loth were we to give up our pious belief
in ghosts and witches, because we liked to persecute the
one, and frighten ourselves to death with the other! It
is not the quality so much as the quantity of excitement
that we are anxious about: we cannot bear a state of
indifference and *ennui :* the mind seems to abhor a *vacuum*
as much as ever nature[1] was supposed to do. Even
when the spirit of the age (that is, the progress of intellectual refinement, warring with our natural infirmities)
no longer allows us to carry our vindictive and headstrong humours into effect, we try to revive them in
description, and keep up the old bugbears, the phantoms
of our terror and our hate, in imagination. We burn
Guy Fawx in effigy, and the hooting and buffeting and
maltreating that poor tattered figure of rags and straw
makes a festival in every village in England once a year.
Protestants and Papists do not now burn one another at
the stake: but we subscribe to new editions of Fox's
Book of Martyrs ; and the secret of the success of the
Scotch Novels is much the same—they carry us back to
the feuds, the heart-burnings, the havoc, the dismay, the

---

[1] The orig. edit. reads *matter.*—W. C. H.

wrongs, and the revenge of a barbarous age and people—
to the rooted prejudices and deadly animosities of sects
and parties in politics and religion, and of contending
chiefs and clans in war and intrigue. We feel the full
force of the spirit of hatred with all of them in turn. As
we read, we throw aside the trammels of civilization, the
flimsy veil of humanity. " Off, you lendings! " The wild
beast resumes its sway within us, we feel like hunting-
animals, and as the hound starts in his sleep and rushes
on the chase in fancy, the heart rouses itself in its native
lair, and utters a wild cry of joy, at being restored once
more to freedom and lawless, unrestrained impulses.
Every one has his full swing, or goes to the Devil his own
way. Here are no Jeremy Bentham Panopticons, none
of Mr. Owen's impassable Parallelograms (Rob Roy would
have spurned and poured a thousand curses on them),
no long calculations of self-interest—the will takes its
instant way to its object, as the mountain-torrent flings
itself over the precipice: the greatest possible good of
each individual consists in doing all the mischief he can
to his neighbour: that is charming, and finds a sure
and sympathetic chord in every breast! So Mr. Irving,
the celebrated preacher, has rekindled the old, original,
almost exploded hell-fire in the aisles of the Caledonian
Chapel, as they introduce the real water of the New River
at Sadler's Wells, to the delight and astonishment of his
fair audience. '*Tis pretty, though a plague*, to sit and peep
into the pit of Tophet, to play at *snap-dragon* with flames
and brimstone (it gives a smart electrical shock, a lively
filip to delicate constitutions), and to see Mr. Irving,
like a huge Titan, looking as grim and swarthy as if
he had to forge tortures for all the damned! What a
strange being man is! Not content with doing all he can
to vex and hurt his fellows here, " upon this bank and
shoal of time," where one would think there were heart-
aches, pain, disappointment, anguish, tears, sighs, and

groans enough, the bigoted maniac takes him to the top of the high peak of school divinity to hurl him down the yawning gulf of penal fire; his speculative malice asks eternity to wreak its infinite spite in, and calls on the Almighty to execute its relentless doom! The cannibals burn their enemies and eat them in good-fellowship with one another: meek Christian divines cast those who differ from them but a hair's-breadth, body and soul into hell-fire for the glory of God and the good of His creatures! It is well that the power of such persons is not co-ordinate with their wills: indeed, it is from the sense of their weakness and inability to control the opinions of others, that they thus " outdo termagant," and endeavour to frighten them into conformity by big words and monstrous denunciations.

The pleasure of hating, like a poisonous mineral, eats into the heart of religion, and turns it to rankling spleen and bigotry; it makes patriotism an excuse for carrying fire, pestilence, and famine into other lands: it leaves to virtue nothing but the spirit of censoriousness, and a narrow, jealous, inquisitorial watchfulness over the actions and motives of others. What have the different sects, creeds, doctrines in religion been but so many pretexts set up for men to wrangle, to quarrel, to tear one another in pieces about, like a target as a mark to shoot at? Does any one suppose that the love of country in an Englishman implies any friendly feeling or disposition to serve another bearing the same name? No, it means only hatred to the French or the inhabitants of any other country that we happen to be at war with for the time. Does the love of virtue denote any wish to discover or amend our own faults? No, but it atones for an obstinate adherence to our own vices by the most virulent intolerance to human frailties. This principle is of a most universal application. It extends to good as well as evil: if it makes us hate folly, it makes us no less dissatisfied with distinguished merit. If it inclines us to resent the wrongs of others, it impels us to be as impatient of their prosperity. We revenge injuries: we repay benefits with ingratitude. Even our strongest partialities and likings soon take this turn. " That which was luscious as locusts, anon becomes bitter as coloquintida; " and love and friendship melt in their own fires. We hate old friends: we hate old books: we hate old opinions; and at last we come to hate ourselves.

I have observed that few of those whom I have formerly known most intimate, continue on the same friendly footing, or combine the steadiness with the warmth of attachment. I have been acquainted with two or three knots of inseparable companions, who saw each other " six days in the week," that have broken up and dispersed. I have quarrelled with almost all my old friends, (they might say this is owing to my bad temper, but) they have also quarrelled with one another. What is become of " that set of whist-players," celebrated by ELIA in his notable *Epistle to Robert Southey, Esq.*[1] (and now I think of it—that I myself have celebrated in this very volume)[2] " that for so many years called Admiral Burney friend? " They are scattered, like last year's snow. Some of them are dead, or gone to live at a distance, or pass one another in the street like strangers, or if they stop to speak, do it as coolly and try to *cut* one another as soon as possible. Some of us have grown rich, others poor. Some have got places under Government, others a *niche* in the *Quarterly Review*. Some of us have dearly earned a name in the world; whilst others remain in their original privacy. We despise the one, and envy and are glad to mortify the other. Times are changed; we cannot revive our old feelings; and we avoid the sight,

---

[1] In the *London Magazine* for October, 1823.—W. C. H.

[2] *The Plain Speaker*, essay " On the Conversation of Authors." [Ed.]

and are uneasy in the presence of, those who remind us of our infirmity, and put us upon an effort at seeming cordiality which embarrasses ourselves, and does not impose upon our *quondam* associates. Old friendships are like meats served up repeatedly, cold, comfortless, and distasteful. The stomach turns against them. Either constant intercourse and familiarity breed weariness and contempt; or, if we meet again after an interval of absence, we appear no longer the same. One is too wise, another too foolish, for us; and we wonder we did not find this out before. We are disconcerted and kept in a state of continual alarm by the wit of one, or tired to death of the dullness of another. The *good things* of the first (besides leaving stings behind them) by repetition grow stale, and lose their startling effect; and the insipidity of the last becomes intolerable. The most amusing or instructive companion is at best like a favourite volume, that we wish after a time to *lay upon the shelf ;* but as our friends are not willing to be laid there, this produces a misunderstanding and ill-blood between us. Or if the zeal and integrity of friendship is not abated, [n]or its career interrupted by any obstacle arising out of its own nature, we look out for other subjects of complaint and sources of dissatisfaction. We begin to criticize each other's dress, looks, and general character. " Such a one is a pleasant fellow, but it is a pity he sits so late ! " Another fails to keep his appointments, and that is a sore that never heals. We get acquainted with some fashionable young men or with a mistress, and wish to introduce our friend; but he is awkward and a sloven, the interview does not answer, and this throws cold water on our intercourse. Or he makes himself obnoxious to opinion; and we shrink from our own convictions on the subject as an excuse for not defending him. All or any of these causes mount up in time to a ground of coolness or irritation; and at last they break out into open violence as the only amends we can make ourselves for suppressing them so long, or the readiest means of banishing recollections of former kindness so little compatible with our present feelings. We may try to tamper with the wounds or patch up the carcase of departed friendship; but the one will hardly bear the handling, and the other is not worth the trouble of embalming! The only way to be reconciled to old friends is to part with them for good: at a distance we may chance to be thrown back (in a waking dream) upon old times and old feelings: or at any rate we should not think of renewing our intimacy, till we have fairly *spit our spite*, or said, thought, and felt all the ill we can of each other. Or if we can pick a quarrel with some one else, and make him the scape-goat, this is an excellent contrivance to heal a broken bone. I think I must be friends with Lamb again, since he has written that magnanimous Letter to Southey, and told him a piece of his mind! I don't know what it is that attaches me to H——[1] so much, except that he and I, whenever we meet, sit in judgment on another set of old friends, and " carve them as a dish fit for the Gods." There was L[eigh] [Hunt], John Scott, Mrs. [Montagu], whose dark raven locks make a picturesque background to our discourse, B——,[2] who is grown fat, and is, they say, married, R[ickman]; these had all separated long ago, and their foibles are the common link that holds us together. We do not affect to condole or whine over their follies; we enjoy, we laugh at them, till we are ready to burst our sides, " *sans* intermission, for hours by the dial." We serve up a course of anecdotes, *traits*, master-strokes of character, and cut and hack at them till we are weary. Perhaps some of them are even with us. For my own part, as I once said, I like a friend the better for having faults that one can talk about.

[1] W. C. Hazlitt suggests that this initial stands for Joseph Hume, but more probably it is for B. R. Haydon. [Ed.]

[2] Query. Martin Burney.—W. C. H.

" Then," said Mrs. [Montagu], " you will never cease to be a philanthropist! " Those in question were some of the choice-spirits of the age, not " fellows of no mark or likelihood "; and we so far did them justice: but it is well they did not hear what we sometimes said of them. I care little what any one says of me, particularly behind my back, and in the way of critical and analytical discussion: it is looks of dislike and scorn that I answer with the worst venom of my pen. The expression of the face wounds me more than the expressions of the tongue. If I have in one instance mistaken this expression, or resorted to this remedy where I ought not, I am sorry for it. But the face was too fine over which it mantled, and I am too old to have misunderstood it! . . . I sometimes go up to ——'s;[1] and as often as I do, resolve never to go again. I do not find the old homely welcome. The ghost of friendship meets me at the door, and sits with me all dinner-time. They have got a set of fine notions and new acquaintance. Allusions to past occurrences are thought trivial, nor is it always safe to touch upon more general subjects. M. does not begin as he formerly did every five minutes, " Fawcett used to say," &c. That topic is something worn. The girls are grown up, and have a thousand accomplishments. I perceive there is a jealousy on both sides. They think I give myself airs, and I fancy the same of them. Every time I am asked, " If I do not think Mr. Washington Irving a very fine writer? " I shall not go again till I receive an invitation for Christmas Day in company with Mr. Liston. The only intimacy I never found to flinch or fade was a purely intellectual one. There was none of the cant of candour in it, none of the whine of mawkish sensibility. Our mutual acquaintance were considered merely as subjects of conversation and knowledge, not at all of affection. We regarded them no

[1] W. C. Hazlitt again suggests Hume's name for this space, though the initial *M.* occurs below. [Ed.]

more in our experiments than " mice in an air-pump: "
or like malefactors, they were regularly cut down and
given over to the dissecting-knife. We spared neither
friend nor foe. We sacrificed human infirmities at the
shrine of truth. The skeletons of character might be seen,
after the juice was extracted, dangling in the air like flies
in cobwebs: or they were kept for future inspection in
some refined acid. The demonstration was as beautiful as
it was new. There is no surfeiting on gall: nothing keeps
so well as a decoction of spleen. We grow tired of every
thing but turning others into ridicule, and congratulating
ourselves on their defects.

We take a dislike to our favourite books, after a time,
for the same reason. We cannot read the same works for
ever. Our honey-moon, even though we wed the Muse,
must come to an end; and is followed by indifference, if
not by disgust. There are some works, those indeed that
produce the most striking effect at first by novelty and
boldness of outline, that will not bear reading twice:
others of a less extravagant character, and that excite and
repay attention by a greater nicety of details, have hardly
interest enough to keep alive our continued enthusiasm.
The popularity of the most successful writers operates to
wean us from them, by the cant and fuss that is made
about them, by hearing their names everlastingly repeated, and by the number of ignorant and indiscriminate
admirers they draw after them:—we as little like to have
to drag others from their unmerited obscurity, lest we
should be exposed to the charge of affectation and singularity of taste. There is nothing to be said respecting an
author that all the world have made up their minds about:
it is a thankless as well as hopeless task to recommend one
that nobody has ever heard of. To cry up Shakespear
as the god of our idolatry, seems like a vulgar national
prejudice: to take down a volume of Chaucer, or Spenser,
or Beaumont and Fletcher, or Ford, or Marlowe, has very

much the look of pedantry and egotism. I confess it
makes me hate the very name of Fame and Genius, when
works like these are " gone into the wastes of time," while
each successive generation of fools is busily employed in
reading the trash of the day, and women of fashion gravely
join with their waiting-maids in discussing the preference
between the *Paradise Lost* and Mr. Moore's *Loves of the
Angels*. I was pleased the other day on going into a shop
to ask, " If they had any of the *Scotch Novels* ? " to be
told—" That they had just sent out the last, *Sir Andrew
Wylie !* "—Mr. Galt will also be pleased with this answer!
The reputation of some books is raw and *unaired :* that
of others is worm-eaten and mouldy. Why fix our affections on that which we cannot bring ourselves to have
faith in, or which others have long ceased to trouble themselves about? I am half afraid to look into *Tom Jones*, lest
it should not answer my expectations at this time of day;
and if it did not, I should certainly be disposed to fling it
into the fire, and never look into another novel while I
lived. But surely, it may be said, there are some works
that, like nature, can never grow old; and that must
always touch the imagination and passions alike! Or
there are passages that seem as if we might brood over
them all our lives, and not exhaust the sentiments of love
and admiration they excite: they become favourites, and
we are fond of them to a sort of dotage. Here is one:

> ——" Sitting in my window
> Printing my thoughts in lawn, I saw a god,
> I thought (but it was you), enter our gates ;
> My blood flew out and back again, as fast
> As I had puffed it forth and sucked it in
> Like breath ; then was I called away in haste
> To entertain you : never was a man
> Thrust from a sheepcote to a sceptre, raised
> So high in thoughts as I ; you left a kiss
> Upon these lips then, which I mean to keep
> From you for ever. I did hear you talk
> Far above singing ! "

A passage like this, indeed, leaves a taste on the palate like nectar, and we seem in reading it to sit with the Gods at their golden tables: but if we repeat it often in ordinary moods, it loses its flavour, becomes vapid, " the wine of *poetry* is drank, and but the lees remain." Or, on the other hand, if we call in the aid of extraordinary circumstances to set it off to advantage, as the reciting it to a friend, or after having our feelings excited by a long walk in some romantic situation, or while we

> ——" play with Amaryllis in the shade,
> Or with the tangles of Neæra's hair "—

we afterwards miss the accompanying circumstances, and instead of transferring the recollection of them to the favourable side, regret what we have lost, and strive in vain to bring back " the irrevocable hour "—wondering in some instances how we survive it, and at the melancholy blank that is left behind! The pleasure rises to its height in some moment of calm solitude or intoxicating sympathy, declines ever after, and from the comparison and a conscious falling-off, leaves rather a sense of satiety and irksomeness behind it. . . . " Is it the same in pictures? " I confess it is, with all but those from Titian's hand. I don't know why, but an air breathes from his landscapes, pure, refreshing, as if it came from other years; there is a look in his faces that never passes away. I saw one the other day. Amidst the heartless desolation and glittering finery of Fonthill, there is a portfolio of the Dresden Gallery. It opens, and a young female head looks from it; a child, yet woman grown; with an air of rustic innocence and the graces of a princess, her eyes like those of doves, the lips about to open, a smile of pleasure dimpling the whole face, the jewels sparkling in her crisped hair, her youthful shape compressed in a rich antique dress, as the bursting leaves contain the April buds! Why do I not call up this image of gentle sweetness, and place it as a perpetual barrier between mischance and me?—It is because pleasure asks a greater effort of the mind to support it than pain; and we turn after a little idle dalliance from what we love to what we hate!

As to my old opinions, I am heartily sick of them. I have reason, for they have deceived me sadly. I was taught to think, and I was willing to believe, that genius was not a bawd, that virtue was not a mask, that liberty was not a name, that love had its seat in the human heart. Now I would care little if these words were struck out of the dictionary, or if I had never heard them. They are become to my ears a mockery and a dream. Instead of patriots and friends of freedom, I see nothing but the tyrant and the slave, the people linked with kings to rivet on the chains of despotism and superstition. I see folly join with knavery, and together make up public spirit and public opinions. I see the insolent Tory, the blind Reformer, the coward Whig! If mankind had wished for what is right, they might have had it long ago. The theory is plain enough; but they are prone to mischief, "to every good work reprobate." I have seen all that had been done by the mighty yearnings of the spirit and intellect of men, "of whom the world was not worthy," and that promised a proud opening to truth and good through the vista of future years, undone by one man, with just glimmering of understanding enough to feel that he was a king, but not to comprehend how he could be king of a free people! I have seen this triumph celebrated by poets, the friends of my youth and the friends of man, but who were carried away by the infuriate tide that, setting in from a throne, bore down every distinction of right reason before it; and I have seen all those who did not join in applauding this insult and outrage on humanity proscribed, hunted down (they and their friends made a byword of), so that it has become an understood thing that no one can live by his talents or knowledge who is

not ready to prostitute those talents and that knowledge
to betray his species, and prey upon his fellow-man.
" This was some time a mystery: but the time gives
evidence of it." The echoes of liberty had awakened once
more in Spain, and the morning of human hope dawned
again: but that dawn has been overcast by the foul breath of
bigotry, and those reviving sounds stifled by fresh cries
from the time-rent towers of the Inquisition—man yielding
(as it is fit he should) first to brute force, but more to the
innate perversity and dastard spirit of his own nature
which leaves no room for farther hope or disappointment.
And England, that arch-reformer, that heroic deliverer,
that mouther about liberty, and tool of power, stands
gaping by, not feeling the blight and mildew coming over
it, nor its very bones crack and turn to a paste under the
grasp and circling folds of this new monster, Legitimacy!
In private life do we not see hypocrisy, servility, selfishness, folly, and impudence succeed, while modesty shrinks
from the encounter, and merit is trodden under foot?
How often is " the rose plucked from the forehead of a
virtuous love to plant a blister there!" What chance is
there of the success of real passion? What certainty of
its continuance? Seeing all this as I do, and unravelling
the web of human life into its various threads of meanness, spite, cowardice, want of feeling, and want of understanding, of indifference towards others, and ignorance of
ourselves—seeing custom prevail over all excellence, itself
giving way to infamy—mistaken as I have been in my
public and private hopes, calculating others from myself,
and calculating wrong; always disappointed where I
placed most reliance; the dupe of friendship, and the fool
of love;—have I not reason to hate and to despise myself?
Indeed I do; and chiefly for not having hated and despised
the world enough.[1]

[1] The only exception to the general drift of this Essay (and
that is an exception in theory—I know of none in practice)

HOT AND COLD

(W R I T T E N   A B O U T   1 8 2 6)

——" Hot, cold, moist, and dry, four champions
  fierce,
Strive here for mastery."—MILTON.

" T H E Protestants are much cleaner than the Catholics,"
said a shopkeeper of Vevey to me. " They are so," I
replied; " but why should they? " A prejudice appeared
to him a matter-of-fact, and he did not think it necessary
to assign reasons for a matter-of-fact. That is not my
way. He had not bottomed his proposition on proofs,
nor rightly defined it.

Nearly the same remark, as to the extreme cleanliness
of the people in this part of the country, had occurred to
me as soon as I got to Brigg, where, however, the inhabitants are Catholics. So the original statement requires

is, that in reading we always take the right side, and make the
case properly our own. Our imaginations are sufficiently
excited, we have nothing to do with the matter but as a pure
creation of the mind, and we therefore yield to the natural,
unwarped impression of good and evil. Our own passions,
interests, and prejudices out of the question, or in an abstracted
point of view, we judge fairly and conscientiously ; for conscience is nothing but the abstract idea of right and wrong.
But no sooner have we to act or suffer, than the spirit of contradiction or some other demon comes into play, and there is
an end of common sense and reason. Even the very strength
of the speculative faculty, or the desire to square things
with an *ideal* standard of perfection (whether we can or no)
leads perhaps to half the absurdities and miseries of mankind.
We are hunting after what we cannot find, and quarrelling with
the good within our reach. Among the thousands that have
read *The Heart of Midlothian* there assuredly never was a single
person who did not wish Jeanie Deans success. Even Gentle
George was sorry for what he had done, when it was over,
though he would have played the same prank the next day :
and the *unknown* author, in his immediate character of contri-
butor to *Blackwood* and the *Sentinel*, is about as respectable
a personage as Daddy Ratton himself. On the stage, every one
takes part with Othello against Iago. Do boys at school, in
reading Homer, generally side with the Greeks or Trojans ?

some qualification as to the mode of enunciation. I had no sooner arrived in this village, which is situated just under the Simplon, and where you are surrounded with *glaciers* and *goitres*, than the genius of the place struck me on looking out at the pump under my window the next morning, where the " neat-handed Phyllises " were washing their greens in the water, that not a caterpillar could crawl on them, and scouring their pails and tubs that not a stain should be left in them. The raw, clammy feeling of the air was in unison with the scene. I had not seen such a thing in Italy. They have there no delight in splashing and dabbling in fresh streams and fountains— they have a dread of ablutions and abstersions, almost amounting to *hydrophobia*. Heat has an antipathy in nature to cold. The sanguine Italian is chilled and shudders at the touch of cold water, while the Helvetian boor, whose humours creep through his veins like the dank mists along the sides of his frozen mountains, is " native and endued unto that element." Here everything is purified and filtered: there it is baked and burnt up, and sticks together in a most amicable union of filth and laziness. There is a little mystery and a little contradiction in the case—let us try if we cannot get rid of both by means of caution and daring together. It is not that the difference of latitude between one side of the Alps and the other can signify much: but the phlegmatic blood of their German ancestors is poured down the valleys of the Swiss like water, and *iced* in its progress; whereas that of the Italians, besides its vigorous origin, is enriched and ripened by basking in more genial plains. A single Milanese market-girl (to go no farther south) appeared to me to have more blood in her body, more fire in her eye (as if the sun had made a burning *lens* of it), more spirit, and probably more mischief about her than all the nice, *tidy*, good-looking, hard-working girls I have seen in Switzerland. To turn this physiognomical observation to a metaphysical account, I should say, then, that Northern people are clean and Southern people are dirty as a general rule, because where the principle of life is more cold, weak, and impoverished, there is a greater shyness and aversion to come in contact with external matter (with which it does not so easily amalgamate), a greater fastidiousness and delicacy in choosing its sensations, a greater desire to know surrounding objects and to keep them clear of each other, than where this principle being more warm and active, it may be supposed to absorb outward impressions in itself, to melt them into its own essence, to impart its own vital impulses to them, and in fine, instead of shrinking from everything, to be shocked at nothing. The Southern temperament is (so to speak) more sociable with matter, more gross, impure, indifferent, from relying on its own strength; while that opposed to it, from being less able to react on external applications, is obliged to be more cautious and particular as to the kind of excitement to which it renders itself liable. Hence the timidity, reserve, and occasional hypocrisy of Northern manners; the boldness, freedom, levity, and frequent licentiousness of Southern ones. It would be too much to say, that if there is anything of which a genuine Italian has a horror, it is of cleanliness; or that if there is anything which seems ridiculous to a thorough-bred Italian woman, it is modesty: but certainly the degree to which nicety is carried by some people is a *bore* to an Italian imagination, as the excess of delicacy which is pretended or practised by some women is quite incomprehensible to the females of the South. It is wrong, however, to make the greater confidence or forwardness of manners an absolute test of morals: the love of virtue is a different thing from the fear or even hatred of vice. The squeamishness and prudery in the one case have a more plausible appearance; but it does not follow that there may not be more native goodness and even habitual refinement in the other, though accompanied with stronger nerves and a less morbid imagination. But to return to the first question.[1] —I can readily understand how a Swiss peasant should stand a whole morning at a pump, washing cabbages, cauliflowers, salads, and getting rid half a dozen times over of the sand, dirt, and insects they contain, because I myself should not only be *gravelled* by meeting with the one at table, but should be in horrors at the other. A Frenchman or an Italian would be thrown into convulsions of laughter at this superfluous delicacy, and would think his repast enriched or none the worse for such additions. The reluctance to prey on life, or on what once had it, seems to arise from a sense of incongruity, from the repugnance between life and death—from the cold, clammy feeling which belongs to the one, and which is enhanced by the contrast to its former warm, lively state, and by the circumstance of its being taken into the mouth, and devoured as food. Hence the desire to get rid of the idea of the living animal even in ordinary cases by all the disguises of cookery, of boiled and roast, and by the artifice of changing the name of the animal into something different when it becomes food.[2] Hence sportsmen are not devourers of game, and hence the aversion to kill

---

[1] Women abroad (generally speaking) are more like men in the tone of their conversation and habits of thinking, so that from the same premises you cannot draw the same conclusions as in England.

[2] This circumstance is noticed in *Ivanhoe*, though a different turn is given to it by the philosopher of Rotherwood.

" Nay, I can tell you more," said Wamba in the same tone ; " there is old Alderman Ox continues to hold his Saxon epithet, while he is under the charge of serfs and bondsmen such as thou ; but becomes Beef, a fiery French gallant, when he arrives before the worshipful jaws that are destined to consume him. Mynheer Calf, too, becomes Monsieur de Veau in like manner : he is Saxon when he requires tendance, and takes a Norman name when he becomes matter of enjoyment."—Vol. I, Chap. I.

the animals we eat.[1] There is a contradiction between
the animate and the inanimate, which is felt as matter of
peculiar annoyance by the more cold and congealed
temperament which cannot so well pass from one to the
other; but this objection is easily swallowed by the
inhabitant of gayer and more luxurious regions, who is so
full of life himself that he can at once impart it to all that
comes in his way, or never troubles himself about the
difference. So the Neapolitan bandit takes the life of his
victim with little remorse, because he has enough and to
spare in himself: his pulse still beats warm and vigorous,
while the blood of a more humane native of the frozen
North would run cold with horror at the sight of the
stiffened corse, and this makes him pause before he stops
in another the gushing source, of which he has such feeble
supplies in himself. The wild Arab of the Desert can
hardly entertain the idea of death, neither dreading it
for himself nor regretting it for others. The Italians,
Spaniards, and people of the South swarm alive without
being sick or sorry at the circumstance: they hunt the
accustomed prey in each other's tangled locks openly in
the streets and on the highways, without manifesting
shame or repugnance: combs are an invention of our
Northern climes. Now I can comprehend this, when I
look at the dirty, dingy, greasy, sun-burnt complexion of
an Italian peasant or beggar, whose body seems alive all
over with a sort of tingling, oily sensation, so that from
any given particle of his shining skin to the beast " whose
name signifies love " the transition is but small. This
populousness is not unaccountable where all teems with
life, where all is glowing and in motion, and every pore
thrills with an exuberance of feeling. Not so in the dearth

---

[1] Hence the peculiar horror of cannibalism from the stronger
sympathy with our own sensations, and the greater violence that
is done to it by the sacrilegious use of what once possessed
human life and feeling.

of life and spirit, in the drossy, dry, material texture, the
clear complexions and fair hair of the Saxon races, where
the puncture of an insect's sting is a solution of their
personal identity, and the idea of life attached to and
courting an intimacy with them in spite of themselves,
naturally produces all the revulsions of the most violent
antipathy and nearly drives them out of their wits. How
well the smooth ivory comb and auburn hair agree—
while the Greek *dandy*, on entering a room, applies his
hand to brush a cloud of busy stragglers from his hair
like powder, and gives himself no more concern about
them than about the motes dancing in the sun-beams!
The dirt of the Italians is as it were baked into them, and
so ingrained as to become a part of themselves, and
occasion no discontinuity of their being.

I can forgive the dirt and sweat of a gipsy under a
hedge, when I consider that the earth is his mother, the
sun is his father. He hunts vermin for food: he is himself
hunted like vermin for prey. His existence is not one of
choice, but of necessity. The hungry Arab devours the
raw shoulder of a horse. This again I can conceive. His
feverish blood seethes it, and the virulence of his own
breath carries off the disagreeableness of the smell. I do
not see that the horse should be reckoned among unclean animals, according to any notions I have of the
matter. The dividing of the hoof or the contrary, I should
think, has not anything to do with the question. I can
understand the distinction between beasts of prey and
the herbivorous and domestic animals, but the horse is
tame. The natural distinction between clean and unclean
animals (which has been sometimes made into a religious
one) I take to depend on two circumstances, viz., the
claws and bristly hide, which generally, though not
always, go together. One would not wish to be torn in
pieces instead of making a comfortable meal, " to be
supped upon " where we thought of supping. With

respect to the wolf, the tiger, and other animals of the
same species, it seems a question which of us should
devour the other: this baulks our appetite by distracting
our attention, and we have so little relish for being eaten
ourselves, or for the fangs and teeth of these shocking
animals, that it gives us a distaste for their whole bodies.
The horror we conceive at preying upon them arises in
part from the fear we had of being preyed upon by them.
No such apprehension crosses the mind with respect to
the deer, the sheep, the hare—" here all is conscience and
tender heart." These gentle creatures (whom we compliment as useful) offer no resistance to the knife, and there
is therefore nothing shocking or repulsive in the idea of
devoting them to it. There is no confusion of ideas, but
a beautiful simplicity and uniformity in our relation to
each other, we as the slayers, they as the slain. A perfect
understanding subsists on the subject. The hair of
animals of prey is also strong and bristly, and forms an
obstacle to our Epicurean designs. The calf or fawn is
sleek and smooth: the bristles on a dog's or a cat's back
are like " the quills upon the fretful porcupine," a very
impracticable repast to the imagination, that stick in the
throat and turn the stomach. Who has not read and been
edified by the account of the supper in *Gil Blas* ? Besides,
there is also in all probability the practical consideration
urged by Voltaire's traveller, who being asked " which
he preferred—black mutton or white? " replied, " Either,
provided it was tender." The greater rankness in the
flesh is, however, accompanied by a corresponding irritability of surface, a tenaciousness, a pruriency, a soreness
to attack, and not that fine, round, pampered passiveness
to impressions which cuts up into handsome joints and
entire pieces without any fidgety process, and with an
obvious view to solid, wholesome nourishment. Swine's
flesh, the abomination of the Jewish law, certainly comes
under the objection here stated; and the bear with its

shaggy fur is only smuggled into the Christian larder as half-brother to the wild boar, and because from its lazy, lumpish character and appearance, it seems matter of indifference whether it eats or is eaten. The horse, with sleek round haunches, is fair game, except from custom; and I think I could survive having swallowed part of an ass's foal without being utterly loathsome to myself.[1] Mites in a rotten cheese are endurable, from being so small and dry that they are scarce distinguishable from the atoms of the cheese itself, " so drossy and divisible are they: " but the Lord deliver me from their more thriving next-door neighbours! Animals that are made use of as food should either be so small as to be imperceptible, or else we should dig into the quarry of life, hew away the masses, and not leave the form standing to reproach us with our gluttony and cruelty. I hate to see a rabbit trussed, or a hare brought to table in the form which it occupied while living: they seem to me apparitions of the burrowers in the earth or the rovers in the wood, sent to scare away appetite. One reason why toads and serpents are disgusting, is from the way in which they run against or suddenly cling to the skin: the encountering them causes a solution of continuity, and we

---

[1] Thomas Cooper of Manchester, the able logician and political partisan, tried the experiment some years ago, when he invited a number of gentlemen and officers quartered in the town to dine with him on an ass's foal instead of a calf's-head, on the anniversary of the 30th of January. The circumstance got wind, and gave great offence. Mr. Cooper had to attend a county-meeting soon after at Boulton-le-Moors, and one of the country magistrates coming to the inn for the same purpose, and when he asked " If any one was in the room ? " receiving for answer—" No one but Mr. Cooper of Manchester "—ordered out his horse and immediately rode home again. Some verses made on the occasion by Mr. Scarlett and Mr. Shepherd of Gateacre explained the story thus—

> " The reason how this came to pass is
> The Justice had heard that Cooper ate asses ! "

shudder to feel a life which is not ours in contact with us. It is this disjointed or imperfect sympathy which in the recoil produces the greatest antipathy. Sterne asks why a sword, which takes away life, may be named without offence, though other things, which contribute to perpetuate it, cannot? Because the idea in the one case is merely painful, and there is no mixture of the agreeable to lead the imagination on to a point from which it must make a precipitate retreat. The morally indecent arises from the doubtful conflict between temptation and duty: the physically revolting is the product of alternate attraction and repulsion, of partial adhesion, or of something that is foreign to us sticking closer to our persons than we could wish. The nastiest tastes and smells are not the most pungent and painful, but a compound of sweet and bitter, of the agreeable and disagreeable; where the sense, having been relaxed and rendered effeminate as it were by the first, is unable to contend with the last, faints and sinks under it, and has no way of relieving itself but by violently throwing off the load that oppresses it. Hence loathing and sickness. But these hardly ever arise without something contradictory or *impure* in the objects, or unless the mind, having been invited and prepared to be gratified at first, this expectation is turned to disappointment and disgust. Mere pains, mere pleasures do not have this effect, save from an excess of the first causing insensibility and then a faintness ensues, or of the last, causing what is called a surfeit. Sea-sickness has some analogy to this. It comes on with that unsettled motion of the ship, which takes away the ordinary footing or firm hold we have of things, and by relaxing our perceptions, unbraces the whole nervous system. The giddiness and swimming of the head on looking down a precipice, when we are ready with every breath of imagination to topple down into the abyss, has its source in the same uncertain and rapid whirl of the fancy through possible extremes.

K

Thus we find that for cases of fainting, sea-sickness, &c., a glass of brandy is recommended as " the sovereign'st thing on earth," because by grappling with the coats of the stomach and bringing our sensations to a *focus*, it does away that nauseous fluctuation and suspense of feeling which is the root of the mischief. I do not know whether I make myself intelligible, for the utmost I can pretend is to suggest some very subtle and remote analogies: but if I have at all succeeded in opening up the train of argument I intend, it will at least be possible to conceive how the sanguine Italian is less nice in his intercourse with material objects, less startled at incongruities, less liable to take offence, than the more literal and conscientious German, because the more headstrong current of his own sensations fills up the gaps and " makes the odds all even." He does not care to have his cabbages and salads washed ten times over, or his beds cleared of vermin: he can lend or borrow satisfaction from all objects indifferently. The air over his head is full of life, of the hum of insects; the grass under his feet rings and is loud with the cry of the grasshopper; innumerable green lizards dart from the rocks and sport before him: what signifies it if any living creature approaches nearer his own person, where all is one vital glow? The Indian even twines the forked serpent round his hand unharmed, copper-coloured like it, his veins as heated; and the Brahmin cherishes life and disregards his own person as an act of his religion— the religion of fire and of the sun! Yet how shall we reconcile to this theory the constant ablutions (five times a day) of the Eastern nations, and the squalid customs of some Northern people, the dirtiness of the Russians and of the Scotch? Superstition may perhaps account for the one, and poverty and barbarism for the other.[1]

---

[1] What a plague Moses had with his Jews to make them " reform and live cleanly ! " To this day (according to a learned traveller) the Jews, wherever scattered, have an aversion to

Laziness has a great deal to do in the question, and this again is owing to a state of feeling sufficient to itself, and rich in enjoyment without the help of action. Clothilde (the finest and darkest of the Gensano girls) fixes herself at her door about noon (when her day's work is done): her smile reflects back the brightness of the sun, she darts upon a little girl with a child in her arms, nearly over-turns both, devours it with kisses, and then resumes her position at the door, with her hands behind her back and her shoes down at heel. This slatternliness and negligence is the more remarkable in so fine a girl, and one whose ordinary costume is a gorgeous picture, but it is a part of the character; her dress would never have been so rich, if she could take more pains about it—they have no nervous or fidgety feeling whether a thing is coming off or not: all their sensations, as it were, sit loose upon them. Their clothes are no part of themselves,—they even fling their limbs about as if they scarcely belonged to them; the heat in summer requires the utmost freedom and airiness (which becomes a habit), and they have nothing tight-bound or straight-laced about their minds or bodies. The same girl in winter (for " dull, cold winter *does* inhabit here " also) would have a *scaldaletto* (an earthen pan with coals in it) dangling at her wrists for four months together, without any sense of incumbrance or distraction, or any other feeling but of the heat it communicated to her hands. She does not mind its chilling the rest of her body or disfiguring her hands, making her fingers look like " long purples "—these children of nature " take the good the Gods provide them," and trouble themselves little about consequences or appearances. Their self-will is much stronger than their vanity—they have as

agriculture and almost to its products ; and a Jewish girl will refuse to accept a flower—if you offer her a piece of money, of jewelry or embroidery, she knows well enough what to make of the proffered courtesy.—See Hacquet's *Travels in Carpathia*, etc.

little curiosity about others as concern for their good
opinion. Two Italian peasants talking by the roadside
will not so much as turn their heads to look at an English
carriage that is passing. They have no interest except in
what is personal, sensual. Hence they have as little
tenaciousness on the score of property as in the acquisition
of ideas. They want neither. Their good spirits are
food, clothing, and books to them. They are fond of
comfort too, but their notion of it differs from ours—ours
consists in accumulating the means of enjoyment, theirs
is being free to enjoy, in the dear *far niente*. What need
have they to encumber themselves with furniture or
wealth or business, when all they require (for the most
part) is air, a bunch of grapes, bread, and stone-walls?
The Italians, generally speaking, have nothing, do nothing, want nothing,—to the surprise of foreigners, who
ask how they live? The men are too lazy to be thieves,
the women to be something else. The dependence of the
Swiss and English on their comforts, that is, on all
" appliances and means to boot," as helps to enjoyment or
hindrances to annoyance, makes them not only eager to
procure different objects of accommodation and luxury,
but makes them take such pains in their preservation and
embellishment, and *pet* them so when acquired. " A man,"
says Yorick, " finds an apple, spits upon it, and calls it
his." The more any one finds himself clinging to material
objects for existence or gratification, the more he will take
a personal interest in them, and the more will he clean,
repair, polish, scrub, scour, and tug at them without end,
as if it were his own soul that he was keeping clear from
spot or blemish. A Swiss dairy-maid scours the very heart
out of a wooden pail; a scullion washes the taste as well as
the worms out of a dish of brocoli. The wenches are in
like manner neat and clean in their own persons, but
insipid. The most coarse and ordinary furniture in
Switzerland has more pains bestowed upon it to keep it

in order than the finest works of art in Italy. There the
pictures are suffered to moulder on the walls; and the
Claudes in the Doria Palace at Rome are black with age
and dirt. We set more store by them in England, where
we have scarce any other sunshine! At the common inns
on this side the Simplon, the very sheets have a character
for whiteness to lose: the rods and testers of the beds are
like a peeled wand. On the opposite side you are thankful
when you are not shewn into an apartment resembling
a three-stalled stable, with horse-cloths for coverlids to
hide the dirt, and beds of horse-hair or withered leaves as
harbourage for vermin. The more, the merrier; the
dirtier, the warmer; live and let live, seem maxims
inculcated by the climate. Wherever things are not kept
carefully apart from foreign admixtures and contamination, the distinctions of property itself will not, I conceive,
be held exceedingly sacred. This feeling is strong as the
passions are weak. A people that are remarkable for cleanliness, will be so for industry, for honesty, for avarice,
and *vice versa*. The Italians cheat, steal, rob (when they
think it worth their while to do so) with licensed impunity: the Swiss, who feel the value of property, and
labour incessantly to acquire it, are afraid to lose it. At
Brigg I first heard the cry of watchmen at night, which
I had not heard for many months. I was reminded of
the traveller who after wandering in remote countries saw
a gallows near at hand, and knew by this circumstance
that he approached the confines of civilization. The
police in Italy is both secret and severe, but it is directed
chiefly to political and not to civil matters. Patriot sighs
are heaved unheard in the dungeons of St. Angelo:
the Neapolitan bandit breathes the free air of his native
mountains!

It may by this time be conjectured why Catholics are
less cleanly than Protestants, because in fact they are less
scrupulous, and swallow whatever is set before them in

matters of faith as well as other things. Protestants, as such, are captious and scrutinizing, try to pick holes and find fault,—have a dry, meagre, penurious imagination. Catholics are buoyed up over doubts and difficulties by a greater redundance of fancy, and make religion sub-servient to a sense of enjoyment. The one are for detect-ing and weeding out all corruptions and abuses in doctrine or worship: the others enrich theirs with the dust and cobwebs of antiquity, and think their ritual none the worse for the tarnish of age. Those of the Catholic Com-munion are willing to take it for granted that everything is right; the professors of the Reformed religion have a pleasure in believing that everything is wrong, in order that they may have to set it right. In morals, again, Protestants are more precise than their Catholic brethren. The creed of the latter absolves them of half their duties, of all those that are a clog on their inclinations, atones for all slips, and patches up all deficiencies. But though this may make them less censorious and sour, I am not sure that it renders them less in earnest in the part they do perform. When more is left to freedom of choice, perhaps the service that is voluntary will be purer and more effectual. That which is not so may as well be done by proxy; or if it does not come from the heart, may be suffered to exhale merely from the lips. If less is owing in this case to a dread of vice and fear of shame, more will proceed from a love of virtue, free from the least sinister construction. It is asserted that Italian women are more gross; I can believe it, and that they are at the same time more refined than others. Their religion is in the same manner more sensual: but is it not to the full as visionary and imaginative as any? I have heard Italian women say things that others would not—it does not therefore follow that they would do them: partly because the knowledge of vice that makes it familiar renders it indifferent; and because the same masculine tone of thinking that enables them to confront vice, may raise them above it into a higher sphere of sentiment. If their senses are more inflammable, their passions (and their love of virtue and of religion among the rest) may glow with proportionable ardour. Indeed the truest virtue is that which is least susceptible of contamination from its opposite. I may admire a Raphael, and yet not swoon at sight of a daub. Why should there not be the same taste in morals as in pictures or poems? Granting that vice has more votaries here, at least it has fewer mercenary ones, and this is no trifling advantage. As to manners, the Catholics must be allowed to carry it all over the world. The better sort not only say nothing to give you pain; they say nothing of others that it would give them pain to hear repeated. Scandal and tittle-tattle are long banished from good society. After all, to be wise is to be humane. What would our English *blue-stockings* say to this? The fault and the excellence of Italian society is, that the shocking or disagreeable is not supposed to have an existence in the nature of things.[1]

ON DEPTH AND SUPERFICIALITY

(WRITTEN ABOUT 1826)

I WISH to make this Essay a sort of study of the meaning of several words, which have at different times a good deal puzzled me. Among these are the words, *wicked*,

---

[1] The dirt and comparative want of conveniences among Catholics is often attributed to the number of their Saints' days and festivals, which divert them from labour, and give them an idle and disorderly turn of mind.

false, and *true,* as applied to feeling; and lastly, *depth* and *shallowness.* It may amuse the reader to see the way in which I work out some of my conclusions underground, before throwing them up on the surface.

A great but useless thinker[1] once asked me, if I had ever known a child of a naturally wicked disposition? and I answered, " Yes, that there was one in the house with me that cried from morning to night, *for spite.*" I was laughed at for this answer, but still I do not repent it. It appeared to me that this child took a delight in tormenting itself and others; that the love of tyrannising over others and subjecting them to its caprices was a full compensation for the beating it received, that the screams it uttered soothed its peevish, turbulent spirit, and that it had a positive pleasure in pain from the sense of power accompanying it. *His principiis nascuntur tyranni, his carnifex animus.* I was supposed to magnify and over-rate the symptoms of the disease, and to make a childish humour into a bugbear; but, indeed, I have no other idea of what is commonly understood by wickedness than that perversion of the will or love of mischief for its own sake, which constantly displays itself (though in trifles and on a ludicrously small scale) in early childhood. I have often been reproached with extravagance for considering things only in their abstract principles, and with heat and ill-temper, for getting into a passion about what no ways concerned me. If any one wishes to see me quite calm, they may cheat me in a bargain, or tread upon my toes; but a truth repelled, a sophism repeated, totally disconcerts me, and I lose all patience. I am not, in the ordinary acceptation of the term, *a good-natured man ;* that is, many things annoy me besides what interferes with my own ease and interest. I hate a lie; a piece of injustice wounds me to the quick, though nothing but the report of it reach me. Therefore I have made many

[1] Coleridge.—W. C. H.

enemies and few friends; for the public know nothing of well-wishers, and keep a wary eye on those that would reform them. Coleridge used to complain of my irascibility in this respect, and not without reason. Would that he had possessed a little of my tenaciousness and jealousy of temper; and then, with his eloquence to paint the wrong, and acuteness to detect it, his country and the cause of liberty might not have fallen without a struggle! The craniologists give me *the organ of local memory*, of which faculty I have not a particle, though they may say that my frequent allusions to conversations that occurred many years ago prove the contrary. I once spent a whole evening with Dr. Spurzheim, and I utterly forgot all that passed, except that the Doctor *waltzed* before we parted! The only faculty I do possess is that of a certain morbid interest in things, which makes me equally remember or anticipate by nervous analogy whatever touches it; and for this our nostrum-mongers have no specific organ, so that I am quite left out of their system. No wonder that I should pick a quarrel with it! It vexes me beyond all bearing to see children kill flies for sport; for the principle is the same as in the most deliberate and profligate acts of cruelty they can afterwards exercise upon their fellow-creatures. And yet I let moths burn themselves to death in the candle, for it makes me mad; and I say it is in vain to prevent fools from rushing upon destruction. The author of the *Rime of the Ancient Mariner* (who sees farther into such things than most people) could not understand why I should bring a charge of *wickedness* against an infant before it could speak, merely for squalling and straining its lungs a little. If the child had been in pain or in fear, I should have said nothing, but it cried only to vent its passion and alarm the house, and I saw in its frantic screams and gestures that great baby, the world, tumbling about in its swaddling-clothes, and tormenting itself and others for the last six thousand

K *

years! The plea of ignorance, of folly, of grossness, or selfishness makes nothing either way: it is the downright love of pain and mischief for the interest it excites, and the scope it gives to an abandoned will, that is the root of all the evil, and the original sin of human nature. There is a love of power in the mind independent of the love of good, and this love of power, when it comes to be opposed to the spirit of good, and is leagued with the spirit of evil to commit it with greediness, is wickedness. I know of no other definition of the term. A person who does not foresee consequences is a fool: he who cheats others to serve himself is a knave: he who is immersed in sensual pleasure is a brute; but he alone, who has a pleasure in injuring another, or in debasing himself, that is, who does a thing with a particular relish because he ought not, is properly wicked. This character implies the fiend at the bottom of it; and is mixed up pretty plenti- fully (according to my philosophy) in the untoward composition of human nature. It is this craving after what is prohibited, and the force of contrast adding its zest to the violations of reason and propriety, that accounts for the excesses of pride, of cruelty, and lust; and at the same time frets and vexes the surface of life with petty evils, and plants a canker in the bosom of our daily enjoyments. Take away the enormities dictated by the wanton and pampered pride of human will, glutting itself with the sacrifice of the welfare of others, or with the desecration of its own best feelings, and also the endless bickerings, heart-burnings, and disappointments produced by the spirit of contradiction on a smaller scale, and the life of man would " spin round on its soft axle," unharmed and free, neither appalled by huge crimes nor infested by insect follies. It might, indeed, be monotonous and in- sipid; but it is the hankering after mischievous and violent excitement that leads to this result, that causes that indifference to good and proneness to evil, which is the

very thing complained of. The griefs we suffer are for
the most part of our own seeking and making; or we incur
or inflict them, not to avert other impending evils, but to
drive off *ennui*. There must be a spice of mischief and
wilfulness thrown into the cup of our existence to give it
its sharp taste and sparkling colour. I shall not go into
a formal argument on this subject, for fear of being
tedious, nor endeavour to enforce it by extreme cases, for
fear of being disgusting; but shall content myself with
some desultory and familiar illustrations of it.

I laugh at those who deny that we ever wantonly or
unnecessarily inflict pain upon others, when I see how
fond we are of ingeniously tormenting ourselves. What
is sullenness in children or grown people but revenge
against ourselves? We had rather be the victims of this
absurd and headstrong feeling, than give up an inveterate
purpose, retract an error, or relax from the intensity of
our will, whatever it may cost us. A surly man is his own
enemy, and knowingly sacrifices his interest to his ill-
humour, because he would at any time rather disoblige
you than serve himself, as I believe I have already shewn
in another place. The reason is, he has a natural aversion
to everything agreeable or happy—he turns with disgust
from every such feeling, as not according with the severe
tone of his mind—and it is in excluding all interchange
of friendly affections or kind offices that the ruling bias
and the chief satisfaction of his life consist. Is not every
country town supplied with its scolds and scandal-
mongers? The first cannot cease from plaguing themselves and everybody about them with their senseless
clamour, because the rage of words has become by habit
and indulgence a thirst, a fever on their parched tongue;
and the others continue to make enemies by some smart
hit or sly insinuation at every third word they speak,
because with every new enemy there is an additional
sense of power. One man will sooner part with his friend

than his joke, because the stimulus of saying a good thing is irritated, instead of being repressed, by the fear of giving offence, and by the imprudence or unfairness of the remark. Malice often takes the garb of truth. We find a set of persons who pride themselves on being *plain-spoken people,* that is, who blurt out everything disagreeable to your face, by way of wounding your feelings and relieving their own, and this they call honesty. Even among philosophers we may have noticed those who are not contented to inform the understandings of their readers, unless they can shock their prejudices; and among poets those who tamper with the rotten parts of their subject, adding to their fancied pretensions by trampling on the sense of shame. There are rigid reasoners who will not be turned aside from following up a logical argument by any regard to consequences, or the " compunctious visitings of nature " (such is their love of truth)—I never knew one of these scrupulous and hard-mouthed logicians who would not falsify the facts and distort the inference in order to arrive at a distressing and repulsive conclusion. Such is the fascination of what releases our own will from thraldom, and compels that of others reluctantly to submit to terms of our dictating! We feel our own power, and disregard their weakness and effeminacy with prodigious self-complacency. Lord Clive, when a boy, saw a butcher passing with a calf in a cart. A companion whom he had with him said, " I should not like to be that butcher! "—" I should not like to be that calf," replied the future Governor of India, laughing at all sympathy but that with his own sufferings. The " wicked " Lord Lyttleton (as he was called) dreamt a little before his death that he was confined in a huge subterranean vault (the inside of this round globe) where as far as eye could see, he could discern no living object, till at last he saw a female figure coming towards him, and who should it turn out to be, but Mother Brownrigg,

whom of all people he most hated! That was the very
reason why he dreamt of her.

> " You ask her crime : she whipp'd two 'prentices to
> death,
> And hid them in the coal-hole."
>
> POETRY OF THE ANTI-JACOBIN.

I do not know that hers is exactly a case in point; but
I conceive that in the well-known catastrophe here alluded
to, words led to blows, bad usage brought on worse from
mere irritation and opposition, and that, probably, even
remorse and pity urged on to aggravated acts of cruelty
and oppression, as the only means of drowning reflection
on the past in the fury of present passion. I believe that
remorse for past offences has sometimes made the greatest
criminals, as the being unable to appease a wounded conscience renders men desperate; and if I hear a person
express great impatience and uneasiness at some error that
he is liable to, I am tolerably sure that the conflict will
end in a repetition of the offence. If a man who got drunk
over-night, repents bitterly next morning, he will get
drunk again at night; for both in his repentance and his
self-gratification he is led away by the feeling of the
moment. But this is not wickedness, but despondency and
want of strength of mind: and I only attribute wickedness
to those who carry their wills in their hands, and who
wantonly and deliberately suffer them to tyrannize over
conscience, reason, and humanity, and who even draw an
additional triumph from this degrading conquest. The
wars, persecutions, and bloodshed occasioned by religion
have generally turned on the most trifling differences in
forms and ceremonies; which shews that it was not the
vital interests of the questions that were at stake, but that
these were made a handle and pretext to exercise cruelty
and tyranny on the score of the most trivial and doubtful
points of faith. There seems to be a love of absurdity and

falsehood as well as mischief in the human mind, and the
most ridiculous as well as barbarous superstitions have on
this account been the most acceptable to it. A lie is
welcome to it, for it is, as it were, its own offspring; and
it likes to believe, as well as act, whatever it pleases, and
in the pure spirit of contradiction. The old idolatry took
vast hold of the earliest ages; for to believe that a piece of
painted stone or wood was a God (in the teeth of the fact)
was a fine exercise of the imagination; and modern fana-
ticism thrives in proportion to the quantity of contradictions and nonsense it pours down the throats of the gaping
multitude, and the jargon and mysticism it offers to their
wonder and credulity. *Credo quia impossibile est*, is the
standing motto of bigotry and superstition; that is, I
believe, because to do so is a favourite act of the will, and
to do so in defiance of common sense and reason enhances
the pleasure and the merit (tenfold) of this indulgence of
blind faith and headstrong imagination. Methodism, in
particular, which at once absolves the understanding
from the rules of reasoning, and the conscience from the
restraints of morality, throwing the whole responsibility
upon a vicarious righteousness and an abstract belief,
must, besides its rant, its vulgarity, and its amatory style,
have a double charm both for saints and sinners. I have
also observed a sort of *fatuity*, an indolence or indocility
of the will to circumstances, which I think has a considerable share in the common affairs of life. I would willingly
compound for all the mischiefs that are done me voluntarily, if I could escape those which are done me without
any motive at all, or even with the best intentions. For
instance, if I go to a distance where I am anxious to
receive an answer to my letters, I am sure to be kept in
suspense. My friends are aware of this, as also of my
impatience and irritability; and they cannot prevail on
themselves to put an end to this dramatic situation of the
parties. There is pleasure (an innocent and well-meaning

one) in keeping a friend in suspense, in not putting oneself out of one's way for his ill humours and apprehensions (though one would not for the world do him a serious
injury), as there is in dangling the finny prey at the end of
a hook, or in twirling round a cock-chaffer after sticking a
pin through him at the end of a string,—there is no malice
in the case, no deliberate cruelty, but the buzzing noise
and the secret consciousness of superiority to any annoyance of inconvenience ourselves lull the mind into a
delightful state of listless torpor and indifference. If a
letter requires an immediate answer, send it by a private
hand to save postage. If our messenger falls sick or
breaks a leg and begs us to forward it by some other
means, return it him again, and insist on its being conveyed according to its first destination. His cure may be
slow but sure. In the meantime our friend can wait. We
have done our duty in writing the letter, and are in no
hurry to *receive* it! We know the contents, and they are
matters of perfect indifference to us. No harm is meant
by all this, but a great deal of mischief may accrue.
There is, in short, a sluggishness and untractableness
about the will, that does not easily put itself in the situation of others, and that consults its own bias best by giving
itself no trouble about them. Human life is so far a game
of cross-purposes. If we wish a thing to be kept secret, it
is sure to transpire: if we wish it to be known, not a
syllable is breathed about it. This is not meant; but it
happens so from mere simplicity and thoughtlessness. No
one has ever yet seen through all the intricate folds and
delicate involutions of our self-love, which is wrapped up
in a set of smooth flimsy pretexts like some precious jewel
in covers of silver paper.

I proceed to say something of the words *false* and *true*,
as applied to moral feelings. It may be argued that this
is a distinction without a difference; for that as feelings
only exist by being *felt*, wherever, and in so far as they

exist, they must be true, and that there can be no falsehood or deception in the question. The distinction between true and false pleasure, between real and seeming good, would be thus done away with; for the reality
and the appearance are here the same. And this would be
the case if our sensations were simple and detached, and
one had no influence on another. But it is in their secret
and close dependence one on another, that the distinction
here spoken of takes its rise. That then is *true* or *pure*
pleasure that has no alloy or drawback in some other consideration; that is free from remorse and alarm; and that
will bear the soberest reflection; because there is nothing
that, upon examination, can be found acting indirectly to
check and throw a damp upon it. On the other hand, we
justly call those pleasures *false* and *hollow*, not merely
which are momentary and ready to elude our grasp, but
which, even at the time, are accompanied with such a
consciousness of other circumstances as must embitter and
undermine them. For instance, putting morality quite out
of the question; is there not an undeniable and wide
difference between the gaiety and animal spirits of one
who indulges in a drunken debauch to celebrate some
unexpected stroke of good fortune, and his who does
the same thing to drown care for the loss of all he is
worth? The outward objects, the immediate and more
obvious sensations are, perhaps, very much the same
in the latter case as in the former,—the rich viands,
the sparkling wines, the social merriment, the wit, the
loud laughter, and the maddening brain, but the still
small voice is wanting, there is a reflection at bottom, that,
however stifled and kept down, poisons and spoils all,
even by the violent effort to keep it from intruding; the
mirth in the one case is forced, in the other is natural;
the one reveller is (we all know by experience) a gay,
laughing wretch, the other a happy man. I profess to
speak of human nature as I find it; and the circumstance

that any distinction I can make may be favourable to the
theories of virtue, will not prevent me from setting it
down, from the fear of being charged with cant and prejudice. Even in a case less palpable than the one supposed,
where " some sweet oblivious antidote " has been applied
to the mind, and it is lulled to temporary forgetfulness of
its immediate cause of sorrow, does it therefore cease to
gnaw the heart by stealth; are no traces of it left in the
care-worn brow or face; is the state of mind the same as
it was; or is there the same buoyancy, freedom, and erectness of spirit as in more prosperous circumstances? On
the contrary, it is torpid, vexed, and sad, enfeebled or
harassed, and weighed down by the corroding pressure of
care, whether it thinks of it or not. The pulse beats slow
and languid, the eye is dead; no object strikes us with the
same alacrity; the avenues to joy or content are shut;
and life becomes a burthen and a perplexing mystery.
Even in sleep, we are haunted with the broken images of
distress or the mockery of bliss, and we in vain try to still
the idle tumult of the heart. The constantly tampering
with the truth, the putting off the day of reckoning, the
fear of looking our situation in the face, gives the mind a
wandering and unsettled turn, makes our waking thoughts
a troubled dream, or sometimes ends in madness, without
any violent paroxysm, without any severe pang, without
any *overt act*, but from that silent operation of the mind
which preys internally upon itself, and works the decay
of its powers the more fatally, because we dare not give
it open and avowed scope. Do we not, in case of any
untoward accident or event, know, when we wake in the
morning, that something is the matter, before we recollect
what it is? The mind no more recovers its confidence
and serenity after a staggering blow, than the haggard
cheek and sleepless eye their colour and vivacity, because
we do not see them in the glass. Is it to be supposed that
there is not a firm and healthy tone of the mind as well as

of the body; or that when this has been deranged, we do not feel pain, lassitude, and fretful impatience, though the local cause or impression may have been withdrawn? Is the state of the mind or of the nervous system, and its disposition or indisposition to receive certain impressions from the remains of others still vibrating on it, nothing? Shall we say that the laugh of a madman is sincere; or that the wit we utter in our dreams is sterling? We often feel uneasy at something, without being able to tell why, or attribute it to a wrong cause. Our unconscious impressions necessarily give a colour to, and re-act upon our conscious ones; and it is only when these two sets of feeling are in accord, that our pleasures are true and sincere; where there is a discordance and misunderstanding in this respect, they are said (not absurdly as is pretended) to be false and hollow. There is then a serenity of virtue, a peace of conscience, a confidence in success, and a pride of intellect, which subsist and are a strong source of satisfaction independently of outward and immediate objects, as the general health of the body gives a glow and animation to the whole frame, notwithstanding a scratch we may have received in our little finger, and certainly very different from a state of sickness and infirmity. The difficulty is not so much in supposing one mental cause or phenomenon to be affected and imperceptibly moulded by another, as in setting limits to the everlasting ramifications of our impressions, and in defining the obscure and intricate ways in which they communicate together. Suppose a man to labour under an habitual indigestion. Does it not oppress the very sun in the sky, beat down all his powers of enjoyment, and imprison all his faculties in a living tomb? Yet he perhaps long laboured under this disease, and felt its withering effects, before he was aware of the cause. It was not the less real on this account; nor did it interfere the less with the sincerity of his other pleasures, tarnish the face of

nature, and throw a gloom over everything. " He was
hurt, and knew it not." Let the pressure be removed, and
he breathes freely again; his spirits run with a livelier
current, and he greets nature with smiles; yet the change
is in him, not in her. Do we not pass the same scenery
that we have visited but a little before, and wonder that no
object appears the same, because we have some secret
cause of dissatisfaction? Let any one feel the force of disappointed affection, and he may forget and scorn his error,
laugh and be gay to all outward appearance, but the heart
is not the less seared and blighted ever after. The splendid banquet does not supply the loss of appetite, nor
the spotless ermine cure the itching palm, nor gold nor
jewels redeem a lost name, nor pleasure fill up the void
of affection, nor passion stifle conscience. Moralists and
divines say true, when they talk of the " unquenchable
fire, and the worm that dies not." The human soul is not
an invention of priests, whatever fables they have engrafted
on it; nor is there an end of all our natural sentiments
because French philosophers have not been able to account
for them! Hume, I think, somewhere contends that all
satisfactions are equal,[1] because the cup can be no more
than full. But surely, though this is the case, one cup
holds more than another. As to mere negative satisfaction,
the argument may be true. But as to positive satisfaction
or enjoyment, I see no more how this must be equal, than
how the heat of a furnace must in all cases be equally
intense. Thus, for instance, there are many things with
which we are contented, so as not to feel an uneasy desire
after more, but yet we have a much higher relish of others.
We may eat a mutton-chop without complaining, though
we should consider a haunch of venison as a greater luxury
if we had it. Again, in travelling abroad, the mind ac-
quires a restless and vagabond habit. There is more of

---

[1] See also Search's [i.e. Abraham Tucker's] *Light of Nature
Pursued*, in which the same sophism is insisted on.

hurry and novelty, but less of sincerity and certainty in our pursuits than at home. We snatch hasty glances of a great variety of things, but want some central point of view. After making the grand tour, and seeing the finest sights in the world, we are glad to come back at last to our native place and our own fireside. Our associations with it are the most steadfast and habitual, we there feel most at home and at our ease, we have a resting-place for the sole of our foot, the flutter of hope, anxiety, and disappointment is at an end, and whatever our satisfactions may be, we feel most confidence in them, and have the strongest conviction of their truth and reality. There is then a true and a false or spurious in sentiment as well as in reasoning, and I hope the train of thought I have here gone into may serve in some respects as a clue to explain it.

The hardest question remains behind. What is *depth* and what is *superficiality?* It is easy to answer that the one is what is obvious, familiar, and lies on the surface, and that the other is recondite and hid at the bottom of a subject. The difficulty recurs—What is meant by lying on the surface, or being concealed below it, in moral and metaphysical questions? Let us try for an analogy. *Depth* consists then in tracing any number of particular effects to a general principle, or in distinguishing an unknown cause from the individual and varying circumstances with which it is implicated, and under which it lurks unsuspected. It is in fact resolving the concrete into the abstract. Now this is a task of difficulty, not only because the abstract naturally merges in the concrete, and we do not well know how to set about separating what is thus jumbled or cemented together in a single object, and presented under a common aspect; but being scattered over a larger surface, and collected from a number of undefined sources, there must be a strong feeling of its weight and pressure, in order to dislocate it from the object and bind it into a principle. The impression of an abstract principle is faint and doubtful in each individual instance; it becomes powerful and certain only by the repetition of the experiment, and by adding the last results to our first hazardous conjectures. We thus gain a distinct hold or clue to the demonstration, when a number of vague and imperfect reminiscences are united and drawn out together, by tenaciousness of memory and conscious feeling, in one continued act. So that the depth of the understanding or reasoning in such cases may be explained to mean, that there is a pile of *implicit* distinctions analysed from a great variety of facts and observations, each supporting the other, and that the mind, instead of being led away by the last or first object or detached view of the subject that occurs, connects all these into a whole from the top to the bottom, and by its intimate sympathy with the most obscure and random impressions that tend to the same result, evolves a principle of abstract truth. Two circumstances are combined in a particular object to produce a given effect: how shall I know which is the true cause, but by finding it in another instance? But the same effect is produced in a third object, which is without the concomitant circumstance of the first or second case. I must then look out for some other latent cause in the rabble of contradictory pretensions huddled together, which I had not noticed before, and to which I am eventually led by finding a necessity for it. But if my memory fails me, or I do not seize on the true character of different feelings, I shall make little progress, or be quite thrown out in my reckoning. Insomuch that according to the general diffusion of any element of thought or feeling, and its floating through the mixed mass of human affairs, do we stand in need of a greater quantity of that refined experience I have spoken of, and of a quicker and firmer tact in connecting or distinguishing its results. However, I must make a reservation here. Both knowledge and sagacity are required, but sagacity abridges and anticipates the labour of knowledge, and sometimes jumps instinctively at a conclusion; that is, the strength or fineness of the feeling, by association or analogy, sooner elicits the recollection of a previous and forgotten one in different circumstances, and the two together, by a sort of internal evidence and collective force, stamp any proposed solution with the character of truth or falsehood. Original strength of impression is often (in usual questions at least) a substitute for accumulated weight of experience; and intensity of feeling is so far synonymous with depth of understanding. It is that which here gives us a contentious and palpable consciousness of whatever affects it in the smallest or remotest manner, and leaves to us the hidden springs of thought and action through our sensibility and jealousy of whatever touches them.—To give illustration or two of this very abstruse subject.

Elegance is a word that means something different from ease, grace, beauty, dignity; yet it is akin to all these; but it seems more particularly to imply a sparkling brilliancy of effect with finish and precision. We do not apply the term to great things; we should not call an epic poem or a head of Jupiter *elegant*, but we speak of an elegant copy of verses, an elegant headdress, an elegant fan, an elegant diamond brooch, or bunch of flowers. In all these cases (and others where the same epithet is used) there is something little and comparatively trifling in the objects and the interest they inspire. So far I deal chiefly in examples, conjectures, and negatives. But this is far from a definition. I think I know what personal beauty is, because I can say in one word what I mean by it, viz., *harmony of form;* and this idea seems to me to answer to all the cases to which the term personal beauty is ever applied. Let us see if we cannot come to something equally definitive with respect to the other phrase. Sparkling effect, finish, and precision are characteristic, as I think, of elegance, but as yet I see no reason why they should be so, any more than why blue, red, and yellow should form the colours of the rainbow. I want a common idea as a link to connect them, or to serve as a substratum for the others. Now suppose I say that elegance is beauty, or at least *the pleasurable* in little things: we then have a ground to rest upon at once. For elegance being beauty or pleasure in little or slight impressions, precision, finish, and polished smoothness follow from this definition as matters of course. In other words, for a thing that is little to be beautiful, or at any rate to please,[1] it must have precision of outline, which in larger masses and gigantic forms is not so indispensable. In what is small, the parts must be finished, or they will offend. Lastly, in what is momentary and evanescent, as in dress, fashions, &c., there must be a glossy and sparkling effect, for brilliancy is the only virtue of novelty. That is to say, by getting the primary conditions or essential qualities of elegance in all circumstances whatever, we see how these branch off into minor divisions in relation to form, details, colour, surface, &c., and rise from a common ground of abstraction into all the variety of consequences and examples. The Hercules is not elegant; the Venus is simply beautiful. The French, whose ideas of beauty or grandeur never amount to more than an elegance, have no relish for Rubens, nor will they understand this definition.

When Sir Isaac Newton saw the apple fall, it was a very simple and common observation, but it suggested to his mind the law that holds the universe together. What then was the process in this case? In general, when we see anything fall, we have the idea of a particular direction, of *up* and *down* associated with the motion by invariable and every day's experience. The earth is always (as we conceive) under our feet, and the sky above our

---

[1] I have said before that this is a study, not a perfect demonstration. I am no merchant in metaphysics.

heads, so that according to this local and habitual feeling, all heavy bodies must everlastingly fall in the same direction downwards, or parallel to the upright position of our bodies. Sir Isaac Newton by a bare effort of abstraction, or by a grasp of mind comprehending all the possible relations of things, got rid of this prejudice, turned the world as it were on its back, and saw the apple fall not *downwards*, but simply *towards* the earth, so that it would fall *upwards* on the same principle, if the earth were above it, or towards it at any rate in whatever direction it lay. This highly abstracted view of the case answered to all the phenomena of nature, and no other did; and this view he arrived at by a vast power of comprehension, retaining and reducing the contradictory phenomena of the universe under one law, and counteracting and banishing from his mind that almost invincible and instinctive association of *up* and *down* as it relates to the position of our own bodies and the gravitation of all others to the earth in the same direction. From a circumscribed and partial view we make that, which is general, particular: the great mathematician here spoken of, from a wide and comprehensive one, made it general again, or he perceived the essential condition or cause of a general effect, and that which acts indispensably in all circumstances, separate from other accidental and arbitrary ones.

I lately heard an anecdote related of an American lady (one of two sisters) who married young and well, and had several children; her sister, however, was married soon after herself to a richer husband, and had a larger (if not finer) family, and after passing several years of constant repining and wretchedness, she died at length of pure envy. The circumstance was well known, and generally talked of. Some one said on hearing this, that it was a thing that could only happen in America; that it was a trait of the republican character and institutions, where alone the principle of mutual jealousy, having no high and distant objects to fix upon, and divert it from immediate and private mortifications, seized upon the happiness or outward advantages even of the nearest connexions as its natural food, and having them constantly before its eyes, gnawed itself to death upon them. I assented to this remark, and I confess it struck me as shewing a deep insight into human nature. Here was a sister envying a sister, and that not for objects that provoke strong passion, but for common and contentional advantages, till it ends in her death. They were also represented as good and respectable people. How then is this extraordinary development of an ordinary human frailty to be accounted for? From the peculiar circumstances? These were the country and state of society. It was in America that it happened. The democratic level, the flatness of imagery, the absence of those towering and artificial heights that in old and monarchical states act as conductors to attract and carry off the splenetic humours and rancorous hostilities of a whole people, and to make common and petty advantages sink into perfect insignificance, were full in the mind of the person who suggested the solution; and in this dearth of every other mark or vent for it, it was felt intuitively, that the natural spirit of envy and discontent would fasten upon those that were next to it, and whose advantages, there being no great difference in point of elevation, would gall in proportion to their proximity and repeated recurrence. The remote and exalted advantages of birth and station in countries where the social fabric is constructed of lofty and unequal materials, necessarily carry the mind out of its immediate and domestic circle; whereas, take away those objects of imaginary spleen and moody speculation, and they leave, as the inevitable alternative, the envy and hatred of our friends and neighbours at every advantage we possess, as so many eye-sores and stumbling-blocks in their way, where these selfish principles have not been curbed or given way altogether to charity and benevolence. The fact, as stated in itself, is an anomaly: as thus explained, by combining it with a general state of feeling in a country, it seems to point out a great principle in society. Now this solution would have been attained but for the deep impression which the operation of certain general causes of moral character had recently made, and the quickness with which the consequences of its removal were felt. I might give other instances, but these will be sufficient to explain the argument, or set others upon elucidating it more clearly.

Acuteness is depth, or sagacity in connecting individual effects with individual causes, or *vice versa*, as in stratagems of war, policy, and a knowledge of character and the world. Comprehension is the power of combining a vast number of particulars in some one view, as in mechanics, or the game of chess, but without referring them to any abstract or general principle. A *common-place* differs from an abstract discourse in this, that it is trite and vague, instead of being new and profound. It is a common-place at present to say that heavy bodies fall by attraction. It would always have been one to say that this falling is the effect of a law of nature, or the will of God. This is assigning a general but not adequate cause.

The depth of passion is where it takes hold of circumstances too remote or indifferent for notice from the force of association or analogy, and turns the current of other passions by its own. Dramatic power in the depth of the knowledge of the human heart, is chiefly shewn in tracing this effect. For instance, the fondness displayed by a mistress for a lover (as she is about to desert him for a rival) is not mere hypocrisy or art to deceive him, but nature, or the reaction of her pity, or parting tenderness towards a person she is about to injure, but does not absolutely hate. Shakespear is the only dramatic author who has laid open this reaction or involution of the passions in a manner worth speaking of. The rest are commonplace declaimers, and may be very fine poets, but not deep philosophers. There is a depth even in superficiality, that is, the affections cling round obvious and familiar objects, not recondite and remote ones; and the intense continuity of feeling thus obtained, forms the depth of sentiment. It is that that redeems poetry and romance from the charge of superficiality. The habitual impressions of things are, as to feeling, the most refined ones. The painter also in his mind's eye penetrates beyond the surface or husk of the object, and sees into a labyrinth of forms, an abyss of colour. My head has grown giddy in following the windings of the drawing in Raphael, and I have gazed on the breadth of Titian, where infinite imperceptible gradations were blended in a common mass, as into a dazzling mirror. This idea is more easily transferred to Rembrandt's chiaro-scura, where the greatest clearness and the nicest distinctions are observed in the midst of obscurity. In a word, I suspect depth to be that strength and at the same time subtlety of impression, which will not suffer the slightest indication of thought or feeling to be lost, and gives warning of them, over whatever extent of surface they are diffused, or under whatever disguises of circumstances they lurk.

ON THE WANT OF MONEY

(MONTHLY MAGAZINE, JAN., 1827)

I T is hard to be without money. To get on without it is like travelling in a foreign country without a passport —you are stopped, suspected, and made ridiculous at every turn, besides being subjected to the most serious inconveniences. The want of money I here allude to is not altogether that which arises from absolute poverty— for where there is a downright absence of the common necessaries of life, this must be remedied by incessant hard labour, and the least we can receive in return is a supply of our daily wants—but that uncertain, casual, precarious mode of existence, in which the temptation to spend remains after the means are exhausted, the want of money joined with the hope and possibility of getting it, the intermediate state of difficulty and suspense between the last guinea or shilling and the next that we may have the good luck to encounter. This gap, this unwelcome interval constantly recurring, however shab- bily got over, is really full of many anxieties, misgivings, mortifications, meannesses, and deplorable embarrass- ments of every description. I may attempt (this Essay is not a fanciful speculation) to enlarge upon a few of them.

It is hard to go without one's dinner through sheer distress, but harder still to go without one's breakfast. Upon the strength of that first and aboriginal meal, one may muster courage to face the difficulties before one, and to dare the worst: but to be roused out of one's warm bed, and perhaps a profound oblivion of care, with golden dreams (for poverty does not prevent golden dreams), and told there is nothing for breakfast, is cold comfort for which one's half-strung nerves are not prepared, and throws a damp upon the prospects of the day. It is a bad beginning. A man without a breakfast is a poor creature, unfit to go in search of one, to meet the frown of the world, or to borrow a shilling of a friend. He may beg at the corner of a street—nothing is too mean for the tone of his feelings—robbing on the highway is out of the question, as requiring too much courage, and some opinion of a man's self. It is, indeed, as old Fuller, or some worthy of that age, expresses it, "the heaviest stone which melancholy can throw at a man," to learn,

the first thing after he rises in the morning, or even to be
dunned with it in bed, that there is no loaf, tea, or butter
in the house, and that the baker, the grocer, and butter-
man have refused to give any farther credit. This is
taking one sadly at a disadvantage. It is striking at one's
spirit and resolution in their very source,—the stomach—
it is attacking one on the side of hunger and mortification
at once; it is casting one into the very mire of humility and
Slough of Despond. The worst is, to know what face to
put upon the matter, what excuse to make to the servants,
what answer to send to the tradespeople; whether to
laugh it off, or be grave, or angry, or indifferent; in
short, to know how to parry off an evil which you cannot
help. What a luxury, what a God's-send in such a
dilemma, to find a half-crown which had slipped through
a hole in the lining of your waistcoat, a crumpled bank-
note in your breeches-pocket, or a guinea clinking in the
bottom of your trunk, which had been thoughtlessly left
there out of a former heap! Vain hope! Unfounded
illusion! The experienced in such matters know better,
and laugh in their sleeves at so improbable a suggestion.
Not a corner, not a cranny, not a pocket, not a drawer
has been left unrummaged, or has not been subjected over
and over again to more than the strictness of a custom-
house scrutiny. Not the slightest rustle of a piece of
bank-paper, not the gentlest pressure of a piece of hard
metal, but would have given notice of its hiding-place
with electrical rapidity, long before, in such circumstances. All the variety of pecuniary resources, which
form a legal tender in the current coin of the realm, are
assuredly drained, exhausted to the last farthing before
this time. But is there nothing in the house that one can
turn to account? Is there not an old family-watch, or
piece of plate, or a ring, or some worthless trinket that
one could part with? nothing belonging to one's-self or a
friend, that one could raise the wind upon, till something

better turns up? At this moment an old-clothes man passes, and his deep, harsh tones sound like a premeditated insult on one's distress, and banish the thought of applying for his assistance, as one's eye glances furtively at an old hat or a great coat, hung up behind a closet-door. Humiliating contemplations! Miserable uncertainty! One hesitates, and the opportunity is gone by; for without one's breakfast, one has not the resolution to do any thing!—The late Mr. Sheridan was often reduced to this unpleasant predicament. Possibly he had little appetite for breakfast himself; but the servants complained bitterly on this head, and said that Mrs. Sheridan was sometimes kept waiting for a couple of hours, while they had to hunt through the neighbourhood, and beat up for coffee, eggs, and French rolls. The same perplexity in this instance appears to have extended to the providing for the dinner; for so sharp-set were they, that to cut short a debate with a butcher's apprentice about leaving a leg of mutton without the money, the cook clapped it into the pot: the butcher's boy, probably used to such encounters, with equal coolness took it out again, and marched off with it in his tray in triumph. It required a man to be the author of *The School for Scandal*, to run the gauntlet of such disagreeable occurrences every hour of the day.[1]

[1] Taylor, of the Opera House, used to say of Sheridan, that he could not pull off his hat to him in the street without its costing him fifty pounds ; and if he stopped to speak to him, it was a hundred. No one could be a stronger instance than he was of what is called *living from hand to mouth*. He was always in want of money, though he received vast sums which he must have disbursed ; and yet nobody can tell what became of them, for he paid nobody. He spent his wife's fortune (sixteen hundred pounds) in a six weeks' jaunt to Bath, and returned to town as poor as a rat. Whenever he and his son were invited out into the country, they always went in two post-chaises and four ; he in one, and his son Tom following in another. This is the secret of those who live in a round of extravagance, and are at the same time always in debt and difficulty—they throw away all the ready money they get upon any new-

The going without a dinner is another of the miseries of wanting money, though one can bear up against this calamity better than the former, which really "blights the tender blossom and promise of the day." With one good meal, one may hold a parley with hunger and moralize upon temperance. One has time to turn one's-self and look about one—to "screw one's courage to the sticking-place," to graduate the scale of disappointment, and stave off appetite till supper-time. You gain time, and time in this weather-cock world is everything. You may dine at two, or at six, or seven—as most convenient.

fangled whim or project that comes in their way, and never think of paying off old scores, which of course accumulate to a dreadful amount. "Such gain the cap of him who makes them fine, yet keeps his book uncrossed." Sheridan once wanted to take Mrs. Sheridan a very handsome dress down into the country, and went to Barber and Nunn's to order it, saying he must have it by such a day, but promising they should have ready money. Mrs. Barber (I think it was) made answer that the time was short, but that ready money was a very charming thing, and that he should have it. Accordingly, at the time appointed she brought the dress, which came to five-and-twenty pounds, and it was sent in to Mr. Sheridan, who sent out a Mr. Grimm (one of his jackalls) to say he admired it exceedingly and that he was sure Mrs. Sheridan would be delighted with it, but he was sorry to have nothing under a hundred pound bank-note in the house. She said she had come provided for such an accident, and could give change for a hundred, two hundred, or five hundred pound note, if it were necessary. Grimm then went back to his principal for farther instructions; who made an excuse that he had no stamped receipt by him. For this, Mrs. B. said she was also provided; she had brought one in her pocket. At each message, she could hear them laughing heartily in the next room, at the idea of having met with their match for once; and presently after, Sheridan came out in high good humour, and paid her the amount of her bill, in ten, five, and one pound notes. Once when a creditor brought him a bill for payment, which had often been presented before, and the man complained of its soiled and tattered state, and said he was quite ashamed to see it, "I'll tell you what I'd advise you to do with it, my friend," said Sheridan, "take it home, and write it upon *parchment!*" He once mounted a

You may in the meanwhile receive an invitation to dinner, or some one (not knowing how you are circumstanced) may send you a present of a haunch of venison or a brace of pheasants from the country, or a distant relation may die and leave you a legacy, or a patron may call and overwhelm you with his smiles and bounty,

"As kind as kings upon their coronation-day;"

or there is no saying what may happen. One may wait for dinner—breakfast admits of no delay, of no interval

horse which a horse-dealer was showing off near a coffee-house at the bottom of St. James's Street, rode it to Tatter-sall's, and sold it, and walked quietly back to the spot from which he set out. The owner was furious, swore he would be the death of him; and, in a quarter of an hour afterwards they were seen sitting together over a bottle of wine in the coffee-house, the horse-jockey with the tears running down his face at Sheridan's jokes, and almost ready to hug him as an honest fellow. Sheridan's house and lobby were beset with duns every morning, who were told that Mr. Sheridan was not yet up, and shewn into the several rooms on each side of the entrance. As soon as he had breakfasted, he asked, "Are those doors all shut, John?" and, being assured they were, marched out very deliberately between them, to the astonishment of his self-invited guests, who soon found the bird was flown. I have heard one of his old city friends declare, that such was the effect of his frank, cordial manner, and insinuating eloquence, that he was always afraid to go to ask him for a debt of long standing, lest he should borrow twice as much. A play had been put off one night, or a favourite actor did not appear, and the audience demanded to have their money back again: but when they came to the door, they were told by the check-takers there was none for them, for that Mr. Sheridan had been in the meantime, and had carried off all the money in the till. He used often to get the old cobbler who kept a stall under the ruins of Drury Lane to broil a beef-steak for him, and take their dinner together. On the night that Drury Lane was burnt down, Sheridan was in the House of Commons, making a speech, though he could hardly stand without leaning his hands on the table, and it was with some difficulty he was forced away, urging the plea, "What signified the concerns of a private individual, compared to the good of the State?" When he

interposed between that and our first waking thoughts.[1]
Besides, there are shifts and devices, shabby and mortifying
enough, but still available in case of need. How
many expedients are there in this great city, time out of
mind and times without number, resorted to by the
dilapidated and thrifty speculator, to get through this
grand difficulty without utter failure! One may dive
into a cellar, and dine on boiled beef and carrots for
tenpence, with the knives and forks chained to the table,
and jostled by greasy elbows that seem to make such a

got to Covent Garden, he went into the Piazza Coffee-house, to
steady himself with another bottle, and then strolled out to the
end of the Piazza to look at the progress of the fire. Here he
was accosted by Charles Kemble and Fawcett, who complimented him on the calmness with which he seemed to regard
so great a loss. He declined this praise, and said : " Gentlemen, there are but three things in human life that in my opinion
ought to disturb a wise man's patience. The first of these is
bodily pain, and that (whatever the ancient stoics may have said
to the contrary) is too much for any man to bear without flinch-
ing ; this I have felt severely, and I know it to be the case.
The second is the loss of a friend whom you have dearly loved ;
that, gentlemen, is a great evil : this I have also felt, and I
know it to be too much for any man's fortitude. And the
third is the consciousness of having done an unjust action.
That, gentlemen, is a great evil, a very great evil, too much for
any man to endure the reflection of ; but that " (laying his
hand upon his heart) " but that, thank God, I have never felt ! "
I have been told that these were nearly the very words, except
that he appealed to the *mens conscia recti* very emphatically
three or four times over, by an excellent authority, Mr.
Mathews, the player, who was on the spot at the time,—a
gentleman whom the public admire deservedly, but with whose
real talents and nice discrimination of character his friends
only are acquainted. Sheridan's reply to the watchman
who had picked him up in the street, and who wanted to know
who he was, " I am Mr. Wilberforce ! " is well known, and
shews that, however frequently he might be at a loss for money,
he never wanted wit !

[1] In Scotland, it seems, the draught of ale or whiskey with
which you commence the day, is emphatically called " taking
your *morning*."

L

precaution not unnecessary (hunger is proof against
indignity!)—or one may contrive to part with a superfluous article of wearing apparel, and carry home a mutton-
chop and cook it in a garret; or one may drop in at a
friend's at the dinner-hour, and be asked to stay or not;
or one may walk out and take a turn in the Park, about
the time, and return home to tea, so as at least to avoid the
sting of the evil—the appearance of not having dined.
You then have the laugh on your side, having deceived
the gossips, and can submit to the want of a sumptuous
repast without murmuring, having saved your pride, and
made a virtue of necessity. I say all this may be done by
a man without a family (for what business has a man
without money with one?—*See English Malthus and
Scotch Macculloch*)—and it is only my intention here to
bring forward such instances of the want of money as are
tolerable both in theory and practice. I once lived on
coffee (as an experiment) for a fortnight together, while I
was finishing the copy of a half-length portrait of a
Manchester manufacturer, who died worth a plum. I
rather slurred over the coat, which was a reddish brown,
" of formal cut," to receive my five guineas, with which
I went to market myself, and dined on sausages and
mashed potatoes, and while they were getting ready, and
I could hear them hissing in the pan, read a volume of
Gil Blas, containing the account of the fair Aurora. This
was in the days of my youth. Gentle reader, do not
smile! Neither Monsieur de Véry, nor Louis XVIII, over
an oyster-pâté, nor Apicius himself, ever understood
the meaning of the word *luxury* better than I did at that
moment! If the want of money has its drawbacks and
disadvantages, it is not without its contrasts and counter-
balancing effects, for which I fear nothing else can make
us amends. Amelia's *hashed mutton* is immortal; and there
is something amusing, though carried to excess and
caricature (which is very unusual with the author) in the

contrivance of old Caleb, in *The Bride of Lammermuir*, for raising the wind at breakfast, dinner, and supper-time. I recollect a ludicrous instance of a disappointment in a dinner which happened to a person of my acquaintance some years ago. He was not only poor but a very poor creature, as will be imagined. His wife had laid by fourpence (their whole remaining stock) to pay for the baking of a shoulder of mutton and potatoes, which they had in the house, and on her return home from some errand, she found he had expended it in purchasing a new string for a guitar. On this occasion a witty friend quoted the lines from Milton:

> " And ever against *eating* cares,
> Lap me in soft Lydian airs ! "

Defoe, in his *Life of Colonel Jack*, gives a striking picture of his young beggarly hero sitting with his companion for the first time in his life at a three-penny ordinary, and the delight with which he relished the hot smoking soup, and the airs with which he called about him —" and every time," he says, " we called for bread, or beer, or whatever it might be, the waiter answered, ' coming, gentlemen, coming; ' and this delighted me more than all the rest! " It was about this time, as the same pithy author expresses it, " the Colonel took upon him to wear a shirt! " Nothing can be finer than the whole of the feeling conveyed in the commencement of this novel, about wealth and finery from the immediate contrast of privation and poverty. One would think it a labour, like the Tower of Babel, to build up a beau and a fine gentleman about town. The little vagabond's admiration of the old man at the banking-house, who sits surrounded by heaps of gold as if it were a dream or poetic vision, and his own eager anxious visits, day by day, to the hoard he had deposited in the hollow tree, are in the very foremost style of truth and nature. See the same intense

feeling expressed in Luke's address to his riches, in the
City Madam, and in the extraordinary raptures of the
" Spanish Rogue " in contemplating and hugging his
ingots of pure gold and Spanish pieces of eight: to which
Mr. Lamb has referred in excuse for the rhapsodies of
some of our elder poets on this subject, which to our
present more refined and tamer apprehensions sound
like blasphemy.[1] In earlier times, before the diffusion of
luxury, of knowledge, and other sources of enjoyment had
become common, and acted as a diversion to the cravings
of avarice, the passionate admiration, the idolatry, the
hunger and thirst of wealth and all its precious symbols,
was a kind of madness or hallucination, and Mammon
was truly worshipped as a god!

It is among the miseries of the want of money, not to
be able to pay your reckoning at an inn—or, if you have
just enough to do that, to have nothing left for the waiter;
—to be stopped at a turnpike gate, and forced to turn
back;—not to venture to call a hackney-coach in a shower
of rain—(when you have only one shilling left yourself,
it is a *bore* to have it taken out of your pocket by a friend,
who comes into your house eating peaches in a hot
summer's-day, and desiring you to pay for the coach in
which he visits you);—not to be able to purchase a
lottery-ticket, by which you might make your fortune,
and get out of all your difficulties;—or to find a letter
lying for you at a country post-office, and not to have
money in your pocket to free it, and be obliged to return
for it the next day. The letter so unseasonably withheld
may be supposed to contain money, and in this case
there is a foretaste, a sort of actual possession taken
through the thin folds of the paper and the wax, which
in some measure indemnifies us for the delay: the bank-
note, the post-bill seems to smile upon us, and shake

---

[1] Shylock's lamentation over the loss of " his daughter and
his ducats," is another case in point.

hands through its prison bars;—or it may be a love-letter, and then the tantalization is at its height: to be deprived in this manner of the only consolation that can make us amends for the want of money, by this very want—to fancy you see the name—to try to get a peep at the hand-writing—to touch the seal, and yet not dare to break it open—is provoking indeed—the climax of amorous and gentlemanly distress. Players are some-times reduced to great extremity, by the seizure of their scenes and dresses, or (what is called) *the property of the theatre*, which hinders them from acting; as authors are prevented from finishing a work, for want of money to buy the books necessary to be consulted on some material point or circumstance, in the progress of it. There is a set of poor devils, who live upon a printed *prospectus* of a work that never will be written, for which they solicit your name and half-a-crown. Decayed actresses take an annual benefit at one of the theatres; there are patriots who live upon periodical subscriptions, and critics who go about the country lecturing on poetry. I confess I envy none of these; but there are persons who, pro-vided they can live, care not how they live—who are fond of display, even when it implies exposure; who court notoriety under every shape, and embrace the public with demonstrations of wantonness. There are genteel beggars, who send up a well-penned epistle requesting the loan of a shilling. Your snug bachelors and retired old-maids pretend they can distinguish the knock of one of these at their door. I scarce know which I dislike the most—the patronage that affects to bring premature genius into notice, or that extends its piecemeal, formal charity towards it in its decline. I hate your Literary Funds, and Funds for Decayed Artists—they are cor-porations for the encouragement of meanness, pretence, and insolence. Of all people, I cannot tell how it is, but players appear to me the best able to do without money.

They are a privileged class. If not exempt from the common calls of necessity and business, they are enabled " by their so potent art " to soar above them. As they make imaginary ills their own, real ones become imaginary, sit light upon them, and are thrown off with comparatively little trouble. Their life is theatrical—its various accidents are the shifting scenes of a play—rags and finery, tears and laughter, a mock-dinner or a real one, a crown of jewels or of straw, are to them nearly the same. I am sorry I cannot carry on this reasoning to actors who are past their prime. The gilding of their profession is then worn off, and shows the false metal beneath; vanity and hope (the props of their existence) have had their day; their former gaiety and carelessness serve as a foil to their present discouragements; and want and infirmities press upon them at once. " We know what we are," as Ophelia says, " but we know not what we shall be." A workhouse seems the last resort of poverty and distress—a *parish-pauper* is another name for all that is mean and to be deprecated in human existence. But that name is but an abstraction, an average term—" within that lowest deep, a lower deep may open to receive us." I heard not long ago of a poor man, who had been for many years a respectable tradesman in London, and who was compelled to take shelter in one of those receptacles of age and wretchedness, and who said he could be contented with it—he had his regular meals, a nook in the chimney, and a coat to his back—but he was forced to lie three in a bed, and one of the three was out of his mind and crazy, and his great delight was, when the others fell asleep, to tweak their noses, and flourish his night-cap over their heads, so that they were obliged to lie awake, and hold him down between them. One should be quite mad to bear this. To what a point of insignificance may not human life dwindle! To what fine, agonizing threads will it not cling! Yet this man had been a lover in his youth, in a humble way, and still begins his letters to an old maid (his former flame), who sometimes comforts him by listening to his complaints, and treating him to a dish of weak tea, " MY DEAR MISS NANCY! "

Another of the greatest miseries of a want of money, is the tap of a dun at your door, or the previous silence when you expect it—the uneasy sense of shame at the approach of your tormentor; the wish to meet, and yet to shun the encounter; the disposition to bully, yet the fear of irritating; the real and the sham excuses; the submission to impertinence; the assurances of a speedy supply; the disingenuousness you practise on him and on yourself; the degradation in the eyes of others and your own. Oh! it is wretched to have to confront a just and oft-repeated demand, and to be without the means to satisfy it; to deceive the confidence that has been placed in you; to forfeit your credit; to be placed at the power of another, to be indebted to his lenity; to stand convicted of having played the knave or the fool; and to have no way left to escape contempt but by incurring pity. The suddenly meeting a creditor on turning the corner of a street, whom you have been trying to avoid for months and had persuaded you were several hundred miles off, discomposes the features and shatters the nerves for some time. It is also a serious annoyance to be unable to repay a loan to a friend, who is in want of it—nor is it very pleasant to be so hard run, as to be induced to request a repayment. It is difficult to decide the preference between debts of honour and legal demands; both are bad enough, and almost a fair excuse for driving any one into the hands of money-lenders—to whom an application, if successful, is accompanied with a sense of being in the vulture's gripe—a reflection akin to that of those who formerly sold themselves to the devil—or, if unsuccessful, is rendered doubly galling by the smooth, civil leer of cool contempt with which you are dismissed, as if they

had escaped from your clutches—not you from theirs.
If anything can be added to the mortification and distress
arising from straitened circumstances, it is when vanity
comes in to barb the dart of poverty—when you have a
picture on which you had calculated, rejected from an
exhibition, or a manuscript returned on your hands, or
a tragedy damned, at the very instant when your cash and
credit are at the lowest ebb. This forlorn and helpless
feeling has reached its *acme* in the prison-scene in
Hogarth's *Rake's Progress*, where his unfortunate hero
has just dropped the Manager's letter from his hands,
with the laconic answer written in it:—" Your play has
been read, and won't do."[1] To feel poverty is bad; but to
feel it with the additional sense of our incapacity to shake
it off, and that we have not merit enough to retrieve our
circumstances—and, instead of being held up to admiration, are exposed to persecution and insult—is the last
stage of human infirmity. We have heard it remarked,
that the most pathetic story in the world is that of
Smollett's fine gentleman and lady in gaol, who have been
roughly handled by the mob for some paltry attempt at
raising the wind, and she exclaims in extenuation of the
pitiful figure he cuts, " Ah! he was a fine fellow once! "

It is justly remarked by the poet, that poverty has no
greater inconvenience attached to it than that of making
men ridiculous. It not only has this disadvantage with
respect to ourselves, but it often shews us others in a
very contemptible point of view. People are not soured
by misfortune, but by the reception they meet with in it.
When we do not want assistance, every one is ready to
obtrude it on us, as if it were advice. If we do, they shun
us instantly. They anticipate the increased demand on
their sympathy or bounty, and escape from it as from

---

[1] It is provoking enough, and makes one look like a fool,
to receive a printed notice of a blank in the last lottery, with a
postscript hoping for your future favours.

a falling house. It is a mistake, however, that we court the society of the rich and prosperous, merely with a view to what we can get from them. We do so, because there is something in external rank and splendour that gratifies and imposes on the imagination; just as we prefer the company of those who are in good health and spirits to that of the sickly and hypochondriacal, or as we would rather converse with a beautiful woman than with an ugly one. I never knew but one man who would lend his money freely and fearlessly in spite of circumstances (if you were likely to pay him, he grew peevish, and would pick a quarrel with you). I can only account for this from a certain sanguine buoyancy and magnificence of spirit, not deterred by distant consequences, or damped by untoward appearances. I have been told by those who shared of the same bounty, that it was not owing to generosity, but ostentation—if so, he kept his ostentation a secret from me, for I never received a hint or a look from which I could infer that I was not the lender, and he the person obliged. Neither was I expected to keep in the background or play an under-part. On the contrary, I was encouraged to do my best; my dormant faculties roused, the ease of my circumstances was on condition of the freedom and independence of my mind, my lucky hits were applauded, and I was paid to shine. I am not ashamed of such patronage as this, nor do I regret any circumstance relating to it but its termination. People endure existence even in Paris: the rows of chairs on the Boulevards are gay with smiles and dress: the saloons are brilliant; at the theatre there is Mademoiselle Mars— what is all this to me? After a certain period, we live only in the past. Give me back one single evening at Boxhill, after a stroll in the deep-empurpled woods, before Buonaparte was yet beaten, " with wine of attic taste," when wit, beauty, friendship presided at the board! But no! Neither the time nor friends that are fled can

L *

be recalled!—Poverty is the test of sincerity, the touch-stone of civility. Even abroad, they treat you scurvily if your remittances do not arrive regularly, and though you have hitherto lived like a *Milord Anglais*. The want of money loses us friends not worth the keeping, mistresses who are naturally jilts or coquets; it cuts us out of society, to which dress and equipage are the only introduction; and deprives us of a number of luxuries and advantages of which the only good is, that they can only belong to the possessors of a large fortune. Many people are wretched because they have not money to buy a fine horse, or to hire a fine house, or to keep a carriage, or to purchase a diamond necklace, or to go to a race-ball, or to give their servants new liveries. I cannot myself enter into all this. If I can *live to think, and think to live*, I am satisfied. Some want to possess pictures, others to collect libraries. All I wish is, sometimes, to see the one and read the other. Gray was mortified because he had not a hundred pounds to bid for a curious library; and the Duchess of —— has immortalized herself by her liberality on that occasion, and by the handsome compliment she addressed to the poet, that " if it afforded him any satisfaction, she had been more than paid, by her pleasure in reading the *Elegy in a Country Church-yard*."

Literally and truly, one cannot get on well in the world without money. To be in want of it, is to pass through life with little credit or pleasure; it is to live out of the world, or to be despised if you come into it; it is not to be sent for to court, or asked out to dinner, or noticed in the street; it is not to have your opinion consulted or else rejected with contempt, to have your acquirements carped at and doubted, your good things disparaged, and at last to lose the wit and the spirit to say them; it is to be scrutinized by strangers, and neglected by friends; it is to be a thrall to circumstances, an exile in one's own country; to forego leisure, freedom, ease of body and mind, to be dependent on the good-will and caprice of others, or earn a precarious and irksome livelihood by some laborious employment; it is to be compelled to stand behind a counter, or to sit at a desk in some public office, or to marry your landlady, or not the person you would wish; or to go out to the East or West Indies, or to get a situation as judge abroad, and return home with a liver-complaint; or to be a law-stationer, or a scrivener or scavenger, or newspaper reporter; or to read law and sit in court without a brief; or to be deprived of the use of your fingers by transcribing Greek manuscripts, or to be a seal-engraver and pore yourself blind; or to go upon the stage, or try some of the Fine Arts; with all your pains, anxiety, and hopes, most probably to fail, or, if you succeed, after the exertions of years, and undergoing constant distress of mind and fortune, to be assailed on every side with envy, back-biting, and falsehood, or to be a favourite with the public for awhile, and then thrown into the background—or a gaol, by the fickleness of taste and some new favourite; to be full of enthusiasm and extravagance in youth, of chagrin and disappointment in after-life; to be jostled by the rabble because you do not ride in your coach, or avoided by those who know your worth and shrink from it as a claim on their respect or their purse; to be a burden to your relations, or unable to do anything for them; to be ashamed to venture into crowds; to have cold comfort at home; to lose by degrees your confidence and any talent you might possess; to grow crabbed, morose, and querulous, dissatisfied with every one, but most so with yourself; and plagued out of your life, to look about for a place to die in, and quit the world without any one's asking after your will. The *wiseacres* will possibly, however, crowd round your coffin, and raise a monument at a considerable expense, and after a lapse of time, to commemorate your genius and your misfortunes!

The only reason why I am disposed to envy the professions of the church or army is, that men can afford to be poor in them without being subjected to insult. A girl with a handsome fortune in a country town may marry a poor lieutenant without degrading herself. An officer is always a gentleman; a clergyman is something more. Echard's book *On the Contempt of the Clergy* is unfounded. It is surely sufficient for any set of individuals, raised above actual want, that their characters are not merely respectable, but sacred. Poverty, when it is voluntary, is never despicable, but takes an heroical aspect. What are the begging friars? Have they not put their base feet upon the necks of princes? Money as a luxury is valuable only as a passport to respect. It is one instrument of power. Where there are other admitted and ostensible claims to this, it becomes superfluous, and the neglect of it is even admired and looked up to as a mark of superiority over it. Even a strolling beggar is a popular character, who makes an open profession of his craft and calling, and who is neither worth a doit nor in want of one. The Scotch are proverbially poor and proud: we know they can remedy their poverty when they set about it. No one is sorry for them. The French emigrants were formerly peculiarly situated in England. The priests were obnoxious to the common people on account of their religion; both they and the nobles, for their politics. Their poverty and dirt subjected them to many rebuffs; but their privations being voluntarily incurred, and also borne with the characteristic patience and good-humour of the nation, screened them from contempt. I little thought, when I used to meet them walking out in the summer's-evenings at Somers' Town, in their long great coats, their beards covered with snuff, and their eyes gleaming with mingled hope and regret in the rays of the setting sun, and regarded them with pity bordering on respect, as the last filmy vestige of the *ancien regime,* as shadows of loyalty and superstition still flitting about the earth and shortly to disappear from it for ever, that they would one day return over the bleeding corpse of their country, and sit like harpies, a polluted triumph, over the tomb of human liberty! To be a lord, a papist, and poor, is perhaps to some temperaments a consummation devoutly to be wished. There is all the subdued splendour of external rank, the pride of self-opinion, irritated and goaded on by petty privations and vulgar obloquy to a degree of morbid acuteness. Private and public annoyances must perpetually remind him of what he is, of what his ancestors were (a circumstance which might otherwise be forgotten); must narrow the circle of conscious dignity more and more, and the sense of personal worth and pretension must be exalted by habit and contrast into a refined abstraction—" pure in the last recesses of the mind "—unmixed with, or unalloyed by " baser matter! "—It was an hypothesis of the late Mr. Thomas Wedgewood, that there is a principle of compensation in the human mind which equalizes all situations, and by which the absence of anything only gives us a more intense and intimate perception of the reality; that insult adds to pride, that pain looks forward to ease with delight, that hunger already enjoys the unsavoury morsel that is to save it from perishing; that want is surrounded with imaginary riches, like the poor poet in Hogarth, who has a map of the mines of Peru hanging on his garret walls; in short, that " we can hold a fire in our hand by thinking on the frosty Caucasus "— but this hypothesis, though ingenious and to a certain point true, is to be admitted only in a limited and qualified sense.

There are two classes of people that I have observed who are not so distinct as might be imagined—those who cannot keep their own money in their hands, and those who cannot keep their hands from other people's.

The first are always in want of money, though they do not know what they do with it. They *muddle* it away, without method or object, and without having anything to shew for it. They have not, for instance, a fine house, but they hire two houses at a time; they have not a hothouse in their garden, but a shrubbery within doors; they do not gamble, but they purchase a library, and dispose of it when they move house. A princely benefactor provides them with lodgings, where, for a time, you are sure to find them at home: and they furnish them in a handsome style for those who are to come after them. With all this sieve-like economy, they can only afford a leg of mutton and a single bottle of wine, and are glad to get a lift in a common stage; whereas with a little management and the same disbursements, they might entertain a round of company and drive a smart tilbury. But they set no value upon money, and throw it away on any object or in any manner that first presents itself, merely to have it off their hands, so that you wonder what has become of it. The second class above spoken of not only make away with what belongs to themselves, but you cannot keep any thing you have from their rapacious grasp. If you refuse to lend them what you want, they insist that you *must:* if you let them have anything to take charge of for a time (a print or a bust) they swear that you have given it them, and that they have too great a regard for the donor ever to part with it. You express surprise at their having run so largely in debt; but where is the singularity while others continue to lend? And how is this to be helped, when the manner of these sturdy beggars amounts to dragooning you out of your money, and they will not go away without your purse, any more than if they came with a pistol in their hand? If a person has no delicacy, he has you in his power, for you necessarily feel some towards him; and since he will take no denial, you must comply with his peremptory demands, or send for a constable, which out of respect for his character you will not do. These persons are also poor—*light come, light go*—and the bubble bursts at last. Yet if they had employed the same time and pains in any laudable art or study that they have in raising a surreptitious livelihood, they would have been respectable, if not rich. It is their facility in borrowing money that has ruined them. No one will set heartily to work, who has the face to enter a strange house, ask the master of it for a considerable loan, on some plausible and pompous pretext, and walk off with it in his pocket. You might as well suspect a highwayman of addicting himself to hard study in the intervals of his profession.

There is only one other class of persons I can think of, in connexion with the subject of this Essay—those who are always in want of money from the want of spirit to make use of it. Such persons are perhaps more to be pitied than all the rest. They live in want, in the midst of plenty—dare not touch what belongs to them, are afraid to say that their soul is their own, have their wealth locked up from them by fear and meanness as effectually as by bolts and bars, scarcely allow themselves a coat to their backs or a morsel to eat, are in dread of coming to the parish all their lives, and are not sorry when they die, to think that they shall no longer be an expense to themselves—according to the old epigram:

> " Here lies Father Clarges,
> Who died to save charges ! "

ON THE FEELING OF IMMORTALITY IN YOUTH

(MONTHLY MAGAZINE, MARCH, 1827)

NO young man believes he shall ever die. It was a saying of my brother's, and a fine one. There is a feeling

of Eternity in youth which makes us amends for everything. To be young is to be as one of the Immortals.
One half of time indeed is spent—the other half remains
in store for us with all its countless treasures, for there
is no line drawn, and we see no limit to our hopes and
wishes. We make the coming age our own—

> " The vast, the unbounded prospect lies before us."

Death, old age, are words without a meaning, a dream,
a fiction, with which we have nothing to do. Others may
have undergone, or may still undergo them—we " bear
a charmed life," which laughs to scorn all such idle
fancies. As, in setting out on a delightful journey, we
strain our eager sight forward,

> " Bidding the lovely scenes at distance hail,"

and see no end to prospect after prospect, new objects
presenting themselves as we advance, so in the outset of
life we see no end to our desires nor to the opportunities
of gratifying them. We have as yet found no obstacle,
no disposition to flag, and it seems that we can go on so
for ever. We look round in a new world, full of life and
motion, and ceaseless progress, and feel in ourselves all
the vigour and spirit to keep pace with it, and do not
foresee from any present signs how we shall be left
behind in the race, decline into old age, and drop into
the grave. It is the simplicity and, as it were, abstracted-
ness of our feelings in youth that (so to speak) identifies
us with Nature and (our experience being weak and our
passions strong) makes us fancy ourselves immortal like
it. Our short-lived connexion with being, we fondly
flatter ourselves, is an indissoluble and lasting union.
As infants smile and sleep, we are rocked in the cradle of
our desires, and hushed into fancied security by the roar
of the universe around us—we quaff the cup of life with
eager thirst without draining it, and joy and hope seem

ever mantling to the brim—objects press around us, filling the mind with their magnitude and with the throng of desires that wait upon them, so that there is no room for the thoughts of death. We are too much dazzled by the gorgeousness and novelty of the bright waking dream about us to discern the dim shadow lingering for us in the distance. Nor would the hold that life has taken of us permit us to detach our thoughts that way, even if we could. We are too much absorbed in present objects and pursuits. While the spirit of youth remains unimpaired, ere " the wine of life is drunk," we are like people intoxicated or in a fever, who are hurried away by the violence of their own sensations: it is only as present objects begin to pall upon the sense, as we have been disappointed in our favourite pursuits, cut off from our closest ties, that we by degrees become weaned from the world, that passion loosens its hold upon futurity, and that we begin to contemplate as in a glass darkly the possibility of parting with it for good. Till then, the example of others has no effect upon us. Casualties we avoid; the slow approaches of age we play at *hide and seek* with. Like the foolish fat scullion in Sterne, who hears that Master Bobby is dead, our only reflection is, " So am not I! " The idea of death, instead of staggering our confidence, only seems to strengthen and enhance our sense of the possession and enjoyment of life. Others may fall around us like leaves, or be mowed down by the scythe of Time like grass: these are but metaphors to the unreflecting, buoyant ears and overweening presumption of youth. It is not till we see the flowers of Love, Hope, and Joy withering around us, that we give up the flattering delusions that before led us on, and that the emptiness and dreariness of the prospect before us reconciles us hypothetically to the silence of the grave.

Life is indeed a strange gift, and its privileges are

most mysterious. No wonder when it is first granted to us, that our gratitude, our admiration, and our delight should prevent us from reflecting on our own nothingness, or from thinking it will ever be recalled. Our first and strongest impressions are borrowed from the mighty scene that is opened to us, and we unconsciously transfer its durability as well as its splendour to ourselves. So newly found, we cannot think of parting with it yet, or at least put off that consideration *sine die*. Like a rustic at a fair, we are full of amazement and rapture, and have no thought of going home, or that it will soon be night. We know our existence only by ourselves, and confound our knowledge with the objects of it. We and Nature are therefore one. Otherwise the illusion, the " feast of reason and the flow of soul," to which we are invited, is a mockery and a cruel insult. We do not go from a play till the last act is ended, and the lights are about to be extinguished. But the fairy face of Nature still shines on: shall we be called away before the curtain falls, or ere we have scarce had a glimpse of what is going on? Like children, our step-mother Nature holds us up to see the raree-show of the universe, and then, as if we were a burden to her to support, lets us fall down again. Yet what brave sublunary things does not this pageant present, like a ball or fête of the universe!

To see the golden sun, the azure sky, the outstretched ocean; to walk upon the green earth, and be lord of a thousand creatures; to look down yawning precipices or over distant sunny vales; to see the world spread out under one's feet on a map; to bring the stars near; to view the smallest insects through a microscope; to read history, and consider the revolutions of empire and the successions of generations; to hear of the glory of Tyre, of Sidon, of Babylon, and of Susa, and to say all these were before me and are now nothing; to say I exist in such a point of time, and in such a point of space; to be a spectator

and a part of its ever-moving scene; to witness the change
of season, of spring and autumn, of winter and summer;
to feel hot and cold, pleasure and pain, beauty and
deformity, right and wrong; to be sensible to the accidents
of Nature; to consider the mighty world of eye and ear;
to listen to the stock-dove's notes amid the forest deep;
to journey over moor and mountain; to hear the midnight
sainted choir; to visit lighted halls, or the cathedral's
gloom, or sit in crowded theatres and see life itself
mocked; to study the works of art and refine the sense of
beauty to agony; to worship fame, and to dream of
immortality; to look upon the Vatican, and to read
Shakespear; to gather up the wisdom of the ancients,
and to pry into the future; to listen to the trump of war,
the shout of victory; to question history as to the movements of the human heart; to seek for truth; to plead the
cause of humanity; to overlook the world as if time and
Nature poured their treasures at our feet—to be and to
do all this, and then in a moment to be nothing—to have
it all snatched from us as by a juggler's trick, or a phantasmagoria! There is something in this transition from
all to nothing that shocks us and damps the enthusiasm
of youth new flushed with hope and pleasure, and we
cast the comfortless thought as far from us as we can.
In the first enjoyment of the estate of life we discard the
fear of debts and duns, and never think of the final
payment of our great debt to Nature. Art we know is
long; life, we flatter ourselves, should be so too. We see
no end of the difficulties and delays we have to encounter:
perfection is slow of attainment, and we must have time
to accomplish it in. The fame of the great names we look
up to is immortal: and shall not we who contemplate it
imbibe a portion of ethereal fire, the *divinæ particula
auræ*, which nothing can extinguish? A wrinkle in
Rembrandt or in Nature takes whole days to resolve
itself into its component parts, its softenings and its

sharpnesses; we refine upon our perfections, and unfold
the intricacies of Nature. What a prospect for the future!
What a task have we not begun! And shall we be arrested
in the middle of it? We do not count our time thus
employed lost, or our pains thrown away; we do not flag
or grow tired, but gain new vigour at our endless task.
Shall Time, then, grudge us to finish what we have begun,
and have formed a compact with Nature to do? Why
not fill up the blank that is left us in this manner? I have
looked for hours at a Rembrandt without being conscious
of the flight of time, but with ever new wonder and
delight, have thought that not only my own but another
existence I could pass in the same manner. This rarefied,
refined existence seemed to have no end, nor stint, nor
principle of decay in it. The print would remain long
after I who looked on it had become the prey of worms.
The thing seems in itself out of all reason: health, strength,
appetite are opposed to the idea of death, and we are not
ready to credit it till we have found our illusions vanished,
and our hopes grown cold. Objects in youth, from novelty,
etc., are stamped upon the brain with such force and
integrity that one thinks nothing can remove or obliterate
them. They are riveted there, and appear to us as an
element of our nature. It must be a mere violence that
destroys them, not a natural decay. In the very strength
of this persuasion we seem to enjoy an age by anticipation.
We melt down years into a single moment of intense
sympathy, and by anticipating the fruits defy the ravages
of time. If, then, a single moment of our lives is worth
years, shall we set any limits to its total value and extent?
Again, does it not happen that so secure do we think
ourselves of an indefinite period of existence, that at
times, when left to ourselves, and impatient of novelty,
we feel annoyed at what seems to us the slow and creeping
progress of time, and argue that if it always moves at
this tedious snail's pace it will never come to an end?

How ready are we to sacrifice any space of time which separates us from a favourite object, little thinking that before long we shall find it move too fast.

For my part, I started in life with the French Revolution, and I have lived, alas! to see the end of it. But I did not foresee this result. My sun arose with the first dawn of liberty, and I did not think how soon both must set. The new impulse to ardour given to men's minds imparted a congenial warmth and glow to mine; we were strong to run a race together, and I little dreamed that long before mine was set, the sun of liberty would turn to blood, or set once more in the night of despotism. Since then, I confess, I have no longer felt myself young, for with that my hopes fell.

I have since turned my thoughts to gathering up some of the fragments of my early recollections, and putting them into a form to which I might occasionally revert. The future was barred to my progress, and I turned for consolation and encouragement to the past. It is thus that, while we find our personal and substantial identity vanishing from us, we strive to gain a reflected and vicarious one in our thoughts: we do not like to perish wholly, and wish to bequeath our names, at least, to posterity. As long as we can make our cherished thoughts and nearest interests live in the minds of others, we do not appear to have retired altogether from the stage. We still occupy the breasts of others, and exert an influence and power over them, and it is only our bodies that are reduced to dust and powder. Our favourite speculations still find encouragement, and we make as great a figure in the eye of the world, or perhaps a greater than in our lifetime. The demands of our self-love are thus satisfied, and these are the most imperious and unremitting. Besides, if by our intellectual superiority we survive ourselves in this world, by our virtues and faith we may attain an interest in another, and a higher state of being,

and may thus be recipients at the same time of men and
of angels.

> " E'en from the tomb the voice of Nature cries,
>   E'en in our ashes live their wonted fires."

As we grow old, our sense of the value of time becomes
vivid. Nothing else, indeed, seems of any consequence.
We can never cease wondering that that which has ever
been should cease to be. We find many things remain
the same: why then should there be change in us. This
adds a convulsive grasp of whatever is, a sense of
fallacious hollowness in all we see. Instead of the full,
pulpy feeling of youth tasting existence and every object
in it, all is flat and vapid,—a whited sepulchre, fair
without but full of ravening and all uncleanness within.
The world is a witch that puts us off with false shows
and appearances. The simplicity of youth, the confiding
expectation, the boundless raptures, are gone: we only
think of getting out of it as well as we can, and without
any great mischance or annoyance. The flush of illusion,
even the complacent retrospect of past joys and hopes,
is over: if we can slip out of life without indignity, can
escape with little bodily infirmity, and frame our minds
to the calm and respectable composure of *still-life* before
we return to absolute nothingness, it is as much as we
can expect. We do not die wholly at our deaths: we have
mouldered away gradually long before. Faculty after
faculty, interest after interest, attachment after attachment
disappear: we are torn from ourselves while living, year
after year sees us no longer the same, and death only
consigns the last fragment of what we were to the grave.
That we should wear out by slow stages, and dwindle at
last into nothing, is not wonderful, when even in our
prime our strongest impressions leave little trace but for
the moment; and we are the creatures of petty circumstance. How little effect is made on us in our best days

by the books we have read, the scenes we have witnessed, the sensations we have gone through! Think only of the feelings we experience in reading a fine romance (one of Sir Walter's, for instance); what beauty, what sublimity, what interest, what heart-rending emotions! You would suppose the feelings you then experienced would last for ever, or subdue the mind to their own harmony and tone: while we are reading it seems as if nothing could ever put us out of our way, or trouble us:—the first splash of mud that we get on entering the street, the first twopence we are cheated out of, the feeling vanishes clean out of our minds, and we become the prey of petty and annoying circumstance. The mind soars to the lofty: it is at home in the grovelling, the disagreeable, and the little. And yet we wonder that age should be feeble and querulous,— that the freshness of youth should fade away. Both worlds would hardly satisfy the extravagance of our desires and of our presumption.

ON DISAGREEABLE PEOPLE

(MONTHLY MAGAZINE, AUG., 1827)

THOSE people who are uncomfortable in themselves are disagreeable to others. I do not here mean to speak of persons who offend intentionally, or are obnoxious to dislike from some palpable defect of mind or body, ugliness, pride, ill-humour, etc.; but of those who are disagreeable in spite of themselves, and, as it might appear, with almost every qualification to recommend them to others. This want of success is owing chiefly to something in what is called their *manner;* and this again has its foundation in a certain cross-grained and unsociable state of feeling on their part, which influences us, perhaps, without our distinctly adverting to it. The mind is a finer instrument than we sometimes suppose it, and is not only swayed by overt acts and tangible proofs, but has an instinctive feeling of the air of truth. We find many individuals in whose company we pass our time, and have no particular fault to find with their understandings or character, and yet we are never thoroughly satisfied with them: the reason will turn out to be, upon examination, that they are never thoroughly satisfied with themselves, but uneasy and out of sorts all the time; and this makes us uneasy with them, without our reflecting on, or being able to discover the cause.

Thus, for instance, we meet with persons who do us a number of kindnesses, who shew us every mark of respect and good-will, who are friendly and serviceable —and yet we do not feel grateful to them, after all. We reproach ourselves with this as caprice or insensibility, and try to get the better of it; but there is something in their way of doing things that prevents us from feeling cordial or sincerely obliged to them. We think them very worthy people, and would be glad of an opportunity to do them a good turn if it were in our power; but we cannot get beyond this: the utmost we can do is to save appearances, and not come to an open rupture with them. The truth is, in all such cases, we do not sympathize (as we ought) with them, because they do not sympathize (as they ought) with us. They have done what they did from a sense of duty in a cold dry manner, or from a meddlesome busy-body humour; or to shew their superiority over us, or to patronize our infirmity; or they have dropped some hint by the way, or blundered upon some topic they should not, and have shewn, by one means or other, that they were occupied with anything but the pleasure they were affording us, or a delicate attention to our feelings. Such persons may be styled *friendly grievances*. They are commonly people of low spirits and disappointed views, who see the discouraging side of human life, and, with the best intentions in the world, contrive to make everything they have to do with uncomfortable. They are alive to your distress, and take pains to remove it; but they have no satisfaction in the gaiety and ease they have communicated, and are on the *look-out* for some new occasion of signalizing their zeal; nor are they backward to insinuate that you will soon have need of their assistance, to guard you against running into fresh difficulties, or to extricate you from them. From large benevolence of soul and " discourse of reason, looking before and after," they are continually reminding you of something that has gone wrong in time past, or that may do so in that which is to come, and are surprised that their awkward hints, sly innuendos, blunt questions, and solemn features do not excite all the complacency and mutual good understanding in you which it is intended that they should. When they make themselves miserable on your account, it is hard that you will not lend them your countenance and support. This deplorable humour of theirs does not hit any one else. They are useful, but not agreeable people; they may assist you in your affairs, but they depress and tyrannize over your feelings. When they have made you happy, they will not let you be so—have no enjoyment of the good they have done—will on no account part with their melancholy and desponding tone—and, by their mawkish insensibility and doleful grimaces, throw a damp over the triumph they are called upon to celebrate. They would keep you in hot water, that they may help you out of it. They will nurse you in a fit of sickness (congenial sufferers !)—arbitrate a law-suit for you, and embroil you deeper—procure you a loan of money;—but all the while they are only delighted with rubbing the sore place, and casting the colour of your mental or other disorders. " The whole need not a physician "; and, being once placed at ease and comfort, they have no farther use for you as subjects for their singular beneficence, and you are not sorry to be quit of their tiresome interference. The old proverb, *A friend in need is a friend indeed*, is not verified in them. The class of persons here spoken of are the very reverse of *summer-friends*, who court you in prosperity, flatter your vanity, are the humble servants of your follies, never see or allude to anything wrong, minister to your gaiety, smooth over every difficulty, and, with the slightest approach of misfortune or of anything unpleasant, take French leave—

> " As when, in prime of June, a burnish'd fly,
> Sprung from the meads, o'er which he sweeps along,
> Cheer'd by the breathing bloom and vital sky,
> Tunes up, amid these airy halls, his song,
> Soothing at first the gay reposing throng ;
> And oft he sips their bowl, or, nearly drown'd,
> He thence recovering drives their beds among,
> And scares their tender sleep with trump profound ;
> Then out **again** he flies, to wing his mazy round." [1]

However we may despise such triflers, yet we regret them more than those well-meaning friends on whom a dull melancholy vapour hangs, that drags them and every one about them to the ground.

Again, there are those who might be very agreeable people, if they had but spirit to be so; but there is a narrow, unaspiring, under-bred tone in all they say or do. They have great sense and information—abound in a knowledge of character—have a fund of anecdote—are unexceptionable in manners and appearance—and yet we cannot make up our minds to like them: we are not glad to see them, nor sorry when they go away. Our familiarity with them, however great, wants the principle of cement, which is a certain appearance of frank cordiality and social enjoyment. They have no pleasure in the subjects of their own thoughts, and therefore can com-

[1] Thomson's *Castle of Indolence*, Canto i., st. 64.

municate none to others. There is a dry, husky, grating manner—a pettiness of detail—a tenaciousness of particulars, however trifling or unpleasant—a disposition to cavil—an aversion to enlarged and liberal views of things —in short, a hard, painful, unbending *matter-of-factness*, from which the spirit and effect are banished, and the letter only is attended to, which makes it impossible to sympathize with their discourse. To make conversation interesting or agreeable, there is required either the habitual tone of good company, which gives a favourable colouring to everything—or the warmth and enthusiasm of genius, which, though it may occasionally offend or be thrown off its guard, makes amends by its rapturous flights, and flings a glancing light upon all things. The literal and *dogged* style of conversation resembles that of a French picture, or its mechanical fidelity is like evidence given in a court of justice, or a police report.

From the literal to the plain-spoken, the transition is easy. The most efficient weapon of offence is truth. Those who deal in dry and repulsive matters-of-fact, tire out their friends; those who blurt out hard and home truths, make themselves mortal enemies wherever they come. There are your blunt, honest creatures, who omit no opportunity of letting you know their minds, and are sure to tell you all the ill, and conceal all the good they hear of you. They would not flatter you for the world, and to caution you against the malice of others, they think the province of a friend. This is not candour, but impudence; and yet they think it odd you are not charmed with their unreserved communicativeness of disposition. Gossips and tale-bearers, on the contrary, who supply the *tittle-tattle* of the neighbourhood, flatter you to your face, and laugh at you behind your back, are welcome and agreeable guests in all companies. Though you know it will be your turn next, yet for the sake of the immediate gratification, you are contented to pay your share of the public tax upon character, and are better pleased with the falsehoods that never reach your ears, than with the truths that others (less complaisant and more sincere) utter to your face—so short-sighted and willing to be imposed upon is our self-love! There is a man, who has the air of not being convinced without an argument: you avoid him as if he were a lion in your path. There is another, who asks you fifty questions as to the commonest things you advance: you would sooner pardon a fellow who held a pistol to your breast and demanded your money. No one regards a turnpike-keeper, or a custom-house officer with a friendly eye: he who stops you in an excursion of fancy, or ransacks the articles of your belief obstinately and churlishly, to distinguish the spurious from the genuine, is still more your foe. These inquisitors and cross-examiners upon system make ten enemies for every controversy in which they engage. The world dread nothing so much as being convinced of their errors. In doing them this piece of service, you make war equally on their prejudices, their interests, their pride, and indolence. You not only set up for a superiority of understanding over them, which they hate, but you deprive them of their ordinary grounds of action, their topics of discourse, of their confidence in themselves, and those to whom they have been accustomed to look up to for instruction and advice. It is making children of them. You unhinge all their established opinions and trains of thought; and after leaving them in this listless, vacant, unsettled state—dissatisfied with their own notions and shocked at yours—you expect them to court and be delighted with your company, because, forsooth, you have only expressed your sincere and conscientious convictions. Mankind are not deceived by professions, unless they choose. They think that this pill of true doctrine, however it may be gilded over, is full of gall and bitterness to them; and, again, it is a maxim of which the vulgar are firmly persuaded, that plain-speaking (as it is called), nine parts in ten, is spleen and self-opinion; and the other part, perhaps, honesty. Those who will not abate an inch in argument, and are always seeking to recover the wind of you, are, in the eye of the world, disagreeable, unconscionable people, who ought to be *sent to Coventry*, or left to wrangle by themselves. No persons, however, are more averse to contradiction than these same dogmatists. What shews our susceptibility on this point is, that there is no flattery so adroit or effectual as that of implicit assent. Any one, however mean his capacity or ill-qualified to judge, who gives way to all our sentiments, and never seems to think but as we do, is indeed an *alter idem*—another self; and we admit him without scruple into our entire confidence, " yea, into our heart of hearts."

It is the same in books. Those which, under the disguise of plain speaking, vent paradoxes, and set their faces against the " common sense " of mankind, are neither " the volumes

> " that enrich the shops,
> That pass with approbation through the land ; "

nor, I fear, can it be added—

> " That bring their authors an immortal fame."

They excite a clamour and opposition at first, and are in general soon consigned to oblivion. Even if the opinions are in the end adopted, the authors gain little by it, and their names remain in their original obloquy; for the public will own no obligations to such ungracious benefactors. In like manner, there are many books written in a very delightful vein, though with little in them, and that are accordingly popular. Their principle is to please, and not to offend; and they succeed in both objects. We are contented with the deference shewn to our feelings for the time, and grant a truce both to wit and wisdom. The " courteous reader " and the good-natured author are well matched in this instance, and find their account in mutual tenderness and forbearance to each other's infirmities. I am not sure that Walton's *Angler* is not a book of this last description—

> " That dallies with the innocence of thought,
> Like the old time."

Hobbes and Mandeville are in the opposite extreme, and have met with a correspondent fate. The *Tatler* and *Spectator* are in the golden mean, carry instruction as far as it can go without shocking, and give the most exquisite pleasure without one particle of pain. " *Desire to please, and you will infallibly please*," is a maxim equally applicable to the study or the drawing-room. Thus, also, we see actors of very small pretensions, and who have scarce any other merit than that of being on good terms with themselves, and in high good humour with their parts (though they hardly understand a word of them), who are universal favourites with the audience. Others, who are masters of their art, and in whom no slip or flaw can be detected, you have no pleasure in seeing, from something dry, repulsive, and unconciliating in their manner; and you almost hate the very mention of their names, as an unavailing appeal to your candid decision in their favour, and as taxing you with injustice for refusing it.

We may observe persons who seem to take a particular delight in the *disagreeable*. They catch all sorts of uncouth tones and gestures, the manners and dialect of clowns and hoydens, and aim at vulgarity as desperately as others ape gentility. [This is what is often understood by a *love of low life*.] They say the most unwarrantable things, without meaning or feeling what they say. What startles or shocks other people, is to them a sport—an amusing excitement—a filip to their constitutions; and from the bluntness of their perceptions, and a certain wilfulness of spirit, not being able to enter into the refined and agreeable, they make a merit of despising everything of the kind. Masculine women, for example, are those who, not being distinguished by the charms and delicacy of the sex, affect a superiority over it by throwing aside all decorum. We also find another class, who continually do and say what they ought not, and what they do not intend, and who are governed almost entirely by an instinct of absurdity. Owing to a perversity of imagination or irritability of nerve, the idea that a thing is improper acts as a provocation to it: the fear of committing a blunder is so strong, that in their agitation they *bolt* out whatever is uppermost in their minds, before they are aware of the consequence. The dread of something wrong haunts and rivets their attention to it; and an uneasy, morbid apprehensiveness of temper takes away their self-possession, and hurries them into the very mistakes they are most anxious to avoid.

If we look about us, and ask who are the agreeable and disagreeable people in the world, we shall see that it does not so much depend on their virtues or vices—their understanding or stupidity—as on the degree of pleasure or pain they seem to feel in ordinary social intercourse. What signify all the good qualities any one possesses, if he is none the better for them himself? If the cause is so delightful, the effect ought to be so too. We enjoy a friend's society only in proportion as he is satisfied with ours. Even wit, however it may startle, is only agreeable as it is sheathed in good-humour. There are a kind of *intellectual stammerers*, who are delivered of their good things with pain and effort; and consequently what costs them such evident uneasiness does not impart unmixed delight to the bystanders. There are those, on the contrary, whose sallies cost them nothing—who abound in a

flow of pleasantry and good-humour; and who float down
the stream with them carelessly and triumphantly—

" Wit at the helm, and Pleasure at the prow."

Perhaps it may be said of English wit in general, that it
too much resembles pointed lead: after all, there is
something heavy and dull in it! The race of small wits
are not the least agreeable people in the world. They
have their little joke to themselves, enjoy it, and do not
set up any preposterous pretensions to thwart the current
of our self-love. Toad-eating is accounted a thriving
profession; and a *butt*, according to the *Spectator*, is a
highly useful member of society—as one who takes
whatever is said of him in good part, and as necessary
to conduct off the spleen and superfluous petulance of
the company. Opposed to these are the swaggering
bullies—the licensed wits—the free-thinkers—the loud
talkers, who, in the jockey phrase, have *lost their mouths*,
and cannot be reined in by any regard to decency or
common-sense. The more obnoxious the subject, the
more are they charmed with it, converting their want of
feeling into a proof of superiority to vulgar prejudice and
squeamish affectation. But there is an unseemly exposure
of the mind, as well as of the body. There are some objects
that shock the sense, and cannot with propriety be
mentioned: there are naked truths that offend the mind,
and ought to be kept out of sight as much as possible.
For human nature cannot bear to be too hardly pressed
upon. One of these cynical truisms, when brought forward to the world, may be forgiven as a slip of the pen:
a succession of them, denoting a deliberate purpose
and *malice prepense*, must ruin any writer. Lord Byron
had got into an irregular course of these a little before his
death—seemed desirous, in imitation of Mr. Shelley, to
run the gauntlet of public obloquy—and, at the same time,
wishing to screen himself from the censure he defied,

dedicated his *Cain* to Sir Walter Scott—a pretty god-father to such a bantling!

Some persons are of so teasing and fidgety a turn of mind, that they do not give you a moment's rest. Everything goes wrong with them. They complain of a headache or the weather. They take up a book, and lay it down again—venture an opinion, and retract it before they have half done—offer to serve you, and prevent some, one else from doing it. If you dine with them at a tavern, in order to be more at your ease, the fish is too little done—the sauce is not the right one; they ask for a sort of wine which they think is not to be had, or if it is, after some trouble, procured, do not touch it; they give the waiter fifty contradictory orders, and are restless and sit on thorns the whole of dinner-time. All this is owing to a want of robust health, and of a strong spirit of enjoyment: it is a fastidious habit of mind, produced by a valetudinary habit of body: they are out of sorts with everything, and of course their ill-humour and captiousness communicates itself to you, who are as little delighted with them as they are with other things. Another sort of people, equally objectionable with this helpless class, who are disconcerted by a shower of rain or stopped by an insect's wing, are those who, in the opposite spirit, will have everything their own way, and carry all before them—who cannot brook the slightest shadow of opposition—who are always in the heat of an argument—who knit their brows and clench their teeth in some speculative discussion, as if they were engaged in a personal quarrel—and who, though successful over almost every competitor, seem still to resent the very offer of resistance to their supposed authority, and are as angry as if they had sustained some premeditated injury. There is an impatience of temper and an intolerance of opinion in this that concilates neither our affection nor esteem. To such persons nothing appears of any

M

moment but the indulgence of a domineering intellectual superiority, to the disregard and discomfiture of their own and every body else's comfort. Mounted on an abstract proposition, they trample on every courtesy and decency of behaviour; and though, perhaps, they do not intend the gross personalities they are guilty of, yet they cannot be acquitted of a want of due consideration for others, and of an intolerable egotism in the support of truth and justice. You may hear one of these Quixotic declaimers pleading the cause of humanity in a voice of thunder, or expatiating on the beauty of a Guido with features distorted with rage and scorn. This is not a very amiable or edifying spectacle.

There are persons who cannot make friends. Who are they? Those who cannot be friends. It is not the want of understanding or good-nature, of entertaining or useful qualities, that you complain of: on the contrary, they have probably many points of attraction; but they have one that neutralizes all these—they care nothing about you, and are neither the better nor worse for what you think of them. They manifest no joy at your approach; and when you leave them, it is with a feeling that they can do just as well without you. This is not sullenness, nor indifference, nor absence of mind; but they are intent solely on their own thoughts, and you are merely one of the subjects they exercise them upon. They live in society as in a solitude; and, however their brain works, their pulse beats neither faster nor slower for the common accidents of life. There is, therefore, something cold and repulsive in the air that is about them—like that of marble. In a word, they are *modern philosophers;* and the modern philosopher is what the pedant was of old—a being who lives in a world of his own, and has no correspondence with this. It is not that such persons have not done you services—you acknowledge it; it is not that they have said severe things of you—you submit to it as a necessary evil: but it is the cool manner in which the whole is done that annoys you —the speculating upon you, as if you were nobody— the regarding you, with a view to an experiment *in corpore vili*—the principle of dissection—the determination to spare no blemishes—to cut you down to your real standard;—in short, the utter absence of the partiality of friendship, the blind enthusiasm of affection, or the delicacy of common decency, that whether they " hew you as a carcase fit for hounds, or carve you as a dish fit for the gods," the operation on your feelings and your sense of obligation is just the same; and, whether they are demons or angels in themselves, you wish them equally *at the devil!*

Other persons of worth and sense give way to mere violence of temperament (with which the understanding has nothing to do)—are burnt up with a perpetual fury —repel and throw you to a distance by their restless, whirling motion—so that you dare not go near them, or feel as uneasy in their company as if you stood on the edge of a volcano. They have their *tempora mollia fandi;* but then what a stir may you not expect the next moment! Nothing is less inviting or less comfortable than this state of uncertainty and apprehension. Then there are those who never approach you without the most alarming advice or information, telling you that you are in a dying way, or that your affairs are on the point of ruin, by way of disburthening their consciences; and others, who give you to understand much the same thing as a good joke, out of sheer impertinence, constitutional vivacity, and want of something to say. All these, it must be confessed, are disagreeable people; and you repay their over-anxiety or total forgetfulness of you, by a determination to *cut* them as speedily as possible. We meet with instances of persons who overpower you by a sort of boisterous mirth and rude animal spirits,

with whose ordinary state of excitement it is as impossible
to keep up as with that of any one really intoxicated; and
with others who seem scarce alive—who take no pleasure
or interest in anything—who are born to exemplify the
maxim,

> " Not to admire is all the art I know
> To make men happy, or to keep them so,"—

and whose mawkish insensibility or sullen scorn are
equally annoying. In general, all people brought up in
remote country places, where life is crude and harsh
—all sectaries—all partisans of a losing cause, are discontented and disagreeable. Commend me above all
to the Westminster School of Reform, whose blood runs
as cold in their veins as the torpedo's, and whose touch
jars like it. Catholics are, upon the whole, more amiable
than Protestants—foreigners than English people. Among
ourselves, the Scotch, as a nation, are particularly disagreeable. They hate every appearance of comfort themselves
and refuse it to others. Their climate, their religion, and
their habits are equally averse to pleasure. Their manners
are either distinguished by a fawning sycophancy (to
gain their own ends, and conceal their natural defects),
that makes one sick; or by a morose, unbending callous-
ness, that makes one shudder. I had forgot to mention
two other descriptions of persons who fall under the
scope of this essay:—those who take up a subject, and
run on with it interminably, without knowing whether
their hearers care one word about it, or in the least
minding what reception their oratory meets with—
these are pretty generally voted *bores* (mostly German
ones);—and others, who may be designated as practical
paradox-mongers—who discard the " milk of human
kindness," and an attention to common observances,
from all their actions, as effeminate and puling—who
wear an out-of-the-way hat as a mark of superior under-

standing, and carry home a handkerchief-full of mush-rooms in the top of it as an original discovery—who give you craw-fish for supper instead of lobsters; seek their company in a garret and over a gin-bottle, to avoid the imputation of affecting genteel society; and discard their friends after a term of years, and warn others against them, as being *honest fellows,* which is thought a vulgar prejudice. This is carrying the harsh and repulsive even beyond the disagreeable—to the hateful. Such persons are generally people of common-place understandings, obtuse feelings, and inordinate vanity. They are formidable if they get you in their power —otherwise, they are only to be laughed at.

There are a vast number who are disagreeable from meanness of spirit, downright insolence, from slovenli-ness of dress or disgusting tricks, from folly or igno-rance; but these causes are positive moral or physical defects, and I only meant to speak of that repulsiveness of manners which arises from want of tact and sympathy with others. So far of friendship: a word, if I durst, of love. Gallantry to women (the sure road to their favour) is nothing but the appearance of extreme devotion to all their wants and wishes—a delight in their satisfaction, and a confidence in yourself, as being able to contribute towards it. The slightest indifference with regard to them, or distrust of yourself, are equally fatal. The amiable is the voluptuous in looks, manner, or words. No face that exhibits this kind of expression—whether lively or serious, obvious or suppressed, will be thought ugly—no address, awkward—no lover who approaches every woman he meets as his mistress, will be unsuccess-ful. Diffidence and awkwardness are the two antidotes to love.

To please universally, we must be pleased with our-selves and others. There should be a tinge of the cox-comb, an oil of self-complacency, an anticipation of success—there should be no gloom, no moroseness, no shyness—in short, there should be very little of the Englishman, and a good deal of the Frenchman. But though, I believe, this is the receipt, we are none the nearer making use of it. It is impossible for those who are naturally disagreeable ever to become otherwise. This is some consolation, as it may save a world of useless pains and anxiety. "*Desire to please, and you will infallibly please*," is a true maxim; but it does not follow that it is in the power of all to practise it. A vain man, who thinks he is endeavouring to please, is only endeavouring to shine, and is still farther from the mark. An irritable man, who puts a check upon himself, only grows dull, and loses spirit to be anything. Good temper and a happy turn of mind (which are the indispensable requisites) can no more be commanded than good health or good looks; and though the plain and sickly need not distort their features, and may abstain from excess, this is all they can do. The utmost a disagreeable person can do is to hope, by care and study, to become less disagreeable than he is, and to pass unnoticed in society. With this negative character he should be contented, and may build his fame and happiness on other things.

I will conclude with a description of men who neither please nor aspire to please anybody, and who can come in nowhere so properly as at the fag-end of an essay:— I mean that class of discontented but amusing persons, who are infatuated with their own ill success, and reduced to despair by a lucky turn in their favour. While all goes well, they are *like fish out of water*. They have no reliance on or sympathy with their good fortune, and look upon it as a momentary delusion. Let a doubt be thrown on the question, and they begin to be full of lively apprehensions again: let all their hopes vanish, and they feel themselves on firm ground once more.

From want of spirit, or from habit, their imaginations cannot rise above the low ground of humility—cannot reflect the gay, flaunting tints of the fancy—flag and droop into despondency—and can neither indulge the expectation, nor employ the means of success. Even when it is within their reach, they dare not lay hands upon it; and shrink from unlooked-for bursts of prosperity, as something of which they are both ashamed and unworthy. The class of *croakers* here spoken of are less delighted with other people's misfortunes than with their own. Their neighbours may have some pretensions —they have none. Querulous complaints and anticipations of discomfort are the food on which they live; and they at last acquire a passion for that which is the favourite theme of their thoughts, and can no more do without it than without the pinch of snuff with which they season their conversation, and enliven the pauses of their daily prognostics.

ON A SUN-DIAL

(NEW MONTHLY MAGAZINE, OCT., 1827)

" To carve out dials quaintly, point by point."
SHAKESPEAR.

H O R A S non numero nisi serenas—is the motto of a sundial near Venice. There is a softness and a harmony in the words and in the thought unparalleled. Of all conceits it is surely the most classical. " I count only the hours that are serene." What a bland and care-dispelling feeling! How the shadows seem to fade on the dial-plate as the sky lours, and time presents only a blank unless as its progress is marked by what is joyous, and all that is not happy sinks into oblivion! What a

fine lesson is conveyed to the mind—to take no note of
time but by its benefits, to watch only for the smiles
and neglect the frowns of fate, to compose our lives of
bright and gentle moments, turning always to the sunny
side of things, and letting the rest slip from our imaginations, unheeded or forgotten! How different from the
common art of self-tormenting! For myself, as I rode
along the Brenta, while the sun shone hot upon its
sluggish, slimy waves, my sensations were far from
comfortable; but the reading this inscription on the
side of a glaring wall in an instant restored me to myself; and still, whenever I think of or repeat it, it has
the power of wafting me into the region of pure and
blissful abstraction. I cannot help fancying it to be a
legend of Popish superstition. Some monk of the dark
ages must have invented and bequeathed it to us, who,
loitering in trim gardens and watching the silent march
of time, as his fruits ripened in the sun or his flowers
scented the balmy air, felt a mild languor pervade his
senses, and having little to do or to care for, determined
(in imitation of his sun-dial) to efface that little from
his thoughts or draw a veil over it, making of his life
one long dream of quiet! *Horas non numero nisi serenas*
—he might repeat, when the heavens were overcast and
the gathering storm scattered the falling leaves, and
turn to his books and wrap himself in his golden studies!
Out of some such mood of mind, indolent, elegant,
thoughtful, this exquisite device (speaking volumes)
must have originated.

Of the several modes of counting time, that by the
sun-dial is perhaps the most apposite and striking, if
not the most convenient or comprehensive. It does
not obtrude its observations, though it "morals on
the time," and, by its stationary character, forms a
contrast to the most fleeting of all essences. It stands
sub dio—under the marble air, and there is some con-

nexion between the image of infinity and eternity. I should also like to have a sun-flower growing near it with bees fluttering round.[1] It should be of iron to denote duration, and have a dull, leaden look. I hate a sun-dial made of wood, which is rather calculated to show the variations of the seasons, than the progress of time, slow, silent, imperceptible, chequered with light and shade. If our hours were all serene, we might probably take almost as little note of them, as the dial does of those that are clouded. It is the shadow thrown across, that gives us warning of their flight. Otherwise, our impressions would take the same undistinguishable hue; we should scarce be conscious of our existence. Those who have had none of the cares of this life to harass and disturb them, have been obliged to have recourse to the hopes and fears of the next to vary the prospect before them. Most of the methods for measuring the lapse of time have, I believe, been the contrivance of monks and religious recluses, who, finding time hang heavy on their hands, were at some pains to see how they got rid of it. The hour-glass is, I suspect, an older invention; and it is certainly the most defective of all. Its creeping sands are not indeed an unapt emblem of the minute, countless portions of our existence; and the manner in which they gradually slide through the hollow glass and diminish in number till not a single one is left, also illustrates the way in which our years slip from us by stealth: but as a mechanical invention, it is rather a hindrance than a help, for it requires to have the time, of which it pretends to count the precious moments, taken up in attention to itself, and in seeing that when one end of the glass is empty, we turn it round, in order that it may go on again, or else all our labour is

[1] Is this a verbal fallacy? Or in the close, retired, sheltered scene which I have imagined to myself, is not the sun-flower a natural accompaniment of the sun-dial?

M *

lost, and we must wait for some other mode of ascertaining the time before we can recover our reckoning and proceed as before. The philosopher in his cell, the cottager at her spinning-wheel must, however, find an invaluable acquisition in this " companion of the lonely hour," as it has been called,[1] which not only serves to tell how the time goes, but to fill up its vacancies. What a treasure must not the little box seem to hold, as if it were a sacred deposit of the very grains and fleeting sands of life ! What a business, in lieu of other more important avocations, to see it out to the last sand, and then to renew the process again on the instant, that there may not be the least flaw or error in the account! What a strong sense must be brought home to the mind of the value and irrecoverable nature of the time that is fled; what a thrilling, incessant consciousness of the slippery tenure by which we hold what remains of it! Our very existence must seem crumbling to atoms, and running down (without a miraculous reprieve) to the last fragment. " Dust to dust and ashes to ashes " is a text that might be fairly inscribed on an hour-glass: it is ordinarily associated with the scythe of Time and a Death's-head, as a *memento mori;* and has, no doubt, furnished many a tacit hint to the apprehensive and visionary enthusiast in favour of a resurrection to another life!

The French give a different turn to things, less *sombre* and less edifying. A common and also a very pleasing ornament to a clock, in Paris, is a figure of Time seated in a boat which Cupid is rowing along, with the motto, *L'Amour fait passer le Temps*—which the wits again have travestied into *Le Temps fait passer l'Amour.* All this is ingenious and well; but it wants sentiment. I like a

---

[1] " Once more, companion of the lonely hour,
    I'll turn thee up again."
    Bloomfield's Poems—The Widow to her Hour-glass.

people who have something that they love and something
that they hate, and with whom everything is not alike a
matter of indifference or *pour passer le temps*. The French
attach no importance to anything, except for the moment;
they are only thinking how they shall get rid of one
sensation for another; all their ideas are *in transitu*.
Everything is detached, nothing is accumulated. It would
be a million of years before a Frenchman would think
of the *Horas non numero nisi serenas*. Its impassioned
repose and *ideal* voluptuousness are as far from their
breasts as the poetry of that line in Shakespear—"How
sweet the moonlight sleeps upon that bank!" They
never arrive at the classical—or the romantic. They
blow the bubbles of vanity, fashion, and pleasure; but
they do not expand their perceptions into refinement,
or strengthen them into solidity. Where there is nothing
fine in the groundwork of the imagination, nothing fine
in the superstructure can be produced. They are light,
airy, fanciful (to give them their due)—but when they
attempt to be serious (beyond mere good sense) they are
either dull or extravagant. When the volatile salt has
flown off, nothing but a *caput mortuum* remains. They
have infinite crotchets and caprices with their clocks and
watches, which seem made for anything but to tell the
hour—gold repeaters, watches with metal covers, clocks
with hands to count the seconds. There is no escaping
from quackery and impertinence, even in our attempts
to calculate the waste of time. The years gallop fast
enough for me, without remarking every moment as it
flies; and farther, I must say I dislike a watch (whether
of French or English manufacture) that comes to me
like a footpad with its face muffled, and does not present
its clear, open aspect like a friend, and point with its
finger to the time of day. All this opening and shutting
of dull, heavy cases (under pretence that the glass lid
is liable to be broken, or lets in the dust or air and

obstructs the movements of the watch,) is not to husband time, but to give trouble. It is mere pomposity and self-importance, like consulting a mysterious oracle that one carries about with one in one's pocket, instead of asking a common question of an acquaintance or companion. There are two clocks which strike the hour in the room where I am. This I do not like. In the first place, I do not want to be reminded twice how the time goes (it is like the second tap of a saucy servant at your door when perhaps you have no wish to get up): in the next place, it is starting a difference of opinion on the subject, and I am averse to every appearance of wrangling and disputation. Time moves on the same, whatever disparity there may be in our mode of keeping count of it, like true fame in spite of the cavils and contradictions of the critics. I am no friend to repeating watches. The only pleasant association I have with them is the account given by Rousseau of some French lady, who sat up reading the *New Eloise* when it first came out, and ordering her maid to sound the repeater, found it was too late to go to bed, and continued reading on till morning. Yet how different is the interest excited by this story from the account which Rousseau somewhere else gives of his sitting up with his father reading romances, when a boy, till they were startled by the swallows twittering in their nests at day-break, and the father cried out, half angry and ashamed—" *Allons, mon fils; je suis plus enfant que toi!* " In general, I have heard repeating watches sounded in stage-coaches at night, when some fellow-traveller suddenly awaking and wondering what was the hour, another has very deliberately taken out his watch, and pressing the spring, it has counted out the time; each petty stroke acting like a sharp puncture on the ear, and informing me of the dreary hours I had already passed, and of the more dreary ones I had to wait till morning.

The great advantage, it is true, which clocks have over watches and other dumb reckoners of time is, that for the most part they strike the hour—that they are as it were the mouth-pieces of time; that they not only point it to the eye, but impress it on the ear; that they " lend it both an understanding and a tongue." Time thus speaks to us in an audible and warning voice. Objects of sight are easily distinguished by the sense, and suggest useful reflections to the mind; sounds, from their inter-mittent nature, and perhaps other causes, appeal more to the imagination, and strike upon the heart. But to do this, they must be unexpected and involuntary—there must be no trick in the case—they should not be squeezed out with a finger and thumb; there should be nothing optional, personal in their occurrence; they should be like stern, inflexible monitors, that nothing can prevent from discharging their duty. Surely, if there is any-thing with which we should not mix up our vanity and self-consequence, it is with Time, the most independent of all things. All the sublimity, all the superstition that hang upon this palpable mode of announcing its flight, are chiefly attached to this circumstance. Time would lose its abstracted character, if we kept it like a curiosity or a jack-in-a-box: its prophetic warnings would have no effect, if it obviously spoke only at our prompting like a paltry ventriloquism. The clock that tells the coming, dreaded hour—the castle bell, that " with its brazen throat and iron tongue, sounds *one* unto the drowsy ear of night "—the curfew, " swinging slow with sullen roar " o'er wizard stream or fountain, are like a voice from other worlds, big with unknown events. The last sound, which is still kept up as an old custom in many parts of England, is a great favourite with me. I used to hear it when a boy. It tells a tale of other times. The days that are past, the generations that are gone, the tangled forest glades and hamlets brown of my native country, the woodsman's art, the Norman warrior armed for the battle or in his festive hall, the conqueror's iron rule and peasant's lamp extinguished, all start up at the clamorous peal, and fill my mind with fear and wonder. I confess, nothing at present interests me but what has been—the recollection of the impressions of my early life, or events long past, of which only the dim traces remain in a mouldering ruin or half-obsolete custom. That *things should be that are now no more,* creates in my mind the most unfeigned astonishment. I cannot solve the mystery of the past, nor exhaust my pleasure in it. The years, the generations to come, are nothing to me. We care no more about the world in the year 2300 than we do about one of the planets. We might as well make a voyage to the moon as think of stealing a march upon Time with impunity. *De non apparentibus et non existentibus eadem est ratio.* Those who are to come after us and push us from the stage seem like upstarts and pretenders, that may be said to exist *in vacuo,* we know not upon what, except as they are blown up with vanity and self-conceit by their patrons among the moderns. But the ancients are true and *bona fide* people, to whom we are bound by aggregate knowledge and filial ties, and in whom, seen by the mellow light of history, we feel our own existence doubled and our pride consoled, as we ruminate on the vestiges of the past. The public in general, however, do not carry this speculative indifference about the future to what is to happen to themselves, or to the part they are to act in the busy scene. For my own part, I do; and the only wish I can form, or that ever prompts the passing sigh, would be to live some of my years over again—they would be those in which I enjoyed and suffered most!

The ticking of a clock in the night has nothing very interesting nor very alarming in it, though superstition has magnified it into an omen. In a state of vigilanc-

or debility, it preys upon the spirits like the persecution of a teazing, pertinacious insect; and haunting the imagination after it has ceased in reality, is converted into the death-watch. Time is rendered vast by contemplating its minute portions thus repeatedly and painfully urged upon its attention, as the ocean in its immensity is composed of water-drops. A clock striking with a clear and silver sound is a great relief in such circumstances, breaks the spell, and resembles a sylph-like and friendly spirit in the room. Foreigners, with all their tricks and contrivances upon clocks and time-pieces, are strangers to the sound of village bells, though perhaps a people that can dance may dispense with them. They impart a pensive, wayward pleasure to the mind, and are a kind of chronology of happy events, often serious in the retrospect—births, marriages, and so forth. Coleridge calls them " the poor man's only music." A village spire in England peeping from its cluster of trees, is always associated in imagination with this cheerful accompaniment, and may be expected to pour its joyous tidings on the gale. In Catholic countries, you are stunned with the everlasting tolling of bells to prayers or for the dead. In the Apennines, and other wild and mountainous districts of Italy, the little chapel-bell with its simple tinkling sound has a romantic and charming effect. The monks in former times appear to have taken a pride in the construction of bells as well as churches; and some of those of the great cathedrals abroad (as at Cologne and Rouen) may be fairly said to be hoarse with counting the flight of ages. The chimes in Holland are a nuisance. They dance in the hours and the quarters. They leave no respite to the imagination. Before one set has done ringing in your ears, another begins. You do not know whether the hours move or stand still, go backwards or forwards, so fantastical and perplexing are their accompaniments. Time is a more

staid personage, and not so full of gambols. It puts you
in mind of a tune with variations, or of an embroidered
dress. Surely, nothing is more simple than Time. His
march is straightforward; but we should have leisure
allowed us to look back upon the distance we have come,
and not be counting his steps every moment. Time in
Holland is a foolish old fellow with all the antics of a
youth, who " goes to church in a coranto, and lights his
pipe in a cinque-pace." The chimes with us, on the
contrary, as they come in every three or four hours, are
like stages in the journey of the day. They give a fillip
to the lazy, creeping hours, and relieve the lassitude of
country-places. At noon, their desultory, trivial song is
diffused through the hamlet with the odour of rashers
of bacon; at the close of day they send the toil-worn
sleepers to their beds. Their discontinuance would be a
great loss to the thinking or unthinking public. Mr.
Wordsworth has painted their effect on the mind when
he makes his friend Matthew, in a fit of inspired dotage,

> " Sing those witty rhymes
> About the crazy old church-clock
> And the bewilder'd chimes."

The tolling of the bell for deaths and executions is a
fearful summons, though, as it announces, not the
advance of time but the approach of fate, it happily makes
no part of our subject. Otherwise, the " sound of the
bell " for Macheath's execution in the *Beggar's Opera*,
or for that of the Conspirators in *Venice Preserved*, with
the roll of the drum at a soldier's funeral, and a digression
to that of my Uncle Toby, as it is so finely described by
Sterne, would furnish ample topics to descant upon. If
I were a moralist, I might disapprove the ringing in the
new and ringing out the old year.

> " Why dance ye, mortals, o'er the grave of Time ? "

St. Paul's bell tolls only for the death of our English

kings, or a distinguished personage or two, with long intervals between.[1]

Those who have no artificial means of ascertaining the progress of time, are in general the most acute in discerning its immediate signs, and are most retentive of individual dates. The mechanical aids to knowledge are not sharpeners of the wits. The understanding of a savage is a kind of natural almanac, and more true in its prognostication of the future. In his mind's eye he sees what has happened or what is likely to happen to him, "as in a map the voyager his course." Those who read the times and seasons in the aspect of the heavens and the configuration of the stars, who count by moons and know when the sun rises and sets, are by no means ignorant of their own affairs or of the common concatenation of events. People in such situations have not their faculties distracted by any multiplicity of inquiries beyond what befalls themselves, and the outward appearances that mark the change. There is, therefore, a simplicity and clearness in the knowledge they possess, which often puzzles the more learned. I am sometimes surprised at a shepherd-boy by the road-side, who sees nothing but the earth and sky, asking me the time of day—he ought to know so much better than any one how far the sun is above the horizon. I suppose he wants to ask a question of a passenger, or to see if he has a watch. Robinson Crusoe lost his reckoning in the monotony of his life and that bewildering dream of solitude, and was fain to have recourse to the notches in a piece of wood. What a diary was his! And how time must have spread its circuit round him, vast and pathless as the ocean!

For myself, I have never had a watch nor any other

---

[1] Rousseau has admirably described the effect of bells on the imagination in a passage in the *Confessions*, beginning, "*Le son des cloches m'a toujours singulièrement affecté*," etc.

mode of keeping time in my possession, nor ever wish
to learn how time goes. It is a sign I have had little to
do, few avocations, few engagements. When I am in
a town, I can hear the clock; and when I am in the
country, I can listen to the silence. What I like best is
to lie whole mornings on a sunny bank on Salisbury
Plain, without any object before me, neither knowing nor
caring how time passes, and thus " with light-winged
toys of feathered Idleness " to melt down hours to moments. Perhaps some such thoughts as I have here set
down float before me like motes before my half-shut eyes,
or some vivid image of the past by forcible contrast rushes
by me—" Diana and her fawn, and all the glories of the
antique world "; then I start away to prevent the iron
from entering my soul, and let fall some tears into that
stream of time which separates me farther and farther
from all I once loved! At length I rouse myself from
my reverie, and home to dinner, proud of killing time
with thought, nay even without thinking. Somewhat of
this idle humour I inherit from my father, though he
had not the same freedom from *ennui*, for he was not a
metaphysician; and there were stops and vacant intervals in his being which he did not well know how to fill
up. He used in these cases, and as an obvious resource,
carefully to wind up his watch at night, and " with lack-
lustre eye " more than once in the course of the day
look to see what o'clock it was. Yet he had nothing else
in his character in common with the elder Mr. Shandy.
Were I to attempt a sketch of him, for my own or the
reader's satisfaction, it would be after the following
manner——But now I recollect I have done something
of the kind once before, and were I to resume the subject
here, some bat or owl of a critic, with spectacled gravity,
might swear I had stolen the whole of this Essay from
myself—or (what is worse) from him! So I had better
let it go as it is.

THE LETTER-BELL

(MONTHLY MAGAZINE, MARCH, 1831)

COMPLAINTS are frequently made of the vanity and shortness of human life, when, if we examine its smallest details, they present a world by themselves. The most trifling objects, retraced with the eye of memory, assume the vividness, the delicacy, and importance of insects seen through a magnifying glass. There is no end of the brilliancy or the variety. The habitual feeling of the love of life may be compared to " one entire and perfect chrysolite," which, if analysed, breaks into a thousand shining fragments. Ask the sum-total of the value of human life, and we are puzzled with the length of the account, and the multiplicity of items in it: take any one of them apart, and it is wonderful what matter for reflection will be found in it! As I write this, the *Letter-Bell* passes; it has a lively, pleasant sound with it, and not only fills the street with its importunate clamour, but rings clear through the length of many half-forgotten years. It strikes upon the ear, it vibrates to the brain, it wakes me from the dream of time, it flings me back upon my first entrance into life, the period of my first coming up to town, when all around was strange, uncertain, adverse—a hubbub of confused noises, a chaos of shifting objects—and when this sound alone, startling me with the recollection of a letter I had to send to the friends I had lately left, brought me as it were to myself, made me feel that I had links still connecting me with the universe, and gave me hope and patience to persevere. At that loud-tinkling, interrupted sound, the long line of blue hills near the place where I was brought up waves in the horizon, a golden sunset hovers over them, the dwarf-oaks rustle their red leaves in the evening breeze, and the road from Wem to Shrewsbury, by which I first set out on my journey through life, stares me in the face as plain, but, from time and change, not less visionary and mysterious than the pictures in the *Pilgrim's Progress*. Or if the Letter-Bell does not lead me a dance into the country, it fixes me in the thick of my town recollections, I know not how long ago. It was a kind of alarm to break off from my work when there happened to be company to dinner or when I was going to the play. *That* was going to the play, indeed, when I went twice a year, and had not been more than half a dozen times in my life. Even the idea that any one else in the house was going, was a sort of reflected enjoyment, and conjured up a lively anticipation of the scene. I remember a Miss D——, a maiden lady from Wales (who in her youth was to have been married to an earl), tantalized me greatly in this way, by talking all day of going to see Mrs. Siddons' " airs and graces " at night in some favourite part; and when the Letter-Bell announced that the time was approaching, and its last receding sound lingered on the ear, or was lost in silence, how anxious and uneasy I became, lest she and her companion should not be in time to get good places—lest the curtain should draw up before they arrived—and lest I should lose one line or look in the intelligent report which I should hear the next morning! The punctuating of time at that early period—everything that gives it an articulate voice—seems of the utmost consequence; for we do not know what scenes in the *ideal* world may run out of them: a world of interest may hang upon every instant, and we can hardly sustain the weight of future years which are contained in embryo in the most minute and inconsiderable passing events. How often have I put off writing a letter till it was too late! How often have I had to run after the postman with it—now missing, now recovering the sound of his bell —breathless, angry with myself—then hearing the welcome sound come full round a corner—and seeing the scarlet costume which set all my fears and self-reproaches at rest! I do not recollect having ever repented giving a letter to the postman or wishing to retrieve it after he had once deposited it in his bag. What I have once set my hand to, I take the consequences of, and have been always pretty much of the same humour in this respect. I am not like the person who, having sent off a letter to his mistress, who resided a hundred and twenty miles in the country, and disapproving, on second thoughts, of some expressions contained in it, took a post-chaise and four to follow and intercept it the next morning. At other times, I have sat and watched the decaying embers in a little back painting-room (just as the wintry day declined), and brooded over the half-finished copy of a Rembrandt, or a landscape by Vangoyen, placing it where it might catch a dim gleam of light from the fire; while the Letter-Bell was the only sound that drew my thoughts to the world without, and reminded me that I had a task to perform in it. As to that landscape, methinks I see it now—

> " The slow canal, the yellow-blossomed vale,
> The willow-tufted bank, the gliding sail."

There was a windmill, too, with a poor low clay-built cottage beside it: how delighted I was when I had made the tremulous, undulating reflection in the water, and saw the dull canvas become a lucid mirror of the commonest features of nature! Certainly, painting gives one a strong interest in nature and humanity (it is not the *dandy-school* of morals or sentiment)—

> " While with an eye made quiet by the power
> Of harmony and the deep power of joy,
> We see into the life of things."

Perhaps there is no part of a painter's life (if we must tell " the secrets of the prison-house ") in which he has

more enjoyment of himself and his art, than that in
which, after his work is over, and with furtive, sidelong
glances at what he has done, he is employed in washing
his brushes and cleaning his pallet for the day. Afterwards, when he gets a servant in livery to do this for
him, he may have other and more ostensible sources of
satisfaction—greater splendour, wealth, or fame; but he
will not be so wholly in his art, nor will his art have
such a hold on him as when he was too poor to transfer
its meanest drudgery to others—too humble to despise
aught that had to do with the object of his glory and his
pride, with that on which all his projects of ambition or
pleasure were founded. " Entire affection scorneth nicer
hands." When the professor is above this mechanical
part of his business, it may have become a *stalking-horse*
to other worldly schemes, but is no longer his *hobby-horse*
and the delight of his inmost thoughts.

I used sometimes to hurry through this part of my
occupation, while the Letter-Bell (which was my dinner-
bell) summoned me to the fraternal board, where youth
and hope

> " Made good digestion wait on appetite
> And health on both ; "

or oftener I put it off till after dinner, that I might loiter
longer and with more luxurious indolence over it, and
connect it with the thoughts of my next day's labours.

The dustman's-bell, with its heavy monotonous noise,
and the brisk, lively tinkle of the muffin-bell, have something in them, but not much. They will bear dilating
upon with the utmost licence of inventive prose. All
things are not alike *conductors* to the imagination. A
learned Scotch professor found fault with an ingenious
friend and arch-critic for cultivating a rookery on his
grounds: the professor declared " he would as soon
think of encouraging a *froggery*." This was barbarous

as it was senseless. Strange, that a country that has produced the *Scotch Novels* and *Gertrude of Wyoming* should want sentiment!

The postman's double-knock at the door the next morning is "more germain to the matter." How that knock often goes to the heart! We distinguish to a nicety the arrival of the Twopenny or the General Post. The summons of the latter is louder and heavier, as bringing news from a greater distance, and as, the longer it has been delayed, fraught with a deeper interest. We catch the sound of what is to be paid—eight-pence, nine-pence, a shilling—and our hopes generally rise with the postage. How we are provoked at the delay in getting change—at the servant who does not hear the door! Then if the postman passes, and we do not hear the expected knock, what a pang is there! It is like the silence of death—of hope! We think he does it on purpose, and enjoys all the misery of our suspense. I have sometimes walked out to see the Mail-Coach pass, by which I had sent a letter, or to meet it when I expected one. I never see a Mail-Coach, for this reason, but I look at it as the bearer of glad tidings—the messenger of fate. I have reason to say so. The finest sight in the metropolis is that of the Mail-Coaches setting off from Piccadilly. The horses paw the ground, and are impatient to be gone, as if conscious of the precious burden they convey. There is a peculiar secresy and despatch, significant and full of meaning, in all the proceedings concerning them. Even the outside passengers have an erect and supercilious air, as if proof against the accidents of the journey. In fact, it seems indifferent whether they are to encounter the summer's heat or winter's cold, since they are borne on through the air in a winged chariot. The Mail-Carts drive up; the transfer of packages is made; and, at a signal given, they start off, bearing the irrevocable scrolls that give wings to thought, and that bind or sever hearts

for ever. How we hate the Putney and Brentford stages
that draw up in a line after they are gone! Some persons
think the sublimest object in nature is a ship launched
on the bosom of the ocean; but give me, for my private
satisfaction, the Mail-Coaches that pour down Piccadilly
of an evening, tear up the pavement, and devour the
way before them to the Land's-End!

In Cowper's time, Mail-Coaches were hardly set up;
but he has beautifully described the coming-in of the
Post-Boy:—

> " Hark ! 'tis the twanging horn o'er yonder bridge,
>   That with its wearisome but needful length
>   Bestrides the wintry flood, in which the moon
>   Sees her unwrinkled face reflected bright :
>   He comes, the herald of a noisy world,
>   With spattered boots, strapped waist, and frozen
>   locks ;
>   News from all nations lumbering at his back.
>   True to his charge, the close-packed load behind.
>   Yet careless what he brings, his one concern
>   Is to conduct it to the destined inn ;
>   And having dropped the expected bag, pass on.
>   He whistles as he goes, light-hearted wretch !
>   Cold and yet cheerful ; messenger of grief
>   Perhaps to thousands, and of joy to some ;
>   To him indifferent whether grief or joy.
>   Houses in ashes and the fall of stocks,
>   Births, deaths, and marriages, epistles wet
>   With tears that trickled down the writer's cheeks
>   Fast as the periods from his fluent quill,
>   Or charged with amorous sighs of absent swains
>   Or nymphs responsive, equally affect
>   His horse and him, unconscious of them all."

And yet, notwithstanding this, and so many other
passages that seem like the very marrow of our being,
Lord Byron denies that Cowper was a poet!—The Mail-
Coach is an improvement on the Post-Boy; but I fear
it will hardly bear so poetical a description. The
picturesque and dramatic do not keep pace with the

useful and mechanical. The telegraphs that lately communicated the intelligence of the new revolution to all France within a few hours, are a wonderful contrivance; but they are less striking and appalling than the beacon-fires (mentioned by Æschylus), which, lighted from hill-top to hill-top, announced the taking of Troy, and the return of Agamemnon.

ON CANT AND HYPOCRISY

(LONDON WEEKLY REVIEW, DEC. 6, 13, 1828)

If to do were as easy as to teach others what were good to be done, chapels had been churches, and poor men's cottages princes' palaces.

MR. ADDISON, it is said, was fond of tippling; and Curll, it is added, when he called on him in the morning, used to ask as a particular favour for a glass of Canary, by way of ingratiating himself, and that the other might have a pretence to join him and finish the bottle. He fell a martyr to this habit, and *yet* (some persons more nice than wise exclaim) he desired that the young Earl of Warwick might attend him on his death-bed, " to see how a Christian could die! " I see no inconsistency nor hypocrisy in this. A man may be a good Christian, a sound believer, and a sincere lover of virtue, and have, notwithstanding, one or more failings. If he had recommended it to others to get drunk, then I should have said he was a hypocrite, and that his pretended veneration for the Christian religion was a mere cloak put on to suit the purposes of fashion or convenience. His doing what it condemned was no proof of any such thing: " The spirit was willing, but the flesh was weak." He is a hypocrite who professes what he does not believe; not he who does not practise all he wishes or approves. It might on the same ground be argued, that a man is a hypocrite who admires Raphael or Shakespear, because he cannot paint like the one, or write like the other. If any one really despised what he affected outwardly to admire, this would be hypocrisy. If he affected to admire it a great deal more than he really did, this would be cant. Sincerity has to do with the connexion between our words and thoughts, and not between our belief and actions. The last constantly belie the strongest convictions and resolutions in the best of men; it is only the base and dishonest who give themselves credit with their tongue, for sentiments and opinions which in their hearts they disown.

I do not therefore think that the old theological maxim —" The greater the sinner, the greater the saint "—is so utterly unfounded. There is some mixture of truth in it. For as long as man is composed of two parts, body and soul, and while these are allowed to pull different ways, I see no reason why, in proportion to the length the one goes, the opposition or reaction of the other should not be more violent. It is certain, for example, that no one makes such good resolutions as the sot and the gambler in their moments of repentance, or can be more impressed with the horrors of their situation;— should this disposition, instead of a transient, idle pang, by chance become lasting, who can be supposed to feel the beauty of temperance and economy more, or to look back with greater gratitude to their escape from the trammels of vice and passion? Would the ingenious and elegant author of the *Spectator* feel less regard for the Scriptures, because they denounced in pointed terms the infirmity that " most easily beset him," that was the torment of his life, and the cause of his death? Such reasoning would be true, if man was a simple animal or a logical machine, and all his faculties and impulses were in strict unison; instead of which they are eternally at variance, and no one hates or takes part against himself more heartily or heroically than does the same individual. Does he not pass sentence on his own conduct? Is not his conscience both judge and accuser? What else is the meaning of all our resolutions against ourselves, as well as of our exhortations to others? *Video meliora proboque, deteriora sequor*, is not the language of hypocrisy, but of human nature.

The hypocrisy of priests has been a butt for ridicule in all ages; but I am not sure that there has not been more wit than philosophy in it. A priest, it is true, is obliged to affect a greater degree of sanctity than ordinary men, and probably more than he possesses; and this is so far, I am willing to allow, hypocrisy and solemn grimace. But I cannot admit, that though he may exaggerate, or even make an ostentatious display of religion and virtue through habit and spiritual pride, that this is a proof he has not these sentiments in his heart, or that his whole behaviour is the mere acting of a part. His character, his motives, are not altogether pure and sincere: are they therefore all false and hollow? No such thing. It is contrary to all our observation and experience so to interpret it. We all wear some disguise —make some professions—use some artifice to set ourselves off as being better than we are; and yet it is not denied that we have some good intentions and praise-worthy qualities at bottom, though we may endeavour to keep some others that we think less to our credit as much as possible in the background:—why then should we not extend the same favourable construction to monks and priests, who may be sometimes caught tripping as well as other men—with less excuse, no doubt; but if it is also with greater remorse of conscience, which probably often happens, their pretensions are not all downright, barefaced imposture. Their sincerity, compared with that of other men, can only be judged of by

the proportion between the degree of virtue they profess,
and that which they practise, or at least carefully seek to
realize. To conceive it otherwise is to insist that characters
must be all perfect, or all vicious—neither of which
suppositions is even possible. If a clergyman is notoriously
a drunkard, a debauchee, a glutton, or a scoffer, then for
him to lay claim at the same time to extraordinary inspirations of faith or grace, is both scandalous and ridiculous. The scene between the Abbot and the poor brother
in the *Duenna* is an admirable exposure of this double-
faced dealing. But because a parson has a relish for the
good things of this life, or what is commonly called a
liquorish tooth in his head (beyond what he would have it
supposed by others, or even by himself), that he has
therefore no fear or belief of the next, I hold for a crude
and vulgar prejudice. If a poor half-starved parish priest
pays his court to an *olla podrida*, or a venison pasty, with
uncommon *gusto*, shall we say that he has no other
sentiments in offering his devotions to a crucifix, or in
counting his beads? I see no more ground for such an
inference, than for affirming that Handel was not in
earnest when he sat down to compose a Symphony,
because he had at the same time perhaps a bottle of
cordials in his cupboard; or that Raphael was not entitled
to the epithet of *divine*, because he was attached to the
Fornarina. Everything has its turn in this chequered
scene of things, unless we prevent it from taking its turn
by over-rigid conditions, or drive men to despair or the
most callous effrontery by erecting a standard of perfection, to which no one can conform in reality. Thomson,
in his *Castle of Indolence* (a subject on which his pen ran
riot), has indulged in rather a free description of " a little
round, fat, oily man of God," who—

> " Shone all glittering with ungodly dew,
> If a tight damsel chanced to trippen by ;
> Which when observed, he shrunk into his mew,
> And straight would recollect his piety anew."

Now, was the piety in this case the less real, because it had been forgotten for a moment? Or even if this motive should not prove the strongest in the end, would this therefore shew that it was none, which is necessary to the argument here combated, or to make out our little plump priest a very knave? A priest may be honest, and yet err; as a woman may be modest, and yet half-inclined to be a rake. So the virtue of prudes may be suspected, though not their sincerity. The strength of their passions may make them more conscious of their weakness, and more cautious of exposing themselves; but not more to blind others than as a guard upon themselves. Again, suppose a clergyman hazards a jest upon sacred subjects, does it follow that he does not believe a word of the matter? Put the case that any one else, encouraged by his example, takes up the banter or levity, and see what effect it will have upon the reverend divine. He will turn round like a serpent trod upon, with all the vehemence and asperity of the most bigoted orthodoxy. Is this dictatorial and exclusive spirit then put on merely as a mask and to browbeat others? No; but he thinks he is privileged to trifle with the subject safely himself, from the store of evidence he has in reserve, and from the nature of his functions; but he is afraid of serious consequences being drawn from what others might say, or from his seeming to countenance it; and the moment the Church is in danger, or his own faith brought in question, his attachment to each becomes as visible as his hatred to those who dare to impugn either the one or the other. A woman's attachment to her husband is not to be suspected, if she will allow no one to abuse him but herself. It has been remarked, that with the spread of liberal opinions, or a more general scepticism on articles of faith, the clergy and religious persons in general have become more squeamish and jealous of any objections to their favourite doctrines: but this is what must follow in the natural course of things—the resistance being always in proportion to the danger; and arguments and books that were formerly allowed to pass unheeded, because it was supposed impossible they could do any mischief, are now denounced or prohibited with the most zealous vigilance, from a knowledge of the contagious nature of their influence and contents. So in morals, it is obvious that the greatest nicety of expression and allusion must be observed, where the manners are the most corrupt, and the imagination most easily excited, not out of mere affectation, but as a dictate of common sense and decency.

One of the finest remarks that have been made in modern times, is that of Lord Shaftesbury, that there is no such thing as a perfect Theist, or an absolute Atheist; that whatever may be the general conviction entertained on the subject, the evidence is not and cannot be at all times equally present to the mind; that even if it were, we are not in the same humour to receive it: a fit of the gout, a shower of rain shakes our best-established conclusions; and according to circumstances and the frame of mind we are in, our belief varies from the most sanguine enthusiasm to lukewarm indifference, or the most gloomy despair. There is a point of conceivable faith which might prevent any lapse from virtue, and reconcile all contrarieties between theory and practice; but this is not to be looked for in the ordinary course of nature, and is reserved for the abodes of the blest. Here, " upon this bank and shoal of time," the utmost we can hope to attain is, a strong habitual belief in the excellence of virtue, or the dispensations of Providence; and the conflict of the passions, and their occasional mastery over us, far from disproving or destroying this general, rational conviction, often fling us back more forcibly upon it, and like other infidelities and misunderstandings, produce all the alternate remorse and raptures of repentance and reconciliation.

It has been frequently remarked that the most obstinate heretic or confirmed sceptic, witnessing the service of the Roman Catholic Church, the elevation of the host amidst the sounds of music, the pomp of ceremonies, the embellishments of art, feels himself spellbound; and is almost persuaded to become a renegado to his reason or his religion. Even in hearing a vespers chanted on the stage, or in reading an account of a torch-light procession in a romance, a superstitious awe creeps over the frame, and we are momentarily charmed out of ourselves. When such is the obvious and involuntary influence of circumstances on the imagination, shall we say that a monkish recluse surrounded from his childhood by all this pomp, a stranger to any other faith, who has breathed no other atmosphere, and all whose meditations are bent on this one subject both by interest and habit and duty, is to be set down as a rank and heartless mountebank in the professions he makes of belief in it, because his thoughts may sometimes wander to forbidden subjects, or his feet stumble on forbidden ground? Or shall not the deep shadows of the woods in Vallombrosa enhance the solemnity of this feeling, or the icy horrors of the Grand Chartreux add to its elevation and its purity? To argue otherwise is to misdeem of human nature, and to limit its capacities for good or evil by some narrow-minded standard of our own. Man is neither a god nor a brute; but there is a prosaic and a poetical side to everything concerning him, and it is as impossible absolutely and for a constancy to exclude either one or the other from the mind, as to make him live without air or food. The *ideal*, the empire of thought and aspiration after truth and good, is inseparable from the nature of an intellectual being—what right have we then to catch at every strife, which in the mortified professors of religion the spirit wages with the flesh, as grossly vicious? or at every doubt, the bare suggestion of which fills them with consternation and despair, as a proof of the most glaring hypocrisy? The grossnesses of religion and its stickling for mere forms as its essence, have given a handle, and a just one, to its impugners. At the feast of Ramadan (says Voltaire) the Mussulmans wash and pray five times a day, and then fall to cutting one another's throats again with the greatest deliberation and goodwill. The two things, I grant, are sufficiently at variance; but they are, I contend, equally sincere in both. The Mahometans are savages, but they are not the less true believers— they hate their enemies as heartily as they revere the Koran. This, instead of shewing the fallacy of the *ideal* principle, shews its universality and indestructible essence. Let a man be as bad as he will, as little refined as possible, and indulge whatever hurtful passions or gross vices he thinks proper, these cannot occupy the whole of his time; and in the intervals between one scoundrel action and another he may and must have better thoughts, and may have recourse to those of religion (true or false) among the number, without in this being guilty of hypocrisy or of making a jest of what is considered as sacred This, I take it, is the whole secret of Methodism, which is a sort of modern vent for the ebullitions of the spirit through the gaps of uprighteousness.

We often see that a person condemns in another the very thing he is guilty of himself. Is this hypocrisy? It may, or it may not. If he really feels none of the disgust and abhorrence he expresses, this is quackery and impudence. But if he really expresses what he feels (and he easily may, for it is the abstract idea he contemplates in the case of another, and the immediate temptation to which he yields in his own, so that he probably is not even conscious of the identity or connexion between the two), then this is not hypocrisy, but want of strength and keeping in the moral sense. All morality consists in squaring our actions and sentiments

to our ideas of what is fit and proper; and it is the
incessant struggle and alternate triumph of the two
principles, the *ideal* and the physical, that keeps up this
" mighty coil and pudder " about vice and virtue, and
is one great source of all the good and evil in the world.
The mind of man is like a clock that is always running
down, and requires to be as constantly wound up. The
ideal principle is the master-key that winds it up, and
without which it would come to a stand: the sensual
and selfish feelings are the dead weights that pull it
down to the gross and grovelling. Till the intellectual
faculty is destroyed (so that the mind sees nothing beyond
itself, or the present moment), it is impossible to have
all brutal depravity; till the material and physical are
done away with (so that it shall contemplate everything
from a purely spiritual and disinterested point of view),
it is impossible to have all virtue. There must be a mixture
of the two, as long as man is compounded of opposite
materials, a contradiction and an eternal competition
for the mastery. I by no means think a single bad action
condemns a man, for he probably condemns it as much as
you do; nor a single bad habit, for he is probably trying
all his life to get rid of it. A man is only thoroughly
profligate when he has lost the sense of right and wrong;
or a thorough hypocrite, when he has not even the wish
to be what he appears. The greatest offence against
virtue is to speak ill of it. To recommend certain things
is worse than to practise them. There may be an excuse
for the last in the frailty of passion; but the former can
arise from nothing but an utter depravity of disposition.
Any one may yield to temptation, and yet feel a sincere
love and aspiration after virtue: but he who maintains
vice in theory, has not even the conception or capacity
for virtue in his mind. Men err: fiends only make a
mock at goodness.

We sometimes deceive ourselves, and think worse

N

of human nature than it deserves, in consequence of judging of character from names, and classes, and modes of life. No one is simply and absolutely any one thing, though he may be branded with it as a name. Some persons have expected to see his crimes written in the face of a murderer, and have been disappointed because they did not, as if this impeached the distinction between virtue and vice. Not at all. The circumstance only shewed that the man was other things, and had other feelings besides those of a murderer. If he had nothing else—if he fed on nothing else—if he had dreamt of nothing else but schemes of murder, his features would have expressed nothing else: but this perfection in vice is not to be expected from the contradictory and mixed nature of our motives. Humanity is to be met with in a den of robbers; nay, modesty in a brothel. Even among the most abandoned of the other sex, there is not unfrequently found to exist (contrary to all that is generally supposed) one strong and individual attachment, which remains unshaken to the last. Virtue may be said to steal, like a guilty thing, into the secret haunts of vice and infamy; it clings to their devoted victim, and will not be driven quite away. Nothing can destroy the human heart. Again, there is a heroism in crime, as well as in virtue. Vice and infamy have also their altars and their religion. This makes nothing in their favour, but is a proof of the heroical disinterestedness of man's nature, and that whatever he does, he must fling a dash of romance and sublimity into it; just as some grave biographer has said of Shakespear, that " even when he killed a calf, he made a speech and did it in a great style."

It is then impossible to get rid of this original distinction and contradictory bias, and to reduce everything to the system of French levity and Epicurean indifference. Wherever there is a capacity of conceiving of things as

different from what they are, there must be a principle
of taste and selection—a disposition to make them better,
and a power to make them worse. Ask a Parisian milliner
if she does not think one bonnet more becoming than
another—a Parisian dancing-master if French grace is
not better than English awkwardness—a French cook
if all sauces are alike—a French *blacklegs* if all throws are
equal on the dice? It is curious that the French nation
restrict rigid rules and fixed principles to cookery and the
drama, and maintain that the great drama of human
life is entirely a matter of caprice and fancy. No one
will assert that Raphael's histories, that Claude's landscapes are not better than a daub: but if the expression
in one of Raphael's faces is better than the most mean
and vulgar, how resist the consequence that the feeling
so expressed is better also? It does not appear to me
that all faces or all actions are alike. If goodness were
only a theory, it were a pity it should be lost to the
world. There are a number of things, the idea of which
is a clear gain to the mind. Let people, for instance,
rail at friendship, genius, freedom, as long as they will—
the very names of these despised qualities are better
than anything else that could be substituted for them,
and embalm even the most envenomed satire against
them. It is no small consideration that the mind is
capable even of feigning such things. So I would contend
against that reasoning which would have it thought that
if religion is not true, there is no difference between
mankind and the beasts that perish;—I should say,
that this distinction is equally proved, if religion is
supposed to be a mere fabrication of the human mind;
the capacity to conceive it makes the difference. The
idea alone of an over-ruling Providence, or of a future
state, is as much a distinctive mark of a superiority of
nature, as the invention of the mathematics, which are
true—or of poetry, which is a fable. Whatever the truth

or falsehood of our speculations, the power to make them is peculiar to ourselves.

The contrariety and warfare of different faculties and dispositions within us has not only given birth to the Manichean and Gnostic heresies, and to other superstitions of the East, but will account for many of the mummeries and dogmas both of Popery and Calvinism —confession, absolution, justification by faith, etc.; which, in the hopelessness of attaining perfection, and our dissatisfaction with ourselves for falling short of it, are all substitutes for actual virtue, and an attempt to throw the burden of a task, to which we are unequal or only half disposed, on the merits of others, or on outward forms, ceremonies, and professions of faith. Hence the crowd of

> " Eremites and friars,
> White, black, and grey, with all their trumpery."

If we do not conform to the law, we at least acknowledge the jurisdiction of the court. A person does wrong; he is sorry for it; and as he still feels himself liable to error, he is desirous to make atonement as well as he can, by ablutions, by tithes, by penance, by sacrifices, or other voluntary demonstrations of obedience, which are in his power, though his passions are not, and which prove that his will is not refractory, and that his understanding is right towards God. The stricter tenets of Calvinism, which allow of no medium between grace and reprobation, and doom man to eternal punishment for every breach of the moral law, as an equal offence against infinite truth and justice, proceed (like the paradoxical doctrine of the Stoics) from taking a half-view of this subject, and considering man as amenable only to the dictates of his understanding and his conscience, and not excusable from the temptations and frailty of human ignorance and passion. The mixing up of religion and morality together, or the making us accountable for every word, thought, or action, under no less a responsibility than our everlasting future welfare or misery, has also added incalculably to the difficulties of self-knowledge, has superinduced a violent and spurious state of feeling, and made it almost impossible to distinguish the boundaries between the true and false, in judging of human conduct and motives. A religious man is afraid of looking into the state of his soul, lest at the same time he should reveal it to Heaven; and tries to persuade himself that by shutting his eyes to his true character and feelings, they will remain a profound secret, both here and hereafter. This is a strong engine and irresistible inducement to self-deception; and the more zealous any one is in his convictions of the truth of religion, the more we may suspect the sincerity of his pretensions to piety and morality.

Thus, though I think there is very little downright hypocrisy in the world, I do think there is a great deal of *cant*—" cant religious, cant political, cant literary," etc., as Lord Byron said. Though few people have the face to set up for the very thing they in their hearts despise, we almost all want to be thought better than we are, and affect a greater admiration or abhorrence of certain things than we really feel. Indeed, some degree of affectation is as necessary to the mind as dress is to the body ; we must overact our part in some measure, in order to produce any effect at all. There was formerly the two hours' sermon, the long-winded grace, the nasal drawl, the uplifted hands and eyes; all which, though accompanied with some corresponding emotion, expressed more than was really felt, and were in fact intended to make up for the conscious deficiency. As our interest in anything wears out with time and habit, we exaggerate the outward symptoms of zeal as mechanical helps to devotion, dwell the longer on our words as they are less felt, and hence the very origin of the term, *cant*. The cant of sentimentality has succeeded to that of religion. There is a cant of humanity, of patriotism and loyalty—not that people do not feel these emotions, but they make too great a *fuss* about them, and drawl out the expression of them till they tire themselves and others. There is a cant about Shakespear. There is a cant about *Political Economy* just now. In short, there is and must be a cant about everything that excites a considerable degree of attention and interest, and that people would be thought to know and care rather more about them than they actually do. Cant is the voluntary overcharging or prolongation of a real sentiment; hypocrisy is the setting up a pretension to a feeling you never had and have no wish for. There are people who are made up of *cant*, that is, of mawkish affectation and sensibility ; but who have not sincerity enough to be *hypocrites*, that is, have not hearty dislike or contempt enough for anything, to give the lie to their puling professions of admiration and esteem for it.

THE FRENCH REVOLUTION

(THE LIFE OF NAPOLEON, VOL. I, 1828)

BUONAPARTE was not quite twenty years old, when the French Revolution broke out in 1789. From the time of his being employed at the siege of Toulon and in the war of Italy which followed, he may be considered as its sword-arm. From that time, its fate became in a manner bound up with his. It awaited his appearance to triumph and to perish with him. It will be therefore not improper in this place to give some account of its origin and progress up to that period.

The French Revolution might be described as a remote

but inevitable result of the invention of the art of printing. The gift of speech, or the communication of thought by words, is that which distinguishes man from other animals. But this faculty is limited and imperfect without the intervention of books, which render the knowledge possessed by every one in the community accessible to all. There is no doubt, then, that the press (as it has existed in modern times) is the great organ of intellectual improvement and civilization.[1] It was impossible in this point of view, that those institutions, which were founded in a state of society and manners long anterior to this second breathing of understanding into the life of man, should remain on the same proud footing after it, with all their disproportions and defects. Many of these, indeed, must be softened by the lapse of time and influence of opinion, and give way of their own accord: but others are too deeply rooted in the passions and interests of men to be wrenched asunder without violence, or by the mutual consent of the parties concerned; and it is this which makes revolutions necessary, with their train of lasting good and present evil. When a government, like an old-fashioned building, has become crazy and rotten, stops the way of improvement, and only serves to collect diseases and corruption, and the proprietors refuse to come to any compromise, the community proceed in this as in some other cases; they set summarily to work—" they pull down the house, they abate the nuisance." All other things had changed: why then should governments remain the same, an excrescence

---

[1] The free states of antiquity, or the republics in the middle ages, were single cities, where the spirit of liberty and independence was called forth, and strengthened by personal intercourse and communication. The towns in different parts of Europe, on the same principle, obtained several immunities before the *villains* or country people thought of throwing off their yoke. In Spain the cities are ripe for a revolution, while the peasantry are averse to any change.

and incumbrance on the state? It is only because they have most power and most interest to continue their abuses. This circumstance is a reason why it is doubly incumbent on those who are aggrieved by them to get rid of them; and makes the shock the greater, when opinion at last becomes a match for arbitrary power.

The feudal system was in full vigour almost up to the period of the discovery of printing. Much had been done since that time: but it was the object of the French Revolution to get rid at one blow of the frame-work and of the last relics of that system. Before the diffusion of knowledge and inquiry, governments were for the most part the growth of brute force or of barbarous superstition. Power was in the hands of a few, who used it only to gratify their own pride, cruelty, or avarice, and who took every means to extend and cement it by fear and favour. The lords of the earth, disdaining to rule by the choice or for the benefit of the mass of the community, whom they regarded and treated as no better than a herd of cattle, derived their title from the skies, pretending to be accountable for the exercise or abuse of their authority to God only—the throne rested on the altar, and every species of atrocity or wanton insult having power on its side, received the sanction of religion, which it was thenceforth impiety and rebellion against the will of Heaven to impugn. This state of things continued and grew worse and worse, while knowledge and power were confined within mere local and personal limits. Each petty sovereign shut himself up in his castle or fortress, and scattered havoc and dismay over the unresisting country around him. In an age of ignorance and barbarism, when force and interest decided every thing, and reason had no means of making itself heard, what was to prevent this or act as a check upon it? The lord himself had no other measure of right than his own will: his pride and passions would blind him to every

consideration of conscience or humanity; he would regard
every act of disobedience as a crime of the deepest die,
and to give unbridled sway to his lawless humours, would
become the ruling passion and sole study of his life.
How would it stand with those within the immediate
circle of his influence or his vengeance? Fear would
make them cringe, and lick the feet of their haughty and
capricious oppressor: the hope of reward or the dread of
punishment would stifle the sense of justice or pity;
despair of success would make them cowards, habit would
confirm them into slaves, and they would look up with
bigoted devotion (the boasted *loyalty* of the good old
times) to the right of the strongest as the only law. A
king would only be the head of a confederation of such
petty despots, and the happiness or rights of the people
would be equally disregarded by them both. Religion,
instead of curbing this state of rapine and licentiousness,
became an accomplice and a party in the crime; gave
absolution and plenary indulgence for all sorts of enormities; granting the forgiveness of Heaven in return for a
rich jewel or fat abbey-lands, and setting up a regular
(and what in the end proved an intolerable) traffic in
violence, cruelty, and lust. As to the restraints of law,
there was none but what resided in the breast of the
Grand Seigneur, who hung up in his court-yard, without
judge or jury, any one who dared to utter the slightest
murmur against the most flagrant wrong. Such must be
the consequence, as long as there was no common
standard or impartial judge to appeal to; and this could
only be found in public opinion, the offspring of books.
As long as any unjust claim or transaction was confined
to the knowledge of the parties concerned, the tyrant and
the slave, which is the case in all unlettered states of
society, *might* must prevail over *right;* for the strongest
would bully, and the weakest must submit, even in his
own defence, and persuade himself that he was in the

N *

wrong, even in his own despite: but the instant the world (that dread jury) are impanelled, and called to look on and be umpires in the scene, so that nothing is done by connivance or in a corner, then reason mounts the judgment-seat in lieu of passion or interest, and opinion becomes law, instead of arbitrary will; and farewell feudal lord and sovereign king!

From the moment that the press opens the eyes of the community beyond the actual sphere in which each moves, there is from that time inevitably formed the germ of a body of opinion directly at variance with the selfish and servile code that before reigned paramount, and approximating more and more to the manly and disinterested standard of truth and justice. Hitherto force, fraud, and fear decided every question of individual right or general reasoning; the possessor of rank and influence, in answer to any censure or objection to his conduct, appealed to God and to his sword:—now a new principle is brought into play which had never been so much as dreamt of, and before which he must make good his pretensions, or it will shatter his strongholds of pride and prejudice to atoms, as the pent-up air shatters whatever resists its expansive force. This power is public opinion, exercised upon men, things, and general principles, and to which mere physical power must conform, or it will crumble it to powder. Books alone teach us to judge of truth and good in the abstract: without a knowledge of things at a distance from us, we judge like savages or animals from our senses and appetites only; but by the aid of books and of an inter-course with the world of ideas, we are purified, raised, ennobled from savages into intellectual and rational beings. Our impressions of what is near to us are false, of what is distant feeble; but the last gaining strength from being united in public opinion, and expressed by the public voice, are like the congregated roar of many waters, and quail the hearts of princes. Who but the tyrant does not hate the tyrant? Who but the slave does not despise the slave? The first of these looks upon himself as a God, upon his vassal as a clod of the earth, and forces him to be of the same opinion: the philosopher looks upon them both as men, and instructs the world to do so. While they had to settle their pretensions by themselves, and in the night of ignorance, it is no wonder no good was done; while pride intoxicated the one, and fear stupefied the other. But let them be brought out of that dark cave of despotism and superstition, and let a thousand other persons, who have no interest but that of truth and justice, be called on to determine between them, and the plea of the lordly oppressor to make a beast of burden of his fellow-man becomes as ridiculous as it is odious. All that the light of philosophy, the glow of patriotism, all that the brain wasted in midnight study, the blood poured out upon the scaffold or in the field of battle can do or have done, is to take this question in all cases from before the first gross, blind, and iniquitous tribunal, where power insults over weakness, and place it before the last more just, disinterested, and in the end more formidable one, where each individual is tried by his peers, and according to rules and principles which have received the common examination and the common consent. A public sense is thus formed, free from slavish awe or the traditional assumption of insolent superiority, which the more it is exercised becomes the more enlightened and enlarged, and more and more requires equal rights and equal laws. This new sense acquired by the people, this new organ of opinion and feeling, is like bringing a battering-train to bear upon some old Gothic castle, long the den of rapine and crime, and must finally prevail against all absurd and antiquated institutions, unless it is violently suppressed, and this engine of political reform turned by bribery and terror against

itself. Who in reading history, where the characters are
laid open and the circumstances fairly stated, and where
he himself has no false bias to mislead him, does not
take part with the oppressed against the oppressor? Who
is there that admires Nero at the distance of two thousand
years? Did not the *Tartuffe* in a manner hoot religious
hypocrisy out of France; and was it not on this account
constantly denounced by the clergy? What do those,
who read the annals of the Inquisition, think of that dread
tribunal? And what has softened its horrors but those
annals being read? What figure does the massacre of
St. Bartholomew make in the eyes of posterity? But books
anticipate and conform the decision of the public, of
individuals, and even of the actors in such scenes, to that
lofty and irrevocable standard, mould and fashion the
heart and inmost thoughts upon it, so that something
manly, liberal, and generous grows out of the fever of
passion and the palsy of base fear; and this is what is
meant by the progress of modern civilization and modern
philosophy. An individual in a barbarous age and
country throws another who has displeased him (without
other warrant than his will) into a dungeon, where he
pines for years, and then dies; and perhaps only the
mouldering bones of the victim, discovered long after,
disclose his fate: or if known at the time, the confessor
gives absolution, and the few who are let into the secret
are intimidated from giving vent to their feelings, and
hardly dare disapprove in silence. Let this act of violence
be repeated afterwards in story, and there is not an
individual in the whole nation whose bosom does not
swell with pity, or whose blood does not curdle within
him at the recital of so foul a wrong. Why then should
there be an individual in a nation privileged to do what
no other individual in the nation can be found to approve?
But he has the power, and will not part with it in spite of
public opinion. Then that public opinion must become

active, and break the moulds of prescription in which his right derived from his ancestors is cast, and this will be a Revolution. Is that a state of things to regret or bring back, the bare mention of which makes one shudder? But the form, the shadow of it only was left: then why keep up that form, or cling to a shadow of injustice, which is no less odious than contemptible, except to make an improper use of it? Let all the wrongs public and private produced in France by arbitrary power and exclusive privileges for a thousand years be collected in a volume, and let this volume be read by all who have hearts to feel or capacity to understand, and the strong, stifling sense of oppression and kindling burst of indignation that would follow will be that impulse of public opinion that led to the French Revolution. Let all the victims that have perished under the mild, paternal sway of the ancient *régime*, in dungeons, and in agony, without a trial, without an accusation, without witnesses, be assembled together, and their chains struck off, and the shout of jubilee and exultation they would make, or that nature would make at the sight, will be the shout that was heard when the Bastille fell! The dead pause that ensued among the Gods of the earth, the rankling malice, the panic-fear, when they saw law and justice raised to an equality with their sovereign will, and mankind no longer doomed to be their sport, was that of fiends robbed of their prey: their struggles, their arts, their unyielding perseverance, and their final triumph was that of fiends when it is restored to them!

DEATH OF THE EMPEROR NAPOLEON

(LIFE OF NAPOLEON, VOL. IV, 1830)

NAPOLEON lay in state in his little bedroom which had been converted into a funeral chamber. It was hung with black cloth brought from the town. It was this circumstance which first apprised the inhabitants of his death; for till then every one had believed in the report of the Governor that " General Buonaparte was doing well." The corpse, which had not been embalmed for want of means and which was of an extraordinary whiteness, was placed on one of the camp-beds, surrounded with little white curtains which served for a sarcophagus. The blue cloak which Napoleon had worn at the battle of Marengo covered it. The feet and the hands were free; the sword on the left side, and a crucifix on the breast. At some distance was the silver vase containing the heart and stomach which were not allowed to be removed. At the back of the head was an altar, where the priest in his stole and surplice recited the customary prayers. All the individuals of Napoleon's suite, officers and domestics, dressed in mourning, remained standing on the left. Dr. Arnott had been charged to see that no attempt was made to convey away the body.

For some hours the crowd had besieged the doors; they were admitted, and beheld the inanimate remains of Napoleon without disorder, and in respectful silence. The officers of the 20th and 66th Regiments were admitted first: then the others. The following day (the 7th) the throng was greater; the troops, the inhabitants, even women came, in spite of a ridiculous order to the contrary. Antommarchi was not allowed to take the heart of Napoleon to Europe with him; he deposited that and the stomach in two vases, filled with alcohol and hermetically sealed, in the corners of the coffin in which the corpse was laid. This was a case of tin, lined with a mattress, furnished with a pillow, and covered with white satin. There not being room for the hat to remain on his head, it was placed at his feet, with some eagles, the pieces of French money coined during his reign, a plate engraved with his arms, etc. The coffin was closed, carefully soldered up, and then fixed in another case of mahogany, which was enclosed in a third, made of lead, which last was fastened in a fourth of mahogany, which was sealed up, and fastened with iron-screws. The coffin was exposed in the same place as the body had been, and was covered with the cloak that Napoleon had worn at the battle of Marengo. The funeral was ordered for the morrow; and the troops were to attend in the morning by break of day.

This took place accordingly: the Governor arrived first, the Rear-Admiral soon after; and shortly all the authorities, civil and military, were assembled at Longwood. The day was fine, the people crowded the roads, music resounded from the heights; never spectacle so sad and solemn had been witnessed in these remote regions. At half-past twelve, the grenadiers took hold of the coffin, lifted it with difficulty, and succeeded in removing it into the great walk in the garden, where the hearse awaited them. It was placed in the carriage, covered with a pall of purple velvet and with the cloak which the hero wore at Marengo. The Emperor's household were in mourning. The cavalcade was arranged by order of the Governor in the following manner: The Abbé Vignali in his sacerdotal robes, with young Henry Bertrand at his side, bearing a holy-water sprinkle: Doctors Arnott and Antommarchi; the persons entrusted with the superintendence of the hearse, drawn by four horses, led by grooms, and escorted by twelve grenadiers without arms, on each side: these last were to carry the coffin on their shoulders as soon as the ruggedness of the road prevented the hearse from advancing: young Napoleon Bertrand and Marchand, both on foot and by the side of the hearse; Counts Bertrand and Montholon on horseback close behind the hearse; a part of the household of the Emperor; Countess Bertrand with her daughter Hortense, in a calash drawn by two horses, led by hand by her domestics, who walked by the side of the precipice; the Emperor's horse led by his equerry Archambaud; the officers of marine on horseback and on foot; the officers of the staff on horseback; the members of the council of the island, in like manner; General Coffin and the Marquis Montchenu on horseback; the Rear-Admiral and the Governor on horseback; the inhabitants of the island.

The train set out in this order from Longwood, passed by the barracks, and was met by the garrison, about two thousand five hundred in number, drawn up on the left of the road as far as *Hut's-Gate*. Groups of musicians placed at different distances added still more, by the mournful airs which they played, to the striking solemnity of the occasion. When the train had passed, the troops followed and accompanied it to the burying-place. The dragoons marched first. Then came the 20th Regiment of Infantry, the marines, the 66th, the volunteers of St. Helena, and lastly the company of royal artillery with fifteen pieces of cannon. Lady Lowe and her daughter were on the road-side at Hut's-Gate, in an open carriage drawn by two horses. They were attended by some domestics in mourning, and followed the procession at a distance. The fifteen pieces of artillery were ranged along the road, and the cannoneers were at their posts, ready to fire. Having advanced about a quarter of a mile beyond Hut's-Gate, the hearse stopped, the troops halted, and drew up in line of battle by the road-side. The grenadiers then raised the coffin on their shoulders, and bore it thus to the place of interment, by the new route which had been made on purpose on the declivity of the mountain.

All the attendants alighted, the ladies descended from their carriages, and the procession followed the corpse without observing any regular order.—Counts Bertrand and Montholon, Marchand and young Napoleon Bertrand carried the four corners of the pall. The coffin was put down on the side of the tomb, which was hung with black. Near were seen the cords and pulleys which were to lower it into the earth. Every thing had a *sombre* aspect, all conspired to increase the melancholy and silent grief of the attendants. The coffin was then uncovered, the Abbé Vignali repeated the usual prayers, and the body was let down into the grave, with the feet to the east. The Artillery then fired three salutes in succession of fifteen discharges each. The Admiral's vessel had fired during the march twenty-five cannon-shot from time to time. A huge stone, which was to have been employed in the building of the new house of the Emperor, was made use of to close his grave. This was also strengthened by a stone-wall with a covering of cement. While this was doing, the crowd fell upon the willows, which the former presence of Napoleon had already rendered objects of veneration. Every one was ambitious to possess a branch or some leaves of these trees, which were henceforth to shadow the tomb of this great man; and to preserve them as a precious relic of so memorable a scene. The Governor and Admiral endeavoured to prevent this mark of enthusiasm, but in vain. The Governor, however, took his revenge by interdicting all access to the tomb, and surrounding it with a barricade, where he placed a guard to keep off all intruders. The tomb of the Emperor is about a league from Longwood. It is of a quadrangular shape, wider at top than at bottom: the depth is about twelve feet. The coffin is fixed on two strong pieces of wood, and is detached in its whole circumference. The French were not allowed to mark the spot with a tomb-stone or with any inscription. The

Governor opposed this, as if a tomb-stone or an inscription could tell the world more than they knew already. Sir Hudson Lowe had committed Buonaparte to the ground; his task was ended; but he proceeded to ransack his effects with the same rage and jealousy as if he had been still alive, and refused the smallest trifle found among them, and that could be of no use to any one else, to the entreaties of his faithful followers. To make amends, however, he assured them that they should soon be dismissed from the island with every attention; and he sent them home in a crazy store-ship. Antommarchi, on his return to the Continent, could not procure an interview with Maria-Louisa; but he saw the Princess Pauline at Rome, and gave his mother an account of all that her son had gone through.

ON WRITERS AND
WRITING

ON COMMON-PLACE CRITICS

(EXAMINER, NOV. 24, 1816)

" Nor can I think what thoughts they can conceive."

WE have already given some account of common-place
people; we shall in this number attempt a description of
another class of the community, who may be called (by
way of distinction) common-place critics. The former
are a set of people who have no opinions of their own,
and do not pretend to have any; the latter are a set of
people who have no opinions of their own, but who affect
to have one upon every subject you can mention. The
former are a very honest, good sort of people, who are
contented to pass for what they are; the latter are a very
pragmatical, troublesome sort of people, who would pass
for what they are not, and try to put off their common-
place notions in all companies and on all subjects, as
something of their own. They are of both species, the
grave and the gay; and it is hard to say which is the most
tiresome.

A common-place critic has something to say upon every
occasion, and he always tells you either what is not true,
or what you knew before, or what is not worth knowing.
He is a person who thinks by proxy, and talks by rote.
He differs with you, not because he thinks you are in the
wrong, but because he thinks somebody else will think
so. Nay, it would be well if he stopped here; but he will
undertake to misrepresent you by anticipation, lest
others should misunderstand you, and will set you right,
not only in opinions which you have, but in those which
you may be supposed to have. Thus, if you say that
Bottom the weaver is a character that has not had justice
done to it, he shakes his head, is afraid you will be
thought extravagant, and wonders you should think the

Midsummer Night's Dream the finest of all Shakespear's plays. He judges of matters of taste and reasoning as he does of dress and fashion, by the prevailing tone of good company; and you would as soon persuade him to give up any sentiment that is current there, as to wear the hind part of his coat before. By the best company, of which he is perpetually talking, he means persons who live on their own estates, and other people's ideas. By the opinion of the world, to which he pays and expects you to pay great deference, he means that of a little circle of his own, where he hears and is heard. Again, *good sense* is a phrase constantly in his mouth, by which he does not mean his own sense or that of anybody else, but the opinions of a number of persons who have agreed to take their opinions on trust from others. If any one observes that there is something better than common sense, viz. *uncommon* sense, he thinks this a bad joke. If you object to the opinions of the majority, as often arising from ignorance or prejudice, he appeals from them to the sensible and well-informed; and if you say that there may be other persons as sensible and well-informed as himself and his friends, he smiles at your presumption. If you attempt to prove anything to him, it is in vain, for he is not thinking of what you say, but of what will be thought of it. The stronger your reasons, the more incorrigible he thinks you; and looks upon any attempt to expose his gratuitous assumptions as the wandering of a disordered imagination. His notions are like plaster figures cast in a mould, as brittle as they are hollow; but they will break before you can make them give way. In fact, he is the representative of a large part of the community, the shallow, the vain, and indolent, of those who have time to talk, and are not bound to think; and he considers any deviation from the select forms of commonplace, or the accredited language of conventional impertinence, as compromising the authority under which he acts in his diplomatic capacity. It is wonderful how this class of people agree with one another; how they herd together in all their opinions; what a tact they have for folly; what an instinct for absurdity; what a sympathy in sentiment; how they find one another out by infallible signs, like Freemasons! The secret of this unanimity and strict accord is, that not any one of them ever admits any opinion that can cost the least effort of mind in arriving at, or of courage in declaring it. Folly is as consistent with itself as wisdom: there is a certain level of thought and sentiment, which the weakest minds, as well as the strongest, find out as best adapted to them; and you as regularly come to the same conclusions, by looking no farther than the surface, as if you dug to the centre of the earth! You know beforehand what a critic of this class will say on almost every subject the first time he sees you, the next time, the time after that, and so on to the end of the chapter. The following list of his opinions may be relied on:—It is pretty certain that before you have been in the room with him ten minutes, he will give you to understand that Shakespear was a great but irregular genius. Again, he thinks it a question whether any one of his plays, if brought out now for the first time, would succeed. He thinks that *Macbeth* would be the most likely, from the music which has been since introduced into it. He has some doubts as to the superiority of the French school over us in tragedy, and observes, that Hume and Adam Smith were both of that opinion. He thinks Milton's pedantry a great blemish in his writings, and that *Paradise Lost* has many prosaic passages in it. He conceives that genius does not always imply taste, and that wit and judgment are very different faculties. He considers Dr. Johnson as a great critic and moralist, and that his Dictionary was a work of prodigious erudition and vast industry; but that some of the anecdotes of him in Boswell are trifling. He conceives that

Mr. Locke was a very original and profound thinker. He thinks Gibbon's style vigorous but florid. He wonders that the author of *Junius* was never found out. He thinks Pope's translation of the *Iliad* an improvement on the simplicity of the original, which was necessary to fit it to the taste of modern readers. He thinks there is a great deal of grossness in the old comedies; and that there has been a great improvement in the morals of the higher classes since the reign of Charles II. He thinks the reign of Queen Anne the golden period of our literature; but that, upon the whole, we have no English writer equal to Voltaire. He speaks of Boccaccio as a very licentious writer, and thinks the wit in Rabelais quite extravagant, though he never read either of them. He cannot get through Spenser's *Fairy Queen*, and pronounces all allegorical poetry tedious. He prefers Smollett to Fielding, and discovers more knowledge of the world in *Gil Blas* than in *Don Quixote*. Richardson he thinks very minute and tedious. He thinks the French Revolution has done a great deal of harm to the cause of liberty; and blames Buonaparte for being so ambitious. He reads the *Edinburgh* and *Quarterly Reviews*, and thinks as they do. He is shy of having an opinion on a new actor or a new singer; for the public do not always agree with the newspapers. He thinks that the moderns have great advantages over the ancients in many respects. He thinks Jeremy Bentham a greater man than Aristotle. He can see no reason why artists of the present day should not paint as well as Raphael or Titian. For instance, he thinks there is something very elegant and classical in Mr. Westall's drawings. He has no doubt that Sir Joshua Reynolds's Lectures were written by Burke. He considers Horne Tooke's account of the conjunction *That* very ingenious, and holds that no writer can be called elegant who uses the present for the subjunctive mood, who says, *If it is* for *If it be*. He thinks Hogarth a great master of low, comic humour; and Cobbett a coarse, vulgar writer. He often talks of men of liberal education, and men without education, as if that made much difference. He judges of people by their pretensions; and pays attention to their opinions according to their dress and rank in life. If he meets with a fool, he does not find him out; and if he meets with any one wiser than himself, he does not know what to make of him. He thinks that manners are of great consequence to the common intercourse of life. He thinks it difficult to prove the existence of any such thing as original genius, or to fix a general standard of taste. He does not think it possible to define what wit is. In religion, his opinions are liberal. He considers all enthusiasm as a degree of madness, particularly to be guarded against by young minds; and believes that truth lies in the middle, between the extremes of right and wrong. He thinks that the object of poetry is to please; and that astronomy is a very pleasing and useful study. He thinks all this, and a great deal more, that amounts to nothing. We wonder we have remembered one half of it.

" For true no-meaning puzzles more than wit."

Though he has an aversion to all new ideas, he likes all new plans and matters-of-fact; the new Schools for All, the Penitentiary, the New Bedlam, the new Steam-Boats, the Gas-Lights, the new Patent Blacking; everything of that sort, but the Bible Society. The Society for the Suppression of Vice he thinks a great nuisance, as every honest man must.

In a word, a common-place critic is the pedant of polite conversation. He refers to the opinion of Lord M. or Lady G. with the same air of significance that the learned pedant does to the authority of Cicero or Virgil; retails the wisdom of the day, as the anecdote-monger does the

wit; and carries about with him the sentiments of people
of a certain respectability in life, as the dancing-master
does their air, or their valets their clothes.

ON POETRY IN GENERAL

(LECTURES ON THE ENGLISH POETS, 1818)

THE best general notion which I can give of poetry is,
that it is the natural impression of any object or event,
by its vividness exciting an involuntary movement of
imagination and passion, and producing, by sympathy,
a certain modulation of the voice, or sounds, expressing it.

In treating of poetry, I shall speak first of the subject-
matter of it, next of the forms of expression to which it
gives birth, and afterwards of its connection with harmony
of sound.

Poetry is the language of the imagination and the
passions. It relates to whatever gives immediate pleasure
or pain to the human mind. It comes home to the bosoms
and businesses of men; for nothing but what so comes
home to them in the most general and intelligible shape,
can be a subject for poetry. Poetry is the universal
language which the heart holds with nature and itself.
He who has a contempt for poetry, cannot have much
respect for himself, or for anything else. It is not a mere
frivolous accomplishment, (as some persons have been
led to imagine), the trifling amusement of a few idle
readers or leisure hours—it has been the study and
delight of mankind in all ages. Many people suppose
that poetry is something to be found only in books,
contained in lines of ten syllables, with like endings : but
wherever there is a sense of beauty, or power, or harmony,
as in the motion of a wave of the sea, in the growth of a

flower that "spreads its sweet leaves to the air, and dedicates its beauty to the sun,"—*there* is poetry, in its birth. If history is a grave study, poetry may be said to be a graver: its materials lie deeper, and are spread wider. History treats, for the most part, of the cumbrous and unwieldy masses of things, the empty cases in which the affairs of the world are packed, under the heads of intrigue or war, in different states, and from century to century: but there is no thought or feeling that can have entered into the mind of man, which he would be eager to communicate to others, or which they would listen to with delight, that is not a fit subject for poetry. It is not a branch of authorship: it is "the stuff of which our life is made." The rest is "mere oblivion," a dead letter: for all that is worth remembering in life, is the poetry of it. Fear is poetry, hope is poetry, love is poetry, hatred is poetry; contempt, jealousy, remorse, admiration, wonder, pity, despair, or madness, are all poetry. Poetry is that fine particle within us, that expands, rarefies, refines, raises our whole being: without it "man's life is poor as beast's." Man is a poetical animal: and those of us who do not study the principles of poetry, act upon them all our lives, like Molière's *Bourgeois Gentilhomme*, who had always spoken prose without knowing it. The child is a poet in fact, when he first plays at hide-and-seek, or repeats the story of Jack the Giant-killer; the shepherd-boy is a poet, when he first crowns his mistress with a garland of flowers; the countryman, when he stops to look at the rainbow; the city-apprentice, when he gazes after the Lord-Mayor's show; the miser, when he hugs his gold; the courtier, who builds his hopes upon a smile; the savage, who paints his idol with blood; the slave, who worships a tyrant, or the tyrant, who fancies himself a god;—the vain, the ambitious, the proud, the choleric man, the hero and the coward, the beggar and the king, the rich and the poor, the young and the old, all live in a world of their own making; and the poet does no more than describe what all the others think and act. If his art is folly and madness, it is folly and madness at second hand. "There is warrant for it." Poets alone have not "such seething brains, such shaping fantasies, that apprehend more than cooler reason" can.

> "The lunatic, the lover, and the poet
> Are of imagination all compact.
> One sees more devils than vast hell can hold :
> The madman. While the lover, all as frantic,
> Sees Helen's beauty in a brow of Egypt.
> The poet's eye in a fine frenzy rolling,
> Doth glance from heav'n to earth, from earth to
>   heav'n ;
> And as imagination bodies forth
> The forms of things unknown, the poet's pen
> Turns them to shape, and gives to airy nothing
> A local habitation and a name.
> Such tricks hath strong imagination."

If poetry is a dream, the business of life is much the same. If it is a fiction, made up of what we wish things to be, and fancy that they are, because we wish them so, there is no other nor better reality. Ariosto has described the loves of Angelica and Medoro : but was not Medoro, who carved the name of his mistress on the barks of trees, as much enamoured of her charms as he? Homer has celebrated the anger of Achilles : but was not the hero as mad as the poet? Plato banished the poets from his Commonwealth, lest their descriptions of the natural man should spoil his mathematical man, who was to be without passions and affections, who was neither to laugh nor weep, to feel sorrow nor anger, to be cast down nor elated by anything. This was a chimera, however, which never existed but in the brain of the inventor; and Homer's poetical world has outlived Plato's philosophical Republic.

Poetry then is an imitation of Nature, but the imagination and the passions are a part of man's nature. We shape things according to our wishes and fancies, without poetry; but poetry is the most emphatical language that can be found for those creations of the mind " which ecstasy is very cunning in." Neither a mere description of natural objects, nor a mere delineation of natural feelings, however distinct or forcible, constitutes the ultimate end and aim of poetry, without the heightenings of the imagination. The light of poetry is not only a direct but also a reflected light, that while it shews us the object, throws a sparkling radiance on all around it: the flame of the passions, communicated to the imagination, reveals to us, as with a flash of lightning, the inmost recesses of thought, and penetrates our whole being. Poetry represents forms chiefly as they suggest other forms; feelings, as they suggest forms or other feelings. Poetry puts a spirit of life and motion into the universe. It describes the flowing, not the fixed. It does not define the limits of sense, or analyse the distinctions of understanding, but signifies the excess of the imagination beyond the actual or ordinary impression of any object or feeling. The poetical impression of any object is that uneasy, exquisite sense of beauty or power that cannot be contained within itself; that is impatient of all limit; that (as flame bends to flame) strives to link itself to some other image of kindred beauty or grandeur; to enshrine itself, as it were, in the highest forms of fancy, and to relieve the aching sense of pleasure by expressing it in the boldest manner, and by the most striking examples of the same quality in other instances. Poetry, according to Lord Bacon, for this reason, " has something divine in it, because it raises the mind and hurries it into sublimity, by conforming the shows of things to the desires of the soul, instead of subjecting the soul to external things, as reason and history do." It is strictly the language of the imagination; and the imagination is that

faculty which represents objects, not as they are in themselves, but as they are moulded by other thoughts and
feelings, into an infinite variety of shapes and combinations of power. This language is not the less true to
nature, because it is false in point of fact; but so much the
more true and natural, if it conveys the impression which
the object under the influence of passion makes on the
mind. Let an object, for instance, be presented to the
senses in a state of agitation or fear—and the imagination
will distort or magnify the object, and convert it into the
likeness of whatever is most proper to encourage the fear.
" Our eyes are made the fools " of our other faculties.
This is the universal law of the imagination,

> " That if it would but apprehend some joy,
> It comprehends some bringer of that joy :
> Or in the night imagining some fear,
> How easy is each bush suppos'd a bear ! "

When Iachimo says of Imogen,

> ——" The flame o' th' taper
> Bows towards her, and would under-peep her lids
> To see the enclosed lights "—

this passionate interpretation of the motion of the flame
to accord with the speaker's own feelings, is true poetry.
The lover, equally with the poet, speaks of the auburn
tresses of his mistress as locks of shining gold, because
the least tinge of yellow in the hair, has, from novelty
and a sense of personal beauty, a more lustrous effect to
the imagination than the purest gold. We compare a
man of gigantic stature to a tower: not that he is anything
like so large, but because the excess of his size beyond
what we are accustomed to expect, or the usual size of
things of the same class, produces by contrast a greater feeling of magnitude and ponderous strength than another
object of ten times the same dimensions. The intensity of
the feeling makes up for the disproportion of the objects.

Things are equal to the imagination, which have the power
of affecting the mind with an equal degree of terror,
admiration, delight, or love. When Lear calls upon the
heavens to avenge his cause, " for they are old like him,"
there is nothing extravagant or impious in this sublime
identification of his age with theirs; for there is no other
image which could do justice to the agonizing sense of
his wrongs and his despair!

Poetry is the high-wrought enthusiasm of fancy and
feeling. As in describing natural objects, it impregnates
sensible impressions with the forms of fancy, so it
describes the feelings of pleasure or pain, by blending
them with the strongest movements of passion, and the
most striking forms of nature. Tragic poetry, which is
the most impassioned species of it, strives to carry on the
feeling to the utmost point of sublimity or pathos, by all
the force of comparison or contrast; loses the sense of
present suffering in the imaginary exaggeration of it;
exhausts the terror or pity by an unlimited indulgence
of it; grapples with impossibilities in its desperate
impatience of restraint; throws us back upon the past,
forward into the future; brings every moment of our
being or object of nature in startling review before us;
and in the rapid whirl of events, lifts us from the depths
of woe to the highest contemplations on human life.
When Lear says of Edgar, " Nothing but his unkind
daughters could have brought him to this; " what a
bewildered amazement, what a wrench of the imagination,
that cannot be brought to conceive of any other cause of
misery than that which has bowed it down, and absorbs
all other sorrow in its own! His sorrow, like a flood,
supplies the sources of all other sorrow. Again, when he
exclaims in the mad scene, " The little dogs and all,
Tray, Blanche, and Sweetheart, see, they bark at me! "
it is passion lending occasion to imagination to make
every creature in league against him, conjuring up

ingratitude and insult in their least looked-for and most
galling shapes, searching every thread and fibre of his
heart, and finding out the last remaining image of respect
or attachment in the bottom of his breast, only to torture
and kill it! In like manner, the " So I am " of Cordelia
gushes from her heart like a torrent of tears, relieving
it of a weight of love and of supposed ingratitude, which
had pressed upon it for years. What a fine return of the
passion upon itself is that in Othello—with what a
mingled agony of regret and despair he clings to the last
traces of departed happiness—when he exclaims,

> ——" Oh now, for ever
> Farewel the tranquil mind. Farewel content ;
> Farewel the plumed troops and the big war,
> That make ambition virtue ! Oh farewel !
> Farewel the neighing steed, and the shrill trump,
> The spirit-stirring drum, th' ear-piercing fife,
> The royal banner, and all quality,
> Pride, pomp, and circumstance of glorious war :
> And O you mortal engines, whose rude throats
> Th' immortal Jove's dread clamours counterfeit,
> Farewel ! Othello's occupation's gone ! "

How his passion lashes itself up and swells and rages
like a tide in its sounding course, when in answer to the
doubts expressed of his returning love, he says,

> " Never, Iago. Like to the Pontic sea,
> Whose icy current and compulsive course
> Ne'er feels retiring ebb, but keeps due on
> To the Propontic and the Hellespont :
> Even so my bloody thoughts, with violent pace,
> Shall ne'er look back, ne'er ebb to humble love,
> Till that a capable and wide revenge
> Swallow them up."—

The climax of his expostulation afterwards with Des-
demona is at that line,

> " But there where I had garner'd up my heart,
> To be discarded thence ! "—

One mode in which the dramatic exhibition of passion excites our sympathy without raising our disgust is, that in proportion as it sharpens the edge of calamity and disappointment, it strengthens the desire of good. It enhances our consciousness of the blessing, by making us sensible of the magnitude of the loss. The storm of passion lays bare and shews us the rich depths of the human soul: the whole of our existence, the sum total of our passions and pursuits, of that which we desire and that which we dread, is brought before us by contrast; the action and re-action are equal; the keenness of immediate suffering only gives us a more intense aspiration after, and a more intimate participation with the antagonist world of good; makes us drink deeper of the cup of human life; tugs at the heart-strings; loosens the pressure about them; and calls the springs of thought and feeling into play with tenfold force.

Impassioned poetry is an emanation of the moral and intellectual part of our nature, as well as of the sensitive —of the desire to know, the will to act, and the power to feel; and ought to appeal to these different parts of our constitution, in order to be perfect. The domestic or prose tragedy, which is thought to be the most natural, is in this sense the least so, because it appeals almost exclusively to one of these faculties, our sensibility. The tragedies of Moore and Lillo, for this reason, however affecting at the time, oppress and lie like a dead weight upon the mind, a load of misery which it is unable to throw off; the tragedy of Shakspeare, which is true poetry, stirs our inmost affections; abstracts evil from itself by combining it with all the forms of imagination, and with the deepest workings of the heart, and rouses the whole man within us.

The pleasure, however, derived from tragic poetry, is not anything peculiar to it as poetry, as a fictitious and

o

fanciful thing. It is not an anomaly of the imagination. It has its source and ground-work in the common love of strong excitement. As Mr. Burke observes, people flock to see a tragedy; but if there were a public execution in the next street, the theatre would very soon be empty. It is not then the difference between fiction and reality that solves the difficulty. Children are satisfied with the stories of ghosts and witches in plain prose: nor do the hawkers of full, true, and particular accounts of murders and executions about the streets, find it necessary to have them turned into penny ballads, before they can dispose of these interesting and authentic documents. The grave politician drives a thriving trade of abuse and calumnies poured out against those whom he makes his enemies for no other end than that he may live by them. The popular preacher makes less frequent mention of heaven than of hell. Oaths and nicknames are only a more vulgar sort of poetry or rhetoric. We are as fond of indulging our violent passions as of reading a description of those of others. We are as prone to make a torment of our fears, as to luxuriate in our hopes of good. If it be asked, Why we do so? the best answer will be, Because we cannot help it. The sense of power is as strong a principle in the mind as the love of pleasure. Objects of terror and pity exercise the same despotic control over it as those of love or beauty. It is as natural to hate as to love, to despise as to admire, to express our hatred or contempt, as our love or admiration.

> " Masterless passion sways us to the mood
>   Of what it likes or loathes."

Not that we like what we loathe; but we like to indulge our hatred and scorn of it; to dwell upon it, to exasperate our idea of it by every refinement of ingenuity and extravagance of illustration; to make it a bugbear to ourselves, to point it out to others in all the splendour of deformity, to embody it to the senses, to stigmatize it by name, to grapple with it in thought, in action, to sharpen our intellect, to arm our will against it, to know the worst we have to contend with, and to contend with it to the utmost. Poetry is only the highest eloquence of passion, the most vivid form of expression that can be given to our conception of anything, whether pleasurable or painful, mean or dignified, delightful or distressing. It is the perfect coincidence of the image and the words with the feeling we have, and of which we cannot get rid in any other way, that gives an instant " satisfaction to the thought." This is equally the origin of wit and fancy, of comedy and tragedy, of the sublime and pathetic. When Pope says of the Lord Mayor's show,—

> " Now night descending, the proud scene is o'er,
> But lives in Settle's numbers one day more ! "

—when Collins makes Danger, " with limbs of giant mould,"

> ——" Throw him on the steep
> Of some loose hanging rock asleep : "

when Lear calls out in extreme anguish,

> " Ingratitude, thou marble-hearted fiend,
> How much more hideous shew'st in a child
> Than the sea-monster ! "

—the passion of contempt in the one case, of terror in the other, and of indignation in the last, is perfectly satisfied. We see the thing ourselves, and shew it to others as we feel it to exist, and as, in spite of ourselves, we are compelled to think of it. The imagination, by thus embodying and turning them to shape, gives an obvious relief to the indistinct and importunate cravings of the will.—We do not wish the thing to be so; but we wish it to appear such as it is. For knowledge is conscious power; and the mind is no longer, in this case, the dupe, though it may be the victim of vice or folly.

Poetry is in all its shapes the language of the imagination and the passions, of fancy and will. Nothing, therefore, can be more absurd than the outcry which has been sometimes raised by frigid and pedantic critics, for reducing the language of poetry to the standard of common sense and reason: for the end and use of poetry, " both at the first and now, was and is to hold the mirror up to nature," seen through the medium of passion and imagination, not divested of that medium by means of literal truth or abstract reason. The painter of history might as well be required to represent the face of a person who has just trod upon a serpent with the still-life expression of a common portrait, as the poet to describe the most striking and vivid impressions which things can be supposed to make upon the mind, in the language of common conversation. Let who will strip nature of the colours and the shapes of fancy, the poet is not bound to do so; the impressions of common sense and strong imagination, that is, of passion and indifference, cannot be the same, and they must have a separate language to do justice to either. Objects must strike differently upon the mind, independently of what they are in themselves, as long as we have a different interest in them, as we see them in a different point of view, nearer or at a greater distance (morally or physically speaking), from novelty, from old acquaintance, from our ignorance of them, from our fear of their consequences, from contrast, from unexpected likeness. We can no more take away the faculty of the imagination, than we can see all objects without light or shade. Some things must dazzle us by their preternatural light; others must hold us in suspense, and tempt our curiosity to explore their obscurity. Those who would dispel these various illusions, to give us their drab-coloured creation in their stead, are not very wise. Let the naturalist, if he will, catch the glow-worm, carry it home with him in a box, and find it next morning nothing but a little grey worm; let the poet or the lover of poetry visit it at evening, when beneath the scented hawthorn and the crescent moon it has built itself a palace of emerald light. This is also one part of nature, one appearance which the glow-worm presents, and that not the least interesting; so poetry is one part of the history of the human mind, though it is neither science nor philosophy. It cannot be concealed, however, that the progress of knowledge and refinement has a tendency to circumscribe the limits of the imagination, and to clip the wings of poetry. The province of the imagination is principally visionary, the unknown and undefined: the understanding restores things to their natural boundaries, and strips them of their fanciful pretensions. Hence the history of religious and poetical enthusiasm is much the same; and both have received a sensible shock from the progress of experimental philosophy. It is the undefined and uncommon that gives birth and scope to the imagination; we can only fancy what we do not know. As in looking into the mazes of a tangled wood we fill them with what shapes we please, with ravenous beasts, with caverns vast, and drear enchantments, so in our ignorance of the world about us, we make gods or devils of the first object we see, and set no bounds to the wilful suggestions of our hopes and fears.

> "And visions, as poetic eyes avow,
>   Hang on each leaf and cling to every bough."

There can never be another Jacob's dream. Since that time, the heavens have gone farther off, and grown astronomical. They have become averse to the imagination, nor will they return to us on the squares of the distances, or on Doctor Chalmers's Discourses. Rembrandt's picture brings the matter nearer to us.—It is not only the progress of mechanical knowledge, but the necessary advances of civilization that are unfavourable

to the spirit of poetry. We not only stand in less awe of
the preternatural world, but we can calculate more
surely, and look with more indifference, upon the regular
routine of this. The heroes of the fabulous ages rid the
world of monsters and giants. At present we are less
exposed to the vicissitudes of good or evil, to the incur-
sions of wild beasts or " bandit fierce," or to the unmitigated fury of the elements. The time has been that
" our fell of hair would at a dismal treatise rouse and stir
as life were in it." But the police spoils all; and we now
hardly so much as dream of a midnight murder. *Macbeth*
is only tolerated in this country for the sake of the
music; and in the United States of America, where the
philosophical principles of government are carried still
farther in theory and practice, we find that the *Beggar's
Opera* is hooted from the stage. Society, by degrees, is
constructed into a machine that carries us safely and
insipidly from one end of life to the other, in a very
comfortable prose style.

> " Obscurity her curtain round them drew,
>   And siren Sloth a dull quietus sung."

The remarks which have been here made, would, in
some measure, lead to a solution of the question of the
comparative merits of painting and poetry. I do not
mean to give any preference, but it should seem that the
argument which has been sometimes set up, that painting
must affect the imagination more strongly, because it
represents the image more distinctly, is not well founded.
We may assume without much temerity, that poetry is
more poetical than painting. When artists or con-
noisseurs talk on stilts about the poetry of painting, they
shew that they know little about poetry, and have little
love for the art. Painting gives the object itself; poetry
what it implies. Painting embodies what a thing contains
in itself: poetry suggests what exists out of it, in any

manner connected with it. But this last is the proper province of the imagination. Again, as it relates to passion, painting gives the event, poetry the progress of events: but it is during the progress, in the interval of expectation and suspense, while our hopes and fears are strained to the highest pitch of breathless agony, that the pinch of the interest lies.

> " Between the acting of a dreadful thing
> And the first motion, all the interim is
> Like a phantasma or a hideous dream.
> The mortal instruments are then in council;
> And the state of man, like to a little kingdom,
> Suffers then the nature of an insurrection."

But by the time that the picture is painted, all is over. Faces are the best part of a picture; but even faces are not what we chiefly remember in what interests us most. —But it may be asked then, Is there anything better than Claude Lorraine's landscapes, than Titian's portraits, than Raphael's cartoons, or the Greek statues? Of the two first I shall say nothing, as they are evidently picturesque, rather than imaginative. Raphael's cartoons are certainly the finest comments that ever were made on the Scriptures. Would their effect be the same if we were not acquainted with the text? But the New Testament existed before the cartoons. There is one subject of which there is no cartoon, Christ washing the feet of the disciples the night before his death. But that chapter does not need a commentary! It is for want of some such resting place for the imagination that the Greek statues are little else than specious forms. They are marble to the touch and to the heart. They have not an informing principle within them. In their faultless excellence they appear sufficient to themselves. By their beauty they are raised above the frailties of passion or suffering. By their beauty they are deified. But they are not objects of religious faith to us, and their forms are a reproach to common humanity. They seem to have no sympathy with us, and not to want our admiration.

Poetry in its matter and form is natural imagery or feeling, combined with passion and fancy. In its mode of conveyance, it combines the ordinary use of language with musical expression. There is a question of long standing, in what the essence of poetry consists; or what it is that determines why one set of ideas should be expressed in prose, another in verse. Milton has told us his idea of poetry in a single line—

> " Thoughts that voluntary move
> Harmonious numbers."

As there are certain sounds that excite certain movements, and the song and dance go together, so there are, no doubt, certain thoughts that lead to certain tones of voice, or modulations of sound, and change "the words of Mercury into the songs of Apollo." There is a striking instance of this adaptation of the movement of sound and rhythm to the subject, in Spenser's description of the Satyrs accompanying Una to the cave of Sylvanus.

> " So from the ground she fearless doth arise
>   And walketh forth without suspect of crime.
> They, all as glad as birds of joyous prime,
>   Thence lead her forth, about her dancing round,
> Shouting and singing all a shepherd's rhyme ;
>   And with green branches strewing all the ground,
> Do worship her as queen with olive garland crown'd.
>
> And all the way their merry pipes they sound,
>   That all the woods and doubled echoes ring ;
> And with their horned feet do wear the ground,
>   Leaping like wanton kids in pleasant spring ;
> So towards old Sylvanus they her bring,
>   Who with the noise awaked, cometh out."
>   *Faery Queen*, b.i., c. vi.

On the contrary, there is nothing either musical or natural in the ordinary construction of language. It is a thing altogether arbitrary and conventional. Neither in the sounds themselves, which are the voluntary signs of certain ideas, nor in their grammatical arrangements in common speech, is there any principle of natural imitation, or correspondence to the individual ideas, or to the tone of feeling with which they are conveyed to others. The jerks, the breaks, the inequalities, and harshnesses of prose, are fatal to the flow of a poetical imagination, as a jolting road or a stumbling horse disturbs the reverie of an absent man. But poetry makes these odds all even. It is the music of language, answering to the music of the mind, untying as it were " the secret soul of harmony." Wherever any object takes such a hold of the mind as to make us dwell upon it, and brood over it, melting the heart in tenderness, or kindling it to a sentiment of enthusiasm;—wherever a movement of imagination or passion is impressed on the mind, by which it seeks to prolong and repeat the emotion, to bring all other objects into accord with it, and to give the same movement of harmony, sustained and continuous, or gradually varied according to the occasion, to the sounds that express it— this is poetry. The musical in sound is the sustained and continuous; the musical in thought is the sustained and continuous also. There is a near connection between music and deep-rooted passion. Mad people sing. As often as articulation passes naturally into intonation, there poetry begins. Where one idea gives a tone and colour to others, where one feeling melts others into it, there can be no reason why the same principle should not be extended to the sounds by which the voice utters these emotions of the soul, and blends syllables and lines into each other. It is to supply the inherent defect of harmony in the customary mechanism of language, to make the sound an echo to the sense, when the sense becomes a sort of echo to itself—to mingle the tide of verse, " the golden cadences of poetry," with the tide of feeling,

o *

flowing and murmuring as it flows—in short, to take the language of the imagination from off the ground, and enable it to spread its wings where it may indulge its own impulses—

> " Sailing with supreme dominion
> Through the azure deep of air "—

without being stopped, or fretted, or diverted with the abruptness and petty obstacles, and discordant flats and sharps of prose, that poetry was invented. It is to common language, what springs are to a carriage, or wings to feet. In ordinary speech we arrive at a certain harmony by the modulations of the voice: in poetry the same thing is done systematically by a regular collocation of syllables. It has been well observed, that every one who declaims warmly, or grows intent upon a subject, rises into a sort of blank verse or measured prose. The merchant, as described in Chaucer, went on his way " sounding always the increase of his winning." Every prose-writer has more or less of rhythmical adaptation, except poets, who, when deprived of the regular mechanism of verse, seem to have no principle of modulation left in their writings.

An excuse might be made for rhyme in the same manner. It is but fair that the ear should linger on the sounds that delight it, or avail itself of the same brilliant coincidence and unexpected recurrence of syllables, that have been displayed in the invention and collocation of images. It is allowed that rhyme assists the memory; and that a man of wit and shrewdness has been heard to say, that the only four good lines of poetry are the well-known ones which tell the number of days in the months of the year.

> "Thirty days hath September," etc.

But if the jingle of names assists the memory, may it not also quicken the fancy? and there are other things worth having at our fingers' ends, besides the contents of the almanac.—Pope's versification is tiresome, from its excessive sweetness and uniformity. Shakspeare's blank verse is the perfection of dramatic dialogue.

All is not poetry that passes for such: nor does verse make the whole difference between poetry and prose. The *Iliad* does not cease to be poetry in a literal translation; and Addison's *Campaign* has been very properly denominated a Gazette in rhyme. Common prose differs from poetry, as treating for the most part either of such trite, familiar, and irksome matters of fact, as convey no extraordinary impulse to the imagination, or else of such difficult and laborious processes of the understanding, as do not admit of the wayward or violent movements either of the imagination or the passions.

I will mention three works which come as near to poetry as possible without absolutely being so, namely, the *Pilgrim's Progress, Robinson Crusoe,* and the *Tales of Boccaccio.* Chaucer and Dryden have translated some of the last into English rhyme, but the essence and power of poetry was there before. That which lifts the spirit above the earth, which draws the soul out of itself with indescribable longings, is poetry in kind, and generally fit to become so in name, by being " married to immortal verse." If it is of the essence of poetry to strike and fix the imagination, whether we will or no, to make the eye of childhood glisten with the starting tear, to be never thought of afterwards with indifference, John Bunyan and Daniel Defoe may be permitted to pass for poets in their way. The mixture of fancy and reality in the *Pilgrim's Progress* was never equalled in any allegory. His pilgrims walk above the earth, and yet are on it. What zeal, what beauty, what truth of fiction! What deep feeling in the description of Christian's swimming across the water at last, and in the picture of the Shining Ones within the gates, with wings at their backs and garlands on their heads, who are to wipe all tears from his eyes! The writer's genius, though not " dipped in dews of Castalie," was baptised with the Holy Spirit and with fire. The prints in this book are no small part of it. If the confinement of Philoctetes in the island of Lemnos was a subject for the most beautiful of all the Greek tragedies, what shall we say to Robinson Crusoe in his? Take the speech of the Greek hero on leaving his cave, beautiful as it is, and compare it with the reflections of the English adventurer in his solitary place of confinement. The thoughts of home, and of all from which he is for ever cut off, swell and press against his bosom, as the heaving ocean rolls its ceaseless tide against the rocky shore, and the very beatings of his heart become audible in the eternal silence that surrounds him. Thus he says:

" As I walked about, either in my hunting, or for viewing the country, the anguish of my soul at my condition would break out upon me on a sudden, and my very heart would die within me to think of the woods, the mountains, the deserts I was in ; and how I was a prisoner, locked up with the eternal bars and bolts of the ocean, in an uninhabited wilderness, without redemption. In the midst of the greatest composures of my mind, this would break out upon me like a storm, and make me wring my hands, and weep like a child. Sometimes it would take me in the middle of my work, and I would immediately sit down and sigh, and look upon the ground for an hour or two together, and this was still worse to me, for if I could burst into tears or vent myself in words, it would go off, and the grief having exhausted itself would abate." P. 50.

The story of his adventures would not make a poem like the *Odyssey*, it is true; but the relator had the true genius of a poet. It has been made a question whether Richardson's romances are poetry; and the answer perhaps is, that they are not poetry, because they are not romance. The interest is worked up to an inconceivable height; but it is by an infinite number of little things, by incessant labour and calls upon the attention, by a repetition of blows that have no rebound in them. The sympathy excited is not a voluntary contribution, but a tax. Nothing is unforced and spontaneous. There is a want of elasticity and motion. The story does not " give an echo to the seat where love is throned." The heart does not answer of itself like a chord in music. The fancy does not run on before the writer with breathless expectation, but is dragged along with an infinite number of pins and wheels, like those with which the Lilliputians dragged Gulliver pinioned to the royal palace.—Sir Charles Grandison is a coxcomb. What sort of a figure would he cut, translated into an epic poem, by the side of Achilles? Clarissa, the divine Clarissa, is too interesting by half. She is interesting in her ruffles, in her gloves, her samplers, her aunts and uncles—she is interesting in all that is uninteresting. Such things, however intensely they may be brought home to us, are not conductors to the imagination. There is infinite truth and feeling in Richardson; but it is extracted from a *caput mortuum* of circumstances: it does not evaporate of itself. His poetical genius is like Ariel confined in a pinetree, and requires an artificial process to let it out. Shakspeare says—

> " Our poesy is as a gum
> Which issues whence 'tis nourished, our gentle flame
> Provokes itself, and like the current flies
> Each bound it chafes."[1]

[1] Burke's writings are not poetry, notwithstanding the vividness of the fancy, because the subject matter is abstruse and dry, not natural, but artificial. The difference between poetry and eloquence is, that the one is the eloquence of the imagination, and the other of the understanding. Eloquence tries to persuade the will, and convince the reason : poetry produces its effect by instantaneous sympathy. Nothing is a subject for poetry that admits of a dispute. Poets are in general bad prose-writers, because their images, though fine in themselves, are not to the purpose, and do not carry on the argument. The French poetry wants the forms of the imagination. It is didactic more than dramatic. And some of our own poetry which has been most admired, is only poetry in the rhyme, and in the studied use of poetic diction.

I shall conclude this general account with some remarks on four of the principal works of poetry in the world, at different periods of history—Homer, the Bible, Dante, and let me add, Ossian. In Homer, the principle of action or life is predominant; in the Bible, the principle of faith and the idea of Providence; Dante is a personification of blind will; and in Ossian we see the decay of life, and the lag end of the world. Homer's poetry is the heroic: it is full of life and action: it is bright as the day, strong as a river. In the vigour of his intellect, he grapples with all the objects of nature, and enters into all the relations of social life. He saw many countries, and the manners of many men; and he has brought them all together in his poem. He describes his heroes going to battle with a prodigality of life, arising from an exuberance of animal spirits: we see them before us, their number, and their order of battle, poured out upon the plain " all plumed like estriches, like eagles newly bathed, wanton as goats, wild as young bulls, youthful as May, and gorgeous as the sun at midsummer," covered with glittering armour, with dust and blood; while the Gods quaff their nectar in golden cups, or mingle in the fray; and the old men assembled on the walls of Troy rise up with reverence as Helen passes by them. The multitude of things in Homer is wonderful; their splendour, their truth, their force, and variety. His poetry is, like his religion, the poetry of number and form: he describes the bodies as well as the souls of men.

The poetry of the Bible is that of imagination and of faith: it is abstract and disembodied: it is not the poetry of form, but of power ; not of multitude, but of immensity. It does not divide into many, but aggrandizes into one. Its ideas of Nature are like its ideas of God. It is not the poetry of social life, but of solitude: each man seems alone in the world, with the original forms of nature, the rocks, the earth, and the sky. It is not the poetry of action or heroic enterprise, but of faith in a supreme Providence, and resignation to the power that governs the universe. As the idea of God was removed farther from humanity, and a scattered polytheism, it became more profound and intense, as it became more universal, for the Infinite is present to everything: "If we fly into the uttermost parts of the earth, it is there also; if we turn to the east or the west, we cannot escape from it." Man is thus aggrandized in the image of his Maker. The history of the patriarchs is of this kind ; they are founders of a chosen race of people, the inheritors of the earth; they exist in the generations which are to come after them. Their poetry, like their religious creed, is vast, unformed, obscure, and infinite; a vision is upon it—an invisible hand is suspended over it. The spirit of the Christian religion consists in the glory hereafter to be revealed; but in the Hebrew dispensation, Providence took an immediate share in the affairs of this life. Jacob's dream arose out of this intimate communion between heaven and earth: it was this that let down, in the sight of the youthful patriarch, a golden ladder from the sky to the earth, with angels ascending and descending upon it, and shed a light upon the lonely place, which can never pass away. The story of Ruth, again, is as if all the depth of natural affection in the human race was involved in her breast. There are descriptions in the book of Job more prodigal of imagery, more intense in passion, than anything in Homer, as that of the state of his prosperity, and of the vision that came upon him by night. The metaphors in the Old Testament are more boldly figurative. Things were collected more into masses, and gave a greater *momentum* to the imagination.

Dante was the father of modern poetry, and he may therefore claim a place in this connection. His poem is the first great step from Gothic darkness and barbarism;

and the struggle of thought in it to burst the thraldom in which the human mind had been so long held, is felt in every page. He stood bewildered, not appalled, on that dark shore which separates the ancient and the modern world; and saw the glories of antiquity dawning through the abyss of time, while revelation opened its passage to the other world. He was lost in wonder at what had been done before him, and he dared to emulate it. Dante seems to have been indebted to the Bible for the gloomy tone of his mind, as well as for the prophetic fury which exalts and kindles his poetry; but he is utterly unlike Homer. His genius is not a sparkling flame, but the sullen heat of a furnace. He is power, passion, self-will personified. In all that relates to the descriptive or fanciful part of poetry, he bears no comparison to many who had gone before, or who have come after him; but there is a gloomy abstraction in his conceptions, which lies like a dead weight upon the mind; a benumbing stupor, a breathless awe, from the intensity of the impression; a terrible obscurity, like that which oppresses us in dreams; an identity of interest, which moulds every object to its own purposes, and clothes all things with the passions and imaginations of the human soul,—that make amends for all other deficiencies. The immediate objects he presents to the mind are not much in themselves, they want grandeur, beauty, and order; but they become everything by the force of the character he impresses upon them. His mind lends its own power to the objects which it contemplates, instead of borrowing it from them. He takes advantage even of the nakedness and dreary vacuity of his subject. His imagination peoples the shades of death, and broods over the silent air. He is the severest of all writers, the most hard and impenetrable, the most opposite to the flowery and glittering; who relies most on his own power, and the sense of it in others, and who leaves most room to the imagination of his readers. Dante's only endeavour is to interest; and he interests by exciting our sympathy with the emotion by which he is himself possessed. He does not place before us the objects by which that emotion has been created; but he seizes on the attention, by shewing us the effect they produce on his feelings; and his poetry accordingly gives the same thrilling and overwhelming sensation, which is caught by gazing on the face of a person who has seen some object of horror. The improbability of the events, the abruptness and monotony in the *Inferno*, are excessive : but the interest never flags, from the continued earnestness of the author's mind. Dante's great power is in combining internal feelings with external objects. Thus the gate of hell, on which that withering inscription is written, seems to be endowed with speech and consciousness, and to utter its dread warning, not without a sense of mortal woes. This author habitually unites the absolutely local and individual with the greatest wildness and mysticism. In the midst of the obscure and shadowy regions of the lower world, a tomb suddenly rises up with the inscription, " I am the tomb of Pope Anastasius the Sixth ": and half the personages whom he has crowded into the *Inferno* are his own acquaintance. All this, perhaps, tends to heighten the effect by the bold intermixture of realities, and by an appeal, as it were, to the individual knowledge and experience of the reader. He affords few subjects for picture. There is, indeed, one gigantic one, that of Count Ugolino, of which Michael Angelo made a bas-relief, and which Sir Joshua Reynolds ought not to have painted.

Another writer whom I shall mention last, and whom I cannot persuade myself to think a mere modern in the groundwork, is Ossian. He is a feeling and a name that can never be destroyed in the minds of his readers. As Homer is the first vigour and lustihood, Ossian is the decay

and old age of poetry. He lives only in the recollection
and regret of the past. There is one impression which
he conveys more entirely than all other poets, namely,
the sense of privation, the loss of all things, of friends,
of good name, of country—he is even without God in the
world. He converses only with the spirits of the departed;
with the motionless and silent clouds. The cold moonlight sheds its faint lustre on his head; the fox peeps
out of the ruined tower; the thistle waves its beard to the
wandering gale; and the strings of his harp seem, as
the hand of age, as the tale of other times, passes over
them, to sigh and rustle like the dry reeds in the winter's
wind! The feeling of cheerless desolation, of the loss
of the pith and sap of existence, of the annihilation of
the substance, and the clinging to the shadow of all
things as in a mock-embrace, is here perfect. In this
way, the lamentation of Selma for the loss of Salgar is
the finest of all. If it were indeed possible to shew that
this writer was nothing, it would only be another instance
of mutability, another blank made, another void left in
the heart, another confirmation of that feeling which
makes him so often complain, " Roll on, ye dark brown
years, ye bring no joy on your wing to Ossian! "

ON WIT AND HUMOUR

(LECTURES ON THE ENGLISH COMIC WRITERS, 1818)

M A N is the only animal that laughs and weeps; for
he is the only animal that is struck with the difference
between what things are, and what they ought to be.
We weep at what thwarts or exceeds our desires in
serious matters: we laugh at what only disappoints

our expectations in trifles. We shed tears from sympathy with real and necessary distress; as we burst into laughter from want of sympathy with that which is unreasonable and unnecessary, the absurdity of which provokes our spleen or mirth, rather than any serious reflections on it.

To explain the nature of laughter and tears, is to account for the condition of human life; for it is in a manner compounded of these two! It is a tragedy or a comedy—sad or merry, as it happens. The crimes and misfortunes that are inseparable from it, shock and wound the mind when they once seize upon it, and when the pressure can no longer be borne, seek relief in tears: the follies and absurdities that men commit, or the odd accidents that befall them, afford us amusement from the very rejection of these false claims upon our sympathy, and end in laughter. If everything that went wrong, if every vanity or weakness in another gave us a sensible pang, it would be hard indeed: but as long as the dis-agreeableness of the consequences of a sudden disaster is kept out of sight by the immediate oddity of the circumstances, and the absurdity or unaccountableness of a foolish action is the most striking thing in it, the ludicrous prevails over the pathetic, and we receive pleasure instead of pain from the farce of life which is played before us, and which discomposes our gravity as often as it fails to move our anger or our pity!

Tears may be considered as the natural and involuntary resource of the mind overcome by some sudden and violent emotion, before it has had time to reconcile its feelings to the change of circumstances: while laughter may be defined to be the same sort of convulsive and involuntary movement, occasioned by mere surprise or contrast (in the absence of any more serious emotion), before it has time to reconcile its belief to contradictory appearances. If we hold a mask before our face, and approach a child with this disguise on, it will at first, from the oddity and incongruity of the appearance, be inclined to laugh; if we go nearer to it, steadily, and without saying a word, it will begin to be alarmed, and be half-inclined to cry: if we suddenly take off the mask, it will recover from its fears, and burst out a-laughing; but if, instead of presenting the old well-known countenance, we have concealed a satyr's head or some frightful caricature behind the first mask, the suddenness of the change will not in this case be a source of merriment to it, but will convert its surprise into an agony of consternation, and will make it scream out for help, even though it may be convinced that the whole is a trick at bottom.

The alternation of tears and laughter, in this little episode in common life, depends almost entirely on the greater or less degree of interest attached to the different changes of appearance. The mere suddenness of the transition, the mere baulking our expectations, and turning them abruptly into another channel, seems to give additional liveliness and gaiety to the animal spirits; but the instant the change is not only sudden, but threatens serious consequences, or calls up the shape of danger, terror supersedes our disposition to mirth, and laughter gives place to tears. It is usual to play with infants, and make them laugh by clapping your hands suddenly before them; but if you clapped your hands too loud, or too near their sight, their countenances immediately change, and they hide them in the nurse's arms. Or suppose the same child, grown up a little older, comes to a place, expecting to meet a person it is particularly fond of, and does not find that person there, its countenance suddenly falls, its lips begin to quiver, its cheek turns pale, its eye glistens, and it vents its little sorrow (grown too big to be concealed) in a flood of tears. Again, if the child meets the same person unexpectedly after a long absence, the same effect will be produced by an excess of joy, with different accompaniments; that is, the surprise and the emotion excited will make the blood come into his face, his eyes sparkle, his tongue falter or be mute, but in either case the tears will gush to his relief, and lighten the pressure about his heart. On the other hand, if a child is playing at hide-and-seek, or blind-man's-buff, with persons it is ever so fond of, and either misses them where it had made sure of finding them, or suddenly runs up against them where it had least expected it, the shock or additional impetus given to the imagination by the disappointment or the discovery, in a matter of this indifference, will only vent itself in a fit of laughter.[1] The transition here is not from one thing of importance to another, or from a state of indifference to a state of strong excitement; but merely from one impression to another that we did not at all expect, and when we had expected just the contrary. The mind having been led to form a certain conclusion, and the result producing an immediate solution of continuity in the chain of our ideas, this alternate excitement and relaxation of the imagination, the object also striking upon the mind more vividly in its loose unsettled state, and before it has had time to recover and collect itself, causes that alternate excitement and relaxation, or irregular convulsive movement of the muscular and nervous system, which constitutes physical laughter. The *discontinuous* in our sensations produces a correspondent jar and discord in the frame. The steadiness of our faith and of our features begins to give way at the same time. We turn with an incredulous smile from a story that staggers our belief: and we are ready to split our sides with laughing at an

---

[1] A child that has hid itself out of the way in sport, is under a great temptation to laugh at the unconsciousness of others as to its situation. A person concealed from assassins, is in no danger of betraying his situation by laughing.

extravagance that sets all common sense and serious concern at defiance.

To understand or define the ludicrous, we must first know what the serious is. Now the serious is the habitual stress which the mind lays upon the expectation of a given order of events, following one another with a certain regularity and weight of interest attached to them. When this stress is increased beyond its usual pitch of intensity, so as to overstrain the feelings by the violent opposition of good to bad, or of objects to our desires, it becomes the pathetic or tragical. The ludicrous, or comic, is the unexpected loosening or relaxing this stress below its usual pitch of intensity, by such an abrupt trans-position of the order of our ideas, as taking the mind unawares, throws it off its guard, startles it into a lively sense of pleasure, and leaves no time nor inclination for painful reflections.

The essence of the laughable then is the incongruous, the disconnecting one idea from another, or the jostling of one feeling against another. The first and most obvious cause of laughter is to be found in the simple succession of events, as in the sudden shifting of a disguise, or some unlooked-for accident, without any absurdity of character or situation. The accidental con-tradiction between our expectations and the event can hardly be said, however, to amount to the ludicrous; it is merely laughable. The ludicrous is where there is the same contradiction between the object and our expectations, heightened by some deformity or inconvenience, that is, by its being contrary to what is customary or desirable; as the ridiculous, which is the highest degree of the laughable, is that which is contrary not only to custom but to sense and reason, or is a voluntary departure from what we have a right to expect from those who are conscious of absurdity and propriety in words, looks, and actions.

Of these different kinds or degrees of the laughable,

the first is the most shallow and short-lived; for the instant the immediate surprise of a thing's merely happening one way or another is over, there is nothing to throw us back upon our former expectation, and renew our wonder at the event a second time. The second sort, that is, the ludicrous arising out of the improbable or distressing, is more deep and lasting, either because the painful catastrophe excites a greater curiosity, or because the old impression, from its habitual hold on the imagination, still recurs mechanically, so that it is longer before we can seriously make up our minds to the unaccountable deviation from it. The third sort, or the ridiculous arising out of absurdity as well as improbability, that is, where the defect or weakness is of a man's own seeking, is the most refined of all, but not always so pleasant as the last, because the same contempt and disapprobation which sharpens and subtilises our sense of the impropriety, adds a severity to it inconsistent with perfect ease and enjoyment. This last species is properly the province of satire. The principle of contrast is, however, the same in all the stages, in the simply laughable, the ludicrous, the ridiculous; and the effect is only the more complete, the more durably and pointedly this principle operates.

To give some examples in these different kinds. We laugh, when children, at the sudden removing of a paste-board mask: we laugh, when grown up, more gravely at the tearing off the mask of deceit. We laugh at absurdity; we laugh at deformity. We laugh at a bottle-nose in a caricature; at a stuffed figure of an alderman in a pantomime, and at the tale of Slaukenbergius. A dwarf standing by a giant makes a contemptible figure enough Rosinante and Dapple are laughable from contrast, as their masters from the same principle make two for a pair. We laugh at the dress of foreigners, and they at ours. Three chimney-sweepers meeting three Chinese in Lincoln's-inn Fields, they laughed at one another till they were ready to drop down. Country people laugh at a person because they never saw him before. Any one dressed in the height of the fashion, or quite out of it, is equally an object of ridicule. One rich source of the ludicrous is distress with which we cannot sympathize from its absurdity or insignificance. Women laugh at their lovers. We laugh at a damned author, in spite of our teeth, and though he may be our friend. " There is something in the misfortunes of our best friends that pleases us." We laugh at people on the top of a stage-coach, or in it, if they seem in great extremity. It is hard to hinder children from laughing at a stammerer, at a negro, at a drunken man, or even at a madman. We laugh at mischief. We laugh at what we do not believe. We say that an argument or an assertion that is very absurd, is quite ludicrous. We laugh to show our satisfaction with ourselves, or our contempt for those about us, or to conceal our envy or our ignorance. We laugh at fools, and at those who pretend to be wise—at extreme simplicity, awkwardness, hypocrisy, and affectation. " They were talking of me," says Scrub, " for they laughed *consumedly*." Lord Foppington's insensibility to ridicule, and airs of ineffable self-conceit, are no less admirable; and Joseph Surface's cant maxims of morality, when once disarmed of their power to do hurt, become sufficiently ludicrous. We laugh at that in others which is a serious matter to ourselves; because our self-love is stronger than our sympathy, sooner takes the alarm, and instantly turns our heedless mirth into gravity, which only enhances the jest to others. Some one is generally sure to be the sufferer by a joke. What is sport to one, is death to another. It is only very sensible or very honest people who laugh as freely at their own absurdities as at those of their neighbours. In general the contrary rule holds, and we only laugh at those misfortunes in which we are spectators, not sharers. The injury, the disappointment, shame, and vexation that we feel, put a stop to our mirth; while the disasters that come home to us, and excite our repugnance and dismay, are an amusing spectacle to others. The greater resistance we make, and the greater the perplexity into which we are thrown, the more lively and *piquant* is the intellectual display of cross-purposes to the by-standers. Our humiliation is their triumph. We are occupied with the disagreeableness of the result instead of its oddity or unexpectedness. Others see only the conflict of motives and the sudden alternation of events—we feel the pain as well, which more than counterbalances the speculative entertainment we might receive from the contemplation of our abstract situation.

You cannot force people to laugh, you cannot give a reason why they should laugh;—they must laugh of themselves, or not at all. As we laugh from a spontaneous impulse, we laugh the more at any restraint upon this impulse. We laugh at a thing merely because we ought not. If we think we must not laugh, this perverse impediment makes our temptation to laugh the greater; for by endeavouring to keep the obnoxious image out of sight, it comes upon us more irresistibly and repeatedly, and the inclination to indulge our mirth, the longer it is held back, collects its force, and breaks out the more violently in peals of laughter. In like manner anything we must not think of makes us laugh, by its coming upon us by stealth and unawares, and from the very efforts we make to exclude it. A secret, a loose word, a wanton jest, makes people laugh. Aretine laughed himself to death at hearing a lascivious story. Wickedness is often made a substitute for wit; and in most of our good old comedies the intrigue of the plot and the double meaning of the dialogue go hand-in-hand, and keep up the ball with wonderful spirit between them.

The consciousness, however it may arise, that there is something that we ought to look grave at, is almost always a signal for laughter outright: we can hardly keep our countenance at a sermon, a funeral, or a wedding. What an excellent old custom was that of throwing the stocking! What a deal of innocent mirth has been spoiled by the disuse of it! It is not an easy matter to preserve decorum in courts of justice; the smallest circumstance that interferes with the solemnity of the proceedings, throws the whole place into an uproar of laughter. People at the point of death often say smart things. Sir Thomas More jested with his executioner: Rabelais and Wycherley both died with a *bon-mot* in their mouths.

Misunderstandings (*malentendus*), where one person means one thing, and another is aiming at something else, are another great source of comic humour, on the same principle of ambiguity and contrast. There is a high-wrought instance of this in the dialogue between Aimwell and Gibbet, in the *Beaux' Stratagem*, where Aimwell mistakes his companion for an officer in a marching regiment, and Gibbet takes it for granted that the gentleman is a highwayman. The alarm and consternation occasioned by some one saying to him in the course of common conversation, " I apprehend you," is the most ludicrous thing in that admirably natural and powerful performance, Mr. Emery's Robert Tyke. Again, unconsciousness in the person himself of what he is about, or of what others think of him, is also a great heightener of the sense of absurdity. It makes it come the fuller home upon us from his insensibility to it. His simplicity sets off the satire, and gives it a finer edge. It is a more extreme case still where the person is aware of being the object of ridicule, and yet seems perfectly reconciled to it as a matter of course. So wit is often the more forcible and pointed for being dry and serious, for it then seems as if the speaker himself had no intention in it, and we were the first to find it out. Irony, as a species of wit, owes its force to the same principle. In such cases it is the contrast between the appearance and the reality, the suspense of belief, and the seeming incongruity, that gives point to the ridicule, and makes it enter the deeper when the first impression is overcome. Excessive impudence, as in the *Liar;* or excessive modesty, as in the hero of *She Stoops to Conquer;* or a mixture of the two, as in the *Busy Body*, are equally amusing. Lying is a species of wit and humour. To lay anything to a person's charge from which he is perfectly free, shews spirit and invention; and the more incredible the effrontery, the greater is the joke.

There is nothing more powerfully humorous than what is called *keeping* in comic character, as we see it very finely exemplified in Sancho Panza and Don Quixote. The proverbial phlegm and the romantic gravity of these two celebrated persons may be regarded as the height of this kind of excellence. The deep feeling of character strengthens the sense of the ludicrous. Keeping in comic character is consistency in absurdity; a determined and laudable attachment to the incongruous and singular. The regularity completes the contradiction; for the number of instances of deviation from the right line, branching out in all directions, shews the inveteracy of the original bias to any extravagance or folly, the natural improbability, as it were, increasing every time with the multiplication of chances for a return to common sense, and in the end mounting up to an incredible and unaccountably ridiculous height, when we find our expectations as invariably baffled. The most curious problem of all, is this truth of absurdity to itself. That reason and good sense should be consistent, is not wonderful: but that caprice, and whim, and fantastical prejudice, should be uniform and infallible in their results, is the surprising thing. But while this characteristic clue to absurdity helps on the ridicule, it also softens and harmonizes its excesses; and the ludicrous is here blended with a certain beauty and decorum, from this very truth of habit and sentiment, or from the principle of similitude in dissimilitude. The devotion to nonsense, and enthusiasm about trifles, is highly affecting as a moral lesson: it is one of the striking weaknesses and greatest happinesses of our nature. That which excites so lively and lasting an interest in itself, even though it should not be wisdom, is not despicable in the sight of reason and humanity. We cannot suppress the smile on the lip; but the tear should also stand ready to start from the eye. The history of hobby-horses is equally instructive and delightful; and after the pair I have just alluded to, My Uncle Toby's is one of the best and gentlest that " ever lifted leg! " The inconveniences, odd accidents, falls, and bruises to which they expose their riders, contribute their share to the amusement of the spectators; and the blows and wounds that the Knight of the Sorrowful Countenance received in his many perilous adventures, have applied their healing influence to many a hurt mind.—In what relates to the laughable, as it arises from unforeseen accidents or self-willed scrapes, the pain, the shame, the mortification, and utter helplessness of situation, add to the joke, provided they are momentary, or overwhelming only to the imagination of the sufferer. Malvolio's punishment and apprehensions are as comic, from our knowing that they are not real, as Christopher Sly's drunken transformation and short-lived dream of happiness are for the like reason. Parson Adams's fall into the tub at the 'Squire's, or his being discovered in bed with Mrs. Slipslop, though pitiable, are laughable accidents; nor do we read with much gravity of the loss of his Æschylus, serious as it was to him at the time. A

Scotch clergyman, as he was going to church, seeing a spruce, conceited mechanic, who was walking before him, suddenly covered all over with dirt, either by falling into the kennel, or by some other calamity befalling him, smiled and passed on; but afterwards seeing the same person, who had stopped to refit, seated directly facing him in the gallery, with a look of perfect satisfaction and composure, as if nothing of the sort had happened to him, the idea of his late disaster and present self-complacency struck him so powerfully, that, unable to resist the impulse, he flung himself back in the pulpit, and laughed till he could laugh no longer. I remember reading a story in an odd number of the *European Magazine*, of an old gentleman who used to walk out every afternoon with a gold-headed cane, in the fields opposite Baltimore House, which were then open, only with foot-paths crossing them. He was frequently accosted by a beggar with a wooden leg, to whom he gave money, which only made him more importunate. One day, when he was more troublesome than usual, a well-dressed person happening to come up, and observing how saucy the fellow was, said to the gentleman, " Sir, if you will lend me your cane for a moment, I'll give him a good thrashing for his impertinence." The old gentleman, smiling at the proposal, handed him his cane, which the other no sooner was going to apply to the shoulders of the culprit, than he immediately whipped off his wooden leg, and scampered off with great alacrity, and his chastiser after him as hard as he could go. The faster the one ran, the faster the other followed him, brandishing the cane, to the great astonishment of the gentleman who owned it, till having fairly crossed the fields, they suddenly turned a corner, and nothing more was seen of either of them.

In the way of mischievous adventure, and a wanton exhibition of ludicrous weakness in character, nothing is superior to the comic parts of the *Arabian Nights'*

Entertainments. To take only the set of stories of the
Little Hunchback, who was choked with a bone, and
the Barber of Bagdad and his seven brothers—there
is that of the tailor who was persecuted by the miller's
wife, and who, after toiling all night in the mill, got
nothing for his pains—of another who fell in love with a
fine lady, who pretended to return his passion, and inviting
him to her house, as the preliminary condition of her
favour, had his eyebrows shaved, his clothes stripped off,
and being turned loose into a winding gallery, he was to
follow her, and by overtaking obtain all his wishes, but
after a turn or two stumbled on a trap-door, and fell plump
into the street, to the great astonishment of the spectators
and his own, shorn of his eyebrows, naked, and without
a ray of hope left:—that of the castle-building pedlar,
who in kicking his wife, the supposed daughter of an
emperor, kicks down his basket of glass, the brittle
foundation of his ideal wealth, his good fortune, and
his arrogance:—that, again, of the beggar who dined
with the Barmecide, and feasted with him on the names
of wines and dishes: and, last and best of all, the inimitable story of the Impertinent Barber, himself one of
the seven, and worthy to be so; his pertinacious, incredible,
teasing, deliberate, yet unmeaning folly, his wearing
out the patience of the young gentleman whom he is sent
for to shave, his preparations and his professions of speed,
his taking out an astrolabe to measure the height of the
sun while his razors are getting ready, his dancing the
dance of Zimri and singing the song of Zamtout, his dis-
appointing the young man of an assignation, following him
to the place of rendezvous, and alarming the master of the
house in his anxiety for his safety, by which his unfortunate patron loses his hand in the affray, and this is felt
as an awkward accident. The danger which the same
loquacious person is afterwards in of losing his head
for want of saying who he was, because he would not

forfeit his character of being " justly called the Silent," is a consummation of the jest, though, if it had really taken place, it would have been carrying the joke too far. There are a thousand instances of the same sort in the *Thousand and One Nights*, which are an inexhaustible mine of comic humour and invention, and which, from the manners of the East which they describe, carry the principle of callous indifference in a jest as far as it can go. The serious and marvellous stories in that work, which have been so much admired and so greedily read, appear to me monstrous and abortive fictions, like disjointed dreams, dictated by a preternatural dread of arbitrary and despotic power, as the comic and familiar stories are rendered proportionally amusing and interesting from the same principle operating in a different direction, and producing endless uncertainty and vicissitude, and an heroic contempt for the untoward accidents and petty vexations of human life. It is the gaiety of despair, the mirth and laughter of a respite during pleasure from death. The strongest instances of effectual and harrowing imagination are in the story of Amine and her three sisters, whom she led by her side as a leash of hounds, and of the *goul* who nibbled grains of rice for her dinner, and preyed on human carcasses. In this condemnation of the serious parts of the *Arabian Nights*, I have nearly all the world, and in particular the author of the *Ancient Mariner*, against me, who must be allowed to be a judge of such matters, and who said, with a subtlety of philosophical conjecture which he alone possesses, that " if I did not like them, it was because I did not dream." On the other hand, I have Bishop Atterbury on my side, who in a letter to Pope, fairly confesses that " he could not read them in his old age."

There is another source of comic humour which has been but little touched on or attended to by the critics —not the infliction of casual pain, but the pursuit of uncertain pleasure and idle gallantry. Half the business and gaiety of comedy turns upon this. Most of the adventures, difficulties, demurs, hair-breadth 'scapes, disguises, deceptions, blunders, disappointments, successes, excuses, all the dextrous manœuvres, artful innuendoes, assignations, billets-doux, *double entendres*, sly allusions, and elegant flattery, have an eye to this—to the obtaining of those " favours secret, sweet, and precious," in which love and pleasure consist, and which when attained, and the *equivoque* is at an end, the curtain drops, and the play is over. All the attractions of a subject that can only be glanced at indirectly, that is a sort of forbidden ground to the imagination, except under severe restrictions, which are constantly broken through; all the resources it supplies for intrigue and invention; the bashfulness of the clownish lover, his looks of alarm and petrified astonishment; the foppish affectation and easy confidence of the happy man; the dress, the airs, the languor, the scorn, and indifference of the fine lady; the bustle, pertness, loquaciousness, and tricks of the chambermaid; the impudence, lies, and roguery of the valet; the match-making and unmaking; the wisdom of the wise; the sayings of the witty; the folly of the fool; " the soldier's, scholar's, courtier's eye, tongue, sword, the glass of fashion and the mould of form," have all a view to this. It is the closet of Blue-Beard. It is the life and soul of Wycherley, Congreve, Vanbrugh, and Farquhar's plays. It is the salt of comedy, without which it would be worthless and insipid. It makes Horner decent, and Millamant divine. It is the jest between Tattle and Miss Prue. It is the bait with which Olivia, in the *Plain Dealer*, plays with honest Manly. It lurks at the bottom of the catechism which Archer teaches Cherry, and which she learns by heart. It gives the finishing grace to Mrs. Amlet's confession—" Though I'm old, I'm chaste." Valentine and his

Angelica would be nothing without it; Miss Peggy would not be worth a gallant; and Slender's " sweet Anne Page " would be no more! " The age of comedy would be gone, and the glory of our play-houses extinguished for ever." Our old comedies would be invaluable, were it only for this, that they keep alive this sentiment, which still survives in all its fluttering grace and breathless palpitations on the stage.

Humour is the describing the ludicrous as it is in itself; wit is the exposing it, by comparing or contrasting it with something else. Humour is, as it were, the growth of nature and accident; wit is the product of art and fancy. Humour, as it is shewn in books, is an imitation of the natural or acquired absurdities of mankind, or of the ludicrous in accident, situation, and character; wit is the illustrating and heightening the sense of that absurdity by some sudden and unexpected likeness or opposition of one thing to another, which sets off the quality we laugh at or despise in a still more contemptible or striking point of view. Wit, as distinguished from poetry, is the imagination or fancy inverted, and so applied to given objects, as to make the little look less, the mean more light and worthless; or to divert our admiration or wean our affections from that which is lofty and impressive, instead of producing a more intense admiration and exalted passion, as poetry does. Wit may sometimes, indeed, be shewn in compliments as well as satire; as in the common epigram—

> " Accept a miracle, instead of wit :
> See two dull lines with Stanhope's pencil writ."

But then the mode of paying it is playful and ironical, and contradicts itself in the very act of making its own performance an humble foil to another's. Wit hovers round the borders of the light and trifling, whether in matters of pleasure or pain; for as soon as it describes

P

the serious seriously, it ceases to be wit, and passes
into a different form. Wit is, in fact, the eloquence
of indifference, or an ingenious and striking exposition
of those evanescent and glancing impressions of objects
which affect us more from surprise or contrast to the
train of our ordinary and literal preconceptions, than
from anything in the objects themselves exciting our
necessary sympathy or lasting hatred. The favourite
employment of wit is to add littleness to littleness, and
heap contempt on insignificance by all the arts of petty
and incessant warfare; or if it ever affects to aggrandise,
and use the language of hyperbole, it is only to betray
into derision by a fatal comparison, as in the mock-heroic;
or if it treats of serious passion, it must do it so as to lower
the tone of intense and high-wrought sentiment by the
introduction of burlesque and familiar circumstances. To
give an instance or two. Butler, in his *Hudibras*, compares
the change of night into day to the change of colour in a
boiled lobster.

> " The sun had long since, in the lap
>   Of Thetis, taken out his nap ;
>   And, like a lobster boil'd, the morn
>   From black to red began to turn :
>   When Hudibras, whom thoughts and aching
>   'Twixt sleeping kept all night and waking,
>   Began to rub his drowsy eyes,
>   And from his couch prepared to rise,
>   Resolving to dispatch the deed
>   He vow'd to do with trusty speed."

Compare this with the following stanzas in Spenser,
treating of the same subject:—

> " By this the Northern Waggoner had set
>   His seven-fold team behind the stedfast star,
>   That was in ocean waves yet never wet,
>   But firm is fix'd and sendeth light from far
>   To all that in the wide deep wand'ring are :
>   And cheerful chanticleer with his note shrill,
>   Had warned once that Phœbus' fiery car

In haste was climbing up the eastern hill,
Full envious that night so long his room did fill.

  At last the golden oriental gate
  Of greatest heaven 'gan to open fair,
  And Phœbus, fresh as bridegroom to his mate,
  Came dancing forth, shaking his dewy hair,
  And hurl'd his glist'ring beams through gloomy air :
  Which when the wakeful elf perceived, straitway
  He started up, and did himself prepare
  In sun-bright arms and battailous array,
For with that pagan proud he combat will that day."

In this last passage every image is brought forward that
can give effect to our natural impressions of the beauty,
the splendour, and solemn grandeur of the rising sun;
pleasure and power wait on every line and word: whereas,
in the other, the only memorable thing is a grotesque and
ludicrous illustration of the alteration which takes place
from darkness to gorgeous light, and that brought from
the lowest instance, and with associations that can only
disturb and perplex the imagination in its conception of
the real object it describes. There cannot be a more witty,
and at the same time degrading comparison, than that
in the same author, of the Bear turning round the pole-
star to a bear tied to a stake :—

  " But now a sport more formidable
  Had raked together village rabble ;
  'Twas an old way of recreating
  Which learned butchers call bear-baiting,
  A bold adventurous exercise
  With ancient heroes in high prize,
  For authors do affirm it came
  From Isthmian or Nemæan game ;
  Others derive it from the Bear
  That's fixed in northern hemisphere,
  And round about his pole does make
  A circle like a bear at stake,
  That at the chain's end wheels about
  And overturns the rabble rout."

I need not multiply examples of this sort. Wit or

ludicrous invention produces its effect oftenest by comparison, but not always. It frequently effects its purposes by unexpected and subtle distinctions. For instance, in the first kind, Mr. Sheridan's description of Mr. Addington's administration as the fag-end of Mr. Pitt's, who had remained so long on the treasury bench that, like Nicias in the fable, " he left the sitting part of the man behind him," is as fine an example of metaphorical wit as any on record. The same idea seems, however, to have been included in the old well-known nickname of the *Rump* Parliament. Almost as happy an instance of the other kind of wit, which consists in sudden retorts, in turns upon an idea, and diverting the train of your adversary's argument abruptly and adroitly into another channel, may be seen in the sarcastic reply of Porson, who hearing some one observe, that " certain modern poets would be read and admired when Homer and Virgil were forgotten," made answer—" And not till then! " Sir Robert Walpole's definition of the gratitude of place-expectants, that " it is a lively sense of *future* favours," is no doubt wit, but it does not consist in the finding out any coincidence or likeness, but in suddenly transposing the order of time in the common account of this feeling, so as to make the professions of those who pretend to it correspond more with their practice. It is filling up a blank in the human heart with a word that explains its hollowness at once. Voltaire's saying, in answer to a stranger who was observing how tall his trees grew—" That they had nothing else to do,"—was a quaint mixture of wit and humour, making it out as if they really led a lazy, laborious life; but there was here neither allusion nor metaphor. Again, that master-stroke in *Hudibras* is sterling wit and profound satire, where, speaking of certain religious hypocrites, he says, that they

> " Compound for sins they are inclin'd to
>   By damning those they have no mind to ; "

but the wit consists in the truth of the character, and in the happy exposure of the ludicrous contradiction between the pretext and the practice; between their lenity towards their own vices, and their severity to those of others. The same principle of nice distinction must be allowed to prevail in those lines of the same author, where he is professing to expound the dreams of judicial astrology.

> " There's but a twinkling of a star
> Betwixt a man of peace and war,
> A thief and justice, fool and knave,
> A huffing officer and a slave ;
> A crafty lawyer and pickpocket ;
> A great philosopher and a blockhead ;
> A formal preacher and a player ;
> A learned physician and man-slayer."

The finest piece of wit I know of, is in the lines of Pope on the Lord Mayor's show—

> " Now night descending, the proud scene is o'er ;
> But lives in Settle's numbers one day more."

This is certainly as mortifying an inversion of the idea of poetical immortality as could be thought of: it fixes the *maximum* of littleness and insignificance; but it is not by likeness to anything else that it does this, but by literally taking the lowest possible duration of ephemeral reputation, marking it (as with a slider) on the scale of endless renown, and giving a rival credit for it as his loftiest praise. In a word, the shrewd separation or disentangling of ideas that seem the same, or where the secret contradiction is not sufficiently suspected, and is of a ludicrous and whimsical nature, is wit just as much as the bringing together those that appear at first sight totally different. There is then no sufficient ground for admitting Mr. Locke's celebrated definition of wit, which he makes to consist in the finding out striking and unexpected resemblances in things so as to make pleasant pictures in the fancy, while judgment and reason, according to him, lie the clean contrary way, in separating and nicely distinguishing those wherein the smallest difference is to be found.[1]

[1] His words are—" If in having our ideas in the memory ready at hand consists quickness of parts, in this of having them unconfused, and being able nicely to distinguish one thing from another, where there is but the least difference, consists in a great measure the exactness of judgment and clearness of reason, which is to be observed in one man above another. And hence, perhaps, may be given some reason of that common observation, that men who have a great deal of wit and prompt memories, have not always the clearest judgment or deepest reason. For wit lying mostly in the assemblage of ideas, and putting them together with quickness and variety, wherein can be found any resemblance or congruity, thereby to make up pleasant pictures and agreeable visions in the fancy; judgment, on the contrary, lies quite on the other side, in separating carefully one from another, ideas wherein can be found the least difference, thereby to avoid being misled by similitude, and by affinity to take one thing for another." (Essay, vol. i. p. 143.) This definition, such as it is, Mr. Locke took without acknowledgment from Hobbes, who says in his Leviathan : " This difference of quickness in imagining is caused by the difference of men's passions, that love and dislike some one thing, some another, and therefore some men's thoughts run one way, some another, and are held to and observe differently the things that pass through their imagination. And whereas in this succession of thoughts there is nothing to observe in the things they think on, but either in what they be like one another, or in what they be unlike, those that observe their similitudes, in case they be such as are but rarely observed by others, are said to have a good wit, by which is meant on this occasion a good fancy. But they that observe their differences and dissimilitudes, which is called distinguishing and discerning, and judging between thing and thing; in case such discerning be not easy, are said to have a good judgment; and particularly in matter of conversation and business, wherein times, places, and persons are to be discerned, this virtue is called discretion. The former, that is, fancy, without the help of judgment, is not commended for a virtue ; but the latter, which is judgment or discretion, is commended for itself, without the help of fancy."—Leviathan, p. 32.

On this definition, Harris, the author of *Hermes*, has very well observed, that the demonstrating the equality of the three angles of a right-angled triangle to two right ones, would, upon the principle here stated, be a piece of wit instead of an act of the judgment or understanding, and Euclid's Elements a collection of epigrams. On the contrary, it has appeared that the detection and exposure of difference, particularly where this implies nice and subtle observation, as in discriminating between pretence and practice, between appearance and reality, is common to wit and satire with judgment and reasoning, and certainly the comparing and connecting our ideas together is an essential part of reason and judgment, as well as of wit and fancy. Mere wit, as opposed to reason or argument, consists in striking out some casual and partial coincidence which has nothing to do, or at least implies no necessary connection with the nature of the things, which are forced into a seeming analogy by a play upon words, or some irrelevant conceit, as in puns, riddles, alliteration, etc. The jest, in all such cases, lies in the sort of mock-identity, or nominal resemblance, established by the intervention of the same words expressing different ideas, and countenancing, as it were, by a fatality of language, the mischievous insinuation which the person who has the wit to take advantage of it wishes to convey. So when the disaffected French wits applied to the new order of the *Fleur du lys* the *double entendre* of *Compagnons d'Ulysse*, or companions of Ulysses, meaning the animal into which the fellow-travellers of the hero of the *Odyssey* were transformed, this was a shrewd and biting intimation of a galling truth (if truth it were) by a fortuitous concourse of letters of the alphabet, jumping in " a foregone conclusion," but there was no proof of the thing, unless it was self-evident. And, indeed, this may be considered as the best defence of the contested maxim, that *ridicule is the test of truth;* viz. that it does not contain or attempt a formal proof of it, but owes its power of conviction to the bare suggestion of it, so that if the thing when once hinted is not clear in itself, the satire fails of its effect and falls to the ground. The sarcasm here glanced at the character of the new or old French noblesse may not be well-founded; but it is so like truth, and " comes in such a questionable shape," backed with the appearance of an identical proposition, that it would require a long train of facts and laboured arguments to do away the impression, even if we were sure of the honesty and wisdom of the person who undertook to refute it. A flippant jest is as good a test of truth as a solid bribe; and there are serious sophistries,

    " Soul-killing lies, and truths that work small good,"

as well as idle pleasantries. Of this we may be sure, that ridicule fastens on the vulnerable points of a cause, and finds out the weak sides of an argument; if those who resort to it sometimes rely too much on its success, those who are chiefly annoyed by it almost always are so with reason, and cannot be too much on their guard against deserving it. Before we can laugh at a thing, its absurdity must at least be open and palpable to common apprehension. Ridicule is necessarily built on certain supposed facts, whether true or false, and on their incon- sistency with certain acknowledged maxims, whether right or wrong. It is, therefore, a fair test, if not of philosophical or abstract truth, at least of what is truth according to public opinion and common sense; for it can only expose to instantaneous contempt that which is condemned by public opinion, and is hostile to the common sense of mankind. Or, to put it differently, it is the test of the quantity of truth that there is in our favourite prejudices. To shew how nearly allied wit is thought to be to truth, it is not unusual to say of any person—" Such a one is a man of sense, for though he said nothing, he laughed in the right place "—Alliteration comes in here under the head of a certain sort of verbal wit; or, by pointing the expression, sometimes points the sense. Mr. Grattan's wit or eloquence (I don't know by what name to call it) would be nothing without this accompaniment. Speaking of some ministers whom he did not like, he said, " Their only means of government are the guinea and the gallows." There can scarcely, it must be confessed, be a more effectual mode of political conversion than one of these applied to a man's friends, and the other to himself. The fine sarcasm of Junius on the effect of the supposed ingratitude of the Duke of Grafton at court—" The instance might be painful, but the principle would please "—notwithstanding the profound insight into human nature it implies, would hardly pass for wit without the alliteration, as some poetry would hardly be acknowledged as such without the rhyme to clench it. A quotation or a hackneyed phrase, dexterously turned or wrested to another purpose, has often the effect of the liveliest wit. An idle fellow who had only fourpence left in the world, which had been put by to pay for the baking some meat for his dinner, went and laid it out to buy a new string for a guitar. An old acquaintance, on hearing this story, repeated those lines out of the *Allegro*—

> " And ever against *eating* cares
> Lap me in soft Lydian airs."

The reply of the author of the periodical paper called the *World* to a lady at church, who seeing him look thoughtful, asked what he was thinking of—" The next World,"—is a perversion of an established formula of language, something of the same kind.—Rhymes are sometimes a species of wit, where there is an alternate combination and resolution or decomposition of the

P *

elements of sound, contrary to our usual division and
classification of them in ordinary speech, not unlike the
sudden separation and re-union of the component parts
of the machinery in a pantomime. The author who excels
infinitely the most in this way is the writer of *Hudibras*. He
also excels in the invention of single words and names,
which have the effect of wit by sounding big, and meaning
nothing:—" full of sound and fury, signifying nothing."
But of the artifices of this author's burlesque style I shall
have occasion to speak hereafter.—It is not always
easy to distinguish between the wit of words and that
of things, " For thin partitions do their bounds divide."
Some of the late Mr. Curran's *bon mots*, or *jeux d'esprit*,
might be said to owe their birth to this sort of equivocal generation; or were a happy mixture of verbal
wit and a lively and picturesque fancy, of legal acuteness in detecting the variable applications of words,
and of a mind apt at perceiving the ludicrous in external
objects. " Do you see anything ridiculous in this wig? "
said one of his brother judges to him. " Nothing but the
head," was the answer. Now here instantaneous advantage
was taken of the slight technical ambiguity in the construction of language, and the matter-of-fact is flung into
the scale as a thumping makeweight. After all, verbal and
accidental strokes of wit, though the most surprising
and laughable, are not the best and most lasting. That wit
is the most refined and effectual, which is founded on the
detection of unexpected likeness or distinction in things,
rather than in words. It is more severe and galling, that is,
it is more unpardonable though less surprising, in proportion as the thought suggested is more complete and
satisfactory, from its being inherent in the nature of the
things themselves. *Hæret lateri lethalis arundo.* Truth
makes the greatest libel, and it is that which barbs the
darts of wit. The Duke of Buckingham's saying, " Laws
are not, like women, the worse for being old," is an

instance of a harmless truism and the utmost malice of wit united. This is, perhaps, what has been meant by the distinction between true and false wit. Mr. Addison, indeed, goes so far as to make it the exclusive test of true wit that it will bear translation into another language, that is to say, that it does not depend at all on the form of expression. But this is by no means the case. Swift would hardly have allowed of such a strait-laced theory, to make havoc with his darling conundrums; though there is no one whose serious wit is more that of things, as opposed to a mere play either of words or fancy. I ought, I believe, to have noticed before, in speaking of the difference between wit and humour, that wit is often pretended absurdity, where the person overacts or exaggerates a certain part with a conscious design to expose it as if it were another person, as when Mandrake in the *Twin Rivals* says, " This glass is too big, carry it away, I'll drink out of the bottle." On the contrary, when Sir Hugh Evans says very innocently, " 'Od's plessed will, I will not be absent at the grace," though there is here a great deal of humour, there is no wit. This kind of wit of the humorist, where the person makes a butt of himself, and exhibits his own absurdities or foibles purposely in the most pointed and glaring lights, runs through the whole of the character of Falstaff, and is, in truth, the principle on which it is founded. It is an irony directed against one's-self. Wit is, in fact, a voluntary act of the mind, or exercise of the invention, shewing the absurd and ludicrous consciously, whether in ourselves or another. Cross-readings, where the blunders are designed, are wit; but if any one were to light upon them through ignorance or accident, they would be merely ludicrous.

It might be made an argument of the intrinsic superiority of poetry or imagination to wit, that the former does not admit of mere verbal combinations. Whenever

they do occur, they are uniformly blemishes. It requires
something more solid and substantial to raise admiration
or passion. The general forms and aggregate masses of our
ideas must be brought more into play, to give weight and
magnitude. Imagination may be said to be the finding out
something similar in things generally alike, or with like
feelings attached to them; while wit principally aims at
finding out something that seems the same, or amounts to
a momentary deception where you least expected it, viz.
in things totally opposite. The reason why more slight
and partial, or merely accidental and nominal resemblances, serve the purposes of wit, and indeed characterise
its essence as a distinct operation and faculty of the mind,
is, that the object of ludicrous poetry is naturally to let
down and lessen; and it is easier to let down than to raise
up, to weaken than to strengthen, to disconnect our
sympathy from passion and power, than to attach and rivet
it to any object of grandeur or interest; to startle and shock
our preconceptions, by incongruous and equivocal combinations, than to confirm, enforce, and expand them by
powerful and lasting associations of ideas, or striking
and true analogies. A slight cause is sufficient to produce
a slight effect. To be indifferent or sceptical, requires no
effort; to be enthusiastic and in earnest, requires a strong
impulse, and ·collective power. Wit and humour (comparatively speaking, or taking the extremes to judge of the
gradations by) appeal to our indolence, our vanity, our
weakness, and insensibility; serious and impassioned
poetry appeals to our strength, our magnanimity, our
virtue, and humanity. Anything is sufficient to heap
contempt upon an object; even the bare suggestion of a
mischievous allusion to what is improper, dissolves the
whole charm, and puts an end to our admiration of the
sublime or beautiful. Reading the finest passage in Milton's
Paradise Lost in a false tone, will make it seem insipid and
absurd. The cavilling at, or invidiously pointing out,

a few slips of the pen, will embitter the pleasure, or
alter our opinion of a whole work, and make us throw
it down in disgust. The critics are aware of this vice
and infirmity in our nature, and play upon it with
periodical success. The meanest weapons are strong
enough for this kind of warfare, and the meanest hands
can wield them. Spleen can subsist on any kind of food.
The shadow of a doubt, the hint of an inconsistency, a
word, a look, a syllable, will destroy our best-formed
convictions. What puts this argument in as striking a
point of view as anything, is the nature of parody or
burlesque, the secret of which lies merely in transposing
or applying at a venture to anything, or to the lowest
objects, that which is applicable only to certain given
things, or to the highest matters. " From the sublime to
the ridiculous, there is but one step." The slightest want
of unity of impression destroys the sublime; the detection
of the smallest incongruity is an infallible ground to rest
the ludicrous upon. But in serious poetry, which aims at
riveting our affections, every blow must tell home. The
missing a single time is fatal, and undoes the spell.
We see how difficult it is to sustain a continued flight
of impressive sentiment: how easy it must be then to
travesty or burlesque it, to flounder into nonsense, and
be witty by playing the fool. It is a common mistake,
however, to suppose that parodies degrade, or imply a
stigma on the subject: on the contrary, they in general
imply something serious or sacred in the originals.
Without this, they would be good for nothing; for the
immediate contrast would be wanting, and with this they
are sure to tell. The best parodies are, accordingly, the
best and the most striking things reversed. Witness the
common travesties of Homer and Virgil. Mr. Canning's
court parodies on Mr. Southey's popular odes are also an
instance in point (I do not know which were the cleverest);
and the best of the *Rejected Addresses* is the parody on

Crabbe though I do not certainly think that Crabbe is the most ridiculous poet now living.

Lear and the Fool are the sublimest instance I know of passion and wit united, or of imagination unfolding the most tremendous sufferings, and of burlesque on passion playing with it, aiding and relieving its intensity by the most pointed, but familiar and indifferent illustrations of the same thing in different objects, and on a meaner scale. The Fool's reproaching Lear with " making his daughters his mothers," his snatches of proverbs and old ballads, " The hedge-sparrow fed the cuckoo so long, that it had its head bit off by its young," and " Whoop jug, I know when the horse follows the cart," are a running commentary of trite truisms, pointing out the extreme folly of the infatuated old monarch, and in a manner reconciling us to its inevitable consequences.

Lastly, there is a wit of sense and observation, which consists in the acute illustration of good sense and practical wisdom by means of some far-fetched conceit or quaint imagery. The matter is sense, but the form is wit. Thus the lines in Pope—

> " 'Tis with our judgments as our watches, none
>   Go just alike ; yet each believes his own "—

are witty rather than poetical; because the truth they convey is a mere dry observation on human life, without elevation or enthusiasm, and the illustration of it is of that quaint and familiar kind that is merely curious and fanciful. Cowley is an instance of the same kind in almost all his writings. Many of the jests and witticisms in the best comedies are moral aphorisms and rules for the conduct of life, sparkling with wit and fancy in the mode of expression. The ancient philosophers also abounded in the same kind of wit, in telling home truths in the most unexpected manner.—In this sense Æsop was the greatest wit and

moralist that ever lived. Ape and slave, he looked
askance at human nature, and beheld its weaknesses
and errors transferred to another species. Vice and
virtue were to him as plain as any objects of sense.
He saw in man a talking, absurd, obstinate, proud,
angry animal; and clothed these abstractions with wings,
or a beak, or tail, or claws, or long ears, as they appeared
embodied in these hieroglyphics in the brute creation. His
moral philosophy is natural history. He makes an ass bray
wisdom, and a frog croak humanity. The store of moral
truth, and the fund of invention in exhibiting it in eternal
forms, palpable and intelligible, and delightful to children
and grown persons, and to all ages and nations, are
almost miraculous. The invention of a fable is to me
the most enviable exertion of human genius: it is the
discovering a truth to which there is no clue, and which,
when once found out, can never be forgotten. I would
rather have been the author of *Æsop's Fables* than of
Euclid's Elements! That popular entertainment, Punch
and the Puppet-show, owes part of its irresistible and
universal attraction to nearly the same principle of inspiring inanimate and mechanical agents with sense and
consciousness. The drollery and wit of a piece of wood is
doubly droll and farcical. Punch is not merry in himself,
but " he is the cause of heartfelt mirth in other men."
The wires and pulleys that govern his motions are conductors to carry off the spleen, and all " that perilous stuff
that weighs upon the heart." If we see a number of people
turning the corner of a street, ready to burst with secret
satisfaction, and with their faces bathed in laughter, we
know what is the matter—that they are just come from a
puppet-show. Who can see three little painted, patched-
up figures, no bigger than one's thumb, strut, squeak, and
gibber, sing, dance, chatter, scold, knock one another
about the head, give themselves airs of importance, and
" imitate humanity most abominably," without laughing

immoderately? We overlook the farce and mummery of
human life in little, and for nothing; and what is still
better, it costs them who have to play in it nothing. We
place the mirth, and glee, and triumph, to our own account;
and we know that the bangs and blows they have received
go for nothing, as soon as the showman puts them up in
his box and marches off quietly with them, as jugglers of a
less amusing description sometimes march off with the
wrongs and rights of mankind in their pockets! I have
heard no bad judge of such matters say, that " he liked a
comedy better than a tragedy, a farce better than a comedy,
a pantomime better than a farce, but a puppet-show best
of all." I look upon it, that he who invented puppet-
shows was a greater benefactor to his species, than he who
invented Operas!

I shall conclude this imperfect and desultory sketch
of wit and humour with Barrow's celebrated description
of the same subject. He says, " —But first it may be
demanded, what the thing we speak of is, or what this
facetiousness doth import; to which question I might
reply, as Democritus did to him that asked the definition
of a man—*'tis that which we all see and know;* and one
better apprehends what it is by acquaintance than I
can inform him by description. It is, indeed, a thing
so versatile and multiform, appearing in so many
shapes, so many postures, so many garbs, so variously
apprehended by several eyes and judgments, that it
seemeth no less hard to settle a clear and certain notice
thereof, than to make a portrait of Proteus, or to define
the figure of fleeting air. Sometimes it lieth in pat
allusion to a known story, or in seasonable application
of a trivial saying, or in forging an apposite tale; sometimes it playeth in words and phrases, taking advantage
from the ambiguity of their sense, or the affinity of their
sound; sometimes it is wrapped in a dress of luminous
expression; sometimes it lurketh under an odd similitude.

Sometimes it is lodged in a sly question, in a smart answer; in a quirkish reason; in a shrewd intimation; in cunningly diverting or cleverly restoring an objection: sometimes it is couched in a bold scheme of speech; in a tart irony; in a lusty hyperbole; in a startling metaphor; in a plausible reconciling of contradictions, or in acute nonsense: sometimes a scenical representation of persons or things, a counterfeit speech, a mimical look or gesture passeth for it; sometimes an affected simplicity, sometimes a presumptuous bluntness giveth it being; sometimes it riseth only from a lucky hitting upon what is strange; sometimes from a crafty wresting obvious matter to the purpose; often it consisteth in one knows not what, and springeth up one can hardly tell how. Its ways are unaccountable and inexplicable, being answerable to the numberless rovings of fancy and windings of language. It is, in short, a manner of speaking out of the simple and plain way (such as reason teacheth and knoweth things by), which by a pretty surprising un-couthness in conceit or expression doth affect and amuse the fancy, shewing in it some wonder, and breathing some delight thereto. It raiseth admiration, as signify-ing a nimble sagacity of apprehension, a special felicity of invention, a vivacity of spirit, and reach of wit more than vulgar: it seeming to argue a rare quickness of parts, that one can fetch in remote conceits applicable; a notable skill that he can dexterously accommodate them to a purpose before him, together with a lively brisk-ness of humour, not apt to damp those sportful flashes of imagination. (Whence in Aristotle such persons are termed ἐπιδέξιοι, dexterous men, and εὔτροποι, men of facile or versatile manners, who can easily turn them-selves to all things, or turn all things to themselves.) It also procureth delight by gratifying curiosity with its rareness or semblance of difficulty (as monsters, not for their beauty but their rarity; as juggling tricks, not for their use but their abstruseness, are beheld with pleasure); by diverting the mind from its road of serious thoughts; by instilling gaiety and airiness of spirit; by provoking to such dispositions of spirit, in way of emulation or complaisance, and by seasoning matter, otherwise distasteful or insipid, with an unusual and thence grateful tang."—*Barrow's Works, Serm.* 14.

I will only add, by way of general caution, that there is nothing more ridiculous than laughter without a cause, nor anything more troublesome than what are called laughing people. A professed laugher is as contemptible and tiresome a character as a professed wit: the one is always contriving something to laugh at, the other is always laughing at nothing. An excess of levity is as impertinent as an excess of gravity. A character of this sort is well personified by Spenser, in the *Damsel of the Idle Lake*—

> ——" Who did assay
> To laugh at shaking of the leaves light."

Any one must be mainly ignorant or thoughtless, who is surprised at everything he sees; or wonderfully conceited, who expects everything to conform to his standard of propriety. Clowns and idiots laugh on all occasions; and the common failing of wishing to be thought satirical often runs through whole families in country places, to the great annoyance of their neighbours. To be struck with incongruity in whatever comes before us, does not argue great comprehension or refinement of perception, but rather a looseness and flippancy of mind and temper, which prevents the individual from connecting any two ideas steadily or consistently together. It is owing to a natural crudity and precipitateness of the imagination, which assimilates nothing properly to itself. People who are always laughing, at length laugh on the wrong side of their faces; for they cannot get others to laugh with them.

In like manner, an affectation of wit by degrees hardens the heart, and spoils good company and good manners. A perpetual succession of good things puts an end to common conversation. There is no answer to a jest, but another; and even where the ball can be kept up in this way without ceasing, it tires the patience of the by-standers, and runs the speakers out of breath. Wit is the salt of conversation, not the food.

The four chief names for comic humour out of our own language are Aristophanes and Lucian among the ancients, Molière and Rabelais among the moderns. Of the two first I shall say, for I know but little. I should have liked Aristophanes better if he had treated Socrates less scurvily, for he has treated him most scurvily both as to wit and argument. His *Plutus* and his *Birds* are striking instances, the one of dry humour, the other of airy fancy.—Lucian is a writer who appears to deserve his full fame: he has the licentious and extravagant wit of Rabelais, but directed more uniformly to a purpose; and his comic productions are interspersed with beautiful and eloquent descriptions, full of sentiment, such as the exquisite account of the fable of the halcyon put into the mouth of Socrates, and the heroic eulogy on Bacchus, which is conceived in the highest strain of glowing panegyric.

The two other authors I proposed to mention are modern, and French. Molière, however, in the spirit of his writings, is almost as much an English as a French author—quite a *barbare* in all in which he really excelled. He was unquestionably one of the greatest comic geniuses that ever lived; a man of infinite wit, gaiety, and invention —full of life, laughter, and whim. But it cannot be denied that his plays are in general mere farces, without scrupulous adherence to nature, refinement of character, or common probability. The plots of several of them could not be carried on for a moment without a perfect collusion

between the parties to wink at contradictions, and act
in defiance of the evidence of their senses. For instance,
take the *Médecin malgré lui* (*The Mock Doctor*), in which a
common wood-cutter takes upon himself, and is made
successfully to support through a whole play, the character of a learned physician, without exciting the least
suspicion; and yet, notwithstanding the absurdity of the
plot, it is one of the most laughable and truly comic productions that can well be imagined. The rest of his lighter
pieces, the *Bourgeois Gentilhomme*, *Monsieur Pourceaugnac*,
George Dandin (or *Barnaby Brittle*), etc., are of the
same description—gratuitous assumptions of character,
and fanciful and outrageous caricatures of nature. He
indulges at his peril in the utmost licence of burlesque
exaggeration; and gives a loose rein to the intoxication of
his animal spirits. With respect to his two most laboured
comedies, the *Tartuffe* and *Misanthrope*, I confess that I
find them rather hard to get through: they have much of
the improbability and extravagance of the others, united
with the endless common-place prosing of French declamation. What can exceed, for example, the absurdity of the
Misanthrope, who leaves his mistress, after every proof
of her attachment and constancy, for no other reason than
that she will not submit to the *technical formality* of going
to live with him in a wilderness? The characters, again,
which Celimene gives of her female friends, near the
opening of the play, are admirable satires (as good as
Pope's characters of women), but not exactly in the
spirit of comic dialogue. The strictures of Rousseau
on this play, in his *Letter to D'Alembert*, are a fine
specimen of the best philosophical criticism.—The same
remarks apply in a greater degree to the *Tartuffe*. The long
speeches and reasonings in this play tire one almost to
death: they may be very good logic, or rhetoric, or
philosophy, or anything but comedy. If each of the
parties had retained a special pleader to speak his senti-

ments, they could not have appeared more verbose or intricate. The improbability of the character of Orgon is wonderful. This play is in one point of view invaluable, as a lasting monument of the credulity of the French to all verbal professions of wisdom or virtue; and its existence can only be accounted for from that astonishing and tyrannical predominance which words exercise over things in the mind of every Frenchman. The *École des Femmes,* from which Wycherley has borrowed his *Country Wife,* with the true spirit of original genius, is, in my judgment, the masterpiece of Molière. The set speeches in the original play, it is true, would not be borne on the English stage, nor indeed on the French, but that they are carried off by the verse. The *Critique de l'École des Femmes,* the dialogue of which is prose, is written in a very different style. Among other things, this little piece contains an exquisite, and almost unanswerable defence of the superiority of comedy over tragedy. Molière was to be excused for taking this side of the question.

A writer of some pretensions among ourselves has reproached the French with " an equal want of books and men." There is a common French print, in which Molière is represented reading one of his plays in the presence of the celebrated Ninon de l'Enclos, to a circle of the wits and first men of his own time. Among these are the great Corneille; the tender, faultless Racine; Fontaine, the artless old man, unconscious of immortality; the accomplished St. Evremond; the Duke de la Rochefoucault, the severe anatomiser of the human breast; Boileau, the flatterer of courts and judge of men! Were these men nothing? They have passed for men (and great ones) hitherto, and though the prejudice is an old one, I should hope it may still last our time.

Rabelais is another name that might have saved this unjust censure. The wise sayings and heroic deeds of

Gargantua and Pantagruel ought not to be set down as nothing. I have already spoken my mind at large of this author; but I cannot help thinking of him here, sitting in his easy-chair, with an eye languid with excess of mirth, his lip quivering with a new-born conceit, and wiping his beard after a well-seasoned jest, with his pen held carelessly in his hand, his wine-flagons, and his books of law, of school divinity, and physic before him, which were his jest-books, whence he drew endless stores of absurdity; laughing at the world and enjoying it by turns, and making the world laugh with him again, for the last three hundred years, at his teeming wit and its own prolific follies. Even to those who have never read his works, the name of Rabelais is a cordial to the spirits, and the mention of it cannot consist with gravity or spleen!

ON THE CONVERSATION
OF AUTHORS

(LONDON MAGAZINE, SEPT., 1820)

A N author is bound to write—well or ill, wisely or foolishly: it is his trade. But I do not see that he is bound to talk, any more than he is bound to dance, or ride, or fence better than other people. Reading, study, silence, thought, are a bad introduction to loquacity. It would be sooner learnt of chambermaids and tapsters. He understands the art and mystery of his own profession, which is book-making: what right has anyone to expect or require him to do more—to make a bow gracefully on entering or leaving a room, to make love charmingly, or to make a fortune at all? In all things there is a division of labour. A lord is no less amorous for writing ridiculous love-letters, nor a General less successful for wanting wit and honesty. Why, then, may not a poor author say nothing, and yet pass muster? Set him on the top of a stage-coach, he will make no figure; he is *mumchance*, while the slang-wit flies about as fast as the dust, with the crack of the whip and the clatter of the horses' heels: put him in a ring of boxers, he is a poor creature—

"And of his port as meek as is a maid."

Introduce him to a tea-party of milliners' girls, and they are ready to split their sides with laughing at him: over his bottle, he is dry: in the drawing-room, rude or awkward: he is too refined for the vulgar, too clownish for the fashionable:—" he is one that cannot make a good leg, one that cannot eat a mess of broth cleanly, one that cannot ride a horse without spur-galling, one that cannot salute a woman, and look on her directly:"—in courts, in camps, in town and country, he is a cypher or a butt: he is good for nothing but a laughing-stock or a scare-crow. You can scarcely get a word out of him for love or money. He knows nothing. He has no notion of pleasure or business, or of what is going on in the world; he does not understand cookery (unless he is a doctor in divinity), nor surgery, nor chemistry (unless he is a *Quidnunc*), nor mechanics, nor husbandry and tillage (unless he is as great an admirer of Tull's *Husbandry*, and has profited as much by it as the philosopher of Botley)—no, nor music, painting, the Drama, nor the Fine Arts in general.

"What the deuce is it then, my good sir, that he does understand, or know anything about?"

"BOOKS, VENUS, BOOKS!"

"What books?"

"Not receipt-books, Madona, nor account-books, nor books of pharmacy, or the veterinary art (they belong to their respective callings and handicrafts), but books of liberal taste and general knowledge."

" What do you mean by that general knowledge which implies not a knowledge of things in general, but an ignorance (by your own account) of every one in particular: or by that liberal taste which scorns the pursuits and acquirements of the rest of the world in succession, and is confined exclusively, and by way of excellence, to what nobody takes an interest in but yourself, and a few idlers like yourself? Is this what the critics mean by the *belles-lettres*, and the study of humanity?"

Book-knowledge, in a word, then, is knowledge *communicable by books:* and it is general and liberal for this reason, that it is intelligible and interesting on the bare suggestion. That to which anyone feels a romantic attachment, merely from finding it in a book, must be interesting in itself: that which he constantly forms a lively and entire conception of, from seeing a few marks and scratches upon paper, must be taken from common nature: that which, the first time you meet with it, seizes upon the attention as a curious speculation, must exercise the general faculties of the human mind. There are certain broader aspects of society and views of things common to every subject, and more or less cognizable to every mind; and these the scholar treats, and founds his claims to general attention upon them, without being chargeable with pedantry. The minute descriptions of fishing-tackle, of baits and flies in Walton's *Complete Angler*, make that work a great favourite with sportsmen: the alloy of an amiable humanity, and the modest but touching descriptions of familiar incidents and rural objects scattered through it, have made it an equal favourite with every reader of taste and feeling. Montaigne's *Essays*, Dilworth's *Spelling Book*, and Fearn's *Treatise on Contingent Remainders*, are all equally books, but not equally adapted for all classes of readers. The two last are of no use but to school-masters and lawyers: but the first is a work we may recommend to anyone to read who has ever thought

at all, or who would learn to think justly on any subject.
Persons of different trades and professions—the mechanic,
the shop-keeper, the medical practitioner, the artist, etc.,
may all have great knowledge and ingenuity in their
several vocations, the details of which will be very edifying to themselves, and just as incomprehensible to their
neighbours: but over and above this professional and
technical knowledge, they must be supposed to have a
stock of common sense and common feeling to furnish
subjects for common conversation, or to give them any
pleasure in each other's company. It is to this common
stock of ideas, spread over the surface, or striking its roots
into the very centre of society, that the popular writer
appeals, and not in vain; for he finds readers. It is of
this finer essence of wisdom and humanity " etherial
mould, sky-tinctured," that books of the better sort are
made. They contain the language of thought. It must
happen that, in the course of time and the variety of
human capacity, some persons will have struck out finer
observations, reflections, and sentiments than others.
These they have committed to books of memory, have
bequeathed as a lasting legacy to posterity; and such
persons have become standard authors. We visit at the
shrine, drink in some measure of the inspiration, and
cannot easily " breathe in other air less pure, accustomed
to immortal fruits." Are we to be blamed for this because
the vulgar and illiterate do not always understand
us? The fault is rather in them who are " confined and
cabin'd in " each in their own particular sphere and com-
partment of ideas, and have not the same refined medium
of communication or abstracted topics of discourse.
Bring a number of literary, or of illiterate persons together, perfect strangers to each other, and see which
party will make the best company. " Verily, we have our
reward." We have made our election, and have no reason
to repent it, if we were wise. But the misfortune is, we

wish to have all the advantages on one side. We grudge, and cannot reconcile it to ourselves, that anyone " should go about to cozen fortune, without the stamp of learning!" We think " because we are *scholars*, there shall be no more cakes and ale!" We don't know how to account for it, that bar-maids should gossip, or ladies whisper, or bullies roar, or fools laugh, or knaves thrive, without having gone through the same course of select study that we have! This vanity is preposterous, and carries its own punishment with it. Books are a world in themselves, it is true; but they are not the only world. The world it-self is a volume larger than all the libraries in it. Learn-ing is a sacred deposit from the experience of ages; but it has not put all future experience on the shelf, or debarred the common herd of mankind from the use of their hands, tongues, eyes, ears, or understandings. Taste is a luxury for the privileged few: but it would be hard upon those who have not the same standard of refinement in their own minds that we suppose ourselves to have, if this should prevent them from having recourse, as usual, to their old frolics, coarse jokes, and horse-play, and getting through the wear and tear of the world, with such homely sayings and shrewd helps as they may. Happy is it, that the mass of mankind eat and drink, and sleep, and perform their several tasks, and do as they like with-out us—caring nothing for our scribblings, our carpings, and our quibbles; and moving on the same, in spite of our fine-spun distinctions, fantastic theories, and lines of demarcation, which are like chalk-figures drawn on ball-room floors to be danced out before morning! In the field opposite the window where I write this, there is a country-girl picking stones: in the one next it, there are several poor women weeding the blue and red flowers from the corn: farther on, are two boys, tending a flock of sheep. What do they know or care about what I am writing about them, or ever will?—or what would they be the better for it, if they did? Or why need we despise

> " The wretched slave,
> Who like a lackey, from the rise to the set,
> Sweats in the eye of Phœbus, and all night
> Sleeps in Elysium ; next day, after dawn,
> Doth rise, and help Hyperion to his horse ;
> And follows so the ever-running year
> With profitable labour to his grave ? "

Is not this life as sweet as writing Ephemerides? But we put that which flutters the brain idly for a moment and then is heard no more, in competition with nature, which exists everywhere, and lasts always. We not only under-rate the force of nature, and make too much of art —but we also over-rate our own accomplishments and advantages derived from art. In the presence of clownish ignorance, or of persons without any great pretensions, real or affected, we are very much inclined to take upon ourselves, as the virtual representatives of science, art, and literature. We have a strong itch to show off and do the honours of civilization for all the great men whose works we have ever read, and whose names our auditors have never heard of, as noblemen's lacqueys, in the absence of their masters, give themselves airs of superiority over everyone else. But though we have read Congreve, a stage-coachman may be an over-match for us in wit: though we are deep-versed in the excellence of Shakspeare's colloquial style, a village beldam may outscold us: though we have read Machiavel in the original Italian, we may be easily outwitted by a clown: and though we have cried our eyes out over the *New Eloise*, a poor shepherd-lad, who hardly knows how to spell his own name, may " tell his tale, under the hawthorn in the dale," and prove a more thriving wooer. What then is the advantage we possess over the meanest of the mean? Why this, that we have read Congreve,

Shakspeare, Machiavel, the *New Eloise* ;—not that we are to
have their wit, genius, shrewdness, or melting tenderness.

From speculative pursuits we must be satisfied with
speculative benefits. From reading too, we learn to write.
If we have had the pleasure of studying the highest
models of perfection in their kind, and can hope to leave
anything ourselves, however slight, to be looked upon
as a model, or even a good copy in its way, we may
think ourselves pretty well off, without engrossing all the
privileges of learning, and all the blessings of ignorance
into the bargain.

It has been made a question whether there have not
been individuals in common life of greater talents and
powers of mind than the most celebrated writers—
whether, for instance, such or such a Liverpool merchant,
or Manchester manufacturer, was not a more sensible
man than Montaigne, of a longer reach of understanding
than the Viscount of St. Albans. There is no saying,
unless some of these illustrious obscure had communicated
their important discoveries to the world. But then they
would have been authors! On the other hand, there is a
set of critics who fall into the contrary error; and suppose
that unless the proof of capacity is laid before all the
world, the capacity itself cannot exist; looking upon
all those who have not commenced authors, as literally
" stocks and stones, and worse then senseless things." I
remember trying to convince a person of this class, that a
young lady, whom he knew nothing of, the niece of a
celebrated authoress, had just the same sort of fine *tact*
and ironical turn in conversation, that her relative had
shewn in her writings when young. The only answer I
could get was an incredulous smile, and the observation
that when she wrote anything as good as [*Evelina*], or
[*Cecilia*], he might think her as clever. I said all I meant
was, that she had the same family talents, and asked
whether he thought that if Miss [Burney] had not been very

clever, as a mere girl, before she wrote her novels, she would ever have written them? It was all in vain. He still stuck to his text, and was convinced that the niece was a little fool compared to her aunt at the same age; and if he had known the aunt formerly, he would have had just the same opinion of *her*. My friend was one of those who have a settled persuasion that it is the book that makes the author, and not the author the book. That's a strange opinion for a great philosopher to hold. But he wilfully shuts his eyes to the germs and indistinct workings of genius, and treats them with supercilious indifference, till they stare him in the face through the press; and then takes cognizance only of the overt acts and published evidence. This is neither a proof of wisdom, nor the way to be wise. It is partly pedantry and prejudice, and partly feebleness of judgment, and want of magnanimity. He dare as little commit himself on the character of books, as of individuals, till they are stamped by the public. If you shew him any work for his approbation, he asks, " Whose is the superscription? " —He judges of genius by its shadow, reputation—of the metal by the coin. He is just the reverse of another person whom I know—for, as G[odwin] never allows a particle of merit to anyone till it is acknowledged by the whole world, C[oleridge] withholds his tribute of applause from every person in whom any mortal but himself can descry the least glimpse of understanding. He would be thought to look farther into a millstone than anybody else. He would have others see with his eyes and take their opinions from him on trust, in spite of their senses. The more obscure and defective the indications of merit, the greater his sagacity and candour in being the first to point them out. He looks upon what he nicknames *a man of genius*, but as the breath of his nostrils, and the clay in the potter's hands. If any such inert, unconscious mass, under the fostering care of the modern Prometheus,

is kindled into life,—begins to see, speak, and move, so
as to attract the notice of other people,—our jealous
patroniser of latent worth in that case throws aside, scorns,
and hates his own handy-work; and deserts his intellectual
offspring from the moment they can go alone and shift
for themselves.—But to pass on to our more immediate
subject.

. The conversation of authors is not so good as might be
imagined: but, such as it is (and with rare exceptions) it
is better than any other. The proof of which is, that,
when you are used to it, you cannot put up with any
other. That of mixed company becomes utterly intolerable—you cannot sit out a common tea and card party, at
least, if they pretend to talk at all. You are obliged in
despair to cut all your old acquaintances who are not
au fait on the prevailing and most smartly contested
topics, who are not imbued with the high gusto of
criticism and *virtù*. You cannot bear to hear a friend
whom you have not seen for many years, tell at how
much a yard he sells his laces and tapes, when he means
to move into his next house, when he heard last from
his relations in the country, whether trade is alive or
dead, or whether Mr. Such-a-one gets to look old. This
sort of neighbourly gossip will not go down after the high-
raised tone of literary conversation. The last may be
absurd, very unsatisfactory, and full of turbulence
and heart-burnings; but it has a zest in it which more
ordinary topics of news or family-affairs do not supply.
Neither will the conversation of what we understand
by *gentlemen* and men of fashion, do after that of men of
letters. It is flat, insipid, stale, and unprofitable, in the
comparison. They talk about much the same things—
pictures, poetry, politics, plays; but they do it worse, and
at a sort of vapid secondhand. They, in fact, talk out of
newspapers and magazines, what *we write there*. They do
not feel the same interest in the subjects they affect to

handle with an air of fashionable condescension, nor have they the same knowledge of them, if they were ever so much in earnest in displaying it. If it were not for the wine and the dessert, no author in his senses would accept an invitation to a well-dressed dinner-party, except out of pure good-nature and unwillingness to disoblige by his refusal. Persons in high life talk almost entirely by rote. There are certain established modes of address, and certain answers to them expected as a matter of course, as a point of etiquette. The studied forms of politeness do not give the greatest possible scope to an exuberance of wit and fancy. The fear of giving offence destroys sincerity, and without sincerity there can be no true enjoyment of society, nor unfettered exertion of intellectual activity.— Those who have been accustomed to live with the great are hardly considered as conversible persons in literary society. They are not to be talked with, any more than puppets or echoes. They have no opinions but what will please; and you naturally turn away, as a waste of time and words, from attending to a person who just before assented to what you said, and whom you find the moment after, from something that unexpectedly or perhaps by design drops from him, to be of a totally different way of thinking. This *bush-fighting* is not regarded as fair play among scientific men. As fashionable conversation is a sacrifice to politeness, so the conversation of low life is nothing but rudeness. They contradict you without giving a reason, or if they do, it is a very bad one—swear, talk loud, repeat the same thing fifty times over, get to calling names, and from words proceed to blows. You cannot make companions of servants, or persons in an inferior station in life. You may talk to them on matters of business, and what they have to do for you (as lords talk to bruisers on subjects of *fancy*, or country squires to their grooms on horse-racing), but out of that narrow sphere, to any general topic, you cannot lead them; the conversation soon flags, and you go back to the old question, or are obliged to break up the sitting for want of ideas in common.

The conversation of authors is better than that of most professions. It is better than that of lawyers, who talk nothing but *double entendre*—than that of physicians, who talk of the approaching deaths of the College, or the marriage of some new practitioner with some rich widow —than that of divines, who talk of the last place they dined at—than that of University-men, who make stale puns, repeat the refuse of London newspapers, and affect an ignorance of Greek and mathematics; it is better than that of players, who talk of nothing but the Green-room, and rehearse the scholar, the wit, or the fine gentleman, like a part on the stage—or than that of ladies, who, whatever you talk of, think of nothing, and expect you to think of nothing, but themselves. It is not easy to keep up a conversation with women in company. It is thought a piece of rudeness to differ from them: it is not quite fair to ask them a reason for what they say. You are afraid of pressing too hard upon them: but where you cannot differ openly and unreservedly, you cannot heartily agree. It is not so in France. There the women talk of things in general, and reason better than the men in this country. They are mistresses of the intellectual foils. They are adepts in all the topics. They know what is to be said for and against all sorts of questions, and are lively and full of mischief into the bargain. They are very subtle. They put you to your trumps immediately. Your logic is more in requisition even than your gallantry. You must argue as well as bow yourself into the good graces of these modern Amazons. What a situation for an Englishman to be placed in![1]

The fault of literary conversation in general is its too

---

[1] The topics of metaphysical argument having got into female society in France, is a proof how much they must have been discussed there generally, and how unfounded the charge

great tenaciousness. It fastens upon a subject, and will not let it go. It resembles a battle rather than a skirmish, and makes a toil of a pleasure. Perhaps it does this from necessity, from a consciousness of wanting the more familiar graces, the power to sport and trifle, to touch lightly and adorn agreeably, every view or turn of a question *en passant*, as it arises. Those who have a reputation to lose are too ambitious of shining, to please. " To excel in conversation," said an ingenious man, " one must not be always striving to say good things: to say one good thing, one must say many bad, and more indifferent ones." This desire to shine without the means at hand, often makes men silent:—

> " The fear of being silent strikes us dumb."

A writer who has been accustomed to take a connected view of a difficult question and to work it out gradually in all its bearings, may be very deficient in that quickness and ease which men of the world, who are in the habit of hearing a variety of opinions, who pick up an observation on one subject, and another on another, and who care about none any farther than the passing away of an idle hour, usually acquire. An author has studied a particular point—he has read, he has inquired, he has thought a great deal upon it: he is not contented to take it up casually in common with others, to throw out a hint, to propose an objection: he will either remain silent, uneasy, and dissatisfied, or he will begin at the beginning, and go through with it to the end. He is for taking the whole responsibility upon himself. He would be thought to understand the subject better than others, or indeed would shew that nobody else knows anything about it. There are always three or four points on which the literary novice

is which we bring against them of excessive thoughtlessness and frivolity. The French (taken all together) are a more sensible, reflecting, and better informed people than the English. [1826.]

Q

at his first outset in life fancies he can enlighten every
company, and bear down all opposition: but he is cured
of this Quixotic and pugnacious spirit, as he goes more
into the world, where he finds that there are other
opinions and other pretensions to be adjusted besides his
own. When this asperity wears off, and a certain scholastic
precocity is mellowed down, the conversation of men of
letters becomes both interesting and instructive. Men of
the world have no fixed principles, no ground-work of
thought: mere scholars have too much an object, a theory
always in view, to which they wrest everything, and not
unfrequently, common sense itself. By mixing with
society, they rub off their hardness of manner, and
impracticable, offensive singularity, while they retain a
greater depth and coherence of understanding. There is
more to be learnt from them than from their books. This
was a remark of Rousseau's, and it is a very true one. In
the confidence and unreserve of private intercourse, they
are more at liberty to say what they think, to put the
subject in different and opposite points of view, to illustrate it more briefly and pithily by familiar expressions,
by an appeal to individual character and personal knowledge—to bring in the limitation, to obviate misconcep-
tion, to state difficulties on their own side of the
argument, and answer them as well as they can. This
would hardly agree with the prudery, and somewhat
ostentatious claims of authorship. Dr. Johnson's conversation in Boswell's *Life* is much better than his published works: and the fragments of the opinions of
celebrated men, preserved in their letters or in anecdotes
of them, are justly sought after as invaluable for the same
reason. For instance, what a fund of sense there is in
Grimm's *Memoirs!* We thus get at the essence of what
is contained in their more laboured productions, without
the affectation or formality. Argument, again, is the death
of conversation, if carried on in a spirit of hostility: but

discussion is a pleasant and profitable thing, where you advance and defend your opinions as far as you can, and admit the truth of what is objected against them with equal impartiality: in short, where you do not pretend to set up for an oracle, but freely declare what you really know about any question, or suggest what has struck you as throwing a new light upon it, and let it pass for what it is worth. This tone of conversation was well described by Dr. Johnson, when he said of some party at which he had been present the night before—" We had good talk, sir!" As a general rule, there is no conversation worth anything but between friends, or those who agree in the same leading views of a subject. Nothing was ever learnt by either side in a dispute. You contradict one another, will not allow a grain of sense in what your adversary advances, are blind to whatever makes against yourself, dare not look the question fairly in the face, so that you cannot avail yourself even of your real advantages, insist most on what you feel to be the weakest points of your argument, and get more and more absurd, dogmatical, and violent every moment. Disputes for victory generally end to the dissatisfaction of all parties; and the one recorded in *Gil Blas* breaks up just as it ought. I once knew a very ingenious man, than whom, to take him in the way of common chit-chat or fireside gossip, no one could be more entertaining or rational. He would make an apt classical quotation, propose an explanation of a curious passage in Shakspeare's *Venus and Adonis*, detect a metaphysical error in Locke, would infer the volatility of the French character from the chapter in Sterne where the Count mistakes the feigned name of Yorick for a proof of his being the identical imaginary character in Hamlet (*Et vous êtes Yorick!*)— thus confounding words with things twice over—but let a difference of opinion be once hitched in, and it was all over with him. His only object from that time was to shut out common sense, and to be proof against conviction. He would argue the most ridiculous point (such as that there were two original languages) for hours together, nay, through the horologe. You would not suppose it was the same person. He was like an obstinate run-away horse, that takes the bit in his mouth, and becomes mischievous and unmanageable. He had made up his mind to one thing—not to admit a single particle of what any one else said for or against him. It was all the difference between a man drunk and sober, sane or mad. It is the same when he once gets the pen in his hand. He has been trying to prove a contradiction in terms for the last ten years of his life, viz., that the Bourbons have the same right to the throne of France that the Brunswick family have to the throne of England. Many people think there is a want of honesty or a want of understanding in this. There is neither. But he will persist in an argument to the last pinch; he will yield, in absurdity, to no man!

This litigious humour is bad enough: but there is one character still worse—that of a person who goes into company, not to contradict, but to *talk at* you. This is the greatest nuisance in civilised society. Such a person does not come armed to defend himself at all points, but to unsettle, if he can, and throw a slur on all your favourite opinions. If he has a notion that any one in the room is fond of poetry, he immediately volunteers a contemptuous tirade against the idle jingle of verse. If he suspects you have a delight in pictures, he endeavours, not by fair argument, but by a side-wind, to put you out of conceit with so frivolous an art. If you have a taste for music, he does not think much good is to be done by this tickling of the ears. If you speak in praise of a comedy, he does not see the use of wit: if you say you have been to a tragedy, he shakes his head at this mockery of human misery, and thinks it ought to be prohibited. He tries to find out beforehand whatever it is that you take a particular pride or pleasure in, that he may annoy your self-love in the tenderest point (as if he were probing a wound) and make you dissatisfied with yourself and your pursuits for several days afterwards. A person might as well make a practice of throwing out scandalous aspersions against your dearest friends or nearest relations, by way of ingratiating himself into your favour. Such ill-timed impertinence is " villainous, and shews a pitiful ambition in the fool that uses it."

The soul of conversation is sympathy.—Authors should converse chiefly with authors, and their talk should be of books. " When Greek meets Greek, then comes the tug of war." There is nothing so pedantic as pretending not to be pedantic. No man can get above his pursuit in life: it is getting above himself, which is impossible. There is a Free-masonry in all things. You can only speak to be understood, but this you cannot be, except by those who are in the secret. Hence an argument has been drawn to supersede the necessity of conversation altogether; for it has been said, that there is no use in talking to people of sense, who know all that you can tell them, nor to fools, who will not be instructed. There is, however, the smallest encouragement to proceed, when you are conscious that the more you really enter into a subject, the farther you will be from the comprehension of your hearers—and that the more proofs you give of any position, the more odd and out-of-the-way they will think your notions. C[oleridge] is the only person who can talk to all sorts of people, on all sorts of subjects, without caring a farthing for their understanding one word he says—and *he* talks only for admiration and to be listened to, and accordingly the least interruption puts him out. I firmly believe he would make just the same impression on half his audiences, if he purposely repeated absolute nonsense with the same voice and manner and inexhaustible flow of undulating speech! In general,

wit shines only by reflection. You must take your cue
from your company—must rise as they rise, and sink as
they fall. You must see that your good things, your
knowing allusions, are not flung away, like the pearls in
the adage. What a check it is to be asked a foolish
question; to find that the first principles are not understood! You are thrown on your back immediately, the
conversation is stopped like a country-dance by those
who do not know the figure. But when a set of adepts, of
illuminati, get about a question, it is worth while to hear
them talk. They may snarl and quarrel over it, like
dogs; but they pick it bare to the bone, they masticate
it thoroughly.

This was the case formerly at L[amb]'s—where we used
to have many lively skirmishes at their Thursday evening
parties. I doubt whether the Small-coal man's musical
parties could exceed them.[1] Oh! for the pen of John
Buncle to consecrate a *petit souvenir* to their memory!—
There was L[amb] himself, the most delightful, the most
provoking, the most witty and sensible of men. He
always made the best pun, and the best remark in the
course of the evening. His serious conversation, like his
serious writing, is his best. No one ever stammered out
such fine, piquant, deep, eloquent things in half a dozen
half-sentences as he does. His jests scald like tears:
and he probes a question with a play upon words. What
a keen, laughing, hair-brained vein of home-felt truth!
What choice venom! How often did we cut into the
haunch of letters, while we discussed the haunch of
mutton on the table! How we skimmed the cream of
criticism! How we got into the heart of controversy!
How we picked out the marrow of authors! " And, in our
flowing cups, many a good name and true was freshly

---

[1] Thomas Britton. He was a native of Wellingborough,
county Northampton. See a good account of him in *Reliquiae
Hearnianae*, 1857, p. 339.—W. C. H.

remembered." Recollect (most sage and critical reader) that in all this I was but a guest! Need I go over the names? They were but the old everlasting set—Milton and Shakspeare, Pope and Dryden, Steele and Addison, Swift and Gay, Fielding, Smollett, Sterne, Richardson, Hogarth's prints, Claude's landscapes, the Cartoons at Hampton Court, and all those things that, having once been, must ever be. The Scotch Novels had not then been heard of: so we said nothing about them. In general, we were hard upon the moderns. The author of the *Rambler* was only tolerated in Boswell's *Life* of him; and it was as much as anyone could do to edge in a word for *Junius*. L[amb] could not bear *Gil Blas*. This was a fault. I remember the greatest triumph I ever had was in persuading him, after some years' difficulty, that Fielding was better than Smollett. On one occasion, he was for making out a list of persons famous in history that one would wish to see again—at the head of whom were Pontius Pilate, Sir Thomas Browne, and Dr. Faustus—but we black-balled most of his list. But with what a gusto would he describe his favourite authors, Donne, or Sir Philip Sidney, and call their most crabbed passages *delicious!* He tried them on his palate as epicures taste olives, and his observations had a smack in them, like a roughness on the tongue. With what discrimination he hinted a defect in what he admired most— as in saying that the display of the sumptuous banquet in *Paradise Regained* was not in true keeping, as the simplest fare was all that was necessary to tempt the extremity of hunger—and stating that Adam and Eve in *Paradise Lost* were too much like married people. He has furnished many a text for C[oleridge] to preach upon. There was no fuss or cant about him: nor were his sweets or his sours ever diluted with one particle of affectation. I cannot say that the party at L[amb]'s were all of one description. There were honorary members, lay-brothers. Wit and good fellowship was the motto inscribed over the door. When a stranger came in, it was not asked, " Has he written anything?"—we were above that pedantry; but we waited to see what he could do. If he could take a hand at piquet, he was welcome to sit down. If a person liked anything, if he took snuff heartily, it was sufficient. He would understand, by analogy, the pungency of other things besides Irish blackguard or Scotch rappee. A character was good any-where, in a room or on paper. But we abhorred insipidity, affectation, and fine gentlemen. There was one of our party who never failed to mark " two for his Nob " at cribbage, and he was thought no mean person. This was Ned P[hillips], and a better fellow in his way breathes not.. There was [Rickman], who asserted some in-credible matter of fact as a likely paradox, and settled all controversies by an *ipse dixit*, a *fiat* of his will, hammering out many a hard theory on the anvil of his brain—the Baron Munchausen of politics and practical philosophy: there was Captain [Burney], who had you at an advantage by never understanding you:—there was Jem White, the Author of *Falstaff's Letters*, who the other day left this dull world to go in search of more kindred spirits, " turn-ing like the latter end of a lover's lute: "—there was A[yrton], who sometimes dropped in, the Will Honey-comb of our set—and Mrs. R[eynolds], who being of a quiet turn, loved to hear a noisy debate. An utterly uninformed person might have supposed this a scene of vulgar confusion and uproar. While the most critical question was pending, while the most difficult problem in philosophy was solving, P[hillips] cried out, " That's game," and M[artin] B[urney] muttered a quotation over the last remains of a veal-pie at a side table. Once, and once only, the literary interest overcame the general. For C[oleridge] was riding the high German horse, and demon-strating the Categories of the Transcendental Philosophy to the Author of the *Road to Ruin;* who insisted on his knowledge of German, and German metaphysics, having read the *Critique of Pure Reason* in the original. " My dear Mr. Holcroft," said C[oleridge], in a tone of infinitely provoking conciliation, " you really put me in mind of a sweet pretty German girl, about fifteen, that I met with in the Hartz forest in Germany—and who one day, as I was reading the *Limits of the Knowable and the Unknowable,* the profoundest of all his works, with great attention, came behind my chair, and leaning over, said, ' What, *you* read Kant? Why, *I* that am a German born, don't understand him!' " This was too much to bear, and Holcroft, starting up, called out in no measured tone, " Mr. C[oleridge], you are the most eloquent man I ever met with, and the most troublesome with your eloquence!" P[hillips] held the cribbage-peg that was to mark him game, suspended in his hand; and the whist table was silent for a moment. I saw Holcroft downstairs, and, on coming to the landing-place at Mitre Court, he stopped me to observe, that " he thought Mr. C[oleridge] a very clever man, with a great command of language, but that he feared he did not always affix very precise ideas to the words he used." After he was gone, we had our laugh out, and went on with the argument on the nature of Reason, the Imagination, and the Will. I wish I could find a publisher for it: it would make a supplement to the *Biographia Literaria* in a volume-and-a-half octavo.

Those days are over! An event, the name of which I wish never to mention, broke up our party, like a bomb-shell thrown into the room: and now we seldom meet——

" Like angels' visits, short and far between."

There is no longer the same set of persons, nor of associations. L[amb] does not live where he did. By shifting his abode, his notions seem less fixed. He does not wear his old snuff-coloured coat and breeches. It looks like an

Q *

alteration in his style. An author and a wit should have a separate costume, a particular cloth: he should present something positive and singular to the mind, like Mr. Douce of the Museum. Our faith in the religion of letters will not bear to be taken to pieces, and put together again by caprice or accident. L[eigh] H[unt] goes there sometimes. He has a fine vinous spirit about him, and tropical blood in his veins: but he is better at his own table. He has a great flow of pleasantry and delightful animal spirits: but his hits do not tell like L[amb]'s; you cannot repeat them the next day. He requires not only to be appreciated but to have a select circle of admirers and devotees, to feel himself quite at home. He sits at the head of a party with great gaiety and grace; has an elegant manner and turn of features; is never at a loss—*aliquando sufflaminandus erat*—has continual sportive sallies of wit or fancy; tells a story capitally; mimics an actor or an acquaintance to admiration; laughs with great glee and good humour at his own or other people's jokes; understands the point of an equivoque, or an observation immediately; has a taste and knowledge of books, of music, of medals; manages an argument adroitly; is genteel and gallant, and has a set of bye-phrases and quaint allusions always at hand to produce a laugh:—if he has a fault, it is that he does not listen so well as he speaks, is impatient of interruption, and is fond of being looked up to, without considering by whom. I believe, however, he has pretty well seen the folly of this. Neither is his ready display of personal accomplishment and variety of resources an advantage to his writings. They sometimes present a desultory and slipshod appearance, owing to this very circumstance. The same things that tell, perhaps, best to a private circle round the fireside, are not always intelligible to the public, nor does he take pains to make them so. He is too confident and secure of his audience. That which may be entertaining enough with the assistance of a certain

liveliness of manner, may read very flat on paper, because
it is abstracted from all the circumstances that had set it
off to advantage. A writer should recollect that he has
only to trust to the immediate impression of words, like a
musician who sings without the accompaniment of an instrument. There is nothing to help out, or slubber over,
the defects of the voice in the one case, nor of the style in
the other. The reader may, if he pleases, get a very good
idea of L[eigh] [Hunt]'s conversation from a very agreeable
paper he has lately published, called the *Indicator*, than
which nothing can be more happily conceived or executed.

The art of conversation is the art of hearing as well as
of being heard. Authors in general are not good list-
eners. Some of the best talkers are, on this account, the
worst company; and some who are very indifferent, but
very great talkers, are as bad. It is sometimes wonderful
to see how a person, who has been entertaining or tiring
a company by the hour together, drops his countenance as
if he had been shot, or had been seized with a sudden
lock-jaw, the moment anyone interposes a single observation. The best converser I know is, however, the best
listener. I mean Mr. Northcote, the painter. Painters by
their profession are not bound to shine in conversation,
and they shine the more. He lends his ear to an observation as if you had brought him a piece of news, and
enters into it with as much avidity and earnestness as if
it interested himself personally. If he repeats an old
remark or story, it is with the same freshness and point
as for the first time. It always arises out of the occasion,
and has the stamp of originality. There is no parroting
of himself. His look is a continual, ever-varying history-
piece of what passes in his mind. His face is as a book.
There need no marks of interjection or interrogation to
what he says. His manner is quite picturesque. There
is an excess of character and *naïveté* that never tires. His
thoughts bubble up and sparkle like beads on old wine.

The fund of anecdote, the collection of curious particulars, is enough to set up any common retailer of jests that dines out every day; but these are not strung together like a row of galley-slaves, but are always introduced to illustrate some argument or bring out some fine distinction of character. The mixture of spleen adds to the sharpness of the point, like poisoned arrows. Mr. Northcote enlarges with enthusiasm on the old painters, and tells good things of the new. The only thing he ever vexed me in was his liking the *Catalogue Raisonnée*. I had almost as soon hear him talk of Titian's pictures (which he does with tears in his eyes, and looking just like them) as see the originals, and I had rather hear him talk of Sir Joshua's than see them. He is the last of that school who knew Goldsmith and Johnson. How finely he describes Pope! His elegance of mind, his figure, his character were not unlike his own. He does not resemble a modern Englishman, but puts one in mind of a Roman Cardinal or a Spanish Inquisitor. I never ate or drank with Mr. Northcote; but I have lived on his conversation with undiminished relish ever since I can remember,— and when I leave it, I come out into the street with feelings lighter and more ethereal than I have at any other time. One of his *tête-à-têtes* would at any time make an Essay; but he cannot write himself, because he loses himself, in the connecting passages, is fearful of the effect, and wants the habit of bringing his ideas into one focus or point of view. A *lens* is necessary to collect the diverging rays, the refracted and broken angular lights of conversation on paper. Contradiction is half the battle in talking—the being startled by what others say, and having to answer on the spot. You have to defend yourself, paragraph by paragraph, parenthesis within parenthesis. Perhaps it might be supposed that a person who excels in conversation and cannot write, would succeed better in dialogue. But the stimulus, the immediate irritation would be wanting; and the work would read flatter than ever, from not having the very thing it pretended to have.

Lively sallies and connected discourse are very different things. There are many persons of that impatient and restless turn of mind, that they cannot wait a moment for a conclusion, or follow up the thread of any argument. In the hurry of conversation their ideas are somehow huddled into sense; but in the intervals of thought, leave a great gap between. Montesquieu said, he often lost an idea before he could find words for it: yet he dictated, by way of saving time, to an amanuensis. This last is, in my opinion, a vile method, and a solecism in authorship. Horne Tooke, among other paradoxes, used to maintain, that no one could write a good style who was not in the habit of talking and hearing the sound of his own voice. He might as well have said that no one could relish a good style without reading it aloud, as we find common people do to assist their apprehension. But there is a method of trying periods on the ear, or weighing them with the scales of the breath, without any articulate sound. Authors, as they write, may be said to " hear a sound so fine, there's nothing lives 'twixt it and silence." Even musicians generally compose in their heads. I agree that no style is good that is not fit to be spoken or read aloud with effect. This holds true not only of emphasis and cadence, but also with regard to natural idiom and colloquial freedom. Sterne's was in this respect the best style that ever was written. You fancy that you hear the people talking. For a contrary reason, no college-man writes a good style, or understands it when written. Fine writing is with him all verbiage and monotony—a translation into classical centos or hexameter-lines.

That which I have just mentioned is among many instances I could give of ingenious absurdities advanced by Mr. Tooke in the heat and pride of controversy. A person who knew him well, and greatly admired his talents, said of him that he never (to his recollection) heard him defend an opinion which he thought right, or in which he believed him to be himself sincere. He indeed provoked his antagonists into the toils by the very extravagance of his assertions, and the teasing sophistry by which he rendered them plausible. His temper was prompter to his skill. He had the manners of a man of the world, with great scholastic resources. He flung every one else off his guard, and was himself immovable. I never knew any one who did not admit his superiority in this kind of warfare. He put a full-stop to one of C[oleridge]'s long-winded prefatory apologies for his youth and inexperience, by saying abruptly, " Speak up, young man!" and, at another time, silenced a learned professor by desiring an explanation of a word which the other frequently used, and which, he said, he had been many years trying to get at the meaning of,—the copulative Is! He was the best intellectual fencer of his day. He made strange havoc of Fuseli's fantastic hieroglyphics, violent humours, and oddity of dialect. Curran, who was sometimes of the same party, was lively and animated in convivial conversation, but dull in argument; nay, averse to anything like reasoning or serious observation, and had the worst taste I ever knew. His favourite critical topics were to abuse Milton's *Paradise Lost,* and *Romeo and Juliet.* Indeed, he confessed a want of sufficient acquaintance with books when he found himself in literary society in London. He and Sheridan once dined at John Kemble's with Mrs. Inchbald and Mary Woolstonecroft, when the discourse almost wholly turned on Love " from noon to dewy eve, a summer's day!" What a subject! What speakers, and what hearers! What would I not give to have been there, had I not learned it all from the bright eyes of Amaryllis, and may one day make a *Table-talk* of it! Peter Pindar was rich in anecdote and grotesque humour, and profound in technical knowledge both of music, poetry, and painting, but he was gross and overbearing. Wordsworth sometimes talks like a man inspired on subjects of poetry (his own out of the question)—Coleridge well on every subject, and G[o]dwin on none. To finish this subject—Mrs. M[ontagu]'s conversation is as fine-cut as her features, and I like to sit in the room with that sort of coronet face. What she says leaves a flavour, like fine green tea. H[un]t's is like champagne, and N[orthcote]'s like anchovy sandwiches. H[a]yd[o]n's is like a game at trap-ball: L[amb]'s like snap-dragon: and my own (if I do not mistake the matter) is not very much unlike a game at ninepins! . . . One source of the conversation of authors is the character of other authors, and on that they are rich indeed. What things they say! What stories they tell of one another, more particularly of their friends! If I durst only give some of these confidential communications! . . . The reader may perhaps think the foregoing a specimen of them—but indeed he is mistaken.

I do not know of any greater impertinence, than for an obscure individual to set about pumping a character of celebrity. " Bring him to me," said a Doctor Tronchin, speaking of Rousseau, " that I may see whether he has anything in him." Before you can take measure of the capacity of others, you ought to be sure that they have not taken measure of yours. They may think you a spy on them, and may not like their company. If you really want to know whether another person can talk well, begin by saying a good thing yourself, and you will have a right to look for a rejoinder. " The best tennis-players," says Sir Fopling Flutter, " make the best matches."

————————" For wit is like a rest
Held up at tennis, which men do the best
With the best players."

We hear it often said of a great author, or a great
actress, that they are very stupid people in private. But
he was a fool that said so. *Tell me your company, and I'll
tell you your manners.* In conversation, as in other things,
the action and reaction should bear a certain proportion
to each other. Authors may, in some sense, be looked
upon as foreigners, who are not naturalized even in their
native soil. L[amb] once came down into the country to
see us.[1] He was " like the most capricious poet Ovid
among the Goths." The country people thought him an
oddity, and did not understand his jokes. It would be
strange if they had; for he did not make any while he
stayed. But when we crossed the country to Oxford, then
he spoke a little. He and the old colleges were hail-
fellow well met; and in the quadrangles, he " walked
gowned."

There is a character of a gentleman; so there is a
character of a scholar, which is no less easily recognised.
The one has an air of books about him, as the other has
of good-breeding. The one wears his thoughts as the
other does his clothes, gracefully; and even if they are a
little old-fashioned, they are not ridiculous: they have
had their day. The gentleman shews, by his manner,
that he has been used to respect from others: the scholar
that he lays claim to self-respect and to a certain independence of opinion. The one has been accustomed to
the best company; the other has passed his time in cultivating an intimacy with the best authors. There is
nothing forward or vulgar in the behaviour of the one;
nothing shrewd or petulant in the observations of the
other, as if he should astonish the bye-standers, or was
astonished himself at his own discoveries. Good taste
and good sense, like common politeness, are, or are supposed to be, matters of course. One is distinguished by
an appearance of marked attention to every one present;

[1] At Winterslow in 1809. [W. H., jun.]

the other manifests an habitual air of abstraction and absence of mind. The one is not an upstart, with all the self-important airs of the founder of his own fortune; nor the other a self-taught man, with the repulsive self-sufficiency which arises from an ignorance of what hundreds have known before him. We must excuse perhaps a little conscious family-pride in the one, and a little harmless pedantry in the other. As there is a class of the first character which sinks into the mere gentleman, that is, which has nothing but this sense of respectability and propriety to support it—so the character of a scholar not unfrequently dwindles down into the shadow of a shade, till nothing is left of it but the mere book-worm. There is often something amiable as well as enviable in this last character. I know one such instance, at least. The person I mean has an admiration for learning, if he is only dazzled by its light. He lives among old authors, if he does not enter much into their spirit. He handles the covers, and turns over the page, and is familiar with the names and dates. He is busy and self-involved. He hangs like a film and cobweb upon letters, or is like the dust upon the outside of knowledge, which should not be rudely brushed aside. He follows learning as its shadow; but as such, he is respectable. He browzes on the husk and leaves of books, as the young fawn browzes on the bark and leaves of trees. Such a one lives all his life in a dream of learning, and has never once had his sleep broken by a real sense of things. He believes implicitly in genius, truth, virtue, liberty, because he finds the names of these things in books. He thinks that love and friendship are the finest things imaginable, both in practice and theory. The legend of good women is to him no fiction. When he steals from the twilight of his cell, the scene breaks upon him like an illuminated missal, and all the people he sees are but so many figures in a *camera obscura*. He reads the world, like a favourite volume, only

to find beauties in it, or like an edition of some old work
which he is preparing for the press, only to make emenda-
tions in 'it, and correct the errors that have inadvertently
slipt in. He and his dog Tray are much the same honest,
simple-hearted, faithful, affectionate creatures—if Tray
could but read! His mind cannot take the impression of
vice: but the gentleness of his nature turns gall to milk.
He would not hurt a fly. He draws the picture of mankind from the guileless simplicity of his own heart: and
when he dies, his spirit will take its smiling leave, without having ever had an ill thought of others, or the
consciousness of one in itself!

ON FAMILIAR STYLE

(WRITTEN AFTER JULY, 1821)

IT is not easy to write a familiar style. Many people
mistake a familiar for a vulgar style, and suppose that
to write without affectation is to write at random. On
the contrary, there is nothing that requires more precision, and, if I may so say, purity of expression, than
the style I am speaking of. It utterly rejects not only
all unmeaning pomp, but all low, cant phrases, and
loose, unconnected, *slipshod* allusions. It is not to take
the first word that offers, but the best word in common
use ; it is not to throw words together in any combinations we please, but to follow and avail ourselves of the
true idiom of the language. To write a genuine familiar
or truly English style, is to write as any one would speak
in common conversation who had a thorough command
and choice of words, or who could discourse with ease,
force, and perspicuity, setting aside all pedantic and
oratorical flourishes. Or, to give another illustration, to

write naturally is the same thing in regard to common
conversation as to read naturally is in regard to common
speech. It does not follow that it is an easy thing to give
the true accent and inflection to the words you utter,
because you do not attempt to rise above the level of
ordinary life and colloquial speaking. You do not assume,
indeed, the solemnity of the pulpit, or the tone of stage-
declamation ; neither are you at liberty to gabble on at a
venture, without emphasis or discretion, or to resort to
vulgar dialect or clownish pronunciation. You must
steer a middle course. You are tied down to a given
and appropriate articulation, which is determined by
the habitual associations between sense and sound, and
which you can only hit by entering into the author's
meaning, as you must find the proper words and style
to express yourself by fixing your thoughts on the
subject you have to write about. Any one may mouth
out a passage with a theatrical cadence, or get upon
stilts to tell his thoughts ; but to write or speak with
propriety and simplicity is a more difficult task. Thus
it is easy to affect a pompous style, to use a word twice
as big as the thing you want to express : it is not so
easy to pitch upon the very word that exactly fits it.
Out of eight or ten words equally common, equally
intelligible, with nearly equal pretensions, it is a matter
of some nicety and discrimination to pick out the very
one the preferableness of which is scarcely perceptible,
but decisive. The reason why I object to Dr. Johnson's
style is that there is no discrimination, no selection, no
variety in it. He uses none but " tall, opaque words,"
taken from the " first row of the rubric "—words with the
greatest number of syllables, or Latin phrases with merely
English terminations. If a fine style depended on this sort
of arbitrary pretension, it would be fair to judge of an
author's elegance by the measurement of his words and
the substitution of foreign circumlocutions (with no precise

associations) for the mother-tongue.[1] How simple is it to
be dignified without ease, to be pompous without meaning! Surely, it is but a mechanical rule for avoiding what
is low, to be always pedantic and affected. It is clear you
cannot use a vulgar English word if you never use a common English word at all. A fine tact is shewn in adhering
to those which are perfectly common, and yet never falling
into any expressions which are debased by disgusting circumstances, or which owe their signification and point to
technical or professional allusions. A truly natural or
familiar style can never be quaint or vulgar, for this reason,
that it is of universal force and applicability, and that
quaintness and vulgarity arise out of the immediate connection of certain words with coarse and disagreeable, or
with confined ideas. The last form what we understand
by *cant* or *slang* phrases.—To give an example of what is
not very clear in the general statement. I should say that
the phrase *To cut with a knife*, or *To cut a piece of wood*, is
perfectly free from vulgarity, because it is perfectly common; but to *cut an acquaintance* is not quite unexceptionable, because it is not perfectly common or intelligible,
and has hardly yet escaped out of the limits of slang
phraseology. I should hardly, therefore, use the word in
this sense without putting it in italics as a license of expression, to be received *cum grano salis*. All provincial or
bye-phrases come under the same mark of reprobation—all
such as the writer transfers to the page from his fireside or
a particular *coterie*, or that he invents for his own sole use
and convenience. I conceive that words are like money,
not the worse for being common, but that it is the stamp of
custom alone that gives them circulation or value. I am
fastidious in this respect, and would almost as soon coin the

---

[1] I have heard of such a thing as an author who makes it a
rule never to admit a monosyllable into his vapid verse. Yet
the charm and sweetness of Marlowe's lines depended often on
their being made up almost entirely of monosyllables.

currency of the realm as counterfeit the King's English. I never invented or gave a new and unauthorised meaning to any word but one single one (the term *impersonal* applied to feelings), and that was in an abstruse metaphysical discussion to express a very difficult distinction. I have been (I know) loudly accused of revelling in vulgarisms and broken English. I cannot speak to that point ; but so far I plead guilty to the determined use of acknowledged idioms and common elliptical expressions. I am not sure that the critics in question know the one from the other, that is, can distinguish any medium between formal pedantry and the most barbarous solecism. As an author I endeavour to employ plain words and popular modes of construction, as, were I a chapman and dealer, I should common weights and measures.

The proper force of words lies not in the words themselves, but in their application. A word may be a fine-sounding word, of an unusual length, and very imposing from its learning and novelty, and yet in the connection in which it is introduced may be quite pointless and irrelevant. It is not pomp or pretension, but the adaptation of the expression to the idea, that clenches a writer's meaning :—as it is not the size or glossiness of the materials, but their being fitted each to its place, that gives strength to the arch ; or as the pegs and nails are as necessary to the support of the building as the larger timbers, and more so than the mere shewy, unsubstantial ornaments. I hate anything that occupies more space than it is worth. I hate to see a load of band-boxes go along the street, and I hate to see a parcel of big words without anything in them. A person who does not deliberately dispose of all his thoughts alike in cumbrous draperies and flimsy disguises, may strike out twenty varieties of familiar every-day language, each coming somewhat nearer to the feeling he wants to convey, and at last not hit upon that particular and only one which may be said to be identical with the exact·

impression in his mind. This would seem to shew that
Mr. Cobbett is hardly right in saying that the first word
that occurs is always the best. It may be a very good one ;
and yet a better may present itself on reflection or from
time to time. It should be suggested naturally, however,
and spontaneously, from a fresh and lively conception of
the subject. We seldom succeed by trying at improvement, or by merely substituting one word for another that
we are not satisfied with, as we cannot recollect the name
of a place or person by merely plaguing ourselves about it.
We wander farther from the point by persisting in a
wrong scent ; but it starts up accidentally in the memory
when we least expected it, by touching some link in the
chain of previous association.

There are those who hoard up and make a cautious
display of nothing but rich and rare phraseology—ancient
medals, obscure coins, and Spanish pieces of eight. They
are very curious to inspect, but I myself would neither
offer nor take them in the course of exchange. A sprinkling of archaisms is not amiss, but a tissue of obsolete
expressions is more fit *for keep than wear*. I do not say I
would not use any phrase that had been brought into
fashion before the middle or the end of the last century,
but I should be shy of using any that had not been employed by any approved author during the whole of that
time. Words, like clothes, get old-fashioned, or mean and
ridiculous, when they have been for some time laid aside.
Mr. Lamb is the only imitator of old English style I can
read with pleasure ; and he is so thoroughly imbued with
the spirit of his authors that the idea of imitation is almost
done away. There is an inward unction, a marrowy vein,
both in the thought and feeling, an intuition, deep and
lively, of his subject, that carries off any quaintness or
awkwardness arising from an antiquated style and dress.
The matter is completely his own, though the manner is
assumed. Perhaps his ideas are altogether so marked and

individual as to require their point and pungency to be neutralised by the affectation of a singular but traditional form of conveyance. Tricked out in the prevailing costume, they would probably seem more startling and out of the way. The old English authors, Burton, Fuller, Coryate, Sir Thomas Browne, are a kind of mediators between us and the more eccentric and whimsical modern, reconciling us to his peculiarities. I do not, however, know how far this is the case or not, till he condescends to write like one of us. I must confess that what I like best of his papers under the signature of Elia (still I do not presume, amidst such excellence, to decide what is most excellent) is the account of " Mrs. Battle's Opinions on Whist," which is also the most free from obsolete allusions and turns of expression—

" A well of native English undefiled."

To those acquainted with his admired prototypes, these *Essays* of the ingenious and highly gifted author have the same sort of charm and relish that Erasmus's *Colloquies* or a fine piece of modern Latin have to the classical scholar. Certainly, I do not know any borrowed pencil that has more power or felicity of execution than the one of which I have here been speaking.

It is as easy to write a gaudy style without ideas as it is to spread a pallet of shewy colours or to smear in a flaunting transparency. " What do you read ? " " Words, words, words."—" What is the matter ? " " *Nothing*," it might be answered. The florid style is the reverse of the familiar. The last is employed as an unvarnished medium to convey ideas ; the first is resorted to as a spangled veil to conceal the want of them. When there is nothing to be set down but words, it costs little to have them fine. Look through the dictionary, and cull out a *florilegium*, rival the *tulippomania*. *Rouge* high enough, and never mind the natural complexion. The vulgar, who are not in the secret, will admire the look of preternatural health and vigour ; and the fashionable, who regard only appearances, will be delighted with the imposition. Keep to your sounding generalities, your tinkling phrases, and all will be well. Swell out an unmeaning truism to a perfect tympany of style. A thought, a distinction is the rock on which all this brittle cargo of verbiage splits at once. Such writers have merely *verbal* imaginations, that retain nothing but words. Or their puny thoughts have dragon-wings, all green and gold. They soar far above the vulgar failing of the *Sermo humi obrepens*—their most ordinary speech is never short of an hyperbole, splendid, imposing, vague, incomprehensible, magniloquent, a cento of sounding common-places. If some of us, whose " ambition is more lowly," pry a little too narrowly into nooks and corners to pick up a number of " unconsidered trifles," they never once direct their eyes or lift their hands to seize on any but the most gorgeous, tarnished, thread-bare, patch-work set of phrases, the left-off finery of poetic extrava-gance, transmitted down through successive generations of barren pretenders. If they criticise actors and actresses, a huddled phantasmagoria of feathers, spangles, floods of light, and oceans of sound float before their morbid sense, which they paint in the style of Ancient Pistol. Not a glimpse can you get of the merits or defects of the per-formers : they are hidden in a profusion of barbarous epithets and wilful rhodomontade. Our hypercritics are not thinking of these little fantoccini beings—

" That strut and fret their hour upon the stage— "

but of tall phantoms of words, abstractions, *genera* and *species*, sweeping clauses, periods that unite the Poles, forced alliterations, astounding antitheses—

" And on their pens *Fustian* sits plumed."

If they describe kings and queens, it is an Eastern pageant.

The Coronation at either House is nothing to it. We get at four repeated images—a curtain, a throne, a sceptre, and a foot-stool. These are with them the wardrobe of a lofty imagination ; and they turn their servile strains to servile uses. Do we read a description of pictures ? It is not a reflection of tones and hues which " nature's own sweet and cunning hand laid on," but piles of precious stones, rubies, pearls, emeralds, Golconda's mines, and all the blazonry of art. Such persons are in fact besotted with words, and their brains are turned with the glittering but empty and sterile phantoms of things. Personifications, capital letters, seas of sunbeams, visions of glory, shining inscriptions, the figures of a transparency, Britannia with her shield, or Hope leaning on an anchor, make up their stock-in-trade. They may be considered as *hieroglyphical* writers. Images stand out in their minds isolated and important merely in themselves, without any ground-work of feeling—there is no context in their imaginations. Words affect them in the same way, by the mere sound, that is, by their possible, not by their actual application to the subject in hand. They are fascinated by first appearances, and have no sense of consequences. Nothing more is meant by them than meets the ear : they understand or feel nothing more than meets their eye. The web and texture of the universe, and of the heart of man, is a mystery to them : they have no faculty that strikes a chord in unison with it. They cannot get beyond the daubings of fancy, the varnish of sentiment. Objects are not linked to feelings, words to things, but images revolve in splendid mockery, words represent themselves in their strange rhapsodies. The categories of such a mind are pride and ignorance—pride in outside show, to which they sacrifice everything, and ignorance of the true worth and hidden structure both of words and things. With a sovereign contempt for what is familiar and natural, they are the slaves of vulgar affectation—of a

routine of high-flown phrases. Scorning to imitate
realities, they are unable to invent anything, to strike out
one original idea. They are not copyists of nature, it is
true ; but they are the poorest of all plagiarists, the plagiarists of words. All is far-fetched, dear bought, artificial,
oriental in subject and allusion ; all is mechanical, conventional, vapid, formal, pedantic in style and execution.
They startle and confound the understanding of the reader
by the remoteness and obscurity of their illustrations ;
they soothe the ear by the monotony of the same everlasting round of circuitous metaphors. They are the
mock-school in poetry and prose. They flounder about
between fustian in expression and bathos in sentiment.
They tantalise the fancy, but never reach the head nor
touch the heart. Their Temple of Fame is like a shadowy
structure raised by Dulness to Vanity, or like Cowper's
description of the Empress of Russia's palace of ice, " as
worthless as in show 'twas glittering "—

"It smiled, and it was cold ! "

ON THE PROSE STYLE
OF POETS

(WRITTEN IN AUG., 1822)

" Do you read or sing ? If you sing, you sing very ill."

I HAVE but an indifferent opinion of the prose-style of
poets: not that it is not sometimes good, nay, excellent;
but it is never the better, and generally the worse, from
the habit of writing verse. Poets are winged animals, and
can cleave the air, like birds, with ease to themselves and
delight to the beholders; but like those " feathered, two-
legged things," when they light upon the ground of prose

and matter-of-fact, they seem not to have the same use of their feet.

What is a little extraordinary, there is a want of *rhythmus* and cadence in what they write without the help of metrical rules. Like persons who have been accustomed to sing to music, they are at a loss in the absence of the habitual accompaniment and guide to their judgment. Their style halts, totters, is loose, disjointed, and without expressive pauses or rapid movements. The measured cadence and regular *sing-song* of rhyme or blank verse have destroyed, as it were, their natural ear for the mere characteristic harmony which ought to subsist between the sound and the sense. I should almost guess the Author of *Waverley* to be a writer of ambling verses from the desultory vacillation and want of firmness in the march of his style. There is neither *momentum* nor elasticity in it; I mean as to the *score*, or effect upon the ear. He has improved since in his other works: to be sure, he has had practice enough.[1] Poets either get into this incoherent, undetermined, shuffling style, made up of " unpleasing flats and sharps," of unaccountable starts and pauses, of doubtful odds and ends, flirted about like straws in a gust of wind; or, to avoid it and steady themselves, mount into a sustained and measured prose (like the translation of Ossian's *Poems*, or some parts of Shaftesbury's *Characteristics*) which is more odious still, and as bad as being at sea in a calm. Dr. Johnson's style (particularly in his *Rambler*) is not free from the last objection. There is a tune in it, a mechanical recurrence of the same rise and fall in the clauses of his sentences, independent of any reference to the meaning of the text, or progress or inflection of the sense. There is the

[1] Is it not a collateral proof that Sir Walter Scott is the Author of *Waverley*, that ever since these novels began to appear, his Muse has been silent, till the publication of *Halidon Hill* ?

alternate roll of his cumbrous cargo of words; his periods complete their revolutions at certain stated intervals, let the matter be longer or shorter, rough or smooth, round or square, different or the same. This monotonous and balanced mode of composition may be compared to that species of portrait-painting which prevailed about a century ago, in which each face was cast in a regular and preconceived mould. The eye-brows were arched mathematically as if with a pair of compasses, and the distances between the nose and mouth, the forehead and chin, determined according to a " fore-gone conclusion," and the features of the identical individual were afterwards accommodated to them, how they could![1]

Horne Tooke used to maintain that no one could write a good prose style, who was not accustomed to express himself *vivâ voce*, or to talk in company. He argued that this was the fault of Addison's prose, and that its smooth, equable uniformity, and want of sharpness and spirit, arose from his not having familiarised his ear to the sound of his own voice, or at least only among his friends and admirers, where there was but little collision, dramatic fluctuation, or sudden contrariety of opinion to provoke animated discussion, and give birth to different intonations and lively transitions of speech. His style (in this view of it) was not indented, nor did it project from the surface. There was no stress laid on one word more than another—it did not hurry on or stop short, or sink or swell with the occasion: it was throughout equally insipid, flowing, and harmonious, and had the effect of a studied recitation rather than of a natural discourse. This would not have happened (so the Member for Old Sarum contended) had Addison laid himself out to argue at his club, or to speak in public; for then his ear would have caught the necessary modulations of sound arising out of the feeling of the moment, and he would have

[1] See the Portraits of Kneller, Richardson, and others.

transferred them unconsciously to paper. Much might be said on both sides of this question:[1] but Mr. Tooke was himself an unintentional confirmation of his own argument; for the tone of his written compositions is as flat and unraised as his manner of speaking was hard and dry. Of the poet it is said by some one, that

> " He murmurs by the running brooks
> A music sweeter than their own."

On the contrary, the celebrated person just alluded to might be said to grind the sentences between his teeth which he afterwards committed to paper, and threw out crusts to the critics, or *bon-mots* to the Electors of Westminster (as we throw bones to the dogs) without altering a muscle, and without the smallest tremulousness of voice or eye![2] I certainly so far agree with the above theory as to conceive that no style is worth a farthing that is not calculated to be read out, or that is not allied to spirited conversation: but I at the same time think the process of modulation and inflection may be quite as complete, or more so, without the external enunciation; and that an author had better try the effect of his sentences on his stomach than on his ear. He may be deceived by the last, not by the first. No person, I imagine, can dictate a good style, or spout his own compositions with impunity. In the former case, he will flounder on before the sense or words are ready, sooner than suspend his voice in air; and

---

[1] Goldsmith was not a talker, though he blurted out his good things now and then : yet his style is gay and voluble enough. Pope was also a silent man ; and his prose is timid and constrained, and his verse inclining to the monotonous.

[2] As a singular example of steadiness of nerves, Mr. Tooke on one occasion had got upon the table at a public dinner to return thanks for his health having been drank. He held a bumper of wine in his hand, but he was received with considerable opposition by one party, and at the end of the disturbance, which lasted for a quarter of an hour, he found the wine-glass still full to the brim.

in the latter, he can supply what intonation he pleases, without consulting his readers. Parliamentary speeches sometimes read well aloud; but we do not find, when such persons sit down to write, that the prose-style of public speakers and great orators is the best, most natural, or varied of all others. It has almost always either a professional twang, a mechanical rounding off, or else is stunted and unequal. Charles Fox was the most rapid and even *hurried* of speakers; but his written style halts and creeps slowly along the ground.[1] A speaker is necessarily kept within bounds in expressing certain things, or in pronouncing a certain number of words, by the limits of the breath or power of respiration: certain sounds are observed to join in harmoniously or happily with others: an emphatic phrase must not be placed where the power of utterance is enfeebled or exhausted, etc. All this must be attended to in writing (and will be so unconsciously by a practised hand), or there will be *hiatus in manuscriptis*. The words must be so arranged, in order to make an efficient readable style, as " to come trippingly off the tongue." Hence it seems that there is a natural measure

---

[1] I have been told, that when Sheridan was first introduced to Mr. Fox, what cemented an immediate intimacy between them was the following circumstance. Mr. Sheridan had been the night before to the House of Commons ; and being asked what his impression was, said he had been principally struck with the difference of manner between Mr. Fox and Lord Stormont. The latter began by declaring in a slow, solemn, drawling, nasal tone that " when he considered the enormity and the unconstitutional tendency of the measures just proposed, he was hurried away in a torrent of passion and a whirlwind of impetuosity," pausing between every word and syllable ; while the first said (speaking with the rapidity of lightning, and with breathless anxiety and impatience), that " such was the magnitude, such the importance, such the vital interest of this question, that he could not help imploring, he could not help adjuring the House to come to it with the utmost calmness, the utmost coolness, the utmost deliberation." This trait of discrimination instantly won Mr. Fox's heart.

of prose in the feeling of the subject and the power of expression in the voice, as there is an artificial one of verse in the number and co-ordination of the syllables; and I conceive that the trammels of the last do not (where they have been long worn) greatly assist the freedom or the exactness of the first.

Again, in poetry, from the restraints in many respects, a greater number of inversions, or a latitude in the transposition of words is allowed, which is not conformable to the strict laws of prose. Consequently, a poet will be at a loss, and flounder about for the common or (as we understand it) *natural* order of words in prose composition. Dr. Johnson endeavoured to give an air of dignity and novelty to his diction by affecting the order of words usual in poetry. Milton's prose has not only this drawback, but it has also the disadvantage of being formed on a classic model. It is like a fine translation from the Latin; and indeed, he wrote originally in Latin. The frequency of epithets and ornaments, too, is a resource for which the poet finds it difficult to obtain an equivalent. A direct, or simple prose-style seems to him bald and flat; and instead of forcing an interest in the subject by severity of description and reasoning, he is repelled from it altogether by the absence of those obvious and meretricious allurements by which his senses and his imagination have been hitherto stimulated and dazzled. Thus there is often at the same time a want of splendour and a want of energy in what he writes, without the invocation of the Muse—*invita Minervâ.* It is like setting a rope-dancer to perform a tumbler's tricks—the hardness of the ground jars his nerves; or it is the same thing as a painter's attempting to carve a block of marble for the first time—the coldness chills him, the colourless uniformity distracts him, the precision of form demanded disheartens him. So in prose-writing, the severity of composition required damps the enthusiasm, and cuts off the resources of the poet. He is

looking for beauty, when he should be seeking for truth;
and aims at pleasure, which he can only communicate by
increasing the sense of power in the reader. The poet
spreads the colours of fancy, the illusions of his own
mind, round every object, *ad libitum;* the prose-writer is
compelled to extract his materials patiently and bit by
bit, from his subject. What he adds of ornament, what
he borrows from the pencil, must be sparing, and judiciously inserted. The first pretends to nothing but the
immediate indulgence of his feelings: the last has a remote
practical purpose. The one strolls out into the adjoining
fields or groves to gather flowers: the other has a journey
to go, sometimes through dirty roads, and at others
through untrodden and difficult ways. It is this effeminacy, this immersion in sensual ideas, or craving after
continual excitement, that spoils the poet for his prose-
tasks. He cannot wait till the effect comes of itself, or
arises out of the occasion: he must force it upon all
occasions, or his spirit droops and flags under a supposed
imputation of dulness. He can never drift with the
current, but is always hoisting sail, and has his streamers
flying. He has got a striking simile on hand; he *lugs* it in
with the first opportunity, and with little connexion, and
so defeats his object. He has a story to tell: he tells it in
the first page, and where it would come in well, has
nothing to say; like Goldsmith, who having to wait upon
a Noble Lord, was so full of himself and of the figure he
should make, that he addressed a set speech, which he
had studied for the occasion, to his Lordship's butler, and
had just ended as the nobleman made his appearance.
The prose-ornaments of the poet are frequently beautiful
in themselves, but do not assist the subject. They are
pleasing excrescences—hindrances, not helps in an argument. The reason is, his embellishments in his own walk
grow out of the subject by natural association; that is,
beauty gives birth to kindred beauty, grandeur leads the

mind on to greater grandeur But in treating a common subject, the link is truth, force of illustration, weight of argument, not a graceful harmony in the immediate ideas; and hence the obvious and habitual clue which before guided him is gone, and he hangs on his patch-work, tinsel finery at random, in despair, without propriety, and without effect. The poetical prose-writer stops to describe an object, if he admires it, or thinks it will bear to be dwelt on: the genuine prose-writer only alludes to or characterizes it in passing, and with reference to his subject. The prose-writer is master of his materials: the poet is the slave of his style. Everything showy, everything extraneous tempts him, and he reposes idly on it: he is bent on pleasure, not on business. He aims at effect, at captivating the reader, and yet is contented with commonplace ornaments, rather than none. Indeed, this last result must necessarily follow, where there is an ambition to shine, without the effort to dig for jewels in the mine of truth. The habits of a poet's mind are not those of industry or research: his images come to him, he does not go to them; and in prose-subjects, and dry matters of fact and close reasoning, the natural stimulus that at other times warms and rouses, deserts him altogether. He sees no unhallowed visions, he is inspired by no daydreams. All is tame, literal, and barren, without the Nine. Nor does he collect his strength to strike fire from the flint by the sharpness of collision, by the eagerness of his blows. He gathers roses, he steals colours from the rainbow. He lives on nectar and ambrosia. He " treads the primrose path of dalliance," or ascends " the highest heaven of invention," or falls flat to the ground. *He is nothing, if not fanciful !*

I shall proceed to explain these remarks, as well as I can, by a few instances in point.

It has always appeared to me that the most perfect prose-style, the most powerful, the most dazzling, the

R

most daring, that which went the nearest to the verge of poetry, and yet never fell over, was Burke's. It has the solidity, and sparkling effect of the diamond: all other *fine writing* is like French paste or Bristol-stones in the comparison. Burke's style is airy, flighty, adventurous, but it never loses sight of the subject; nay, is always in contact with, and derives its increased or varying impulse from it. It may be said to pass yawning gulfs " on the unstedfast footing of a spear: " still it has an actual resting-place and tangible support under it—it is not suspended on nothing. It differs from poetry, as I conceive, like the chamois from the eagle: it climbs to an almost equal height, touches upon a cloud, overlooks a precipice, is picturesque, sublime—but all the while, instead of soaring through the air, it stands upon a rocky cliff, clambers up by abrupt and intricate ways, and browzes on the roughest bark, or crops the tender flower. The principle which guides his pen is truth, not beauty— not pleasure, but power. He has no choice, no selection of subject to flatter the reader's idle taste, or assist his own fancy: he must take what comes, and make the most of it. He works the most striking effects out of the most unpromising materials, by the mere activity of his mind. He rises with the lofty, descends with the mean, luxuriates in beauty, gloats over deformity. It is all the same to him, so that he loses no particle of the exact, characteristic, extreme impression of the thing he writes about, and that he communicates this to the reader, after exhausting every possible mode of illustration, plain or abstracted, figurative or literal. Whatever stamps the original image more distinctly on the mind, is welcome. The nature of his task precludes continual beauty; but it does not preclude continual ingenuity, force, originality. He had to treat of political questions, mixed modes, abstract ideas, and his fancy (or poetry, if you will) was ingrafted on these artificially, and as it might sometimes be thought, violently, instead of growing naturally out of them, as it would spring of its own accord from individual objects and feelings. There is a resistance in the *matter* to the illustration applied to it—the concrete and abstract are hardly co-ordinate; and therefore it is that, when the first difficulty is overcome, they must agree more closely in the essential qualities, in order that the coincidence may be complete. Otherwise, it is good for nothing; and you justly charge the author's style with being loose, vague, flaccid, and imbecile. The poet has been said

> " To make us heirs
> Of truth and pure delight in endless lays."

Not so the prose-writer, who always mingles clay with his gold, and often separates truth from mere pleasure. He can only arrive at the last through the first. In poetry, one pleasing or striking image obviously suggests another: the increasing the sense of beauty or grandeur is the principle of composition: in prose, the professed object is to impart conviction, and nothing can be admitted by way of ornament or relief, that does not add new force or clearness to the original conception. The two classes of ideas brought together by the orator or impassioned prose-writer, to wit, the general subject and the particular image, are so far incompatible, and the identity must be more strict, more marked, more determinate, to make them coalesce to any practical purpose. Every word should be a blow: every thought should instantly grapple with its fellow. There must be a weight, a precision, a conformity from association in the tropes and figures of animated prose to fit them to their place in the argument, and make them *tell*, which may be dispensed with in poetry, where there is something much more congenial between the subject-matter and the illustration—

> " Like beauty making beautiful old rime ! "

What can be more remote, for instance, and at the same
time more apposite, more *the same*, than the following
comparison of the English Constitution to " the proud
Keep of Windsor," in the celebrated *Letter to a Noble
Lord?*

" Such are *their* ideas; such *their* religion, and such
their law. But as to *our* country and *our* race, as long as
the well-compacted structure of our church and state,
the sanctuary, the holy of holies of that ancient law,
defended by reverence, defended by power—a fortress at
once and a temple[1]—shall stand inviolate on the brow of
the British Sion; as long as the British Monarchy—not
more limited than fenced by the orders of the State—
shall, like the proud Keep of Windsor, rising in the
majesty of proportion, and girt with the double belt of
its kindred and coeval towers; as long as this awful
structure shall oversee and guard the subjected land, so
long the mounds and dykes of the low, fat, Bedford level
will have nothing to fear from all the pickaxes of all the
levellers of France. As long as our Sovereign Lord the
King, and his faithful subjects, the Lords and Commons
of this realm—the triple cord which no man can break;
the solemn, sworn, constitutional frank-pledge of this
nation; the firm guarantees of each other's being, and
each other's rights; the joint and several securities, each
in its place and order, for every kind, and every quality
of property and of dignity—As long as these endure, so
long the Duke of Bedford is safe: and we are all safe
together—the high from the blights of envy and the
spoliations of rapacity; the low from the iron hand of
oppression and the insolent spurn of contempt. Amen!
and so be it: and so it will be,

> Dum domus Æneæ Capitoli immobile saxum
> Accolet; imperiumque pater Romanus habebit."

[1] " *Templum in modum arcis.*"
Tacitus, *of the Temple of Jerusalem.*

Nothing can well be more impracticable to a simile than the vague and complicated idea which is here embodied in one; yet how finely, how nobly it stands out, in natural grandeur, in royal state, with double barriers round it to answer for its identity, with " buttress, frieze, and coigne of 'vantage " for the imagination to " make its pendant bed and procreant cradle," till the idea is confounded with the object representing it—the wonder of a kingdom; and then how striking, how determined the descent, " at one fell swoop," to the " low, fat, Bedford level! " Poetry would have been bound to maintain a certain decorum, a regular balance between these two ideas; sterling prose throws aside all such idle respect to appearances, and with its pen, like a sword, " sharp and sweet," lays open the naked truth! The poet's Muse is like a mistress, whom we keep only while she is young and beautiful, *durante bene placito ;* the Muse of prose is like a wife, whom we take during life, *for better, for worse.* Burke's execution, like that of all good prose, savours of the texture of what he describes, and his pen slides or drags over the ground of his subject, like the painter's pencil. The most rigid fidelity and the most fanciful extravagance meet, and are reconciled in his pages. I never pass Windsor but I think of this passage in Burke, and hardly know to which I am indebted most for enriching my moral sense, that or the fine picturesque stanza in Gray,

> " From Windsor's heights the expanse below
> Of mead, of lawn, of wood survey," etc.

I might mention that the so-much-admired description in one of the India speeches, of Hyder Ally's army (I think it is) which " now hung like a cloud upon the mountain, and now burst upon the plain like a thunder-bolt," would do equally well for poetry or prose. It is a bold and striking illustration of a naturally impressive object. This is not the case with the Abbé Sieyès's far-famed " pigeon-holes," nor with the comparison of the Duke of Bedford to "the Leviathan, tumbling about his unwieldy bulk in the ocean of royal bounty." Nothing here saves the description but the force of the invective; the startling truth, the vehemence, the remoteness, the aptitude, the perfect peculiarity and coincidence of the allusion. No writer would ever have thought of it but himself; no reader can ever forget it. What is there in common, one might say, between a Peer of the Realm, and "that sea-beast," of those

> "Created hugest that swim the ocean-stream?"

Yet Burke has knit the two ideas together, and no man can put them asunder. No matter how slight and precarious the connexion, the length of line it is necessary for the fancy to give out in keeping hold of the object on which it has fastened, he seems to have "put his hook in the nostrils" of this enormous creature of the crown, that empurples all its track through the glittering expanse of a profound and restless imagination!

In looking into the *Iris* of last week, I find the following passages, in an article on the death of Lord Castlereagh:

"The splendour of Majesty leaving the British metropolis, careering along the ocean, and landing in the capital of the North, is distinguished only by glimpses through the dense array of clouds in which Death hid himself, while he struck down to the dust the stateliest courtier near the throne, and the broken train of which pursues and crosses the Royal progress wherever its glories are presented to the eye of imagination. . . .

"The same indefatigable mind—a mind of all work— which thus ruled the Continent with a rod of iron, the sword—within the walls of the House of Commons ruled a more distracted region with a more subtle and finely-tempered weapon, the tongue; and truly, if this *was* the only weapon his Lordship wielded there, where he had daily to encounter, and frequently almost alone, enemies more formidable than Buonaparte, it must be acknowledged that he achieved greater victories than Demosthenes or Cicero ever gained in far more easy fields of strife; nay, he wrought miracles of speech, outvying those miracles of song, which Orpheus is said to have performed, when not only men and brutes, but rocks, woods, and mountains, followed the sound of his voice and lyre. . . .

" But there was a worm at the root of the gourd that flourished over his head in the brightest sunshine of a court; both perished in a night, and in the morning, that which had been his glory and his shadow, covered him like a shroud; while the corpse, notwithstanding all his honours, and titles, and offices, lay unmoved in the place where it fell, till a judgment had been passed upon him, which the poorest peasant escapes when he dies in the ordinary course of nature."[1]

This, it must be confessed, is very unlike Burke: yet Mr. Montgomery is a very pleasing poet, and a strenuous politician. The whole is *travelling out of the record*, and to no sort of purpose. The author is constantly getting away from the impression of his subject, to envelop himself in a cloud of images, which weaken and perplex, instead of adding force and clearness to it. Provided he is figurative, he does not care how commonplace or irrelevant the figures are, and he wanders on, delighted in a labyrinth of words, like a truant school-boy, who is only glad to have escaped from his task. He has a very slight hold of his subject, and is tempted to let it go for any fallacious ornament of style. How obscure and circuitous is the allusion to " the clouds in which Death hid himself, to strike down the stateliest courtier near the throne! " How hackneyed is the reference to Demosthenes and Cicero, and how utterly quaint and unmeaning is the ringing the changes upon Orpheus and his train of men,

[1] *Sheffield Advertiser*, Aug. 20, 1822.

beasts, woods, rocks, and mountains in connexion with Lord Castlereagh! But he is better pleased with this classical fable than with the death of the Noble Peer, and delights to dwell upon it, to however little use. So he is glad to take advantage of the scriptural idea of a gourd; not to enforce, but as a relief to his reflections; and points his conclusion with a puling sort of common-place—that a peasant, who dies a natural death, has no Coroner's Inquest to sit upon him. All these are the faults of the ordinary poetical style. Poets think they are bound, by the tenour of their indentures to the Muses, to " elevate and surprise " in every line; and not having the usual resources in common or abstracted subjects, aspire to the end without the means. They make, or pretend, an extraordinary interest where there is none. They are ambitious, vain, and indolent—more busy in preparing idle ornaments, which they take their chance of bringing in somehow or other, than intent on eliciting truths by fair and honest inquiry. It should seem as if they considered prose as a sort of waiting-maid to poetry, that could only be expected to wear her mistress's cast-off finery. Poets have been said to succeed best in fiction; and the account here given may in part explain the reason. That is to say, they must choose their own subject, in such a manner as to afford them continual opportunities of appealing to the senses and exciting the fancy. Dry details, abstruse speculations do not give scope to vividness of description; and, as they cannot bear to be considered dull, they become too often affected, extravagant, and insipid.

I am indebted to Mr. Coleridge for the comparison of poetic prose to the second-hand finery of a lady's-maid (just made use of). He himself is an instance of his own observation, and (what is even worse) of the opposite fault—an affectation of quaintness and originality. With bits of tarnished lace and worthless frippery, he assumes a sweeping oriental costume, or borrows the stiff dresses of our ancestors, or starts an eccentric fashion of his own. He is swelling and turgid—everlastingly aiming to be greater than his subject; filling his fancy with fumes and vapours in the pangs and throes of miraculous parturition, and bringing forth only *still-births*. He has an incessant craving, as it were, to exalt every idea into a metaphor, to expand every sentiment into a lengthened mystery, voluminous and vast, confused and cloudy. His style is not succinct, but incumbered with a train of words and images that have no practical, and only a possible relation to one another—that add to its stateliness, but impede its march. One of his sentences winds its " forlorn way obscure " over the page like a patriarchal procession with camels laden, wreathed turbans, household wealth, the whole riches of the author's mind poured out upon the barren waste of his subject. The palm-tree spreads its sterile branches overhead, and the land of promise is seen in the distance. All this is owing to his wishing to overdo everything—to make something more out of everything than it is, or than it is worth. The simple truth does not satisfy him—no direct proposition fills up the moulds of his understanding. All is foreign, far-fetched, irrelevant, laboured, unproductive. To read one of his disquisitions is like hearing the variations to a piece of music without the score. Or, to vary the simile, he is not like a man going a journey by the stage-coach along the high-road, but is always getting into a balloon, and mounting into the air, above the plain ground of prose. Whether he soars to the empyrean, or dives to the centre (as he sometimes does), it is equally to get away from the question before him, and to prove that he owes everything to his own mind. His object is to invent; he scorns to imitate. The business of prose is the contrary. But Mr. Coleridge is a poet, and his thoughts are free.

I think the poet-laureate is a much better prose-writer. His style has an antique quaintness, with a modern

R *

familiarity. He has just a sufficient sprinkling of *archaisms*, of allusions to old Fuller, and Burton, and Latimer, to set off or qualify the smart flippant tone of his apologies for existing abuses, or the ready, galling virulence of his personal invectives. Mr. Southey is a faithful historian, and no inefficient partisan. In the former character, his mind is tenacious of facts; and in the latter, his spleen and jealousy prevent the " extravagant and erring spirit " of the poet from losing itself in Fancy's endless maze. He " stoops to *earth*," at least, and prostitutes his pen to some purpose (not at the same time losing his own soul, and gaining nothing by it)—and he vilifies Reform, and praises the reign of George III in good set terms, in a straightforward, intelligible, practical, pointed way. He is not buoyed up by conscious power out of the reach of common apprehensions, but makes the most of the obvious advantages he possesses. You may complain of a pettiness and petulance of manner, but certainly there is no want of spirit or facility of execution. He does not waste powder and shot in the air, but loads his piece, takes a level aim, and hits his mark. One would say (though his Muse is ambidexter) that he wrote prose with his right hand; there is nothing awkward, circuitous, or feeble in it. " The words of Mercury are harsh after the songs of Apollo: " but this would not apply to him. His prose-lucubrations are pleasanter reading than his poetry. Indeed, he is equally practised and voluminous in both; and it is no improbable conjecture, that Mr. Southey may have had some idea of rivalling the reputation of Voltaire in the extent, the spirit, and the versatility of his productions in prose and verse, except that he has written no tragedies but Wat Tyler!

To my taste, the Author of *Rimini*, and Editor of the *Examiner*, is among the best and least corrupted of our poetical prose-writers. In his light but well-supported columns we find the raciness, the sharpness, and sparkling effect of poetry, with little that is extravagant or far-fetched, and no turgidity or pompous pretension. Perhaps there is too much the appearance of relaxation and trifling (as if he had escaped the shackles of rhyme), a caprice, a levity, and a disposition to innovate in words and ideas. Still the genuine master-spirit of the prose-writer is there; the tone of lively, sensible conversation; and this may in part arise from the author's being himself an animated talker. Mr. Hunt wants something of the heat and earnestness of the political partisan; but his familiar and miscellaneous papers have all the ease, grace, and point of the best style of Essay-writing. Many of his effusions in the *Indicator* shew, that if he had devoted himself exclusively to that mode of writing, he inherits more of the spirit of Steele than any man since his time.

Lord Byron's prose is bad; that is to say, heavy, laboured, and coarse: he tries to knock some one down with the butt-end of every line, which defeats his object— and the style of the Author of *Waverley* (if he comes fairly into this discussion) as mere style, is villainous. It is pretty plain he is a poet; for the sound of names runs mechanically in his ears, and he rings the changes unconsciously on the same words in a sentence, like the same rhymes in a couplet.

Not to spin out this discussion too much, I would conclude by observing, that some of the old English prose-writers (who were not poets) are the best, and, at the same time, the most *poetical* in the favourable sense. Among these we may reckon some of the old divines, and Jeremy Taylor at the head of them. There is a flush like the dawn over his writings; the sweetness of the rose, the freshness of the morning dew. There is a softness in his style, proceeding from the tenderness of his heart: but his head is firm, and his hand is free. His materials are as finely wrought up as they are original and attractive in themselves. Milton's prose-style savours too much of poetry, and, as I have already hinted, of an imitation of the Latin. Dryden's is perfectly unexceptionable, and a model, in simplicity, strength, and perspicuity, for the subjects he treated of.

MY FIRST ACQUAINTANCE WITH POETS

(THE LIBERAL, APRIL, 1823)

M Y father was a Dissenting Minister, at Wem, in Shropshire; and in the year 1798 (the figures that compose the date are to me like the " dreaded name of Demogorgon ") Mr. Coleridge came to Shrewsbury, to succeed Mr. Rowe in the spiritual charge of a Unitarian Congregation there. He did not come till late on the Saturday afternoon before he was to preach; and Mr. Rowe, who himself went down to the coach, in a state of anxiety and expectation, to look for the arrival of his successor, could find no one at all answering the description but a round-faced man, in a short black coat (like a shooting-jacket) which hardly seemed to have been made for him, but who seemed to be talking at a great rate to his fellow-passengers. Mr. Rowe had scarce returned to give an account of his disappointment when the round-faced man in black entered, and dissipated all doubts on the subject by beginning to talk. He did not cease while he stayed; nor has he since, that I know of. He held the good town of Shrewsbury in delightful suspense for three weeks that he remained there, " fluttering the *proud Salopians*, like an eagle in a dove-cote "; and the Welsh mountains that skirt the horizon with their tempestuous confusion, agree to have heard no such mystic sounds since the days of

" High-born Hoel's harp or soft Llewellyn's lay."

As we passed along between Wem and Shrewsbury, and
I eyed their blue tops seen through the wintry branches,
or the red rustling leaves of the sturdy oak-trees by the
road-side, a sound was in my ears as of a Siren's song;
I was stunned, startled with it, as from deep sleep; but
I had no notion then that I should ever be able to express
my admiration to others in motley imagery or quaint
allusion, till the light of his genius shone into my soul,
like the sun's rays glittering in the puddles of the road.
I was at that time dumb, inarticulate, helpless, like a worm
by the way-side, crushed, bleeding, lifeless; but now,
bursting from the deadly bands that " bound them,

> " With Styx nine times round them,"

my ideas float on winged words, and as they expand their
plumes, catch the golden light of other years. My soul
has indeed remained in its original bondage, dark, obscure,
with longings infinite and unsatisfied; my heart, shut up
in the prison-house of this rude clay, has never found,
nor will it ever find, a heart to speak to; but that my
understanding also did not remain dumb and brutish, or
at length found a language to express itself, I owe to
Coleridge. But this is not to my purpose.

My father lived ten miles from Shrewsbury, and was in
the habit of exchanging visits with Mr. Rowe, and with
Mr. Jenkins of Whitchurch (nine miles farther on),
according to the custom of Dissenting Ministers in each
other's neighbourhood. A line of communication is thus
established, by which the flame of civil and religious
liberty is kept alive, and nourishes its smouldering fire unquenchable, like the fires in the *Agamemnon* of Æschylus,
placed at different stations, that waited for ten long years
to announce with their blazing pyramids the destruction
of Troy. Coleridge had agreed to come over and see my
father, according to the courtesy of the country, as Mr.
Rowe's probable successor; but in the meantime, I had

gone to hear him preach the Sunday after his arrival. A poet and a philosopher getting up into a Unitarian pulpit to preach the gospel, was a romance in these degenerate days, a sort of revival of the primitive spirit of Christianity, which was not to be resisted.

It was in January of 1798, that I rose one morning before day-light, to walk ten miles in the mud, to hear this celebrated person preach. Never, the longest day I have to live, shall I have such another walk as this cold, raw, comfortless one, in the winter of the year 1798. *Il y a des impressions que ni le tems ni les circonstances peuvent effacer. Dussé-je vivre des siecles entiers, le doux tems de ma jeunesse ne peut renaître pour moi, ni s'effacer jamais dans ma mémoire.* When I got there, the organ was playing the 100th Psalm, and when it was done, Mr. Coleridge rose and gave out his text, " And he went up into the mountain to pray, HIMSELF, ALONE." As he gave out this text, his voice " rose like a steam of rich distilled perfumes," and when he came to the two last words, which he pronounced loud, deep, and distinct, it seemed to me, who was then young, as if the sounds had echoed from the bottom of the human heart, and as if that prayer might have floated in solemn silence through the universe. The idea of St. John came into my mind, " of one crying in the wilderness, who had his loins girt about, and whose food was locusts and wild honey." The preacher then launched into his subject, like an eagle dallying with the wind. The sermon was upon peace and war; upon church and state—not their alliance, but their separation— on the spirit of the world and the spirit of Christianity, not as the same, but as opposed to one another. He talked of those who had " inscribed the cross of Christ on banners dripping with human gore." He made a poetical and pastoral excursion—and to shew the fatal effects of war, drew a striking contrast between the simple shepherd-boy, driving his team afield, or sitting under the hawthorn, piping to his flock, " as though he should never be old," and the same poor country-lad, crimped, kidnapped, brought into town, made drunk at an alehouse, turned into a wretched drummer-boy, with his hair sticking on end with powder and pomatum, a long cue at his back, and tricked out in the loathsome finery of the profession of blood:

> " Such were the notes our once-loved poet sung."

And for myself, I could not have been more delighted if I had heard the music of the spheres. Poetry and Philosophy had met together. Truth and Genius had embraced, under the eye and with the sanction of Religion. This was even beyond my hopes. I returned home well satisfied. The sun that was still labouring pale and wan through the sky, obscured by thick mists, seemed an emblem of the *good cause*; and the cold dank drops of dew, that hung half melted on the beard of the thistle, had something genial and refreshing in them; for there was a spirit of hope and youth in all nature, that turned everything into good. The face of nature had not then the brand of JUS DIVINUM on it:

> " Like to that sanguine flower inscrib'd with woe."

On the Tuesday following, the half-inspired speaker came. I was called down into the room where he was, and went half-hoping, half-afraid. He received me very graciously, and I listened for a long time without uttering a word. I did not suffer in his opinion by my silence. " For those two hours," he afterwards was pleased to say, " he was conversing with William Hazlitt's forehead! " His appearance was different from what I had anticipated from seeing him before. At a distance, and in the dim light of the chapel, there was to me a strange wildness in his aspect, a dusky obscurity, and I thought him pitted

with the small-pox. His complexion was at that time clear,
and even bright—

> " As are the children of yon azure sheen."

His forehead was broad and high, light as if built of
ivory, with large projecting eyebrows, and his eyes
rolling beneath them, like a sea with darkened lustre.
" A certain tender bloom his face o'erspread," a purple
tinge as we see it in the pale thoughtful complexions of
the Spanish portrait-painters, Murillo and Valasquez.
His mouth was gross, voluptuous, open, eloquent; his
chin good-humoured and round; but his nose, the rudder
of the face, the index of the will, was small, feeble,
nothing—like what he has done. It might seem that the
genius of his face as from a height surveyed and projected
him (with sufficient capacity and huge aspiration) into
the world unknown of thought and imagination, with
nothing to support or guide his veering purpose, as if
Columbus had launched his adventurous course for the
New World in a scallop, without oars or compass. So,
at least, I comment on it after the event. Coleridge, in
his person, was rather above the common size, inclining
to the corpulent, or like Lord Hamlet, " somewhat fat
and pursy." His hair (now, alas! grey) was then black
and glossy as the raven's, and fell in smooth masses over
his forehead. This long pendulous hair is peculiar to
enthusiasts, to those whose minds tend heavenward;
and is traditionally inseparable (though of a different
colour) from the pictures of Christ. It ought to belong,
as a character, to all who preach *Christ crucified*, and
Coleridge was at that time one of those!

It was curious to observe the contrast between him
and my father, who was a veteran in the cause, and then
declining into the vale of years. He had been a poor
Irish lad, carefully brought up by his parents, and sent
to the University of Glasgow (where he studied under
Adam Smith) to prepare him for his future destination.

It was his mother's proudest wish to see her son a Dissenting Minister. So, if we look back to past generations (as far as eye can reach), we see the same hopes, fears, wishes, followed by the same disappointments, throbbing in the human heart; and so we may see them (if we look forward) rising up for ever, and disappearing, like vapourish bubbles, in the human breast! After being tossed about from congregation to congregation in the heats of the Unitarian controversy, and squabbles about the American war, he had been relegated to an obscure village, where he was to spend the last thirty years of his life, far from the only converse that he loved, the talk about disputed texts of Scripture, and the cause of civil and religious liberty. Here he passed his days, repining, but resigned, in the study of the Bible, and the perusal of the Commentators—huge folios, not easily got through, one of which would outlast a winter! Why did he pore on these from morn to night (with the exception of a walk in the fields or a turn in the garden to gather broccoli-plants or kidney beans of his own rearing, with no small degree of pride and pleasure)? Here were " no figures nor no fantasies " —neither poetry nor philosophy—nothing to dazzle, nothing to excite modern curiosity; but to his lacklustre eyes there appeared within the pages of the ponderous, unwieldy, neglected tomes, the sacred name of JEHOVAH in Hebrew capitals: pressed down by the weight of the style, worn to the last fading thinness of the understanding, there were glimpses, glimmering notions of the patriarchal wanderings, with palm-trees hovering in the horizon, and processions of camels at the distance of three thousand years; there was Moses with the Burning Bush, the number of the Twelve Tribes, types, shadows, glosses on the law and the prophets ; there were discussions (dull enough) on the age of Methuselah, a mighty speculation! there were outlines, rude guesses at the shape of Noah's Ark and of the riches of Solomon's

Temple; questions as to the date of the creation, predictions of the end of all things; the great lapses of time, the strange mutations of the globe were unfolded with the voluminous leaf, as it turned over; and though the soul might slumber with an hieroglyphic veil of inscrutable mysteries drawn over it, yet it was in a slumber ill-exchanged for all the sharpened realities of sense, wit, fancy, or reason. My father's life was comparatively a dream ; but it was a dream of infinity and eternity, of death, the resurrection, and a judgment to come!

No two individuals were ever more unlike than were the host and his guest. A poet was to my father a sort of nondescript; yet whatever added grace to the Unitarian cause was to him welcome. He could hardly have been more surprised or pleased, if our visitor had worn wings. Indeed, his thoughts had wings: and as the silken sounds rustled round our little wainscoted parlour, my father threw back his spectacles over his forehead, his white hairs mixing with its sanguine hue; and a smile of delight beamed across his rugged, cordial face, to think that Truth had found a new ally in Fancy![1] Besides, Coleridge seemed to take considerable notice of me, and that of itself was enough. He talked very familiarly, but agreeably, and glanced over a variety of subjects. At dinner-time he grew more animated, and dilated in a very edifying manner on Mary Wolstonecraft and Mackintosh. The last, he said, he considered (on my father's speaking of his *Vindiciæ Gallicæ* as a capital performance) as a clever, scholastic man—a master of the topics—or, as the ready warehouseman of letters, who knew exactly where to lay his hand on what he wanted, though the goods were

---

[1] My father was one of those who mistook his talent, after all. He used to be very much dissatisfied that I preferred his Letters to his Sermons. The last were forced and dry ; the first came naturally from him. For ease, half-plays on words, and a supine, monkish, indolent pleasantry, I have never seen them equalled.

not his own. He thought him no match for Burke, either in style or matter. Burke was a metaphysician, Mackintosh a mere logician. Burke was an orator (almost a poet) who reasoned in figures, because he had an eye for nature: Mackintosh, on the other hand, was a rhetorician, who had only an eye to common-places. On this I ventured to say that I had always entertained a great opinion of Burke, and that (as far as I could find) the speaking of him with contempt might be made the test of a vulgar, democratical mind. This was the first observation I ever made to Coleridge, and he said it was a very just and striking one. I remember the leg of Welsh mutton and the turnips on the table that day had the finest flavour imaginable. Coleridge added that Mackintosh and Tom Wedgwood (of whom, however, he spoke highly) had expressed a very indifferent opinion of his friend Mr. Wordsworth, on which he remarked to them—" He strides on so far before you, that he dwindles in the distance!" Godwin had once boasted to him of having carried on an argument with Mackintosh for three hours with dubious success; Coleridge told him—" If there had been a man of genius in the room, he would have settled the question in five minutes." He asked me if I had ever seen Mary Wolstonecraft, and I said, I had once for a few moments, and that she seemed to me to turn off Godwin's objections to something she advanced with quite a playful, easy air. He replied, that " this was only one instance of the ascendancy which people of imagination exercised over those of mere intellect." He did not rate Godwin very high[1] (this was caprice or prejudice, real or affected), but he had a great idea of Mrs. Wolstonecraft's

---

[1] He complained in particular of the presumption of his attempting to establish the future immortality of man, " without " (as he said) " knowing what Death was or what Life was "—and the tone in which he pronounced these two words seemed to convey a complete image of both.

powers of conversation ; none at all of her talent for
book-making. We talked a little about Holcroft. He
had been asked if he was not much struck *with* him, and
he said, he thought himself in more danger of being
struck *by* him. I complained that he would not let me get
on at all, for he required a definition of even the commonest word, exclaiming, " What do you mean by a
sensation, Sir? What do you mean by an *idea?* " This,
Coleridge said, was barricadoing the road to truth; it
was setting up a turnpike-gate at every step we took.   I
forget a great number of things, many more than I
remember; but the day passed off pleasantly, and the
next morning Mr. Coleridge was to return to Shrewsbury.
When I came down to breakfast, I found that he had just
received a letter from his friend, T. Wedgwood, making
him an offer of 150*l*. a-year if he chose to waive his
present pursuit, and devote himself entirely to the study
of poetry and philosophy. Coleridge seemed to make up
his mind to close with this proposal in the act of tying
on one of his shoes. It threw an additional damp on his
departure. It took the wayward enthusiast quite from us
to cast him into Deva's winding vales, or by the shores
of old romance. Instead of living at ten miles' distance,
of being the pastor of a Dissenting congregation at
Shrewsbury, he was henceforth to inhabit the Hill of
Parnassus, to be a Shepherd on the Delectable Mountains.
Alas! I knew not the way thither, and felt very little
gratitude for Mr. Wedgwood's bounty. I was presently
relieved from this dilemma; for Mr. Coleridge, asking
for a pen and ink, and going to a table to write something
on a bit of card, advanced towards me with undulating
step, and giving me the precious document, said that
that was his address, *Mr. Coleridge, Nether-Stowey,
Somersetshire*; and that he should be glad to see me there
in a few weeks' time, and, if I chose, would come half-
way to meet me. I was not less surprised than the shepherd-

boy (this simile is to be found in *Cassandra*), when he sees a thunder-bolt fall close at his feet. I stammered out my acknowledgments and acceptance of this offer (I thought Mr. Wedgwood's annuity a trifle to it) as well as I could; and this mighty business being settled, the poet-preacher took leave, and I accompanied him six miles on the road. It was a fine morning in the middle of winter, and he talked the whole way. The scholar in Chaucer is described as going

—" Sounding on his way."

So Coleridge went on his. In digressing, in dilating, in passing from subject to subject, he appeared to me to float in air, to slide on ice. He told me in confidence (going along) that he should have preached two sermons before he accepted the situation at Shrewsbury, one on Infant Baptism, the other on the Lord's Supper, shewing that he could not administer either, which would have effectually disqualified him for the object in view. I observed that he continually crossed me on the way by shifting from one side of the foot-path to the other. This struck me as an odd movement; but I did not at that time connect it with any instability of purpose or involuntary change of principle, as I have done since. He seemed unable to keep on in a straight line. He spoke slightingly of Hume (whose *Essay on Miracles* he said was stolen from an objection started in one of South's sermons— *Credat Judæus Apella!*). I was not very much pleased at this account of Hume, for I had just been reading, with infinite relish, that completest of all metaphysical *choke-pears*, his *Treatise on Human Nature*, to which the *Essays*, in point of scholastic subtility and close reasoning, are mere elegant trifling, light summer reading. Coleridge even denied the excellence of Hume's general style, which I think betrayed a want of taste or candour. He however made me amends by the manner in which he spoke of Berkeley. He dwelt particularly on his *Essay on Vision* as a masterpiece of analytical reasoning. So it undoubtedly is. He was exceedingly angry with Dr. Johnson for striking the stone with his foot, in allusion to this author's *Theory of Matter and Spirit*, and saying, "Thus I confute him, Sir." Coleridge drew a parallel (I don't know how he brought about the connexion) between Bishop Berkeley and Tom Paine. He said the one was an instance of a subtle, the other of an acute mind, than which no two things could be more distinct. The one was a shop-boy's quality, the other the characteristic of a philosopher. He considered Bishop Butler as a true philosopher, a profound and conscientious thinker, a genuine reader of nature and his own mind. He did not speak of his *Analogy*, but of his *Sermons at the Rolls' Chapel*, of which I had never heard. Coleridge somehow always contrived to prefer the *unknown* to the *known*. In this instance, he was right. The *Analogy* is a tissue of sophistry, of wire-drawn, theological special-pleading; the *Sermons* (with the preface to them) are in a fine vein of deep, matured reflection, a candid appeal to our observation of human nature, without pedantry and without bias. I told Coleridge I had written a few remarks, and was sometimes foolish enough to believe that I had made a discovery on the same subject (the *Natural Disinterestedness of the Human Mind*)—and I tried to explain my view of it to Coleridge, who listened with great willingness, but I did not succeed in making myself understood. I sat down to the task shortly afterwards for the twentieth time, got new pens and paper, determined to make clear work of it, wrote a few meagre sentences in the skeleton-style of a mathematical demonstration, stopped half-way down the second page; and, after trying in vain to pump up any words, images, notions, apprehensions, facts, or observations, from that gulph of abstraction in which I had plunged myself for four or five years preceding, gave up the attempt as labour in vain, and shed tears of helpless despondency on the blank, unfinished paper. I can write fast enough now. Am I better than I was then? Oh no! One truth discovered, one pang of regret at not being able to express it, is better than all the fluency and flippancy in the world. Would that I could go back to what I then was! Why can we not revive past times as we can revisit old places? If I had the quaint Muse of Sir Philip Sidney to assist me, I would write a *Sonnet to the Road between Wem and Shrewsbury*, and immortalise every step of it by some fond enigmatical conceit. I would swear that the very milestones had ears, and that Harmer-hill stooped with all its pines, to listen to a poet, as he passed! I remember but one other topic of discourse in this walk. He mentioned Paley, praised the naturalness and clearness of his style, but condemned his sentiments, thought him a mere time-serving casuist, and said that " the fact of his work on Moral and Political Philosophy being made a text-book in our Universities was a disgrace to the national character." We parted at the six-mile stone; and I returned homeward, pensive, but much pleased. I had met with unexpected notice from a person whom I believed to have been prejudiced against me. " Kind and affable to me had been his condescension, and should be honoured ever with suitable regard." He was the first poet I had known, and he certainly answered to that inspired name. I had heard a great deal of his powers of conversation, and was not disappointed. In fact, I never met with anything at all like them, either before or since. I could easily credit the accounts which were circulated of his holding forth to a large party of ladies and gentlemen, an evening or two before, on the Berkeleian Theory, when he made the whole material universe look like a transparency of fine words; and another story (which I believe he has somewhere told himself) of his being asked

to a party at Birmingham, of his smoking tobacco and
going to sleep after dinner on a sofa, where the company
found him, to their no small surprise, which was increased
to wonder when he started up of a sudden, and rubbing
his eyes, looked about him, and launched into a three
hours' description of the third heaven, of which he had
had a dream, very different from Mr. Southey's *Vision
of Judgment*, and also from that other *Vision of Judgment*,
which Mr. Murray, the Secretary of the Bridge-street
Junto, took into his especial keeping!

On my way back, I had a sound in my ears—it was the
voice of Fancy; I had a light before me—it was the face
of Poetry. The one still lingers there, the other has not
quitted my side! Coleridge, in truth, met me half-way
on the ground of philosophy, or I should not have been
won over to his imaginative creed. I had an uneasy,
pleasurable sensation all the time, till I was to visit him.
During those months the chill breath of winter gave me
a welcoming; the vernal air was balm and inspiration
to me. The golden sun-sets, the silver star of evening,
lighted me on my way to new hopes and prospects. *I was
to visit Coleridge in the Spring*. This circumstance was
never absent from my thoughts, and mingled with all
my feelings. I wrote to him at the time proposed, and
received an answer postponing my intended visit for a
week or two, but very cordially urging me to complete
my promise then. This delay did not damp, but rather
increased my ardour. In the meantime, I went to Llangollen Vale, by way of initiating myself in the mysteries
of natural scenery; and I must say I was enchanted with
it. I had been reading Coleridge's description of England
in his fine *Ode on the Departing Year*, and I applied it,
con amore, to the objects before me. That valley was to
me (in a manner) the cradle of a new existence: in the
river that winds through it, my spirit was baptised in the
waters of Helicon!

I returned home, and soon after set out on my journey with unworn heart, and untried feet. My way lay through Worcester and Gloucester, and by Upton, where I thought of Tom Jones and the adventure of the muff. I remember getting completely wet through one day, and stopping at an inn (I think it was at Tewkesbury) where I sat up all night to read *Paul and Virginia*. Sweet were the showers in early youth that drenched my body, and sweet the drops of pity that fell upon the books I read! I recollect a remark of Coleridge's upon this very book— that nothing could shew the gross indelicacy of French manners and the entire corruption of their imagination more strongly than the behaviour of the heroine in the last fatal scene, who turns away from a person on board the sinking vessel, that offers to save her life, because he has thrown off his clothes to assist him in swimming. Was this a time to think of such a circumstance? I once hinted to Wordsworth, as we were sailing in his boat on Grasmere lake, that I thought he had borrowed the idea of his *Poems on the Naming of Places* from the local inscriptions of the same kind in *Paul and Virginia*. He did not own the obligation, and stated some distinction without a difference, in defence of his claim to originality. Any the slightest variation would be sufficient for this purpose in his mind; for whatever *he* added or altered would inevitably be worth all that any one else had done, and contain the marrow of the sentiment.—I was still two days before the time fixed for my arrival, for I had taken care to set out early enough. I stopped these two days at Bridgewater; and when I was tired of sauntering on the banks of its muddy river, returned to the inn and read *Camilla*. So have I loitered my life away, reading books, looking at pictures, going to plays, hearing, thinking, writing on what pleased me best. I have wanted only one thing to make me happy; but wanting that, have wanted everything!

I arrived, and was well received. The country about
Nether Stowey is beautiful, green and hilly, and near the
sea-shore. I saw it but the other day, after an interval
of twenty years, from a hill near Taunton. How was the
map of my life spread out before me, as the map of the
country lay at my feet! In the afternoon, Coleridge took
me over to All-Foxden, a romantic old family mansion
of the St. Aubins, where Wordsworth lived. It was then
in the possession of a friend of the poet's, who gave him
the free use of it. Somehow, that period (the time just
after the French Revolution) was not a time when *nothing
was given for nothing*. The mind opened and a softness
might be perceived coming over the heart of individuals,
beneath " the scales that fence " our self-interest. Wordsworth himself was from home, but his sister kept house,
and set before us a frugal repast; and we had free access
to her brother's poems, the *Lyrical Ballads*, which were
still in manuscript, or in the form of *Sybilline Leaves*.
I dipped into a few of these with great satisfaction, and
with the faith of a novice. I slept that night in an old
room with blue hangings, and covered with the round-
faced family-portraits of the age of George I and II, and
from the wooded declivity of the adjoining park that
overlooked my window, at the dawn of day, could

———" hear the loud stag speak."

In the outset of life (and particularly at this time I felt
it so) our imagination has a body to it. We are in a state
between sleeping and waking, and have indistinct but
glorious glimpses of strange shapes, and there is always
something to come better than what we see. As in our
dreams the fulness of the blood gives warmth and reality
to the coinage of the brain, so in youth our ideas are
clothed, and fed, and pampered with our good spirits;
we breathe thick with thoughtless happiness, the weight
of future years presses on the strong pulses of the heart,

and we repose with undisturbed faith in truth and good. As we advance, we exhaust our fund of enjoyment and of hope. We are no longer wrapped in *lamb's-wool*, lulled in Elysium. As we taste the pleasures of life, their spirit evaporates; the sense palls; and nothing is left but the phantoms, the lifeless shadows of what *has been!*

That morning, as soon as breakfast was over, we strolled out into the park, and seating ourselves on the trunk of an old ash-tree that stretched along the ground, Coleridge read aloud with a sonorous and musical voice, the ballad of *Betty Foy*. I was not critically or sceptically inclined. I saw touches of truth and nature, and took the rest for granted. But in the *Thorn*, the *Mad Mother*, and the *Complaint of a Poor Indian Woman*, I felt that deeper power and pathos which have been since acknowledged,

> " In spite of pride, in erring reason's spite,"

as the characteristics of this author; and the sense of a new style and a new spirit in poetry came over me. It had to me something of the effect that arises from the turning up of the fresh soil, or of the first welcome breath of Spring:

> " While yet the trembling year is unconfirmed."

Coleridge and myself walked back to Stowey that evening, and his voice sounded high

> " Of Providence, foreknowledge, will, and fate,
> Fix'd fate, free-will, foreknowledge absolute,"

as we passed through echoing grove, by fairy stream or waterfall, gleaming in the summer moonlight! He lamented that Wordsworth was not prone enough to believe in the traditional superstitions of the place, and that there was a something corporeal, a *matter-of-fact-ness*, a clinging to the palpable, or often to the petty, in his poetry, in consequence. His genius was not a spirit that

descended to him through the air; it sprung out of the
ground like a flower, or unfolded itself from a green
spray, on which the goldfinch sang. He said, however
(if I remember right), that this objection must be confined
to his descriptive pieces, that his philosophic poetry had
a grand and comprehensive spirit in it, so that his soul
seemed to inhabit the universe like a palace, and to
discover truth by intuition, rather than by deduction.
The next day Wordsworth arrived from Bristol at
Coleridge's cottage. I think I see him now. He answered
in some degree to his friend's description of him, but was
more gaunt and Don Quixote-like. He was quaintly
dressed (according to the *costume* of that unconstrained
period) in a brown fustian jacket and striped pantaloons.
There was something of a roll, a lounge in his gait, not
unlike his own *Peter Bell*. There was a severe, worn
pressure of thought about his temples, a fire in his eye
(as if he saw something in objects more than the outward
appearance), an intense, high, narrow forehead, a Roman
nose, cheeks furrowed by strong purpose and feeling,
and a convulsive inclination to laughter about the mouth,
a good deal at variance with the solemn, stately expression
of the rest of his face. Chantrey's bust wants the marking
traits; but he was teazed into making it regular and
heavy: Haydon's head of him, introduced into the
Entrance of Christ into Jerusalem, is the most like his
drooping weight of thought and expression. He sat down
and talked very naturally and freely, with a mixture of
clear, gushing accents in his voice, a deep guttural
intonation, and a strong tincture of the northern *burr*,
like the crust on wine. He instantly began to make havoc
of the half of a Cheshire cheese on the table, and said,
triumphantly, that " his marriage with experience had
not been so productive as Mr. Southey's in teaching him
a knowledge of the good things of this life." He had
been to see the *Castle Spectre* by Monk Lewis, while at

Bristol, and described it very well. He said " it fitted the taste of the audience like a glove." This *ad captandum* merit was however by no means a recommendation of it, according to the severe principles of the new school, which reject rather than court popular effect. Wordsworth, looking out of the low, latticed window, said, " How beautifully the sun sets on that yellow bank! " I thought within myself, " With what eyes these poets see nature! " and ever after, when I saw the sun-set stream upon the objects facing it, conceived I had made a discovery, or thanked Mr. Wordsworth for having made one for me! We went over to All-Foxden again the day following, and Wordsworth read us the story of *Peter Bell* in the open air; and the comment made upon it by his face and voice was very different from that of some later critics! Whatever might be thought of the poem, " his face was as a book where men might read strange matters," and he announced the fate of his hero in prophetic tones. There is a *chaunt* in the recitation both of Coleridge and Wordsworth, which acts as a spell upon the hearer, and disarms the judgment. Perhaps they have deceived themselves by making habitual use of this ambiguous accompaniment. Coleridge's manner is more full, animated, and varied; Wordsworth's more equable, sustained, and internal. The one might be termed more *dramatic*, the other more *lyrical*. Coleridge has told me that he himself liked to compose in walking over uneven ground, or breaking through the straggling branches of a copse-wood; whereas Wordsworth always wrote (if he could) walking up and down a straight gravel-walk, or in some spot where the continuity of his verse met with no collateral interruption. Returning that same evening, I got into a metaphysical argument with Wordsworth, while Coleridge was explaining the different notes of the nightingale to his sister, in which we neither of us succeeded in making ourselves perfectly clear and intelligible. Thus I passed three weeks at Nether Stowey and in the neighbourhood, generally devoting the afternoons to a delightful chat in an arbour made of bark by the poet's friend Tom Poole, sitting under two fine elm-trees, and listening to the bees humming round us, while we quaffed our *flip*. It was agreed, among other things, that we should make a jaunt down the Bristol Channel, as far as Linton. We set off together on foot, Coleridge, John Chester, and I. This Chester was a native of Nether Stowey, one of those who were attracted to Coleridge's discourse as flies are to honey, or bees in swarming-time to the sound of a brass pan. He "followed in the chace like a dog who hunts, not like one that made up the cry." He had on a brown cloth coat, boots, and corduroy breeches, was low in stature, bow-legged, had a drag in his walk like a drover, which he assisted by a hazel switch, and kept on a sort of trot by the side of Coleridge, like a running footman by a state coach, that he might not lose a syllable or sound that fell from Coleridge's lips. He told me his private opinion, that Coleridge was a wonderful man. He scarcely opened his lips, much less offered an opinion the whole way: yet of the three, had I to choose during that journey, I would be John Chester. He afterwards followed Coleridge into Germany, where the Kantean philosophers were puzzled how to bring him under any of their categories. When he sat down at table with his idol, John's felicity was complete; Sir Walter Scott's, or Mr. Blackwood's, when they sat down at the same table with the King, was not more so. We passed Dunster on our right, a small town between the brow of a hill and the sea. I remember eyeing it wistfully as it lay below us: contrasted with the woody scene around, it looked as clear, as pure, as *embrowned* and ideal as any landscape I have seen since, of Gaspar Poussin's or Domeni-chino's. We had a long day's march—(our feet kept time to the echoes of Coleridge's tongue)—through Minehead and by the Blue Anchor, and on to Linton, which we did not reach till near midnight, and where we had some difficulty in making a lodgment. We, however, knocked the people of the house up at last, and we were repaid for our apprehensions and fatigue by some excellent rashers of fried bacon and eggs. The view in coming along had been splendid. We walked for miles and miles on dark brown heaths overlooking the Channel, with the Welsh hills beyond, and at times descended into little sheltered valleys close by the sea-side, with a smuggler's face scowling by us, and then had to ascend conical hills with a path winding up through a coppice to a barren top, like a monk's shaven crown, from one of which I pointed out to Coleridge's notice the bare masts of a vessel on the very edge of the horizon, and within the red-orbed disk of the setting sun, 'like his own spectre-ship in the *Ancient Mariner*. At Linton the character of the sea-coast becomes more marked and rugged. There is a place called the *Valley of Rocks* (I suspect this was only the poetical name for it), bedded among precipices overhanging the sea, with rocky caverns beneath, into which the waves dash, and where the sea-gull for ever wheels its screaming flight. On the tops of these are huge stones thrown transverse, as if an earthquake had tossed them there, and behind these is a fretwork of perpendicular rocks, something like the *Giant's Causeway*. A thunderstorm came on while we were at the inn, and Coleridge was running out bare-headed to enjoy the commotion of the elements in the *Valley of Rocks*, but as if in spite, the clouds only muttered a few angry sounds, and let fall a few refreshing drops. Coleridge told me that he and Wordsworth were to have made this place the scene of a prose-tale, which was to have been in the manner of, but far superior to, the *Death of Abel*, but they had relinquished the design. In the morning of the second day, we breakfasted luxuriously in an old-fashioned parlour on tea, toast, eggs, and honey, in the very sight of the bee-hives from which it had been taken, and a garden full of thyme and wild flowers that had produced it. On this occasion Coleridge spoke of Virgil's *Georgics*, but not well. I do not think he had much feeling for the classical or elegant. It was in this room that we found a little worn-out copy of the *Seasons*, lying in a window-seat, on which Coleridge exclaimed, " *That* is true fame! " He said Thomson was a great poet, rather than a good one; his style was as meretricious as his thoughts were natural. He spoke of Cowper as the best modern poet. He said the *Lyrical Ballads* were an experiment about to be tried by him and Wordsworth, to see how far the public taste would endure poetry written in a more natural and simple style than had hitherto been attempted; totally discarding the artifices of poetical diction, and making use only of such words as had probably been common in the most ordinary language since the days of Henry II. Some comparison was introduced between Shakspeare and Milton. He said " he hardly knew which to prefer. Shakspeare appeared to him a mere stripling in the art; he was as tall and as strong, with infinitely more activity than Milton, but he never appeared to have come to man's estate; or if he had, he would not have been a man, but a monster." He spoke with contempt of Gray, and with intolerance of Pope. He did not like the versification of the latter. He observed that " the ears of these couplet-writers might be charged with having short memories, that could not retain the harmony of whole passages." He thought little of Junius as a writer; he had a dislike of Dr. Johnson; and a much higher opinion of Burke as an orator and politician, than of Fox or Pitt. He, however, thought him very inferior in richness of style and imagery to some of our elder prose-writers, particularly Jeremy Taylor. He liked Richardson, but not Fielding;

nor could I get him to enter into the merits of *Caleb Williams*.[1] In short, he was profound and discriminating with respect to those authors whom he liked, and where he gave his judgment fair play; capricious, perverse, and prejudiced in his antipathies and distastes. We loitered on the " ribbed sea-sands," in such talk as this a whole morning, and, I recollect, met with a curious sea-weed, of which John Chester told us the country name! A fisherman gave Coleridge an account of a boy that had been drowned the day before, and that they had tried to save him at the risk of their own lives. He said " he did not know how it was that they ventured, but, Sir, we have a *nature* towards one another." This expression, Coleridge remarked to me, was a fine illustration of that theory of disinterestedness which I (in common with Butler) had adopted. I broached to him an argument of mine to prove that *likeness* was not mere association of ideas. I said that the mark in the sand put one in mind of a man's foot, not because it was part of a former impression of a man's foot (for it was quite new), but because it was like the shape of a man's foot. He assented to the justness of this distinction (which I have explained at length elsewhere, for the benefit of the curious) and John Chester listened; not from any interest in the subject, but because he was astonished that I should be able to suggest anything to Coleridge that he did not already know. We returned on the third morning, and Coleridge remarked the silent cottage-smoke curling up the valleys where, a few evenings before, we had seen the lights gleaming through the dark.

[1] He had no idea of pictures, of Claude or Raphael, and at this time I had as little as he. He sometimes gives a striking account at present of the Cartoons at Pisa by Buffamalco and others ; of one in particular, where Death is seen in the air brandishing his scythe, and the great and mighty of the earth shudder at his approach, while the beggars and the wretched kneel to him as their deliverer. He would, of course, understand so broad and fine a moral as this at any time.

s

In a day or two after we arrived at Stowey, we set out,
I on my return home, and he for Germany. It was a
Sunday morning, and he was to preach that day for
Dr. Toulmin of Taunton. I asked him if he had prepared
anything for the occasion? He said he had not even
thought of the text, but should as soon as we parted.
I did not go to hear him—this was a fault—but we met
in the evening at Bridgewater. The next day we had a
long day's walk to Bristol, and sat down, I recollect, by
a well-side on the road, to cool ourselves and satisfy
our thirst, when Coleridge repeated to me some descriptive lines of his tragedy of *Remorse;* which I must say
became his mouth and that occasion better than they,
some years after, did Mr. Elliston's and the Drury-lane
boards—

> " Oh, memory ! shield me from the world's poor
> strife,
> And give those scenes thine everlasting life."

I saw no more of him for a year or two, during which
period he had been wandering in the Hartz Forest, in
Germany; and his return was cometary, meteorous,
unlike his setting out. It was not till some time after
that I knew his friends Lamb and Southey. The last
always appears to me (as I first saw him) with a common-
place book under his arm, and the first with a *bon-mot*
in his mouth. It was at Godwin's that I met him with
Holcroft and Coleridge, where they were disputing
fiercely which was the best—*Man as he was, or man as
he is to be.* " Give me," says Lamb, " man as he is *not*
to be." This saying was the beginning of a friendship
between us, which I believe still continues.—Enough of
this for the present.

> " But there is matter for another rhyme,
> And I to this may add a second tale."

OF PERSONS ONE WOULD
WISH TO HAVE SEEN

(NEW MONTHLY MAGAZINE, JAN., 1826)

"Come like shadows—so depart."

L A M B[1] it was, I think, who suggested this subject, as
well as the defence of Guy Faux, which I urged him to
execute. As, however, he would undertake neither, I
suppose I must do both, a task for which he would have
been much fitter, no less from the temerity than the
felicity of his pen—

"Never so sure our rapture to create
    As when it touched the brink of all we hate."

Compared with him, I shall, I fear, make but a common-
place piece of business of it; but I should be loth the idea
was entirely lost, and besides I may avail myself of some
hints of his in the progress of it. I am sometimes, I
suspect, a better reporter of the ideas of other people
than expounder of my own. I pursue the one too far into
paradox or mysticism; the others I am not bound to follow
farther than I like, or than seems fair and reasonable.

On the question being started, A[yrton] said, "I suppose
the two first persons you would choose to see would be
the two greatest names in English literature, Sir Isaac
Newton and Mr. Locke?" In this A[yrton], as usual,
reckoned without his host. Every one burst out a laughing
at the expression of Lamb's face, in which impatience
was restrained by courtesy. "Yes, the greatest names,"
he stammered out hastily, "but they were not persons—
not persons."—"Not persons?" said A[yrton], looking
wise and foolish at the same time, afraid his triumph
might be premature. "That is," rejoined Lamb, "not
characters, you know. By Mr. Locke and Sir Isaac

---

[1] Lamb's name is given as *B.* throughout in the original text.
The other names are supplied by W. H., jun.

Newton, you mean the *Essay on the Human Understanding*, and the *Principia*, which we have to this day. Beyond their contents there is nothing personally interesting in the men. But what we want to see any one *bodily* for, is when there is something peculiar, striking in the individuals, more than we can learn from their writings, and yet are curious to know. I dare say Locke and Newton were very like Kneller's portraits of them. But who could paint Shakspeare?"—"Ay," retorted A[yrton], "there it is; then I suppose you would prefer seeing him and Milton instead?"—"No," said Lamb, "neither. I have seen so much of Shakspeare on the stage and on book-stalls, in frontispieces and on mantel-pieces, that I am quite tired of the everlasting repetition: and as to Milton's face, the impressions that have come down to us of it I do not like; it is too starched and puritanical; and I should be afraid of losing some of the manna of his poetry in the leaven of his countenance and the precisian's band and gown."—"I shall guess no more," said A[yrton]. "Who is it, then, you would like to see ' in his habit as he lived,' if you had your choice of the whole range of English literature?" Lamb then named Sir Thomas Browne and Fulke Greville, the friend of Sir Philip Sidney, as the two worthies whom he should feel the greatest pleasure to encounter on the floor of his apartment in their nightgown and slippers, and to exchange friendly greeting with them. At this A[yrton] laughed outright, and conceived Lamb was jesting with him; but as no one followed his example, he thought there might be something in it, and waited for an explanation in a state of whimsical suspense. Lamb then (as well as I can remember a conversation that passed twenty years ago—how time slips!) went on as follows. "The reason why I pitch upon these two authors is, that their writings are riddles, and they themselves the most mysterious of personages. They resemble the soothsayers

of old, who dealt in dark hints and doubtful oracles; and
I should like to ask them the meaning of what no mortal
but themselves, I should suppose, can fathom. There
is Dr. Johnson: I have no curiosity, no strange uncertainty
about him; he and Boswell together have pretty well let
me into the secret of what passed through his mind. He
and other writers like him are sufficiently explicit: my
friends whose repose I should be tempted to disturb
(were it in my power), are implicit, inextricable, inscrutable.

" When I look at that obscure but gorgeous prose-
composition, the *Urn-burial*, I seem to myself to look
into a deep abyss, at the bottom of which are hid pearls
and rich treasure; or it is like a stately labyrinth of doubt
and withering speculation, and I would invoke the spirit
of the author to lead me through it. Besides, who would
not be curious to see the lineaments of a man who, having
himself been twice married, wished that mankind were
propagated like trees! As to Fulke Greville, he is like
nothing but one of his own ' Prologues spoken by the
ghost of an old king of Ormus,' a truly formidable and
inviting personage: his style is apocalyptical, cabalistical,
a knot worthy of such an apparition to untie; and for the
unravelling a passage or two, I would stand the brunt of
an encounter with so portentous a commentator! "—
" I am afraid, in that case," said A[yrton], " that if the
mystery were once cleared up, the merit might be lost ";
and turning to me, whispered a friendly apprehension,
that while Lamb continued to admire these old crabbed
authors, he would never become a popular writer.
Dr. Donne was mentioned as a writer of the same period,
with a very interesting countenance, whose history was
singular, and whose meaning was often quite as *uncome-
atable*, without a personal citation from the dead, as that
of any of his contemporaries. The volume was produced;
and while some one was expatiating on the exquisite

simplicity and beauty of the portrait prefixed to the old
edition, A[yrton] got hold of the poetry, and exclaiming
" What have we here?" read the following:

> " Here lies a shee Sunne and a hee Moone here,
> She gives the best light to his Spheare,
> Or each is both, and all, and so
> They unto one another nothing owe."

There was no resisting this, till Lamb, seizing the
volume, turned to the beautiful *Lines to his Mistress*, dis-
suading her from accompanying him abroad, and read
them with suffused features and a faltering tongue:

> " By our first strange and fatall interview,
> By all desires which thereof did ensue,
> By our long starving hopes, by that remorse
> Which my words' masculine perswasive force
> Begot in thee, and by the memory
> Of hurts, which spies and rivals threatned me,
> I calmly beg. But by thy father's wrath,
> By all paines which want and divorcement hath,
> I conjure thee; and all the oathes which I
> And thou have sworne to seale joynt constancy
> Here I unsweare, and oversweare them thus—
> Thou shalt not love by wayes so dangerous.
> Temper, O faire love ! love's impetuous rage,
> Be my true Mistris still, not my faign'd Page;
> I'll goe, and, by thy kinde leave, leave behinde
> Thee, onely worthy to nurse in my minde,
> Thirst to come backe; O, if thou die before,
> My soule from other lands to thee shall soare.
> Thy (else Almighty) beautie cannot move
> Rage from the Seas, nor thy love teach them love.
> Nor tame wild Boreas' harshnesse; thou hast reade
> How roughly hee in pieces shivered
> Fair Orithea, whom he swore he lov'd.
> Fall ill or good, 'tis madnesse to have prov'd
> Dangers unurg'd : Feed on this flattery,
> That absent Lovers one in th' other be.
> Dissemble nothing, not a boy; nor change
> Thy bodie's habite, nor minde's; be not strange

To thy selfe onely. All will spie in thy face
A blushing, womanly, discovering grace.
Richly cloath'd Apes are call'd Apes, and as soone
Eclips'd as bright, we call the Moone the Moon.
Men of France, changeable Camelions,
Spittles of diseases, shops of fashions,
Love's fuellers, and the rightest company
Of Players, which upon the world's stage be,
Will quickly know thee . . .
. . . O stay here ! for, for thee
England is onely a worthy Gallerie,
To walke in expectation ; till from thence
Our greatest King call thee to his presence.
When I am gone, dreame me some happinesse,
Nor let thy lookes our long hid love confesse,
Nor praise, nor dispraise me ; nor blesse, nor curse
Openly love's force, nor in bed fright thy Nurse
With midnight's startings, crying out, oh, oh,
Nurse, o, my love is slaine, I saw him goe
O'er the white Alpes alone ; I saw him, I,
Assail'd, fight, taken, stabb'd, bleed, fall, and die.
Augure me better chance, except dread Jove
Thinke it enough for me to'have had thy love."

Some one then inquired of Lamb if we could not see
from the window the Temple walk in which Chaucer
used to take his exercise ; and on his name being put to
the vote, I was pleased to find that there was a general
sensation in his favour in all but A[yrton], who said something about the ruggedness of the metre, and even objected to the quaintness of the orthography. I was vexed
at this superficial gloss, pertinaciously reducing everything to its own trite level, and asked " if he did not think
it would be worth while to scan the eye that had first
greeted the Muse in that dim twilight and early dawn of
English literature; to see the head round which the
visions of fancy must have played like gleams of inspiration or a sudden glory; to watch those lips that
' lisped in numbers, for the numbers came '—as by a
miracle, or as if the dumb should speak? Nor was it

alone that he had been the first to tune his native tongue
(however imperfectly to modern ears); but he was himself a noble, manly character, standing before his age and
striving to advance it; a pleasant humourist withal, who
has not only handed down to us the living manners of his
time, but had, no doubt, store of curious and quaint
devices, and would make as hearty a companion as Mine
Host of the Tabard. His interview with Petrarch is
fraught with interest. Yet I would rather have seen
Chaucer in company with the author of the *Decameron*,
and have heard them exchange their best stories together
—the *Squire's Tale* against the *Story of the Falcon*, the
Wife of Bath's Prologue against the *Adventures of Friar
Albert*. How fine to see the high mysterious brow which
learning then wore, relieved by the gay, familiar tone of
men of the world, and by the courtesies of genius! Surely,
the thoughts and feelings which passed through the
minds of these great revivers of learning, these Cadmuses
who sowed the teeth of letters, must have stamped an
expression on their features as different from the moderns
as their books, and well worth the perusal. Dante," I
continued, " is as interesting a person as his own Ugolino,
one whose lineaments curiosity would as eagerly devour
in order to penetrate his spirit, and the only one of the
Italian poets I should care much to see. There is a fine
portrait of Ariosto by no less a hand than Titian's; light,
Moorish, spirited, but not answering our idea. The same
artist's large colossal profile of Peter Aretine is the only
likeness of the kind that has the effect of conversing with
' the mighty dead'; and this is truly spectral, ghastly,
necromantic." Lamb put it to me if I should like to see
Spenser as well as Chaucer; and I answered, without
hesitation, " No; for that his beauties were ideal, visionary, not palpable or personal, and therefore connected
with less curiosity about the man. His poetry was the
essence of romance, a very halo round the bright orb of

fancy; and the bringing in the individual might dissolve the charm. No tones of voice could come up to the mellifluous cadence of his verse; no form but of a winged angel could vie with the airy shapes he has described. He was (to my apprehension) rather a ' creature of the element, that lived in the rainbow and played in the plighted clouds,' than an ordinary mortal. Or if he did appear, I should wish it to be as a mere vision, like one of his own pageants, and that he should pass by unquestioned like a dream or sound—

> ——' *That* was Arion crown'd :
> So went he playing on the wat'ry plain.' "

Captain [Burney] muttered something about Columbus, and M[artin Burney] hinted at the Wandering Jew; but the last was set aside as spurious, and the first made over to the New World.

" I should like," said [Mrs. Reynolds], " to have seen Pope talk with Patty Blount; and I *have* seen Goldsmith." Every one turned round to look at [Mrs. Reynolds], as if by so doing they could get a sight at Goldsmith.

" Where," asked a harsh, croaking voice, " was Dr. Johnson in the years 1745–6? He did not write anything that we know of, nor is there any account of him in Boswell during those two years. Was he in Scotland with the Pretender? He seems to have passed through the scenes in the Highlands in company with Boswell, many years after, ' with lack-lustre eye,' yet as if they were familiar to him, or associated in his mind with interests that he durst not explain. If so, it would be an additional reason for my liking him; and I would give something to have seen him seated in the tent with the youthful Majesty of Britain, and penning the Proclamation to all true subjects and adherents of the legitimate Government."

" I thought," said A[yrton], turning short round upon Lamb, " that you of the Lake School did not like Pope? "

s *

—" Not like Pope! My dear sir, you must be under a mistake—I can read him over and over for ever! "— " Why, certainly, the *Essay on Man* must be allowed to be a masterpiece."—" It may be so, but I seldom look into it."—" Oh! then it's his Satires you admire? "— " No, not his Satires, but his friendly Epistles and his compliments."—" Compliments! I did not know he ever made any."—" The finest," said Lamb, " that were ever paid by the wit of man. Each of them is worth an estate for life—nay, is an immortality. There is that superb one to Lord Cornbury:

> ' Despise low joys, low gains ;
>   Disdain whatever Cornbury disdains ;
>   Be virtuous, and be happy for your pains.'

Was there ever more artful insinuation of idolatrous praise? And then that noble apotheosis of his friend Lord Mansfield (however little deserved), when, speaking of the House of Lords, he adds:

> ' Conspicuous scene ! another yet is nigh,
>   (More silent far) where kings and poets lie ;
>   Where Murray (long enough his country's pride)
>   Shall be no more than Tully or than Hyde.'

And with what a fine turn of indignant flattery he addresses Lord Bolingbroke:

> ' Why rail they then, if but one wreath of mine,
>   Oh ! all accomplish'd St. John, deck thy shrine ? '

Or turn," continued Lamb, with a slight hectic on his cheek and his eye glistening, " to his list of early friends:

> ' But why then publish ? Granville the polite,
>   And knowing Walsh, would tell me I could write ;
>   Well-natured Garth inflamed with early praise,
>   And Congreve loved, and Swift endured my lays :
>   The courtly Talbot, Somers, Sheffield read,
>   Ev'n mitred Rochester would nod the head ;

And St. John's self (great Dryden's friend before)
Received with open arms one poet more.
Happy my studies, if by these approved !
Happier their author, if by these beloved !
From these the world will judge of men and books,
Not from the Burnets, Oldmixons, and Cooks.' "

Here his voice totally failed him, and throwing down the
book, he said, " Do you think I would not wish to have
been friends with such a man as this? "

" What say you to Dryden? "—" He rather made a
show of himself, and courted popularity in that lowest
temple of fame, a coffee-shop, so as in some measure to
vulgarize one's idea of him. Pope, on the contrary,
reached the very *beau ideal* of what a poet's life should
be; and his fame while living seemed to be an emanation
from that which was to circle his name after death. He
was so far enviable (and one would feel proud to have
witnessed the rare spectacle in him) that he was almost
the only poet and man of genius who met with his reward
on this side of the tomb, who realized in friends, fortune,
the esteem of the world, the most sanguine hopes of a
youthful ambition, and who found that sort of patronage
from the great during his lifetime which they would be
thought anxious to bestow upon him after his death.
Read Gay's verses to him on his supposed return from
Greece, after his translation of Homer was finished, and
say if you would not gladly join the bright procession
that welcomed him home, or see it once more land at
Whitehall stairs."—" Still," said [Mrs. Reynolds], " I
would rather have seen him talking with Patty Blount,
or riding by in a coronet-coach with Lady Mary Wortley
Montagu! "

E[rasmus Phillips], who was deep in a game of piquet
at the other end of the room, whispered to M[artin Burney]
to ask if Junius would not be a fit person to invoke from
the dead. " Yes," said Lamb, " provided he would agree
to lay aside his mask."

We were now at a stand for a short time, when Fielding was mentioned as a candidate; only one, however, seconded the proposition. " Richardson? "—" By all means, but only to look at him through the glass-door of his back-shop, hard at work upon one of his novels (the most extraordinary contrast that ever was presented between an author and his works), but not to let him come behind his counter, lest he should want you to turn customer, nor to go upstairs with him, lest he should offer to read the first manuscript of Sir Charles Grandison, which was originally written in eight-and-twenty volumes octavo, or get out the letters of his female correspondents, to prove that Joseph Andrews was low."

There was but one statesman in the whole of English history that anyone expressed the least desire to see— Oliver Cromwell, with his fine, frank, rough, pimply face; and wily policy; and one enthusiast, John Bunyan, the immortal author of the *Pilgrim's Progress*. It seemed that if he came into the room, dreams would follow him, and that each person would nod under his golden cloud, "nigh-sphered in heaven," a canopy as strange and stately as any in Homer.

Of all persons near our own time, Garrick's name was received with the greatest enthusiasm, who was proposed by [Barron] F[ield]. He presently superseded both Hogarth and Handel, who had been talked of, but then it was on condition that he should act in tragedy and comedy, in the play and the farce, *Lear* and *Wildair* and *Abel Drugger*. What a *sight for sore eyes* that would be! Who would not part with a year's income at least, almost with a year of his natural life, to be present at it? Besides, as he could not act alone, and recitations are unsatisfactory things, what a troop he must bring with him—the silver-tongued Barry, and Quin, and Shuter and Weston, and Mrs. Clive and Mrs. Pritchard, of whom I have heard my father speak as so great a favourite when he was young. This would indeed be a revival of the dead, the restoring of art; and so much the more desirable, as such is the lurking scepticism mingled with our overstrained admiration of past excellence, that though we have the speeches of Burke, the portraits of Reynolds, the writings of Goldsmith, and the conversation of Johnson, to shew what people could do at that period, and to confirm the universal testimony to the merits of Garrick; yet, as it was before our time, we have our misgivings, as if he was probably, after all, little better than a Bartlemy-fair actor, dressed out to play Macbeth in a scarlet coat and laced cocked-hat. For one, I should like to have seen and heard with my own eyes and ears. Certainly, by all accounts, if any one was ever moved by the true histrionic *æstus*, it was Garrick. When he followed the Ghost in *Hamlet*, he did not drop the sword, as most actors do, behind the scenes, but kept the point raised the whole way round, so fully was he possessed with the idea, or so anxious not to lose sight of his part for a moment. Once at a splendid dinner-party at Lord ——'s, they suddenly missed Garrick, and could not imagine what was become of him, till they were drawn to the window by the convulsive screams and peals of laughter of a young negro boy, who was rolling on the ground in an ecstasy of delight to see Garrick mimicking a turkey-cock in the court-yard, with his coat-tail stuck out behind, and in a seeming flutter of feathered rage and pride. Of our party only two persons present had seen the British Roscius; and they seemed as willing as the rest to renew their acquaintance with their old favourite.

We were interrupted in the hey-day and mid-career of this fanciful speculation, by a grumbler in a corner, who declared it was a shame to make all this rout about a mere player and farce-writer, to the neglect and exclusion of the fine old dramatists, the contemporaries and rivals of Shakspeare. Lamb said he had anticipated this objection when he had named the author of *Mustapha* and *Alaham;*

and, out of caprice, insisted upon keeping him to represent the set, in preference to the wild, hare-brained enthusiast, Kit Marlowe; to the sexton of St. Ann's, Webster, with his melancholy yew-trees and death's-heads; to Decker, who was but a garrulous proser; to the voluminous Heywood; and even to Beaumont and Fletcher, whom we might offend by complimenting the wrong author on their joint productions. Lord Brooke, on the contrary, stood quite by himself, or, in Cowley's words, was " a vast species alone." Some one hinted at the circumstance of his being a lord, which rather startled Lamb, but he said a *ghost* would perhaps dispense with strict etiquette, on being regularly addressed by his title. Ben Jonson divided our suffrages pretty equally. Some were afraid he would begin to traduce Shakspeare, who was not present to defend himself. " If he grows disagreeable," it was whispered aloud, " there is G[odwin] can match him." At length, his romantic visit to Drummond of Hawthornden was mentioned, and turned the scale in his favour.

Lamb inquired if there was any one that was hanged that I would choose to mention? And I answered, Eugene Aram.[1] The name of the "Admirable Crichton " was suddenly started as a splendid example of *waste* talents, so different from the generality of his countrymen. This choice was mightily approved by a North-Briton present, who declared himself descended from that prodigy of learning and accomplishment, and said he had family plate in his possession as vouchers for the fact, with the initials A. C.—*Admirable Crichton!* H—— laughed, or rather roared, as heartily at this as I should think he has done for many years.

The last-named Mitre-courtier[2] then wished to know

[1] See *Newgate Calendar* for 1758.
[2] Lamb at this time occupied chambers in Mitre-court, Temple.

whether there were any metaphysicians to whom one might be tempted to apply the wizard spell? I replied, there were only six in modern times deserving the name—Hobbes, Berkeley, Butler, Hartley, Hume, Leibnitz; and perhaps Jonathan Edwards, a Massachusetts man.[1] As to the French, who talked fluently of having *created* this science, there was not a tittle in any of their writings that was not to be found literally in the authors I had mentioned. [Horne Tooke, who might have a claim to come in under the head of Grammar, was still living.] None of these names seemed to excite much interest, and I did not plead for the re-appearance of those who might be thought best fitted by the abstracted nature of their studies for the present spiritual and disembodied state, and who, even while on this living stage, were nearly divested of common flesh and blood. As A[yrton], with an uneasy, fidgety face, was about to put some question about Mr. Locke and Dugald Stewart, he was prevented by M[artin Burney], who observed, " If J—— was here, he would undoubtedly be for having up those profound and redoubted scholiasts, Thomas Aquinas and Duns Scotus." I said this might be fair enough in him who had read, or fancied he had read, the original works, but I did not see how we could have any right to call up these authors to give an account of themselves in person, till we had looked into their writings.

By this time it should seem that some rumour of our

[1] Lord Bacon is not included in this list, nor do I know where he should come in. It is not easy to make room for him and his reputation together. This great and celebrated man in some of his works recommends it to pour a bottle of claret into the ground of a morning, and to stand over it, inhaling the perfumes. So he sometimes enriched the dry and barren soil of speculation with the fine aromatic spirit of his genius. His *Essays* and his *Advancement of Learning* are works of vast depth and scope of observation. The last, though it contains no positive discoveries, is a noble chart of the human intellect, and a guide to all future inquirers.

whimsical deliberation had got wind, and had disturbed
the *irritabile genus* in their shadowy abodes, for we received
messages from several candidates that we had just been
thinking of. Gray declined our invitation, though he had
not yet been asked: Gay offered to come, and bring in his
hand the Duchess of Bolton, the original Polly: Steele
and Addison left their cards as Captain Sentry and Sir
Roger de Coverley: Swift came in and sat down without
speaking a word, and quitted the room as abruptly:
Otway and Chatterton were seen lingering on the opposite
side of the Styx, but could not muster enough between
them to pay Charon his fare: Thomson fell asleep in the
boat, and was rowed back again—and Burns sent a low
fellow, one John Barleycorn, an old companion of his,
who had conducted him to the other world, to say that he
had during his lifetime been drawn out of his retirement
as a show, only to be made an excise-man of, and that he
would rather remain where he was. He desired, however,
to shake hands by his representative—the hand, thus held
out, was in a burning fever, and shook prodigiously.

The room was hung round with several portraits of
eminent painters. While we were debating whether we
should demand speech with these masters of mute
eloquence, whose features were so familiar to us, it
seemed that all at once they glided from their frames, and
seated themselves at some little distance from us. There
was Leonardo, with his majestic beard and watchful eye,
having a bust of Archimedes before him; next him was
Raphael's graceful head turned round to the Fornarina;
and on his other side was Lucretia Borgia, with calm,
golden locks; Michael Angelo had placed the model of
St. Peter's on the table before him; Correggio had an
angel at his side; Titian was seated with his mistress
between himself and Giorgione; Guido was accompanied
by his own Aurora, who took a dice-box from him;
Claude held a mirror in his hand; Rubens patted a

beautiful panther (led in by a satyr) on the head; Vandyke
appeared as his own Paris, and Rembrandt was hid under
firs, gold chains, and jewels, which Sir Joshua eyed closely,
holding his hand so as to shade his forehead. Not a word
was spoken; and as we rose to do them homage, they still
presented the same surface to the view. Not being *bonâ-
fide* representations of living people, we got rid of the
splendid apparitions by signs and dumb show. As soon
as they had melted into thin air, there was a loud noise
at the outer door, and we found it was Giotto, Cimabue,
and Ghirlandaio, who had been raised from the dead by
their earnest desire to see their illustrious successors—

> " Whose names on earth
> In Fame's eternal records live for aye ! "

Finding them gone, they had no ambition to be seen
after them, and mournfully withdrew. " Egad! " said
Lamb, " these are the very fellows I should like to have
had some talk with, to know how they could see to paint
when all was dark around them."

" But shall we have nothing to say," interrogated
G. J——, " to the *Legend of Good Women*? "—" Name,
name, Mr. J——," cried H—— in a boisterous tone of
friendly exultation, " name as many as you please, without reserve or fear of molestation! " J—— was perplexed
between so many amiable recollections, that the name of
the lady of his choice expired in a pensive whiff of his
pipe ; and Lamb impatiently declared for the Duchess of
Newcastle. Mrs. Hutchinson was no sooner mentioned,
than she carried the day from the Duchess. We were the
less solicitous on this subject of filling up the posthumous
lists of Good Women, as there was already one in the
room as good, as sensible, and in all respects as exemplary,
as the best of them could be for their lives! " I should
like vastly to have seen Ninon de l'Enclos," said that in-
comparable person; and this immediately put us in mind

that we had neglected to pay honour due to our friends on the other side of the Channel: Voltaire, the patriarch of levity, and Rousseau, the father of sentiment; Montaigne and Rabelais (great in wisdom and in wit); Molière and that illustrious group that are collected round him (in the print of that subject) to hear him read his comedy of the *Tartuffe* at the house of Ninon; Racine, La Fontaine, Rochefoucault, St. Evremont, etc.

"There is one person," said a shrill, querulous voice, "I would rather see than all these—Don Quixote!"

"Come, come!" said H——; "I thought we should have no heroes, real or fabulous. What say you, Mr. Lamb? Are you for eking out your shadowy list with such names as Alexander, Julius Cæsar, Tamerlane, or Ghengis Khan?"—"Excuse me," said Lamb, "on the subject of characters in active life, plotters and disturbers of the world, I have a crotchet of my own, which I beg leave to reserve."—"No, no! come, out with your worthies!"—"What do you think of Guy Fawkes and Judas Iscariot?" H—— turned an eye upon him like a wild Indian, but cordial and full of smothered glee. "Your most exquisite reason!" was echoed on all sides; and A[yrton] thought that Lamb had now fairly entangled himself. "Why I cannot but think," retorted he of the wistful countenance, "that Guy Fawkes, that poor, fluttering annual scare-crow of straw and rags, is an ill-used gentleman. I would give something to see him sitting pale and emaciated, surrounded by his matches and his barrels of gunpowder, and expecting the moment that was to transport him to Paradise for his heroic self-devotion; but if I say any more, there is that fellow G[odwin] will make something of it. And as to Judas Iscariot, my reason is different. I would fain see the face of him who, having dipped his hand in the same dish with the Son of Man, could afterwards betray him. I have no conception of such a thing; nor have I ever seen

any picture (not even Leonardo's very fine one) that gave
me the least idea of it."—" You have said enough, Mr.
Lamb, to justify your choice."

" Oh! ever right, Menenius—ever right! "

" There is only one other person I can ever think of
after this," continued H——; but without mentioning
a name that once put on a semblance of mortality. " If
Shakspeare was to come into the room, we should all rise
up to meet him; but if that person was to come into it, we
should all fall down and try to kiss the hem of his garment! "

As a lady present seemed now to get uneasy at the
turn the conversation had taken, we rose up to go. The
morning broke with that dim, dubious light by which
Giotto, Cimabue, and Ghirlandaio must have seen to paint
their earliest works; and we parted to meet again and
renew similar topics at night, the next night, and the night
after that, till that night overspread Europe which saw
no dawn. The same event, in truth, broke up our little
Congress that broke up the great one. But that was to
meet again: our deliberations have never been resumed.

ON THE DIFFERENCE
BETWEEN WRITING AND
SPEAKING

(WRITTEN ABOUT 1825)

Some minds are proportioned to that which may be dis-
patched at once, or within a short return of time : others to that
which begins afar off, and is to be won with length of pursuit.—
BACON.

IT is a common observation, that few persons can be
found who speak and write equally well. Not only is it
obvious that the two faculties do not always go together

in the same proportions: but they are not unusually in
direct opposition to each other. We find that the greatest
authors often make the worst company in the world;
and again, some of the liveliest fellows imaginable in
conversation, or extempore speaking, seem to lose all
their vivacity and spirit the moment they set pen to paper.
For this a greater degree of quickness or slowness of
parts, education, habit, temper, turn of mind, and a
variety of collateral and predisposing causes are necessary
to account. The subject is at least curious, and worthy
of an attempt to explain it. I shall endeavour to illustrate
the difference by familiar examples rather than by
analytical reasonings. The philosopher of old was not
unwise who defined motion by getting up and walking.

The great leading distinction between writing and
speaking is, that more time is allowed for the one than
the other; and hence different faculties are required
for, and different objects attained by, each. He is properly
the best speaker who can collect together the greatest
number of apposite ideas at a moment's warning: he
is properly the best writer who can give utterance to
the greatest quantity of valuable knowledge in the course
of his whole life. The chief requisite for the one, then,
appears to be quickness and facility of perception—for
the other, patience of soul, and a power increasing with
the difficulties it has to master. He cannot be denied
to be an expert speaker, a lively companion, who is never
at a loss for something to say on every occasion or subject
that offers: he, by the same rule, will make a respectable
writer, who, by dint of study, can find out anything good
to say upon any one point that has not been touched upon
before, or who, by asking for time, can give the most
complete and comprehensive view of any question. The
one must be done off-hand, at a single blow: the other
can only be done by a repetition of blows, by having time
to think and do better. In speaking, less is required of

you, if you only do it at once, with grace and spirit: in writing, you stipulate for all that you are capable of, but you have the choice of your own time and subject. You do not expect from the manufacturer the same despatch in executing an order that you do from a shopman or warehouseman. The difference of *quicker* and *slower*, however, is not all: that is merely a difference of comparison in doing the same thing. But the writer and speaker have to do things essentially different. Besides habit, and greater or less facility, there is also a certain reach of capacity, a certain depth or shallowness, grossness or refinement of intellect, which marks out the distinction between those whose chief ambition is to shine by producing an immediate effect, or who are thrown back, by a natural bias, on the severer researches of thought and study.

We see persons of that standard or texture of mind that they can do nothing, but on the spur of the occasion: if they have time to deliberate, they are lost. There are others who have no resource, who cannot advance a step by any efforts or assistance, beyond a successful arrangement of commonplaces: but these they have always at command, at everybody's service. There is [Fletcher?]— meet him where you will in the street, he has his topic ready to discharge in the same breath with the customary forms of salutations; he is hand and glove with it; on it goes and off, and he manages it like Wart his caliver.

> " Hear him but reason in divinity,
>   And, all-admiring, with an inward wish
>   You would desire that he were made a prelate.
>   Let him but talk of any state-affair,
>   You'd say it had been all in all his study.
>   Turn him to any cause of policy,
>   The Gordian knot of it he will unloose,
>   Familiar as his garter. When he speaks,
>   The air, a charter'd libertine, stands still "—

but, ere you have time to answer him, he is off like a shot,

to repeat the same rounded, fluent observations to others:
—a perfect master of the sentences, a walking polemic
wound up for the day, a smartly bound political pocket-
book! Set the same person to write a common paragraph,
and he cannot get through it for very weariness: ask him
a question, ever so little out of the common road, and he
stares you in the face. What does all this bustle, animation, plausibility, and command of words amount to? A
lively flow of animal spirits, a good deal of confidence, a
communicative turn, and a tolerably tenacious memory
with respect to floating opinions and current phrases.
Beyond the routine of the daily newspapers and coffee-
house criticism, such persons do not venture to think
at all: or if they did, it would be so much the worse
for them, for they would only be perplexed in the
attempt, and would perform their part in the mechanism
of society with so much the less alacrity and easy
volubility.

The most dashing orator I ever heard is the flattest
writer I ever read. In speaking, he was like a volcano
vomiting out *lava;* in writing, he is like a volcano burnt
out. Nothing but the dry cinders, the hard shell remains.
The tongues of flame, with which, in haranguing a mixed
assembly, he used to illuminate his subject, and almost
scorched up the panting air, do not appear painted on
the margin of his works. He was the model of a flashy,
powerful demagogue—a madman blest with a fit audience.
He was possessed, infuriated with the patriotic *mania;*
he seemed to rend and tear the rotten carcase of corruption with the remorseless, indecent rage of a wild beast:
he mourned over the bleeding body of his country,
like another Antony over the dead body of Cæsar, as if
he would " move the very stones of Rome to rise and
mutiny:" he pointed to the " Persian abodes, the
glittering temples " of oppression and luxury, with prophetic exultation ; and like another Helen, had almost

fired another Troy! The lightning of national indignation
flashed from his eye; the workings of the popular mind
were seen labouring in his bosom: it writhed and swelled
with its rank " fraught of aspics' tongues," and the poison
frothed over at his lips. Thus qualified, he " wielded at
will the fierce democracy, and fulmin'd over " an area of
souls, of no mean circumference. He who might be said
to have " roared you in the ears of the groundlings an
'twere any lion, aggravates his voice " on paper, " like
any sucking-dove." It is not merely that the same individual cannot sit down quietly in his closet, and produce
the same, or a correspondent effect—that what he delivers
over to the compositor is tame, and trite, and tedious—that
he cannot by any means, as it were, " create a soul under
the ribs of death "—but sit down yourself, and read one
of these very popular and electrical effusions (for they
have been published), and you would not believe it to be
the same! The thunder-and-lightning mixture of the
orator turns out a mere drab-coloured suit in the person
of the prose-writer. We wonder at the change, and think
there must be some mistake, some leger-de-main trick
played off upon us, by which what before appeared so fine
now appears to be so worthless. The deception took
place *before;* now it is removed. " Bottom! thou art
translated! " might be placed as a motto under most
collections of printed speeches that I have had the good
fortune to meet with, whether originally addressed to the
people, the senate, or the bar. Burke's and Windham's
form an exception: Mr. Coleridge's *Conciones ad Populum* do not, any more than Mr. Thelwall's *Tribune.* What
we read is the same: what we hear and see is different—
" the self-same words, but *not* to the self-same tune." The
orator's vehemence of gesture, the loudness of the voice,
the speaking eye, the conscious attitude, the inexplicable
dumb show and noise,—all " those brave sublunary
things that made his raptures clear,"—are no longer there,

and without these he is nothing;—his "fire and air" turn to puddle and ditch-water, and the God of eloquence and of our idolatry sinks into a common mortal, or an image of lead, with a few labels, nicknames, and party watch-words stuck in his mouth. The truth is, that these always made up the stock of his intellectual wealth; but a certain exaggeration and extravagance of *manner* covered the nakedness and swelled out the emptiness of the *matter*: the sympathy of angry multitudes with an impassioned theatrical declaimer supplied the place of argument or wit; while the physical animation and ardour of the speaker evaporated in " sound and fury, signifying nothing," and leaving no trace behind it. A popular speaker (such as I have been here describing) is like a vulgar actor off the stage—take away his cue, and he has nothing to say for himself. Or he is so accustomed to the intoxication of popular applause, that without that stimulus he has no motive or power of exertion left— neither imagination, understanding, liveliness, common sense, words, or ideas—he is fairly cleared out; and in the intervals of sober reason, is the dullest and most imbecile of all mortals.

An orator can hardly get beyond *commonplaces*: if he does, he gets beyond his hearers. The most successful speakers, even in the House of Commons, have not been the best scholars or the finest writers—neither those who took the most profound views of their subject, nor who adorned it with the most original fancy, or the richest combinations of language. Those speeches that in general told the best at the time, are not now readable. What were the materials of which they were chiefly composed? An imposing detail of passing events, a formal display of official documents, an appeal to established maxims, an echo of popular clamour, some worn-out metaphor newly vamped-up,—some hackneyed argument used for the hundredth, nay thousandth time, to fall in with the interests, the passions, or prejudices of listening and devoted admirers;—some truth or falsehood, repeated as the Shibboleth of party time out of mind, which gathers strength from sympathy as it spreads, because it is understood or assented to by the million, and finds, in the increased action of the minds of numbers, the weight and force of an instinct. A COMMON-PLACE does not leave the mind " sceptical, puzzled, and undecided in the moment of action ':"—" it gives a body to opinion, and a permanence to fugitive belief." It operates mechanically, and opens an instantaneous and infallible communication between the hearer and speaker. A set of cant-phrases, arranged in sounding sentences, and pronounced " with good emphasis and discretion," keep the gross and irritable humours of an audience in constant fermentation; and levy no tax on the understanding. To give a reason for anything is to breed a doubt of it, which doubt you may not remove in the sequel; either because your reason may not be a good one, or because the person to whom it is addressed may not be able to comprehend it, or because *others* may not be able to comprehend it. He who offers to go into the grounds of an acknowledged axiom, risks the unanimity of the company " by most admired disorder," as he who digs to the foundation of a building to shew its solidity, risks its falling. But a common-place is enshrined in its own unquestioned evidence, and constitutes its own immortal basis. Nature, it has been said, abhors a *vacuum*; and the House of Commons, it might be said, hates everything but a common-place ! Mr. Burke did not often shock the prejudices of the House: he endeavoured to *account for them*, to " lay the flattering unction " of philosophy " to their souls." They could not endure him. Yet he did not attempt this by dry argument alone; he called to his aid the flowers of poetical fiction, and strewed the most dazzling colours of language over the Standing Orders of the House. It

was a double offence to them—an aggravation of the
encroachments of his genius. They would rather " hear
a cat mew or an axle-tree grate," than hear a man talk
philosophy by the hour—

> " Not harsh and crabbed, as dull fools suppose,
> But musical as is Apollo's lute,
> And a perpetual feast of nectar'd sweets,
> Where no crude surfeit reigns."

He was emphatically called the *Dinner-Bell*. They went
out by shoals when he began to speak. They coughed and
shuffled him down. While he was uttering some of the
finest observations (to speak in compass) that ever were
delivered in that House, they walked out, not as the beasts
came out of the ark, by twos and by threes, but in droves
and companies of tens, of dozens, and scores! Oh! it is
" the heaviest stone which melancholy can throw at a
man," when you are in the middle of a delicate speculation
to see " a robusteous periwig-pated fellow " deliberately
take up his hat and walk out. But what effect could
Burke's finest observations be expected to have on the
House of Commons in their corporate capacity? On the
supposition that they were original, refined, comprehensive, his auditors had never heard, and assuredly they had
never thought of them before: how then should they
know that they were good or bad, till they had time to
consider better of it, or till they were told what to think?
In the meantime, their effect would be to stop the question:
they were blanks in the debate : they could at best only
be laid aside and left *ad referendum*. What would it signify
if four or five persons, at the utmost, felt their full force
and fascinating power the instant they were delivered?
They would be utterly unintelligible to nine-tenths of
the persons present, and their impression upon any particular individual, more knowing than the rest, would be
involuntarily paralysed by the torpedo touch of the elbow
of a country-gentleman or city-orator. There is a reaction

in insensibility as well as in enthusiasm; and men in society judge not by their own convictions, but by sympathy with others. In reading, we may go over the page again, whenever anything new or questionable " gives us pause:" besides we are by ourselves, and it is *a word to the wise*. We are not afraid of understanding too much, and being called upon to unriddle. In hearing, we are (saving the mark!) in the company of fools; and time presses. Was the debate to be suspended while Mr. Fox or Mr. Windham took this or that Honourable Member aside, to explain to them *that fine observation* of Mr. Burke's, and to watch over the new birth of their understandings, the dawn of this new light! If we were to wait till Noble Lords and Honourable Gentlemen were inspired with a relish for abstruse thinking, and a taste for the loftier flights of fancy, the business of this great nation would shortly be at a stand. No: it is too much to ask that our good things should be duly appreciated by the first person we meet, or in the next minute after their disclosure; if the world are a little, a very little, the wiser or better for them a century hence, it is full as much as can be modestly expected! The impression of anything delivered in a large assembly must be comparatively null and void, unless you not only understand and feel its value yourself, but are conscious that it is felt and understood by the meanest capacity present. Till that is the case, the speaker is in your power, not you in his. The eloquence that is effectual and irresistible must stir the inert mass of prejudice, and pierce the opaquest shadows of ignorance. Corporate bodies move slow in the progress of intellect, for this reason, that they must keep back, like convoys, for the heaviest sailing vessels under their charge. The sinews of the wisest councils are, after all, impudence and interest: the most enlightened bodies are often but slaves of the weakest intellects they reckon among them, and the best-intentioned are but tools of

the greatest hypocrites and knaves.—To conclude what I
had to say on the character of Mr. Burke's parliamentary
style, I will just give an instance of what I mean in
affirming that it was too recondite for his hearers; and
it shall be even in so obvious a thing as a quotation.
Speaking of the newfangled French Constitution, and
in particular of the King (Louis XVI) as the chief power
in form and appearance only, he repeated the famous
lines in Milton describing Death, and concluded with
peculiar emphasis,

> ——" What *seem'd* its head,
> The *likeness* of a kingly crown had on."

The person who heard him make the speech said, that
if ever a poet's language had been finely applied by an
orator to express his thoughts and make out his purpose,
it was in this instance. The passage, I believe, is not in
his reported speeches; and I should think, in all likelihood, it " fell still-born " from his lips; while one of
Mr. Canning's well-thumbed quotations out of Virgil
would electrify the Treasury Benches, and be echoed by
all the politicians of his own standing, and the tyros of
his own school, from Lord Liverpool in the Upper down
to Mr. William Ward in the Lower House.

Mr. Burke was an author before he was a Member of
Parliament: he ascended to that practical eminence from
" the platform " of his literary pursuits. He walked out
of his study into the House. But he never became a
thorough-bred debater. He was not " native to that
element," nor was he ever " subdued to the quality " of
that motley crew of knights, citizens, and burgesses. The
late Lord Chatham was made for, and by it. He seemed
to vault into his seat there, like Hotspur, with the excla-
mation in his mouth—" that Roan shall be my throne."
Or he sprang out of the genius of the House of Commons,
like Pallas from the head of Jupiter, completely armed.

He assumed an ascendancy there from the very port and stature of his mind—from his aspiring and fiery temperament. He vanquished, because he could not yield. He controlled the purposes of others, because he was strong in his own obdurate self-will. He convinced his followers by never doubting himself. He did not argue, but assert; he took what he chose for granted, instead of making a question of it. He was not a dealer in *moot-points*. He seized on some stronghold in the argument, and held it fast with a convulsive grasp—or wrested the weapons out of his adversaries' hands by main force. He entered the lists like a gladiator. He made political controversy a combat of personal skill and courage. He was not for wasting time in long-winded discussions with his opponents, but tried to disarm them by a word, by a glance of his eye, so that they should not dare to contradict or confront him again. He did not wheedle, or palliate, or circumvent, or make a studied appeal to the reason or the passions—he *dictated* his opinions to the House of Commons. " He spoke as one having authority, and not as the Scribes." But if he did not produce such an effect either by reason or imagination, how did he produce it? The principle by which he exerted his influence over others (and it is a principle of which some speakers that I might mention seem not to have an idea, even in possibility) was sympathy. He himself evidently had a strong possession of his subject, a thorough conviction, an intense interest; and this communicated itself from his *manner*, from the tones of his voice, from his commanding attitudes and eager gestures, instinctively and unavoidably to his hearers. His will was surcharged with electrical matter like a Voltaic battery; and all who stood within its reach felt the full force of the shock. Zeal will do more than knowledge. To say the truth, there is little knowledge, —no ingenuity, no parade of individual details, not much attempt at general argument, neither wit nor fancy in his

speeches—but there are a few plain truths told home:
whatever he says, he does not mince the matter, but
clenches it in the most unequivocal manner, and with the
fullest sense of its importance, in clear, short, pithy old
English sentences. The most obvious things, as he puts
them, read like axioms—so that he appears, as it were, the
genius of common sense personified; and in turning to his
speeches you fancy that you have met with (at least) one
honest statesman! Lord Chatham commenced his career
in the intrigues of a camp and the bustle of a mess-room;
where he probably learnt that the way to govern others is
to make your will your warrant, and your word a law. If
he had spent the early part of his life, like Mr. Burke,
in writing a treatise on the *Sublime and Beautiful*, and in
dreaming over the abstract nature and causes of things, he
would never have taken the lead he did in the British Senate.

Both Mr. Fox and Mr. Pitt (though as opposite to each
other as possible) were essentially speakers, not authors,
in their mode of oratory. Beyond the moment, beyond the
occasion, beyond the immediate power shewn, astonishing as that was, there was little remarkable or worth preserving in their speeches. There is no thought in them
that implies a habit of deep and refined reflection (more
than we are accustomed ordinarily to find in people of
education); there is no knowledge that does not lie
within the reach of obvious and mechanical search; and
as to the powers of language, the chief miracle is, that a
source of words so apt, forcible, and well-arranged, so
copious and unfailing, should have been found constantly
open to express their ideas without any previous preparation. Considered as written style, they are not far out of
the common course of things; and perhaps it is assuming
too much, and making the wonder greater than it is, with
a very natural love of indulging our admiration of extraordinary persons, when we conceive that parliamentary
speeches are in general delivered without any previous

preparation. They do not, it is true, allow of preparation at the moment, but they have the preparation of the
preceding night, and of the night before that, and of
nights, weeks, months, and years of the same endless
drudgery and routine, in going over the same subjects,
argued (with some paltry difference) on the same grounds.
Practice makes perfect. He who has got a speech by heart
on any particular occasion, cannot be much gravelled for
lack of matter on any similar occasion in future. Not
only are the topics the same; the very same phrases—
whole batches of them,—are served up as the Order of the
Day; the same parliamentary bead-roll of grave impertinence is twanged off, in full cadence, by the Honourable
Member or his Learned and Honourable Friend; and the
well-known, voluminous, calculable periods roll over the
drowsy ears of the auditors, almost before they are
delivered from the vapid tongue that utters them! It
may appear, at first sight, that here are a number of
persons got together, picked out from the whole nation,
who can speak at all times upon all subjects in the most
exemplary manner; but the fact is, they only repeat the
same things over and over on the same subjects,—and
they obtain credit for general capacity and ready wit, like
Chaucer's Monk, who, by having three words of Latin
always in his mouth, passed for a great scholar.

> " A few termes coude he, two or three,
>   That he had learned out of som decree ;
>   No wonder is, he herd it all the day."

Try them on any other subject *out of doors,* and see how
soon the extempore wit and wisdom " will halt for it."
See how few of those who have distinguished themselves
in the House of Commons have done anything *out of it;*
how few that have, shine *there!* Read over the collections
of old Debates, twenty, forty, eighty, a hundred years ago;
they are the same *mutatis mutandis,* as those of yesterday.

You wonder to see how little has been added; you grieve that so little has been lost. Even in their own favourite topics, how much are they to seek! They still talk gravely of the Sinking Fund in St. Stephen's Chapel, which has been for some time exploded as a juggle by Mr. Place of Charing-Cross; and a few of the principles of Adam Smith, which every one else had been acquainted with long since, are just now beginning to dawn on the collective understanding of the two Houses of Parliament. Instead of an exuberance of sumptuous matter, you have the same meagre standing dishes for every day in the year. You must serve an apprenticeship to a want of originality, to a suspension of thought and feeling. You are in a go-cart of prejudices, in a regularly constructed machine of pretexts and precedents; you are not only to wear the livery of other men's thoughts, but there is a House-of-Commons jargon which must be used for everything. A man of simplicity and independence of mind cannot easily reconcile himself to all this formality and mummery; yet woe to him that shall attempt to discard it! You can no more move against the stream of custom than you can make head against a crowd of people; the mob of lords and gentlemen will not let you speak or think but as they do. You are hemmed in, stifled, pinioned, pressed to death,—and if you make one false step, are " trampled under the hoofs of a swinish multitude! " Talk of mobs! Is there any body of people that has this character in a more consummate degree than the House of Commons? Is there any set of men that determines more by acclamation, and less by deliberation and individual conviction?—that is moved more *en masse*, in its aggregate capacity, as brute force and physical number?—that judges with more Midas ears, blind and sordid, without discrimination of right and wrong? The greatest test of courage I can conceive, is to speak truth in the House of Commons. I have heard Sir Francis Burdett say things there which I

could not enough admire; and which he could not have
ventured upon saying, if, besides his honesty, he had not
been a man of fortune, of family, of character,—aye, and a
very good-looking man into the bargain! Dr. Johnson had
a wish to try his hand in the House of Commons. An
elephant might as well have been introduced there, in all
the forms: Sir William Curtis makes a better figure.
Either he or the Speaker (Onslow) must have resigned.
The orbit of his intellect was not the one in which the
intellect of the House moved by ancient privilege. *His*
common-places were not *their* common-places. Even
Horne Tooke failed, with all his *tact*, his self-possession,
his ready talent, and his long practice at the hustings.
He had weapons of his own, with which he wished to
make play, and did not lay his hand upon the established
levers for wielding the House of Commons. A succession
of dry, sharp-pointed sayings, which come in excellently
well in the pauses or quick turns of conversation, do not
make a speech. A series of drops is not a stream.
Besides, he had been in the practice of rallying his guests
and tampering with his subject; and this ironical tone
did not suit his new situation. He had been used to " give
his own little Senate laws," and when he found the resistance of the great one more than he could manage, he
shrunk back from the attempt, disheartened and powerless. It is nothing that a man can talk (the better, the
worse it is for him) unless he can talk in trammels; he
must be drilled into the regiment; he must not run out of
the course! The worse thing a man can do is to set up
for a wit there—or rather (I should say) for a humorist
—to say odd out-of-the-way things, to ape a character, to
play the clown or the wag in the House. This is the
very forlorn hope of a parliamentary ambition. They
may tolerate it till they know what you are at, but no
longer. It may succeed once or twice, but the third time
you will be sure to break your neck. They know nothing

T

of you, or your whims, nor have they time to look at a
puppet-show. " They look only at the stop-watch, my
Lord!" We have seen a very lively sally of this sort
which failed lately. The House of Commons is the last
place where a man will draw admiration by making a jest
of his own character. But if he has a mind to make a
jest of humanity, of liberty, and of common sense and
decency, he will succeed well enough!

The only person who ever " hit the House between
wind and water " in this way,—who made sport for the
Members, and kept his own dignity (in our time at least),
was Mr. Windham. He carried on the traffic in parliamentary conundrums and enigmas with great *éclât* for
more than one season. He mixed up a vein of characteristic eccentricity with a succession of far-fetched and
curious speculations, very pleasantly. Extremes meet;
and Mr. Windham overcame the obstinate attachment of
his hearers to fixed opinions by the force of paradoxes.
He startled his bed-rid audience effectually. A paradox
was a treat to them, on the score of novelty at least; " the
sight of one," according to the Scotch proverb, " was
good for sore eyes." So Mr. Windham humoured them
in the thing for once. He took all sorts of commonly-
received doctrines and notions (with an understood
reserve)—reversed them, and set up a fanciful theory of
his own instead. The changes were like those in a pantomime. Ask the first old woman you meet her opinion on
any subject, and you could get at the statesman's; for his
would be just the contrary. He would be wiser than the
old woman at any rate. If a thing had been thought
cruel, he would prove that it was humane; if barbarous,
manly; if wise, foolish; if sense, nonsense. His creed
was the antithesis of common sense, loyalty excepted.
Economy he could turn into ridicule, " as a saving of
cheese-parings and candle-ends; "—and total failure was
with him " negative success." He had no occasion, in

thus setting up for original thinking, to inquire into the
truth or falsehood of any proposition, but to ascertain
whether it was currently believed in, and then to contradict it point-blank. He made the vulgar prejudices of
others " servile ministers " to his own solecism. It was
not easy always to say whether he was in jest or earnest—
but he contrived to hitch his extravagances into the midst
of some grave debate; the House had their laugh for
nothing; the question got into shape again, and Mr.
Windham was allowed to have been more *brilliant* than
ever.[1]

Mr. Windham was, I have heard, a silent man in
company. Indeed his whole style was an artificial and
studied imitation, or capricious caricature of Burke's bold,
natural, discursive manner. This did not imply much
spontaneous power or fertility of invention; he was an
intellectual posture-master, rather than a man of real
elasticity and vigour of mind. Mr. Pitt was also, I
believe, somewhat taciturn and reserved. There was
nothing clearly in the subject-matter of his speeches to
connect with the ordinary topics of discourse, or with any
given aspect of human life. One would expect him to be
quite as much in the clouds as the automaton chess-player
or the last new Opera-singer. Mr. Fox said little in
private, and complained that in writing he had no style.
So (to compare great things with small) Jack Davies, the
unrivalled racket-player, never said anything at all in
company, and was what is understood by a modest man.
When the racket was out of his hand, his occupation,

---

[1] It must be granted, however, that there was something
piquant and provoking in his manner of " making the worse
appear the better reason." In keeping off the ill odour of a
bad cause, he applied hartshorn and burnt feathers to the
offended sense ; and did not, like Mr. Canning, treat us with
the faded flowers of his oratory, like the faint smell of a per-
fumer's shop, or try to make Government " love-locks " of
dead men's hair !

his delight, his glory — that which he excelled all
mankind in — was gone! So when Mr. Fox had no
longer to keep up the ball of debate, with the floor of
Saint Stephen's for a stage, and the world for spectators
of the game, it is hardly to be wondered at that he felt a
little at a loss—without his usual train of subjects, the
same crowd of associations, the same spirit of competition,
or stimulus to extraordinary exertion.   The excitement of
leading in the House of Commons (which, in addition to
the immediate attention and applause that follows, is a
sort of whispering gallery to all Europe) must act upon
the brain like brandy or laudanum upon the stomach;
and must, in most cases, produce the same debilitating
effects afterwards.   A man's faculties must be quite
exhausted, his virtue gone out of him.   That any one
accustomed all his life to the tributary roar of applause
from the great council of the nation, should think of
dieting himself with the prospect of posthumous fame as
an author, is like offering a confirmed dram-drinker a glass
of fair water for his morning's draught. Charles Fox is not
to be blamed for having written an indifferent history of
James II, but for having written a history at all. It was
not his business to write a history—his business was *not
to have made any more Coalitions!* But he found writing
so dull, he thought it better to be a colleague of Lord
Grenville! He did not want style (to say so is nonsense,
because the style of his speeches was just and fine)—he
wanted a sounding-board in the ear of posterity to try his
periods upon. If he had gone to the House of Commons
in the morning, and tried to make a speech fasting, when
there was nobody to hear him, he might have been equally
disconcerted at his want of style. The habit of speaking
is the habit of being heard, and of wanting to be heard;
the habit of writing is the habit of thinking aloud, but
without the help of an echo. The orator sees his subject in
the eager looks of his auditors; and feels doubly conscious,

doubly impressed with it in the glow of their sympathy; the author can only look for encouragement in a blank piece of paper. The orator feels the impulse of popular enthusiasm,

> ——" like proud seas under him : "

the only Pegasus the writer has to boast, is the hobby-horse of his own thoughts and fancies. How is he to get on, then? From the lash of necessity. We accordingly see persons of rank and fortune continually volunteer into the service of oratory—and the State; but we have few authors who are not paid by the sheet! I myself have heard Charles Fox engaged in familiar conversation. It was in the Louvre. He was describing the pictures to two persons that were with him. He spoke rapidly, but very unaffectedly. I remember his saying—" All those blues and greens and reds are the Guercinos; you may know them by the colours." He set Opie right as to Domenichino's Saint Jerome. " You will find," he said, " though you may not be struck with it at first, that there is a great deal of truth and good sense in that picture." There was a person at one time a good deal with Mr. Fox, who, when the opinion of the latter was asked on any subject, very frequently interposed to give the answer. This sort of tantalizing interruption was ingeniously enough compared by some one, to walking up Ludgate-hill, and having the spire of St. Martin's constantly getting in your way, when you wished to see the dome of St. Paul's! Burke, it is said, conversed as he spoke in public, and as he wrote. He was communicative, diffuse, magnificent. " What is the use," said Mr. Fox to a friend, " of Sheridan's trying to swell himself out in this manner, like the frog in the fable? "—alluding to his speech on Warren Hastings's trial. " It is very well for Burke to express himself in that figurative way. It is natural to him; he talks so to his wife, to his servants, to his children; but as for Sheridan, he either never opens his mouth at all, or if he does, it is to utter some joke. It is out of the question for him to affect these *Oriental-isms*." Burke once came into Sir Joshua Reynolds's painting-room, when one of his pupils was sitting for one of the sons of Count Ugolino; this gentleman was personally introduced to him;—" Ah! then," said Burke, " I find that Mr. N[orthcote] has not only a head that would do for Titian to paint, but is himself a painter." At another time, he came in when Goldsmith was there, and poured forth such a torrent of violent personal abuse against the King, that they got to high words, and Goldsmith threatened to leave the room if he did not desist. Goldsmith bore testimony to his powers of conversation. Speaking of Johnson, he said, " Does he wind into a subject like a serpent, as Burke does? " With respect to his facility in composition, there are contradictory accounts. It has been stated by some, that he wrote out a plain sketch first, like a sort of dead colouring, and added the ornaments and tropes afterwards. I have been assured by a person who had the best means of knowing, that the *Letter to a Noble Lord* (the most rapid, impetuous, glancing, and sportive of all his works) was printed off, and the proof sent to him: and that it was returned to the printing-office with so many alterations and passages interlined, that the compositors refused to correct it as it was—took the whole matter in pieces, and re-set the copy. This looks like elaboration and after-thought. It was also one of Burke's latest compositions.[1] A regularly bred speaker would have made up his mind beforehand; but Burke's mind being, as originally constituted and by its first bias, that of an author, never became set. It was in further

---

[1] Tom Paine, while he was busy about any of his works, used to walk out, compose a sentence or paragraph in his head, come home and write it down, and never altered it afterwards. He then added another, and so on, till the whole was completed.

search and progress. It had an internal spring left. It was not tied down to the printer's form. It could still project itself into new beauties, and explore strange regions from the unwearied impulse of its own delight or curiosity. Perhaps among the passages interlined, in this case, were the description of the Duke of Bedford, as " the Leviathan among all the creatures of the crown,"—the *catalogue raisonnée* of the Abbé Sieyes's pigeon-holes,—or the comparison of the English Monarchy to " the proud keep of Windsor, with its double belt of kindred and coeval towers." Were these to be given up? If he had had to make his defence of his pension in the House of Lords, they would not have been ready in time, it appears; and, besides, would have been too difficult of execution on the spot: a speaker must not set his heart on such forbidden fruit. But Mr. Burke was an author, and the press did not " shut the gates of *genius* on mankind." A set of oratorical flourishes, indeed, is soon exhausted, and is generally all that the extempore speaker can safely aspire to. Not so with the resources of art or nature, which are inexhaustible, and which the writer has time to seek out, to embody, and to fit into shape and use, if he has the strength, the courage, and patience to do so.

There is then a certain range of thought and expression beyond the regular rhetorical routine, on which the author, to vindicate his title, must trench somewhat freely. The proof that this is understood to be so, is, that what is called an oratorical style is exploded from all good writing; that we immediately lay down an article, even in a common newspaper, in which such phrases occur as " the Angel of Reform," " the drooping Genius of Albion; " and that a very brilliant speech at a loyal dinner-party makes a very flimsy, insipid pamphlet. The orator has to get up for a certain occasion a striking compilation of partial topics, which, " to leave no rubs or botches in the work," must be pretty familiar as well as palatable to his hearers; and in doing this, he may avail himself of all the resources of an artificial memory. The writer must be original, or he is nothing. He is not to take up with ready-made goods; for he has time allowed him to create his own materials, to make novel combinations of thought and fancy, to contend with unforeseen difficulties of style and execution, while we look on, and admire the growing work in secret and at leisure. There is a degree of finishing as well as of solid strength in writing which is not to be got at every day, and we can wait for perfection. The author owes a debt to truth and nature which he cannot satisfy at sight, but he has pawned his head on redeeming it. It is not a string of clap-traps to answer a temporary or party-purpose,— violent, vulgar, and illiberal,—but general and lasting truth that we require at his hands. We go to him as pupils, not as partisans. We have a right to expect from him profounder views of things; finer observations; more ingenious illustrations; happier and bolder expressions. He is to give the choice and picked results of a whole life of study; what he has struck out in his most felicitous moods, has treasured up with most pride, has laboured to bring to light with most anxiety and confidence of success. He may turn a period in his head fifty different ways, so that it comes out smooth and round at last. He may have caught a glimpse of a simile, and it may have vanished again: let him be on the watch for it, as the idle boy watches for the lurking-place of the adder. We can wait. He is not satisfied with a reason he has offered for something: let him wait till he finds a better reason. There is some word, some phrase, some idiom that expresses a particular idea better than any other, but he cannot for the life of him recollect it: let him wait till he does. Is it strange that among twenty thousand words in the English language, the one of all others that he most needs should have escaped him? There are more things in nature than there are words in the English language, and he must not expect to lay rash hands on them all at once.

> " Learn to *write* slow : all other graces
> Will follow in their proper places."

You allow a writer a year to think of a subject; he should not put you off with a truism at last. You allow him a year more to find out words for his thoughts; he should not give us an echo of all the fine things that have been said a hundred times.[1] All authors, however, are not so squeamish; but take up with words and ideas as they find them delivered down to them. Happy are they who write Latin verses!—who copy the style of Dr. Johnson!— who hold up the phrase of ancient Pistol! They do not trouble themselves with those hair-breadth distinctions of thought or meaning that puzzle nicer heads;—let us leave them to their repose! A person in habits of composition often hesitates in conversation for a particular word: it is because he is in search of the best word, and *that* he cannot hit upon. In writing he would stop till it came.[2] It is not true, however, that the scholar could avail himself of a more ordinary word if he chose, or readily acquire a command of ordinary language; for his associations are habitually intense, not vague and shallow; and words occur to him only as *tallies* to certain modifications of feeling. They are links in the chain of thought. His imagination is fastidious, and rejects all those that are " of no mark or likelihood." Certain words are in his mind indissolubly wedded to certain things; and none are admitted at the *levée* of his thoughts but those of which

[1] Just as a poet ought not to cheat us with lame metre and defective rhymes, which might be excusable in an improvisatori versifier.

[2] That is essentially a bad style which seems as if the person writing it never stopped for breath, nor gave himself a moment's pause, but strove to make up by redundancy and fluency for want of choice and correctness of expression.

T *

the banns have been solemnized with scrupulous propriety. Again, the student finds a stimulus to literary exertion, not in the immediate *éclat* of his undertaking, but in the difficulty of his subject, and the progressive nature of his task. He is not wound up to a sudden and extraordinary effort of presence of mind; but is for ever awake to the silent influxes of things, and his life is one long labour. Are there no sweeteners of his toil? No reflections, in the absence of popular applause or social indulgence, to cheer him on his way? Let the reader judge. *His* pleasure is the counterpart of, and borrowed from the same source as the writer's. A man does not read out of vanity, nor in company, but to amuse his own thoughts. If the reader, from disinterested and merely intellectual motives, relishes an author's "fancies and good nights," the last may be supposed to have relished them no less. If he laughs at a joke, the inventor chuckled over it to the full as much. If he is delighted with a phrase, he may be sure the writer jumped at it; if he is pleased to cull a straggling flower from the page, he may believe that it was plucked with no less fondness from the face of nature. Does he fasten, with gathering brow and looks intent, on some difficult speculation? He may be convinced that the writer thought it a fine thing to split his brain in solving so curious a problem, and to publish his discovery to the world. There is some satisfaction in the contemplation of power; there is also a little pride in the conscious possession of it. With what pleasure do we read books! If authors could but feel this, or remember what they themselves once felt, they would need no other temptation to persevere.

To conclude this account with what perhaps I ought to have set out with,—a definition of the character of an author. There are persons who in society, in public intercourse, feel no excitement,

"Dull as the lake that slumbers in the storm,"

but who, when left alone, can lash themselves into a foam.
They are never less alone than when alone. Mount them
on a dinner-table, and they have nothing to say; shut
them up in a room by themselves, and they are inspired.
They are " made fierce with dark keeping." In revenge
for being tongue-tied, a torrent of words flows from their
pens, and the storm which was so long collecting comes
down apace. It never rains but it pours. Is not this
strange, unaccountable? Not at all so. They have a real
interest, a real knowledge of the subject, and they cannot
summon up all that interest, or bring all that knowledge
to bear, while they have anything else to attend to. Till
they can do justice to the feeling they have, they can do
nothing. For this they look into their own minds, not in
the faces of a gaping multitude. What they would say (if
they could) does not lie at the orifices of the mouth ready
for delivery, but is wrapped in the folds of the heart and
registered in the chambers of the brain. In the sacred
cause of truth that stirs them, they would put their whole
strength, their whole being into requisition; and as it
implies a greater effort to drag their words and ideas from
their lurking-places, so there is no end when they are
once set in motion. The whole of a man's thoughts and
feelings cannot lie on the surface, made up for use; but
the whole must be a greater quantity, a mightier power, if
they could be got at, layer under layer, and brought into
play by the levers of imagination and reflection. Such a
person then sees farther and feels deeper than most others.
He plucks up an argument by the roots, he tears out the
very heart of his subject. He has more pride in conquer-
ing the difficulties of a question, than vanity in courting
the favour of an audience. He wishes to satisfy himself
before he pretends to enlighten the public. He takes an
interest in things in the abstract more than by common
consent. Nature is his mistress, truth his idol. The
contemplation of a pure idea is the ruling passion of his

breast. The intervention of other people's notions, the being the immediate object of their censure or their praise, puts him out. What will tell, what will produce an effect, he cares little about; and therefore he produces the greatest. The *personal* is to him an impertinence ; so he conceals himself and writes. Solitude " becomes his glittering bride, and airy thoughts his children." Such a one is a true author; and not a member of any Debating Club, or Dilettanti Society whatever! [1]

ON OLD ENGLISH WRITERS
AND SPEAKERS

(NEW MONTHLY MAGAZINE, JAN., 1825)

WHEN I see a whole row of standard French authors piled up on a Paris book-stall, to the height of twenty or thirty volumes, shewing their mealy coats to the sun,

---

[1] I have omitted to dwell on some other differences of body and mind that often prevent the same person from shining in both capacities of speaker and writer. There are natural impediments to public speaking, such as the want of a strong voice and steady nerves. A high authority of the present day (Mr. Canning) has thought this a matter of so much importance, that he goes so far as even to let it affect the constitution of Parliament, and conceives that gentlemen who have not bold foreheads, and brazen lungs, but modest pretensions and patriotic views, should be allowed to creep into the great assembly of the nation through the avenue of close boroughs, and not be called upon " to face the storms of the hustings." In this point of view, Stentor was a man of genius, and a noisy jack-pudding may cut a considerable figure in the "Political House that Jack built." I fancy Mr. C. Wynne is the only person in the kingdom who has fully made up his mind that a total defect of voice is the most necessary qualification for a Speaker in the House of Commons!

pink, blue, and yellow, they seem to me a wall built up
to keep out the intrusion of foreign letters. There is
scarcely such a thing as an English book to be met with,
unless, perhaps, a dusty edition of *Clarissa Harlowe* lurks
in an obscure corner, or a volume of the *Sentimental
Journey* perks its well-known title in your face.[1] But
there is a huge column of Voltaire's works complete in
sixty volumes, another (not so frequent) of Rousseau's in
fifty, Racine in ten volumes, Molière in about the same
number, La Fontaine, Marmontel, *Gil Blas*, for ever;
Madame Sevigné's *Letters*, Pascal, Montesquieu, Crebillon,
Marivaux, with Montaigne, Rabelais, and the grand
Corneille more rare ; and eighteen full-sized volumes of
La Harpe's criticism, towering vain-gloriously in the
midst of them, furnishing the streets of Paris with a
graduated scale of merit for all the rest, and teaching
the very *garçons perruquiers* how to measure the length of
each act of each play by a stop-watch, and to ascertain
whether the angles at the four corners of each classic
volumes are right ones. How climb over this lofty pile
of taste and elegance to wander down into the bogs and
wastes of English or of any other literature, " to this
obscure and wild? " Must they " on that fair mountain
leave to feed, to batten on this moor? " Or why should
they? Have they not literature enough of their own, and
to spare, without coming to us? Is not the public mind
crammed, choked with French books, pictures, statues,
plays, operas, newspapers, parties, and an incessant
farrago of words, so that it has not a moment left to look
at home into itself, or abroad into nature? Must they

----

[1] A splendid edition of Goldsmith has been lately got up
under the superintendence of Mr. Washington Irving, with a
preface and a portrait of each author. By what concatenation
of ideas that gentleman arrived at the necessity of placing his
own portrait before a collection of Goldsmith's works, one must
have been early imprisoned in Transatlantic solitudes to understand.

cross the Channel to increase the vast stock of impertinence, to acquire foreign tastes, suppress native prejudices,
and reconcile the opinions of the *Edinburgh* and *Quarterly
Reviews?* It is quite needless. There is a project at
present entertained in certain circles, to give the French
a taste for Shakespear. They should really begin
with the English.[1] Many of their own best authors are
neglected; others, of whom new Editions have been
printed, lie heavy on the booksellers' hands. It is by an
especial dispensation of Providence that languages wear
out; as otherwise we should be buried alive under a load
of books and knowledge. People talk of a philosophical
and universal language. We have enough to do to understand our own, and to read a thousandth part (perhaps not
the best) of what is written in it. It is ridiculous and
monstrous vanity. We would set up a standard of general
taste and of immortal renown; we would have the benefits
of science and of art universal, because we suppose our
own capacity to receive them unbounded; and we would
have the thoughts of others never die, because we flatter
ourselves that our own will last for ever; and like the
frog imitating the ox in the fable, we burst in the vain
attempt. Man, whatever he may think, is a very limited
being; the world is a narrow circle drawn about him; the
horizon limits our immediate view; immortality means a
century or two. Languages happily restrict the mind to

[1] I would as soon try to remove one side of the Seine or of the
Thames to the other. By the time an author begins to be much
talked of abroad, he is going out of fashion at home. We have
many little Lord Byrons among ourselves, who think they can
write nearly, if not quite as well. I am not anxious to spread
Shakespear's fame, or to increase the number of his admirers.
" What's he that wishes for more men from England ? " etc.
It is enough if he is admired by all those who understand
him. He may be very inferior to many French writers, for
what I know; but I am quite sure he is superior to all
English ones. We may say that, without national prejudice or
vanity.

what is of its own native growth and fitted for it, as
rivers and mountains bound countries; or the empire of
learning, as well as states, would become unwieldly and
overgrown. A little importation from foreign markets
may be good; but the home production is the chief thing
to be looked to.

"The proper study of the *French* is *French!*"

No people can act more uniformly upon a conviction of
this maxim, and in that respect I think they are much to
be commended.

Mr. Lamb has lately taken it into his head to read
St. Evremont, and works of that stamp. I neither praise
nor blame him for it. He observed, that St. Evremont
was a writer half-way between Montaigne and Voltaire,
with a spice of the wit of the one and the sense of the
other. I said I was always of opinion that there had been
a great many clever people in the world, both in France
and England, but I had been sometimes rebuked for it.
Lamb took this as a slight reproach; for he has been a
little exclusive and national in his tastes. He said that
Coleridge had lately given up all his opinions respecting
German literature, that all their high-flown pretensions
were in his present estimate sheer cant and affectation,
and that none of their works were worth anything but
Schiller's and the early ones of Goethe. "What," I said,
"my old friend Werter! How many battles have I had
in my own mind, and compunctious visitings of criticism
to stick to my old favourite, because Coleridge thought
nothing of it! It is hard to find one's-self right at last!"
I found they were of my mind with respect to the
celebrated *Faust*—that is a mere piece of abortive per-
verseness, a wilful evasion of the subject and omission of
the characters; that it is written on the absurd principle
that as to produce a popular and powerful effect is not a
proof of the highest genius, so to produce no effect at all

is an evidence of the highest poetry—and in fine, that the
German play is not to be named in a day with Marlowe's.
Poor Kit! How Lord Byron would have sneered at
this comparison between the boasted modern and a contemporary of Shakespear's! Captain Medwin or his
Lordship must have made a mistake in the enumeration
of plays of that period still acted. There is one of Ben
Jonson's, *Every Man in his Humour;* and one of Massinger's, *A New Way to Pay Old Debts;* but there is
none of Ford's either acted or worth acting, except
'Tis Pity She's a Whore, and that would no more bear
acting than Lord Byron and Goethe together could have
written it.

This account of Coleridge's vacillations of opinion on
such subjects might be adduced to shew that our love for
foreign literature is an acquired or rather an assumed
taste; that it is, like a foreign religion, adopted for the
moment, to answer a purpose or to please an idle humour;
that we do not enter into the *dialect* of truth and nature
in their works as we do in our own; and that consequently
our taste for them seldom becomes a part of ourselves,
that " grows with our growth, and strengthens with our
strength," and only quits us when we die. Probably it
is this acquaintance with, and pretended admiration of,
extraneous models, that adulterates and spoils our native
literature, that polishes the surface but undermines its
basis, and by taking away its original simplicity, character,
and force, makes it just tolerable to others, and a matter
of much indifference to ourselves. When I see Lord
Byron's poems stuck all over Paris, it strikes me as
ominous of the decline of English genius: on the contrary,
when I find the Scotch Novels in still greater request, I
think it augurs well for the improvement of French taste.[1]

[1] I have heard the popularity of Sir Walter Scott in France
ingeniously, and somewhat whimsically, traced to Buonaparte.
He did not like the dissipation and frivolity of Paris, and rele-

There was advertised not long ago in Paris an Elegy on the Death of Lord Byron, by his friend Sir Thomas More,—evidently confounding the living bard with the old statesman. It is thus the French in their light, salient way transpose everything. The mistake is particularly ludicrous to those who have ever seen Mr. Moore, or Mr. Shee's portrait of him in Mr. Hookham's shop, and who chance to see Holbein's head of Sir Thomas More in the Louvre. There is the same difference that there is between a surly English mastiff and a little lively French pug. Mr. Moore's face is gay and smiling enough, old Sir Thomas's is severe, not to say sour. It seems twisted awry with difficult questions, and bursting asunder with a ponderous load of meaning. Mr. Moore has nothing of this painful and puritanical cast. He floats idly and fantastically on the top of the literature of his age; his renowned and almost forgotten namesake has nearly sunk to the bottom of his. The Author of *Utopia* was no flincher, he was a martyr to his opinions, and was burnt to death for them—the most heroic action of Mr. Moore's life is, the having burnt the Memoirs of his friend!

The expression in Holbein's pictures conveys a faithful

gated the country-gentlemen to their seats for eight months in the year. Here they yawn and gasp for breath, and would not know what to do without the aid of the Author of *Waverley*. They ask impatiently when the *Tales of the Crusaders* will be out; and what you think of *Red Gauntlet?* To the same cause is to be attributed the change of manners. *Messieurs, je veux des mœurs*, was constantly in the French Ruler's mouth. Manners, according to my informant, were necessary to consolidate his plans of tyranny;—how, I do not know. Forty years ago no man was ever seen in company with *Madame sa femme*. A comedy was written on the *ridicule* of a man being in love with his wife. Now he must be with her three-and-twenty hours out of the four-and-twenty; it is from this that they date the decline of happiness in France; and the unfortunate couple endeavour to pass the time and get rid of *ennui* as well as they can by reading the Scotch Novels together.

but not very favourable notion of the literary character of that period. It is painful, dry, and laboured. Learning was then an ascetic, but recluse and profound. You see a weight of thought and care in the studious heads of the time of the Reformation, a sincerity, an integrity, a sanctity of purpose, like that of a formal dedication to a religious life, or the inviolability of monastic vows. They had their work to do; we reap the benefits of it. We skim the surface, and travel along the high road. They had to explore dark recesses, to dig through mountains, and make their way through pathless wildernesses. It is no wonder they looked grave upon it. The seriousness, indeed, amounts to an air of devotion; and it has to me something fine, manly, and *old English* about it. There is a heartiness and determined resolution; a willingness to contend with opposition; a superiority to ease and pleasure; some sullen pride, but no trifling vanity. They addressed themselves to study as to a duty, and were ready to " leave all and follow it." In the beginning of such an era, the difference between ignorance and learning, between what was commonly known and what was possible to be known, would appear immense; and no pains or time would be thought too great to master the difficulty. Conscious of their own deficiencies and the scanty information of those about them, they would be glad to look out for aids and support, and to put themselves apprentices to time and nature. This temper would lead them to exaggerate rather than to make light of the difficulties of their undertaking; and would call forth sacrifices in proportion. Feeling how little they knew, they would be anxious to discover all that others had known, and instead of making a display of themselves, their first object would be to dispel the mist and darkness that surrounded them. They did not cull the flowers of learning, or pluck a leaf of laurel for their own heads, but tugged at the roots and very heart of their subject, as the woodman tugs at the roots of the gnarled oak. The sense of the arduousness of their enterprise braced their courage, so that they left nothing half done. They inquired *de omne scibile et quibusdam aliis.* They ransacked libraries, they exhausted authorities. They acquired languages, consulted books, and decyphered manuscripts. They devoured learning, and swallowed antiquity whole, and (what is more) digested it. They read incessantly, and remembered what they read, from the zealous interest they took in it. Repletion is only bad when it is accompanied with apathy and want of exercise. They laboured hard, and shewed great activity both of reasoning and speculation. Their fault was that they were too prone to unlock the secrets of nature with the key of learning, and often to substitute authority in the place of argument. They were also too polemical; as was but naturally to be expected in the first breaking up of established prejudices and opinions. It is curious to observe the slow progress of the human mind in loosening and getting rid of its trammels, link by link, and how it crept on its hands and feet, and with its eyes bent on the ground, out of the cave of Bigotry, making its way through one dark passage after another; those who gave up one half of an absurdity contending as strenuously for the remaining half, the lazy current of tradition stemming the tide of innovation, and making an endless struggle between the two. But in the dullest minds of this period there was a deference to the opinions of their leaders; an imposing sense of the importance of the subject, of the necessity of bringing all the faculties to bear upon it; a weight either of armour or of internal strength, a zeal either *for* or *against;* a head, a heart, and a hand, a holding out to the death for conscience sake, a strong spirit of proselytism—no flippancy, no indifference, no compromising, no pert shallow scepticism, but truth was supposed indissolubly knit to good, knowledge to usefulness, and the temporal and eternal welfare of mankind to hang in the balance. The pure springs of a lofty faith (so to speak) had not then descended by various gradations from their skyey regions and cloudy height, to find their level in the smooth, glittering expanse of modern philosophy, or to settle in the stagnant pool of stale hypocrisy! A learned man of that day, if he knew no better than others, at least knew all that they did. He did not come to his subject, like some dapper barrister who has never looked at his brief, and trusts to the smartness of his wit and person for the agreeable effect he means to produce, but like an old and practised counsellor, covered over with the dust and cobwebs of the law. If it was a speaker in Parliament, he came prepared to handle his subject, armed with cases and precedents, the constitution and history of Parliament from the earliest period, a knowledge of the details of business and the local interests of the country; in short, he had taken up *the freedom of the House*, and did not treat the question like a cosmopolite, or a writer in a Magazine. If it were a divine, he knew the Scriptures and the Fathers, and the Councils and the Commentators by heart, and thundered them in the ears of his astonished audience. Not a trim essay or a tumid oration, patronizing religion by modern sophisms, but the Law and the Prophets, the chapter and the verse. If it was a philosopher, Aristotle and the Schoolmen were drawn out in battle-array against you:—if an antiquarian, the Lord bless us! There is a passage in Selden's notes on Drayton's *Poly-Olbion*, in which he elucidates some point of topography by a reference not only to Stowe and Holinshed and Camden and Saxo-Grammaticus and Dugdale and several other authors that we are acquainted with, but to twenty obscure names, that no modern reader ever heard of; and so on through the notes to a folio volume, written apparently for relaxation. Such were the intellectual amusements of our ancestors! Learning then ordinarily lay-in of folio volumes: now she litters octavos and duodecimos, and will soon, as in France, miscarry of half sheets! Poor Job Orton! why should I not record a jest of his (perhaps the only one he ever made), emblematic as it is of the living and the learning of the good old times? The Rev. Job Orton was a Dissenting Minister in the middle of the last century, and had grown heavy and gouty by sitting long at dinner and at his studies. He could only get downstairs at last by spreading the folio volumes of Caryl's *Commentaries upon Job* on the steps and sliding down them. Surprised one day in his descent, he exclaimed, " You have often heard of Caryl upon Job— now you see Job upon Caryl! " This same quaint-witted gouty old gentleman seems to have been one of those " superior, happy spirits," who slid through life on the rollers of learning, enjoying the good things of the world and laughing at them, and turning his infirmities to a livelier account than his patriarchal name-sake. Reader, didst thou ever hear either of Job Orton or of Caryl on Job? I daresay not. Yet the one did not therefore slide down his theological staircase the less pleasantly; nor did the other compile his Commentaries in vain! For myself, I should like to browze on folios, and have to deal chiefly with authors that I have scarcely strength to lift, that are as solid as they are heavy, and if dull, are full of matter. It is delightful to repose on the wisdom of the ancients; to have some great name at hand, besides one's own initials always staring one in the face: to travel out of one's-self into the Chaldee, Hebrew, and Egyptian characters; to have the palm-trees waving mystically in the margin of the page, and the camels moving slowly on in the distance of three thousand years. In that dry desert of learning, we gather strength and patience, and a strange and insatiable thirst of knowledge. The ruined monuments of antiquity are also there, and the fragments of buried cities (under which the adder lurks) and cool

springs, and green sunny spots, and the whirlwind and the
lion's roar, and the shadow of angelic wings. To those
who turn with supercilious disgust from the ponderous
tomes of scholastic learning, who never felt the witchery
of the Talmuds and the Cabbala, of the Commentators and
the Schoolmen, of texts and authorities, of types and
anti-types, hieroglyphics and mysteries, dogmas and
contradictions, and endless controversies and doubtful
labyrinths, and quaint traditions, I would recommend the
lines of Warton written in a Blank Leaf of Dugdale's
Monasticon:

> " Deem not devoid of elegance the sage,
>   By fancy's genuine feelings unbeguiled,
>   Of painful pedantry the poring child,
>   Who turns of these proud domes the historic page,
>   Now sunk by time and Henry's fiercer rage.
>   Think'st thou the warbling Muses never smiled
>   On his lone hours ? Ingenious views engage
>   His thoughts, on themes (unclassic falsely styled)
>   Intent. While cloister'd piety displays
>   Her mouldering scroll, the piercing eye explores
>   New manners and the pomp of elder days ;
>   Whence culls the pensive bard his pictured stores.
>   Nor rough nor barren are the winding ways
>   Of hoar Antiquity, but strewn with flowers."

This Sonnet, if it were not for a certain intricacy in
the style, would be a perfect one: at any rate, the
thought it contains is fine and just. Some of the *caput
mortuum* of learning is a useful ballast and relief to the
mind. It must turn back to the acquisitions of others as
its natural sustenance and support; facts must go hand in
hand with feelings, or it will soon prey like an empty
stomach on itself, or be the sport of the windy impertinence of ingenuity self-begotten. Away, then, with this
idle cant, as if everything were barbarous and without
interest that is not the growth of our own times and of
our own taste; with this everlasting evaporation of mere

sentiment, this affected glitter of style, this equivocal generation of thought out of ignorance and vanity, this total forgetfulness of the subject, and display of the writer, as if every possible train of speculation must originate in the pronoun *I*, and the world had nothing to do but to look on and admire. It will not do to consider all truth or good as a reflection of our own pampered and inordinate self-love; to resolve the solid fabric of the universe into an essence of Della-Cruscan witticism and conceit. The perpetual search after effect, the premature and effeminate indulgence of nervous sensibility, defeats and wears itself out. We cannot make an abstraction of the intellectual ore from the material dross, of feelings from objects, of results from causes. We must get at the kernel of pleasure through the dry and hard husk of truth. We must wait Nature's time. These false births weaken the constitution. It has been observed that men of science live longer than mere men of letters. They exercise their understandings more, their sensibility less. There is with them less *wear and tear* of the irritable fibre, which is not shattered and worn to a very thread. On the hill of science, they keep an eye intent on truth and fame:

> " Calm pleasures there abide, majestic pains,"—

while the man of letters mingles in the crowd below, courting popularity and pleasure. His is a frail and feverish existence accordingly, and he soon exhausts himself in the tormenting pursuit—in the alternate excitement of his imagination and gratification of his vanity.

> ————————" Earth destroys
> Those raptures duly : Erebus disdains ! "

Lord Byron appears to me to have fairly run himself out in his debilitating intercourse with the wanton Muse He had no other idea left but that of himself and the public—he was uneasy unless he was occupied in administering repeated provocatives to idle curiosity, and receiving strong doses of praise or censure in return: the irritation at last became so violent and importunate, that he could neither keep on with it nor take any repose from it. The glistering orb of heated popularity

" Glared round his soul and mocked his closing eye-lids."

The successive endless Cantos of *Don Juan* were the quotidian that killed him! Old Sir Walter will last long enough, stuffing his wallet and his " wame," as he does, with mouldy fragments and crumbs of comfort. He does not " spin his brains," but something much better. The cunning *chield*, the old *canty gaberlunzie* has got hold of another clue—that of nature and history—and long may he spin it, " even to the crack of doom," watching the threads as they are about to break through his fringed eye-lids, catching a tradition in his mouth like a trap, and heaping his forehead with facts, till it shoves up the Baronet's blue bonnet into a Baron's crown, and then will the old boy turn in his chair, rest his chin upon his crutch, give a last look to the Highlands, and with his latest breath thank God that he leaves the world as he found it! And so he will pretty nearly with one exception —the Scotch Novels. They are a small addition to this round world of ours. We and they shall jog on merrily together for a century or two, I hope, till some future Lord Byron asks, " Who reads Sir Walter Scott now? " There is the last and almost worst of them. I would take it with me into a wilderness. Three pages of poor *Peter Peebles* will at any time redeem three volumes of *Red Gauntlet*. And Nanty Ewart is even better with his steady walk upon the deck of the *Jumping Jenny* and his story of himself, " and her whose foot (whether he came in or went out) was never off the stair." There you came near me, there you touched me, old truepenny! And then again the catch that blind Willie and his wife and the boy sing in the hollow of the heath—there is more mirth and heart's ease in it than in all Lord Byron's *Don Juan*, or Mr. Moore's *Lyrics*. And why? Because the author is thinking of beggars and a beggar's brat, and not of himself while he writes it. He looks at nature, sees it, hears it, feels it, and believes that it exists, before it is printed, hot-pressed, and labelled on the back, *By the Author of Waverley*. He does not fancy, nor would he for one moment have it supposed, that his name and fame compose all that is worth a moment's consideration in the universe. This is the great secret of his writings—a perfect indifference to self. Whether it is the same in his politics, I cannot say. I see no comparison between his prose writing and Lord Byron's poems. The only writer that I should hesitate about is Wordsworth. There are thoughts and lines of his that to me shew as fine a mind, a subtler sense of beauty than anything of Sir Walter's, such as those above quoted, and that other line in the *Laodamia*

"Elysian beauty, melancholy grace."

I would as soon have written that line as have carved a Greek statue. But in this opinion I shall have three or four with me, and all the rest of the world against me. I do not dislike a House-of-Commons Minority in matters of taste—that is, one that is select, independent, and has a proxy from posterity.—To return to the question with which I set out.

Learning is its own exceeding great reward; and at the period of which we speak, it bore other fruits, not unworthy of it. Genius, when not smothered and kept down by learning, blazed out triumphantly over it; and the Fancy often rose to a height proportioned to the depth to which the Understanding had struck its roots. After the first emancipation of the mind from the trammels of Papal ignorance and superstition, people seemed to be in a state of breathless wonder at the new light that was suffered to break in upon them. They were startled as " at the birth of nature from the un-apparent deep." They seized on all objects that rose in view with a firm and eager grasp, in order to be sure whether they were imposed upon or not. The mind of man, " pawing to get free " from custom and prejudice, struggled and plunged, and like the fabled Pegasus, opened at each spring a new source of truth. Images were piled on heaps, as well as opinions and facts, the ample materials for poetry and prose, to which the bold hand of enthusiasm applied its torch, and kindled it into a flame. The accumulation of past records seemed to form the frame-work of their prose, as the observation of external objects did of their poetry—

> " Whose body nature was, and *man* the soul."

Among poets they have to boast such names, for in-stance, as Shakespear, Spenser, Beaumont and Fletcher, Marlowe, Webster, Decker, and soon after, Milton; among prose-writers, Selden, Bacon, Jeremy Taylor, Baxter, and Sir Thomas Browne; for patriots they have such men as Pym, Hampden, Sydney; and for a witness of their zeal and piety, they have Fox's *Book of Martyrs*, instead of which we have Mr. Southey's *Book of the Church*, and a whole host of renegades! Perhaps Jeremy Taylor and also Beaumont and Fletcher may be men-tioned as rather exceptions to the gravity and severity I have spoken of as characteristic of our earlier literature. It is true, they are florid and voluptuous in their style, but they still keep their state apart, and there is an eloquence of the heart about them, which seems to gush from the " pure well of English undefiled." The one treats of sacred things with a vividness and fervour as if he had a revelation of them: the others speak of human interests with a tenderness as if man's nature were divine. Jeremy

Taylor's pen seems to have been guided by the very spirit of joy and youth, but yet with a sense of what was due to the reverence of age, and " tears of pious awe, that feared to have offended." Beaumont and Fletcher's love-scenes are like the meeting of hearts in Elysium. Let any one have dwelt on any object with the greatest fondness, let him have cherished the feeling to the utmost height, and have it put to the test in the most trying circumstances, and he will find it described to the life in Beaumont and Fletcher. Our modern dramatists (with one exception[1]) appeal not to nature or the heart, but—to the readers of modern poetry. Words and paper, each *couleur de rose*, are the two requisites of a fashionable style. But the glossy splendour, the voluptuous glow of the obsolete, old-fashioned writers just mentioned has nothing artificial, nothing meretricious in it. It is the luxuriance of natural feeling and fancy. I should as soon think of accusing the summer-rose of vanity for unfolding its leaves to the dawn, or the hawthorn that puts forth its blossoms in the genial warmth of spring, of affecting to be fine. We have heard a good deal of the pulpit-eloquence of Bossuet and other celebrated preachers of the time of Fenelon; but I doubt much whether all of them together could produce any number of passages to match the best of those in the *Holy Living and Dying*, or even Baxter's severe but thrilling denunciations of the insignificance and nothingness of life and the certainty of a judgment to come. There is a fine portrait of this last-named powerful controversialist, with his high forehead and black velvet cap, in Calamy's *Non-Conformist's Memorial*, containing an account of the Two Thousand Ejected Ministers at the Restoration of Charles II. This was a proud list for Old England; and the account of their lives, their zeal, their eloquence and sufferings for conscience sake, is one of the most interesting chapters in the history of the human

---

[1] [Sheridan Knowles] the author of *Virginius*.

mind. How high it can soar in faith! How nobly it
can arm itself with resolution and fortitude! How far it
can surpass itself in cruelty and fraud! How incapable
it seems to be of good, except as it is urged on by the
contention with evil! The retired and inflexible descendants of the Two Thousand Ejected Ministers and their
adherents are gone with the spirit of persecution that gave
a soul and body to them; and with them, I am afraid, the
spirit of liberty, of manly independence, and of inward
self-respect is nearly extinguished in England. There
appears to be no natural necessity for evil, but that there
is a perfect indifference to good without it. One thing
exists and has a value set upon it only as it has a foil in
some other; learning is set off by ignorance, liberty by
slavery, refinement by barbarism. The cultivation and
attainment of any art or excellence is followed by its
neglect and decay; and even religion owes its zest to the
spirit of contradiction; for it flourishes most from persecution and hostile factions. Mr. Irving speaks of the great
superiority of religion over every other motive, since it
enabled its professors to " endure having hot molten lead
poured down their throats." He forgets that it was
religion that poured it down their throats, and that this
principle, mixed with the frailty of human passion, has
often been as ready to inflict as to endure. I could make
the world good, wise, happy to-morrow, if, when made, it
would be contented to remain so without the alloy of
mischief, misery, and absurdity: that is, if every possession did not require the principle of contrast, contradiction, and excess, to enliven and set it off and keep it at a
safe distance from sameness and insipidity.

The different styles of art and schools of learning vary
and fluctuate on this principle. After the restoration of
Charles, the grave, enthusiastic, puritanical, " prick-
eared " style became quite exploded, and a gay and
piquant style, the reflection of courtly conversation and

polished manners, and borrowed from the French, came into fashion, and lasted till the Revolution. Some examples of the same thing were given in the time of Charles I by Sir J. Suckling and others, but they were eclipsed and overlaid by the prevalence and splendour of the opposite examples. It was at its height, however, in the reign of the restored monarch, and in the witty and licentious writings of Wycherley, Congreve, Rochester, and Waller. Milton alone stood out as a partisan of the old Elizabethan school. Out of compliment, I suppose, to the Houses of Orange and Hanover, we sobered down, after the Revolution, into a strain of greater demureness, and into a Dutch and German fidelity of imitation of domestic manners and individual character, as in the periodical essayists, and in the works of Fielding and Hogarth. Yet, if the two last-named painters of manners are not English, who are so? I cannot give up my partiality to them for the fag-end of a theory. They have this mark of genuine English intellect, that they constantly combine truth of external observation with strength of internal meaning. The Dutch are patient observers of nature, but want character and feeling. The French, as far as we have imitated them, aim only at the pleasing, and glance over the surfaces of words and things. Thus has our literature descended (according to the foregoing scale) from the tone of the pulpit to that of the court or drawing-room, from the drawing-room into the parlour, and from thence, if some critics say true, into the kitchen and ale-house. It may do even worse than that!

French literature has undergone great changes in like manner, and was supposed to be at its height in the time of Louis XIV. We sympathise less, however, with the pompous and set speeches in the tragedies of Racine and Corneille, or in the serious comedies of Molière, than we do with the grotesque farces of the latter, with the exaggerated descriptions and humour of Rabelais (whose wit was a madness, a drunkenness), or with the accomplished humanity, the easy style, and gentlemanly and scholar-like sense of Montaigne. But these we consider as in a great measure English, or as what the old French character inclined to, before it was corrupted by courts and academies of criticism. The exquisite graces of La Fontaine, the indifferent sarcastic tone of Voltaire and Le Sage, who made light of everything, and who produce their greatest effects with the most imperceptible and rapid touches, we give wholly to the constitutional genius of the French, and despair of imitating. Perhaps in all this we proceed by guess-work at best. Nations (particularly rival nations) are bad judges of one another's literature or physiognomy. The French certainly do not understand *us*: it is most probable we do not understand *them*. How slowly great works, great names make their way across the Channel! M. Tracey's *Ideologie* has not yet been heard of amongst us, and a Frenchman who asks if you have read it, almost subjects himself to the suspicion of being the author. They have also their little sects and parties in literature, and though they do not nickname and vilify their rivals, as is done with us (thanks to the national politeness), yet if you do not belong to the prevailing party, they very civilly suppress all mention of you, your name is not noticed in the Journals, nor your work inquired for at the shops.[1]

Those who explain everything by final causes (that is, who deduce causes from effects) might avail themselves of their privilege on this occasion. There must be some

---

[1] In Paris, to be popular, you must wear out, they say, twenty pair of pumps and twenty pair of silk stockings in calls upon the different Newspaper Editors. In England, you have only to give in your resignation at the Treasury, and you receive your passport to the John Bull Parnassus; otherwise you are shut out and made a bye-word. Literary jealousy and littleness is still the motive, politics the pretext, and blackguardism the mode.

checks to the excessive increase of literature as of population, or we should be overwhelmed by it; and they are happily found in the envy, dulness, prejudices, and vanity of mankind. While we think we are weighing the merits of an author, we are indulging our own national pride, indolence, or ill-humour, by laughing at what we do not understand, or condemning what thwarts our inclinations. The French reduce all philosophy to a set of agreeable sensations: the Germans reduce the commonest things to an abstruse metaphysics. The one are a mystical, the other a superficial people. Both proceed by the severest logic; but the real guide to their conclusions is the proportion of phlegm or mercury in their dispositions. When we appeal to a man's reason against his inclinations, we speak a language without meaning, and which he will not understand. Different nations have favourite modes of feeling and of accounting for things to please themselves and fall in with their ordinary habits; and our different systems of philosophy, literature, and art meet, contend, and repel one another on the confines of opinion, because their elements will not amalgamate with our several humours, and all the while we fancy we settle the question by an abstract exercise of reason, and by laying down some refined and exclusive standard of taste. There is no great harm in this delusion, nor can there be much in seeing through it; for we shall still go on just as we did before.[1]

---

[1] Buonaparte got a committee of the French Institute to draw up a report of the Kantean Philosophy; he might as well have ordered them to draw up a report of the geography of the moon. It is difficult for an Englishman to understand Kant; for a Frenchman impossible. The latter has a certain routine of phrases into which his ideas run habitually as into a mould, and you cannot get him out of them.

PUBLIC OPINION

(CONVERSATIONS OF NORTHCOTE,
NOV. 22, 1830)

NORTHCOTE—I ought to cross myself like the Catholics, when I see you. You terrify me by repeating what I say. But I see you have regulated yourself. There is nothing personally offensive, except what relates to Sir Walter. You make him swear too, which he did not do. He would never use the expression *Egad*. These little things mark the gentleman. I am afraid, if he sees it, he'll say I am a babbler. That is what they dread so at court, that the least word should transpire.

HAZLITT—They may have their reasons for caution. At least, they can gain nothing, and might possibly lose equally by truth or falsehood, as it must be difficult to convey an adequate idea of royalty. But authors are glad to be talked about. If Sir W. Scott has an objection to having his name mentioned, he is singularly unlucky. Enough was said in his praise; and I do not believe he is captious. I fancy he *takes the rough with the smooth*. I did not well know what to do. You seemed to express a wish that the conversations should proceed, and yet you are startled at particular phrases, or I would have brought you what I had done to shew you. I thought it best to take my chance of the general impression.

N.—Why, if kept to be published as a diary after my death, they might do: nobody could then come to ask me questions about them. But I cannot say they appear very striking to me. One reason may be, what I observe myself cannot be very new to me. If others are pleased, they are the best judges. It seems very odd that you who are acquainted with some of the greatest authors of the day cannot find anything of theirs worth setting down.

H.—That by no means pleases them. I understand G——— is angry at the liberty I take with you. He is quite safe in this respect. I might answer him much in the manner of the fellow in the *Country Girl* when his friend introduces his mistress and he salutes her,—" Why, I suppose if I were to introduce my grandmother to you ——" " Sir," replies the other, " I should treat her with the utmost respect." So I shall never think of repeating any of G——'s conversations. My indifference may arise in part, as you say, from their not being very new to me. G—— might, I dare say, argue very well on the doctrine of philosophical necessity or many other questions; but then I have read all this before in Hume or other writers, and I am very little edified, because I have myself had access to the same sources that he has drawn from. But you, as an artist, have been pushed into an intercourse with the world as well as an observation of nature; and combine a sufficient knowledge of general subjects with living illustrations of them. I do not like the conversation of mere men of the world or anecdote-mongers, for there is nothing to bind it together, and the other sort is pedantic and tiresome from repetition, so that there is nobody but you I can come to.

N.—You do not go enough into society, or you would be cured of what I cannot help regarding as a whim. You would there find many people of sense and information whose names you never heard of. It is not those who have made most noise in the world who are persons of the greatest general capacity. It is the making the most of a little, or the being determined to get before others in some one thing (perhaps for want of other recommendations) that brings men into notice. Individuals gain a reputation as they make a fortune, by application and by having set their minds upon it. But you have set out (like other people brought up among books) with such exclusive notions of authors and literary fame, that if you find the least glimmering of common sense out of this pale, you think it a prodigy, and run

U

into the opposite extreme. I do not say that you have not a perception of character, or have not thought as far as you have observed; but you have not had the opportunities. You turn your back on the world, and fancy that they turn their backs on you. This is a very dangerous principle. You become reckless of consequences. It leads to an abandonment of character. By setting the opinion of others at defiance, you lose your self-respect. It is of no use that you still say, you will do what is right; your passions usurp the place of reason, and whisper you, that whatever you are bent upon doing is right. You cannot put this deception on the public, however false or prejudiced their standard may be; and the opinion of the world, therefore, acts as a seasonable check upon wilfulness and eccentricity.

H.—What you have stated is the best excuse I could make for my own faults or blunders. When one is found fault with for nothing, or for doing one's best, one is apt to give the world their revenge. All the former part of my life I was treated as a cipher; and since I have got into notice, I have been set upon as a wild beast. When this is the case, and you can expect as little justice as candour, you naturally in self-defence take refuge in a sort of misanthropy and cynical contempt for mankind. One is disposed to humour them, and to furnish them with some ground for their idle and malevolent censures.

N.—But you should not. If you do nothing to confirm them in their first prejudices, they will come round in time. They are *slow* to admit claims, because they are not *sure* of their validity; and they thwart and cross-examine you to try what temper you are made of. Without some such ordeal or difficulty thrown in the way, every upstart and pretender must be swallowed whole. That would never do. But if you have patience to stand the test, justice is rendered at last, and you are stamped for as much as you are worth. You certainly have not spared others: why should you expect nothing but "the milk of human kindness?" Look to those men behind you (*a collection of portraits on the same frame*)—there is Pope and Dryden—did they fare better than living authors? Had not Dryden his Shadwell, and Pope his Dennis, who fretted him to a shadow, and galled him almost to death? There was Dr. Johnson, who in his writings was a pattern of wisdom and morality—he declared that he had been hunted down as if he had been the great enemy of mankind. But he had strength of mind to look down upon it. Not to do this, is either infirmity of temper, or shews a conscious want of any claims that are worth carrying up to a higher tribunal than the cabal and clamour of the moment. Sir Joshua always despised malicious reports; he knew they would blow over; at the same time, he as little regarded exaggerated praise. Nothing you could say had any effect, if he was not satisfied with himself. He had a great game to play, and only looked to the result. He had studied himself thoroughly; and, besides, had great equanimity of temper, which, to be sure, it is difficult to acquire, if it is not natural. You have two faults: one is a *feud* or quarrel with the world, which makes you despair, and prevents you taking all the pains you might: the other is a careless-ness and mismanagement, which makes you throw away the little you actually do, and brings you into difficulties that way. Sir Joshua used to say it was as wrong for a man to think too little as too much of himself: if the one ran him into extravagance and presumption, the other sank him in sloth and insignificance. You see the same thing in horses: if they cannot stir a load at the first effort, they give it up as a hopeless task; and nothing can rouse them from their sluggish obstinacy but blows and ill-treatment.

H.—I confess all this, but I hardly know how to remedy it: nor do I feel any strong inducement. Taking

one thing with another, I have no great cause to complain. If I had been a merchant, a bookseller, or the
proprietor of a newspaper, instead of what I am, I might
have had more money or possessed a town and country-
house, instead of lodging in a first or second floor, as it
may happen. But what then? I see how the man of
business and fortune passes his time. He is up and in
the city by eight, swallows his breakfast in haste, attends
a meeting of creditors, must read Lloyd's lists, consult
the price of consols, study the markets, look into his
accounts, pay his workmen, and superintend his clerks:
he has hardly a minute in the day to himself, and perhaps
in the four-and-twenty hours does not do a single thing
that he would do if he could help it. Surely, this sacrifice
of time and inclination requires some compensation,
which it meets with. But how am I entitled to make my
fortune (which cannot be done without all this anxiety
and drudgery) who do hardly anything at all, and never
anything but what I like to do? I rise when I please,
breakfast *at length*, write what comes into my head, and
after taking a mutton-chop and a dish of strong tea,
go to the play, and thus my time passes. Mr. —— has
no time to go to the play. It was but the other day that
I had to get up a little earlier than usual to go into the
city about some money transaction, which appeared to
me a prodigious hardship: if so, it was plain that I must
lead a tolerably easy life: nor should I object to passing
mine over again   Till I was twenty, I had no idea of
anything but books, and thought everything else was
worthless and mechanical. The having to study painting
about this time, and finding the difficulties and beauties
it unfolded, opened a new field to me, and I began to conclude that there might be a number of " other things
between heaven and earth that were never dreamt of in
my philosophy." Ask G——, or any other literary man
who has never been taken out of the leading-strings of

learning, and you will perceive that they hold for a settled truth that the universe is built of words. G—— has no interest but in literary fame, of which he is a worshipper: he cannot believe that any one is clever or has even common sense, who has not written a book. If you talk to him of Italian cities, where great poets and patriots lived, he heaves a sigh; and if I were possessed of a fortune, he should go and visit the house where Galileo lived, or the tower where Ugolino was imprisoned. He can see with the eyes of his mind. To all else he is marble. It is like speaking to him of the objects of a *sixth sense;* every other language seems dumb and inarticulate.

DISAPPOINTMENT

(LECTURES CHIEFLY ON THE DRAMATIC LITERATURE OF THE AGE OF ELIZABETH, 1820)

I HAVE done: and if I have done no better, the fault has been in me, not in the subject. My liking to this grew with my knowledge of it: but so did my anxiety to do it justice. I somehow felt it as a point of honour not to make my hearers think less highly of some of these old writers than I myself did of them. If I have praised an author, it was because I liked him: if I have quoted a passage, it was because it pleased me in the reading : if I have spoken contemptuously of any one, it has been reluctantly. It is no easy task, that a writer, even in so humble a class as myself, takes upon him; he is scouted and ridiculed if he fails; and if he succeeds, the enmity and cavils and malice with which he is assailed, are just in proportion to his success. The coldness and jealousy of his friends not unfrequently keep pace with the rancour of his enemies. They do not like you a bit the better for fulfilling the good opinion they always entertained of you. They would wish you to be always promising a great deal, and doing nothing, that they may answer for the performance. That shews their sagacity and does not hurt their vanity. An author wastes his time in painful study and obscure researches, to gain a little breath of popularity, meets with nothing but vexation and disappointment in ninety-nine instances out of a hundred; or when he thinks to grasp the luckless prize, finds it not worth the trouble—the perfume of a minute, fleeting as a shadow, hollow as a sound; " as often got without merit as lost without deserving." He thinks that the attainment of acknowledged excellence will secure him the expression of those feelings in others, which the image and hope of it had excited in his own breast, but instead of that, he meets with nothing (or scarcely nothing) but squint-eyed suspicion, idiot wonder, and grinning scorn.—It seems hardly worth while to have taken all the pains he has been at for this!

In youth we borrow patience from our future years: the spring of hope gives us courage to act and suffer. A cloud is upon our onward path, and we fancy that all is sunshine beyond it. The prospect seems endless, because we do not know the end of it. We think that life is long, because art is so, and that, because we have much to do, it is well worth doing: or that no exertions can be too great, no sacrifices too painful, to overcome the difficulties we have to encounter. Life is a continued struggle to be what we are not, and to do what we cannot. But as we approach the goal, we draw in the reins; the impulse is less, as we have not so far to go; as we see objects nearer, we become less sanguine in the pursuit: it is not the despair of not attaining, so much as knowing that there is nothing worth obtaining, and the fear of having nothing left even to wish for, that damps our ardour and relaxes our efforts; and if the mechanical habit did not increase the facility, would, I believe, take away all inclination or power to do anything. We stagger on the few remaining paces to the end of our journey; make perhaps one final effort; and are glad when our task is done!

A FAREWELL TO ESSAY-WRITING

(LONDON WEEKLY REVIEW, MARCH 29, 1828)

"This life is best, if quiet life is best."

FOOD, warmth, sleep, and a book; these are all I at present ask—the *ultima Thule* of my wandering desires. Do you not then wish for

"A friend in your retreat,
Whom you may whisper, solitude is sweet?"

Expected, well enough:—gone, still better. Such attractions are strengthened by distance. Nor a mistress? "Beautiful mask! I know thee!" When I can judge of the heart from the face, of the thoughts from the lips, I may again trust myself. Instead of these, give me the robin red-breast, pecking the crumbs at the door, or warbling on the leafless spray, the same glancing form that has followed me wherever I have been, and "done its spiriting gently"; or the rich notes of the thrush that startle the ear of winter, and seem to have drunk up the full draught of joy from the very sense of contrast. To these I adhere, and am faithful, for they are true to me; and, dear in themselves, are dearer for the sake of what is departed, leading me back (by the hand) to that dreaming

world, in the innocence of which they sat and made
sweet music, waking the promise of future years, and
answered by the eager throbbings of my own breast.
But now " the credulous hope of mutual minds is o'er,"
and I turn back from the world that has deceived me, to
nature that lent it a false beauty, and that keeps up the
illusion of the past. As I quaff my libations of tea in a
morning, I love to watch the clouds sailing from the
west, and fancy that " the spring comes slowly up this
way." In this hope, while " fields are dank and ways
are mire," I follow the same direction to a neighbouring
wood, where, having gained the dry, level greensward,
I can see my way for a mile before me, closed in on each
side by copse-wood, and ending in a point of light more
or less brilliant, as the day is bright or cloudy. What a
walk is this to me! I have no need of book or companion
—the days, the hours, the thoughts of my youth are at
my side, and blend with the air that fans my cheek. Here
I can saunter for hours, bending my eye forward, stopping
and turning to look back, thinking to strike off into
some less trodden path, yet hesitating to quit the one
I am in, afraid to snap the brittle threads of memory.
I remark the shining trunks and slender branches of the
birch-trees, waving in the idle breeze; or a pheasant
springs up on whirring wing; or I recall the spot where
I once found a wood-pigeon at the foot of a tree, weltering
in its gore, and think how many seasons have flown since
" it left its little life in air." Dates, names, faces come
back—to what purpose? Or why think of them now?
Or rather, why not think of them oftener? We walk
through life, as through a narrow path, with a thin curtain
drawn around it; behind are ranged rich portraits, airy
harps are strung—yet we will not stretch forth our hands
and lift aside the veil, to catch glimpses of the one, or
sweep the chords of the other. As in a theatre, when the
old-fashioned green curtain drew up, groups of figures,

fantastic dresses, laughing faces, rich banquets, stately columns, gleaming vistas appeared beyond; so we have only at any time to " peep through the blanket of the past," to possess ourselves at once of all that has regaled our senses, that is stored up in our memory, that has struck our fancy, that has pierced our hearts:—yet to all this we are indifferent, insensible, and seem intent only on the present vexation, the future disappointment. If there is a Titian hanging up in the room with me, I scarcely regard it: how then should I be expected to strain the mental eye so far, or to throw down, by the magic spells of the will, the stone-walls that enclose it in the Louvre? There is one head there of which I have often thought, when looking at it, that nothing should ever disturb me again, and I would become the character it represents—such perfect calmness and self-possession reigns in it! Why do I not hang an image of this in some dusky corner of my brain, and turn an eye upon it ever and anon, as I have need of some such talisman to calm my troubled thoughts? The attempt is fruitless, if not natural; or, like that of the French, to hang garlands on the grave, and to conjure back the dead by miniature pictures of them while living! It is only some actual coincidence or local association that tends, without violence, to " open all the cells where memory slept." I can easily, by stooping over the long-sprent grass and clay cold clod, recall the tufts of primroses, or purple hyacinths, that formerly grew on the same spot, and cover the bushes with leaves and singing-birds, as they were eighteen summers ago; or prolonging my walk and hearing the sighing gale rustle through a tall, straight wood at the end of it, can fancy that I distinguish the cry of hounds, and the fatal group issuing from it, as in the tale of *Theodore and Honoria*. A moaning gust of wind aids the belief; I look once more to see whether the trees before me answer to the idea of the horror-

U *

stricken grove, and an air-built city towers over their grey tops.

> " Of all the cities in Romanian lands,
> The chief and most renown'd Ravenna stands."

I return home resolved to read the entire poem through, and, after dinner, drawing my chair to the fire, and holding a small print close to my eyes, launch into the full tide of Dryden's couplets (a stream of sound), comparing his didactic and descriptive pomp with the simple pathos and picturesque truth of Boccaccio's story, and tasting with a pleasure, which none but an habitual reader can feel, some quaint examples of pronunciation in this accomplished versifier.

> " Which when Honoria view'd,
> The fresh *impulse* her former fright renew'd."
>
> Dryden's *Theodore and Honoria*.

> " And made th' *insult*, which in his grief appears,
> The means to mourn thee with my pious tears."
>
> Dryden's *Sigismonda and Guiscardo*.

These trifling instances of the wavering and unsettled state of the language give double effect to the firm and stately march of the verse, and make me dwell with a sort of tender interest on the difficulties and doubts of an earlier period of literature. They pronounced words then in a manner which we should laugh at now; and they wrote verse in a manner which we can do anything but laugh at. The pride of a new acquisition seems to give fresh confidence to it; to impel the rolling syllables through the moulds provided for them, and to overflow the envious bounds of rhyme into time-honoured triplets.

What sometimes surprises me in looking back to the past, is, with the exception already stated, to find myself so little changed in the time. The same images and trains of thought stick by me: I have the same tastes, likings, sentiments, and wishes that I had then. One great ground of confidence and support has, indeed, been struck from under my feet; but I have made it up to myself by proportionable pertinacity of opinion. The success of the great cause, to which I had vowed myself, was to me more than all the world: I had a strength in its strength, a resource which I knew not of, till it failed me for the second time.

> " Fall'n was Glenartny's stately tree !
> Oh ! ne'er to see Lord Ronald more ! "

It was not till I saw the axe laid to the root, that I found the full extent of what I had to lose and suffer. But my conviction of the right was only established by the triumph of the wrong; and my earliest hopes will be my last regrets. One source of this unbendingness (which some may call obstinacy), is that, though living much alone, I have never worshipped the Echo. I see plainly enough that black is not white, that the grass is green, that kings are not their subjects; and, in such self-evident cases, do not think it necessary to collate my opinions with the received prejudices. In subtler questions, and matters that admit of doubt, as I do not impose my opinion on others without a reason, so I will not give up mine to them without a better reason; and a person calling me names, or giving himself airs of authority, does not convince me of his having taken more pains to find out the truth than I have, but the contrary. Mr. Gifford once said, that " while I was sitting over my gin and tobacco-pipes, I fancied myself a Leibnitz." He did not so much as know that I had ever read a metaphysical book:—was I therefore, out of complaisance or deference to him, to forget whether I had or not? Leigh Hunt is puzzled to reconcile the shyness of my pretensions with the inveteracy and sturdiness of my principles.

I should have thought they were nearly the same thing. Both from disposition and habit, I can *assume* nothing in word, look, or manner. I cannot steal a march upon public opinion in any way. My standing upright, speaking loud, entering a room gracefully, proves nothing; therefore I neglect these ordinary means of recommending myself to the good graces and admiration of strangers (and, as it appears, even of philosophers and friends). Why? Because I have other resources, or, at least, am absorbed in other studies and pursuits. Suppose this absorption to be extreme, and even morbid—that I have brooded over an idea till it has become a kind of substance in my brain, that I have reasons for a thing which I have found out with much labour and pains, and to which I can scarcely do justice without the utmost violence of exertion (and that only to a few persons)—is this a reason for my playing off my out-of-the-way notions in all companies, wearing a prim and self-complacent air, as if I were " the admired of all observers "? or is it not rather an argument (together with a want of animal spirits) why I should retire into myself, and perhaps acquire a nervous and uneasy look, from a consciousness of the disproportion between the interest and conviction I feel on certain subjects, and my ability to communicate what weighs upon my own mind to others? If my ideas, which I do not avouch, but suppose, lie below the surface, why am I to be always attempting to dazzle superficial people with them, or smiling, delighted, at my own want of success?

In matters of taste and feeling, one proof that my conclusions have not been quite shallow or hasty, is the circumstance of their having been lasting. I have the same favourite books, pictures, passages, that I ever had: I may therefore presume that they will last me my life— nay, I may indulge a hope that my thoughts will survive me. This continuity of impression is the only thing on which I pride myself. Even Lamb, whose relish of certain things is as keen and earnest as possible, takes a surfeit of admiration, and I should be afraid to ask about his select authors or particular friends, after a lapse of ten years. As to myself, any one knows where to have me. What I have once made up my mind to, I abide by to the end of the chapter. One cause of my independence of opinion is, I believe, the liberty I give to others, or the very diffidence and distrust of making converts. I should be an excellent man on a jury. I might say little, but should starve " the other eleven obstinate fellows " out. I remember Mr. Godwin writing to Mr. Wordsworth, that " his tragedy of *Antonio* could not fail of success." It was damned past all redemption. I said to Mr. Wordsworth that I thought this a natural consequence; for how could any one have a dramatic turn of mind who judged entirely of others from himself? Mr. Godwin might be convinced of the excellence of his work; but how could he know that others would be convinced of it, unless by supposing that they were as wise as himself, and as infallible critics of dramatic poetry—so many Aristotles sitting in judgment on Euripides! This shews why pride is connected with shyness and reserve; for the really proud have not so high an opinion of the generality as to suppose that they can understand them, or that there is any common measure between them. So Dryden exclaims of his opponents with bitter disdain—

" Nor can I think what thoughts they can conceive."

I have not sought to make partisans, still less did I dream of making enemies; and have therefore kept my opinions myself, whether they were currently adopted or not. To get others to come into our ways of thinking, we must go over to theirs; and it is necessary to follow, in order to lead. At the time I lived here formerly, I had no suspicion that I should ever become a voluminous writer, yet I had just the same confidence in my feelings before I had ventured to air them in public as I have now. Neither the outcry *for* or *against* moves me a jot: I do not say that the one is not more agreeable than the other.

Not far from the spot where I write, I first read Chaucer's *Flower and Leaf*, and was charmed with that young beauty, shrouded in her bower, and listening with ever-fresh delight to the repeated song of the nightingale close by her—the impression of the scene, the vernal landscape, the cool of the morning, the gushing notes of the songstress,

" And ayen methought she sung close by mine ear,"

is as vivid as if it had been of yesterday; and nothing can persuade me that that is not a fine poem. I do not find this impression conveyed in Dryden's version, and therefore nothing can persuade me that that is as fine. I used to walk out at this time with Mr. and Miss Lamb of an evening, to look at the Claude Lorraine skies over our heads melting from azure into purple and gold, and to gather mushrooms, that sprung up at our feet, to throw into our hashed mutton at supper. I was at that time an enthusiastic admirer of Claude, and could dwell for ever on one or two of the finest prints from him hung round my little room; the fleecy flocks, the bending trees, the winding streams, the groves, the nodding temples, the air-wove hills, and distant sunny vales; and tried to translate them into their lovely living hues. People then told me that Wilson was much superior to Claude: I did not believe them. Their pictures have since been seen together at the British Institution, and all the world have come into my opinion. I have not, on that account, given it up. I will not compare our hashed mutton with Amelia's; but it put us in mind of it, and led to a discussion, sharply seasoned and well sustained, till midnight, the result of which appeared some years after in the *Edinburgh Review*. Have I a better opinion of those criticisms on that account, or should I therefore maintain them with greater vehemence and tenaciousness? Oh no! Both rather with less, now that they are before the public, and it is for them to make their election.

It is in looking back to such scenes that I draw my best consolation for the future. Later impressions come and go, and serve to fill up the intervals; but these are my standing resource, my true classics. If I have had few real pleasures or advantages, my ideas, from their sinewy texture, have been to me in the nature of realities; and if I should not be able to add to the stock, I can live by husbanding the interest. As to my speculations, there is little to admire in them but my admiration of others; and whether they have an echo in time to come or not, I have learned to set a grateful value on the past, and am content to wind up the account of what is personal only to myself and the immediate circle of objects in which I have moved, with an act of easy oblivion,

" And curtain-close such scene from every future view."

WINTERSLOW, *Feb.* 20, 1828.

ON PAINTERS AND
PAINTING

WHY THE ARTS
ARE NOT PROGRESSIVE---
A FRAGMENT

(MORNING CHRONICLE, JAN. II AND 15,
1814)

I T is often made a subject of complaint and surprise, that the arts in this country, and in modern times, have not kept pace with the general progress of society and civilization in other respects, and it has been proposed to remedy the deficiency by more carefully availing ourselves of the advantages which time and circumstances have placed within our reach, but which we have hitherto neglected, the study of the antique, the formation of academies, and the distribution of prizes.

First, the complaint itself, that the arts do not attain that progressive degree of perfection which might reasonably be expected from them, proceeds on a false notion, for the analogy appealed to in support of the regular advances of art to higher degrees of excellence, totally fails; it applies to science, not to art.—Secondly, the expedients proposed to remedy the evil by adven titious means are only calculated to confirm it. The arts hold immediate communication with nature, and are only derived from that source. When that original impulse no longer exists, when the inspiration of genius is fled, all the attempts to recall it are no better than the tricks of galvanism to restore the dead to life. The arts may be said to resemble Antæus in his struggle with Hercules, who was strangled when he was raised above the ground, and only revived and recovered his strength when he touched his mother earth.

Nothing is more contrary to the fact than the supposition that in what we understand by the *fine arts,* as painting and poetry, relative perfection is only the result of repeated efforts, and that what has been once well done constantly leads to something better. What is mechanical, reducible to rule, or capable of demonstration, is progressive, and admits of gradual improvement: what is not mechanical or definite, but depends on genius, taste, and feeling, very soon becomes stationary, or retrograde, and loses more than it gains by transfusion. The contrary opinion is, indeed, a common error, which has grown up, like many others, from transferring an analogy of one kind to something quite distinct, without thinking of the difference in the nature of the things, or attending to the difference of the results. For most persons, finding what wonderful advances have been made in biblical criticism, in chemistry, in mechanics, in geometry, astronomy, &c., i.e. in things depending on mere inquiry and experiment, or on absolute demonstration, have been led hastily to conclude, that there was a general tendency in the efforts of the human intellect to improve by repetition, and in all other arts and institutions to grow perfect and mature by time. We look back upon the theological creed of our ancestors, and their discoveries in natural philosophy, with a smile of pity; science, and the arts connected with it, have all had their infancy, their youth, and manhood, and seem to have in them no principle of limitation or decay; and, inquiring no farther about the matter, we infer, in the height of our self-congratulation, and in the intoxication of our pride, that the same progress has been, and will continue to be, made in all other things which are the work of man. The fact, however, stares us so plainly in the face, that one would think the smallest reflection must suggest the truth, and overturn our sanguine theories. The greatest poets, the ablest orators, the best painters, and the finest sculptors that the world ever saw, appeared soon after the birth of these arts, and lived in a state of society, which was, in other respects, comparatively barbarous. Those arts, which depend on individual genius and incommunicable power, have always leaped at once from infancy to manhood, from the first rude dawn of invention to their meridian height and dazzling lustre, and have in general declined ever after. This is the peculiar distinction and privilege of each, of science and of art; of the one, never to attain its utmost summit of perfection, and of the other, to arrive at it almost at once. Homer, Chaucer, Spenser, Shakspeare, Dante, and Ariosto (Milton alone was of a later age, and not the worse for it), Raphael, Titian, Michael Angelo, Correggio, Cervantes, and Boccaccio—all lived near the beginning of their arts— perfected, and all but created them. These giant sons of genius stand, indeed, upon the earth, but they tower above their fellows, and the long line of their successors does not interpose anything to obstruct their view, or lessen their brightness. In strength and stature they are unrivalled, in grace and beauty they have never been surpassed. In after-ages, and more refined periods, (as they are called,) great men have arisen one by one, as it were by throes and at intervals : though in general the best of these cultivated and artificial minds were of an inferior order, as Tasso and Pope among poets, Guido and Vandyke among painters. But in the earliest stages of the arts, when the first mechanical difficulties had been got over, and the language as it were acquired, they rose by clusters and in constellations, never to rise again.

The arts of painting and poetry are conversant with the world of thought within us, and with the world of sense without us—with what we know, and see, and feel intimately. They flow from the sacred shrine of our own breasts, and are kindled at the living lamp of nature. The pulse of the passions assuredly beats as high, the depths and soundings of the human heart were as well understood three thousand years ago, as they are at present; the face of nature, and " the human face divine," shone as bright then as they have ever done. It is this light, reflected by true genius on art, that marks out its path before it, and sheds a glory round the Muses' feet, like that which " circled Una's angel face,

"And made a sunshine in the shady place."

Nature is the soul of art. There is a strength in the imagination that reposes entirely on nature, which nothing else can supply. There is in the old poets and painters a vigour and grasp of mind, a full possession of their subject, a confidence and firm faith, a sublime simplicity, an elevation of thought, proportioned to their depth of feeling, an increasing force and impetus, which moves, penetrates, and kindles all that come in contact with it, which seems not theirs, but given to them. It is this reliance on the power of nature which has produced those masterpieces by the Prince of Painters, in which expression is all in all, where one spirit—that of truth—pervades every part, brings down heaven to earth, mingles cardinals and popes with angels and apostles, and yet blends and harmonizes the whole by the true touches and intense feeling of what is beautiful and grand in nature. It was the same trust in nature that enabled Chaucer to describe the patient sorrow of Griselda; or the delight of that young beauty, in the Flower and the Leaf, shrouded in her bower, and listening, in the morning of the year, to the singing of the nightingale, while her joy rises with the rising song, and gushes out afresh at every pause, and is borne along with the full tide of pleasure, and still increases and repeats and prolongs itself, and knows no ebb. It is thus that Boccaccio, in the divine story of the the Hawk, has represented Frederigo Alberigi steadily contemplating his favourite Falcon (the wreck and remnant of his fortune), and glad to see how fat and fair a bird she is, thinking what a dainty repast she would make for his Mistress, who had deigned to visit him in his low cell. So Isabella mourns over her pot of Basil, and never asks for anything but that. So Lear calls out for his poor fool, and invokes the heavens, for they are old like him. So Titian impressed on the countenance of that young Neapolitan nobleman in the Louvre, a look that never passed away. So Nicolas Poussin describes some shepherds wandering out in a morning of the spring, and coming to a tomb with this inscription, " I ALSO WAS AN ARCADIAN."

In general, it must happen in the first stages of the Arts, that as none but those who had a natural genius for them would attempt to practise them, so none but those who had a natural taste for them would pretend to judge of or criticize them. This must be an incalculable advantage to the man of true genius, for it is no other than the privilege of being tried by his peers. In an age when connoisseurship had not become a fashion; when religion, war, and intrigue, occupied the time and thoughts of the great, only those minds of superior refinement would be led to notice the works of art, who had a real sense of their excellence; and in giving way to the powerful bent of his own genius, the painter was most likely to consult the taste of his judges. He had not to deal with pretenders to taste, through vanity, affectation, and idleness. He had to appeal to the higher faculties of the soul; to that deep and innate sensibility to truth and beauty, which required only a proper object to have its enthusiasm excited; and to that independent strength of mind, which, in the midst of ignorance and barbarism, hailed and fostered genius, wherever it met with it. Titian was patronised by Charles V. Count Castiglione was the friend of Raphael. These were true patrons, and true critics; and as there were no others, (for the world, in general, merely looked on and wondered) there can be little doubt, that such a period of dearth of factitious patronage would be the most favourable to the full development of the greatest talents, and the attainment of the highest excellence.

The diffusion of taste is not the same thing as the improvement of taste; but it is only the former of these objects that is promoted by public institutions and other artificial means. The number of candidates for fame, and of pretenders to criticism, is thus increased beyond all proportion, while the quantity of genius and feeling remains the same; with this difference, that the man of genius is lost in the crowd of competitors, who would never have become such but from encouragement and example; and that the opinion of those few persons whom nature intended for judges, is drowned in the noisy suffrages of shallow smatterers in taste. The principle of universal suffrage, however applicable to matters of government, which concern the common feelings and common interests of society, is by no means applicable to matters of taste, which can only be decided upon by the most refined understandings. The highest efforts of genius, in every walk of art, can never be properly understood by the generality of mankind: There are numberless beauties and truths which lie far beyond their comprehension. It is only as refinement and sublimity are blended with other qualities of a more obvious and grosser nature, that they pass current with the world. Taste is the highest degree of sensibility, or the impression made on the most cultivated and sensible minds, as genius is the result of the highest powers both of feeling and invention. It may be objected, that the public taste is capable of gradual improvement, because, in the end, the public do justice to works of the greatest merit. This is a mistake. The reputation ultimately, and often slowly affixed to works of genius, is stamped upon them by authority, not by popular consent or the common sense of the world. We imagine that the admiration of the works of celebrated men has become common, because the admiration of their names has become so. But does not every ignorant connoisseur pretend the same veneration, and talk with the same vapid assurance of Michael Angelo, though he has never seen even a copy of any of his pictures, as if he had studied them accurately,— merely because Sir Joshua Reynolds has praised him? Is Milton more popular now than when the *Paradise Lost* was first published? Or does he not rather owe his reputation to the judgment of a few persons in every successive period, accumulating in his favour, and overpowering by its weight the public indifference? Why is Shakspeare popular? Not from his refinement of character or sentiment, so much as from his power of telling a story,— the variety and invention,—the tragic catastrophe and broad farce of his plays? Spenser is not yet understood. Does not Boccaccio pass to this day for a writer of ribaldry, because his jests and lascivious tales were all that caught the vulgar ear, while the story of the Falcon is forgotten!

ON GUSTO

(THE EXAMINER, MAY 26, 1816)

GUSTO in art is power or passion defining any object.— It is not so difficult to explain this term in what relates to expression (of which it may be said to be the highest degree) as in what relates to things without expression, to the natural appearances of objects, as mere colour or form. In one sense, however, there is hardly any object entirely devoid of expression, without some character of power belonging to it, some precise association with pleasure or pain: and it is in giving this truth of character from the truth of feeling, whether in the highest or the lowest degree, but always in the highest degree of which the subject is capable, that gusto consists.

There is a gusto in the colouring of Titian. Not only do his heads seem to think—his bodies seem to feel. This is what the Italians mean by the *morbidezza* of his flesh-colour. It seems sensitive and alive all over; not merely to have the look and texture of flesh, but the feeling in itself. For example, the limbs of his female figures have a luxurious softness and delicacy, which appears conscious of the pleasure of the beholder. As the objects themselves in nature would produce an impression on the sense, distinct from every other object, and having something divine in it, which the heart owns and the imagination consecrates, the objects in the picture preserve the same impression, absolute, unimpaired, stamped with all the truth of passion, the pride of the eye, and the charm of beauty. Rubens makes his flesh-colour like flowers; Albano's is like ivory; Titian's is like flesh, and like nothing else. It is as different from that of other painters, as the skin is from a piece of white or red drapery thrown over it. The blood circulates here and there, the blue veins just appear, the rest is distinguished throughout only by that sort of tingling sensation to the eye, which the body feels within itself. This is gusto.—Vandyke's flesh-colour, though it has great truth and purity, wants gusto. It has not the internal character, the living principle in it. It is a smooth surface, not a warm, moving mass. It is painted without passion, with indifference. The hand only has been concerned. The impression slides off from the eye, and does not, like the tones of Titian's pencil, leave a sting behind it in the mind of the spectator. The eye does not acquire a taste or appetite for what it sees. In a word, gusto in painting is where the impression made on one sense excites by affinity those of another.

Michael Angelo's forms are full of gusto. They every where obtrude the sense of power upon the eye. His limbs convey an idea of muscular strength, of moral grandeur, and even of intellectual dignity: they are firm, commanding, broad, and massy, capable of executing with ease the determined purposes of the will. His faces have no other expression than his figures, conscious power and capacity. They appear only to think what they shall do, and to know that they can do it. This is what is meant by saying that his style is hard and masculine. It is the reverse of Correggio's, which is effeminate. That is, the gusto of Michael Angelo consists in expressing energy of will without proportionable sensibility, Correggio's in expressing exquisite sensibility without energy of will. In Correggio's faces as well as figures we see neither bones nor muscles, but then what a soul is there, full of sweetness and of grace—pure, playful, soft, angelical! There is sentiment enough in a hand painted by Correggio to set up a school of history painters. Whenever we look at the hands of Correggio's women or of Raphael's, we always wish to touch them.

Again, Titian's landscapes have a prodigious gusto, both in the colouring and forms. We shall never forget one that we saw many years ago in the Orleans Gallery of Acteon hunting. It had a brown, mellow, autumnal look. The sky was of the colour of stone. The winds seemed to sing through the rustling branches of the trees, and already you might hear the twanging of bows resound through the tangled mazes of the wood. Mr. West, we understand, has this landscape. He will know if this description of it is just. The landscape background of the St. Peter Martyr is another well-known instance of the power of this great painter to give a romantic interest and an appropriate character to the objects of his pencil, where every circumstance adds to the effect of the scene,—the bold trunks of the tall forest trees, the trailing ground plants, with that cold convent spire rising in the distance, amidst the blue sapphire mountains and the golden sky.

Rubens has a great deal of gusto in his Fauns and Satyrs, and in all that expresses motion, but in nothing else. Rembrandt has it in everything; everything in his pictures has a tangible character. If he puts a diamond in the ear of a Burgomaster's wife, it is of the first water; and his furs and stuffs are proof against a Russian winter. Raphael's gusto was only in expression; he had no idea of the character of anything but the human form. The dryness and poverty of his style in other respects is a phenomenon in the art. His trees are like sprigs of grass stuck in a book of botanical specimens. Was it that Raphael never had time to go beyond the walls of Rome? That he was always in the streets, at church, or in the bath? He was not one of the Society of Arcadians.[1]

Claude's landscapes, perfect as they are, want gusto. This is not easy to explain. They are perfect abstractions of the visible images of things; they speak the visible language of nature truly. They resemble a mirror or microscope. To the eye only they are more perfect than any other landscapes that ever were or will be painted; they give more of nature, as cognizable by one sense alone; but they lay an equal stress on all visible impressions; they do not interpret one sense by another; they do not distinguish the character of different objects as we are taught, and can only be taught, to distinguish them by their effect on the different senses. That is, his eye wanted imagination: it did not strongly sympathize with his other faculties. He saw the atmosphere, but he

---

[1] Raphael not only could not paint a landscape; he could not paint people in a landscape. He could not have painted the heads or the figures, or even the dresses of the St. Peter Martyr. His figures have always an *in-door* look, that is, a set, determined, voluntary, dramatic character, arising from their own passions, or a watchfulness of those of others, and want that wild uncertainty of expression, which is connected with the accidents of nature and the changes of the elements. He has nothing *romantic* about him.

did not feel it. He painted the trunk of a tree or a rock in the foreground as smooth—with as complete an abstraction of the gross, tangible impression, as any other part of the picture; his trees are perfectly beautiful, but quite immoveable; they have a look of enchantment. In short, his landscapes are unequalled imitations of nature, released from its subjection to the elements,—as if all objects were become a delightful fairy vision, and the eye had rarefied and refined away the other senses.

The gusto in the Greek statues is of a very singular kind. The sense of perfect form nearly occupies the whole mind, and hardly suffers it to dwell on any other feeling. It seems enough for them *to be*, without acting or suffering. Their forms are ideal, spiritual. Their beauty is power. By their beauty they are raised above the frailties of pain or passion; by their beauty they are deified.

The infinite quantity of dramatic invention in Shakspeare takes from his gusto. The power he delights to shew is not intense, but discursive. He never insists on any thing as much as he might, except a quibble. Milton has great gusto. He repeats his blow twice; grapples with and exhausts his subject. His imagination has a double relish of its objects, an inveterate attachment to the things he describes, and to the words describing them.

> ——" Or where Chineses drive
> With sails and wind their *cany* waggons *light*."

>   .   .   .   .

" Wild above rule or art, *enormous* bliss."

There is a gusto in Pope's compliments, in Dryden's satires, and Prior's tales; and among prose-writers, Boccaccio and Rabelais had the most of it. We will only mention one other work which appears to us to be full of gusto, and that is the *Beggar's Opera*. If it is not, we are altogether mistaken in our notions on this delicate subject.

ON THE PLEASURE OF PAINTING

(LONDON MAGAZINE, DEC., 1820)

"THERE is a pleasure in painting which none but painters know." In writing, you have to contend with the world; in painting, you have only to carry on a friendly strife with Nature. You sit down to your task, and are happy. From the moment that you take up the pencil, and look Nature in the face, you are at peace with your own heart. No angry passions rise to disturb the silent progress of the work, to shake the hand, or dim the brow; no irritable humours are set afloat: you have no absurd opinions to combat, no point to strain, no adversary to crush, no fool to annoy—you are actuated by fear or favour to no man. There is "no juggling here," no sophistry, no intrigue, no tampering with the evidence, no attempt to make black white, or white black: but you resign yourself into the hands of a greater power, that of Nature, with the simplicity of a child, and the devotion of an enthusiast—"study with joy her manner, and with rapture taste her style." The mind is calm, and full at the same time. The hand and eye are equally employed. In tracing the commonest object, a plant or the stump of a tree, you learn something every moment. You perceive unexpected differences, and discover likenesses where you looked for no such thing. You try to set down what you see —find out your error, and correct it. You need not play tricks, or purposely mistake: with all your pains, you are still far short of the mark. Patience grows out of the endless pursuits, and turns it into a luxury. A streak in a flower, a wrinkle in a leaf, a tinge in a cloud, a stain in an old wall or ruin grey, are seized with avidity as the *spolia opima* of this sort of mental warfare, and furnish out labour for another half day. The hours pass away untold, without chagrin, and without weariness; nor would you ever wish to pass them otherwise. Innocence is joined with industry, pleasure with business; and the mind is satisfied, though it is not engaged in thinking or in doing any mischief.[1]

I have not much pleasure in writing these Essays, or in reading them afterwards; though I own I now and then meet with a phrase that I like, or a thought that strikes me as a true one. But after I begin them, I am only anxious to get to the end of them, which I am not sure I shall do, for I seldom see my way a page or even a sentence beforehand; and when I have as by a miracle escaped, I trouble myself little more about them. I sometimes have to write them twice over: then it is necessary to read the

[1] There is a passage in Werter which contains a very pleasing illustration of this doctrine, and is as follows.

"About a league from the town is a place called Walheim. It is very agreeably situated on the side of a hill : from one of the paths which leads out of the village, you have a view of the whole country ; and there is a good old woman who sells wine, coffee, and tea there : but better than all this are two lime-trees before the church, which spread their branches over a little green, surrounded by barns and cottages. I have seen few places more retired and peaceful. I send for a chair and table from the old woman's, and there I drink my coffee and read Homer. It was by accident that I discovered this place one fine afternoon : all was perfect stillness ; every body was in the fields, except a little boy about four years old, who was sitting on the ground, and holding between his knees a child of about six months ; he pressed it to his bosom with his little arms, which made a sort of great chair for it, and notwithstanding the vivacity which sparkled in his eyes, he sat perfectly still. Quite delighted with the scene, I sat down on a plough opposite, and had great pleasure in drawing this little picture of brotherly tenderness. I added a bit of the hedge, the barn-door, and some broken cart-wheels, without any order, just as they happened to lie ; and in about an hour I found I had made a drawing of great expression and very correct design, without having put in anything of my own. This confirmed me in the resolution I had made before, only to copy nature for the future. Nature is inexhaustible, and alone forms the greatest masters. Say what you will of rules, they alter the true features, and the natural expression." P. 15.

proof, to prevent mistakes by the printer; so that by the time they appear in a tangible shape, and one can con them over with a conscious, sidelong glance to the public approbation, they have lost their gloss and relish, and become " more tedious than a twice-told tale." For a person to read his own works over with any great delight, he ought first to forget that he ever wrote them. Familiarity naturally breeds contempt. It is, in fact, like poring fondly over a piece of blank paper; from repetition, the words convey no distinct meaning to the mind, are mere idle sounds, except that our vanity claims an interest and property in them. I have more satisfaction in my own thoughts than in dictating them to others: words are necessary to explain the impression of certain things upon me to the reader, but they rather weaken and draw a veil over than strengthen it to myself. However, I might say with the poet, " My mind to me a kingdom is," yet I have little ambition " to set a throne or chair of state in the understandings of other men." The ideas we cherish most, exist best in a kind of shadowy abstraction,

" Pure in the last recesses of the mind : "

and derive neither force nor interest from being exposed to public view. They are old familiar acquaintance, and any change in them, arising from the adventitious ornaments of style or dress, is little to their advantage. After I have once written on a subject, it goes out of my mind: my feelings about it have been melted down into words, and *them* I forget. I have, as it were, discharged my memory of its old habitual reckoning, and rubbed out the score of real sentiment. For the future, it exists only for the sake of others.—But I cannot say, from my own experience, that the same process takes place in transferring our ideas to canvas; they gain more than they lose in the mechanical transformation. One is never tired of painting, because you have to set down not what you

knew already, but what you have just discovered. In the
former case, you translate feelings into words; in the
latter, names into things. There is a continual creation
out of nothing going on. With every stroke of the brush,
a new field of inquiry is laid open; new difficulties arise,
and new triumphs are prepared over them. By comparing
the imitation with the original, you see what you have
done, and how much you have still to do. The test of the
senses is severer than that of fancy, and an over-match
even for the delusions of our self-love. One part of a
picture shames another, and you determine to paint up
to yourself, if you cannot come up to Nature. Every
object becomes lustrous from the light thrown back upon
it by the mirror of art: and by the aid of the pencil we
may be said to touch and handle the objects of sight. The
air-drawn visions that hover on the verge of existence
have a bodily presence given them on the canvas: the
form of beauty is changed into a substance: the dream
and the glory of the universe is made " palpable to feeling
as to sight."—And see! a rainbow starts from the canvas,
with all its humid train of glory, as if it were drawn from
its cloudy arch in heaven. The spangled landscape
glitters with drops of dew after the shower. The " fleecy
fools " show their coats in the gleams of the setting sun.
The shepherds pipe their farewell notes in the fresh
evening air. And is this bright vision made from a dead
dull blank, like a bubble reflecting the mighty fabric of
the universe? Who would think this miracle of Rubens'
pencil possible to be performed? Who, having seen it,
would not spend his life to do the like? See how the rich
fallows, the bare stubble-field, the scanty harvest-home,
drag in Rembrandt's landscapes! How often have I
looked at them and Nature, and tried to do the same, till
the very " light thickened," and there was an earthiness
in the feeling of the air! There is no end of the refinements of art and Nature in this respect. One may look

x

at the misty glimmering horizon till the eye dazzles and the imagination is lost, in hopes to transfer the whole interminable expanse at one blow upon canvas. Wilson said, he used to try to paint the effect of the motes dancing in the setting sun. At another time, a friend coming into his painting-room when he was sitting on the ground in a melancholy posture, observed that his picture looked like a landscape after a shower: he started up with the greatest delight, and said, " That is the effect I intended to produce, but thought I had failed." Wilson was neglected; and, by degrees, neglected his art to apply himself to brandy. His hand became unsteady, so that it was only by repeated attempts that he could reach the place, or produce the effect he aimed at; and when he had done a little to a picture, he would say to any acquaintance who chanced to drop in, " I have painted enough for one day: come, let us go somewhere." It was not so Claude left his pictures, or his studies on the banks of the Tiber, to go in search of other enjoyments, or ceased to gaze upon the glittering sunny vales and distant hills; and while his eye drank in the clear sparkling hues and lovely forms of Nature, his hand stamped them on the lucid canvas to last there for ever!—One of the most delightful parts of my life was one fine summer, when I used to walk out of an evening to catch the last light of the sun, gemming the green slopes or russet lawns, and gilding tower or tree, while the blue sky gradually turning to purple and gold, or skirted with dusky grey, hung its broad marble pavement over all, as we see it in the great master of Italian landscape. But to come to a more particular explanation of the subject.

The first head I ever tried to paint was an old woman with the upper part of the face shaded by her bonnet, and I certainly laboured it with great perseverance. It took me numberless sittings to do it. I have it by me still, and sometimes look at it with surprise, to think how much pains were thrown away to little purpose,—yet not altogether in vain if it taught me to see good in everything, and to know that there is nothing vulgar in Nature seen with the eye of science or of true art. Refinement creates beauty everywhere: it is the grossness of the spectator that discovers nothing but grossness in the object. Be this as it may, I spared no pains to do my best. If art was long, I thought that life was so too at that moment. I got in the general effect the first day; and pleased and surprised enough I was at my success. The rest was a work of time—of weeks and months (if need were) of patient toil and careful finishing. I had seen an old head by Rembrandt at Burleigh House, and if I could produce a head at all like Rembrandt in a year, in my life-time, it would be glory and felicity, and wealth and fame enough for me! The head I had seen at Burleigh was an exact and wonderful facsimile of Nature, and I resolved to make mine (as nearly as I could) an exact facsimile of Nature. I did not then, nor do I now believe, with Sir Joshua, that the perfection of art consists in giving general appearances without individual details, but in giving general appearances with individual details. Otherwise, I had done my work the first day. But I saw something more in Nature than general effect, and I thought it worth my while to give it in the picture. There was a gorgeous effect of light and shade: but there was a delicacy as well as depth in the *chiaro scuro*, which I was bound to follow into all its dim and scarce perceptible variety of tone and shadow. Then I had to make the transition from a strong light to as dark a shade, preserving the masses, but gradually softening off the intermediate parts. It was so in Nature: the difficulty was to make it so in the copy. I tried, and failed again and again; I strove harder, and succeeded as I thought. The wrinkles in Rembrandt were not hard lines; but broken and irregular. I saw the same appearance in Nature, and strained every nerve to give it. If I could hit off this edgy appearance, and insert the reflected light in the furrows of old age in half a morning, I did not think I had lost a day. Beneath the shrivelled yellow parchment look of the skin, there was here and there a streak of the blood colour tinging the face; this I made a point of conveying, and did not cease to compare what I saw with what I did (with jealous lynx-eyed watchfulness) till I succeeded to the best of my ability and judgment. How many revisions were there! How many attempts to catch an expression which I had seen the day before! How often did we try to get the old position, and wait for the return of the same light! There was a puckering up of the lips, a cautious introversion of the eye under the shadow of the bonnet, indicative of the feebleness and suspicion of old age, which at last we managed, after many trials and some quarrels, to a tolerable nicety. The picture was never finished, and I might have gone on with it to the present hour.[1] I used to set it on the ground when my day's work was done, and saw revealed to me with swimming eyes the birth of new hopes, and of a new world of objects. The painter thus learns to look at Nature with different eyes. He before saw her " as in a glass darkly, but now face to face." He understands the texture and meaning of the visible universe, and " sees into the life of things," not by the help of mechanical instruments, but of the improved exercise of his faculties, and an intimate sympathy with Nature. The meanest thing is not lost upon him, for he looks at it with an eye to itself, not merely to his own vanity or interest, or the opinion of the world. Even where there is neither beauty nor use— if that ever were—still there is truth, and a sufficient source of gratification in the indulgence of curiosity and

---

[1] It is at present covered with a thick slough of oil and varnish (the perishable vehicle of the English school) like an envelope of gold-beater's skin, so as to be hardly visible.

activity of mind. The humblest painter is a true scholar;
and the best of scholars—the scholar of Nature. For
myself, and for the real comfort and satisfaction of the
thing, I had rather have been Jan Steen, or Gerard Dow,
than the greatest casuist or philologer that ever lived.
The painter does not view things in clouds or " mist, the
common gloss of theologians," but applies the same
standard of truth and disinterested spirit of inquiry, that
influence his daily practice, to other subjects. He perceives form, he distinguishes character. He reads men
and books with an intuitive eye. He is a critic as well as
a connoisseur. The conclusions he draws are clear and
convincing, because they are taken from the things themselves. He is not a fanatic, a dupe, or a slave: for the
habit of seeing for himself also disposes him to judge for
himself. The most sensible men I know (taken as a class)
are painters; that is, they are the most lively observers of
what passes in the world about them, and the closest
observers of what passes in their own minds. From their
profession they in general mix more with the world than
authors; and if they have not the same fund of acquired
knowledge, are obliged to rely more on individual
sagacity. I might mention the names of Opie, Fuseli,
Northcote, as persons distinguished for striking description and acquaintance with the subtle traits of character.[1]
Painters in ordinary society, or in obscure situations
where their value is not known, and they are treated with
neglect and indifference, have sometimes a forward self-
sufficiency of manner: but this is not so much their fault

---

[1] Men in business, who are answerable with their fortunes
for the consequences of their opinions and are therefore accustomed to ascertain pretty accurately the grounds on which they
act, before they commit themselves on the event, are often
men of remarkably quick and sound judgments. Artists in
like manner must know tolerably well what they are about,
before they can bring the result of their observations to the test
of ocular demonstration.

as that of others. Perhaps their want of regular education may also be in fault in such cases. Richardson, who
is very tenacious of the respect in which the profession
ought to be held, tells a story of Michael Angelo, that
after a quarrel between him and Pope Julius II, " upon
account of a slight the artist conceived the pontiff had
put upon him, Michael Angelo was introduced by a
bishop, who, thinking to serve the artist by it, made it
an argument that the Pope should be reconciled to him,
because men of his profession were commonly ignorant,
and of no consequence otherwise: his holiness, enraged
at the bishop, struck him with his staff, and told him, it
was he that was the blockhead, and affronted the man
himself would not offend; the prelate was driven out
of the chamber, and Michael Angelo had the Pope's
benediction accompanied with presents. This bishop had
fallen into the vulgar error, and was rebuked accordingly."

Besides the exercise of the mind, painting exercises
the body. It is a mechanical as well as a liberal art. To
do anything, to dig a hole in the ground, to plant a
cabbage, to hit a mark, to move a shuttle, to work a
pattern,—in a word, to attempt to produce any effect,
and to *succeed*, has something in it that gratifies the love
of power, and carries off the restless activity of the mind
of man. Indolence is a delightful but distressing state:
we must be doing something to be happy. Action is no
less necessary than thought to the instinctive tendencies
of the human frame; and painting combines them both
incessantly.[1] The hand furnishes a practical test of the
correctness of the eye; and the eye thus admonished,
imposes fresh tasks of skill and industry upon the hand.
Every stroke tells, as the verifying of a new truth; and
every new observation, the instant it is made, passes into

[1] The famous Schiller used to say, that he found the great
happiness of life, after all, to consist in the discharge of some
mechanical duty.

an act and emanation of the will. Every step is nearer what we wish, and yet there is always more to do. In spite of the facility, the fluttering grace, the evanescent hues, that play round the pencil of Rubens and Vandyke, however I may admire, I do not envy them this power so much as I do the slow, patient, laborious execution of Correggio, Leonardo da Vinci, and Andrea del Sarto, where every touch appears conscious of its charge, emulous of truth, and where the painful artist has so distinctly wrought,

"that you might almost say his picture thought!"

In the one case, the colours seem breathed on the canvas as by magic, the work and the wonder of a moment; in the other, they seem inlaid in the body of the work, and as if it took the artist years of unremitting labour, and of delightful never-ending progress to perfection.[1] Who would wish ever to come to the close of such works,—not to dwell on them, to return to them, to be wedded to them to the last? Rubens, with his florid, rapid style, complained that when he had just learned his art, he should be forced to die. Leonardo, in the slow advances of his, had lived long enough!

Painting is not, like writing, what is properly understood by a sedentary employment. It requires not indeed a strong, but a continued and steady exertion of muscular power. The precision and delicacy of the manual operation makes up for the want of vehemence,—as to balance himself for any time in the same position the rope-dancer must strain every nerve. Painting for a whole morning gives one as excellent an appetite for one's dinner, as old Abraham Tucker acquired for his by riding over Banstead

---

[1] The rich *impasting* of Titian and Giorgione combines something of the advantages of both these styles, the felicity of the one with the carefulness of the other, and is perhaps to be preferred to either.

Downs. It is related of Sir Joshua Reynolds, that " he took no other exercise than what he used in his painting-room,"—the writer means, in walking backwards and forwards to look at his picture; but the act of painting itself, of laying on the colours in the proper place, and proper quantity, was a much harder exercise than this alternate receding from and returning to the picture. This last would be rather a relaxation and relief than an effort. It is not to be wondered at, that an artist like Sir Joshua, who delighted so much in the sensual and practical part of his art, should have found himself at a considerable loss when the decay of his sight precluded him, for the last year or two of his life, from the following up of his profession,—" the source," according to his own remark, " of thirty years' uninterrupted enjoyment and prosperity to him." It is only those who never think at all, or else who have accustomed themselves to brood incessantly on abstract ideas, that never feel *ennui*.

To give one instance more, and then I will have done with this rambling discourse. One of my first attempts was a picture of my father, who was then in a green old age, with strong-marked features, and scarred with the small-pox. I drew it with a broad light crossing the face, looking down, with spectacles on, reading. The book was Shaftesbury's *Characteristics*, in a fine old binding, with Gribelin's etchings. My father would as lieve it had been any other book; but for him to read was to be content, was " riches fineless." The sketch promised well; and I set to work to finish it, determined to spare no time nor pains. My father was willing to sit as long as I pleased; for there is a natural desire in the mind of man to sit for one's picture, to be the object of continued attention, to have one's likeness multiplied; and besides his satisfaction in the picture, he had some pride in the artist, though he would rather I should have written a sermon than painted like Rembrandt or like Raphael. Those winter days, with the gleams of sunshine coming through the chapel-windows, and cheered by the notes of the robin-redbreast in our garden (that " ever in the haunch of winter sings ")—as my afternoon's work drew to a close,—were among the happiest of my life. When I gave the effect I intended to any part of the picture for which I had prepared my colours, when I imitated the roughness of the skin by a lucky stroke of the pencil, when I hit the clear pearly tone of a vein, when I gave the ruddy complexion of health, the blood circulating under the broad shadows of one side of the face, I thought my fortune made; or rather it was already more than made, in my fancying that I might one day be able to say with Correggio, " *I also am a painter!* " It was an idle thought, a boy's conceit; but it did not make me less happy at the time. I used regularly to set my work in the chair to look at it through the long evenings; and many a time did I return to take leave of it before I could go to bed at night. I remember sending it with a throbbing heart to the Exhibition, and seeing it hung up there by the side of one of the Honourable Mr. Skeffington (now Sir George). There was nothing in common between them, but that they were the portraits of two very good-natured men. I think, but I am not sure, that I finished this portrait (or another afterwards) on the same day that the news of the battle of Austerlitz came; I walked out in the afternoon, and, as I returned, saw the evening star set over a poor man's cottage with other thoughts and feelings than I shall ever have again. Oh for the revolution of the great Platonic year, that those times might come over again! I could sleep out the three hundred and sixty-five thousand intervening years very contentedly!—The picture is left: the table, the chair, the window where I learned to construe Livy, the chapel where my father preached, remain where they were;

x *

but he himself is gone to rest, full of years, of faith, of hope, and charity!

The painter not only takes a delight in Nature, he has a new and exquisite source of pleasure opened to him in the study and contemplation of works of art—

> " Whate'er Lorraine light touch'd with soft'ning hue,
>   Or savage Rosa dash'd, or learned Poussin drew."

He turns aside to view a country-gentleman's seat with eager looks, thinking it may contain some of the rich products of art. There is an air round Lord Radnor's park, for there hang the two Claudes, the Morning and Evening of the Roman Empire—round Wilton-house, for there is Vandyke's picture of the Pembroke family— round Blenheim, for there is his picture of the Duke of Buckingham's children, and the most magnificent collection of Rubenses in the world—at Knowsley, for there is Rembrandt's Hand-writing on the Wall—and at Burleigh, for there are some of Guido's angelic heads. The young artist makes a pilgrimage to each of these places, eyes them wistfully at a distance, " bosomed high in tufted trees," and feels an interest in them of which the owner is scarce conscious: he enters the well-swept walks and echoing arch-ways, passes the threshold, is led through wainscoted rooms, is shown the furniture, the rich hangings, the tapestry, the massy services of plate— and, at last, is ushered into the room where his treasure is, the idol of his vows—some speaking face or bright landscape! It is stamped on his brain, and lives there thenceforward, a tally for Nature, and a test of art. He furnishes out the chambers of the mind from the spoils of time, picks and chooses which shall have the best places—nearest his heart. He goes away richer than he came, richer than the possessor; and thinks that he may one day return, when he perhaps shall have done something like them, or even from failure shall have learned to admire truth and genius more.

My first initiation in the mysteries of the art was at the Orleans Gallery: it was there I formed my taste, such as it is; so that I am irreclaimably of the old school in painting. I was staggered when I saw the works there collected, and looked at them with wondering and with longing eyes. A mist passed away from my sight: the scales fell off. A new sense came upon me, a new heaven and a new earth stood before me. I saw the soul speaking in the face—" hands that the rod of empire had swayed " in mighty ages past—" a forked mountain or blue promontory,"

——" with trees upon't
That nod unto the world and mock our eyes with air."

Old Time had unlocked his treasures, and Fame stood portress at the door. We had all heard of the names of Titian, Raphael, Guido, Domenichino, the Caracci—but to see them face to face, to be in the same room with their deathless productions, was like breaking some mighty spell—was almost an effect of necromancy! From that time I lived in a world of pictures. Battles, sieges, speeches in parliament seemed mere idle noise and fury, " signifying nothing," compared with those mighty works and dreaded names that spoke to me in the eternal silence of thought. This was the more remarkable, as it was but a short time before that I was not only totally ignorant of, but insensible to the beauties of art. As an instance, I remember that one afternoon I was reading the *Provoked Husband* with the highest relish, with a green woody landscape of Ruysdael or Hobbema just before me, at which I looked off the book now and then, and wondered what there could be in that sort of work to satisfy or delight the mind—at the same time asking myself, as a speculative question, whether I should ever feel an interest in it like what I took in reading Vanbrugh and Cibber?

I had made some progress in painting when I went to the Louvre to study, and I never did anything afterwards. I never shall forget conning over the Catalogue which a friend lent me just before I set out. The pictures, the names of the painters, seemed to relish in the mouth. There was one of Titian's Mistress at her toilette. Even the colours with which the painter had adorned her hair were not more golden, more amiable to sight, than those which played round and tantalised my fancy ere I saw the picture. There were two portraits by the same hand— " A young Nobleman with a glove "—another, " A companion to it "—I read the description over and over with fond expectancy, and filled up the imaginary outline with whatever I could conceive of grace, and dignity, and an antique *gusto*—all but equal to the original. There was the Transfiguration too. With what awe I saw it in my mind's eye, and was overshadowed with the spirit of the artist! Not to have been disappointed with these works afterwards, was the highest compliment I can pay to their transcendent merits. Indeed, it was from seeing other works of the same great masters that I had formed a vague, but no disparaging idea of these.— The first day I got there, I was kept for some time in the French Exhibition-room, and thought I should not be able to get a sight of the old masters. I just caught a peep at them through the door (vile hindrance!) like looking out of purgatory into paradise—from Poussin's noble mellow-looking landscapes to where Rubens hung out his gaudy banner, and down the glimmering vista to the rich jewels of Titian and the Italian school. At last, by much importunity I was admitted, and lost not an instant in making use of my new privilege—It was *un beau jour* to me. I marched delighted through a quarter of a mile of the proudest efforts of the mind of man, a whole

creation of genius, a universe of art! I ran the gauntlet
of all the schools from the bottom to the top; and in the
end got admitted into the inner room, where they had
been repairing some of their greatest works. Here the
Transfiguration, the St. Peter Martyr, and the St. Jerome
of Domenichino stood on the floor, as if they had bent
their knees, like camels stooping, to unlade their riches
to the spectator. On one side, on an easel, stood Hippolito
de Medici (a portrait by Titian) with a boar-spear in his
hand, looking through those he saw, till you turned away
from the keen glance: and thrown together in heaps were
landscapes of the same hand, green pastoral hills and
vales, and shepherds piping to their mild mistresses
underneath the flowering shade. Reader, " if thou hast
not seen the Louvre, thou art damned! "—for thou hast
not seen the choicest remains of the works of art; or
thou hast not seen all these together, with their mutually
reflected glories. I say nothing of the statues; for I know
but little of sculpture, and never liked any till I saw the
Elgin Marbles. . . . Here, for four months together, I
strolled and studied, and daily heard the warning sound—
" *Quatres heures passées, il faut fermer, Citoyens,*" (ah!
why did they ever change their style?) muttered in
coarse provincial French; and brought away with me
some loose draughts and fragments, which I have been
forced to part with, like drops of life-blood, for " hard
money." How often, thou tenantless mansion of godlike
magnificence—how often has my heart since gone a
pilgrimage to thee!

It has been made a question, whether the artist, or the
mere man of taste and natural sensibility, receives most
pleasure from the contemplation of works of art? and I
think this question might be answered by another as a
sort of *experimentum crucis*, namely, whether any one out
of that " number numberless " of mere gentlemen and
amateurs, who visited Paris at the period here spoken of,

felt as much interest, as much pride or pleasure in this display of the most striking monuments of art as the humblest student would? The first entrance into the Louvre would be only one of the events of his journey, not an event in his life, remembered ever after with thankfulness and regret. He would explore it with the same unmeaning curiosity and idle wonder as he would the Regalia in the Tower, or the Botanic Garden in the Thuilleries, but not with the fond enthusiasm of an artist. How should he? His is " casual fruition, joyless, un-endeared." But the painter is wedded to his art, the mistress, queen, and idol of his soul. He has embarked his all in it, fame, time, fortune, peace of mind, his hopes in youth, his consolation in age: and shall he not feel a more intense interest in whatever relates to it than the mere indolent trifler? Natural sensibility alone, without the entire application of the mind to that one object, will not enable the possessor to sympathise with all the degrees of beauty and power in the conceptions of a Titian or a Correggio; but it is he only who does this, who follows them into all their force and matchless grace, that does or can feel their full value. Knowledge is pleasure as well as power. No one but the artist who has studied Nature and contended with the difficulties of art, can be aware of the beauties, or intoxicated with a passion for painting. No one who has not devoted his life and soul to the pursuit of art, can feel the same exultation in its brightest ornaments and loftiest triumphs which an artist does. Where the treasure is, there the heart is also. It is now seventeen years since I was studying in the Louvre (and I have long since given up all thoughts of the art as a profession), but long after I returned, and even still, I sometimes dream of being there again—of asking for the old pictures—and not finding them, or finding them changed or faded from what they were, I cry myself awake! What gentleman-amateur ever does this at such a distance of time,—that is, ever received pleasure or took interest enough in them to produce so lasting an impression?

But it is said that if a person had the same natural taste, and the same acquired knowledge as an artist, without the petty interests and technical notions, he would derive a purer pleasure from seeing a fine portrait, a fine landscape, and so on. This however is not so much begging the question as asking an impossibility: he cannot have the same insight into the end without having studied the means; nor the same love of art without the same habitual and exclusive attachment to it. Painters are, no doubt, often actuated by jealousy, partiality, and a sordid attention to that only which they find useful to themselves in painting. W—— has been seen poring over the texture of a Dutch cabinet-picture, so that he could not see the picture itself. But this is the perversion and pedantry of the profession, not its true or genuine spirit. If W—— had never looked at anything but megilps and handling, he never would have put the soul of life and manners into his pictures, as he has done. Another objection is, that the instrumental parts of the art, the means, the first rudiments, paints, oils, and brushes, are painful and disgusting; and that the consciousness of the difficulty and anxiety with which perfection has been attained, must take away from the pleasure of the finest performance. This, however, is only an additional proof of the greater pleasure derived by the artist from his profession; for these things which are said to interfere with and destroy the common interest in works of art, do not disturb him; he never once thinks of them, he is absorbed in the pursuit of a higher object; he is intent, not on the means but the end; he is taken up, not with the difficulties, but with the triumph over them. As in the case of the anatomist, who overlooks many things in the eagerness of his search after abstract truth;

.or the alchemist who, while he is raking into his soot and furnaces, lives in a golden dream; a lesser gives way to a greater object. But it is pretended that the painter may be supposed to submit to the unpleasant part of the process only for the sake of the fame or profit in view. So far is this from being a true state of the case, that I will venture to say, in the instance of a friend of mine who has lately succeeded in an important undertaking in his art, that not all the fame he has acquired, not all the money he has received from thousands of admiring spectators, not all the newspaper puffs,—not even the praise of the *Edinburgh Review*,—not all these, put together, ever gave him at any time the same genuine, undoubted satisfaction as any one half-hour employed in the ardent and propitious pursuit of his art—in finishing to his heart's content a foot, a hand, or even a piece of drapery. What is the state of mind of an artist while he is at work? He is then in the act of realising the highest idea he can form of beauty or grandeur: he conceives, he embodies that which he understands and loves best: that is, he is in full and perfect possession of that which is to him the source of the highest happiness and intellectual excitement which he can enjoy.

In short, as a conclusion to this argument, I will mention a circumstance which fell under my knowledge the other day. A friend had bought a print of Titian's Mistress, the same to which I have alluded above. He was anxious to shew it to me on this account. I told him it was a spirited engraving, but it had not the look of the original. I believe he thought this fastidious, till I offered to shew him a rough sketch of it, which I had by me. Having seen this, he said he perceived exactly what I meant, and could not bear to look at the print afterwards. He had good sense enough to see the difference in the individual instance; but a person better acquainted with Titian's manner and with art in general, that is, of a more cultivated and refined taste, would know that it was a bad print, without having any immediate model to compare it with. He would perceive with a glance of the eye, with a sort of instinctive feeling, that it was hard, and without that bland, expansive, and nameless expression which always distinguished Titian's most famous works. Any one who is accustomed to a head in a picture can never reconcile himself to a print from it: but to the ignorant they are both the same. To a vulgar eye there is no difference between a Guido and a daub, between a penny-print or the vilest scrawl, and the most finished performance. In other words, all that excellence which lies between these two extremes,—all, at least, that marks the excess above mediocrity,—all that constitutes true beauty, harmony, refinement, grandeur, is lost upon the common observer. But it is from this point that the delight, the glowing raptures of the true adept commence. An uninformed spectator may like an ordinary drawing better than the ablest connoisseur; but for that very reason he cannot like the highest specimens of art so well. The refinements not only of execution but of truth and Nature are inaccessible to unpractised eyes. The exquisite gradations in a sky of Claude's are not perceived by such persons, and consequently the harmony cannot be felt. Where there is no conscious apprehension, there can be no conscious pleasure. Wonder at the first sight of works of art may be the effect of ignorance and novelty ; but real admiration and permanent delight in them are the growth of taste and knowledge. " I would not wish to have your eyes," said a good-natured man to a critic, who was finding fault with a picture, in which the other saw no blemish. Why so ? The idea which prevented him from admiring this inferior production was a higher idea of truth and beauty which was ever present with him, and a continual source of pleasing and lofty contemplations. It may be different in a taste for outward luxuries and the privations of mere sense; but the idea of perfection, which acts as an intellectual foil, is always an addition, a support, and a proud consolation!

Richardson, in his *Essays*, which ought to be better known, has left some striking examples of the felicity and infelicity of artists, both as it relates to their external fortune, and to the practice of their art. In speaking of *the knowledge of hands*, he exclaims—" When one is considering a picture or a drawing, one at the same time thinks this was done by him[1] who had many extraordinary endowments of body and mind, but was withal very capricious; who was honoured in life and death, expiring in the arms of one of the greatest princes of that age, Francis I., King of France, who loved him as a friend. Another is of him[2] who lived a long and happy life, beloved of Charles V., emperour; and many others of the first princes of Europe. When one has another in hand, we think that this was done by one[3] who so excelled in three arts, as that any of them in that degree had rendered him worthy of immortality; and one moreover that durst contend with his sovereign (one of the haughtiest popes that ever was) upon a slight offered to him, and extricated himself with honour. Another is the work of him[4] who, without any one exterior advantage but mere strength of genius, had the most sublime imaginations, and executed them accordingly, yet lived and died obscurely. Another we shall consider as the work of him[5] who restored Painting when it had almost sunk; of him whom art made honourable, but who, neglecting and despising greatness with a sort of cynical pride, was treated suitably to the figure he gave himself, not his intrinsic worth; which, not having philosophy enough to bear it, broke his heart. Another is done by one[6] who

[1] Leonardo da Vinci.   [2] Titian.   [3] Michael Angelo.
[4] Correggio.   [5] Annibal Caracci.   [6] Rubens.

(on the contrary) was a fine gentleman, and lived in great magnificence, and was much honoured by his own and foreign princes; who was a courtier, a statesman, and a painter; and so much all these, that when he acted in either character, *that* seemed to be his business, and the others his diversion. I say when one thus reflects, besides the pleasure arising from the beauties and excellences of the work, the fine ideas it gives us of natural things, the noble way of thinking it may suggest to us, an additional pleasure results from the above considerations. But, oh! the pleasure, when a connoisseur and lover of art has before him a picture or drawing, of which he can say this is the hand, these are the thoughts of him[1] who was one of the politest, best-natured gentlemen that ever was; and beloved and assisted by the greatest wits and the greatest men then in Rome: of him who lived in great fame, honour, and magnificence, and died extremely lamented; and missed a Cardinal's hat only by dying a few months too soon; but was particularly esteemed and favoured by two Popes, the only ones who filled the chair of St. Peter in his time, and as great men as ever sat there since that apostle, if at least he ever did : one, in short, who could have been a Leonardo, a Michael Angelo, a Titian, a Correggio, a Parmegiano, an Annibal, a Rubens, or any other whom he pleased, but none of them could ever have been a Rafaelle " (page 251).

The same writer speaks feelingly of the change in the style of different artists from their change of fortune, and as the circumstances are little known, I will quote the passage relating to two of them.

" Guido Reni from a prince-like affluence of fortune (the just reward of his angelic works) fell to a condition like that of a hired servant to one who supplied him with money for what he did at a fixed rate ; and that by his

---

[1] Rafaelle.

being bewitched with a passion for gaming, whereby he lost vast sums of money; and even what he got in this his state of servitude by day, he commonly lost at night: nor could he ever be cured of this cursed madness. Those of his works, therefore, which he did in this unhappy part of his life, may easily be conceived to be in a different style to what he did before, which in some things, that is, in the airs of his heads (in the gracious kind), had a delicacy in them peculiar to himself, and almost more than human. But I must not multiply instances. Parmegiano is one that alone takes in all the several kinds of variation, and all the degrees of goodness, from the lowest of the indifferent up to the sublime. I can produce evident proofs of this in so easy a gradation, that one cannot deny but that he that did this, might do that, and very probably did so; and thus one may ascend and descend, like the angels on Jacob's ladder, whose foot was upon the earth, but its top reached to Heaven.

"And this great man had his unlucky circumstance: he became mad after the philosopher's stone, and did but very little in painting or drawing afterwards. Judge what that was, and whether there was not an alteration of style from what he had done, before this devil possessed him. His creditors endeavoured to exorcise him, and did him some good, for he set himself to work again in his own way: but if a drawing I have of a Lucretia be that he made for his last picture, as it probably is (Vasari says that was the subject of it), it is an evident proof of his decay: it is good indeed, but it wants much of the delicacy which is commonly seen in his works; and so I always thought before I knew or imagined it to be done in this his ebb of genius" (page 153).

We have had two artists of our own country, whose fate has been as singular as it was hard. Gandy was a portrait-painter in the beginning of the last century, whose heads were said to have come near to Rembrandt's,

and he was the undoubted prototype of Sir Joshua
Reynolds's style. Yet his name has scarcely been heard
of; and his reputation, like his works, never extended
beyond his own county. What did he think of himself
and of a fame so bounded! Did he ever dream he was
indeed an artist? Or how did this feeling in him differ
from the vulgar conceit of the lowest pretender? The
best known of his works is a portrait of an alderman of
Exeter, in some public building in that city.

Poor Dan. Stringer! Forty years ago he had the finest
hand and the clearest eye of any artist of his time, and
produced heads and drawings that would not have
disgraced a brighter period in the art. But he fell a
martyr (like Burns) to the society of country-gentlemen,
and then of those whom they would consider as more
his equals. I saw him many years ago, when he treated
the masterly sketches he had by him (one in particular
of the group of citizens in Shakespear " swallowing the
tailor's news ") as " bastards of his genius, not his
children "; and seemed to have given up all thoughts
of his art. Whether he is since dead, I cannot say: the
world do not so much as know that he ever lived!

WHETHER GENIUS IS
CONSCIOUS OF ITS POWERS?

(WRITTEN ABOUT JUNE, 1823)

N O really great man ever thought himself so. The idea
of greatness in the mind answers but ill to our knowledge
—or to our ignorance of ourselves. What living prose-
writer for instance would think of comparing himself

with Burke? Yet would it not have been equal presumption or egotism in him to fancy himself equal to
those who had gone before him—Bolingbroke, or Johnson,
or Sir William Temple? Because his rank in letters is
become a settled point with us, we conclude that it must
have been quite as self-evident to him, and that he must
have been perfectly conscious of his vast superiority to
the rest of the world. Alas! not so. No man is truly
himself but in the idea which others entertain of him.
The mind, as well as the eye, " sees not itself, but by
reflection from some other thing." What parity can there
be between the effect of habitual composition on the mind
of the individual, and the surprise occasioned by first
reading a fine passage in an admired author; between
what we do with ease, and what we thought it next to
impossible ever to be done; between the reverential
awe we have for years encouraged, without seeing reason
to alter it, for distinguished genius, and the slow, reluctant,
unwelcome conviction that after infinite toil and repeated
disappointments, and when it is too late and to little
purpose, we have ourselves at length accomplished what
we at first proposed; between the insignificance of our
petty, personal pretensions, and the vastness and splendour
which the atmosphere of imagination lends to an illustrious name? He who comes up to his own idea of
greatness, must always have had a very low standard of it
in his mind. " What a pity," said some one, " that Milton
had not the pleasure of reading *Paradise Lost!* " He
could not read it, as we do, with the weight of impression
that a hundred years of admiration have added to it—" a
phœnix gazed by all "—with the sense of the number of
editions it has passed through with still increasing reputation, with the tone of solidity, time-proof, which it has
received from the breath of cold, envious maligners, with
the sound which the voice of Fame has lent to every line
of it! The writer of an ephemeral production may be

as much dazzled with it as the public: it may sparkle in
his own eyes for a moment, and be soon forgotten by everyone else. But no one can anticipate the suffrages of
posterity. Every man, in judging of himself, is his own
contemporary. He may feel the gale of popularity, but
he cannot tell how long it will last. His opinion of himself wants distance, wants time, wants numbers, to set it
off and confirm it. He must be indifferent to his own
merits before he can feel a confidence in them. Besides,
everyone must be sensible of a thousand weaknesses and
deficiencies in himself; whereas Genius only leaves
behind it the monuments of its strength. A great name
is an abstraction of some one excellence : but whoever
fancies himself an abstraction of excellence, so far from
being great, may be sure that he is a blockhead, equally
ignorant of excellence or defect, of himself or others.
Mr. Burke, besides being the author of the *Reflections*,
and the *Letter to a Noble Lord*, had a wife and son ; and
had to think as much about them as we do about him.
The imagination gains nothing by the minute details of
personal knowledge.

On the other hand, it may be said that no man knows
so well as the author of any performance what it has
cost him, and the length of time and study devoted to it
This is one, among other reasons, why no man can pronounce an opinion upon himself. The happiness of the
result bears no proportion to the difficulties overcome or
the pains taken. *Materiam superabat opus*, is an old and
fatal complaint. The definition of genius is that it acts
unconsciously ; and those who have produced immortal
works have done so without knowing how or why. The
greatest power operates unseen, and executes its appointed
task with as little ostentation as difficulty. Whatever is
done best, is done from the natural bent and disposition
of the mind. It is only where our incapacity begins,
that we begin to feel the obstacles, and to set an undue

value on our triumph over them. Correggio, Michael Angelo, Rembrandt, did what they did without premeditation or effort—their works came from their minds as a natural birth—if you had asked them why they adopted this or that style, they would have answered, *because they could not help it*, and because they knew of no other. So Shakespear says :—

> " Our poesy is as a gum which oozes
> From whence 'tis nourish'd : the fire i' the flint
> Shews not till it be struck : our gentle flame
> Provokes itself; and, like the current, flies
> Each bound it chafes."

Shakespear himself was an example of his own rule, and appears to have owed almost everything to industry or design. His poetry flashes from him like the lightning from the summer-cloud, or the stroke from the sunflower. When we look at the admirable comic designs of Hogarth, they seem from the unfinished state in which they are left, and from the freedom of the pencilling, to have cost him little trouble; whereas the " Sigismunda " is a very laboured and comparatively feeble performance, and he accordingly set great store by it. He also thought highly of his portraits, and boasted that " he could paint equal to Vandyke, give him his time and let him choose his subject." This was the very reason why he could not. Vandyke's excellence consisted in this, that he could paint a fine portrait of any one at sight: let him take ever so much pains or choose ever so bad a subject, he could not help making something of it. His eye, his mind, his hand was cast in the mould of grace and delicacy. Milton, again, is understood to have preferred *Paradise Regained* to his other works. This, if so, was either because he himself was conscious of having failed in it, or because others thought he had. We are willing to think well of that which we know wants our favourable opinion, and to prop the rickety bantling. Every step taken, *invitâ Minerva*, costs us something, and is set down to account; whereas we are borne on the full tide of genius and success into the very haven of our desires almost imperceptibly. The strength of the impulse by which we are carried along prevents the sense of difficulty or resistance: the true inspiration of the Muse is soft and balmy as the air we breathe; and indeed leaves us little to boast of, for the effect hardly seems to be our own.

There are two persons who always appear to me to have worked under this involuntary, silent impulse more than any others; I mean Rembrandt and Correggio. It is not known that Correggio ever saw a picture of any great master. He lived and died obscurely in an obscure village. We have few of his works, but they are all perfect. What truth, what grace, what angelic sweetness are there! Not one line or tone that is not divinely soft or exquisitely fair; the painter's mind rejecting, by a natural process, all that is discordant, coarse, or unpleasing. The whole is an emanation of pure thought. The work grew under his hand as if of itself, and came out without a flaw, like the diamond from the rock. He knew not what he did; and looked at each modest grace as it stole from the canvas with anxious delight and wonder. Ah! gracious God! not he alone; how many more in all time have looked at their works with the same feelings, not knowing but they too may have done something divine, immortal, and finding in that sole doubt ample amends for pining solitude, for want, neglect, and an untimely fate. Oh! for one hour of that uneasy rapture, when the mind first thinks that it has struck out something that may last for ever; when the germ of excellence bursts from nothing on the startled sight! Take, take away the gaudy triumphs of the world, the long deathless shout of fame, and give back that heartfelt sigh with which the youthful enthusiast first weds immortality as his secret bride! And thou too, Rembrandt! Thou wert a man of genius, if ever painter was a man of genius!—did his dream hang over you as you painted that strange picture of " Jacob's Ladder "? Did your eye strain over those gradual dusky clouds into futurity, or did those white-vested, beaked figures babble to you of fame as they approached? Did you know what you were about, or did you not paint much as it happened? Oh! if you had thought once about yourself, or anything but the subject, it would have been all over with " the glory, the intuition, the amenity," the dream had fled, the spell had been broken. The hills would not have looked like those we see in sleep—that tatterdemalion figure of Jacob, thrown on one side, would not have slept as if the breath was fairly taken out of his body. So much do Rembrandt's pictures savour of the soul and body of reality, that the thoughts seem identical with the objects—if there had been the least question what he should have done, or how he should do it, or how far he had succeeded, it would have spoiled everything. Lumps of light hung upon his pencil and fell upon his canvas like dew-drops: the shadowy veil was drawn over his backgrounds by the dull, obtuse finger of night, making darkness visible by still greater darkness that could only be felt!

Cervantes is another instance of a man of genius, whose work may be said to have sprung from his mind, like Minerva from the head of Jupiter. Don Quixote and Sancho were a kind of twins; and the jests of the latter, as he says, fell from him like drops of rain when he least thought of it. Shakspeare's creations were more multi-form, but equally natural and unstudied. Raphael and Milton seem partial exceptions to this rule. Their productions were of the *composite order;* and those of the latter sometimes even amount to centos. Accordingly, we find Milton quoted among those authors who have left proofs of their entertaining a high opinion of themselves, and of cherishing a strong aspiration after fame. Some of Shak-speare's *Sonnets* have been also cited to the same purpose; but they seem rather to convey wayward and dissatisfied complaints of his untoward fortune than anything like a triumphant and confident reliance on his future renown. He appears to have stood more alone and to have thought less about himself than any living being. One reason for this indifference may have been, that as a writer he was tolerably successful in his life-time, and no doubt produced his works with very great facility.

I hardly know whether to class Claude Lorraine as among those who succeeded most " through happiness or pains." It is certain that he imitated no one, and has had no successful imitator. The perfection of his landscapes seems to have been owing to an inherent quality of harmony, to an exquisite sense of delicacy in his mind. His monotony has been complained of, which is apparently produced from a preconceived idea in his mind; and not long ago I heard a person, not more distinguished for the subtilty than the *naïveté* of his sarcasms, remark, " Oh! I never look at Claude: if one has seen one of his pictures, one has seen them all; they are every one alike: there is the same sky, the same climate, the same time of day, the same tree, and that tree is like a cabbage. To be sure, they say he did pretty well; but when a man is always doing one thing, he ought to do it pretty well." There is no occasion to write the name under this criticism, and the best answer to it is that it is true—his pictures always are the same, but we never wish them to be otherwise. Perfection is one thing. I confess I think that Claude knew this, and felt that his were the finest landscapes in the world—that ever had been, or would ever be.

I am not in the humour to pursue this argument any farther at present, but to write a digression. If the reader is not already apprised of it, he will please to take notice that I write this at Winterslow. My style there is apt to be redundant and excursive. At other times it may be cramped, dry, abrupt; but here it flows like a river, and overspreads its banks. I have not to seek for thoughts or hunt for images: they come of themselves, I inhale them with the breeze, and the silent groves are vocal with a thousand recollections—

> " And visions, as poetic eyes avow,
>   Hang on each leaf, and cling to ev'ry bough."

Here I came fifteen years ago, a willing exile; and as I trod the lengthened greensward by the low woodside, repeated the old line,

> " My mind to me a kingdom is ! "

I found it so then, before, and since; and shall I faint, now that I have poured out the spirit of that mind to the world, and treated many subjects with truth, with freedom, and power, because I have been followed with one cry of abuse ever since *for not being a government-tool ?* Here I returned a few years after to finish some works I had undertaken, doubtful of the event, but determined to do my best; and wrote that character of Millimant[1] which was once transcribed by fingers fairer than Aurora's, but no notice was taken of it, because I was not a government-tool, and must be supposed devoid of taste and elegance by all who aspired to these qualities in their own persons. Here I sketched my account of that old honest Signior Orlando Friscobaldo,[2] which with its fine, racy, acrid tone that old crab-apple, G[i]ff[or]d, would have relished or pretended to relish, had I been a government-tool! Here, too, I have written *Table-Talks* without number, and as

---

[1] See *Lectures on the English Comic Writers*, 1819, pp. 139–142. (Ed.)

[2] See *Lectures on the Literature of the Age of Elizabeth*, etc., 1820, pp. 114–18. (Ed.)

yet without a falling-off, till now that they are nearly done, or I should not make this boast. I could swear (were they not mine) the thoughts in many of them are founded as the rock, free as air, the tone like an Italian picture. What then? Had the style been like polished steel, as firm and as bright, it would have availed me nothing, for I am not a government-tool! I had endeavoured to guide the taste of the English people to the best old English writers; but I had said that English kings did not reign by right divine, and that his present Majesty was descended from an Elector of Hanover in a right line; and no loyal subject would after this look into Webster or Decker because I had pointed them out. I had done something (more than anyone except Schlegel) to vindicate the *Characters of Shakespear's Plays* from the stigma of French criticism: but our Anti-Jacobin and Anti-Gallican writers soon found out that I had said and written that Frenchmen, Englishmen, men were not slaves by birthright. This was enough to *damn* the work. Such has been the head and front of my offending. While my friend Leigh Hunt was writing the *Descent of Liberty*, and strewing the march of the Allied Sovereigns with flowers, I sat by the waters of Babylon and hung my harp upon the willows. I knew all along there was but one alternative —the cause of kings or of mankind. This I foresaw, this I feared; the world see it now, when it is too late. Therefore I lamented, and would take no comfort when the Mighty fell, because we, all men, fell with him, like lightning from heaven, to grovel in the grave of Liberty, in the stye of Legitimacy! There is but one question in the hearts of monarchs,—whether mankind are their property or not. There was but this one question in mine. I had made an abstract, metaphysical principle of this question. I was not the dupe of the voice of the charmers. By my hatred of tyrants I knew what their hatred of the freeborn spirit of man must be, of the semblance, of the very name

of Liberty and Humanity. And while others bowed their
heads to the image of the BEAST, I spat upon it and
buffeted it, and made mouths at it, and pointed at it, and
drew aside the veil that then half concealed it, but has
been since thrown off, and named it by its right name;
and it is not to be supposed that my having penetrated
their mystery would go unrequited by those whose darling
and whose delight the idol, half-brute, half-demon, was,
and who were ashamed to acknowledge the image and
superscription as their own! Two half-friends of mine,
who would not make a whole one between them, agreed
the other day that the indiscriminate, incessant abuse of
what I write was mere prejudice and party-spirit, and that
what I do in periodicals and without a name does well,
pays well, and is " cried out upon in the top of the
compass." It is this indeed that has saved my shallow
skiff from quite foundering on Tory spite and rancour;
for when people have been reading and approving an
article in a miscellaneous journal, it does not do to say
when they discover the author afterwards (whatever might
have been the case before) it is written by a blockhead;
and even Mr. Jerdan recommends the volume of *Characteristics* as an excellent little work, because it has no
cabalistic name in the title-page, and swears " there is a
first-rate article of forty pages in the last number of the
Edinburgh from Jeffrey's own hand," though when he
learns against his will that it is mine, he devotes three
successive numbers of the *Literary Gazette* to abuse " that
strange article in the last number of the *Edinburgh
Review*." Others who had not this advantage have fallen
a sacrifice to the obloquy attached to the suspicion of
doubting, or of being acquainted with anyone who is
known to doubt, the divinity of kings. Poor Keats paid
the forfeit of this *lèse majesté* with his health and life.
What, though his Verses were like the breath of spring,
and many of his thoughts like flowers—would this, with

the circle of critics that beset a throne, lessen the crime of
their having been praised in the *Examiner ?* The lively
and most agreeable Editor of that paper has in like manner
been driven from his country and his friends who delighted in him, for no other reason than having written the
Story of Rimini, and asserted ten years ago, " that the
most accomplished prince in Europe was an Adonis of
fifty !"

> " Return, Alpheus, the dread voice is past
>   That shrunk thy streams ; return, Sicilian Muse ! "

I look out of my window and see that a shower has just
fallen: the fields look green after it, and a rosy cloud
hangs over the brow of the hill; a lily expands its petals
in the moisture, dressed in its lovely green and white; a
shepherd-boy has just brought some pieces of turf with
daisies and grass for his young mistress to make a bed for
her sky-lark, not doomed to dip his wings in the dappled
dawn—my cloudy thoughts draw off, the storm of angry
politics has blown over—Mr. *Blackwood,* I am yours—
Mr. Croker, my service to you—Mr. T. Moore, I am alive
and well—Really, it is wonderful how little the worse I
am for fifteen years' wear-and-tear, how I came upon my
legs again on the ground of truth and nature, and " look
abroad into universality," forgetting that there is any
such person as myself in the world!

I have let this passage stand (however critical) because
it may serve as a practical illustration to shew what
authors really think of themselves when put upon the
defensive—(I confess, the subject has nothing to do with
the title at the head of the Essay!)—and as a warning to
those who may reckon upon their fair portion of popularity
as the reward of the exercise of an independent spirit and
such talents as they possess. It sometimes seems at first
sight as if the low scurrility and jargon of abuse by which
it is attempted to overlay all common sense and decency

by a tissue of lies and nicknames, everlastingly repeated and applied indiscriminately to all those who are not of the regular government-party, was peculiar to the present time, and the anomalous growth of modern criticism; but if we look back, we shall find the same system acted upon as often as power, prejudice, dulness, and spite found their account in playing the game into one another's hands—in decrying popular efforts, and in giving currency to every species of base metal that had their own conventional stamp upon it. The names of Pope and Dryden were assailed with daily and unsparing abuse; the epithet A. P. E. was levelled at the sacred head of the former; and if even men like these, having to deal with the consciousness of their own infirmities and the insolence and spurns of wanton enmity, must have found it hard to possess their souls in patience, any living writer amidst such contradictory evidence can scarcely expect to retain much calm, steady conviction of his own merits, or build himself a secure reversion in immortality.

However one may in a fit of spleen and impatience turn round and assert one's claims in the face of low-bred, hireling malice, I will here repeat what I set out with saying, that there never yet was a man of sense and proper spirit who would not decline rather than court a comparison with any of those names whose reputation he really emulates—who would not be sorry to suppose that any of the great heirs of memory had as many foibles as he knows himself to possess—and who would not shrink from including himself or being included by others in the same praise that was offered to long-established and universally-acknowledged merits, as a kind of profanation. Those who are ready to fancy themselves Raphaels and Homers are very inferior men indeed—they have not even an idea of the mighty names that " they take in vain." They are as deficient in pride as in modesty, and have not so much as served an apprenticeship to a true and honourable am-

bition. They mistake a momentary popularity for lasting
renown, and a sanguine temperament for the inspirations
of genius. The love of fame is too high and delicate a
feeling in the mind to be mixed up with realities—it is a
solitary abstraction, the secret sigh of the soul—

> " It is all one as we should love
>   A bright particular star, and think to wed it."

A name " fast-anchored in the deep abyss of time " is like
a star twinkling in the firmament, cold, silent, distant,
but eternal and sublime; and our transmitting one to posterity is as if we should contemplate our translation to
the skies. If we are not contented with this feeling on
the subject, we shall never sit in Cassiopeia's chair, nor
will our names, studding Ariadne's crown or streaming
with Berenice's locks, ever make

> " the face of heaven so bright,
> That birds shall sing, and think it were not night."

Those who are in love only with noise and show, instead
of devoting themselves to a life of study, had better hire
a booth at Bartlemy-Fair, or march at the head of a recruiting regiment with drums beating and colours flying!

It has been urged, that however little we may be disposed to indulge the reflection at other times or out of
mere self-complacency, yet the mind cannot help being
conscious of the effort required for any great work while
it is about it, of

> " The high endeavour and the glad success."

I grant that there is a sense of power in such cases, with
the exception before stated; but then this very effort and
state of excitement engrosses the mind at the time, and
leaves it listless and exhausted afterwards. The energy
we exert, or the high state of enjoyment we feel, puts us
out of conceit with ourselves at other times: compared to

Y

what we are in the act of composition, we seem dull common-place people, generally speaking; and what we have
been able to perform is rather matter of wonder than of
self-congratulation to us. The stimulus of writing is like
the stimulus of intoxication, with which we can hardly
sympathise in our sober moments, when we are no longer
under the inspiration of the demon, or when the virtue is
gone out of us. While we are engaged in any work, we
are thinking of the subject, and cannot stop to admire ourselves; and when it is done, we look at it with comparative
indifference. I will venture to say, that no one but a
pedant ever read his own works regularly through. They
are not *his*—they are become mere words, waste-paper,
and have none of the glow, the creative enthusiasm, the
vehemence, and natural spirit with which he wrote them.
When we have once committed our thoughts to paper,
written them fairly out, and seen that they are right in
the printing, if we are in our right wits, we have done
with them for ever. I sometimes try to read an article
I have written in some magazine or review—(for when
they are bound up in a volume, I dread the very sight of
them)—but stop after a sentence or two, and never recur
to the task. I know pretty well what I have to say on
the subject, and do not want to go to school to myself.
It is the worst instance of the *bis repetita crambe* in the
world. I do not think that even painters have much
delight in looking at their works after they are done.
While they are in progress, there is a great degree of satisfaction in considering what has been done, or what is still
to do—but this is hope, is reverie, and ceases with the
completion of our efforts. I should not imagine Raphael
or Correggio would have much pleasure in looking at their
former works, though they might recollect the pleasure
they had had in painting them; they might spy defects
in them (for the idea of unattainable perfection still keeps
pace with our actual approaches to it), and fancy that they

were not worthy of immortality. The greatest portrait-painter the world ever saw used to write under his pictures, " *Titianus faciebat*," signifying that they were imperfect; and in his letter to Charles V accompanying one of his most admired works, he only spoke of the time he had been about it. Annibal Caracci boasted that he could do like Titian and Correggio, and, like most boasters, was wrong.[1]

The greatest pleasure in life is that of reading, while we are young. I have had as much of this pleasure as perhaps anyone. As I grow older, it fades; or else, the stronger stimulus of writing takes off the edge of it. At present, I have neither time nor inclination for it: yet I should like to devote a year's entire leisure to a course of the English Novelists; and perhaps clap on that old sly knave, Sir Walter, to the end of the list. It is astonishing how I used formerly to relish the style of certain authors, at a time when I myself despaired of ever writing a single line. Probably this was the reason. It is not in mental as in natural ascent—intellectual objects seem higher when we survey them from below, than when we look down from any given elevation above the common level. My three favourite writers about the time I speak of were Burke, Junius, and Rousseau. I was never weary of admiring and wondering at the felicities of the style, the turns of expression, the refinements of thought and sentiment: I laid the book down to find out the secret of so much strength and beauty, and took it up again in despair, to read on and admire. So I passed whole days, months, and I may add, years; and have only this to say now, that as my life began, so I could wish that it may end. The last time I tasted this luxury in its full perfection was one day after a sultry day's walk in summer between Farnham and Alton. I was fairly tired out; I walked into

[1] See his spirited Letter to his cousin Ludovico, on seeing the pictures at Parma.

an inn-yard (I think at the latter place); I was shewn by the waiter to what looked at first like common out-houses at the other end of it, but they turned out to be a suite of rooms, probably a hundred years old—the one I entered opened into an old-fashioned garden, embellished with beds of larkspur and a leaden Mercury; it was wainscoted, and there was a grave-looking, dark-coloured portrait of Charles II hanging over the tiled chimney-piece. I had *Love for Love* in my pocket, and began to read; coffee was brought in in a silver coffee-pot; the cream, the bread and butter, everything was excellent, and the flavour of Congreve's style prevailed over all. I prolonged the entertainment till a late hour, and relished this divine comedy better even than when I used to see it played by Miss Mellon, as *Miss Prue ;* Bob Palmer, as *Tattle ;* and Bannister, as honest *Ben.* This circumstance happened just five years ago, and it seems like yesterday. If I count my life so by lustres, it will soon glide away; yet I shall not have to repine, if, while it lasts, it is enriched with a few such recollections!

ON SITTING FOR ONE'S PICTURE

(NEW MONTHLY MAGAZINE, NOV., 1823)

THERE is a pleasure in sitting for one's picture, which many persons are not aware of. People are coy on this subject at first, coquet with it, and pretend not to like it, as is the case with other venial indulgences, but they soon get over their scruples, and become resigned to their fate. There is a conscious vanity in it; and vanity is the *aurum potabile* in all our pleasures, the true *elixir* of human life. The sitter at first affects an air of indifference, throws himself into a slovenly or awkward position, like a clown when he goes a courting for the first time, but gradually recovers himself, attempts an attitude, and calls up his best looks, the moment he receives intimation that there is something about him that will do for a picture. The beggar in the street is proud to have his picture painted, and would almost sit for nothing: the finest lady in the land is as fond of sitting to a favourite artist as of seating herself before her looking-glass; and the more so, as the glass in this case is sensible of her charms, and does all it can to fix or heighten them. Kings lay aside their crowns to sit for their portraits, and poets their laurels to sit for their busts! I am sure, my father had as little vanity, and as little love for the art, as most persons: yet when he had sat to me a few times (now some twenty years ago), he grew evidently uneasy when it was a fine day, that is, when the sun shone into the room, so that we could not paint; and when it became cloudy, began to bustle about, and ask me if I was not getting ready. Poor old room! Does the sun still shine into thee, or does Hope fling its colours round thy walls, gaudier than the rainbow? No, never, while thy oak-panels endure, will they inclose such fine movements of the brain as passed through mine, when the fresh hues of nature gleamed from the canvas, and my heart silently breathed the names of Rembrandt and Correggio! Between my father's love of sitting and mine of painting, we hit upon a tolerable likeness at last; but the picture is cracked and gone; and *Megilp* (that bane of the English school) has destroyed as fine an old Nonconformist head as one could hope to see in these degenerate times.

The fact is, that the having one's picture painted is like the creation of another self; and that is an idea, of the repetition or reduplication of which no man is ever tired, to the thousandth reflection. It has been said that lovers are never tired of each other's company, because they are always talking of themselves. This seems to be the bond of connexion (a delicate one it is!) between the painter and the sitter—they are always thinking and talking of the same thing, the picture, in which their self-love finds an equal counter-part. There is always something to be done or to be altered, that touches that sensitive chord—this feature was not exactly hit off, something is wanting to the nose or to the eye-brows, it may perhaps be as well to leave out this mark or that blemish, if it were possible to recall an expression that was remarked a short time before, it would be an indescribable advantage to the picture—a squint or a pimple on the face handsomely avoided may be a link of attachment ever after. He is no mean friend who conceals from ourselves, or only gently indicates, our obvious defects to the world. The sitter, by his repeated, minute, *fidgety* inquiries about himself may be supposed to take an indirect and laudable method of arriving at self-knowledge; and the artist, in self-defence, is obliged to cultivate a scrupulous tenderness towards the feelings of his sitter, lest he should appear in the character of a spy upon him. I do not conceive there is a stronger call upon secret gratitude than the having made a favourable likeness of any one; nor a surer ground of jealousy and dislike than the having failed in the attempt. A satire or a lampoon in writing is bad enough; but here we look doubly foolish, for we are ourselves parties to the plot, and have been at considerable pains to give evidence against ourselves. I have never had a plaster cast taken of myself: in truth, I rather shrink from the experiment; for I know I should be very much mortified if it did not turn out well, and should never forgive the unfortunate artist who had lent his assistance to prove that I looked like a blockhead!

The late Mr. Opie used to remark that the most sensible

people made the best sitters; and I incline to his opinion, especially as I myself am an excellent sitter. Indeed, it seems to me a piece of mere impertinence not to sit as still as one can in these circumstances. I put the best face I can upon the matter, as well out of respect to the artist as to myself. I appear on my trial in the court of physiognomy, and am as anxious to make good a certain idea I have of myself, as if I were playing a part on a stage. I have no notion how people go to sleep, who are sitting for their pictures. It is an evident sign of want of thought and of internal resources. There are some individuals, all whose ideas are in their hands and feet—make them sit still, and you put a stop to the machine altogether. The volatile spirit of quicksilver in them turns to a *caput mortuum*. Children are particularly sensible of this constraint from their thoughtlessness and liveliness. It is the next thing with them to wearing the fool's cap at school: yet they are proud of having their pictures taken, ask when they are to sit again, and are mightily pleased when they are done. Charles the First's children seem to have been good sitters, and the great dog sits like a Lord Chancellor.

The second time a person sits, and the view of the features is determined, the head seems fastened in an imaginary *vice*, and he can hardly tell what to make of his situation. He is continually overstepping the bounds of duty, and is tied down to certain lines and limits chalked out upon the canvas, to him " invisible or dimly seen " on the throne where he is exalted. The painter has now a difficult task to manage—to throw in his gentle admonitions, " A little more this way, sir," or " You bend rather too forward, madam,"—and ought to have a delicate white hand, that he may venture to adjust a straggling lock of hair, or by giving a slight turn to the head, co-operate in the practical attainment of a position. These are the ticklish and tiresome places of the work, before much progress is made, where the sitter grows peevish and abstracted, and the painter more anxious and particular than he was the day before. Now is the time to fling in a few adroit compliments, or to introduce general topics of conversation. The artist ought to be a well-informed and agreeable man—able to expatiate on his art, and abounding in lively and characteristic anecdotes. Yet he ought not to talk too much, or to grow too animated; or the picture is apt to stand still, and the sitter to be aware of it. Accordingly, the best talkers in the profession have not always been the most successful portrait-painters. For this purpose it is desirable to bring a friend, who may relieve guard, or fill up the pauses of conversation, occasioned by the necessary attention of the painter to his business, and by the involuntary reveries of the sitter on what his own likeness will bring forth; or a book, a newspaper, or a port-folio of prints may serve to amuse the time. When the sitter's face begins to flag, the artist may then properly start a fresh topic of discourse, and while his attention is fixed on the graces called out by the varying interest of the subject, and the model anticipates, pleased and smiling, their being transferred every moment to the canvas, nothing is wanting to improve and carry to its height the amicable understanding and mutual satisfaction and good-will subsisting between these two persons so happily occupied with each other!

Sir Joshua must have had a fine time of it with his sitters. Lords, ladies, generals, authors, opera-singers, musicians, the learned and the polite, besieged his doors, and found an unfailing welcome. What a rustling of silks! What a fluttering of flounces and brocades! What a cloud of powder and perfumes! What a flow of periwigs! What an exchange of civilities and of titles! What a recognition of old friendships, and an introduction of new acquaintance and sitters! It must, I think, be allowed that this is the only mode in which genius can form a legitimate union with wealth and fashion. There is a secret and sufficient tie in interest and vanity. Abstract topics of wit or learning do not furnish a connecting link: but the painter, the sculptor, come in close contact with the persons of the Great. The lady of quality, the courtier, and the artist, meet and shake hands on this common ground; the latter exercises a sort of natural jurisdiction and dictatorial power over the pretensions of the first to external beauty and accomplishment, which produces a mild sense and tone of equality; and the opulent sitter pays the taker of flattering likenesses handsomely for his trouble, which does not lessen the sympathy between them. There is even a satisfaction in paying down a high price for a picture—it seems as if one's head was worth something!—During the first sitting, Sir Joshua did little but chat with the new candidate for the fame of portraiture, try an attitude, or remark an expression. His object was to gain time, by not being in haste to commit himself, until he was master of the subject before him. No one ever dropped in but the friends and acquaintance of the sitter—it was a rule with Sir Joshua that from the moment the latter entered, he was at home —the room belonged to him—but what secret whisperings would there be among these, what confidential, inaudible communications! It must be a refreshing moment, when the cake and wine had been handed round, and the artist began again. He, as it were, by this act of hospitality assumed a new character, and acquired a double claim to confidence and respect. In the meantime, the sitter would perhaps glance his eye round the room, and see a Titian or a Vandyke hanging in one corner, with a transient feeling of scepticism whether he should make such a picture. How the ladies of quality and fashion must bless themselves from being made to look like Dr. Johnson or Goldsmith! How proud the first of these would be, how happy the last, to fill the same arm-chair where the

Y *

Bunburys and the Hornecks had sat! How superior the
painter would feel to them all! By "happy alchemy of
mind," he brought out all their good qualities and reconciled their defects, gave an air of studious ease to his
learned friends, or lighted up the face of folly and fashion
with intelligence and graceful smiles. Those portraits,
however, that were most admired at the time, do not
retain their pre-eminence now: the thought remains upon
the brow, while the colour has faded from the cheek, or
the dress grown obsolete; and after all, Sir Joshua's best
pictures are those of his worst sitters—*his Children.* They
suited best with his unfinished style; and are like the
infancy of the art itself—happy, bold, and careless. Sir
Joshua formed the circle of his private friends from the
élite of his sitters; and Vandyke was, it appears, on the
same footing with his. When any of those noble or distinguished persons whom he has immortalised with his pencil,
were sitting to him, he used to ask them to dinner, and
afterwards it was their custom to return to the picture
again, so that it is said that many of his finest portraits
were done in this manner, ere the colours were yet dry,
in the course of a single day. Oh! ephemeral works to
last for ever!

Vandyke married a daughter of Earl Gowrie[1], of whom
there is a very beautiful picture. She was the Œnone,
and he his own Paris. A painter of the name of Astley
married a Lady ——, who sat to him for her picture.
He was a wretched hand, but a fine person of a man, and
a great coxcomb; and on his strutting up and down
before the portrait when it was done with a prodigious air
of satisfaction, she observed, "If he was so pleased with
the copy, he might have the original." This Astley was
a person of magnificent habits and a sumptuous taste in
living; and is the same of whom the anecdote is recorded,

---

[1] The orig. edit. has *Cowper* in the text, altered to *Gower* in
the *errata.* [Ed.]

that when some English students walking out near Rome were compelled by the heat to strip off their coats, Astley displayed a waistcoat with a huge waterfall streaming down the back of it, which was a piece of one of his own canvases that he had converted to this purpose. Sir Joshua fell in love with one of his fair sitters, a young and beautiful girl, who ran out one day in a great panic and confusion, hid her face in her companion's lap who was reading in an outer room, and said, " Sir Joshua had made her an offer!" This circumstance perhaps deserves mentioning the more, because there is a general idea that Sir Joshua Reynolds was a confirmed old bachelor. Goldsmith conceived a fruitless attachment to the same person, and addressed some passionate letters to her. Alas! it is the fate of genius to admire and to celebrate beauty, not to enjoy it! It is a fate, perhaps, not without its compensations—

> " Had Petrarch gained his Laura for a wife,
>   Would he have written Sonnets all his life ? "

This distinguished beauty is still living, and handsomer than Sir Joshua's picture of her when a girl; and inveighs against the freedom of Lord Byron's pen with all the charming prudery of the last age.[1]

The relation between the portrait-painter and his amiable sitters is one of established custom; but it is also one of metaphysical nicety, and is a running *double entendre*. The fixing an inquisitive gaze on beauty, the heightening a momentary grace, the dwelling on the

---

[1] Sir Joshua may be thought to have studied the composition of his female portraits very coolly. There is a picture of his remaining of a Mrs. Symmons, who appears to have been a delicate beauty, pale, with a very little colour in her cheeks: but then to set-off this want of complexion, she is painted in a snow-white satin dress, there is a white marble pillar near her, a white cloud over her head, and by her side stands one white lily.

heaven of an eye, the losing oneself in the dimple of a chin, is a dangerous employment. The painter may chance to slide into the lover—the lover can hardly turn painter. The eye indeed grows critical, the hand is busy: but are the senses unmoved? We are employed to transfer living charms to an inanimate surface; but they may sink into the heart by the way, and the nerveless hand be unable to carry its luscious burthen any further. St. Preux wonders at the rash mortal who had dared to trace the features of his Julia; and accuses him of insensibility without reason. Perhaps he, too, had an enthusiasm and pleasures of his own! Mr. Burke, in his *Sublime and Beautiful*, has left a description of what he terms the most beautiful object in nature—the neck of a lovely and innocent female—which is written very much as if he had himself formerly painted this object, and sacrificed at this formidable shrine. There is no doubt that the perception of beauty becomes more exquisite (" till the sense aches at it ") by being studied and refined upon as an object of art—it is at the same time fortunately neutralised by this means, or the painter would run mad. It is converted into an abstraction, an *ideal* thing, into something intermediate between Nature and art, hovering between a living substance and a senseless shadow. The health and spirit that but now breathed from a speaking face, the next moment breathe with almost equal effect from a dull piece of canvas, and thus distract attention: the eye sparkles, the lips are moist there too; and if we can fancy the picture alive, the face in its turn fades into a picture, a mere object of sight. We take rapturous possession with one sense, the eye; but the artist's pencil acts as a non-conductor to the grosser desires. Besides, the sense of duty, of propriety interferes. It is not the question at issue: we have other work on our hands, and enough to do. Love is the product of ease and idleness: but the painter has an anxious, feverish, never-ending task, to rival the beauty to which he dare not aspire even in thought, or in a dream of bliss. Paints and brushes are not " amorous toys of light-winged Cupid "; a rising sigh evaporates in the aroma of some fine oil-colour or varnish, a kindling blush is transfixed in a bed of vermilion on the palette. A blue vein meandering in a white wrist invites the hand to touch it: but it is better to proceed, and not spoil the picture. The ambiguity becomes more striking in painting from the naked figure. If the wonder occasioned by the object is greater, so is the despair of rivalling what we see. The sense of responsibility increases with the hope of creating an artificial splendour to match the real one. The display of unexpected charms foils our vanity, and mortifies passion. The painting " A Diana and Nymphs " is like plunging into a cold bath of desire: to make a statue of a " Venus " transforms the sculptor himself to stone. The snow on the lap of beauty freezes the soul. The heedless, unsuspecting licence of foreign manners gives the artist abroad an advantage over ours at home. Sir Joshua Reynolds painted only the head of " Iphigene " from a beautiful woman of quality: Canova had innocent girls to sit to him for his " Graces." The Princess Borghese, whose symmetry of form was admirable, sat to him for a model, which he considered as his master-piece and the perfection of the female form; and when asked if she did not feel uncomfortable while it was taking, she replied with great indifference, " No: it was not cold!" I have but one other word to add on this part of the subject: if having to paint a delicate and modest female is a temptation to gallantry, on the other hand the sitting to a lady for one's picture is a still more trying situation, and amounts (almost of itself) to a declaration of love!

Landscape-painting is free from these tormenting dilemmas and embarrassments. It is as full of the feeling of pastoral simplicity and ease, as portrait-painting is of

personal vanity and egotism. Away, then, with those incumbrances to the true liberty of thought—the sitter's
chair, the bag-wig and sword, the drapery, the lay figure
—and let us to some retired spot in the country, take out
our portfolio, plant our easel, and begin. We are all at
once shrouded from observation—

> " The world forgetting, by the world forgot ! "

We enjoy the cool shade, with solitude and silence; or
hear the dashing waterfall,

> " Or stock-dove plain amid the forest deep,
> That drowsy rustles to the sighing gale."

It seems almost a shame to do anything, we are so well
content without it; but the eye is restless, and we must
have something to shew when we get home. We set to
work, and failure or success prompts us to go on. We
take up the pencil, or lay it down again, as we please. We
muse or paint, as objects strike our senses or our reflection.
The perfect leisure we feel turns labour to a luxury. We
try to imitate the grey colour of a rock or of the bark of
a tree: the breeze wafted from its broad foliage gives us
fresh spirits to proceed, we dip our pencil in the sky, or
ask the white clouds sailing over its bosom to sit for their
pictures. We are in no hurry, and have the day before
us. Or else, escaping from the close-embowered scene,
we catch fading distances on airy downs, and seize on
golden sunsets with the fleecy flocks glittering in the
evening ray, after a shower of rain has fallen. Or from
Norwood's ridgy heights, survey the snake-like Thames,
or its smoke-crowned capital;

> " Think of its crimes, its cares, its pain,
> Then shield us in the woods again."

No one thinks of disturbing a landscape-painter at his
task: he seems a kind of magician, the privileged genius

of the place. Wherever a Claude, a Wilson has introduced his own portrait in the foreground of a picture, we look at it with interest (however ill it may be done), feeling that it is the portrait of one who was quite happy at the time, and how glad we should be to change places with him.

Mr. Burke has brought in a striking episode in one of his later works in allusion to Sir Joshua's portrait of Lord Keppel, with those of some other friends, painted in their better days. The portrait is indeed a fine one, worthy of the artist and the critic, and perhaps recalls Lord Keppel's memory oftener than any other circumstance at present does.[1] Portrait-painting is in truth a sort of cement

---

[1] "No man lives too long, who lives to do with spirit, and suffer with resignation, what Providence pleases to command or inflict : but indeed they are sharp incommodities which beset old age. It was but the other day, that in putting in order some things which had been brought here on my taking leave of London for ever, I looked over a number of fine portraits, most of them of persons now dead, but whose society, in my better days, made this a proud and happy place. Amongst these was the picture of Lord Keppel. It was painted by an artist worthy of the subject, the excellent friend of that excellent man from their earliest youth, and a common friend of us both, with whom we lived for many years without a moment of coldness, of peevishness, of jealousy, or of jar, to the day of our final separation.

"I ever looked on Lord Keppel as one of the greatest and best men of his age ; and I loved and cultivated him accordingly. He was much in my heart, and I believe I was in his to the very last beat. It was after his trial at Portsmouth that he gave me this picture. With what zeal and anxious affection I attended him through that his agony of glory ; what part, my son, in early flush and enthusiasm of his virtue and the pious passion with which he attached himself to all my connexions, with what prodigality we both squandered ourselves in courting almost every sort of enmity for his sake, I believe he felt, just as I should have felt, such friendship on such an occasion."
—*Letter to a Noble Lord*, p. 29, Second Edition, printed for T. Williams.

I have given this passage entire here, because I wish to be

of friendship, and a clue to history. That blockhead, Mr. C[roke]r, of the Admiralty, the other day blundered upon some observations of mine relating to this subject, and made the House stare by asserting that portrait-painting was history or history portrait, as it happened; but went on to add, " That those gentlemen who had seen the ancient portraits lately exhibited in Pall-Mall, must have been satisfied that they were strictly *historical*"; which shewed that he knew nothing at all of the matter, and merely talked by rote. There was nothing historical in the generality of those portraits, except that they were portraits of people mentioned in history—there was no more of the spirit of history in them (which is *passion* or *action*) than in their dresses. But this is the way in which that person, by his pettifogging habits and literal understanding, always mistakes a verbal truism for sense, and a misnomer for wit! I was going to observe, that I think the aiding the recollection of our family and friends in our absence may be a frequent and strong inducement to sitting for our pictures; but that I believe the love of posthumous fame, or of continuing our memories after we are dead, has very little to do with it. And one reason I should give for that opinion is this, that we are not naturally very prone to dwell with pleasure on anything that may happen in relation to us after we are dead,

informed, if I could, what is the construction of the last sentence of it. It has puzzled me all my life. One difficulty might be got over by making a pause after " I believe he felt," and leaving out the comma between " have felt " and " such friendship." That is, the meaning would be, " I believe he felt with what zeal and anxious affection," etc., " just as I should have felt such friendship on such an occasion." But then, again, what is to become of the " what part, my son ? " etc. With what does this connect, or to what verb is " my son " the nominative case, or by what verb is " what part " governed ? I should really be glad, if, from any manuscript, printed copy, or marginal correction, this point could be cleared up, and so fine a passage resolved, by any possible ellipsis, into ordinary grammar because we are not fond of thinking of death at all. We shrink equally from the prospect of that fatal event or from any speculation on its consequences. The surviving ourselves in our pictures is but a poor compensation—it is rather adding mockery to calamity. The perpetuating our names in the wide page of history or to a remote posterity is a vague calculation, that may take out the immediate sting of mortality—whereas we ourselves may hope to last (by a fortunate extension of the term of human life) almost as long as an ordinary portrait; and the wounds of lacerated friendship it heals must be still green, and our ashes scarcely cold. I think therefore that the looking forward to this mode of keeping alive the memory of what we were by lifeless hues and discoloured features, is not among the most approved consolations of human life, or favourite dalliances of the imagination. Yet I own I should like some part of me, as the hair or even nails, to be preserved entire, or I should have no objection to lie like Whitfield in a state of petrifaction. This smacks of the bodily reality at least—acts like a deception to the spectator, and breaks the fall from this " warm, kneaded motion to a clod "—from that to nothing—even to the person himself. I suspect that the idea of posthumous fame, which has so unwelcome a condition annexed to it, loses its general relish as we advance in life, and that it is only while we are young that we pamper our imaginations with this bait, with a sort of impunity. The reversion of immortality is then so distant, that we may talk of it without much fear of entering upon immediate possession: death is itself a fable—a sound that dies upon our lips; and the only certainty seems the only impossibility. Fame, at that romantic period, is the first thing in our mouths, and death the last in our thoughts.

THE DULWICH GALLERY

(LONDON MAGAZINE, JAN., 1823)

I T was on the 5th of November that we went to see this Gallery. The morning was mild, calm, pleasant: it was a day to ruminate on the object we had in view. It was the time of year

> " When yellow leaves, or few or none, do hang
> Upon the branches " ;

their scattered gold was strongly contrasted with the dark green spiral shoots of the cedar trees that skirt the road; the sun shone faint and watery, as if smiling his last; Winter gently let go the hand of Summer, and the green fields, wet with the mist, anticipated the return of Spring. At the end of a beautiful little village, Dulwich College appeared in view, with modest state, yet mindful of the olden time; and the name of Allen and his compeers rushed full upon the memory! How many races of school-boys have played within its walls, or stammered out a lesson, or sauntered away their vacant hours in its shade: yet, not one Shakespear is there to be found among them all! The boy is clothed and fed and gets through his accidence: but no trace of his youthful learning, any more than of his saffron livery, is to be met with in the man. Genius is not to be " constrained by mastery."—Nothing comes of these endowments and foundations for learning,—you might as well make dirt-pies, or build houses with cards. Yet something *does* come of them too—a retreat for age, a dream in youth— a feeling in the air around them, the memory of the past, the hope of what will never be. Sweet are the studies of the school-boy, delicious his idle hours! Fresh and gladsome is his waking, balmy are his slumbers, book-pillowed! He wears a green and yellow livery perhaps; but " green and yellow melancholy " comes not near him, or if it does, is tempered with youth and innocence! To thumb his Eutropius, or to knuckle down at taw, are to him equally delightful; for whatever stirs the blood, or inspires thought in him, quickens the pulse of life and joy. He has only to feel, in order to be happy; pain turns smiling from him, and sorrow is only a softer kind of pleasure. Each sensation is but an unfolding of his new being; care, age, sickness, are idle words; the musty records of antiquity look glossy in his sparkling eye, and he clasps immortality as his future bride! The coming years hurt him not—he hears their sound afar off, and is glad. See him there, the urchin, seated in the sun, with a book in his hand, and the wall at his back. He has a thicker wall before him—the wall that parts him from the future. He sees not the archers taking aim at his peace; he knows not the hands that are to mangle his bosom. He stirs not, he still pores upon his book, and, as he reads, a slight hectic flush passes over his cheek, for he sees the letters that compose the word FAME glitter on the page, and his eyes swim, and he thinks that he will one day write a book, and have his name repeated by thousands of readers, and assume a certain signature, and write Essays and Criticisms in a LONDON MAGAZINE, as a consummation of felicity scarcely to be believed. Come hither, thou poor little fellow, and let us change places with thee if thou wilt; here, take the pen and finish this article, and sign what name you please to it; so that we may but change our dress for yours, and sit shivering in the sun, and con over our little task, and feed poor, and lie hard, and be contented and happy, and think what a fine thing it is to be an author and dream of immortality, and sleep o'nights!

There is something affecting and monastic in the sight of this little nursery of learning, simple and retired as it stands, just on the verge of the metropolis, and in the midst of modern improvements. There is a chapel, containing a copy of Raphael's *Transfiguration*, by Julio

Romano; but the great attraction to curiosity at present
is the Collection of pictures left to the College by the late
Sir Francis Bourgeois, who is buried in a mausoleum
close by. He once (it is said) spent an agreeable day here
in company with the Masters of the College and some
other friends; and he determined, in consequence, upon
this singular mode testifying his gratitude and his respect.
Perhaps, also, some such idle thoughts as we have here
recorded might have mingled with this resolution. The
contemplation and the approach of death might have been
softened to his mind by being associated with the hopes
of childhood; and he might wish that his remains should
repose, in monumental state, amidst " the innocence
and simplicity of poor *Charity Boys !* " Might it not have
been so?

The pictures are 356 in number, and are hung on the
walls of a large gallery, built for the purpose, and divided
into five compartments. They certainly looked better
in their old places, at the house of Mr. Desenfans (the
original collector), where they were distributed into a
number of small rooms, and seen separately and close to
the eye. They are mostly cabinet-pictures; and not only
does the height, at which many of them are necessarily
hung to cover a large space, lessen the effect, but the
number distracts and deadens the attention. Besides, the
skylights are so contrived as to " shed a dim," though not
a " religious light " upon them. At our entrance, we were
first struck by our old friends the Cuyps; and just beyond,
caught a glimpse of that fine female head by Carlo Maratti,
giving us a welcome with cordial glances. May we not
exclaim—

> " What a delicious breath *painting* sends forth !
> The violet-bed's not sweeter."

A fine gallery of pictures is a sort of illustration of
Berkeley's *Theory of Matter and Spirit*. It is like a palace
of thought—another universe, built of air, of shadows, of

colours. Everything seems " palpable to feeling as to sight." Substances turn to shadows by the painter's arch-chemic touch; shadows harden into substances. " The eye is made the fool of the other senses, or else worth all the rest." The material is in some sense embodied in the immaterial, or, at least, we see all things in a sort of intellectual mirror. The world of art is an enchanting deception. We discover distance in a glazed surface; a province is contained in a foot of canvas; a thin evanescent tint gives the form and pressure of rocks and trees; an inert shape has life and motion in it. Time stands still, and the dead re-appear, by means of this " so potent art I " Look at the Cuyp next the door (No. 3). It is woven of etherial hues. A soft mist is on it, a veil of subtle air. The tender green of the valleys beyond the gleaming lake, the purple light of the hills, have an effect like the down on an unripe nectarine. You may lay your finger on the canvas; but miles of dewy vapour and sunshine are between you and the objects you survey. It is almost needless to point out that the cattle and figures in the fore-ground, like dark, transparent spots, give an immense relief to the perspective. This is, we think, the finest Cuyp, perhaps, in the world. The landscape opposite to it (in the same room) by Albert Cuyp, has a richer colouring and a stronger contrast of light and shade, but it has not that tender bloom of a spring morning (so delicate, yet so powerful in its effect) which the other possesses. *Two Horses*, by Cuyp (No. 74), is another admirable specimen of this excellent painter. It is hard to say, which is most true to Nature—the sleek, well-fed look of the bay horse, or the bone and spirit of the dappled iron-grey one, or the face of the man who is busy fastening a girth. Nature is scarcely more faithful to itself, than this delightfully *unmannered*, unaffected picture is to it. In the same room there are several good Tenierses, and a small *Head of an Old Man*, by

Rembrandt, which is as smoothly finished as a miniature. No. 10, *Interior of an Ale-house*, by Adrian Brouwer, almost gives one a sick head-ache; particularly, the face and figure of the man leaning against the door, overcome with " potations pottle deep." Brouwer united the depth and richness of Ostade to the spirit and felicity of Teniers. No. 12, *Sleeping Nymph and Satyr*, and 59, *Nymph and Satyr*, by Polemberg, are not pictures to our taste. Why should any one make it a rule never to paint anything but this one subject? Was it to please himself or others? The one shews bad taste, the other wrong judgment. The grossness of the selection is hardly more offensive than the finicalness of the execution. No. 49, a *Mater Dolorosa*, by Carlo Dolce, is a very good specimen of this master; but the expression has too great a mixture of piety and pauperism in it. It is not altogether spiritual. No. 51, *A School with Girls at work*, by Crespi, is a most rubbishy performance, and has the look of a modern picture. It was, no doubt, painted in the fashion of the time, and is now old-fashioned. Everything has this modern, or rather uncouth and obsolete look, which, besides the temporary and local circumstances, has not the free look of nature. Dress a figure in what costume you please (however fantastic, however barbarous), but add the expression which is common to all faces, the properties that are common to all drapery in its elementary principles, and the picture will belong to all times and places. It is not the addition of individual circumstances, but the omission of general truth, that makes the little, the deformed, and the short-lived in art. No. 183, *Religion in the Desert*, a sketch by Sir Francis Bourgeois, is a proof of the remark. There are no details, nor is there any appearance of permanence or sta[bility about it. It][1] seems to have been painted yesterday, and

[1] These words are missing in *The Picture Galleries of England*, 1824, from which this text is printed. [Ed.]

to labour under premature decay. It has a look of being half done, and you have no wish to see it finished. No. 52, *Interior of a Cathedral*, by Sanadram, is curious and fine. From one end of the perspective to the other—and back again—would make a morning's walk.

In the SECOND ROOM, No. 90, a *Sea Storm*, by Backhuysen, and No. 93, *A Calm*, by W. Vandervelde, are equally excellent, the one for its gloomy turbulence, and the other for its glassy smoothness. 92, *Landscape with Cattle and Figures*, is by Both, who is, we confess, no great favourite of ours. We do not like his straggling branches of trees without masses of foliage, continually running up into the sky, merely to let in the landscape beyond. No. 96, *Blowing Hot and Cold*, by Jordaens, is as fine a picture as need be painted. It is full of character, of life, and pleasing colour. It is rich and not gross. 98, *Portrait of a Lady*, said in the printed Catalogue to be by Andrea Sacchi, is surely by Carlo Maratti, to whom it used to be given. It has great beauty, great elegance, great expression, and great brilliancy of execution; but everything in it belongs to a more polished style of art than Andrea Sacchi. Be this as it may, it is one of the most perfect pictures in the collection. Of the portraits of known individuals in this room, we wish to say but little, for we can say nothing good. That of *Mr. Kemble*, by Beechey, is perhaps the most direct and manly. In this room is Rubens' *Sampson and Dalilah*, a coarse daub —at least, it looks so between two pictures by Vandyke, *Charity*, and a *Madonna and Infant Christ*. That painter probably never produced anything more complete than these two compositions. They have the softness of air, the solidity of marble: the pencil appears to float and glide over the features of the face, the folds of the drapery, with easy volubility, but to mark everything with a precision, a force, a grace indescribable. Truth seems to hold the pencil, and elegance to guide it. The attitudes are exquisite, and the expression all but divine. It is not like Raphael's, it is true—but whose else was? Vandyke was born in Holland, and lived most of his time in England!—There are several capital pictures of horses, &c. by Wouvermans, in the same room, particularly the one with a hay-cart loading on the top of a rising ground. The composition is as striking and pleasing as the execution is delicate. There is immense knowledge and character in Wouverman's horses—an ear, an eye turned round, a cropped tail, give you their history and thoughts —but from the want of a little arrangement, his figures look too often like spots on a dark ground. When they are properly relieved and disentangled from the rest of the composition, there is an appearance of great life and bustle in his pictures. His horses, however, have too much of the *manège* in them—he seldom gets beyond the camp or the riding school.—This room is rich in master-pieces. Here is the *Jacob's Dream*, by Rembrandt, with that sleeping figure, thrown like a bundle of clothes in one corner of the picture, by the side of some stunted bushes, and with those winged shapes, not human, nor angelical, but bird-like, dream-like, treading on clouds, ascending, descending through realms of endless light, that loses itself in infinite space! No one else could ever grapple with this subject, or stamp it on the willing canvas in its gorgeous obscurity but Rembrandt! Here also is the *St. Barbara*, of Rubens, fleeing from her persecutors; a noble design, as if she were scaling the steps of some high overhanging turret, moving majestically on, with Fear before her, Death behind her, and Martyrdom crowning her:—and here is an eloquent landscape by the same master-hand, the subject of which is, a shepherd piping his flock homewards through a narrow defile, with a graceful group of autumnal trees waving on the edge of the declivity above, and the rosy evening light streaming through the clouds on the green moist landscape in the still lengthening distance. Here (to pass from one kind of excellence to another with kindly interchange) is a clear sparkling *Waterfall*, by Ruysdael, and Hobbema's *Water-Mill*, with the wheels in motion, and the ducks paddling in the restless stream. Is not this a sad anti-climax from Jacob's Dream to a picture of a Water-Mill? We do not know; and we should care as little, could we but paint either of the pictures.

"Entire affection scorneth nicer hands."

If a picture is admirable in its kind, we do not give our-selves much trouble about the subject. Could we paint as well as Hobbema, we should not envy Rembrandt: nay, even as it is, while we can relish both, we envy neither!

The CENTRE ROOM commences with a *Girl at a Window*, by Rembrandt. The picture is known by the print of it, and is one of the most remarkable and pleasing in the Collection. For clearness, for breadth, for a lively, ruddy look of healthy nature, it cannot be surpassed. The execution of the drapery is masterly. There is a story told of its being his servant-maid looking out of a window, but it is evidently the portrait of a mere child.—*A Farrier shoeing an Ass*, by Berchem, is in his usual manner. There is truth of character and delicate finishing; but the fault of all Berchem's pictures is, that he continues to finish after he has done looking at nature, and his last touches are different from hers. Hence comes that resemblance to *tea-board* painting, which even his best works are chargeable with. We find here one or two small Claudes of no great value; and two very clever specimens of the court-painter, Watteau, the Gainsborough of France. They are marked as Nos. 184 and 194, *Fête Champêtre*, and *Le Bal Champêtre*. There is something exceedingly light, agreeable, and characteristic in this artist's productions. He might almost be said to breathe his figures and his flowers on the canvas—so fragile is their texture, so evanescent is his touch. He unites the court and the country at a sort of salient point—you may fancy yourself with Count Grammont and the beauties of Charles II. in their gay retreat at Tunbridge Wells. His trees have a drawing-room air with them, an appearance of gentility and etiquette, and nod gracefully overhead; while the figures below, thin as air, and *vegetably* clad, in the midst of all their affectation and grimace, seem to have just sprung out of the ground, or to be the fairy inhabitants of the scene in masquerade. They are the Oreads and Dryads of the Luxembourg! Quaint association, happily effected by the pencil of Watteau! In the *Bal Champêtre* we see Louis XIV. himself dancing, looking so like an old beau, his face flushed and puckered up with gay anxiety; but then the satin of his slashed doublet is made of the softest leaves of the water-lily; Zephyr plays wanton with the curls of his wig! We have nobody who could produce a companion to this picture now: nor do we very devoutly wish it. The Louis the Fourteenths are extinct, and we suspect their revival would hardly be compensated even by the re-appearance of a Watteau.—No. 187, *the Death of Cardinal Beaufort,* by Sir Joshua Reynolds, is a very indifferent and rather unpleasant sketch of a very fine picture. One of the most delightful things in this delightful collection is *the Portrait* (195) *of the Prince of the Asturias,* by Velasquez. The easy lightness of the childish Prince contrasts delightfully with the unwieldy figure of the horse, which has evidently been brought all the way from the Low Countries for the amusement of his rider. Velasquez was (with only two exceptions, Titian and Vandyke) as fine a portrait-painter as ever lived! In the centre room also is the *Meeting of Jacob and Rachel,* by Murillo—a sweet picture with a fresh green landscape, and the heart of Love in the midst of it.—There are several heads by

Holbein scattered up and down the different compartments. We need hardly observe that they all have
character in the extreme, so that we may be said to be
acquainted with the people they represent; but then they
give nothing but character, and only one part of that, *viz.*
the dry, the literal, the concrete, and fixed. They want
the addition of passion and beauty; but they are the finest
caput mortuums of expression that ever were made. Hans
Holbein had none of the volatile essence of genius in his
composition. If portrait-painting is the prose of the art,
his pictures are the prose of portrait-painting. Yet he is
" a reverend name " in art, and one of the benefactors of
the human mind. He has left faces behind him that we
would give the world to have seen, and there they are—
stamped on his canvas for ever! Who, in reading over
the names of certain individuals, does not feel a yearning
in his breast to know their features and their lineaments?
We look through a small frame, and lo! at the distance of
three centuries, we have before us the figures of Anne
Boleyn, of the virtuous Cranmer, the bigoted Queen
Mary, the noble Surrey—as if we had seen them in their
life-time, not perhaps in their best moods or happiest
attitudes, but as they sometimes appeared, no doubt.
We know at least what sort of looking people they
were: our minds are made easy on that score; the
" body and limbs " are there, and we may " add what
flourishes " of grace or ornament we please. Holbein's
heads are to the finest portraits what state-papers are to
history.

The first picture in the FOURTH ROOM is the *Prophet
Samuel,* by Sir Joshua. It is not the Prophet Samuel, but
a very charming picture of a little child saying its prayers.
The second is, *The Education of Bacchus,* by Nicholas
Poussin. This picture makes one thirsty to look at it—the
colouring even is dry and adust. It is true *history* in the
technical phrase, that is to say, true *poetry* in the vulgate.

The figure of the infant Bacchus seems as if he would drink up a vintage—he drinks with his mouth, his hands, his belly, and his whole body. Gargantua was nothing to him. In the *Education of Jupiter*, in like manner, we are thrown back into the infancy of mythologic lore. The little Jupiter, suckled by a she-goat, is beautifully conceived and expressed; and the dignity and ascendancy given to these animals in the picture is wonderfully happy. They have a very imposing air of gravity indeed, and seem to be by prescription " grand caterers and wet-nurses of the state " of Heaven! *Apollo giving a Poet a Cup of Water to drink* is elegant and classical; and *The Flight into Egypt* instantly takes the tone of Scripture-history. This is strange, but so it is. All things are possible to a high imagination. All things, about which we have a feeling, may be expressed by true genius. A dark landscape (by the same hand) in a corner of the room is a proof of this. There are trees in the fore-ground, with a paved road and buildings in the distance. The Genius of antiquity might wander here, and feel itself at home. —The large leaves are wet and heavy with dew, and the eye dwells " under the shade of melancholy boughs." In the old Collection (in Mr. Desenfans' time) the Poussins occupied a separate room by themselves, and it was (we confess) a very favourite room with us. —No. 226 is a *Landscape*, by Salvator Rosa. It is one of his very best—rough, grotesque, wild—Pan has struck it with his hoof—the trees, the rocks, the fore-ground, are of a piece, and the figures are subordinate to the landscape. The same dull sky lowers upon the scene, and the bleak air chills the crisp surface of the water. It is a consolation to us to meet with a fine Salvator. His is one of the great names in art, and it is among our sources of regret that we cannot always admire his works as we would do, from our respect to his reputation and our love of the man. Poor Salvator! he was unhappy in his lifetime; and it vexes us to think that we cannot make him amends by fancying him so great a painter as some others, whose fame was not their only inheritance!—227, *Venus and Cupid*, is a delightful copy after Correggio. We have no such regrets or qualms of conscience with respect to him. "He has had his reward." The weight of his renown balances the weight of barbarous coin that sunk him to the earth. Could he live now, and know what others think of him, his misfortunes would seem as dross compared with his lasting glory, and his heart would melt within him at the thought, with a sweetness that only his own pencil could express. 233, *The Virgin, Infant Christ, and St. John*, by Andrea del Sarto, is exceedingly good.—290, Another *Holy Family*, by the same, is an admirable picture, and only inferior to Raphael. It has delicacy, force, thought, and feeling. "What lacks it then," to be equal to Raphael? We hardly know, unless it be a certain firmness and freedom, and glowing animation. The execution is more timid and laboured. It looks like a picture (an exquisite one, indeed), but Raphael's looks like the divine reality itself!—No. 234, *Cocles defending the Bridge*, is by Le Brun. We do not like this picture, nor 271, *The Massacre of the Innocents*, by the same artist. One reason is that they are French, and another that they are not good. They have great merit, it is true, but their merits are only splendid sins. They are mechanical, mannered, colourless, and unfeeling. —No. 237, is Murillo's *Spanish Girl with Flowers*. The sun tinted the young gipsey's complexion, and not the painter.—No. 240 is *The Casatella and Villa of Mæcenas, near Tivoli*, by Wilson, with his own portrait in the foreground. It is an imperfect sketch; but there is a curious anecdote relating to it, that he was so delighted with the waterfall itself, that he cried out, while painting it: "Well done, water, by G—d!"—No. 243, *Saint Cecilia*, by Guercino, is a very pleasing picture, in his least gaudy manner.

No. 251, *Venus and Adonis*, by Titian. We see so many of these Venuses and Adonises, that we should like to know which is the true one. This is one of the best we have seen. We have two Francesco Molas in this room, the *Rape of Proserpine*, and a *Landscape with a Holy Family*. This artist dipped his pencil so thoroughly in Titian's palette, that his works cannot fail to have that rich, mellow look, which is always delightful. —No. 303, *Portrait of Philip the Fourth of Spain*, by Velasquez, is purity and truth itself. We used to like the *Sleeping Nymph*, by Titian, when we saw it formerly in the little entrance-room at Desenfans', but we cannot say much in its praise here.

The FIFTH ROOM is the smallest, but the most precious in its contents.—No. 322, *Spanish Beggar Boys*, by Murillo, is the triumph of this Collection, and almost of painting. In the imitation of common life, nothing ever went beyond it, or as far as we can judge, came up to it. A Dutch picture is mechanical, and mere *still-life* to it. But this is life itself. The boy at play on the ground is miraculous. It is done with a few dragging strokes of the pencil, and with a little tinge of colour; but the mouth, the nose, the eyes, the chin, are as brimful as they can hold of expression, of arch roguery, of animal spirits, of vigorous, elastic health. The vivid, glowing, cheerful look is such as could only be found beneath a southern sun. The fens and dykes of Holland (with all our respect for them) could never produce such an epitome of the vital principle. The other boy, standing up with the pitcher in his hand, and a crust of bread in his mouth, is scarcely less excellent. His sulky, phlegmatic indifference speaks for itself. The companion to this picture, 324, is also very fine. Compared with these imitations of nature, as faultless as they are spirited, Murillo's Virgins and Angels however good in themselves, look vapid, and even vulgar. A *Child Sleeping*, by the same painter, is a beautiful and masterly study.—No. 329, a *Musical Party*, by Giorgione, is well worthy of the notice of the connoisseur. —No. 331, *St. John preaching in the Wilderness*, by Guido, is an extraordinary picture, and very unlike this painter's usual manner. The colour is as if the flesh had been stained all over with brick-dust. There is, however, a wildness about it which accords well with the subject, and the figure of St. John is full of grace and gusto.— No. 344, *The Martyrdom of St. Sebastian*, by the same, is much finer, both as to execution and expression. The face is imbued with deep passion.—No. 345, *Portrait of a Man*, by L. da Vinci, is truly simple and grand, and at once carries you back to that age.—*Boors Merry Making*, by Ostade, is fine; but has no business where it is. Yet it takes up very little room.—No. 347, *Portrait of Mrs. Siddons, in the Character of the Tragic Muse*, by Sir Joshua, appears to us to resemble neither Mrs. Siddons, nor the Tragic Muse. It is in a bastard style of art. Sir Joshua had an importunate theory of improving upon nature. He might improve upon indifferent nature, but when he had got the finest, he thought to improve upon that too, and only spoiled it.—No. 349, *The Virgin and Child*, by Correggio, can only be a copy.—No. 332, *The Judgment of Paris*, by Vanderwerf, is a picture, and by a master, that we hate. He always chooses for his subjects naked figures of women, and tantalises us by making them of coloured ivory. They are like hard-ware toys.— No. 354, *a Cardinal blessing a Priest*, by P. Veronese, is dignified and picturesque in the highest degree.—No. 355, *The Adoration of the Shepherds*, by Annibal Caracci, is an elaborate, but not very successful performance.—No. 356, *Christ bearing His Cross*, by Morales, concludes the list, and is worthy to conclude it.

ON ACTORS AND

ACTING

MRS. SIDDONS

(EXAMINER, JUNE 15TH, 1816)

PLAYERS should be immortal, if their own wishes or ours could make them so; but they are not. They not only die like other people, but like other people they cease to be young, and are no longer themselves, even while living. Their health, strength, beauty, voice, fail them; nor can they, without these advantages, perform the same feats, or command the same applause that they did when possessed of them. It is the common lot: players are only *not* exempt from it. Mrs. Siddons retired once from the stage: why should she return to it again? She cannot retire from it twice with dignity; and yet it is to be wished that she should do all things with dignity. Any loss of reputation to her, is a loss to the world. Has she not had enough of glory? The homage she has received is greater than that which is paid to Queens. The enthusiasm she excited had something idolatrous about it; she was regarded less with admiration than with wonder, as if a being of a superior order had dropped from another sphere to awe the world with the majesty of her appearance. She raised Tragedy to the skies, or brought it down from thence. It was something above nature. We can conceive of nothing grander. She embodied to our imagination the fables of mythology, of the heroic and deified mortals of elder time. She was not less than a goddess, or than a prophetess inspired by the gods. Power was seated on her brow, passion emanated from her breast as from a shrine. She was Tragedy personified. She was the stateliest ornament of the public mind. She was not only the idol of the people, she not only hushed the tumultuous shouts of the pit in breathless expectation, and quenched the blaze of surrounding beauty in silent tears, but to the retired and lonely student, through long years of solitude, her face has shone as if an eye had appeared from heaven; her name has been as if a voice had opened the chambers of the human heart, or as if a trumpet had awakened the sleeping and the dead   To have seen Mrs. Siddons, was an event in everyone's life; and does she think we have forgot her? Or would she remind us of herself by shewing us what *she was not*? Or is she to continue on the stage to the very last, till all her grace and all her grandeur gone, shall leave behind them only a melancholy blank? Or is she merely to be played off as " the baby of a girl " for a few nights?—" Rather than so," come, Genius of Gil Blas, thou that didst inspire him in an evil hour to perform his promise to the Archbishop of Grenada, " and champion us to the utterance " of what we think on this occasion.

It is said that the Princess Charlotte has expressed a desire to see Mrs. Siddons in her best parts, and this, it is said, is a thing highly desirable. We do not know that the Princess has expressed any such wish, and we shall suppose that she has not, because we do not think it altogether a reasonable one. If the Princess Charlotte had expressed a wish to see Mr. Garrick, this would have been a thing highly desirable, but it would have been impossible; or if she had desired to see Mrs. Siddons *in her best days*, it would have been equally so; and yet without this, we do not think it desirable that she should see her at all. It is said to be desirable that a Princess should have a taste for the Fine Arts, and that this is best promoted by seeing the highest models of perfection. But it is of the first importance for Princes to acquire a taste for what is reasonable: and the second thing which it is desirable they should acquire, is a deference to public opinion: and we think neither of these objects likely to be promoted in the way proposed. If it was reasonable that Mrs. Siddons should retire from the stage three years ago, certainly those reasons have not diminished since, nor do we think Mrs. Siddons would consult what is due to her powers or her fame, in commencing a new career. If it is only intended that she should act a few nights in the presence of a particular person, this might be done as well in private. To all other applications she should answer—" Leave me to my repose."

Mrs. Siddons always spoke as slow as she ought: she now speaks slower than she did. " The line too labours, and the words move slow." The machinery of the voice seems too ponderous for the power that wields it. There is too long a pause between each sentence, and between each word in each sentence. There is too much preparation. The stage waits for her. In the sleeping scene, she produced a different impression from what we expected. It was more laboured, and less natural. In coming on formerly, her eyes were open, but the sense was shut. She was like a person bewildered, and unconscious of what she did. She moved her lips involuntarily; all her gestures were involuntary and mechanical. At present she acts the part more with a view to effect. She repeats the action when she says, " I tell you he cannot rise from his grave," with both hands sawing the air, in the style of parliamentary oratory, the worst of all others. There was none of this weight or energy in the way she did the scene the first time we saw her, twenty years ago. She glided on and off the stage almost like an apparition. In the close of the banquet scene, Mrs. Siddons condescended to an imitation which we were sorry for. She said, " Go, go," in the hurried familiar tone of common life, in the manner of Mr. Kean, and without any of that sustained and graceful spirit of con-ciliation towards her guests, which used to characterise her mode of doing it. Lastly, if Mrs. Siddons has to leave the stage again, Mr. Horace Twiss will write another farewell address for her: if she continues on it, we shall have to criticise her performances. We know which of these two evils we shall think the greatest.

Too much praise cannot be given to Mr. Kemble's performance of Macbeth. He was " himself again," and more than himself. His action was decided, his voice audible. His tones had occasionally indeed a learned quaintness, like the colouring of Poussin; but the effect of the whole was fine. His action in delivering the speech, " To-morrow and to-morrow," was particularly striking and expressive, as if he had stumbled by an accident on fate, and was baffled by the impenetrable obscurity of the future.—In that prodigious prosing paper, the *Times*, which seems to be written as well as printed by a steam-engine, Mr. Kemble is compared to the ruin of a magnificent temple, in which the divinity still resides. This is not the case. The temple is unimpaired; but the divinity is sometimes from home.

ON ACTORS AND ACTING

(EXAMINER, JAN. 5, 1817)

PLAYERS are " the abstracts and brief chronicles of the time "; the motley representatives of human nature. They are the only honest hypocrites. Their life is a voluntary dream; a studied madness. The height of their ambition is to be *beside themselves*. To-day kings, to-morrow beggars, it is only when they are themselves, that they are nothing. Made up of mimic laughter and tears, passing from the extremes of joy or woe at the prompter's call, they wear the livery of other men's fortunes; their very thoughts are not their own. They are, as it were, train-bearers in the pageant of life, and hold a glass up to humanity, frailer than itself. We see ourselves at second-hand in them: they shew us all

that we are, all that we wish to be, and all that we dread
to be. The stage is an epitome, a bettered likeness of the
world, with the dull part left out: and, indeed, with this
omission, it is nearly big enough to hold all the rest.
What brings the resemblance nearer is, that, as *they*
imitate us, we, in our turn, imitate them. How many
fine gentlemen do we owe to the stage? How many
romantic lovers are mere Romeos in masquerade? How
many soft bosoms have heaved with Juliet's sighs?
They teach us when to laugh and when to weep, when to
love and when to hate, upon principle and with a good
grace! Wherever there is a playhouse, the world will
go on not amiss. The stage not only refines the manners,
but it is the best teacher of morals, for it is the truest and
most intelligible picture of life. It stamps the image of
virtue on the mind by first softening the rude materials
of which it is composed, by a sense of pleasure. It
regulates the passions by giving a loose to the imagination.
It points out the selfish and depraved to our detestation;
the amiable and generous to our admiration; and if it
clothes the more seductive vices with the borrowed
graces of wit and fancy, even those graces operate as a
diversion to the coarser poison of experience and bad
example, and often prevent or carry off the infection by
inoculating the mind with a certain taste and elegance.
To shew how little we agree with the common declama-
tions against the immoral tendency of the stage on this
score, we will hazard a conjecture, that the acting of the
Beggar's Opera a certain number of nights every year
since it was first brought out, has done more towards
putting down the practice of highway robbery, than all
the gibbets that ever were erected. A person, after seeing
this piece, is too deeply imbued with a sense of humanity,
is in too good humour with himself and the rest of the
world, to set about cutting throats or rifling pockets.
Whatever makes a jest of vice, leaves it too much a matter

of indifference for any one in his senses to rush desperately on his ruin for its sake. We suspect that just the contrary effect must be produced by the representation of George Barnwell, which is too much in the style of the Ordinary's sermon to meet with any better success. The mind, in such cases, instead of being deterred by the alarming consequences held out to it, revolts against the denunciation of them as an insult offered to its free-will, and, in a spirit of defiance, returns a practical answer to them, by daring the worst that can happen. The most striking lesson ever read to levity and licentiousness, is in the last act of the *Inconstant*, where young Mirabel is preserved by the fidelity of his mistress, Orinda, in the disguise of a page, from the hands of assassins, into whose power he has been allured by the temptations of vice and beauty. There never was a rake who did not become in imagination a reformed man, during the representation of the last trying scenes of this admirable comedy.

If the stage is useful as a school of instruction, it is no less so as a source of amusement. It is the source of the greatest enjoyment at the time, and a never-failing fund of agreeable reflection afterwards. The merits of a new play, or of a new actor, are always among the first topics of polite conversation. One way in which public exhibitions contribute to refine and humanise mankind, is by supplying them with ideas and subjects of conversation and interest in common. The progress of civilization is in proportion to the number of common-places current in society. For instance, if we meet with a stranger at an inn or in a stage-coach, who knows nothing but his own affairs, his shop, his customers, his farm, his pigs, his poultry, we can carry on no conversation with him on these local and personal matters : the only way is to let him have all the talk to himself. But if he has fortunately ever seen Mr. Liston act, this is an immediate topic of

mutual conversation, and we agree together the rest of
the evening in discussing the merits of that inimitable
actor, with the same satisfaction as in talking over the
affairs of the most intimate friend.

If the stage thus introduces us familiarly to our contemporaries, it also brings us acquainted with former
times. It is an interesting revival of past ages, manners,
opinions, dresses, persons, and actions,—whether it
carries us back to the wars of York and Lancaster, or
half-way back to the heroic times of Greece and Rome,
in some translation from the French, or quite back to
the age of Charles II., in the scenes of Congreve and of
Etherege, (the gay Sir George!)—happy age, when kings
and nobles led purely ornamental lives, when the utmost
stretch of a morning's study went no farther than the
choice of a sword-knot, or the adjustment of a side-curl;
when the soul spoke out in all the pleasing eloquence
of dress; and beaux and belles, enamoured of themselves
in one another's follies, fluttered like gilded butterflies in
giddy mazes through the walks of St. James's Park!

A good company of comedians, a Theatre-Royal
judiciously managed, is your true Herald's College;
the only Antiquarian Society, that is worth a rush. It
is for this reason that there is such an air of romance
about players, and that it is pleasanter to see them, even
in their own persons, than any of the three learned
professions. We feel more respect for John Kemble in
a plain coat, than for the Lord Chancellor on the wool-
sack. He is surrounded, to our eyes, with a greater number
of imposing recollections: he is a more reverend piece
of formality; a more complicated tissue of costume.
We do not know whether to look upon this accomplished
actor as Pierre or King John or Coriolanus or Cato or
Leontes or the Stranger. But we see in him a stately hieroglyphic of humanity; a living monument of departed
greatness; a sombre comment on the rise and fall of

z *

kings. We look after him till he is out of sight, as we listen to a story of one of Ossian's heroes, to " a tale of other times! "

One of the most affecting things we know is to see a favourite actor take leave of the stage. We were present not long ago when Mr. Bannister quitted it. We do not wonder that his feelings were overpowered on the occasion: ours were nearly so too. We remembered him in the first heyday of our youthful spirits, in the *Prize*, in which he played so delightfully with that fine old croaker Suett, and Madame Storace,—in the farce of *My Grandmother*, in the *Son-in-Law*, in *Autolycus*, and in *Scrub*, in which our satisfaction was at its height. At that time, King and Parsons, and Dodd, and Quick, and Edwin were in the full vigour of their reputation, who are now all gone. We still feel the vivid delight with which we used to see their names in the play-bills, as we went along to the Theatre. Bannister was one of the last of these that remained; and we parted with him as we should with one of our oldest and best friends. The most pleasant feature in the profession of a player, and which, indeed, is peculiar to it, is that we not only admire the talents of those who adorn it, but we contract a personal intimacy with them. There is no class of society whom so many persons regard with affection as actors. We greet them on the stage; we like to meet them in the streets; they almost always recall to us pleasant associations; and we feel our gratitude excited, without the uneasiness of a sense of obligation. The very gaiety and popularity, however, which surround the life of a favourite performer, make the retiring from it a very serious business. It glances a mortifying reflection on the shortness of human life, and the vanity of human pleasures. Something reminds us, that " all the world's a stage, and all the men and women merely players."

CHARACTERS

EDMUND BURKE

(ELOQUENCE OF THE BRITISH SENATE, 1807)

T H E following speech[1] is perhaps the fairest specimen I could give of Mr. Burke's various talents as a speaker; his wisdom, his imagination, his wit, and playfulness of fancy. The subject itself is not the most interesting, nor does it admit of that weight and closeness of reasoning which he displayed on other occasions. But there is no single speech which can convey a satisfactory idea of his powers of mind: to do him justice, it would be necessary to quote all his works; the only specimen of Burke is, *all that he wrote*. With respect to most other speakers, a specimen is generally enough, or more than enough. When you are acquainted with their manner, and see what proficiency they have made in the mechanical exercise of their profession, with what facility they can borrow a simile, or round a period, how dexterously they can argue, and object, and rejoin, you are satisfied; there is no other difference in their speeches than what arises from the difference of the subjects. But this was not the case with Burke. He brought his subjects along with him; he drew his materials from himself. The only limits which circumscribed his variety were the stores of his own mind. His stock of ideas did not consist of a few meagre facts, meagrely stated, of half a dozen common-places tortured in a thousand different ways: but his mine of wealth was a profound understanding, inexhaustible as the human heart, and various as the sources of nature. He therefore enriched every subject to which he applied himself, and new subjects were only the occasions of calling forth fresh powers of mind which had not been before exerted.

[1] His Speech on presenting a Plan for the better security of the Independence of Parliament, and the economical Reformation of the civil and other Establishments, 1780. (Ed.)

It would therefore be in vain to look for the proof of his powers in any one of his speeches or writings: they all contain some additional proof of power. In speaking of Burke, then, I shall speak of the whole compass and circuit of his mind—not of that small part or section of him which I have been able to give: to do otherwise would be like the story of the man who put the brick in his pocket, thinking to show it as the model of a house. I have been able to manage pretty well with respect to all my other speakers, and curtailed them down without remorse. It was easy to reduce them within certain limits, to fix their spirit, and condense their variety; by having a certain quantity given, you might infer all the rest; it was only the same thing over again. But who can bind Proteus, or confine the roving flight of genius?

Burke's writings are better than his speeches, and indeed his speeches are writings. But he seemed to feel himself more at ease, to have a fuller possession of his faculties in addressing the public, than in addressing the house of commons. Burke was *raised* into public life: and he seems to have been prouder of this new dignity than became so great a man. For this reason, most of his speeches have a sort of parliamentary preamble to them: there is an air of affected modesty, and ostentatious trifling in them: he seems fond of coquetting with the house of commons, and is perpetually calling the speaker out to dance a minuet with him, before he begins. There is also something like an attempt to stimulate the superficial dulness of his hearers by exciting their surprise, by running into extravagance: and he sometimes demeans himself by condescending to what may be considered as bordering too much upon buffoonery, for the amusement of the company. Those lines of Milton were admirably applied to him by some one—" The elephant to make them sport wreathed his proboscis lithe." The truth is, that he was out of his place in the house of commons;

he was eminently qualified to shine as a man of genius, as the instructor of mankind, as the brightest luminary of his age: but he had nothing in common with that motley crew of knights, citizens, and burgesses. He could not be said to be " native and endued unto that element." He was above it; and never appeared like himself, but when, forgetful of the idle clamours of party, and of the little views of little men, he appealed to his country, and the enlightened judgment of mankind.

I am not going to make an idle panegyric on Burke (he has no need of it); but I cannot help looking upon him as the chief boast and ornament of the English house of commons. What has been said of him is, I think, strictly true, that " he was the most eloquent man of his time: his wisdom was greater than his eloquence." The only public man that in my opinion can be put in any competition with him, is lord Chatham: and he moved in a sphere so very remote, that it is almost impossible to compare them. But though it would perhaps be difficult to determine which of them excelled most in his particular way, there is nothing in the world more easy than to point out in what their peculiar excellences consisted. They were in every respect the reverse of each other. Chatham's eloquence was popular: his wisdom was altogether plain and practical. Burke's eloquence was that of the poet; of the man of high and unbounded fancy: his wisdom was profound and contemplative. Chatham's eloquence was calculated to make men *act;* Burke's was calculated to make them *think.* Chatham could have roused the fury of a multitude, and wielded their physical energy as he pleased: Burke's eloquence carried conviction into the mind of the retired and lonely student, opened the recesses of the human breast, and lighted up the face of nature around him. Chatham supplied his hearers with motives to immediate action: Burke furnished them with *reasons* for action which might have little effect upon them at the time, but for which they would be the wiser and better all their lives after. In research, in originality, in variety of knowledge, in richness of invention, in depth and comprehension of mind, Burke had as much the advantage of lord Chatham as he was excelled by him in plain common sense, in strong feeling, in steadiness of purpose, in vehemence, in warmth, in enthusiasm, and energy of mind. Burke was the man of genius, of fine sense, and subtle reasoning; Chatham was a man of clear understanding, of strong sense, and violent passions. Burke's mind was satisfied with speculation; Chatham's was essentially *active*: it could not rest without an object. The power which governed Burke's mind was his Imagination; that which gave its *impetus* to Chatham's was Will. The one was almost the creature of pure intellect, the other of physical temperament.

There are two very different ends which a man of genius may propose to himself either in writing or speaking, and which will accordingly give birth to very different styles. He can have but one of these two objects; either to enrich, or strengthen the mind; either to furnish us with new ideas, to lead the mind into new trains of thought, to which it was before unused, and which it was incapable of striking out for itself; or else to collect and embody what we already knew, to rivet our old impressions more deeply; to make what was before plain still plainer, and to give to that which was familiar all the effect of novelty. In the one case we receive an accession to the stock of our ideas; in the other, an additional degree of life and energy is infused into them: our thoughts continue to flow in the same channels, but their pulse is quickened and invigorated. I do not know how to distinguish these different styles better than by calling them severally the inventive and refined, or the impressive and vigorous styles. It is only the subject matter of eloquence, however, which is allowed to be remote or obscure. The things in themselves may be subtle and recondite, but they must be dragged out of their obscurity and brought struggling to the light; they must be rendered plain and palpable (as far as it is in the wit of man to do so) or they are no longer eloquence. That which by its natural impenetrability, and in spite of every effort, remains dark and difficult, which is impervious to every ray, on which the imagination can shed no lustre, which can be clothed with no beauty, is not a subject for the orator or poet. At the same time it cannot be expected that abstract truths or profound observations should ever be placed in the same strong and dazzling points of view as natural objects and mere matters of fact. It is enough if they receive a reflex and borrowed lustre, like that which cheers the first dawn of morning, where the effect of surprise and novelty gilds every object, and the joy of beholding another world gradually emerging out of the gloom of night, "a new creation rescued from his reign," fills the mind with a sober rapture. Philosophical eloquence is in writing what *chiaro scuro* is in painting; he would be a fool who should object that the colours in the shaded part of a picture were not so bright as those on the opposite side; the eye of the connoisseur receives an equal delight from both, balancing the want of brilliancy and effect with the greater delicacy of the tints, and difficulty of the execution. In judging of Burke, therefore, we are to consider first the style of eloquence which he adopted, and secondly the effects which he produced with it. If he did not produce the same effects on vulgar minds, as some others have done, it was not for want of power, but from the turn and direction of his mind.[1]

[1] For instance : he produced less effect on the mob that compose the English House of Commons than Chatham or Fox, or even Pitt ; and he produced less effect on the mob that compose the English Public than Paine, or Joel Barlow, at least at the time.

It was because his subjects, his ideas, his arguments, were less vulgar. The question is not whether he brought certain truths equally *home* to us, but how much nearer he brought them than they were before. In my opinion, he united the two extremes of refinement and strength in a higher degree than any other writer whatever.

The subtlety of his mind was undoubtedly that which rendered Burke a less popular writer and speaker than he otherwise would have been. It weakened the impression of his observations upon others, but I cannot admit that it weakened the observations themselves; that it took anything from their real weight and solidity. Coarse minds think all that is subtle, futile: that because it is not gross and obvious and palpable to the senses, it is therefore light and frivolous, and of no importance in the real affairs of life; thus making their own confined understandings the measure of truth, and supposing that whatever they do not distinctly perceive, is nothing. Seneca, who was not one of the vulgar, also says, that subtle truths are those which have the least substance in them, and consequently approach nearest to non-entity. But for my own part I cannot help thinking that the most important truths must be the most refined and subtle; for that very reason, that they must comprehend a great number of particulars, and instead of referring to any distinct or positive fact, must point out the combined effects of an extensive chain of causes, operating gradually, remotely, and collectively, and therefore imperceptibly. General principles are not the less true or important because from their nature they elude immediate observation; they are like the air, which is not the less necessary because we neither see nor feel it, or like that secret influence which binds the world together, and holds the planets in their orbits. The very same persons, who are the most forward to laugh at all systematic reasoning as idle and impertinent, you will the next moment hear exclaiming bitterly against the baleful effects of new-fangled systems of philosophy, or gravely descanting on the immense importance of instilling sound principles of morality into the mind. It would not be a bold conjecture, but an obvious truism to say, that all the great changes which have been brought about in the moral world, either for the better or worse, have been introduced not by the bare statement of facts, which are things already known, and which must always operate nearly in the same manner, but by the development of certain opinions and abstract principles of reasoning on life and manners, on the origin of society and man's nature in general, which being obscure and uncertain, vary from time to time, and produce correspondent changes in the human mind. They are the wholesome dew and rain, or the mildew and pestilence that silently destroy. To this principle of generalization all religious creeds, the institutions of wise lawgivers, and the systems of philosophers, owe their influence.

It has always been with me a test of the sense and candour of any one belonging to the opposite party, whether he allowed Burke to be a great man. Of all the persons of this description that I have ever known, I never met with above one or two who would make this concession; whether it was that party feelings ran too high to admit of any real candour, or whether it was owing to an essential vulgarity in their habits of thinking, they all seemed to be of opinion that he was a wild enthusiast, or a hollow sophist, who was to be answered by bits of facts, by smart logic, by shrewd questions, and idle songs. They looked upon him as a man of disordered intellect, because he reasoned in a style to which they had not been used and which confounded their dim perceptions. If you said that though you differed with him in sentiment, yet you thought him an admirable reasoner, and a close observer of human nature, you were answered with a loud laugh, and some hackneyed quotation. "Alas! Leviathan was not so tamed!" They did not know whom they had to contend with. The corner stone, which the builders rejected, became the head-corner, though to the Jews a stumbling-block, and to the Greeks foolishness; for indeed I cannot discover that he was much better understood by those of his own party, if we may judge from the little affinity there is between his mode of reasoning and theirs. The simple clue to all his reasonings on this subject is, I think, as follows. He did not agree with some writers, that that mode of government is necessarily the best which is the cheapest. He saw in the construction of society other principles at work, and other capacities of fulfilling the desires, and perfecting the nature of man, besides those of securing the equal enjoyment of the means of animal life, and doing this at as little expense as possible. He thought that the wants and happiness of man were not to be provided for, as we provide for those of a herd of cattle, merely by attending to their physical necessities. He thought more nobly of his fellows. He knew that man had affections and passions and powers of imagination, as well as, hunger and thirst and the sense of heat and cold. He took his idea of political society from the pattern of private life, wishing, as he himself expresses it, to incorporate the domestic charities with the orders of the state, and to blend them together. He strove to establish an analogy between the compact that binds together the community at large, and that which binds together the several families that compose it. He knew that the rules that form the basis of private morality are not founded in reason, that is, in the abstract properties of those things which are the subjects of them, but in the nature of man, and his capacity of being affected by certain things from habit, from imagination, and sentiment, as well as from reason.

Thus, the reason why a man ought to be attached to his wife and children is not, surely, that they are better than others, (for in this case every one else ought to be of the same opinion) but because he must be chiefly interested in those things which are nearest to him, and with which he is best acquainted, since his understanding cannot reach equally to everything; because he must be most attached to those objects which he has known the longest, and which by their situation have actually affected him the most, not those which in themselves are the most affecting, whether they have ever made any impression on him or no; that is, because he is by his nature the creature of habit and feeling, and because it is reasonable that he should act in conformity to his nature. He was therefore right in saying that it is no objection to an institution, that it is founded in *prejudice*, but the contrary, if that prejudice is natural and right; that is, if it arises from those circumstances which are properly subjects of feeling and association, not from any defect or perversion of the understanding in those things which fall properly under its jurisdiction. On this profound maxim he took his stand. Thus he contended, that the prejudice in favour of nobility was natural and proper, and fit to be encouraged by the positive institutions of society; not on account of the real or personal merit of the individuals, but because such an institution has a tendency to enlarge and raise the mind, to keep alive the memory of past greatness, to connect the different ages of the world together, to carry back the imagination over a long tract of time, and feed it with the contemplation of remote events: because it is natural to think highly of that which inspires us with high thought, which has been connected for many generations with splendour, and affluence, and dignity, and power, and permanence. He also conceived, that by transferring the respect from the person to the thing, and thus rendering it steady and permanent, the mind would be habitually formed to sentiments of deference, attachment, and fealty, to whatever else demanded its respect: that it would be led to fix its view on what was elevated and lofty, and be weaned from that low and narrow jealousy which never willingly or heartily admits of any superiority in others, and is glad of every opportunity to bring down all excellence to a level with its own miserable standard. Nobility did not therefore exist to the prejudice of the other orders of the state, but by, and for them. The inequality of the different orders of society did not destroy the unity and harmony of the whole. The health and well-being of the moral world was to be promoted by the same means as the beauty of the natural world; by contrast, by change, by light and shade, by variety of parts, by order and proportion. To think of reducing all mankind to the same insipid level, seemed to him the same absurdity as to destroy the inequalities of surface in a country, for the benefit of agriculture and commerce. In short, he believed that the interests of men in society should be consulted, and their several stations and employments assigned, with a view to their nature, not as physical, but as moral beings, so as to nourish their hopes, to lift their imagination, to enliven their fancy, to rouse their activity, to strengthen their virtue, and to furnish the greatest number of objects of pursuit and means of enjoyment to beings constituted as man is, consistently with the order and stability of the whole.

The same reasoning might be extended farther. I do not say that his arguments are conclusive: but they are profound and *true*, as far as they go. There may be disadvantages and abuses necessarily interwoven with this scheme, or opposite advantages of infinitely greater value, to be derived from another order of things and state of society. This, however, does not invalidate either the truth or importance of Burke's reasoning: since the advantages he points out as connected with the mixed form of government are really and necessarily inherent in it: since they are compatible in the same degree with no other; since the principle itself on which he rests his argument (whatever we may think of the application) is of the utmost weight and moment; and since on which ever side the truth lies, it is impossible to make a fair decision without having the opposite side of the question clearly and fully stated to us. This Burke has done in a masterly manner. He presents to you one view or face of society. Let him, who thinks he can, give the reverse side with equal force, beauty, and clearness. It is said, I know, that truth is *one*; but to this I cannot subscribe, for it appears to me that truth is *many*. There are as many truths as there are things and causes of action and contradictory principles at work in society. In making up the account of good and evil, indeed, the final result must be one way or the other; but the particulars on which that result depends are infinite and various.

It will be seen from what I have said, that I am very far from agreeing with those who think that Burke was a man without understanding, and a merely florid writer. There are two causes which have given rise to this calumny; namely, that narrowness of mind which leads men to suppose that the truth lies entirely on the side of their own opinions, and that whatever does not make for them is absurd and irrational; secondly, a trick we have of confounding reason with judgment, and supposing that it is merely the province of the understanding to pronounce sentence, and not to give in evidence, or argue the case; in short, that it is a passive, not an active faculty. Thus there are persons who never run into any extravagance, because they are so buttressed up with the opinions of others on all sides, that they cannot lean much to one side or the other; they are so little moved with any kind of reasoning, that they remain at an equal distance from every extreme, and are never very far from the truth, because the slowness of their faculties will not suffer them to make much progress in error. These are persons of great judgment. The scales of the mind are pretty sure to remain even, when there is nothing in them. In this sense of the word, Burke must be allowed to have wanted judgment, by all those who think that he was wrong in his conclusion. This accusation of want of judgment, in fact, only means that you yourself are of a different opinion. But if in arriving at one error he discovered a hundred truths, I should consider myself a hundred times more indebted to him than if, stumbling on that which I consider as the right side of the question, he had committed a hundred absurdities in striving to establish his point. I speak of him now merely as an author, or as far as I and other readers are concerned with him; at the same time, I should not differ from any one who may be disposed to contend that the consequences of his writings as instruments of political power have been tremendous, fatal, such as no exertion of wit, or knowledge, or genius, can ever counteract or atone for.

Burke also gave a hold to his antagonist by mixing up sentiment and imagery with his reasoning; so that being unused to such a sight in the region of politics, they were deceived, and could not discern the fruit from the flowers. Gravity is the cloak of wisdom; and those who have nothing else think it an insult to affect the one without the other, because it destroys the only foundation on which their pretensions are built. The easiest part of reason is dulness ; the generality of the world are therefore concerned in discouraging any example of unnecessary brilliancy that might tend to shew that the two things do not always go together. Burke in some measure dissolved the spell. It was discovered, that his gold was not the less valuable for being wrought into elegant shapes and richly embossed with curious figures; that the solidity of a building is not destroyed by adding to it beauty and ornament; and that the strength of man's understanding is not always to be estimated in exact proportion to his want of imagination. His understanding was not the less real, because it was not the only faculty he possessed. He justified the description of the poet,

> " How charming is divine philosophy !
> Not harsh and crabbed as dull fools suppose,
> But musical as is Apollo's lute ! "

Those who object to this union of grace and beauty with reason, are in fact weak-sighted people, who cannot distinguish the noble and majestic form of Truth from that of her sister Folly, if they are dressed both alike! But there is always a difference even in the adventitious ornaments they wear, which is sufficient to distinguish them.

Burke was so far from being a gaudy or flowery writer, that he was one of the *severest* writers we have. His words are the most like things; his style is the most strictly suited to the subject. He unites every extreme and every variety of composition; the lowest and the meanest words and descriptions with the highest. He exults in the display of power, in shewing the extent, the force, and intensity of his ideas; he is led on by the mere impulse and vehemence of his fancy, not by the affectation of dazzling his readers by gaudy conceits or pompous images. He was completely carried away by his subject. He had no other object but to produce the strongest impression on his reader, by giving the truest, the most characteristic, the fullest, and most forcible description of things, trusting to the power of his own mind to mould them into grace and beauty. He did not produce a splendid effect by setting fire to the light vapours that float in the regions of fancy, as the chemists make fine colours with phosphorus, but by the eagerness of his blows struck fire from the flint, and melted the hardest substances in the furnace of his imagination. The wheels of his imagination did not catch fire from the rottenness of the materials, but from the rapidity of their motion. One would suppose, to hear people talk of Burke, that his style was such as would have suited the *Lady's Magazine*; soft, smooth, showy, tender, insipid, full of fine words, without any meaning. The essence of the gaudy or glittering style consists in producing a momentary effect by fine words and images brought together without order or connection. Burke most frequently produced an effect by the remoteness and novelty of his combinations, by the force of contrast, by the striking manner in which the most opposite and unpromising materials were harmoniously blended together; not by laying his hands on all the fine things he could think of, but by bringing together those things which he knew would blaze out into glorious light by their collision. The florid style is a mixture of affectation and commonplace. Burke's was an union of untameable vigour and originality.

Burke was not a verbose writer. If he sometimes multiplies words, it is not for want of ideas, but because there are no words that fully express his ideas, and he tries to do it as well as he can by different ones. He had nothing of the *set* or formal style, the measured cadence, and stately phraseology of Johnson, and most of our modern writers. This style, which is what we understand by the *artificial*, is all in one key. It selects a certain set of words to represent all ideas whatever, as the most dignified and elegant, and excludes all others as low and vulgar. The words are not fitted to the things, but the things to the words. Everything is seen through a false medium. It is putting a mask on the face of nature, which may indeed hide some specks and blemishes, but takes away all beauty, delicacy, and variety. It destroys all dignity or elevation, because nothing can be raised where all is on a level, and completely destroys all force, expression, truth, and character, by arbitrarily confounding the differences of things, and reducing everything to the same insipid standard. To suppose that this stiff uniformity can add anything to real grace or dignity, is like supposing that the human body in order to be perfectly graceful, should never deviate from its upright posture. Another mischief of this method is, that it confounds all ranks in literature. Where there is no room for variety, no discrimination, no nicety to be shewn in matching the idea with its proper word, there can be no room for taste or elegance. A man must easily learn the art of writing, when every sentence is to be cast in the same mould: where he is only allowed the use of one word, he cannot choose wrong, nor will he be in much danger of making himself ridiculous by affectation or false glitter, when, whatever subject he treats of, he must treat of it in the same way. This indeed is to wear golden chains for the sake of ornament.

Burke was altogether free from the pedantry which I have here endeavoured to expose. His style was as original, as expressive, as rich and varied, as it was possible; his combinations were as exquisite, as playful, as happy, as unexpected, as bold and daring, as his fancy. If anything, he ran into the opposite extreme of too great an inequality, if truth and nature could ever be carried to an extreme.

Those who are best acquainted with the writings and speeches of Burke will not think the praise I have here bestowed on them exaggerated. Some proof will be found of this in the following extracts. But the full proof must be sought in his works at large, and particularly in the *Thoughts on the Discontents*; in his *Reflections on the French Revolution*; in his *Letter to the Duke of Bedford*;

and in the *Regicide Peace*. The two last of these are perhaps the most remarkable of all his writings, from the contrast they afford to each other. The one is the most delightful exhibition of wild and brilliant fancy that is to be found in English prose, but it is too much like a beautiful picture painted upon gauze; it wants something to support it: the other is without ornament, but it has all the solidity, the weight, the gravity of a judicial record. It seems to have been written with a certain constraint upon himself, and to shew those who said he could not *reason*, that his arguments might be stripped of their ornaments without losing anything of their force. It is certainly, of all his works, that in which he has shewn most power of logical deduction, and the only one in which he has made any important use of facts. In general he certainly paid little attention to them: they were the playthings of his mind. He saw them as he pleased, not as they were; with the eye of the philosopher or the poet, regarding them only in their general principle, or as they might serve to decorate his subject. This is the natural consequence of much imagination: things that are probable are elevated into the rank of realities. To those who can reason on the essences of things, or who can invent according to nature, the experimental proof is of little value. This was the case with Burke. In the present instance, however, he seems to have *forced* his mind into the service of facts: and he succeeded completely. His comparison between our connection with France or Algiers, and his account of the conduct of the war, are as clear, as convincing, as forcible examples of this kind of reasoning, as are anywhere to be met with. Indeed I do not think there is anything in Fox, (whose mind was purely historical) or in Chatham, (who attended to feelings more than facts) that will bear a comparison with them.

Burke has been compared to Cicero—I do not know

for what reason. Their excellences are as different, and indeed as opposite, as they well can be. Burke had not the polished elegance, the glossy neatness, the artful regularity, the exquisite modulation of Cicero: he had a thousand times more richness and originality of mind, more strength and pomp of diction.

It has been well observed, that the ancients had no word that properly expresses what we mean by the word Genius. They perhaps had not the thing. Their minds appear to have been too exact, too retentive, too minute and subtle, too sensible to the external differences of things, too passive under their impressions, to admit of those bold and rapid combinations, those lofty flights of fancy, which, glancing from heaven to earth, unite the most opposite extremes, and draw the happiest illustrations from things the most remote. Their ideas were kept too confined and distinct by the material form or vehicle in which they were conveyed to unite cordially together, or be melted down in the imagination. Their metaphors are taken from things of the same class, not from things of different classes; the general analogy, not the individual feeling, directs them in their choice. Hence, as Dr. Johnson observed, their figures are either repetitions of the same idea, or so obvious and general as not to lend any additional force to it; as when a huntress is compared to Diana, or a warrior rushing into battle to a lion rushing on his prey. Their *forte* was exquisite art and perfect imitation. Witness their statues and other things of the same kind. But they had not that high and enthusiastic fancy which some of our own writers have shewn. For the proof of this, let anyone compare Milton and Shakespear with Homer and Sophocles, or Burke with Cicero.

It may be asked whether Burke was a poet. He was so only in the general vividness of his fancy, and in richness of invention. There may be poetical passages in his works, but I certainly think that his writings in general are quite distinct from poetry; and that for the reason before given, namely, that the subject matter of them is not poetical. The finest parts of them are illustrations or personifications of dry abstract ideas; and the union between the idea and the illustration is not of that perfect and pleasing kind as to constitute poetry, or indeed to be admissible, but for the effect intended to be produced by it; that is, by every means in our power to give animation and attraction to subjects in themselves barren of ornament, but which at the same time are pregnant with the most important consequences, and in which the understanding and the passions are equally interested.

I have heard it remarked by a person, to whose opinion I would sooner submit than to a general council of critics, that the sound of Burke's prose is not musical; that it wants cadence; and that instead of being so lavish of his imagery as is generally supposed, he seemed to him to be rather parsimonious in the use of it, always expanding and making the most of his ideas. This may be true if we compare him with some of our poets, or perhaps with some of our early prose writers, but not if we compare him with any of our political writers or parliamentary speakers. There are some very fine things of Lord Bolingbroke's on the same subjects, but not equal to Burke's. As for Junius, he is at the head of his class; but that class is not the highest. He has been said to have more dignity than Burke. Yes—if the stalk of a giant is less dignified than the strut of a *petit-maître*. I do not mean to speak disrespectfully of Junius, but grandeur is not the character of his composition; and if it is not to be found in Burke, it is to be found nowhere.

CHARACTER OF COBBETT

(TABLE TALK, 1821)

PEOPLE have about as substantial an idea of Cobbett as they have of Cribb. His blows are as hard, and he himself is as impenetrable. One has no notion of him as making use of a fine pen, but a great mutton-fist; his style stuns his readers, and he "fillips the ear of the public with a three-man beetle." He is too much for any single newspaper antagonist; "lays waste" a city orator or Member of Parliament, and bears hard upon the government itself. He is a kind of *fourth estate* in the politics of the country. He is not only unquestionably the most powerful political writer of the present day, but one of the best writers in the language. He speaks and thinks plain, broad, downright English. He might be said to have the clearness of Swift, the naturalness of Defoe, and the picturesque satirical description of Mandeville; if all such comparisons were not impertinent. A really great and original writer is like nobody but himself. In one sense, Sterne was not a wit, nor Shakespear a poet. It is easy to describe second-rate talents, because they fall into a class, and enlist under a standard; but first-rate powers defy calculation or comparison, and can be defined only by themselves. They are *sui generis*, and make the class to which they belong. I have tried half a dozen times to describe Burke's style without ever succeeding,—its severe extravagance; its literal boldness; its matter-of-fact hyperboles; its running away with a subject, and from it at the same time,—but there is no making it out, for there is no example of the same thing anywhere else. We have no common measure to refer to; and his qualities contradict even themselves.

Cobbett is not so difficult. He has been compared to Paine; and so far it is true there are no two writers who come more into juxta-position from the nature of their subjects, from the internal resources on which they draw, and from the popular effect of their writings and their adaptation (though that is a bad word in the present case) to the capacity of every reader. But still if we turn to a volume of Paine's (his *Common Sense* or *Rights of Man*) we are struck (not to say somewhat refreshed) by the difference. Paine is a much more sententious writer than Cobbett. You cannot open a page in any of his best and earlier works without meeting with some maxim, some antithetical and memorable saying, which is a sort of starting-place for the argument, and the goal to which it returns. There is not a single *bon-mot*, a single sentence in Cobbett that has ever been quoted again. If anything is ever quoted from him, it is an epithet of abuse or a nickname. He is an excellent hand at invention in that way, and has " damnable iteration " in him. What could be better than his pestering Erskine year after year with his second title of Baron Clackmannan? He is rather too fond of *the Sons and Daughters of Corruption*. Paine affected to reduce things to first principles, to announce self-evident truths. Cobbett troubles himself about little but the details and local circumstances. The first appeared to have made up his mind beforehand to certain opinions, and to try to find the most compendious and pointed expressions for them: his successor appears to have no clue, no fixed or leading principles, nor ever to have thought on a question till he sits down to write about it; but then there seems no end of his matters of fact and raw materials, which are brought out in all their strength and sharpness from not having been squared or frittered down or vamped up to suit a theory—he goes on with his descriptions and illustrations as if he would never come to a stop; they have all the force of novelty with all the familiarity of old acquaintance; his knowledge grows out of the subject, and his style is that of a man who has an absolute intuition of what he is talking about, and never thinks of anything else. He deals in premises and speaks to evidence—the coming to a conclusion and summing up (which was Paine's *forte*) lies in a smaller compass. The one could not compose an elementary treatise on politics to become a manual for the popular reader; nor could the other in all probability have kept up a weekly journal for the same number of years with the same spirit, interest, and untired perseverance. Paine's writings are a sort of introduction to political arithmetic on a new plan: Cobbett keeps a day-book, and makes an entry at full of all the occurrences and troublesome questions that start up throughout the year. Cobbett, with vast industry, vast information, and the utmost power of making what he says intelligible, never seems to get at the beginning or come to the end of any question: Paine in a few short sentences seems by his peremptory manner " to clear it from all controversy, past, present, and to come." Paine takes a bird's-eye view of things. Cobbett sticks close to them, inspects the component parts, and keeps fast hold of the smallest advantages they afford him. Or, if I might here be indulged in a pastoral allusion, Paine tries to enclose his ideas in a fold for security and repose; Cobbett lets *his* pour out upon the plain like a flock of sheep to feed and batten. Cobbett is a pleasanter writer for those to read who do not agree with him; for he is less dogmatical, goes more into the common grounds of fact and argument to which all appeal, is more desultory and various, and appears less to be driving at a previous conclusion than urged on by the force of present conviction. He is therefore tolerated by all parties, though he has made himself by turns obnoxious to all; and even those he abuses read him. The Reformers read him when he was a Tory, and the Tories read him now that he is a Reformer. He must, I think, however, be *caviare* to the Whigs.[1]

---

[1] The late Lord Thurlow used to say that Cobbett was the only writer that deserved the name of a political reasoner.

2 A

If he is less metaphysical and poetical than his celebrated prototype, he is more picturesque and dramatic. His episodes, which are numerous as they are pertinent, are striking, interesting, full of life and *naïveté*, minute, double measure running over, but never tedious—*nunquam sufflaminandus erat*. He is one of those writers who can never tire us, not even of himself; and the reason is, he is always "full of matter." He never runs to lees, never gives us the vapid leavings of himself, is never "weary, stale, and unprofitable," but always setting out afresh on his journey, clearing away some old nuisance, and turning up new mould. His egotism is delightful, for there is no affectation in it. He does not talk of himself for lack of something to write about, but because some circumstance that has happened to himself is the best possible illustration of the subject, and he is not the man to shrink from giving the best possible illustration of the subject from a squeamish delicacy. He likes both himself and his subject too well. He does not put himself before it, and say, "Admire me first," but places us in the same situation with himself, and makes us see all that he does. There is no blindman's-buff, no conscious hints, no awkward ventriloquism, no testimonies of applause, no abstract, senseless self-complacency, no smuggled admiration of his own person by proxy: it is all plain and above-board. He writes himself plain William Cobbett, strips himself quite as naked as anybody would wish—in a word, his egotism is full of individuality, and has room for very little vanity in it. We feel delighted, rub our hands, and draw our chair to the fire, when we come to a passage of this sort: we know it will be something new and good, manly and simple, not the same insipid story of self over again. We sit down at table with the writer, but it is to a course of rich viands, flesh, fish, and wild-fowl, and not to a nominal entertainment, like that given by the Barmecide in the *Arabian Nights*, who put off his visitors with calling for a number of exquisite things that never appeared, and with the honour of his company. Mr. Cobbett is not a *make-believe* writer: his worst enemy cannot say that of him. Still less is he a vulgar one: he must be a puny, common-place critic indeed who thinks him so. How fine were the graphical descriptions he sent us from America: what a transatlantic flavour, what a native gusto, what a fine *sauce-piquante* of contempt they were seasoned with! If he had sat down to look at himself in the glass, instead of looking about him like Adam in Paradise, he would not have got up these articles in so capital a style. What a noble account of his first breakfast after his arrival in America! It might serve for a month. There is no scene on the stage more amusing. How well he paints the gold and scarlet plumage of the American birds, only to lament more pathetically the want of the wild wood-notes of his native land! The groves of the Ohio that had just fallen beneath the axe's stroke " live in his description," and the turnips that he transplanted from Botley " look green " in prose! How well at another time he describes the poor sheep that had got the tick and had tumbled down in the agonies of death! It is a portrait in the manner of Bewick, with the strength, the simplicity, and feeling of that great naturalist. What havoc he makes, when he pleases, of the curls of Dr. Parr's wig and of the Whig consistency of Mr. [Coleridge?]! His *Grammar*, too, is as entertaining as a story-book. He is too hard upon the style of others, and not enough (sometimes) on his own.

As a political partisan no one can stand against him. With his brandished club, like Giant Despair in the *Pilgrim's Progress*, he knocks out their brains; and not only no individual, but no corrupt system could hold out against his powerful and repeated attacks, but with the same weapon, swung round like a flail, that he levels his antagonists, he lays his friends low, and puts his own party *hors de combat*. This is a bad propensity, and a worse principle in political tactics, though a common one. If his blows were straightforward and steadily directed to the same object, no unpopular minister could live before him; instead of which he lays about right and left, impartially and remorselessly, makes a clear stage, has all the ring to himself, and then runs out of it, just when he should stand his ground. He throws his head into his adversary's stomach, and takes away from him all inclination for the fight, hits fair or foul, strikes at everything, and as you come up to his aid or stand ready to pursue his advantage, trips up your heels or lays you sprawling, and pummels you when down as much to his heart's content as ever the Yanguesian carriers belaboured Rosinante with their pack-staves. " *He has the back-trick simply the best of any man in Illyria.*" He pays off both scores of old friendship and new-acquired enmity in a breath, in one perpetual volley, one raking fire of " arrowy sleet " shot from his pen. However his own reputation or the cause may suffer in consequence, he cares not one pin about that, so that he disables all who oppose, or who pretend to help him. In fact, he cannot bear success of any kind, not even of his own views or party; and if any principle were likely to become popular, would turn round against it to shew his power in shouldering it on one side. In short, wherever power is, there is he against it: he naturally butts at all obstacles, as unicorns are attracted to oak trees, and feels his own strength only by resistance to the opinions and wishes of the rest of the world. To sail with the stream, to agree with the company, is not his humour. If he could bring about a Reform in Parliament, the odds are that he would instantly fall foul of and try to mar his own handy-work; and he quarrels with his own creatures as soon as he has written them into a little vogue—and a prison. I do not think this is vanity or fickleness so much as a pugnacious disposition, that must have an antagonistic power to contend with, and only finds itself at ease in systematic opposition. If it were not for this, the high towers and rotten places of the world would fall before the battering-ram of his hard-headed reasoning; but if he once found them tottering, he would apply his strength to prop them up, and disappoint the expectations of his followers. He cannot agree to anything established, nor to set up anything else in its stead. While it is established, he presses hard against it, because it presses upon him, at least in imagination. Let it crumble under his grasp, and the motive to resistance is gone. He then requires some other grievance to set his face against. His principle is repulsion, his nature contradiction: he is made up of mere antipathies, an Ishmaelite indeed without a fellow. He is always playing at *hunt-the-slipper* in politics. He turns round upon whoever is next him. The way to wean him from any opinion, and make him conceive an intolerable hatred against it, would be to place somebody near him who was perpetually dinning it in his ears. When he is in England he does nothing but abuse the Boroughmongers and laugh at the whole system; when he is in America he grows impatient of freedom and a republic. If he had stayed there a little longer he would have become a loyal and a loving subject of His Majesty King George IV. He lampooned the French Revolution when it was hailed as the dawn of liberty by millions: by the time it was brought into almost universal ill-odour by some means or other (partly no doubt by himself), he had turned, with one or two or three others, staunch Buona-partist. He is always of the militant, not of the triumphant party: so far he bears a gallant show of magnanimity. But his gallantry is hardly of the right stamp. It wants principle; for though he is not servile or mercenary, he is the victim of self-will. He must pull down and pull in pieces: it is not his disposition to do otherwise. It is a pity; for with his great talents he might do great things, if he would go right forward to any useful object, make thorough stitch-work of any question, or join hand and heart with any principle. He changes his opinions as he does his friends, and much on the same account. He has no comfort in fixed principles: as soon as anything is settled in his own mind, he quarrels with it. He has no satisfaction but in the chase after truth, runs a question down, worries and kills it, then quits it like vermin, and starts some new game, to lead him a new dance, and give him a fresh breathing through bog and brake, with the rabble yelping at his heels and the leaders perpetually at fault. This he calls sport-royal. He thinks it as good as cudgel-playing or single-stick, or anything else that has life in it. He likes the cut and thrust, the falls, bruises, and dry blows of an argument: as to any good or useful results that may come of the amicable settling of it, any one is welcome to them for him. The amusement is over when the matter is once fairly decided.

There is another point of view in which this may be put. I might say that Mr. Cobbett is a very honest man with a total want of principle, and I might explain this paradox thus:—I mean that he is, I think, in downright earnest in what he says, in the part he takes at the time; but in taking that part, he is led entirely by headstrong obstinacy, caprice, novelty, pique, or personal motive of some sort, and not by a steadfast regard for truth, or habitual anxiety for what is right uppermost in his mind. He is not a fee'd, time-serving, shuffling advocate (no man could write as he does who did not believe himself sincere); but his understanding is the dupe and slave of his momentary, violent, and irritable humours. He does not adopt an opinion " deliberately or for money," yet his conscience is at the mercy of the first provocation he receives, of the first whim he takes in his head: he sees things through the medium of heat and passion, not with reference to any general principles, and his whole system of thinking is deranged by the first object that strikes his fancy or sours his temper.—One cause of this phenomenon is perhaps his want of a regular education. He is a self-taught man, and has the faults as well as excellences of that class of persons in their most striking and glaring excess. It must be acknowledged that the editor of the *Political Register* (the *two-penny-trash*, as it was called, till a bill passed the House to raise the price to sixpence) is not " the gentleman and scholar," though he has qualities that, with a little better management, would be worth (to the public) both those titles. For want of knowing what has been discovered before him, he has not certain general landmarks to refer to, or a general standard of thought to apply to individual cases. He relies on his own acuteness and the immediate evidence, without being acquainted with the comparative anatomy or philosophical structure of opinion. He does not view things on a large scale or at the horizon (dim and airy enough perhaps)—but as they affect himself, close, palpable, tangible. Whatever he finds out is his own, and he only knows what he finds out. He is in the constant hurry and fever of gestation; his brain teems incessantly with some fresh project. Every new light is the birth of a new system, the dawn of a new world to him. He is continually outstripping and over-reaching himself. The last opinion is the only true one. He is wiser to-day than he was yesterday. Why should he not be wiser to-morrow than he was to-day?—Men of a learned education are not so sharp-witted as clever men without it; but they know the balance of the human intellect better; if they are more stupid, they are more steady, and are less liable to be led astray by their own sagacity and the over-weening petulance of hard-earned and late-acquired wisdom. They do not fall in love with every meretricious extravagance at first sight, or mistake an old battered hypothesis for a vestal, because they are new to the ways of this old world. They do not seize upon it as a prize, but are safe from gross imposition by being as wise and no wiser than those who went before them.

Paine said on some occasion, "What I have written, I have written"—as rendering any farther declaration of his principles unnecessary. Not so Mr. Cobbett. What he has written is no rule to him what he is to write. He learns something every day, and every week he takes the field to maintain the opinions of the last six days against friend or foe. I doubt whether this outrageous inconsistency, this headstrong fickleness, this understood want of all rule and method, does not enable him to go on with the spirit, vigour, and variety that he does. He is not pledged to repeat himself. Every new *Register* is a kind of new Prospectus. He blesses himself from all ties and shackles on his understanding; he has no mortgages on his brain; his notions are free and unencumbered. If he was in the trammels, he might become a vile hack like so many more. But he gives himself "ample scope and verge enough." He takes both sides of a question, and maintains one as sturdily as the other. If nobody else can argue against him, he is a very good match for himself. He writes better in favour of Reform than anybody else; he used to write better against it. Wherever he is, there is the tug of war, the weight of the argument, the strength of abuse. He is not like a man in danger of being *bed-rid* in his faculties—he tosses and tumbles about his unwieldy bulk, and when he is tired of lying on one side, relieves himself by turning on the other. His shifting his point of view from time to time not merely adds variety and greater compass to his topics (so that the *Political Register* is an armoury and magazine for all the materials and weapons of political warfare), but it gives a greater zest and liveliness to his manner of treating them. Mr. Cobbett takes nothing for granted as what he has proved before; he does not write a book of reference. We see his

ideas in their first concoction, fermenting and overflowing
with the ebullitions of a lively conception. We look on
at the actual process, and are put in immediate possession
of the grounds and materials on which he forms his
sanguine, unsettled conclusions. He does not give us
samples of reasoning, but the whole solid mass, refuse
and all.

> " He pours out all as plain
> As downright Shippen or as old Montaigne."

This is one cause of the clearness and force of his writings. An argument does not stop to stagnate and muddle
in his brain, but passes at once to his paper. His ideas
are served up, like pancakes, hot and hot. Fresh theories
give him fresh courage. He is like a young and lusty
bridegroom that divorces a favourite speculation every
morning, and marries a new one every night. He is not
wedded to his notions, not he. He has not one Mrs.
Cobbett among all his opinions. He makes the most of
the last thought that has come in his way, seizes fast hold
of it, rumples it about in all directions with rough strong
hands, has his wicked will of it, takes a surfeit, and throws
it away.—Our author's changing his opinions for new
ones is not so wonderful; what is more remarkable is his
facility in forgetting his old ones. He does not pretend to
consistency (like Mr. Coleridge); he frankly disavows all
connexion with himself. He feels no personal responsibility in this way, and cuts a friend or principle with the
same decided indifference that Antipholis of Ephesus cuts
Ægeon of Syracuse. It is a hollow thing. The only time
he ever grew romantic was in bringing over the relics of
Mr. Thomas Paine with him from America to go a progress
with them through the disaffected districts. Scarce had
he landed in Liverpool when he left the bones of a great
man to shift for themselves; and no sooner did he arrive
in London than he made a speech to disclaim all participation in the political and theological sentiments of his

2 A *

late idol, and to place the whole stock of his admiration
and enthusiasm towards him to the account of his financial
speculations, and of his having predicted the fate of paper-
money. If he had erected a little gold statue to him, it
might have proved the sincerity of this assertion; but to
make a martyr and a patron-saint of a man, and to dig up
" his canonised bones " in order to expose them as objects
of devotion to the rabble's gaze, asks something that has
more life and spirit in it, more mind and vivifying soul,
than has to do with any calculation of pounds, shillings,
and pence! The fact is, he *ratted* from his own project.
He found the thing not so ripe as he had expected. His
heart failed him; his enthusiasm fled, and he made his
retractation. His admiration is short-lived; his contempt
only is rooted, and his resentment lasting.—The above
was only one instance of his building too much on practical *data*. He has an ill habit of prophesying, and goes on,
though still deceived. The art of prophesying does not
suit Mr. Cobbett's style. He has a knack of fixing names
and times and places. According to him, the Reformed
Parliament was to meet in March 1818—it did not, and
we heard no more of the matter. When his predictions
fail, he takes no farther notice of them, but applies himself to new ones—like the country-people who turn to see
what weather there is in the almanac for the next week,
though it has been out in its reckoning every day of the last.

Mr. Cobbett is great in attack, not in defence; he cannot fight an up-hill battle. He will not bear the least
punishing. If anyone turns upon him (which few people
like to do) he immediately turns tail. Like an overgrown
schoolboy, he is so used to have it all his own way,
that he cannot submit to anything like competition or
a struggle for the mastery; he must lay on all the blows,
and take none. He is bullying and cowardly; a Big Ben in
politics, who will fall upon others and crush them by his
weight, but is not prepared for resistance, and is soon

staggered by a few smart blows. Whenever he has been set upon, he has slunk out of the controversy. The *Edinburgh Review* made (what is called) a dead set at him some years ago, to which he only retorted by an eulogy on the superior neatness of an English kitchen-garden to a Scotch one. I remember going one day into a bookseller's shop in Fleet-Street to ask for the *Review;* and on my expressing my opinion to a young Scotchman, who stood behind the counter, that Mr. Cobbett might hit as hard in his reply, the North Briton said with some alarm, " But you don't think, sir, Mr. Cobbett will be able to injure the Scottish nation? " I said I could not speak to that point, but I thought he was very well able to defend himself. He, however, did not, but has borne a grudge to the *Edinburgh Review* ever since, which he hates worse than the *Quarterly.* I cannot say I do.[1]

COLERIDGE

(LECTURES ON THE ENGLISH POETS, 1818)

I T remains that I should say a few words of Mr. Coleridge; and there is no one who has a better right to say what he thinks of him than I have. " Is there here any dear friend of Cæsar? To him I say, that Brutus's love to Cæsar was

---

[1] Mr. Cobbett speaks almost as well as he writes. The only time I ever saw him he seemed to me a very pleasant man— easy of access, affable, clear-headed, simple and mild in his manner, deliberate and unruffled in his speech, though some of his expressions were not very qualified. His figure is tall and portly. He has a good, sensible face—rather full, with little grey eyes, a hard, square forehead, a ruddy complexion, with hair grey or powdered ; and had on a scarlet broadcloth waistcoat with the flaps of the pockets hanging down, as was the custom for gentlemen-farmers in the last century, or as we see it in the pictures of Members of Parliament in the reign of George I. I certainly did not think less favourably of him for seeing him.

no less than his." But no matter.—His *Ancient Mariner* is his most remarkable performance, and the only one that I could point out to anyone as giving an adequate idea of his great natural powers. It is high German, however, and in it he seems to " conceive of poetry but as a drunken dream, reckless, careless, and heedless, of past, present, and to come." His tragedies (for he has written two) are not answerable to it; they are, except a few poetical passages, drawling sentiment and metaphysical jargon. He has no genuine dramatic talent. There is one fine passage in his *Christobel*, that which contains the description of the quarrel between Sir Leoline and Sir Roland de Vaux of Tryermaine, who had been friends in youth.

It might seem insidious if I were to praise his ode entitled Fire, Famine, and Slaughter, as an effusion of high poetical enthusiasm, and strong political feeling. His Sonnet to Schiller conveys a fine compliment to the author of the Robbers, and an equally fine idea of the state of youthful enthusiasm in which he composed it.[1] His *Conciones ad Populum*, Watchman, &c. are dreary trash. Of his *Friend*, I have spoken the truth elsewhere. But I may say of him here, that he is the only person I ever knew who answered to the idea of a man of genius. He is the only person from whom I ever learnt anything. There is only one thing he could learn from me in return, but *that* he has not. He was the first poet I ever knew. His genius at that time had angelic wings, and fed on manna. He talked on for ever; and you wished him to talk on for ever. His thoughts did not seem to come with labour and effort; but as if borne on the gusts of genius, and as if the wings of his imagination lifted him from off his feet. His voice rolled on the ear like the pealing organ, and its sound alone was the music of thought. His mind was clothed with wings; and raised on them, he lifted

---

[1] Quotations are here omitted. (Ed.)

philosophy to heaven. In his descriptions, you then saw the progress of human happiness and liberty in bright and never-ending succession, like the steps of Jacob's ladder, with airy shapes ascending and descending, and with the voice of God at the top of the ladder. And shall I, who heard him then, listen to him now? Not I! . . . That spell is broke; that time is gone for ever; that voice is heard no more: but still the recollection comes rushing by with thoughts of long-past years, and rings in my ears with never-dying sound.

> " What though the radiance which was once so bright,
>   Be now for ever taken from my sight,
>   Though nothing can bring back the hour
> Of glory in the grass, of splendour in the flow'r;
>   I do not grieve, but rather find
>   Strength in what remains behind;
>   In the primal sympathy,
>   Which having been, must ever be;
>   In the soothing thoughts that spring
>   Out of human suffering;
> In years that bring the philosophic mind! "

MR. COLERIDGE

(THE SPIRIT OF THE AGE, 1825)

THE present is an age of talkers, and not of doers; and the reason is, that the world is growing old. We are so far advanced in the Arts and Sciences, that we live in retrospect, and doat on past achievements. The accumulation of knowledge has been so great, that we are lost in wonder at the height it has reached, instead of attempting to climb or add to it; while the variety of objects distracts and dazzles the looker-on. What *niche* remains unoccupied? What path untried? What is the use of doing anything, unless we could do better than all those who

have gone before us? What hope is there of this? We
are like those who have been to see some noble monument
of art, who are content to admire without thinking of
rivalling it; or like guests after a feast, who praise the
hospitality of the donor " and thank the bounteous Pan "
—perhaps carrying away some trifling fragments; or like
the spectators of a mighty battle, who still hear its sound
afar off, and the clashing of armour and the neighing of
the war-horse and the shout of victory is in their ears,
like the rushing of innumerable waters!

Mr. Coleridge has " a mind reflecting ages past ": his
voice is like the echo of the congregated roar of the " dark
rearward and abyss " of thought. He who has seen a
mouldering tower by the side of a chrystal lake, hid by the
mist, but glittering in the wave below, may conceive the
dim, gleaming, uncertain intelligence of his eye: he who
has marked the evening clouds uprolled (a world of
vapours) has seen the picture of his mind, unearthly, unsubstantial, with gorgeous tints and ever-varying forms—

> " That which was now a horse, even with a thought
> The rack dislimns, and makes it indistinct
> As water is in water."

Our author's mind is (as he himself might express
it) *tangential*. There is no subject on which he has
not touched, none on which he has rested. With an
understanding, fertile, subtle, expansive, " quick, for-
getive, apprehensive," beyond all living precedent, few
traces of it will perhaps remain. He lends himself to all
impressions alike; he gives up his mind and liberty of
thought to none. He is a general lover of art and science,
and wedded to no one in particular. He pursues knowledge as a mistress, with outstretched hands and winged
speed; but as he is about to embrace her, his Daphne
turns—alas! not to a laurel! Hardly a speculation has
been left on record from the earliest time, but it is loosely

folded up in Mr. Coleridge's memory, like a rich, but
somewhat tattered piece of tapestry: we might add (with
more seeming than real extravagance) that scarce a
thought can pass through the mind of man, but its sound
has at some time or other passed over his head with
rustling pinions.

On whatever question or author you speak, he is
prepared to take up the theme with advantage—from
Peter Abelard down to Thomas Moore, from the subtlest
metaphysics to the politics of the *Courier*. There is no
man of genius, in whose praise he descants, but the critic
seems to stand above the author, and " what in him is
weak, to strengthen, what is low, to raise and support ":
nor is there any work of genius that does not come out
of his hands like an illuminated Missal, sparkling even
in its defects. If Mr. Coleridge had not been the most
impressive talker of his age, he would probably have
have been the finest writer; but he lays down his pen to
make sure of an auditor, and mortgages the admiration
of posterity for the stare of an idler. If he had not been a
poet, he would have been a powerful logician; if he had
not dipped his wing in the Unitarian controversy, he
might have soared to the very summit of fancy. But, in
writing verse, he is trying to subject the Muse to *transcendental* theories: in his abstract reasoning, he misses
his way by strewing it with flowers.

All that he has done of moment, he had done twenty
years ago: since then, he may be said to have lived on the
sound of his own voice. Mr. Coleridge is too rich in
intellectual wealth, to need to task himself to any
drudgery: he has only to draw the sliders of his imagination, and a thousand subjects expand before him, startling
him with their brilliancy, or losing themselves in endless
obscurity—

> " And by the force of blear illusion,
>   They draw him on to his confusion."

What is the little he could add to the stock, compared with the countless stores that lie about him, that he should stoop to pick up a name, or to polish an idle fancy? He walks abroad in the majesty of an universal understanding, eyeing the " rich strond " or golden sky above him, and " goes sounding on his way " in eloquent accents, uncompelled and free !

· Persons of the greatest capacity are often those, who for this reason do the least; for surveying themselves from the highest point of view, amidst the infinite variety of the universe, their own share in it seems trifling, and scarce worth a thought; and they prefer the contemplation of all that is, or has been, or can be, to the making a coil about doing what, when done, is no better than vanity. It is hard to concentrate all our attention and efforts on one pursuit, except from ignorance of others; and without this concentration of our faculties no great progress can be made in any one thing. It is not merely that the mind is not capable of the effort; it does not think the effort worth making. Action is one; but thought is manifold. He whose restless eye glances through the wide compass of nature and art, will not consent to have " his own nothings monstered "; but he must do this before he can give his whole soul to them. The mind, after " letting contemplation have its fill," or

> " Sailing with supreme dominion
> Through the azure deep of air,"

sinks down on the ground, breathless, exhausted, powerless, inactive; or if it must have some vent to its feelings, seeks the most easy and obvious; is soothed by friendly flattery, lulled by the murmur of immediate applause: thinks, as it were, aloud, and babbles in its dreams!

A scholar (so to speak) is a more disinterested and abstracted character than a mere author. The first looks at the numberless volumes of a library, and says, " All

these are mine ": the other points to a single volume
(perhaps it may be an immortal one) and says, "My
name is written on the back of it." This is a puny and
grovelling ambition, beneath the lofty amplitude of
Mr. Coleridge's mind. No, he revolves in his wayward
soul, or utters to the passing wind, or discourses to his
own shadow, things mightier and more various!—Let us
draw the curtain, and unlock the shrine.

Learning rocked him in his cradle, and while yet a
child,

"He lisped in numbers, for the numbers came."

At sixteen he wrote his *Ode on Chatterton,* and he still
reverts to that period with delight, not so much as it
relates to himself (for that string of his own early promise
of fame rather jars than otherwise) but as exemplifying
the youth of a poet. Mr. Coleridge talks of himself
without being an egotist; for in him the individual is
always merged in the abstract and general. He distinguished himself at school and at the University by his
knowledge of the classics, and gained several prizes for
Greek epigrams. How many men are there (great
scholars, celebrated names in literature) who, having
done the same thing in their youth, have no other idea all
the rest of their lives but of this achievement, of a fellowship and dinner, and who, installed in academic honours,
would look down on our author as a mere strolling bard!
At Christ's Hospital, where he was brought up, he was
the idol of those among his schoolfellows, who mingled
with their bookish studies the music of thought and of
humanity; and he was usually attended round the cloisters
by a group of these (inspiring and inspired) whose hearts,
even then, burnt within them as he talked, and where the
sounds yet linger to mock ELIA on his way, still turning
pensive to the past!

One of the finest and rarest parts of Mr. Coleridge's

conversation is, when he expatiates on the Greek tragedians (not that he is not well acquainted, when he pleases, with the epic poets, or the philosophers, or orators, or historians of antiquity)—on the subtle reasonings and melting pathos of Euripides, on the harmonious gracefulness of Sophocles, tuning his love-laboured song, like sweetest warblings from a sacred grove; on the high-wrought, trumpet-tongued eloquence of Æschylus, whose *Prometheus*, above all, is like an Ode to Fate and a pleading with Providence, his thoughts being let loose as his body is chained on his solitary rock, and his afflicted will (the emblem of mortality)

" Struggling in vain with ruthless destiny."

As the impassioned critic speaks and rises in his theme, you would think you heard the voice of the Man hated by the Gods, contending with the wild winds as they roar; and his eye glitters with the spirit of Antiquity!

Next, he was engaged with Hartley's tribes of mind, " etherial braid, thought-woven,"—and he busied himself for a year or two with vibrations and vibratiuncles, and the great law of association that binds all things in its mystic chain, and the doctrine of Necessity (the mild teacher of Charity) and the Millennium, anticipative of a life to come; and he plunged deep into the controversy on Matter and Spirit, and, as an escape from Dr. Priestley's Materialism, where he felt himself imprisoned by the logician's spell, like Ariel in the cloven pine-tree, he became suddenly enamoured of Bishop Berkeley's fairy-world,[1] and used in all companies to build the universe, like a brave poetical fiction, of fine words. And he was

[1] Mr. Coleridge named his eldest son (the writer of some beautiful Sonnets) after Hartley, and the second after Berkeley. The third was called Derwent, after the river of that name. Nothing can be more characteristic of his mind than this circumstance. All his ideas indeed are like a river, flowing on for

deep-read in Malebranche, and in Cudworth's Intellectual System (a huge pile of learning, unwieldy, enormous) and in Lord Brook's hieroglyphic theories, and in Bishop Butler's Sermons, and in the Duchess of Newcastle's fantastic folios, and in Clarke and South, and Tillotson, and all the fine thinkers and masculine reasoners of that age; and Leibnitz's *Pre-established Harmony* reared its arch above his head, like the rainbow in the cloud, covenanting with the hopes of man—and then he fell plump, ten thousand fathoms down (but his wings saved him harmless) into the *hortus siccus* of Dissent, where he pared religion down to the standard of reason, and stripped faith of mystery, and preached Christ crucified and the Unity of the Godhead, and so dwelt for a while in the spirit with John Huss and Jerome of Prague and Socinus and old John Zisca, and ran through Neal's *History of the Puritans* and Calamy's *Non-Conformists' Memorial*, having like thoughts and passions with them—but then Spinoza became his God, and he took up the vast chain of being in his hand, and the round world became the centre and the soul of all things in some shadowy sense, forlorn of meaning, and around him he beheld the living traces and the sky-pointing proportions of the mighty Pan—but poetry redeemed him from this spectral philosophy, and he bathed his heart in beauty, and gazed at the golden light of heaven, and drank of the spirit of the universe, and wandered at eve by fairy-stream or fountain,

" ——When he saw nought but beauty,
When he heard the voice of that Almighty One
In every breeze that blew, or wave that murmured "—

and wedded with truth in Plato's shade, and in the

ever, and still murmuring as it flows, discharging its waters and still replenished—

" And so by many winding nooks it strays,
With willing sport to the wild ocean ! "

writings of Proclus and Plotinus saw the ideas of things
in the eternal mind, and unfolded all mysteries with the
Schoolmen and fathomed the depths of Duns Scotus and
Thomas Aquinas, and entered the third heaven with
Jacob Behmen, and walked hand in hand with Swedenborg
through the pavilions of the New Jerusalem, and sung his
faith in the promise and in the word in his *Religious
Musings*—and lowering himself from that dizzy height
poised himself on Milton's wings, and spread out his
thoughts in charity with the glad prose of Jeremy Taylor,
and wept over Bowles's *Sonnets*, and studied Cowper's
blank verse, and betook himself to Thomson's *Castle of
Indolence*, and sported with the wits of Charles the
Second's days and of Queen Anne, and relished Swift's
style and that of the John Bull (Arbuthnot's we mean,
not Mr. Croker's), and dallied with the British Essayists
and Novelists, and knew all qualities of more modern
writers with a learned spirit: Johnson, and Goldsmith,
and Junius, and Burke, and Godwin, and the Sorrows of
Werter, and Jean Jacques Rousseau, and Voltaire, and
Marivaux, and Crebillon, and thousands more—now
"laughed with Rabelais in his easy chair" or pointed
to Hogarth, or afterwards dwelt on Claude's classic
scenes, or spoke with rapture of Raphael, and compared
the women at Rome to figures that had walked out of his
pictures, or visited the Oratory of Pisa, and described
the works of Giotto and Ghirlandaio and Massaccio, and
gave the moral of the picture of the Triumph of Death,
where the beggars and the wretched invoke his dreadful
dart, but the rich and mighty of the earth quail and shrink
before it; and in that land of siren sights and sounds, saw
a dance of peasant girls, and was charmed with lutes and
gondolas,—or wandered into Germany and lost himself
in the labyrinths of the Hartz Forest and of the Kantean
philosophy, and amongst the cabalistic names of Fichtè
and Schelling and Lessing, and God knows who—this

was long after, but all the former while, he had nerved his
heart and filled his eyes with tears, as he hailed the rising
orb of liberty, since quenched in darkness and in blood,
and had kindled his affections at the blaze of the French
Revolution, and sang for joy, when the towers of the
Bastille and the proud places of the insolent and the
oppressor fell, and would have floated his bark, freighted
with fondest fancies, across the Atlantic wave with
Southey and others to seek for peace and freedom—

"In Philarmonia's undivided dale!"

Alas! "Frailty, thy name is *Genius!*"—What is become
of all this mighty heap of hope, of thought, of learning
and humanity? It has ended in swallowing doses of
oblivion and in writing paragraphs in the *Courier.*—Such
and so little is the mind of man!

It was not to be supposed that Mr. Coleridge could
keep on at the rate he set off; he could not realize all he
knew or thought, and less could not fix his desultory
ambition; other stimulants supplied the place, and kept
up the intoxicating dream, the fever and the madness of
his early impressions. Liberty (the philosopher's and the
poet's bride) had fallen a victim, meanwhile, to the
murderous practices of the hag Legitimacy. Proscribed
by court-hirelings, too romantic for the herd of vulgar
politicians, our enthusiast stood at bay, and at last turned
on the pivot of a subtle casuistry to the *unclean side:* but
his discursive reason would not let him trammel himself
into a poet-laureate or stamp-distributor; and he stopped,
ere he had quite passed that well-known "bourne from
whence no traveller returns"—and so has sunk into
torpid, uneasy repose, tantalized by useless resources,
haunted by vain imaginings, his lips idly moving, but
his heart for ever still, or, as the shattered chords vibrate
of themselves, making melancholy music to the ear of
memory! Such is the fate of genius in an age when, in

the unequal contest with sovereign wrong, every man is ground to powder who is not either a born slave, or who does not willingly and at once offer up the yearnings of humanity and the dictates of reason as a welcome sacrifice to besotted prejudice and loathsome power.

Of all Mr. Coleridge's productions, the *Ancient Mariner* is the only one that we could with confidence put into any person's hands, on whom we wished to impress a favourable idea of his extraordinary powers. Let whatever other objections be made to it, it is unquestionably a work of genius—of wild, irregular, overwhelming imagination, and has that rich, varied movement in the verse, which gives a distant idea of the lofty or changeful tones of Mr. Coleridge's voice. In the *Christobel*, there is one splendid passage on divided friendship. The Translation of Schiller's *Wallenstein* is also a masterly production in its kind, faithful and spirited. Among his smaller pieces there are occasional bursts of pathos and fancy, equal to what we might expect from him; but these form the exception, and not the rule. Such, for instance, is his affecting Sonnet to the author of the *Robbers*.

" Schiller ! that hour I would have wish'd to die,
    If through the shudd'ring midnight I had sent
    From the dark dungeon of the tower time-rent,
That fearful voice, a famish'd father's cry—

That in no after-moment aught less vast
    Might stamp me mortal ! A triumphant shout
    Black horror scream'd, and all her goblin rout
From the more with'ring scene diminish'd pass'd.

Ah ! Bard tremendous in sublimity !
    Could I behold thee in thy loftier mood,
Wand'ring at eve, with finely frenzied eye,
    Beneath some vast old tempest-swinging wood !
    Awhile, with mute awe gazing, I would brood,
Then weep aloud in a wild ecstasy."

His Tragedy, entitled *Remorse,* is full of beautiful and striking passages; but it does not place the author in the first rank of dramatic writers. But if Mr. Coleridge's works do not place him in that rank, they injure instead of conveying a just idea of the man; for he himself is certainly in the first class of general intellect.

If our author's poetry is inferior to his conversation, his prose is utterly abortive. Hardly a gleam is to be found in it of the brilliancy and richness of those stores of thought and language that he pours out incessantly, when they are lost like drops of water in the ground. The principal work, in which he has attempted to embody his general views of things, is the FRIEND, of which, though it contains some noble passages and fine trains of thought, prolixity and obscurity are the most frequent characteristics.

No two persons can be conceived more opposite in character or genius than the subject of the present and of the preceding sketch. Mr. Godwin, with less natural capacity and with fewer acquired advantages, by concentrating his mind on some given object, and doing what he had to do with all his might, has accomplished much, and will leave more than one monument of a powerful intellect behind him; Mr. Coleridge, by dissipating his, and dallying with every subject by turns, has done little or nothing to justify to the world or to posterity the high opinion which all who have ever heard him converse, or known him intimately, with one accord entertain of him. Mr. Godwin's faculties have kept at home, and plied their task in the workshop of the brain, diligently and effectually: Mr. Coleridge's have gossiped away their time, and gadded about from house to house, as if life's business were to melt the hours in listless talk. Mr. Godwin is intent on a subject, only as it concerns himself and his reputation; he works it out as a matter of duty, and discards from his mind whatever does not forward his main object as impertinent and vain. Mr. Coleridge, on the other hand, delights in nothing but episodes and digressions, neglects whatever he undertakes to perform, and can act only on spontaneous impulses, without object or method. " He cannot be constrained by mastery." While he should be occupied with a given pursuit, he is thinking of a thousand other things: a thousand tastes, a thousand objects tempt him, and distract his mind, which keeps open house, and entertains all comers; and after being fatigued and amused with morning calls from idle visitors finds the day consumed and its business unconcluded. Mr. Godwin, on the contrary, is somewhat exclusive and unsocial in his habits of mind, entertains no company but what he gives his whole time and attention to, and wisely writes over the doors of his understanding, his fancy, and his senses —" No admittance except on business." He has none of that fastidious refinement and false delicacy, which might lead him to balance between the endless variety of modern attainments. He does not throw away his life (nor a single half hour of it) in adjusting the claims of different accomplishments, and in choosing between them or making himself master of them all. He sets about his task (whatever it may be), and goes through it with spirit and fortitude. He has the happiness to think an author the greatest character in the world, and himself the greatest author in it.

Mr. Coleridge, in writing an harmonious stanza, would stop to consider whether there was not more grace and beauty in a *Pas de trois*, and would not proceed till he had resolved this question by a chain of metaphysical reasoning without end. Not so Mr. Godwin. That is best to him, which he can do best. He does not waste himself in vain aspirations and effeminate sympathies. He is blind, deaf, insensible to all but the trump of Fame. Plays, operas, painting, music, ball-rooms, wealth, fashion, titles, lords, ladies, touch him not—all these are no more to him than to the magician in his cell, and he writes on to the end of the chapter through good report and evil report. *Pingo in eternitatem* is his motto. He neither envies nor admires what others are, but is contented to be what he is, and strives to do the utmost he can. Mr. Coleridge has flirted with the Muses as with a set of mistresses: Mr. Godwin has been married twice, to Reason and to Fancy, and has to boast no short-lived progeny by each.

So to speak, he has *valves* belonging to his mind, to regulate the quantity of gas admitted into it, so that like the bare, unsightly, but well-compacted steam-vessel, it cuts its liquid way, and arrives at its promised end: while Mr. Coleridge's bark, " taught with the little nautilus to sail," the sport of every breath, dancing to every wave,

" Youth at its prow, and Pleasure at its helm,"

flutters its gaudy pennons in the air, glitters in the sun, but we wait in vain to hear of its arrival in the destined harbour. Mr. Godwin, with less variety and vividness, with less subtlety and susceptibility both of thought and feeling, has had firmer nerves, a more determined purpose, a more comprehensive grasp of his subject; and the results are as we find them. Each has met with his reward: for justice has, after all, been done to the pretensions of each: and we must, in all cases, use means to ends!

It was a misfortune to any man of talent to be born in the latter end of the last century. Genius stopped the way of Legitimacy, and therefore it was to be abated, crushed, or set aside as a nuisance. The spirit of the monarchy was at variance with the spirit of the age. The flame of liberty, the light of intellect, was to be extinguished with the sword—or with slander, whose edge is sharper than the sword. The war between power and reason was carried on by the first of these abroad, by the last at home. No quarter was given (then or now) by the Government-critics, the authorised censors of the press, to those who followed the dictates of independence, who listened to the voice of the tempter Fancy. Instead of gathering fruits and flowers, immortal fruits and amaranthine flowers, they soon found themselves beset not only by a host of prejudices, but assailed with all the engines of power: by nicknames, by lies, by all the arts of malice, interest and hypocrisy, without the possibility of their defending themselves " from the pelting of the pitiless storm," that poured down upon them from the strongholds of corruption and authority.

The philosophers, the dry abstract reasoners, submitted to this reverse pretty well, and armed themselves with patience " as with triple steel," to bear discomfiture, persecution, and disgrace. But the poets, the creatures of sympathy, could not stand the frowns both of king and people. They did not like to be shut out when places and pensions, when the critic's praises, and the laurel wreath were about to be distributed. They did not stomach being *sent to Coventry*, and Mr. Coleridge sounded a retreat for them by the help of casuistry and a musical voice.—" His words were hollow, but they pleased the ear " of his friends of the Lake School, who turned back disgusted and panic-struck from the dry desert of unpopularity, like Hassan the camel-driver,

" And curs'd the hour, and curs'd the luckless day,
   When first from Shiraz' walls they bent their way."

They are safely inclosed there, but Mr. Coleridge did not enter with them; pitching his tent upon the barren waste without, and having no abiding place nor city of refuge!

MR. WORDSWORTH

M R . W O R D S W O R T H ' S genius is a pure emanation of the Spirit of the Age. Had he lived in any other period of the world, he would never have been heard of. As it is, he has some difficulty to contend with the hebetude of his intellect and the meanness of his subject. With him " lowliness is young ambition's ladder ": but he finds it a toil to climb in his way the steep of Fame. His homely Muse can hardly raise her wing from the ground, nor spread her hidden glories to the sun. He has " no figures nor no fantasies, which busy *passion* draws in the brains of men ": neither the gorgeous machinery of mythologic lore, nor the splendid colours of poetic diction. His style is vernacular: he delivers household truths. He sees nothing loftier than human hopes, nothing deeper than the human heart. This he probes, this he tampers with, this he poises, with all its incalculable weight of thought and feeling, in his hands, and at the same time calms the throbbing pulses of his own heart by keeping his eye ever fixed on the face of nature. If he can make the life-blood flow from the wounded breast, this is the living colouring with which he paints his verse: if he can assuage the pain or close up the wound with the balm of solitary musing, or the healing power of plants and herbs and " skyey influences," this is the sole triumph of his art. He takes the simplest elements of nature and of the human mind, the mere abstract conditions inseparable from our being, and tries to compound a new system of poetry from them; and has perhaps succeeded as well as any one could. " *Nihil humani a me alienum puto* " is the motto of his works. He thinks nothing low or indifferent of which this can be affirmed: everything that professes to be more than this, that is not an absolute essence of truth and feeling, he holds to be vitiated, false, and spurious. In a word, his poetry is founded on setting up an opposition (and pushing it to the utmost length) between the natural and the artificial, between the spirit of humanity and the spirit of fashion and of the world!

It is one of the innovations of the time. It partakes of, and is carried along with, the revolutionary movement of our age: the political changes of the day were the model on which he formed and conducted his poetical experiments. His Muse (it cannot be denied, and without this we cannot explain its character at all) is a levelling one. It proceeds on a principle of equality, and strives to reduce all things to the same standard. It is distinguished by a proud humility. It relies upon its own resources, and disdains external show and relief. It takes the commonest events and objects, as a test to prove that nature is always interesting from its inherent truth and beauty, without any of the ornaments of dress or pomp of circumstances to set it off. Hence the unaccountable mixture of seeming simplicity and real abstruseness in the *Lyrical Ballads*. Fools have laughed at, wise men scarcely understand, them. He takes a subject or a story merely as pegs or loops to hang thought and feeling on; the incidents are trifling, in proportion to his contempt for imposing appearances: the reflections are profound, according to the gravity and aspiring pretensions of his mind.

His popular, inartificial style gets rid (at a blow) of all the trappings of verse, of all the high places of poetry: " the cloud-capt towers, the solemn temples, the gorgeous palaces," are swept to the ground, and " like the baseless fabric of a vision, leave not a rack behind." All the traditions of learning, all the superstitions of age, are obliterated and effaced. We begin *de novo* on a *tabula rasa* of poetry. The purple pall, the nodding plume of tragedy are exploded as mere pantomime and trick, to return to the simplicity of truth and nature. Kings, queens, priests, nobles, the altar and the throne, the distinctions of rank, birth, wealth, power, "the judge's robe, the marshal's truncheon, the ceremony that to great ones 'longs," are not to be found here. The author tramples on the pride of art with greater pride. The Ode and Epode, the Strophe and the Antistrophe, he laughs to scorn. The harp of Homer, the trump of Pindar and of Alcæus, are still. The decencies of costume, the decorations of vanity are stripped off without mercy as barbarous, idle, and Gothic. The jewels in the crisped hair, the diadem on the polished brow, are thought meretricious, theatrical, vulgar; and nothing contents his fastidious taste beyond a simple garland of flowers. Neither does he avail himself of the advantages which nature or accident holds out to him. He chooses to have his subject a foil to his invention, to owe nothing but to himself. He gathers manna in the wilderness, he strikes the barren rock for the gushing moisture. He elevates the mean by the strength of his own aspirations; he clothes the naked with beauty and grandeur from the stores of his own recollections. No cypress grove loads his verse with funeral pomp: but his imagination lends "a sense of joy

> ' To the bare trees and mountains bare,
> And grass in the green field.' "

No storm, no shipwreck startles us by its horrors: but the rainbow lifts its head in the cloud, and the breeze sighs through the withered fern. No sad vicissitude of fate, no overwhelming catastrophe in nature deforms his page: but the dew-drop glitters on the bending flower, the tear collects in the glistening eye.

> " Beneath the hills, along the flowery vales,
> The generations are prepared ; the pangs,
> The internal pangs are ready ; the dread strife
> Of poor humanity's afflicted will,
> Struggling in vain with ruthless destiny."

As the lark ascends from its low bed on fluttering wing, and salutes the morning skies, so Mr. Wordsworth's unpretending Muse, in russet guise, scales the summits of reflection, while it makes the round earth its footstool and its home!

Possibly a good deal of this may be regarded as the effect of disappointed views and an inverted ambition. Prevented by native pride and indolence from climbing the ascent of learning or greatness, taught by political opinions to say to the vain pomp and glory of the world, " I hate ye," seeing the path of classical and artificial poetry blocked up by the cumbrous ornaments of style and turgid *common-places*, so that nothing more could be achieved in that direction but by the most ridiculous bombast or the tamest servility, he has turned back, partly from the bias of his mind, partly perhaps from a judicious policy—has struck into the sequestered vale of humble life, sought out the Muse among sheep-cotes and hamlets, and the peasant's mountain-haunts, has discarded all the tinsel pageantry of verse, and endeavoured (not in vain) to aggrandise the trivial, and add the charm of novelty to the familiar. No one has shown the same imagination in raising trifles into importance : no one has displayed the same pathos in treating of the simplest feelings of the heart. Reserved, yet haughty, having no unruly or violent passions (or those passions having been early suppressed), Mr. Wordsworth has passed his life in solitary musing or in daily converse with the face of nature. He exemplifies in an eminent degree the power of *association*; for his poetry has no other source or character. He has dwelt among pastoral scenes, till each object has become connected with a thousand feelings, a link in the chain of thought, a fibre of his own heart. Every one is by habit and familiarity strongly attached to the place of his birth, or to objects that recall the most pleasing and eventful circumstances of his life. But to the author

of the *Lyrical Ballads* nature is a kind of home; and
he may be said to take a personal interest in the universe. There is no image so insignificant that it has not
in some mood or other found the way into his heart:
no sound that does not awaken the memory of other
years.—
> " To him the meanest flower that blows can give
> Thoughts that do often lie too deep for tears."

The daisy looks up to him with sparkling eye as an
old acquaintance: the cuckoo haunts him with sounds
of early youth not to be expressed: a linnet's nest
startles him with boyish delight: an old withered thorn
is weighed down with a heap of recollections: a grey
cloak, seen on some wild moor, torn by the wind, or
drenched in the rain, afterwards becomes an object of
imagination to him: even the lichens on the rock have
a life and being in his thoughts. He has described all
these objects in a way and with an intensity of feeling
that no one else had done before him, and has given a
new view or aspect of nature. He is in this sense the most
original poet now living, and the one whose writings could
the least be spared: for they have no substitute elsewhere. The vulgar do not read them; the learned, who
see all things through books, do not understand them,
the great despise, the fashionable may ridicule them:
but the author has created himself an interest in the
heart of the retired and lonely student of nature, which
can never die. Persons of this class will still continue to
feel what he has felt: he has expressed what they might in
vain wish to express, except with glistening eye and faultering tongue! There is a lofty philosophic tone, a thoughtful
humanity, infused into his pastoral vein. Remote from
the passions and events of the great world, he has communicated interest and dignity to the primal movements of
the heart of man, and ingrafted his own conscious reflections on the casual thoughts of hinds and shepherds.

Nursed amidst the grandeur of mountain scenery, he has stooped to have a nearer view of the daisy under his feet, or plucked a branch of white-thorn from the spray: but, in describing it, his mind seems imbued with the majesty and solemnity of the objects around him—the tall rock lifts its head in the erectness of his spirit; the cataract roars in the sound of his verse; and in its dim and mysterious meaning the mists seem to gather in the hollows of Helvellyn, and the forked Skiddaw hovers in the distance. There is little mention of mountainous scenery in Mr. Wordsworth's poetry; but by internal evidence one might be almost sure that it was written in a mountainous country, from its bareness, its simplicity, its loftiness and its depth!

His later philosophic productions have a somewhat different character. They are a departure from, a dereliction of, his first principles. They are classical and courtly. They are polished in style, without being gaudy; dignified in subject, without affectation. They seem to have been composed not in a cottage at Grasmere, but among the half-inspired groves and stately recollections of Cole-Orton. We might allude in particular, for examples of what we mean, to the lines on a Picture by Claude Lorraine, and to the exquisite poem, entitled *Laodamia*. The last of these breathes the pure spirit of the finest fragments of antiquity—the sweetness, the gravity, the strength, the beauty and the languor of death—

> " Calm contemplation and majestic pains."

Its glossy brilliancy arises from the perfection of the finishing, like that of a careful sculpture, not from gaudy colouring—the texture of the thoughts has the smoothness and solidity of marble. It is a poem that might be read aloud in Elysium, and the spirits of departed heroes and sages would gather round to listen to it!

Mr. Wordsworth's philosophic poetry, with a less

glowing aspect and less tumult in the veins than Lord Byron's on similar occasions, bends a calmer and keener eye on mortality; the impression, if less vivid, is more pleasing and permanent; and we confess it (perhaps it is a want of taste and proper feeling) that there are lines and poems of our author's, that we think of ten times for once that we recur to any of Lord Byron's. Or if there are any of the latter's writings, that we can dwell upon in the same way, that is, as lasting and heart-felt sentiments, it is when laying aside his usual pomp and pretension, he descends with Mr. Wordsworth to the common ground of a disinterested humanity. It may be considered as characteristic of our poet's writings, that they either make no impression on the mind at all, seem mere *nonsense-verses*, or that they leave a mark behind them that never wears out. They either

" Fall blunted from the indurated breast "—

without any perceptible result, or they absorb it like a passion. To one class of readers he appears sublime, to another (and we fear the largest) ridiculous. He has probably realised Milton's wish,—" and fit audience found, though few ": but we suspect he is not reconciled to the alternative.

There are delightful passages in the *Excursion*, both of natural description and of inspired reflection (passages of the latter kind that in the sound of the thoughts and of the swelling language resemble heavenly symphonies, mournful *requiems* over the grave of human hopes); but we must add, in justice and in sincerity, that we think it impossible that this work should ever become popular, even in the same degree as the *Lyrical Ballads*. It affects a system without having any intelligible clue to one, and, instead of unfolding a principle in various and striking lights, repeats the same conclusions till they become flat and insipid. Mr. Wordsworth's mind is obtuse, except

2 B

as it is the organ and the receptacle of accumulated feelings; it is not analytic, but synthetic; it is reflecting, rather than theoretical. The *Excursion*, we believe, fell still-born from the press. There was something abortive, and clumsy, and ill-judged in the attempt. It was long and laboured. The personages, for the most part, were low, the fare rustic; the plan raised expectations which were not fulfilled; and the effect was like being ushered into a stately hall and invited to sit down to a splendid banquet in the company of clowns, and with nothing but successive courses of apple-dumplings served up. It was not even *toujours perdrix!*

Mr. Wordsworth, in his person, is above the middle size, with marked features and an air somewhat stately and Quixotic. He reminds one of some of Holbein's heads: grave, saturnine, with a slight indication of sly humour, kept under by the manners of the age or by the pretensions of the person. He has a peculiar sweetness in his smile, and great depth and manliness and a rugged harmony in the tones of his voice. His manner of reading his own poetry is particularly imposing; and in his favourite passages his eye beams with preternatural lustre, and the meaning labours slowly up from his swelling breast. No one who has seen him at these moments could go away with an impression that he was a " man of no mark or likelihood." Perhaps the comment of his face and voice is necessary to convey a full idea of his poetry. His language may not be intelligible; but his manner is not to be mistaken. It is clear that he is either mad or inspired. In company, even in a *tête-à-tête*, Mr. Wordsworth is often silent, indolent and reserved. If he is become verbose and oracular of late years, he was not so in his better days. He threw out a bold or an indifferent remark without either effort or pretension, and relapsed into musing again. He shone most (because he seemed most roused and animated) in reciting his own poetry, or in talking about it. He sometimes gave striking views of his feelings and trains of association in composing certain passages; or if one did not always understand his distinctions, still there was no want of interest—there was a latent meaning worth inquiring into, like a vein of ore that one cannot exactly hit upon at the moment, but of which there are sure indications. His standard of poetry is high and severe, almost to exclusiveness. He admits of nothing below, scarcely of anything above, himself. It is fine to hear him talk of the way in which certain subjects should have been treated by eminent poets, according to his notions of the art. Thus he finds fault with Dryden's description of Bacchus in the *Alexander's Feast*, as if he were a mere good-looking youth or boon companion—

> " Flushed with a purple grace,
> He shows his honest face "—

instead of representing the God returning from the conquest of India, crowned with vine-leaves and drawn by panthers, and followed by troops of satyrs, of wild men and animals that he had tamed. You would think, in hearing him speak on this subject, that you saw Titian's picture of the meeting of *Bacchus and Ariadne*—so classic were his conceptions, so glowing his style.

Milton is his great idol, and he sometimes dares to compare himself with him. His Sonnets, indeed, have something of the same high-raised tone and prophetic spirit. Chaucer is another prime favourite of his, and he has been at the pains to modernize some of the *Canterbury Tales*. Those persons, who look upon Mr. Wordsworth as a merely puerile writer, must be rather at a loss to account for his strong predilection for such geniuses as Dante and Michael Angelo. We do not think our author has any very cordial sympathy with Shakespear. How should he? Shakespear was the least of an egotist of anybody in the world. He does not much relish the variety and scope of dramatic composition. " He hates those interlocutions between Lucius and Caius." Yet Mr. Wordsworth himself wrote a tragedy when he was young; and we have heard the following energetic lines quoted from it, as put into the mouth of a person smit with remorse for some rash crime:

> " ——Action is momentary,
> The motion of a muscle this way or that;
> Suffering is long, obscure and infinite ! "

Perhaps for want of light and shade, and the unshackled spirit of the drama, this performance was never brought forward. Our critic has a great dislike to Gray, and a fondness for Thomson and Collins. It is mortifying to hear him speak of Pope and Dryden whom, because they have been supposed to have all the possible excellences of poetry, he will allow to have none. Nothing, however, can be fairer, or more amusing than the way in which he sometimes exposes the unmeaning verbiage of modern poetry. Thus, in the beginning of Dr. Johnson's *Vanity of Human Wishes*—

> " Let observation with extensive view
> Survey mankind from China to Peru "—

he says there is a total want of imagination accompanying the words; the same idea is repeated three times under the disguise of a different phraseology: it comes to this— " let *observation*, with extensive *observation*, observe mankind "; or take away the first line, and the second,

> " Survey mankind from China to Peru,"

literally conveys the whole. Mr. Wordsworth is, we must say, a perfect Drawcansir as to prose writers. He complains of the dry reasoners and matter-of-fact people for their want of *passion*; and he is jealous of the rhetorical declaimers and rhapsodists as trenching on the province of poetry. He condemns all French writers (as well of poetry as prose) in the lump. His list in this way is indeed small. He approves of Walton's *Angler*, Paley, and some other writers of an inoffensive modesty of pretension. He also likes books of voyages and travels, and *Robinson Crusoe*. In art, he greatly esteems Bewick's woodcuts and Waterloo's sylvan etchings. But he sometimes takes a higher tone, and gives his mind fair play. We have known him enlarge with a noble intelligence and enthusiasm on Nicolas Poussin's fine landscape-compositions, pointing out the unity of design that pervades them, the superintending mind, the imaginative principle that brings all to bear on the same end; and declaring he would not give a rush for any landscape that did not express the time of day, the climate, the period of the world it was meant to illustrate, or had not this character of *wholeness* in it. His eye also does justice to Rembrandt's fine and masterly effects In the way in which that artist works something out of nothing, and transforms the stump of a tree, a common figure, into an *ideal* object by the gorgeous light and shade thrown upon it, he perceives an analogy to his own mode of investing the minute details of nature with an atmosphere of sentiment; and in pronouncing Rembrandt to be a man of genius, feels that he strengthens his own claim to the title. It has been said of Mr. Wordsworth, that " he hates conchology, that he hates the Venus of Medicis." But these, we hope, are mere epigrams and *jeux-d'esprit*, as far from truth as they are free from malice: a sort of running satire or critical clenches—

> " Where one for sense and one for rhyme
> Is quite sufficient at one time."

We think, however, that if Mr. Wordsworth had been a more liberal and candid critic, he would have been a more sterling writer. If a greater number of sources of pleasure had been open to him, he would have communicated pleasure to the world more frequently. Had he been less fastidious in pronouncing sentence on the works of others, his own would have been received more favourably, and treated more leniently. The current of his feelings is deep, but narrow; the range of his understanding is lofty and aspiring rather than discursive. The force, the originality, the absolute truth and identity, with which he feels some things, make him indifferent to so many others. The simplicity and enthusiasm of his feelings, with respect to nature, render him bigoted and intolerant in his judgments of men and things. But it happens to him, as to others, that his strength lies in his weakness; and perhaps we have no right to complain. We might get rid of the cynic and the egotist, and find in his stead a common-place man. We should " take the good the Gods provide us ": a fine and original vein of poetry is not one of their most contemptible gifts; and the rest is scarcely worth thinking of, except as it may be a mortification to those who expect perfection from human nature ; or who have been idle enough at some period of their lives to deify men of genius as possessing claims above it. But this is a chord that jars, and we shall not dwell upon it.

Lord Byron we have called, according to the old proverb, " the spoiled child of fortune ": Mr. Wordsworth might plead, in mitigation of some peculiarities, that he is "the spoiled child of disappointment." We are convinced, if he had been early a popular poet, he would have borne his honours meekly, and would have been a person of great *bonhomie* and frankness of disposition. But the sense of injustice and of undeserved ridicule sours the temper and narrows the views. To have produced works of genius, and to find them neglected or treated with scorn, is one of the heaviest trials of human patience.

We exaggerate our own merits when they are denied by others, and are apt to grudge and cavil at every particle of praise bestowed on those to whom we feel a conscious superiority. In mere self-defence we turn against the world, when it turns against us; brood over the undeserved slights we receive; and thus the genial current of the soul is stopped, or vents itself in effusions of petulance and self-conceit. Mr. Wordsworth has thought too much of contemporary critics and criticism, and less than he ought of the award of posterity and of the opinion, we do not say of private friends, but of those who were made so by their admiration of his genius. He did not court popularity by a conformity to established models, and he ought not to have been surprised that his originality was not understood as a matter of course. He has *gnawed too much on the bridle*, and has often thrown out crusts to the critics, in mere defiance or as a point of honour when he was challenged, which otherwise his own good sense would have withheld. We suspect that Mr. Wordsworth's feelings are a little morbid in this respect, or that he resents censure more than he is gratified by praise. Otherwise, the tide has turned much in his favour of late years—he has a large body of determined partisans—and is at present sufficiently in request with the public to save or relieve him from the last necessity to which a man of genius can be reduced—that of becoming the God of his own idolatry!

MR. GIFFORD

(THE SPIRIT OF THE AGE, 1825)

MR. GIFFORD was originally bred to some handicraft: he afterwards contrived to learn Latin, and was for some time an usher in a school, till he became a tutor in a nobleman's family. The low-bred, self-taught man, the pedant, and the dependent on the great, contribute to form the Editor of the *Quarterly Review*. He is admirably qualified for this situation, which he has held for some years, by a happy combination of defects, natural and acquired; and in the event of his death it will be difficult to provide him a suitable successor.

Mr. Gifford has no pretensions to be thought a man of genius, of taste, or even of general knowledge. He merely understands the mechanical and instrumental part of learning. He is a critic of the last age, when the different editions of an author, or the dates of his several performances were all that occupied the inquiries of a profound scholar, and the spirit of the writer or the beauties of his style were left to shift for themselves, or exercise the fancy of the light and superficial reader. In studying an old author, he has no notion of anything beyond adjusting a point, proposing a different reading, or correcting, by the collation of various copies, an error of the press.

In appreciating a modern one, if it is an enemy, the first thing he thinks of is to charge him with bad grammar: he scans his sentences instead of weighing his sense; or if it is a friend, the highest compliment he conceives it possible to pay him is, that his thoughts and expressions are moulded on some hackneyed model. His standard of *ideal* perfection is what he himself now is, a person of *mediocre* literary attainments: his utmost contempt is shown by reducing any one to what he himself once was, a person without the ordinary advantages of education and learning. It is accordingly assumed with much complacency in his critical pages, that Tory writers are classical and courtly as a matter of course; as it is a standing jest and evident truism, that Whigs and Reformers must be persons of low birth and breeding—imputations from one of which he himself has narrowly escaped, and both of which he holds in suitable abhorrence. He stands over a contemporary performance with all the self-conceit and self-importance of a country schoolmaster, tries it by technical rules, affects not to understand the meaning, examines the hand-writing, the spelling, shrugs up his shoulders and chuckles over a slip of the pen, and keeps a sharp look-out for a false concord and—a flogging. There is nothing liberal, nothing humane in his style of judging: it is altogether petty, captious, and literal. The Editor's political subserviency adds the last finishing to his ridiculous pedantry and vanity. He has all his life been a follower in the train of wealth and power—strives to back his pretensions on Parnassus by a place at court, and to gild his reputation as a man of letters by the smile of greatness. He thinks his works are stamped with additional value by having his name in the *Red-Book*. He looks up to the distinctions of rank and station as he does to those of learning, with the gross and over-weening adulation of his early origin. All his notions are low, upstart, servile. He thinks it the highest honour to a poet to be patronised by a peer or by some dowager of quality. He is prouder of a court-livery than of a laurel-wreath, and is only sure of having established his claims to respectability by having sacrificed those of independence. He is a retainer to the Muses, a door-keeper to learning, a lacquey in the State. He believes that modern literature should wear the fetters of classical antiquity; that truth is to be weighed in the scales of opinion and prejudice; that power is equivalent to right; that genius is dependent on rules; that taste and refinement of language consist in *word-catching*. Many persons suppose that Mr. Gifford knows better than he pretends, and that he is shrewd, artful and designing. But perhaps it may be nearer the mark to suppose that his dulness is guarantee for his sincerity; or that, before he is the tool of the profligacy of others, he

2 B *

is the dupe of his own jaundiced feelings and narrow, hood-winked perceptions.

> " Destroy his fib or sophistry : in vain—
>   The creature's at his dirty work again ! "

But this is less from choice or perversity, than because he cannot help it, and can do nothing else. He damns a beautiful expression less out of spite than because he really does not understand it; any novelty of thought or sentiment gives him a shock from which he cannot recover for some time; and he naturally takes his revenge for the alarm and uneasiness occasioned him, without referring to venal or party motives. He garbles an author's meaning, not so much wilfully, as because it is a pain to him to enlarge his microscopic view to take in the context, when a particular sentence or passage has struck him as quaint and out of the way. He fly-blows an author's style, and picks out detached words and phrases for cynical reprobation, simply because he feels himself at home, or takes a pride and pleasure in this sort of petty warfare. He is tetchy and impatient of contradiction, sore with wounded pride, angry at obvious faults, more angry at unforeseen beauties. He has the *chalk-stones* in his understanding, and from being used to long confinement, cannot bear the slightest jostling or irregularity of motion. He may call out with the fellow in the *Tempest*—" I am not Stephano, but a cramp ! "

He would go back to the standard of opinions, style, faded ornaments and insipid formalities that came into fashion about forty years ago. Flashes of thought, flights of fancy, idiomatic expressions, he sets down among the signs of the times, the extraordinary occurrences of the age we live in. They are marks of a restless and revolutionary spirit: they disturb his composure of mind, and threaten (by implication) the safety of the State. His slow, snail-paced, bed-rid habits of reasoning, cannot keep up with the whirling, eccentric motion, the rapid, perhaps extravagant combinations of modern literature. He has long been stationary himself, and is determined that others shall remain so. The hazarding a paradox is like letting off a pistol close to his ear: he is alarmed and offended. The using an elliptical mode of expression (such as he did not use to find in Guides to the English Tongue) jars him like coming suddenly to a step in a flight of stairs that you were not aware of. He *pishes* and *pshaws* at all this, exercises a sort of interjectional criticism on what excites his spleen, his envy, or his wonder, and hurls his meagre anathemas *ex cathedrâ* at all those writers who are indifferent alike to his precepts and his example!

Mr. Gifford, in short, is possessed of that sort of learning which is likely to result from an over-anxious desire to supply the want of the first rudiments of education: that sort of wit which is the offspring of ill-humour or bodily pain: that sort of sense which arises from a spirit of contradiction and a disposition to cavil at and dispute the opinions of others: and that sort of reputation which is the consequence of bowing to established authority and ministerial influence. He dedicates to some great man, and receives his compliments in return. He appeals to some great name, and the Under-graduates of the two Universities look up to him as an oracle of wisdom. He throws the weight of his verbal criticism and puny discoveries in *black-letter* reading into the gap, that is supposed to be making in the Constitution by Whigs and Radicals, whom he qualifies without mercy as dunces and miscreants, and so entitles himself to the protection of the Church and State. The character of his mind is an utter want of independence and magnanimity in all that he attempts. He cannot go alone; he must have crutches, a go-cart and trammels, or he is timid, fretful, and helpless as a child. He cannot conceive of anything different from what he finds it, and hates those who pretend to a greater reach of intellect or boldness of spirit than himself. He inclines, by a natural and deliberate bias, to the traditional in laws and government, to the orthodox in religion, to the safe in opinion, to the trite in imagination, to the technical in style, to whatever implies a surrender of individual judgment into the hands of authority, and a subjection of individual feeling to mechanic rules. If he finds any one flying in the face of these, or straggling from the beaten path, he thinks he has them at a notable disadvantage, and falls foul of them without loss of time, partly to soothe his own sense of mortified self-consequence, and as an edifying spectacle to his legitimate friends. He takes none but unfair advantages. He *twits* his adversaries (that is, those who are not in the leading-strings of his school or party) with some personal or accidental defect. If a writer has been punished for a political libel, he is sure to hear of it in a literary criticism. If a lady goes on crutches and is out of favour at court, she is reminded of it in Mr. Gifford's manly satire. He sneers at people of low birth or who have not had a college education, partly to hide his own want of certain advantages, partly as well-timed flattery to those who possess them. He has a right to laugh at poor, unfriended, un-titled genius from wearing the livery of rank and letters, as footmen behind a coronet-coach laugh at the rabble. He keeps good company, and forgets himself. He stands at the door of Mr. Murray's shop, and will not let any body pass but the well-dressed mob or some followers of the court. To edge into the *Quarterly* Temple of Fame the candidate must have a diploma from the Universities, a passport from the Treasury. Otherwise, it is a breach of etiquette to let him pass, an insult to the better sort who aspire to the love of letters—and may chance to drop in to the *Feast of the Poets*. Or, if he cannot manage it thus, or get rid of the claim on the bare ground of poverty

or want of school-learning, he *trumps* up an excuse for
the occasion, such as that " a man was confined in Newgate a short time before "—it is not a *lie* on the part of the
critic; it is only an amiable subserviency to the will of his
betters, like that of a menial who is ordered to deny his
master: a sense of propriety, a knowledge of the world, a
poetical and moral licence. Such fellows (such is his cue
from his employers) should at any rate be kept out of
privileged places: persons who have been convicted of
prose-libels ought not to be suffered to write poetry—if
the fact was not exactly as it was stated, it was something
of the kind, or it *ought* to have been so; the assertion was
a pious fraud,—the public, the court, the prince himself
might read the work, but for this mark of opprobrium
set upon it—it was not to be endured that an insolent
plebeian should aspire to elegance, taste, fancy—it was
throwing down the barriers which ought to separate the
higher and the lower classes, the loyal and the disloyal—
the paraphrase of the story of Dante was therefore to
perform quarantine; it was to seem not yet recovered
from the gaol infection; there was to be a taint upon it,
as there was none in it—and all this was performed by a
single slip of Mr. Gifford's pen! We would willingly
believe (if we could) that in this case there was as much
weakness and prejudice as there was malice and cunning.

Again, we do not think it possible that under any
circumstances the writer of the *Verses to Anna* could enter
into the spirit or delicacy of Mr. Keats's poetry. The fate
of the latter somewhat resembled that of

> " a bud bit by an envious worm,
> Ere it could spread its sweet leaves to the air,
> Or dedicate its beauty to the sun."

Mr. Keats's ostensible crime was that he had been praised
in the *Examiner* newspaper; a greater and more unpardonable offence probably was, that he was a true poet, with

all the errors and beauties of youthful genius to answer for. Mr. Gifford was as insensible to the one as he was inexorable to the other. Let the reader judge from the two subjoined specimens how far the one writer could ever, without a presumption equalled only by a want of self-knowledge, set himself in judgment on the other.

" Out went the taper as she hurried in;
  Its little smoke in pallid moonshine died:
She closed the door, she panted, all akin
  To spirits of the air and visions wide:
  No utter'd syllable or woe betide!
  But to her heart, her heart was voluble,
  Paining with eloquence her balmy side;
  As though a tongueless nightingale should swell
Her heart in vain, and die, heart-stifled, in her dell.

  A casement high and triple-arch'd there was,
  All garlanded with carven imag'ries
  Of fruits and flowers, and bunches of knot-grass,
  And diamonded with panes of quaint device,
  Innumerable of stains and splendid dyes,
  As are the tiger-moth's deep-damask'd wings;
  And in the midst, 'mong thousand heraldries,
  And twilight saints and dim emblazonings,
A shielded scutcheon blush'd with blood of queens and
    kings.

  Full on this casement shone the wintry moon,
  And threw warm gules on Madeline's fair breast,
  As down she knelt for Heaven's grace and boon;
  Rose-bloom fell on her hands, together prest,
  And on her silver cross soft amethyst,
  And on her hair a glory, like a saint.
  She seem'd a splendid angel, newly drest,
  Save wings, for Heaven:—Porphyro grew faint:
She knelt, so pure a thing, so free from mortal taint.

  Anon his heart revives : her vespers done,
  Of all its wreathèd pearls her hair she frees;
  Unclasps her warmèd jewels one by one;
  Loosens her fragrant bodice; by degrees

Her rich attire creeps rustling to her knees:
Half-hidden, like a mermaid in sea-weed,
Pensive awhile she dreams awake, and sees,
In fancy, fair St. Agnes in her bed,
But dares not look behind, or all the charm is fled.

Soon trembling in her soft and chilly nest,
In sort of wakeful swoon, perplex'd she lay,
Until the poppied warmth of sleep oppress'd
Her soothèd limbs, and soul fatigued away:
Flown, like a thought, until the morrow-day:
Blissfully haven'd both from joy and pain;
Clasp'd like a missal where swart Paynims pray;
Blinded alike from sunshine and from rain,
As though a rose should shut, and be a bud again."

Eve of St. Agnes.

With the rich beauties and the dim obscurities of lines
like these, let us contrast the Verses addressed *To a Tuft
of early Violets* by the fastidious author of the *Baviad*
and *Mæviad* :—

" Sweet flowers! that from your humble beds
    Thus prematurely dare to rise,
And trust your unprotected heads
    To cold Aquarius' watery skies.

Retire, retire! *These* tepid airs
    Are not the genial brood of May;
That sun with light malignant glares,
    And flatters only to betray.

Stern Winter's reign is not yet past—
    Lo! while your buds prepare to blow,
On icy pinions comes the blast,
    And nips your root, and lays you low.

Alas, for such ungentle doom!
    But I will shield you; and supply
A kindlier soil on which to bloom,
    A nobler bed on which to die.

Come then—ere yet the morning ray
    Has drunk the dew that gems your crest,
And drawn your balmiest sweets away;
    O come and grace my Anna's breast.

Ye droop, fond flowers! But did ye know
  What worth, what goodness there reside,
Your cups with liveliest tints would glow;
  And spread their leaves with conscious pride.

For there has liberal Nature joined
  Her riches to the stores of Art,
And added to the vigorous mind
  The soft, the sympathising heart.

Come then—ere yet the morning ray
  Has drunk the dew that gems your crest,
And drawn your balmiest sweets away;
  O come and grace my Anna's breast.

O! I should think—*that fragrant bed*
  Might I but hope with you to share—[1]
Years of anxiety repaid
  By one short hour of transport there.

More blest than me, thus shall ye live
  Your little day; and when ye die,
Sweet flowers! the grateful Muse shall give
  A verse; the sorrowing maid, a sigh.

While I, alas! no distant date,
  Mix with the dust from whence I came,
Without a friend to weep my fate,
  Without a stone to tell my name."

We subjoin one more specimen of these " wild strains "[2]
said to be " *Written two years after the preceding.*" ECCE
ITERUM CRISPINUS!

  "I wish I was where Anna lies;
    For I am sick of lingering here,
  And every hour Affection cries,
    Go, and partake her humble bier.

---

[1] What an awkward bedfellow for a tuft of violets!
[2] " How oft, O Dart! what time the faithful pair
  Walk'd forth, the fragrant hour of eve to share,
  On thy romantic banks, have my *wild strains*
  (Not yet forgot amidst my native plains)
  While thou hast sweetly gurgled down the vale,
  Filled up the pause of love's delightful tale!

I wish I could! for when she died
    I lost my all; and life has prov'd
Since that sad hour a dreary void,
    A waste unlovely and unlov'd.

But who, when I am turn'd to clay,
    Shall duly to her grave repair,
And pluck the ragged moss away,
    And weeds that have ' no business there' ?

And who, with pious hand, shall bring
    The flowers she cherish'd, snow-drops cold,
And violets that unheeded spring,
    To scatter o'er her hallow'd mould?

And who, while Memory loves to dwell
    Upon her name for ever dear,
Shall feel his heart with passions swell,
    And pour the bitter, bitter tear?

While, ever as she read, the conscious maid,
By faultering voice and downcast looks betray'd,
Would blushing on her lover's neck recline,
And with her finger—point the tenderest line!"
              .   *Mæviad*, pp. 194, 202.

Yet the author assures us just before, that in these " wild strains " " all was plain."
    " Even then (admire, John Bell! my simple ways)
    No heaven and hell danced madly through my lays,
    No oaths, no execrations: *all was plain;*
    Yet trust me, while thy ever jingling train
    Chime their sonorous woes with frigid art,
    And shock the reason and revolt the heart;
    My hopes and fears, in nature's language drest,
    Awakened love in many a gentle breast."
                    Mæviad, v. 185–92.

If any one else had composed these " wild strains," in which " all is plain," Mr. Gifford would have accused them of three things : " 1. Downright nonsense. 2. Downright frigidity. 3. Downright doggrel"; and proceeded to anatomise them very cordially in his way. As it is, he is thrilled with a very pleasing horror at his former scenes of tenderness, and " gasps at the recollection " " of *watery Aquarius!* " *Sed ohe! jam satis est!* " Why rack a grub—a butterfly upon a wheel?"

I did it; and would fate allow,
    Should visit still, should still deplore—
But health and strength have left me now,
    But I, alas! can weep no more.

Take then, sweet maid! this simple strain,
    The last I offer at thy shrine;
Thy grave must then undeck'd remain,
    And all thy memory fade with mine.

And can thy soft persuasive look,
    That voice that might with music vie,
Thy air that every gazer took,
    Thy matchless eloquence of eye—

Thy spirits, frolicsome as good,
    Thy courage, by no ills dismay'd,
Thy patience by no wrongs subdued,
    Thy gay good-humour—can they 'fade'?

Perhaps—but sorrow dims my eye:
    Cold turf, which I no more must view,
Dear name, which I no more must sigh,
    A long, a last, a sad adieu!"

It may be said in extenuation of the low, mechanic
vein of these impoverished lines, that they were written
at an early age—they were the inspired production of a
youthful lover! Mr Gifford was thirty when he wrote
them: Mr. Keats died when he was scarce twenty!
Farther it may be said, that Mr. Gifford hazarded his
first poetical attempts under all the disadvantages of a
neglected education: but the same circumstance, together
with a few unpruned redundancies of fancy and quaint-
nesses of expression, was made the plea on which Mr.
Keats was hooted out of the world, and his fine talents
and wounded sensibilities consigned to an early grave. In
short, the treatment of this heedless candidate for poetical
fame might serve as a warning, and was intended to serve
as a warning, to all unfledged tyros, how they venture
upon any such doubtful experiments, except under the

auspices of some lord of the bedchamber or Government Aristarchus, and how they imprudently associate themselves with men of mere popular talent or independence of feeling!

It is the same in prose works. The Editor scorns to enter the lists of argument with any proscribed writer of the opposite party. He does not refute, but denounces him. He makes no concessions to an adversary, lest they should in some way be turned against him. He only feels himself safe in the fancied insignificance of others: he only feels himself superior to those whom he stigmatizes as the lowest of mankind. All persons are without common-sense and honesty who do not believe implicitly (with him) in the immaculateness of Ministers and the divine origin of Kings. Thus he informed the world that the author of *Table-Talk* was a person who could not write a sentence of common English, and who could hardly spell his own name, because he was not a friend to the restoration of the Bourbons, and had the assurance to write *Characters of Shakespear's Plays* in a style of criticism somewhat different from Mr. Gifford's. He charged this writer with imposing on the public by a flowery style; and when the latter ventured to refer to a work of his, called *An Essay on the Principles of Human Action,* which has not a single ornament in it, as a specimen of his original studies and the proper bias of his mind, the learned critic, with a shrug of great self-satisfaction, said, " It was amusing to see this person, sitting like one of Brouwer's Dutch boors over his gin and tobacco-pipes, and fancying himself a Leibnitz ! " The question was, whether the subject of Mr. Gifford's censure had ever written such a work or not; for if he had, he had amused himself with something besides gin and tobacco-pipes. But our Editor, by virtue of the situation he holds, is superior to facts or arguments: he is accountable neither to the public nor to authors for what he says of them, but owes it to his employers to prejudice the work and vilify the writer, if the latter is not avowedly ready to range himself on the stronger side.

The *Quarterly Review*, besides the political *tirades* and denunciations of suspected writers, intended for the guidance of the heads of families, is filled up with accounts of books of Voyages and Travels for the amusement of the younger branches. The poetical department is almost a sinecure, consisting of mere summary decisions and a list of quotations. Mr. Croker is understood to contribute the St. Helena articles and the liberality, Mr. Canning the practical good sense, Mr. D'Israeli the good-nature, Mr. Jacob the modesty, Mr. Southey the consistency, and the Editor himself the chivalrous spirit and the attacks on Lady Morgan. It is a double crime, and excites a double portion of spleen in the Editor, when female writers are not advocates of passive obedience and non-resistance. This Journal, then, is a depository for every species of political sophistry and personal calumny. There is no abuse or corruption that does not there find a jesuitical palliation or a bare-faced vindication. There we meet the slime of hypocrisy, the varnish of courts, the cant of pedantry, the cobwebs of the law, the iron hand of power. Its object is as mischievous as the means by which it is pursued are odious. The intention is to poison the sources of public opinion and of individual fame, to pervert literature from being the natural ally of freedom and humanity into an engine of priestcraft and despotism, and to undermine the spirit of the English constitution and the independence of the English character. The Editor and his friends systematically explode every principle of liberty, laugh patriotism and public spirit to scorn, resent every pretence to integrity as a piece of singularity or insolence, and strike at the root of all free inquiry or discussion by running down every writer as a vile scribbler and a bad member

of society, who is not a hireling and a slave. No means
are stuck at in accomplishing this laudable end. Strong
in patronage, they trample on truth, justice and decency.
They claim the privilege of court-favourites. They keep
as little faith with the public as with their opponents.
No statement in the *Quarterly Review* is to be trusted:
there is no fact that is not misrepresented in it, no quotation that is not garbled, no character that is not slandered,
if it can answer the purposes of a party to do so. The
weight of power, of wealth, of rank is thrown into the
scale, gives its impulse to the machine; and the whole
is under the guidance of Mr. Gifford's instinctive genius
—of the in-born hatred of servility for independence, of
dulness for talent, of cunning and impudence for truth
and honesty. It costs him no effort to execute his dis-
reputable task; in being the tool of a crooked policy, he
but labours in his natural vocation. He patches up a
rotten system, as he would supply the chasms in a worm-
eaten manuscript, from a grovelling incapacity to do anything better; thinks that if a single iota in the claims
of prerogative and power were lost, the whole fabric of
society would fall upon his head and crush him; and
calculates that his best chance for literary reputation is
by *black-balling* one half of the competitors as Jacobins
and levellers, and securing the suffrages of the other half
in his favour as a loyal subject and trusty partisan!

Mr. Gifford, as a satirist, is violent and abrupt. He
takes obvious or physical defects, and dwells upon them
with much labour and harshness of invective, but with
very little wit or spirit. He expresses a great deal of anger
and contempt; but you cannot tell very well why—except
that he seems to be sore and out of humour. His satire
is mere peevishness and spleen, or something worse—
personal antipathy and rancour. We are in quite as
much pain for the writer as for the object of his resentment. His address to Peter Pindar is laughable from its

outrageousness. He denounces him as a wretch hateful to God and man for some of the most harmless and amusing trifles that ever were written—and the very good-humour and pleasantry of which, we suspect, constituted their offence in the eyes of this Drawcansir.

His attacks on Mrs. Robinson were unmanly, and even those on Mr. Merry and the Della-Cruscan School were very much more ferocious than the occasion warranted. A little affectation and quaintness of style did not merit such severity of castigation[1]. As a translator, Mr. Gifford's version of the Roman satirist is the baldest and, in parts, the most offensive of all others. We do not know why he attempted it, unless he had got it in his head that he should thus follow in the steps of Dryden, as he had already done in those of Pope in the Baviad and Mæviad. As an editor of old authors, Mr. Gifford is entitled to considerable praise for the pains he has taken in revising the text, and for some improvements he has introduced into it. He had better have spared the notes in which, though he has detected the blunders of previous commentators, he has exposed his own ill-temper and narrowness of feeling more. As a critic, he has thrown no light on the character and spirit of his authors. He has shown no striking power of analysis nor of original illustration, though he has chosen to exercise his pen on writers most congenial to his own turn of mind, from their dry and caustic vein—Massinger and Ben Jonson. What he will make of Marlowe, it is difficult to guess. He has none of " the fiery quality " of the poet. Mr. Gifford does not take for his motto on these occasions *Spiritus precipitandus est!* His most successful efforts in this way are barely respectable. In general, his observations are petty, ill-concocted, and discover

---

[1] Mr. Merry was even with our author in personality of abuse. See his Lines on the Story of the Ape that was given in charge to the ex-tutor.

as little *tact*, as they do a habit of connected reasoning. Thus, for instance, in attempting to add the name of Massinger to the list of Catholic poets, our minute critic insists on the profusion of crucifixes, glories, angelic visions, garlands of roses, and clouds of incense scattered through the *Virgin-Martyr*, as evidence of the theological sentiments meant to be inculcated by the play, when the least reflection might have taught him that they proved nothing but the author's poetical conception of the character and *costume* of his subject. A writer might, with the same sinister, short-sighted shrewdness, be accused of Heathenism for talking of Flora and Ceres in a poem on the Seasons! What are produced as the exclusive badges and occult proofs of Catholic bigotry, are nothing but the adventitious ornaments and external symbols, the gross and sensible language—in a word, the *poetry* of Christianity in general. What indeed shows the frivolousness of the whole inference is that Decker, who is asserted by our critic to have contributed some of the most passionate and fantastic of these devotional scenes, is not even suspected of a leaning to Popery. In like manner, he excuses Massinger for the grossness of one of his plots (that of the *Unnatural Combat*) by saying that it was supposed to take place before the Christian era ; by this shallow common-place persuading himself, or fancying he could persuade others, that the crime in question (which yet on the very face of the story is made the ground of a tragic catastrophe) was first made *statutory* by the Christian religion.

The foregoing is a harsh criticism, and may be thought illiberal. But as Mr. Gifford assumes a right to say what he pleases of others, they may be allowed to speak the truth of him!

ELIA, AND GEOFFREY CRAYON

(THE SPIRIT OF THE AGE, 1825)

s o Mr. Charles Lamb and Mr. Washington Irving choose to designate themselves; and as their lucubrations under one or other of these *noms de guerre* have gained considerable notice from the public, we shall here attempt to discriminate their several styles and manner, and to point out the beauties and defects of each in treating of somewhat similar subjects.

Mr. Irving is, we take it, the more popular writer of the two, or a more general favourite: Mr. Lamb has more devoted, and perhaps more judicious partisans. Mr. Irving is by birth an American, and has, as it were, *skimmed the cream,* and taken off patterns with great skill and cleverness, from our best-known and happiest writers, so that their thoughts and almost their reputation are indirectly transferred to his page, and smile upon us from another hemisphere, like " the pale reflex of Cynthia's brow." He succeeds to our admiration and our sympathy by a sort of prescriptive title and traditional privilege. Mr. Lamb, on the contrary, being " native to the manner here," though he too has borrowed from previous sources, instead of availing himself of the most popular and admired, has groped out his way, and made his most successful researches among the more obscure and intricate, though certainly not the least pithy or pleasant of our writers. Mr. Washington Irving has culled and transplanted the flowers of modern literature for the amusement of the general reader: Mr. Lamb has raked among the dust and cobwebs of a more remote period, has exhibited specimens of curious relics, and pored over moth-eaten, decayed manuscripts for the benefit of the more inquisitive and discerning part of the public. Antiquity after a time has the grace of novelty, as old fashions revived are mistaken for new ones; and a certain quaintness and singularity of style is an agreeable relief to the smooth and insipid monotony of modern composition.

Mr. Lamb has succeeded, not by conforming to the *Spirit of the Age*, but in opposition to it. He does not march boldly along with the crowd, but steals off the pavement to pick his way in the contrary direction. He prefers *bye-ways* to *highways*. When the full tide of human life pours along to some festive show, to some pageant of a day, Elia would stand on one side to look over an old book-stall, or stroll down some deserted pathway in search of a pensive description over a tottering doorway, or some quaint device in architecture, illustrative of embryo art and ancient manners. Mr. Lamb has the very soul of an antiquarian, as this implies a reflecting humanity; the film of the past hovers forever before him. He is shy, sensitive, the reverse of everything coarse, vulgar, obtrusive, and *common-place*. He would fain " shuffle off this mortal coil "; and his spirit clothes itself in the garb of elder time, homelier, but more durable. He is borne along with no pompous paradoxes, shines in no glittering tinsel of a fashionable phraseology, is neither fop nor sophist. He has none of the turbulence or froth of new-fangled opinions. His style runs pure and clear, though it may often take an underground course, or be conveyed through old-fashioned conduit-pipes. Mr. Lamb does not court popularity, nor strut in gaudy plumes, but shrinks from every kind of ostentatious and obvious pretension into the retirement of his own mind.

> " The self-applauding bird, the peacock see :—
> Mark what a sumptuous pharisee is he !
> Meridian sun-beams tempt him to unfold
> His radiant glories, azure, green, and gold :
> He treads as if, some solemn music near,
> His measured step were governed by his ear :

And seems to say—' Ye meaner fowl, give place,
I am all splendour, dignity, and grace ! '
Not so the pheasant on his charms presumes,
Though he too has a glory in his plumes.
He, Christian-like, retreats with modest mien ⎫
To the close copse or far sequestered green, ⎬
And shines without desiring to be seen." ⎭

These lines well describe the modest and delicate
beauties of Mr. Lamb's writings, contrasted with the
lofty and vain-glorious pretensions of some of his contemporaries. This gentleman is not one of those who pay
all their homage to the prevailing idol : he thinks that

" New-born gauds are made and moulded of things past,"

nor does he
> " Give to dust that is a little gilt
> More laud than gilt o'er-dusted."

His convictions " do not in broad rumour lie," nor are
they " set off to the world in the glistering foil " of fashion,
but " live and breathe aloft in those pure eyes, and perfect
judgment of all-seeing *time*."

Mr. Lamb rather affects and is tenacious of the obscure
and remote, of that which rests on its own intrinsic and
silent merit; which scorns all alliance, or even the
suspicion of owing anything to noisy clamour, to the
glare of circumstances. There is a fine tone of *chiaro-scuro*,
a moral perspective in his writings. He delights to dwell
on that which is fresh to the eye of memory; he yearns
after and covets what soothes the frailty of human nature.
That touches him most nearly which is withdrawn to a
certain distance, which verges on the borders of oblivion:
that piques and provokes his fancy most, which is hid
from a superficial glance. That which, though gone by,
is still remembered, is in his view more genuine, and has
given more " vital signs that it will live," than a thing of
yesterday, that may be forgotten to-morrow. Death has
in this sense the spirit of life in it; and the shadowy has to

our author something substantial in it. Ideas savour most of reality in his mind; or rather his imagination loiters on the edge of each, and a page of his writings recalls to our fancy the *stranger* on the grate, fluttering in its dusky tenuity, with its idle superstition and hospitable welcome!

Mr. Lamb has a distaste to new faces, to new books, to new buildings, to new customs. He is shy of all imposing appearances, of all assumptions of self-importance, of all adventitious ornaments, of all mechanical advantages, even to a nervous excess. It is not merely that he does not rely upon, or ordinarily avail himself of them; he holds them in abhorrence; he utterly abjures and discards them and places a great gulph between him and them. He disdains all the vulgar artifices of authorship, all the cant of criticism and helps to notoriety. He has no grand swelling theories to attract the visionary and the enthusiast, no passing topics to allure the thoughtless and the vain. He evades the present; he mocks the future. His affections revert to, and settle on the past; but then even this must have something personal and local in it to interest him deeply and thoroughly. He pitches his tent in the surbubs of existing manners; brings down the account of character to the few straggling remains of the last generation; seldom ventures beyond the bills of mortality, and occupies that nice point between egotism and disinterested humanity. No one makes the tour of our southern metropolis, or describes the manners of the last age, so well as Mr. Lamb—with so fine and yet so formal an air—with such vivid obscurity, with such arch piquancy, such picturesque quaintness, such smiling pathos. How admirably he has sketched the former inmates of the South-Sea House; what "fine fretwork he makes of their double and single entries!" With what a firm, yet subtle pencil he has embodied *Mrs. Battle's Opinions on Whist!* How notably he embalms a battered *beau*; how delightfully an amour, that was cold forty years ago, revives in his pages! With what well-disguised humour he introduces us to his relations, and how freely he serves up his friends! Certainly, some of his portraits are *fixtures*, and will do to hang up as lasting and lively emblems of human infirmity. Then there is no one who has so sure an ear for " the chimes at midnight," not even excepting Mr. Justice Shallow; nor could Master Silence himself take his " cheese and pippins " with a more significant and satisfactory air. With what a gusto Mr. Lamb describes the Inns and Courts of law, the Temple and Gray's-Inn, as if he had been a student there for the last two hundred years, and had been as well acquainted with the person of Sir Francis Bacon as he is with his portrait or writings! It is hard to say whether St. John's Gate is connected with more intense and authentic associations in his mind, as a part of old London Wall, or as the frontispiece (time out of mind) of the *Gentleman's Magazine*. He haunts Watling-street like a gentle spirit; the avenues to the play-houses are thick with panting recollections; and Christ's-Hospital still breathes the balmy breath of infancy in his description of it! Whittington and his Cat are a fine hallucination for Mr. Lamb's historic Muse, and we believe he never heartily forgave a certain writer who took the subject of Guy Faux out of his hands. The streets of London are his fairy-land, teeming with wonder, with life and interest to his retrospective glance, as it did to the eager eye of childhood; he has contrived to weave its tritest traditions into a bright and endless romance!

Mr. Lamb's taste in books is also fine, and it is peculiar. It is not the worse for a little *idiosyncrasy*. He does not go deep into the Scotch Novels; but he is at home in Smollett or Fielding. He is little read in Junius or Gibbon, but no man can give a better account of Burton's *Anatomy of Melancholy*, or Sir Thomas Brown's

Urn-Burial, or Fuller's *Worthies,* or John Bunyan's *Holy War.* No one is more unimpressible to a specious declamation; no one relishes a recondite beauty more. His admiration of Shakespear and Milton does not make him despise Pope; and he can read Parnell with patience, and Gay with delight. His taste in French and German literature is somewhat defective; nor has he made much progress in the science of Political Economy or other abstruse studies, though he has read vast folios of controversial divinity, merely for the sake of the intricacy of style, and to save himself the pain of thinking.

Mr. Lamb is a good judge of prints and pictures. His admiration of Hogarth does credit to both, particularly when it is considered that Leonardo da Vinci is his next greatest favourite, and that his love of the *actual* does not proceed from a want of taste for the *ideal.* His worst fault is an over-eagerness of enthusiasm, which occasionally makes him take a surfeit of his highest favourites. Mr. Lamb excels in familiar conversation almost as much as in writing, when his modesty does not overpower his self-possession. He is as little of a proser as possible; but he *blurts* out the finest wit and sense in the world. He keeps a good deal in the back-ground at first, till some excellent conceit pushes him forward, and then he abounds in whim and pleasantry. There is a primitive simplicity and self-denial about his manners, and a Quakerism in his personal appearance, which is, however, relieved by a fine Titian head, full of dumb eloquence!

Mr. Lamb is a general favourite with those who know him. His character is equally singular and amiable. He is endeared to his friends not less by his foibles than his virtues; he insures their esteem by the one, and does not wound their self-love by the other. He gains ground in the opinion of others by making no advances in his own. We easily admire genius where the diffidence of the possessor makes our acknowledgment of merit seem like a sort of patronage, or act of condescension, as we willingly extend our good offices where they are not exacted as obligations, or repaid with sullen indifference.

The style of the Essays of Elia is liable to the charge of a certain *mannerism*. His sentences are cast in the mould of old authors; his expressions are borrowed from them; but his feelings and observations are genuine and original, taken from actual life, or from his own breast; and he may be said (if any one can) " to have coined his heart for *jests*," and to have split his brain for fine distinctions! Mr. Lamb, from the peculiarity of his exterior and address as an author, would probably never have made his way by detached and independent efforts; but, fortunately for himself and others, he has taken advantage of the Periodical Press, where he has been stuck into notice; and the texture of his compositions is assuredly fine enough to bear the broadest glare of popularity that has hitherto shone upon them. Mr. Lamb's literary efforts have procured him civic honours (a thing unheard of in our times), and he has been invited, in his character of Elia, to dine at a select party with the Lord Mayor. We should prefer this distinction to that of being poet-laureat. We would recommend to Mr. Waithman's perusal (if Mr. Lamb has not anticipated us) the *Rosamund Gray* and the *John Woodvil* of the same author, as an agreeable relief to the noise of a City feast and the heat of City elections.

A friend, a short time ago, quoted some lines[1] from the last-mentioned of these works, which meeting Mr. Godwin's eye, he was so struck with the beauty of the passage, and with a consciousness of having seen it before, that he was uneasy till he could recollect where, and after hunting in vain for it in Ben Jonson, Beaumont

---

[1] The description of sports in the forest:

" To see the sun to bed and to arise,
  Like some hot amourist with glowing eyes," etc.

and Fletcher, and other not unlikely places, sent to Mr. Lamb to know if he could help him to the author!

Mr. Washington Irving's acquaintance with English literature begins almost where Mr. Lamb's ends— with the *Spectator*, Tom Brown's works and the wits of Queen Anne. He is not bottomed in our elder writers, nor do we think he has tasked his own faculties much, at least on English ground. Of the merit of his *Knicker-bocker* and New York stories we cannot pretend to judge. But in his *Sketch-book* and *Bracebridge-Hall* he gives us very good American copies of our British Essayists and Novelists, which may be very well on the other side of the water, or as proofs of the capabilities of the national genius, but which might be dispensed with here, where we have to boast of the originals. Not only Mr. Irving's language is with great taste and felicity modelled on that of Addison, Goldsmith, Sterne, or Mackenzie : but the thoughts and sentiments are taken at the rebound, and, as they are brought forward at the present period, want both freshness and probability.

Mr. Irving's writings are literary *anachronisms*. He comes to England for the first time, and being on the spot, fancies himself in the midst of those characters and manners which he had read of in the *Spectator* and other approved authors, and which were the only idea he had hitherto formed of the parent country. Instead of look-ing round to see what *we are*, he sets to work to describe us as *we were*—at second hand. He has Parson Adams or Sir Roger de Coverley in his " *mind's eye* "; and he makes a village curate, or a country 'squire in York-shire or Hampshire sit to these admired models for their portraits in the beginning of the nineteenth century. Whatever the ingenious writer has been most delighted with in the representations of books, he transfers to his port-folio, and swears that he has found it actually existing in the course of his observation and travels through Great Britain. Instead of tracing the changes that have taken place in society since Addison or Fielding wrote, he transcribes their account in a different hand-writing, and thus keeps us stationary, at least in our most attractive and praise-worthy qualities of simplicity, honesty, hospitality, modesty, and good-nature. This is a very flattering mode of turning fiction into history, or history into fiction ; and we should scarcely know ourselves again in the softened and altered likeness, but that it bears the date of 1820, and issues from the press in Albemarle-street. This is one way of complimenting our national and Tory prejudices, and, coupled with literal or exaggerated portraits of *Yankee* peculiarities, could hardly fail to please. The first Essay in the *Sketch-book*, that on National Antipathies, is the best; but, after that, the sterling ore of wit or feeling is gradually spun thinner and thinner, till it fades to the shadow of a shade. Mr. Irving is himself, we believe, a most agreeable and deserving man, and has been led into the natural and pardonable error we speak of by the tempting bait of European popularity, in which he thought there was no more likely method of succeeding than by imitating the style of our standard authors, and giving us credit for the virtues of our forefathers.

ON THE CLERICAL CHARACTER

(THE YELLOW DWARF, JAN. 24, 31 & FEB. 7, 1818)

——————" Now mark a spot or two,
Which so much virtue would do well to clear."
COWPER.

THE clerical character has, no doubt, its excellences, which have been often insisted on: it has also its faults, which cannot be corrected or guarded against, unless they are pointed out. The following are some of them.

The first, and most obvious objection we have to it, arises from the dress. All artificial distinctions of this kind have a tendency to warp the understanding and sophisticate the character. They create egotism. A man is led to think of himself more than he should, who by any outward marks of distinction invites others to fix their attention on him. They create affectation; for they make him study to be not like himself, but like his dress. They create hypocrisy; for as his thoughts and feelings cannot be as uniform and mechanical as his dress, he must be constantly tempted to make use of the one as a cloak to the other, and to conceal the defects or aberrations of his mind by a greater primness of professional costume, or a more mysterious carriage of his person—

——" And in Franciscan think to pass disguised."

No man of the ordinary stamp can retain a downright unaffected simplicity of character who is always reminding others, and reminding himself, of his pretensions to superior piety and virtue by a conventional badge, which implies neither one nor the other, and which must gradually accustom the mind to compromise appearances for reality, the form for the power of godliness. We do not care to meet the Lawyers fluttering about Chancery-lane in their full-bottomed wigs and loose silk gowns: their dress seems to sit as loose upon them as their opinions, and they wear their own hair under the well-powdered dangling curls, as they bury the sense of right and wrong under the intricate and circuitous forms of law: but we hate much more to meet a three-cornered well-pinched clerical hat on a prim expectant pair of shoulders, that seems to announce to half a street before it, that sees the theological puppet coming, with a mingled air of humility and self-conceit—" Stand off, for I am holier than you."

2 c

We are not disposed to submit to this pharisaical appeal; we are more inclined to resent than to sympathise with the claims to our respect, which are thus mechanically perked in our faces. The dress of the bar merely implies a professional indifference to truth or falsehood in those who wear it, and they seldom carry it out of Court: the dress of the pulpit implies a greater gravity of pretension; and they therefore stick to it as closely as to a doublet and hose of religion and morality. If the reverend persons who are thus clothed with righteousness as with a garment, are sincere in their professions, it is well: if they are hypocrites, it is also well. It is no wonder that the class of persons so privileged are tenacious of the respect that is paid to the cloth; that their tenderness on this subject is strengthened by all the incentives of self-love; by the *esprit de corps;* by the indirect implication of religion itself in any slight put upon its authorised Ministers; and that the deliberate refusal to acknowledge the gratuitous claims which are thus set up to our blind homage, is treated as a high offence against the good order of society in the present world, and threatened with exemplary punishment in the next. There is nothing fair or manly in all this. It is levying a tax on our respect under fraudulent, or at best, equivocal pretences. There is no manner of connexion between the thing and the symbol of it, to which public opinion is expected to bow. The whole is an affair of dress—a dull masquerade. There is no proof of the doctrine of the Trinity in a three-cornered hat, nor does a black coat without a cape imply sincerity and candour. A man who wishes to pass for a saint or a philosopher on the strength of a button in his hat or a buckle in his shoes, is not very likely to be either; as the button in the hat or the buckle in the shoes will answer all the same purpose with the vulgar, and save time and trouble. Those who make their dress a principal part of themselves, will, in general, become of no more value than their dress. Their understandings will receive a costume. Their notions will be as stiff and starched as their bands; their morals strait-laced and rickety; their pretended creed formal and out of date; and they themselves a sort of demure lay-figures, sombre Jacks-of-the-Green, to carry about the tattered fragments and hoarded relics of bigotry and superstition, which, when they no longer awe the imagination or impose on credulity, only insult the understanding and excite contempt.—No one who expects you to pay the same regard to the cut or colour of his coat as to what he says or does, will be anxious to set an exclusive value on what can alone entitle him to respect. You are to take his merit for granted on the score of civility, and he will take it for granted himself on the score of convenience. He will do all he can to keep up the farce. These gentlemen find it no hardship

> " To counterfeiten chere
> Of court, and ben estatelich of manere,
> And to ben holden digne of reverence."

On the contrary, if you offer to withhold it from them,

> " Certain so wroth are they,
> That they are out of all charity."

This canonical standard of moral estimation is too flattering to their pride and indolence to be parted with in a hurry; and nothing will try their patience or provoke their humility so much as to suppose that there is any truer stamp of merit than the badge of their profession. It has been contended, that more is made here of the clerical dress than it is meant to imply; that it is simply a mark of distinction, to know the individuals of that particular class of society from others, and that they ought to be charged with affectation, or an assumption of self-importance for wearing it, no more than a waterman, a fireman, or a chimney-sweeper, for appearing in the streets

in their appropriate costume. We do not think " the collusion holds in the exchange." If a chimney-sweeper were
to jostle a spruce divine in the street, which of them would
ejaculate the word " Fellow ? " The humility of the
churchman would induce him to lift up his cane at the
sooty professor, but the latter would hardly take his revenge
by raising his brush and shovel, as equally respectable
insignia of office. As to the watermen and firemen, they
do not, by the badges of their trade, claim any particular
precedence in moral accomplishments, nor are their jackets
and trowsers hieroglyphics of any particular creed, which
others are bound to believe on pain of damnation. It is
there the shoe pinches. Where external dress really
denotes distinction of rank in other cases, as in the dress
of officers in the army, those who might avail themselves
of this distinction lay it aside as soon as possible; and,
unless very silly fellows or very great coxcombs, do not
choose to be made a gazing-stock to women and children.
But there is in the clerical habit something too sacred
to be lightly put on or off: *once a priest, and always a
priest:* it adheres to them as a part of their function; it
is the outward and visible sign of an inward and invisible grace; it is a light that must not be hid; it is a
symbol of godliness, an edifying spectacle, an incentive
to good morals, a discipline of humanity, and a *memento
mori*, which cannot be too often before us. To lay aside
their habit, would be an unworthy compromise of the
interests of both worlds. It would be a sort of denying
Christ. They therefore venture out into the streets with
this gratuitous obtrusion of opinion and unwarrantable
assumption of character wrapped about them, ticketed
and labelled with the Thirty-nine Articles, St. Athan-
asius's Creed, and the Ten Commandments,—with the
Cardinal Virtues and the Apostolic Faith sticking out of
every corner of their dress, and angling for the applause
or contempt of the multitude. A full-dressed ecclesiastic

is a sort of go-cart of divinity; an ethical automaton. A clerical prig is, in general, a very dangerous as well as contemptible character. The utmost that those who thus habitually confound their opinions and sentiments with the outside coverings of their bodies can aspire to, is a negative and neutral character, like wax-work figures, where the dress is done as much to the life as the man, and where both are respectable pieces of pasteboard, or harmless compositions of fleecy hosiery.

The bane of all religions has been the necessity (real or supposed) of keeping up an attention and attaching a value to external forms and ceremonies. It was, of course, much easier to conform to these, or to manifest a reverence for them, than to practise the virtues or understand the doctrines of true religion, of which they were merely the outward types and symbols. The consequence has been, that the greatest stress has been perpetually laid on what was of the least value, and most easily professed. The form of religion has superseded the substance; the means have supplanted the end; and the sterling coin of charity and good works has been driven out of the currency, for the base counterfeits of superstition and intolerance, by all the money-changers and dealers in the temples established to religion throughout the world. Vestments and chalices have been multiplied for the reception of the Holy Spirit; the tagged points of controversy and lackered varnish of hypocrisy have eaten into the solid substance and texture of piety; " and all the inward acts of worship, issuing from the native strength of the soul, run out (as Milton expresses it) lavishly to the upper skin, and there harden into the crust of formality." Hence we have had such shoals of

> " Eremites and friars,
> White, black, and grey, with all their trumpery "—

who have foisted their " idiot and embryo " inventions upon

us for truth, and who have fomented all the bad passions
of the heart, and let loose all the mischiefs of war, of
fire, and famine, to avenge the slightest difference of
opinion on any one iota of their lying creeds, or the
slightest disrespect to any one of those mummeries and
idle pageants which they had set up as sacred idols for
the world to wonder at. We do not forget, in making
these remarks, that there was a time when the persons
who will be most annoyed and scandalized at them,
would have taken a more effectual mode of shewing their
zeal and indignation; when to have expressed a free
opinion on a Monk's cowl or a Cardinal's hat, would have
exposed the writer who had been guilty of such sacrilege,
to the pains and penalties of excommunication: to be
burnt at an *auto da fe*; to be consigned to the dungeons
of the Inquisition, or doomed to the mines of Spanish
America; to have his nose slit, or his ears cut off, or his
hand reduced to a stump. Such were the considerate and
humane proceedings by which the Priests of former times
vindicated their own honour, which they pretended to
be the honour of God. Such was their humility, when
they had the power. Will they complain now, if we only
criticize the colour of a coat, or smile at the circumference
of a Doctor of Divinity's wig, since we can do it with
impunity? We cry them mercy!

ON THE CLERICAL CHARACTER
(*continued*)

——" Now mark a spot or two,
Which so much virtue would do well to clear."
                                        COWPER.

Jan. 31, 1818.

M A N Y people seem to think, that the restraints imposed
on the Clergy by the nature of their profession, take

away from them, by degrees, all temptation to violate the limits of duty, and that the character grows to the cloth. We are afraid that this is not altogether the case.

How little can be done in the way of extracting virtues or intellect from a piece of broad-cloth or a beaver-hat, we have an instance in the Quakers, who are the most remarkable, and the most unexceptionable class of professors in this kind. They bear the same relation to genuine characters, not brought up in the trammels of dress and custom, that a clipped yew-tree, cut into the form of a peacock or an arm-chair, does to the natural growth of a tree in the forest, left to its own energies and luxuriance. The Quakers are docked into form, but they have no spirit left. They are without ideas, except in trade; without vices or virtues, unless we admit among the latter those which we give as a character to servants when we turn them away, viz. " that they are cleanly, sober, and honest." The Quaker is, in short, a negative character, but it is the best that can be formed in this mechanical way. The Priest is not a negative character; he is something positive and disagreeable. He is not, like the Quaker, distinguished from others merely by singularity of dress and manner, but he is distinguished from others by pretensions to superiority over them. His faults arise from his boasted exemption from the opposite vices; he has one vice running through all his others— hypocrisy. He is proud, with an affectation of humility; bigoted, from a pretended zeal for the truth; greedy, with an ostentation of entire contempt for the things of this world; professing self-denial, and always thinking of self-gratification; censorious, and blind to his own faults; intolerant, unrelenting, impatient of opposition, insolent to those below, and cringing to those above him, with nothing but Christian meekness and brotherly love in his mouth. He thinks more of external appearances than of his internal convictions. He is tied down to the opinions and prejudices of the world in every way. The motives of the heart are clogged and checked at the outset, by the fear of idle censure; his understanding is the slave of established creeds and formulas of faith. He can neither act, feel, or think for himself, or from genuine impulse. He plays a part through life. He is an actor upon a stage. The public are a spy upon him, and he wears a mask the better to deceive them. If in this sort of theatrical assumption of character he makes one false step, it may be fatal to him, and he is induced to have recourse to the most unmanly arts to conceal it, if possible. As he cannot be armed at all points against the flesh and the devil, he takes refuge in self-delusion and mental imposture; learns to play at fast and loose with his own conscience, and to baffle the vigilance of the public by dexterous equivocations; sails as near the wind as he can, shuffles with principle, is punctilious in matters of form, and tries to reconcile the greatest strictness of decorum and regularity of demeanour with the least possible sacrifice of his own interest or appetites. Parsons are not drunkards, because it is a vice that is easily detected and immediately offensive; but they are great eaters, which is no less injurious to the health and intellect. They indulge in all the sensuality that is not prohibited in the Decalogue: they monopolize every convenience they can lay lawful hands on: and consider themselves as the peculiar favourites of Heaven, and the rightful inheritors of the earth. They are on a short allowance of sin; and are only the more eager to catch at all the stray bits and nice morsels they can meet. They are always considering how they shall indemnify themselves in smaller things, for their grudging self-denial in greater ones. Satan lies in wait for them in a pinch of snuff, in a plate of buttered toast, or the kidney end of a loin of veal. They lead their cooks the devil of a life. Their dinner is the principal event of the day.

They say a long grace over it, partly to prolong the pleasure of expectation, and to keep others waiting. They are appealed to as the most competent judges, as arbiters *deliciarum* in all questions of the palate. Their whole thoughts are taken up in pampering the flesh, and comforting the spirit with all the little debasing luxuries which do not come under the sentence of damnation, or breed scandal in the parish. You find out their true character in those of them who have quitted the cloth, and think it no longer necessary to practise the same caution or disguise. You there find the dogmatism of the divine ingrafted on the most lax speculations of the philosophical freethinker, and the most romantic professions of universal benevolence made a cover to the most unfeeling and unblushing spirit of selfishness. The mask is taken off, but the character was the same under a more jealous attention to appearances. With respect to one vice from which the Clergy are bound to keep themselves clear, St. Paul has observed, that *it is better to marry than burn*. " Continents," says Hobbes, " have more of what they contain than other things." The Clergy are men: and many of them, who keep a sufficient guard over their conduct, are too apt, from a common law of nature, to let their thoughts and desires wander to forbidden ground. This is not so well. It is not so well to be always thinking of the peccadillos they cannot commit: to be hankering after the fleshpots of Egypt: to have the charms of illicit gratification enhanced by privations, to which others are not liable; to have the fancy always prurient, and the imagination always taking a direction which they themselves cannot follow.

> " Where's that palace, whereunto foul things
>   Sometimes intrude not ? Who has that breast so
>   pure,
>   But some uncleanly apprehensions
>   Keep leets and law-days, and in Sessions sit
>   With meditations lawful ? "

2 C *

But the mind of the Divine and Moralist by profession is a sort of sanctuary for such thoughts. He is bound by his office to be always detecting and pointing out abuses, to describe and conceive of them in the strongest colours, to denounce and abhor vice in others, to be familiar with the diseases of the mind, as the physician is with those of the body. But that this sort of speculative familiarity with vice leads to a proportionable disgust at it, may be made a question. The virtue of prudes has been thought doubtful: the morality of priests, even of those who lead the most regular lives, is not, perhaps, always " pure in the last recesses of the mind." They are obliged, as it were, to have the odious nature of sin habitually in their thoughts, and in their mouths; to wink, to make wry faces at it, to keep themselves in a state of incessant indignation against it. It is like living next door to a brothel, a situation which produces a great degree of irritation against vice, and an eloquent abuse of those who are known to practise it, but is not equally favourable to the growth and cultivation of sentiments of virtue. To keep theoretical watch and ward over vice, to be systematic spies and informers against immorality, " while *they* the supervisors grossly gape on," is hardly decent. It is almost as bad as belonging to the Society for the Suppression of Vice—a Society which appears to have had its origin in much the same feeling as the monkish practice of auricular confession in former times. —Persons who undertake to pry into, or cleanse out all the filth of a common sewer, either cannot have very nice noses, or will soon lose them. Swift used to say, that people of the nicest imaginations have the dirtiest ideas. The virtues of the priesthood are not the virtues of humanity. They are not honest, cordial, unaffected, and sincere. They are the mask, not the man. There is always the feeling of something hollow, assuming, and disagreeable, in them. There is something in the profession that does not sit easy on the imagination. You are not at home with it. Do you, or do you not, seek the society of a man for being a Parson? You would as soon think of marrying a woman for being an old maid!

To proceed to what we at first proposed, which was a consideration of the Clerical Character, less in connexion with private morality than with public principle. We have already spoken of the Dissenting Clergy as, in this respect, an honest exemplary body of men. They are so by the supposition, in what relates to matters of opinion. The Established Clergy of any religion certainly are not so, by the same self-evident rule; on the contrary, they are bound to conform their professions of religious belief to a certain popular and lucrative standard, and bound over to keep the peace by certain articles of faith. It is a rare felicity in any one who gives his attention fairly and freely to the subject, and has read the Scriptures, the Misnah, and the Talmud—the Fathers, the Schoolmen, the Socinian Divines, the Lutheran and Calvinistic controversy, with innumerable volumes appertaining thereto and illustrative thereof, to believe all the Thirty-nine Articles, " except one." If those who are destined for the episcopal office exercise their understandings honestly and openly upon every one of these questions, how little chance is there that they should come to the same conclusion upon them all? If they do not inquire, what becomes of their independence of understanding? If they conform to what they do not believe, what becomes of their honesty? Their estimation in the world, as well as their livelihood, depends on their tamely submitting their understanding to authority at first, and on their not seeing reason to alter their opinion after-wards. Is it likely that a man will intrepidly open his eyes to conviction, when he sees poverty and disgrace staring him in the face as the inevitable consequence? Is it likely, after the labours of a whole life of servility and cowardice—after repeating daily what he does not understand, and what those who require him to repeat it do not believe, or pretend to believe, and impose on others only as a ready test of insincerity, and a compendious shibboleth of want of principle: after doing morning and evening service to the God of this world— after keeping his lips sealed against the indiscreet mention of the plainest truths, and opening them only to utter mental reservations—after breakfasting, dining, and supping, waking and sleeping, being clothed and fed, upon a collusion,—after saying a double grace and washing his hands after dinner, and preparing for a course of smutty jests to make himself good company,— after nodding to Deans, bowing to Bishops, waiting upon Lords, following in the train of Heads of Colleges, watching the gracious eye of those who have presentations in their gift, and the lank cheek of those who are their present incumbents,—after finding favour, patronage, promotion, prizes, praise, promises, smiles, squeezes of the hand, invitations to tea and cards with the ladies, the epithets, " a charming man," " an agreeable creature," " a most respectable character," the certainty of reward, and the hopes of glory, always proportioned to the systematic baseness of his compliance with the will of his superiors, and the sacrifice of every particle of independence, or pretence to manly spirit and honesty of character,—is it likely, that a man so tutored and trammelled, and inured to be his own dupe, and the tool of others, will ever, in one instance out of thousands, attempt to burst the cobweb fetters which bind him in the magic circle of contradictions and enigmas, or risk the independence of his fortunes for the independence of his mind? *Principle* is a word that is not to be found in the *Young Clergyman's Best Companion:* it is a thing he has no idea of, except as something pragmatical, sour, puritanical, and Presbyterian. To oblige is his object, not to offend. He wishes " to be conformed to this world, rather than transformed." He expects one day to be a Court-divine, a dignitary of the Church, an ornament to the State; and he knows all the texts of Scripture, which, tacked to a visitation, an assize, or corporation-dinner sermon, will float him gently, " like little wanton boys that swim on bladders," up to the palace at Lambeth. A hungry poet, gaping for solid pudding or empty praise, may easily be supposed to set about a conscientious revision and change of his unpopular opinions, from the reasonable prospect of a place or pension, and to eat his words the less scrupulously, the longer he has had nothing else to eat. A snug, promising, soft, smiling, orthodox Divine, who has a living attached to the cure of souls, and whose sentiments are beneficed, who has a critical *bonus* for finding out that all the books he cannot understand are written against the Christian Religion, and founds the doctrine of the Trinity, and his hopes of a Bishopric, on the ignorant construction of a Greek particle, cannot be expected to change the opinions to which he has formerly subscribed his belief, with the revolutions of the sun or the changes of the moon. His political, as well as religious creed, is installed in hopes, pampered in expectations; and the longer he winks and shuts his eyes and holds them close, catching only under their drooping lids " glimpses that may make him less forlorn," day-dreams of lawn-sleeves, and nightly beatific visions of episcopal mitres, the less disposed will he be to open them to the broad light of reason, or to forsake the primrose path of preferment, to tear and mangle his sleek tender-skinned conscience, dipped and softened in the milk-bath of clerical complaisance, among the thorns and briars of controversial divinity, or to get out on the other side upon a dark and dreary waste, amidst a crew of hereticks and schismatics, and Unitarian dealers in " potential infidelity "—

"Who far from steeples and their sacred sound,
In fields their sullen conventicles found."

This were too much to expect from the chaplain of an Archbishop.

Take one illustration of the truth of all that has been here said, and of more that might be said upon the subject. It is related in that valuable comment on the present reign and the existing order of things, Bishop Watson's Life, that the late Dr. Paley having at one time to maintain a thesis in the University, proposed to the Bishop, for his approbation, the following:—" That the eternity of Hell torments is contradictory to the goodness of God." The Bishop observed, that he thought this a bold doctrine to maintain in the face of the Church; but Paley persisted in his determination. Soon after, however, having sounded the opinions of certain persons, high in authority, and well read in the orthodoxy of preferment, he came back in great alarm, said he found the thing would not do, and begged, instead of his first thesis, to have the reverse one substituted in its stead, viz.—" That the Eternity of Hell torments is *not* contradictory to the goodness of God."—What burning daylight is here thrown on clerical discipline, and the bias of a University education! This passage is worth all Mosheim's *Ecclesiastical History*, Wood's *Athenæ Oxoniensis*, and Mr. Coleridge's two *Lay Sermons*. This same shuffling Divine is the same Dr. Paley, who afterwards employed the whole of his life, and his moderate second-hand abilities, in tampering with religion, morality, and politics,—in trimming between his convenience and his conscience,—in crawling between heaven and earth, and trying to cajole both. His celebrated and popular work on Moral Philosophy, is celebrated and popular for no other reason, than that it is a somewhat ingenious and amusing apology for existing abuses of every description, by which anything is to be got. It is a very elaborate and consolatory elucidation of the text, *that men should not quarrel with their bread and butter*. It is not an attempt to shew what is right, but to palliate and find out plausible excuses for what is wrong. It is a work without the least value, except as a convenient common-place book or *vade mecum*, for tyro politicians and young divines, to smooth their progress in the Church or the State. This work is a text-book in the University: its morality is the acknowledged morality of the House of Commons. The Lords are above it. They do not affect that sort of casuistry, by which the country gentlemen contrive to oblige the Ministers, and to reconcile themselves to their constituents.

ON THE CLERICAL CHARACTER
(*concluded*)

" Priests were the first deluders of mankind,
Who with vain faith made all their reason blind;
Not Lucifer himself more proud than they,
And yet persuade the world they must obey:
Of avarice and luxury complain,
And practise all the vices they arraign.
Riches and honour they from laymen reap,
And with dull *crambo* feed the silly sheep.
As Killigrew buffoons his master, they
Droll on their god, but a much duller way.
With hocus pocus, and their heavenly light,
They gain on tender consciences at night.
Whoever has an over-zealous wife,
Becomes the priest's Amphitrio during life."
MARVEL'S State Poems.
February 7, 1818.

This then is the secret of the alliance between Church and State—make a man a tool and a hypocrite in one respect, and he will make himself a slave and a pander in every other, that you can make it worth his while. Those who make a regular traffic of their belief in

religion, will not be backward to compromise their sentiments in what relates to the concerns between man and
man. He who is in the habit of affronting his Maker with
solemn mockeries of faith, as the means of a creditable
livelihood, will not bear the testimony of a good conscience before men, if he finds it a losing concern. The
principle of integrity is gone; the patriotism of the
religious sycophant is rotten at the core. Hence we find
that the Established Clergy of all religions have been the
most devoted tools of power. Priest-craft and Despotism
have gone hand in hand—have stood and fallen together.
It is this that makes them so fond and loving; so pious
and so loyal; so ready to play the Court-game into one
another's hands, and so firmly knit and leagued together
against the rights and liberties of mankind. Thus Mr.
Southey sings in laureat strains:—

> " One fate attends the altar and the throne."

Yet the same peremptory versifier qualifies the Church
of Rome with the epithets of that Harlot old,—

> " The same that is, that was, and is to be,"—

without giving us to understand whether in Popish
countries, the best and most " single-hearted " portion
of Europe, the same lofty and abstracted doctrine holds
good. This uncivil laureat has indeed gone so far in one
of his " songs of delight and rustical roundelays ", as to
give the Princess Charlotte the following critical advice:—

> " Bear thou that great Eliza in thy mind,
>   Who from a wreck this fabric edified,
>   AND HER WHO, TO A NATION'S VOICE RESIGNED,
>   WHEN ROME IN HOPE HER WILIEST ENGINES PLIED,
>   BY HER OWN HEART AND RIGHTEOUS HEAV'N APPROVED,
>   STOOD UP AGAINST THE FATHER WHOM SHE LOV'D."

These lines seem to glance at contingent rebellion, at
speculative treason: they have a squint, a strong cast of

the eye, that way. But it is neither our business nor inclination to point out passages in prose or verse, for the animadversion of the Attorney-General. Mr. Croker, we fear, however, must have been greatly scandalised at this specimen of his friend's original mode of thinking for himself in such delicate matters as the cashiering of Kings and encouraging their daughters, as in duty bound, to stand up against them whenever Mr. Southey pleases. *Launce* could not have been more put to it when his dog misbehaved " among the gentlemanlike dogs at the Duke's table " than the Admiralty Secretary at this *faux-pas* of Mr. Southey's reformed Jacobin Muse. It was shewing the lady's breeding to some purpose. This gratuitous piece of advice to a Protestant Princess is, however, just the reverse of that which Cardinal Wolsey gave to a Popish ruler of these realms, Henry VIII, before that Monarch saw reason to change his religious principles for a wife, as Mr. Southey has changed his political ones for a pension. The Cardinal was almost as wise a man in his generation as Mr. Southey is in his; saw as far into reasons of State, and charged by anticipation all the evils of anarchy and rebellion since his time on that very Protestant religion, which the modern courtier under the Protestant succession considers as the only support of passive obedience and non-resistance. Cavendish, in his Memoirs, in the *Harleian Miscellany*, makes Wolsey on his death-bed give this testamentary advice to his Sovereign:—" And, Master Kingston, I desire you further to request his Grace, in God's name, that he have a vigilant eye to suppress the hellish Lutherans, that they increase not through his great negligence, in such a sort as to be compelled to take up arms to subdue them, as the King of Bohemia was; whose commons being infected with Wickliff's heresies, the King was forced to take that course. Let him consider the story of King Richard the Second, the second son of his progenitor, who lived in the time of Wickliff's seditions and heresies: did not the commons, I pray you, in his time, rise against the nobility and chief governors of this realm; and, at the last, some of them were put to death without justice or mercy? And, under pretence of having all things common, did they not fall to spoiling and robbing, and at last took the King's person, and carried him about the city, making him obedient to their proclamations? "—(The author of *Wat Tyler* has given a very different version of this story.)—" Did not also the traitorous heretick, Sir John Oldcastle, Lord Cobham, pitch a field with hereticks against King Henry the Fourth, where the King was in person, and fought against them, to whom God gave the victory? Alas! if these be not plain precedents and sufficient persuasions to admonish a Prince, then God will take away from us our present rulers, and leave us to the hands of our enemies. And then will ensue mischief upon mischief, inconveniences, barrenness, and scarcity, for want of good orders in the commonwealth, from which God of his tender mercy defend us."—*Harleian Miscell.*, vol. iv, p. 556.

The dying Cardinal might here be supposed to have foreseen the grand Rebellion, the glorious Revolution of 1688, the expulsion of the Stuarts, and the Protestant ascendancy, the American and the French Revolutions—as all growing out of Wickliff's heresy, and the doctrines of the hellish Lutherans. Our laurel-honouring laureat cannot see all this after it has happened. Wolsey was a prophet; he is only a poet. Wolsey knew (and so would any man but a poet), that to allow men freedom of opinion in matters of religion, was to make them free in all other things. Mr. Southey, who raves in favour of the Bourbons and against the Pope, is " blind with double darkness." He will assuredly never find that " single-heartedness " which he seeks, but in the bosom of the Church of Rome.

One mischief of this alliance between Church and State (which the old-fashioned Statesman understood so thoroughly and the modern sciolist only by halves) is, that it is tacit and covert. The Church does not profess to take any active share in affairs of State, and by this means is able to forward all the designs of indirect and crooked policy more effectually and without suspicion. The garb of religion is the best cloak for power. There is nothing so much to be guarded against as the wolf in sheep's clothing. The Clergy pretend to be neutral in all such matters, not to meddle with politics. But that is, and always must be, a false pretence. *Those that are not with us, are against us,* is a maxim that always holds true. These pious pastors of the people and accomplices of the government make use of their heavenly calling and demure professions of meekness and humility as an excuse for never committing themselves on the side of the people: but the same sacred and spiritual character, not to be sullied by mixing with worldly concerns, does not hinder them from employing all their arts and influence on the side of power and of their own interest. Their religion is incompatible with a common regard to justice or humanity; but it is compatible with an excess of courtly zeal. The officiating Clergyman at Derby the other day pestered Brandreth to death with importunities to inform against his associates, but put his hand before his mouth when he offered to say what he knew of Oliver, the Government-spy. This is not exactly as it should be; but it cannot be otherwise than it is. Priests are naturally favourers of power, inasmuch as they are dependent on it.—Their power over the mind is hardly sufficient of itself to insure absolute obedience to their authority, without a reinforcement of power over the body. The secular arm must come in aid of the spiritual. The law is necessary to compel the payment of tythes. Kings and conquerors make laws, parcel out lands,

and erect churches and palaces for the priests and digni-
taries of religion: " they will have them to shew their
mitred fronts in Courts and Parliaments "; and in return,
Priests anoint Kings with holy oil, hedge them round
with inviolability, spread over them the mysterious
sanctity of religion, and, with very little ceremony, make
over the whole species as slaves to these Gods upon
earth by virtue of divine right! This is no losing trade.
It aggrandizes those who are concerned in it, and is
death to the rest of the world. It is a solemn league and
covenant fully ratified and strictly carried into effect, to
the very letter, in all countries, Pagan, Mahommedan,
and Christian,—except this. It is time to put an end to
it everywhere. But those who are pledged to its support,
and " by this craft have their wealth ", have unfortunately remained of one opinion, quite " single-hearted "
from the beginning of the world: those who, like Mr.
Southey, are for separating the Man of Sin from the
Scarlet Whore, change their opinions once every five and
twenty years. Need we wonder at the final results?
Kings and priests are not such coxcombs or triflers as
poets and philosophers. The two last are always squab-
bling about their share of reputation; the two first
amicably divide the spoil. It is the opinion, we understand,
of an eminent poet and a minute philosopher of the present
day, that the press ought to be shackled,—severely
shackled; and particularly that the *Edinburgh Review*, the
Examiner, and the *Yellow Dwarf*, as full of *Examinerisms*,
ought to be instantly put down. Another poet or philosopher, who has not been so severely handled in these
works, thinks differently; and so do we. Nay, Mr. ——
himself has been a long time in coming to this opinion;
and no wonder, for he had a long way to come in order
to arrive at it. But all the Kings that ever were, and
ninety-nine out of a hundred of all the Priests that surround them, jump at this conclusion concerning the fatal

consequences of the Liberty of the Press—by instinct. We have never yet seen that greatest calamity that can befal mankind, deprecated by Mr. Burke, namely, literary men acting in *corps*, and making common cause for the benefit of mankind, as another description of persons act in concert and make common cause against them. He himself was an instance how little need be dreaded in this way. If the National Assembly had sent for Burke over, to assist in framing a Constitution for them, this traitor to liberty and apostate from principle, instead of loading the French Revolution with every epithet of obloquy and execration which his irritable vanity and mercenary malice could invent, would have extolled it to the skies, as the highest monument of human happiness and wisdom. But the genius of philosophy, as he said, is not yet known. It is a subject which we shall shortly endeavour to make clear.

> ————" At this day
> When a Tartarean darkness overspreads
> The groaning nations; when the impious rule,
> By will or by established ordinance,
> Their own dire agents, and constrain the good
> To acts which they abhor; though I bewail
> This triumph, yet the pity of my heart
> Prevents me not from owning that the law,
> By which mankind now suffers, is most just.
> FOR BY SUPERIOR ENERGIES; MORE STRICT
> AFFIANCE WITH EACH OTHER; FAITH MORE FIRM
> IN THEIR UNHALLOWED PRINCIPLES; THE BAD
> HAVE FAIRLY EARNED A VICTORY O'ER THE WEAK,
> THE VACILLATING, INCONSISTENT GOOD."
>
> WORDSWORTH.

In another point of view, Priests are a sort of women in the State, and naturally subject to the higher powers. The Church has no means of temporal advancement but through the interest and countenance of the State. It receives what the other is pleased to allow it as a mark of friendship, out of the public purse. The Clergy do not engage in active or lucrative professions: they are occupied with praise and prayer, and the salvation of souls—with heaping up for themselves treasures in heaven, and wrath upon their enemies' heads against the day of judgment. The candidate for Church preferment must therefore look for it as a free gift at the hands of the great and powerful; he must win his way to wealth and honours by " the sufferance of supernal power." The Church can only hope for a comfortable establishment in the world by finding favour, as a handmaid, in the eye of the State: the Church must wed the State, both for protection and a maintenance. The preacher of God's word looks for his reward in heaven, but he must live in the meantime. But he is precluded by his cloth and his spiritual avocations from getting on in the world by the usual means of interest or ambition. His only hope of advancement lies in the Bishop's blessing and his patron's smile. These may in time translate him to a vacant diocese of 10,000*l.* a year. His labours in the cure of souls, or the settling the most difficult point of controversial divinity, would not, on an average calculation, bring him in a 100*l.* Parson Adams could not dispose of his manuscript sermons to the booksellers; and he ruined his hopes of preferment with Lady Booby, by refusing to turn pimp. Finally, the Clergy are lovers of abstract power, for they are themselves the representatives of almighty power: they are ambassadors of religion, delegates of heaven. The authority under which they act is not always respected so readily, cordially, and implicitly, as it ought to be, and they are indignant at the neglect. They become tetchy and imperious, and mingle the irritability of self-love with their zeal for the honour of God. They are not backward to call for fire from heaven, and to put down the Atheist and Schismatic by the strong hand of power. *Fear God and honour the*

King, is the motto of priestcraft; but it is not a sound logical dilemma, for this reason, that God is always the same; but Kings are of all sorts, good, bad, or indifferent —wise, or mad, or foolish—arbitrary tyrants, or constitutional Monarchs, like our own. The rule is absolute in the first case, not in the second. But the Clergy, by a natural infirmity, are disposed to force the two into a common analogy. They are servants of God by profession, and sycophants of power from necessity. They delight to look up with awe to Kings, as to another Providence. It was a Bishop, in the reign of James I, who drew a parallel between " their divine and sacred Majesties ", meaning the pitiful tyrant whom he served, and God Almighty: yet the Attorney-General of that day did not prosecute him for blasphemy. The Clergy fear God more than they love him They think more of his power than of his wisdom or goodness They would make Kings Gods upon earth; and as they cannot clothe them with the wisdom or beneficence of the Deity, would arm them with his power at any rate.[1]

[1] " And for the Bishops (in Edward VI's days), they were so far from any such worthy attempts, as that they suffered themselves to be the common stales to countenance, with their prostituted gravities, every politick fetch that was then on foot, as oft as the potent Statists pleased to employ them. Never do we read that they made use of their authority, and high place of access, to bring the jarring nobility to Christian peace, or to withstand their disloyal projects : but if a toleration for Mass were to be begged of the King for his sister Mary, lest Charles the Fifth should be angry, who but the grave prelates, *Cranmer* and *Ridley*, must be sent to extort it from the young King ! But out of the mouth of that godly and royal child, Christ himself returned such an awful repulse to those halting and time-serving Prelates, that, after much importunity they went their way, not without shame and tears."—*MILTON*—*Of Reformation in England, and the Causes that have hitherto hindered it.*

THE ENGLISHMAN

(NOTES OF A JOURNEY THROUGH FRANCE
AND ITALY, 1826)

T H E R E are two things that an Englishman understands,
hard words and hard blows. Nothing short of this
(generally speaking) excites his attention or interests him
in the least. His neighbours have the benefit of the one
in war time, and his own countrymen of the other in
time of peace. The French express themselves astonished
at the feats which our Jack Tars have so often performed.
A fellow in that class of life in England will strike his
hand through a deal board—first, to shew his strength,
which he is proud of; secondly, to give him a sensation,
which he is in want of; lastly to prove his powers of
endurance, which he also makes a boast of. So qualified,
a controversy with a cannon-ball is not much out of his
way: a thirty-two pounder is rather an *ugly customer*,
but it presents him with a tangible idea (a thing he is
always in search of)—and, should it take off his head or
carry away one of his limbs, he does not feel the want
of the one or care for that of the other. Naturally obtuse,
his feelings become hardened by custom; or if there are
any qualms of repugnance or dismay left, a volley of
oaths, a few coarse jests, and a double allowance of grog
soon turn the affair into a pastime. Stung with wounds,
stunned with bruises, bleeding and mangled, an English
sailor never finds himself so much alive as when he is
flung half dead into the cockpit; for he then perceives
the extreme consciousness of his existence in his conflict
with external matter, in the violence of his will, and his
obstinate contempt for suffering. He feels his personal
identity on the side of the disagreeable and repulsive;
and it is better to feel it so than to be a stock or a stone,
which is his ordinary state. Pain puts life into him; action,
soul: otherwise, he is a mere log. The English are not

like a nation of women. They are not thin-skinned, nervous, or effeminate, but dull and morbid: they look danger and difficulty in the face, and shake hands with death as with a brother. They do not hold up their heads, but they will turn their backs on no man: they delight in doing and in bearing more than others: what every one else shrinks from through aversion to labour or pain, they are attracted to, and go through with, and so far (and so far only) they are a great people. At least, it cannot be denied that they are a *pugnacious* set. Their heads are so full of this, that if a Frenchman speaks of Scribe, the celebrated farce-writer, a young Englishman present will suppose he means Cribb the boxer; and ten thousand people assembled at a prize-fight will witness an exhibition of pugilism with the same breathless attention and delight as the audience at the *Théatre Français* listen to the dialogue of Racine or Molière. Assuredly, *we* do not pay the same attention to Shakespear: but at a boxing-match every Englishman feels his power to give and take blows increased by sympathy, as at a French theatre every spectator fancies that the actors on the stage talk, laugh, and make love as he would. A metaphysician might say, that the English perceive objects chiefly by their mere material qualities of solidity, inertness, and impenetrability, or by their own muscular resistance to them; that they do not care about the colour, taste, smell, the sense of luxury or pleasure:—they require the heavy, hard, and tangible only, something for them to grapple with and resist, to try their strength and their unimpressibility upon. They do not like to smell to a rose, or to taste of made-dishes, or to listen to soft music, or to look at fine pictures, or to make or hear fine speeches, or to enjoy themselves or amuse others; but they will knock any man down who tells them so, and their sole delight is to be as uncomfortable and disagreeable as possible. To them the greatest labour is to be pleased: they hate to have nothing to find fault with: to expect them to smile or to converse on equal terms, is the heaviest tax you can levy on their want of animal spirits or intellectual resources. A drop of pleasure is the most difficult thing to extract from their hard, dry, mechanical, husky frame; a civil word or look is the last thing they can part with. Hence the *matter-of-factness* of their understandings, their tenaciousness of reason or prejudice, their slowness to distinguish, their backwardness to yield, their mechanical improvements, their industry, their courage, their blunt honesty, their dislike to the frivolous and florid, their love of liberty out of hatred to oppression, and their love of virtue from their antipathy to vice. Hence also their philosophy, from their distrust of appearances and unwillingness to be imposed upon; and even their poetry has its probable source in the same repining, discontented humour, which flings them from cross-grained realities into the region of lofty and eager imaginations.[1]—A French gentleman, a man of sense and wit, expressed his wonder that all the English did not go and live in the South of France, where they would have a beautiful country, a fine climate, and every comfort almost for nothing. He

[1] We have five names unrivalled in modern times and in their different ways:—Newton, Locke, Bacon, Shakespear, and Milton—and if to these we were to add a sixth that could not be questioned in his line, perhaps it would be Hogarth. Our wit is the effect not of gaiety, but spleen—the last result of a pertinacious *reductio ad absurdum*. Our greatest wits have been our gravest men. Fielding seems to have produced his *History of a Foundling* with the same deliberation and forethought that Arkwright did his spinning-jenny. The French have no poetry; that is, no combination of internal feeling with external imagery. Their dramatic dialogue is frothy verbiage or a mucilage of sentiment without natural bones or substance: ours constantly clings to the concrete, and has a *purchase* upon matter. Outward objects interfere with and extinguish the flame of their imagination: with us they are the fuel that kindles it into a brighter and stronger blaze.

did not perceive that they would go back in shoals from this scene of fancied contentment to their fogs and sea-coal fires, and that no Englishman can live without something to complain of. Some persons are sorry to see our countrymen abroad cheated, laughed at, quarrelling at all the inns they stop at:—while they are in *hot water*, while they think themselves ill-used and have but the spirit to resent it, they are happy. As long as they can swear, they are excused from being complimentary: if they have to fight, they need not think: while they are provoked beyond measure, they are released from the dreadful obligation of being pleased. Leave them to themselves, and they are dull: introduce them into company, and they are worse. It is the incapacity of enjoyment that makes them sullen and ridiculous; the mortification they feel at not having their own way in everything, and at seeing others delighted without asking their leave, that makes them haughty and distant. An Englishman is silent abroad from having nothing to say; and he looks stupid, because he is so. It is kind words and graceful acts that afflict his soul—an appearance of happiness, which he suspects to be insincere because he cannot enter into it, and a flow of animal spirits which dejects him the more from making him feel the want of it in himself; pictures that he does not understand, music that he does not feel, love that he cannot make, suns that shine out of England, and smiles more radiant than they! Do not stifle him with roses; do not kill him with kindness: leave him some pretext to grumble, to fret, and torment himself. Point at him as he drives an English mail-coach about the streets of Paris or of Rome, to relieve his despair of *éclat* by affording him a pretence to horsewhip some one. Be disagreeable, surly, lying, knavish, impertinent out of compassion; insult, rob him, and he will thank you; take anything from him (nay even his life) sooner than his opinion of himself and his prejudices against others, his moody dissatisfaction and his contempt for every one who is not in as ill a humour as he is.

John Bull is certainly a singular animal. It is the being the beast he is that has made a man of him. If he do not take care what he is about, the same ungoverned humour will be his ruin. He must have something to butt at; and it matters little to him whether it be friend or foe, provided only he can *run-a-muck*. He must have a grievance to solace him, a bug-bear of some sort or other to keep himself in breath: otherwise, he droops and hangs the head—he is no longer John Bull, but John Ox, according to a happy allusion of the Poet-Laureate's. This necessity of John's to be repulsive (right or wrong) has been lately turned against himself, to the detriment of others, and his proper cost. Formerly, the Pope, the Devil, the Inquisition, and the Bourbons, served the turn, with all of whom he is at present sworn friends, unless Mr. Canning should throw out a *tub to a whale* in South America: then Bonaparte took the lead for awhile in John's panic-struck brain; and latterly, the Whigs and the *Examiner* newspaper have borne the bell before all other topics of abuse and obloquy. Formerly, liberty was the word with John,—now it has become a bye-word. Whoever is not determined to make a slave and a drudge of him, he defies, he sets at, he tosses in the air, he tramples under foot; and after having mangled and crushed whom he pleases, stands stupid and melancholy (*fœnum in cornu*) over the lifeless remains of his victim. When his fury is over, he repents of what he has done—too late. In his tame fit, and having made a clear stage of all who would or could direct him right, he is led gently by the nose by Mr. Croker; and the " Stout Gentleman " gets upon his back, making a monster of him. Why is there a tablet stuck up in St. Peter's at Rome, to the memory of the three last of the

Stuarts? Is it a *baisés-mains* to the Pope, or a compromise with legitimacy? Is the dread of usurpation become so strong, that a reigning family are half-ready to acknowledge themselves usurpers, in favour of those who are not likely to come back to assert their claim, and to countenance the principles that may keep them on a throne, in lieu of the paradoxes that placed them there? It is a handsome way of paying for a kingdom with an epitaph, and of satisfying the pretensions of the living and the dead. But we did not expel the slavish and tyrannical Stuarts from our soil by the volcanic eruption of 1688, to send a whining Jesuitical recantation and *writ of error* after them to the other world a hundred years afterwards. But it may be said that the inscription is merely a tribute of respect to misfortune. What! from that quarter? No! it is a " lily-livered ", polished, courtly, pious monument to the fears that have so long beset the hearts of Monarchs, to the pale apparitions of Kings dethroned or beheaded in time past or to come (from that sad example), to the crimson flush of victory, which has put out the light of truth, and to the reviving hope of that deathless night of ignorance and superstition, when they shall once more reign as Gods upon the earth, and make of their enemies their footstool! Foreigners cannot comprehend this bear-garden work of ours at all: they " perceive a fury, but nothing wherefore." They cannot reconcile the violence of our wills with the dulness of our apprehensions, nor account for the fuss we make about nothing; our convulsions and throes without end or object, the pains we take to defeat ourselves and others, and to undo all that we have ever done, sooner than any one else should share the benefit of it. They think it is strange, that out of mere perversity and contradiction we would rather be slaves ourselves, than suffer others to be free; that we *back* out of our most heroic acts and disavow our favourite maxims (the blood-

stained devices in our national coat of arms) the moment
we find others disposed to assent to or imitate us, and
that we would willingly see the last hope of liberty and
independence extinguished, sooner than give the smallest
credit to those who sacrifice everything to keep the spark
alive, or abstain from joining in every species of scurrility,
insult, and calumny against them, if the word is once
given by the whippers-in of power. The English imagination is not *riante:* it inclines to the gloomy and morbid
with a heavy instinctive bias, and when fear and interest
are thrown into the scale, down it goes with a vengeance
that is not to be resisted, and from the effects of which
it is not easy to recover. The enemies of English liberty
are aware of this weakness in the public mind, and make
a notable use of it.

> " But that two-handed engine at the door
> Stands ready to smite once and smite no more."

Give a dog an ill name, and hang him—so says the proverb.
The courtiers say, " Give a *patriot* an ill name, and ruin
him " alike with Whig and Tory—with the last, because
he hates you as a friend to freedom; with the first, because
he is afraid of being implicated in the same obloquy
with you. This is the reason why the Magdalen Muse
of Mr. Thomas Moore finds a taint in the *Liberal;* why
Mr. Hobhouse visits Pisa, to dissuade Lord Byron from
connecting himself with any but gentlemen-born, for the
credit of the popular cause. Set about a false report or insinuation, and the effect is instantaneous and universally
felt—prove that there is nothing in it, and you are just
where you were. Something wrong somewhere, in reality
or imagination, in public or in private, is necessary to
the minds of the English people: bring a charge against
any one, and they hug you to their breasts: attempt to
take it from them, and they resist it as they would an
attack upon their persons or property: a nickname is to

their moody, splenetic humour a freehold estate, from which they will not be ejected by fair means or foul: they conceive they have a *vested right* in calumny. No matter how base the lie, how senseless the jest, it *tells*—because the public appetite greedily swallows whatever is nauseous and disgusting, and refuses, through weakness or obstinacy, to disgorge it again. Therefore, Mr. Croker plies his dirty task—and is a Privy-councillor; Mr. Theodore Hook calls Mr. Waithman "Lord Waithman" once a week, and passes for a wit!

THE END